The regions of Normandie Cotentin

Western Normandy. See the map opposite.

For eastern Normandy, known as Normandie Vallée de la Seine, see the inside back cover.

THeGreenGuide
Normandy

Apple stall in a market, Normandy © Leplat Veronique/Sime/Photononstop

THEGREENGUIDE **NORMANDY**

Editorial Manager	Jonathan P. Gilbert
Principal Writers	Deborah Mends, Paul Murphy
Production Manager	Natasha G. George
Cartography	John Dear
Photo Editor	Yoshimi Kanazawa
Proofreader	Jay Slater
Interior Design	Chris Bell
Layout	Michelin Apa Publications Ltd.
Cover Design	Chris Bell, Christelle Le Déan
Cover Layout	Michelin Apa Publications Ltd.

Contact Us

The Green Guide
Michelin Travel and Lifestyle
One Parkway South
Greenville, SC 29615
USA
www.michelintravel.com

Michelin TravelPartner
Hannay House
39 Clarendon Road
Watford, Herts WD17 1JA
UK
℘01923 205240
www.ViaMichelin.com
travelpubsales@uk.michelin.com

Special Sales

For information regarding bulk sales,
customized editions and premium sales,
please contact our Customer Service
Departments:
USA   1-800-432-6277
UK   01923 205240
Canada 1-800-361-8236

HOW TO USE THIS GUIDE

PLANNING YOUR TRIP

The blue-tabbed PLANNING YOUR TRIP section at the front of the guide gives you **ideas for your trip** and **practical information** to help you organise it. You'll find tours, practical information, a host of outdoor activities, a calendar of events, information on shopping, sightseeing, kids' activities and more.

INTRODUCTION

The orange-tabbed INTRODUCTION section explores Normandy's **Nature** and geology. The **History** section spans Roman times through William the Conqueror to the modern day. The **Art and Culture** section covers architecture, art, literature and music, while **Normandy Today** delves into modern Normandy.

DISCOVERING

The green-tabbed DISCOVERING section features Principal Sights by region, featuring the most interesting local **Sights**, **Walking Tours**, nearby **Excursions**, and detailed **Driving Tours**. Admission prices shown are normally for a single adult.

ADDRESSES

We've selected the best hotels, restaurants, cafés shops, nightlife and entertainment to fit all budgets. See the Legend on the cover flap for an explanation of the price categories. See the back of the guide for an index of where to find hotels and restaurants.

Sidebars

Throughout the guide you will find blue, orange and green-coloured text boxes with lively anecdotes, detailed history and background information.

😊 A Bit of Advice 😊

Green advice boxes found in this guide contain practical tips and handy information relevant to your visit or to a sight in the Discovering section.

STAR RATINGS★★★

Michelin has given star ratings for more than 100 years. If you're pressed for time, we recommend you visit the ★★★, or ★★ sights first:

★★★   **Highly recommended**
★★   **Recommended**
★   **Interesting**

MAPS

- 😊 Principal Sights map.
- 😊 Region maps.
- 😊 Maps for major cities and villages.
- 😊 Local tour maps.

All maps in this guide are oriented north, unless otherwise indicated by a directional arrow. The term "Local Map" refers to a map within the chapter or Tourism Region. A complete list of the maps found in the guide appears at the back of this book.

© Arthur Leroy/Iconotec/Photononstop

INTRODUCTION TO NORMANDY

PLANNING YOUR TRIP

DISCOVERING NORMANDY

CONTENTS

Welcome to Normandy

This former dukedom today incorporates all or part of seven French *départements*, with Rouen as the capital. The Norman coast offers elegant resorts, while cows, orchards and hedgerows provide rural charm. Castles and abbeys such as Mont-St-Michel evoke a long history of power struggles, not least the 1944 Normandy Landings. The cuisine, favouring cream, is justly celebrated.

ROUEN AND THE BOUCLES DE LA SEINE *(pp82-123)*

Rouen, the capital of Normandy, rose from the ashes of World War II to become the dynamic, historic city it is today. The Seine meanders here, bringing trade to towns and villages, nourishing gentle, rich landscapes and inspiring Impressionist painters.

COTE D'ALBÂTRE AND PAYS DE CAUX *(pp124–157)*

The Pays de Caux, lying between Rouen and Le Havre, is charming and intimate. The appealing landscape invites exploration on foot, by bicycle or on horseback; it contrasts sharply with countryside made for walkers, one of seaspray, cliffs, wheeling gulls and endless sky otherwise known as the Alabaster Coast.

VEXIN NORMAND AND PAYS DE BRAY *(pp158–178)*

Richard the Lion Heart and Philippe Auguste clashed in the Vexin Normand for ownership of these lands; today a region of history but also one of art, being the very cradle of Impressionism with the gardens of Giverny. Yet the Pays de Bray offers renewal to nature lovers longing for thick forests and wild landscapes.

CÔTE FLEURIE AND PAYS D'AUGE *(pp179–210)*

Elegant summer holidays are to be had on the fine sand beaches and in the seafood restaurants of the Côte Fleurie, running from the Pays d'Auge to east of Calvados. Gourmets on the lookout for Norman authenticity will be drawn to the Pays d'Auge for its lush greenery and its cream, butter, milk and cheeses.

PLAIN DE L'EURE AND PAYS D'OUCHE *(pp211–232)*

This is where you can glimpse the authentic Normandy. Time is suspended here in a countryside of small farms, enclosed and protected by hedgerows, with little villages nestling around their country church and the occasional horserider out for a canter in the sun.

PERCHE *(pp233–247)*

The Perche is a region of deep forests, hedgerows, gentle hills and valleys, dotted with manor houses like small stone fortresses. The region's name is also that given to the horse that evolved centuries ago in this countryside: the gentle, powerful Percheron. People like to eat and drink here, and cider is a long Perche tradition, now proudly returning to its place of prominence.

CAEN AND THE PLAGES DU DÉBARQUEMENT *(pp248–291)*

With the conquest of England by Duke William, Caen was bound to its powerful neighbour. The region was to become the stage for the greatest battle of the Second World War; Caen was almost completely razed, yet rose from its ashes to become the modern town it is today. The nearby beaches and villages carry the memory of the great sacrifices made here in 1944 with the Normandy Landings, and today have become a place for contemplation and for peace.

Granville

© Andrejs Jegorovs/iStockphoto.com

LE BOCAGE AND PAYS D'ARGENTAN (pp292–312)

The gentle hills and dales of the Bocage stand in sharp contrast with the little mountains sculpted by the rushing rivers of the Suisse Normande. While this part of Normandy suffered as well in the Allied bombings of June 1944, it has been rebuilt and today is a delight for holiday-makers out to enjoy the lush countryside in which the River Orne meanders.

ALENÇON AND THE PARC NORMANDIE-MAINE (pp313–335)

The Parc Régional Normandie-Maine was created in 1975 with a total area of 234,000 hectares (580,000 acres). It contains a vast variety of natural riches; its landscapes range from heath to limestone hills and its wildlife includes many rare species. Alençon, meanwhile, awaits with its history and tradition of lacemaking, and its architectural treasures.

THE NORTH OF THE MAYENNE (pp336–351)

The portion of of the Mayenne *département* that extends into Normandy includes the cities of Laval, with its medieval centre and terraced Perrine Gardens, and Mayenne, with its 8C castle. Ruins of the Roman town of Jublains recall Julius Caesar's Gaul, while the countryside offers forests, castles, and fields where horses graze. Along the River Mayenne, visitors can bathe and rent watercraft.

GRANVILLE AND THE BAY OF MONT-ST-MICHEL (pp352–374)

Granville, on the Cotentin Peninsula at the mouth of the Bosq and Pointe du Roc, closes the Bay of Mont St Michel. Its old town preserves the history of its military and religious past. The Bay of Mont-St-Michel awaits holiday-makers, nature lovers and amateur biologists and botanists alike with the wealth of flora and fauna waiting to be discovered here.

LA PRESQU'ÎLE DU COTENTIN (pp375–413)

Shaped like a snail's head, this rocky peninsula extends into the English Channel with the port of Cherbourg-Octeville at its tip. Lighthouses, bays and splendid views line the coast. A national park offers excellent bird-watching.

CHANNEL ISLANDS (pp414–445)

Off the west coast of Normandy, much closer to France than to Britain, the Channel Islands offer English charm, extensive tourist amenities, bathing beaches, and delightful rambles along country lanes. Principal islands are Alderney, Guernsey and Jersey, as well as little Sark, where cars are banned.

Landscape of the Bocage near Nonant-le-Pin, Pays d'Argentan
© Arthur Leroy/Iconotec/Photononstop

When and Where to Go

SEASONS

The most pleasant time of year here is July to September, although the mildness of the coastal climate makes it possible to visit Normandy at any time of the year. In spring, the blossoming of the apple trees transforms the Normandy countryside. Apples flower last, after the Gaillon cherries and the Domfront pears. Apple blossom time is really without equal, and this would therefore be the ideal time to explore the countryside by driving through the Pays d'Auge and along the Seine Valley.

In summer, the hot weather comes earlier inland than on the coast. The beach season does not begin before June, when the last storms have died away. From Le Tréport to Mont-St-Michel, the coast is taken over by the people in search of sea air, relaxation and amusement. The sky remains hazy, and the sunshine has a special quality, filtered through the light clouds. Inland, the fine weather inspires long rambles through the picturesque countryside, and the many recreational areas along the winding rivers provide opportunities to cool off in bucolic surroundings. The autumn months are the wettest of the year but as soon as November approaches there are many magnificent days. It is the time of year to enjoy the wonderful changing colours of the forest trees. The light is incomparably soft, making the stone buildings appear all the more substantial. It is never very cold.

THEMED TOURS
HERITAGE TRAILS

To help tourists discover France's national heritage in its historical context, municipalities, recently aided by the **Fédération nationale des Routes Historiques**, have set up a number of routes focussing on a given theme. Each itinerary is clearly

Plan Your Itinerary

The website www.normandy-tourism.fr, produced by the Normandy Tourist Board, offers downloadable guidebooks and brochures so you can plan a personalised itinerary.
One booklet covers parks and gardens; another describes historical sites and monuments, yet another lists how to enjoy golf holidays in Normandy. There is also a guidebook devoted to D-Day and the Battle of Normandy.

signposted by panels laid out along the roads and is described in leaflets available from the tourist offices for each *département* or locality. In Calvados, for example, you could choose the Route of the Old Mills, through Fontaine-Henry and Creully; in Orne you could explore the land of Sir Lancelot, around Domfront, Lassay and La Ferté-Macé, or perhaps the Forest Route, taking in the countryside between Essay and Domfront.

THEMATIC ITINERARIES

Driving tours have been prepared for you throughout this guide. Others, on more specific themes, have been mapped out for you by French specialists.

Following in William the Conqueror's Footsteps

A suggested 7-day itinerary, with supporting information and links, follows the career of the Conqueror from Fécamp through 20 towns and sites. Write for information to: President of the Route, 3 pl. du Chauchix-St-Léonard, 22510 Moncontour-de-Bretagne. Or call ☏06 81 87 33 40 or ☏02 96 32 27 97.

Route des Colombiers Cauchois

Visit Normandy's famous dovecotes nestling along the valleys of the Durdent, Valmont or Gonzeville. A website gives a detailed itinerary, in English, as well as photos and links: www.francerama.com/escapade/colombiers cauchois.

Visiting Mont-St-Michel Bay

The bay surrounding Mont-St-Michel, which features on UNESCO's list of World Nature and Culture Heritage Sites, is also an exceptional place on account of its tidal range – the greatest in continental Europe. During spring tides, the sea level can rise up to 15m/49ft between low and high tide. The water recedes 15km/9mi from the coast, then rushes back, accelerating in pace towards the end.

Throughout the year, the **Maison de la Baie** at Le-Vivier-sur-Mer (on the Brittany side) and the Eco-Musée de la Baie in Vains-St Léonard, welcome tourists, organise tours of the bay, provide information and stage exhibits aimed at promoting the heritage of the bay. From July to August they are open every day of the week; weekdays only the rest of the year.

Maison de la Baie (visits to oyster beds by tractor, visits on foot to the bay to explore its landscapes and enjoy its flora and fauna, such as the seals), Pont Le Vivier, Cherrueix, 35960 Le Vivier-sur-Mer. ℘02 99 48 84 38. www.maison-baie.com.

Eco-musée de la Baie (demonstration of salt-making, excursions to discover the bay's flora and fauna), Route du Grouin du Sud, 50300 Vains-St Léonard. ℘02 33 89 06 06. www.patrimoine.manche.fr.

Crossing the Bay to Mont-St-Michel – Visitors should know that it can be very dangerous to cross the Bay alone, even if there are no barriers. Rivers, sand bars and areas of mud and quicksand change place constantly with the currents and winds, and the sea level can rise with the incoming tide at a speed sometimes said to be as fast as a galloping horse. Therefore, for your safety, cross to Mont-St-Michel only with one of the specially licensed Bay guides. Indeed, in the past the first guides were the Bay's fishermen and hunters; they passed their knowledge down to the next generation from which many of today's guides come, making the crossings completely safe and quite unforgettable. To obtain further information, or to make reservations (essential), apply to:

Maison de la Baie (tourist office providing information only), Place de la Mairie, 50 530 Genêts ℘02 33 89 64 00. www.tourismebaiemontstmichel.com.

Two **private guide companies** organise crossings to Mont-St-Michel:

Chemins de la Baie, 34 rue de l'Ortillon, 50530 Genêts. ℘02 33 89 80 88. www.cheminsdelabaie.com.

Découverte de la Baie, La Maison du Guide, 1 rue Montroise, 50530 Genêts. ℘02 33 70 83 49. www.decouvertebaie.com.

There are also a great many private guides conducting interesting specialised tours (nature, history, as a pilgrimage, etc). Call the Maison de la Baie in Genêts or consult the listing at: www.tourismebaiemontstmichel.com.

Walking at the low tide to Mont-St-Michel

L. Vauthier/MICHELIN

Abbaye du Bec-Hellouin

© Gérard Labriet/Photononstop

Route de la Pomme et du Cidre

The countryside stretching from the Pays de Caux and the Pays de Bray is dotted with *cour-masures* planted with venerable apple trees. Leaflets about apples and cider making are available from local tourist offices or www. routeducidre.free.fr.

There is also a Route du Poiré, a sparkling drink made from pears, around the town of Domfront: Maison de la pomme et de la poire – 50720 Baranton. &02 33 59 56 22. www. parc-naturel-normandie-maine.fr.

Route Historique des Abbayes Normandes

This route takes you to 33 abbeys and priories (of 60 surviving in Normandy) as well as 24 châteaux and museums along the valley of the Seine, around Caen and in Basse-Normandie. Contact Route Historique des Abbayes Normandes at 6 r. Couronné, BP 60, 76420 Bihorel. &02 35 12 41 60. www.abbayes-normandes.com.

Route Historique du Patrimoine Cultural Québécois

Three circuits have been developed especially for French Canadians seeking to learn about the land of their ancestors.

Comité Chomedey de Maisonneuve, Centre Culturel Maisonneuve, 10190 Neuville-sur-Vanne, Aube, France.

http://perso.orange.fr/comite. maisonneuve.

MUSEUMS OF NORMANDY

The extraordinary cultural heritage of Normandy is reflected in museums of all types: art, traditional industry and crafts, natural history, etc., many tucked into out-of-the-way villages you might easily miss. The website www.normandie-tourisme.fr lists museums (including those devoted to Impressionist art).

GARDENS OF NORMANDY

The mild climate has long inspired Normans to cultivate lovely gardens which are the perfect setting for a leisurely stroll.

The **Comité Régional de Tourisme de Normandie** (www.normandy-tourism.org) offers a brochure listing some 60 gardens open to the public. The **Comité des Parcs and Jardins de France** has regional associations in Normandy. The excellent website, www.parcsetjardins.fr (in French only), lets you locate gardens by type, region, name or on interactive maps. Local garden organisations, under the umbrella of the national Comité, are:

◆ **Union des Parcs et Jardins de Basse-Normandie**
Maison des Quatrans,
25 r. de Geôle, 14000 Caen.
&02 31 15 57 35.

- **Union des Parcs et Jardins de Haute-Normandie**
  7 r. de Trianon, 76100 Rouen.
  ℰ02 32 18 76 18.

Here is a selection of gardens and parks described in this guide:
- Jardin des Plantes in Avranches.
- Gardens of the Château de Brécy.
- Park and gardens of Thury-Harcourt.
- Botanical gardens in Vauville.
- Parc Emmanuel-Liais and its greenhouses in Cherbourg.
- Jardin des Plantes Quesnel-Morinière in Coutances.
- Jardin Christian-Dior in Granville.
- Park of the Château de Nacqueville.
- Floral park of the Bois des Moustiers at Varengeville-sur-Mer.
- Jardin des Plantes at Rouen.
- Park of the Château de Miromesnil.
- Gardens and terraces of the Château de Sassy.
- Park of the Château d'Acquigny.
- Park of the Château de Beaumesnil.
- Parc zoologique Jean-Delacour at Clères.
- Claude Monet's garden at Giverny.
- Park of the Château de Launay.

BATTLE OF NORMANDY ITINERARIES

Eight themed itineraries, under the general title The Historical Area of the Battle of Normandy (signposted in French along the routes as Normandie: Terre-Liberté) take in the sites, museums and memorials relating to the events of June 1944 in the Manche, Calvados and Orne *départements*. The symbol to follow along the roads is a seagull.
For detailed maps and descriptions of the sights, contact the Tourism Office, Maison du Département, 50008 St-Lô, ℰ02 33 05 98 70 or go to www.manchetourisme.com.
- **Overlord-L'Assaut** *(70km/43.5mi)* from Pegasus Bridge to Bayeux via Sword, Juno and Gold beaches.

😊 D-Day Tours 😊

Normandy Sightseeing Tours *(6 r. Saint-Jean, 14400 Bayeux. ℰ02 31 51 70 52. www.normandywebguide.com)* offer D-Day Tours departing from Bayeux. You can take a half- or full-day tour, taking in such historic sites as Omaha Beach, Ste-Mère-Église, Dead Man's Corner Museum, Canadian Cemetery and Ardenne Abbey. Half-day 50€; full-day 80€.

- **D-Day-Le Choc** *(130km/81mi)* from Bayeux to Carentan taking in Omaha Beach and St-Lô.
- **Objectif-Un Port** *(95km/59mi)* from Carentan to Cherbourg via Ste-Mère-Église and Valognes.
- **L'Affrontement** *(207km/128.6mi)* This itinerary completes the Overlord-L'Assault one and carries on from Bénouville to Vire coming back by Caen.
- **Cobra-La Percée** *(155km/96mi)* from Cherbourg to Avranches via Coutances.
- **La Contre-Attaque** *(162km/100mi)* from Avranches to Alençon via Mortain.
- **L'Encerclement** *(145km/90mi)* from Alençon to L'Aigle via Chambois and Montormel.
- **Le Dénouement** *(122km/76mi)* from Caen to L'Aigle via Montormel and Vimoutiers.

An entry ticket purchased full price at any of the museums of the Espace historique de la bataille de Normandie entitles the holder to a pass (1€) giving reduced fares at all other museums on the tour.

Normandy Campaign

For a day-by-day account of the Normandy Campaign, from the landings on 6 June 1944 to the liberation of Paris on 25 August, with detailed maps, go to the website of the American Battle Monuments Commission, at www.abmc.gov.

What to See and Do

OUTDOOR FUN
CANOEING/KAYAKING

The fast-flowing rivers in the Suisse Normande are particularly good for canoes and kayaks.

Notable sites in Normandy are Pont-d'Ouilly, Clécy, Sillé-le-Guillaume and St-Léonard-des-Bois. The rivers **Eure** (around Dreux-Louviers) and **Risle** (around L'Aigle-Seine estuary) have excellent sites; contact clubs in **Rouen** or **Belbeuf**. You can also practice sea-kayaking out of major nautical centres such as Le Havre and Fécamp.

- **Comité Départemental de Canoë-Kayak Calvados**,
  4 quai Caffarelli, 14000 Caen.
  ✆ 06 82 18 53 19.
  www.calvados-nautisme.com.
- **Fédération Française de Canoë-Kayak**
  87 quai de la Marne,
  94344 Joinville-le-Pont.
  ✆ 01 45 11 08 50.
  www.ffcanoe.asso.fr.

The Fédération works with the French Institut Géographique National which publishes a map, *Canoë-Kayak en France*, showing all good canoeing and kayaking watercourses. It can be obtained by post from the English-speaking bookshop Le Canotier, 206 rue du Moulin à Vent, 76760 Yerville.
✆ 02 35 96 61 31. www.canotier.com.

- **Comité régional de Normandie de Canoë-Kayak** –
  40 r. des Mouettes,
  76960 Notre-Dame-de-Bondeville.
  ✆ 02 35 75 16 10.
  www.crck.org/normandie.

CRUISES ON THE RIVER SEINE

A number of boats able to accommodate between 80 and 350 passengers visit the main harbours (Le Havre, Honfleur, Rouen).

Trips can take half a day or a whole day, including meals on board, or you can opt for luxury cruises between Paris and Honfleur lasting up to a week, with stops along the way.

The following list features the most popular boats offering this type of excursion.

- **CroisiEurope**
  12 r. de la Division-Leclerc,
  67000 Strasbourg.
  ✆ 03 88 76 44 44.
  www.croisieurope.com.
  Cruises between Paris and Honfleur, or the reverse, in 5–7 days.
- **Le Guillaume-le-Conquérant** –
  Contact Rives de Seine Croisières,
  72 r. Scheurer-Kestner,
  76320 Caudebec-lès-Elbeuf.
  ✆ 02 35 78 31 70.
  www.rives-seine-croisieres.fr.

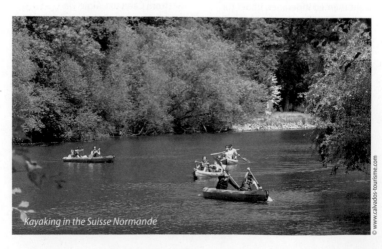

Kayaking in the Suisse Normande

© www.calvados-tourisme.com

Shorter cruises, about 4hr with a meal between Poses and Muids.

CLIMBING

Climbers are attracted to the steep rocky slopes of the Alpes Mancelles and Suisse Normande, particularly the vertical walls of the Rochers des Parcs near Clécy or the Fosse-Arthour northwest of Domfront. For information apply to Tourist Information Centres or to:

- **Club Alpin Français**
  92 r. de Geôle, 14000 Caen.
  𝒞02 31 86 29 55.
  www.ffcam.fr.
- **Fédération française de la montagne et de l'escalade**
  www.ffme.fr.

CYCLING

Good cycling country is found in the Brotonne Forest, Lyons Forest, Eure Valley, Seine Valley and along the Caux coast; there are steeper gradients in the Alpes Mancelles, the Suisse Normande and the Cotentin Peninsula. Voies vertes (ecolo-paths for all-terrain bikes) are being developed throughout the region. Consult tourist offices. You can take the train for part of your circuit; your bike travels for free. Certain train stations even rent bikes, which you can turn in at another station. For up-to-date information, consult:

- **Fédération Française de Cyclotourisme**
  12 r. Louis-Bertrand,
  94207 Ivry-sur-Seine Cedex.
  𝒞01 56 20 88 88.
  www.ffct.org.
  The Fédération supplies itineraries covering most of France, giving mileage, difficult routes and sights to see.
- **Fédération Française de Cyclisme**
  5 r. de Rome,
  93561 Rosny-sous-Bois, Cedex.
  𝒞01 49 35 69 24.
  www.ffc.fr.
  This group produces an annual repertory covering 46,000km/

28,5901mi of marked trails for all-terrain bicycling.

- **Comité Départemental de Cyclotourisme de l'Eure**
  Mme Monique Loride,
  Le Clos Tiger, 27170 Beaumonte.
  𝒞02 32 45 35 06.
  www.codep27.fr.
- **Comité départemental de Cyclotourisme de Seine-Maritime**
  M. Charles Brassart
  12 rue des Acres,
  27110 Le Leubourg.
  𝒞02 32 3618 50.
  www.ffc76.fr.
- **Comité Départemental de Cyclotourisme de la Manche**,
  Maison Tollemer, 50190 Périers.
  𝒞02 33 47 93 51.
  www.cyclisme50.com.

FISHING

For those interested in freshwater fishing, it is necessary to know the dates of the *saison de la pêche*: all over France, the second Saturday in March heralds the start of the fishing season for rivers belonging to the first category *(première catégorie)*, ending on the third Sunday in September. In the case of second-category rivers *(deuxième catégorie)*, fishing is permitted all year round, except for pike, which can usually be caught between July and January, depending on the area. Normandy is dotted with a great many lakes, rivers and ponds of astounding variety. This particular type of topography makes it one of France's most treasured regions for fishing. The fast-flowing rivers abound in fario trout, a local variety, and rainbow trout, brought over from America, whereas the various lakes and ponds are the favourite haunt of carnivorous species such as pike, pikeperch and salmon. The most popular rivers among anglers are the **Risle** (fario trout, carnivores), the **Iton** (pike, rainbow trout), the **Charentonne** (fario trout), the **Huisne** (grayling, fario trout), the **Touques** (fario trout), the **Yères** (fario trout), the

Bresle (sea trout), the **Arques** (salmon and sea trout) and the **Durdent** (fario trout, sea trout).

A leaflet with a map and information called *La Pêche en France* (Fishing in France) is available from the **Office national de l'eau et des milieux aquatiques (ONEMA)** "Le Nadar" Hall C, 5 sq. Félix Nadar, 94300 Vincennes. ℘01 45 14 36 00. www.onema.fr.

ⓘ *Anglers are expected to comply with legislation on fishing, in particular concerning the size of their catch. They are expected to throw back certain fish into rivers if their length does not meet the required standards (40cm/16in in the case of pike; 23cm/9in in the case of trout).*

It is possible to take up sea fishing, both along the coast and on board one of the boats leaving from Trouville, Honfleur, Fécamp, Dieppe, Le Tréport or St-Valery-en-Caux. The waters near Dieppe are said to be teeming with fish and anglers who settle near the piers, often to see their patience rewarded by landing mackerel, pollock, sole or bass. Details are available from regional tourist offices.

ⓘ *Wherever you choose to go fishing, make sure you obey the laws on angling and apply for details from the relevant federations and associations. You have to become a member (for the year in progress) of an affiliated angling association in the **département** of your choice, pay the annual angling tax or buy a day card, and obtain permission from the landowner if you wish to fish on private land.*

- **Fédération de Calvados pour la pêche**
  18 r. de la Girafe, 14000 Caen.
  ℘02 31 44 63 00.
  www.federation-peche14.fr.
- **Fédération de la Manche pour la pêche**,
  16 r. du Pont-l'Abbé, 50190 Périers.
  ℘02 33 46 96 50.
  www.federationpeche.fr/50.
- **Fédération de l'Orne pour la pêche**,
  59 r. Julien, BP 91,

61014 Alençon Cedex.
℘02 33 26 10 66.
www.federationpeche.fr/61.

- **Fédération de l'Eure pour la pêche et la protection du milieu aquatique**
  av. de l'Europe, Immeuble Leipzig, BP 412, 27504 Pont-Audemer Cedex.
  ℘02 32 57 10 73.
  www.eure-peche.com.
- **Fédération de Seine-Maritime pour la pêche**,
  11 cours Clemenceau, 76100 Rouen.
  ℘02 35 62 01 55.
  www.federationpeche.fr/76.

GOLF

Normandy has some 35 golf courses; all the major resorts have clubs, many very beautiful. For information about golf in Calvados, la Manche or Orne *départements*, contact:

- **Ligue de Golf de Basse-Normandie**
  Mairie de Varaville, 2 av. du Grand-Hôtel, 143 Le Home Varaville.
  ℘02 31 28 31 00.
  http://www.lgolfbn.fr.

For information about courses in the Sarthe and La Mayenne départements, contact www.ligue-golf-paysdelaloire.asso.fr. For the Eure and Seine-Maritime contact:

- **Ligue de Golf de Haute-Normandie**
  94 r. St-Jacques, 76600 Le Havre.
  ℘ 02 35 42 71 19. http://liguede golfdehautenormandie.com.
- **Fédération Française de Golf**
  68 r. Anatole-France, 92309 Levallois-Perret Cedex.
  ℘01 41 49 77 00.
  www.ffgolf.org.

HIKING

Walking is one of the best ways of discovering the countryside – the superb beech forests and the occasional manor houses on well-kept farms. Throughout the region there are long-distance footpaths (*sentiers de grande randonnée*, or **GR** – one- or

Hiking with a view to the cliffs of Étretat

© Leroy Arthur/age fotostock

two-day hikes) marked with red-and-white lined posts and shorter, local paths (*petite randonnée* or PR) marked on posts with a single yellow line. Detailed topographical guides are available showing the routes and giving good advice to walkers. The Topo-guides are published by the **Fédération Française de la Randonnée Pédestre** (Comité National des Sentiers de Grande Randonnée) and are on sale at 14 r. Riquet, 75019 Paris. ℘01 44 89 93 90. www.ffrandonnee.fr.

Several of these well-marked footpaths cross Normandy.

- The **GR 2** follows the north bank of the Seine and crosses the Londe and Roumare forests.
- The **GR 21** runs up the Lézarde Valley to meet the coast at Étretat.
- The **GR 22** from Paris to Mont-St-Michel crosses the southwest of Normandy up to Mamers.
- The **GR 23** follows the left bank of the Seine and crosses the Forest of Brotonne.
- The **GR 221** crosses parts of the Suisse Normande and the Cotentin Peninsula.
- The **GR 223** (444km/276mi) runs along the north coast and the Cotentin Peninsula, often following old customs agents' trails with superb views, notably at Cap de la Hague.

- The **GR Sur les traces du chasse-marée** (on the trail of the fishmongers) follows the ancient medieval cart-track that, until the arrival of the railway in 1848, brought fish from Dieppe to Rouen and Paris. Information is available from the Dieppe tourism office ℘02 32 14 40 60 and the tourist office of the *département* of Seine-Maritime (www.seine-maritime-tourisme.com).
- The **Chemins de Saint-Michel** follow routes taken by pilgrims in the years when Mont-St-Michel drew penitents from all over France. These trails, long forgotten, have been progressively traced and marked with bright blue posts. Two 200km/124mi trails in the North Cotentin are collectively named the *Chemins aux Anglais*, while the *Chemin de l'Intérieur* leaves from Barfleur and crosses Ste-Mère-l'Église, Carentan, St-Lô, Coutances, La Haye-Pesnel, to arrive in Genêts. The *Chemin Côtier* links Cherbourg with Genêts following the sea coast. Other trails lead to St-Michel from Caen, Rouen, Chartres and Paris For information, contact: **Les Chemins du Mont-St-Michel**, r. de Picardie, 14500 Vire. ℘02 31 66 10 02.

www.lescheminsdumontsaint
michel.com.

- **Voies vertes, sentiers de
  découverte and sorties natures**
  are shorter, less ambitious trails
  organised locally or in regional
  parks. Contact tourist offices for
  information.

HORSE-RIDING

In such a well-known horse-breeding
region many riding clubs and centres
organise rides on the many miles of
bridle paths through the woodlands
or exhilarating canters along the shore
as well as pony-trekking holidays.
There are many local gymkhanas
and equestrian events and racegoers
are spoiled for choice for a day at
the races. From September to Easter,
experienced riders can hunt in the
forests of Écouves or Andaines to the
sound of the horn. Some *gîtes* will
even put up both you and your horse!

- **Fédération Française
  d'Equitation**
  This governing body for
  horsemanship in France, delivers
  licences, conducts training, is
  responsible for the regulatory
  framework and oversees
  competitions.
  ✆ 02 54 94 46 00.
  www.ffe.com.

- **Comité Départemental de
  Tourisme Équestre du Calvados**
  4, chemin de la grande Bruyère
  14190 St Germain Le Vasson.
  ✆ 02 31 90 52 01.
- **Comité Départemental
  de Tourisme Équestre
  de la Manche**
  Le Presbytère
  50160 Brectouville.
  ✆ 02 33 56 76 84.
- **Comité Départemental
  d'Equitation de l'Orne**
  25, rue des Iris
  61250 Damigny.
  ✆ 02 33 29 19 92.

Horse-drawn Caravans
In the Orne and Calvados *départements*
you can hire a horse-drawn caravan
(roulotte). Enquire at local tourist
information centres.

HUNTING

For all enquiries apply to the various
Fédérations départementales de Chasse:

- **Calvados**
  r. des Compagnons, 14000 Caen.
  ✆ 02 31 44 24 87.
  www.fdc14.fr.
- **Manche**
  La Malherbière, 31 r. des Aumônes,
  50750 St-Romphaire.
  ✆ 02 33 72 63 63.
  www.fdc50.com.

Horse riding on the beach at Cap de la Hague, Presqu'île du Cotentin

© Patrick Escudero/hemis.fr

- **Orne**
  46 r. de Bretagne, BP 177,
  61005 Alençon Cedex.
  ✆02 33 80 05 05.
  www.fdc61.com.
- **Eure**:
  r. de Melleville,
  27930 Angerville-la-Campagne.
  ✆02 32 23 03 15.
  www.fdc27.com.
- **Seine-Maritime**
  Maison de la Chasse et de la
  Nature, r. de l'Étang,
  76890 Belleville-en-Caux.
  ✆02 35 60 35 97.
  www.fdc76.com.
- **Union Nationale des
  Fédérations Départementales
  des Chasseurs**
  48 r. d'Alésia, 75014 Paris.
  ✆01 43 27 85 76.
  www.chasseurdefrance.com.

LAND SAILING

The great stretches of sandy beach
on the Calvados and Cotentin coasts
are ideal for land sailing *(char-à-voile)*,
an exhilarating sport performed on a
three-wheeled cart equipped with a
sail; speeds can reach 100kph/62mph.
Speed sailing, a form of windsurfing
on wheels is also available. Further
information may be obtained from:

- **Fédération Française
  de Char à Voile**
  17 r. Henri-Bocquillon, 75015 Paris.
  ✆01 45 58 75 75.
  www.ffcv.org.
  The federation offers a list of clubs,
  guidebooks and calendars.

REGIONAL NATURE PARKS

Normandy's four regional nature parks
are a popular destination for hikers
and nature lovers alike since they
provide countless opportunities for
a wide range of open-air activities.
In these highly protected areas,
extensive facilities have been set up
to introduce visitors to local flora and
fauna and to increase their awareness
of environmental concerns.
There are a great many sports in which
to indulge, depending on the time of

year. **Boucles de la Seine Normande**
(☙ see Forêt de Brotonne, p110) **Perche**
(☙ see Mortagne-au-Perche, p212),
Normandie-Maine *(☙ see
Château de Carrouges, p323)* and
Marais du Cotentin et du Bessin
(☙ see Presqu'île du Cotentin, p375).

SAILING

The Channel coast is a favourite venue
for boaters and sailors. Many sailing
clubs offer lessons at all levels of
skill, and in the bigger coastal towns,
annual regattas are a glorious sight.
The main moorings and marinas for
visiting yachtspeople are indicated on
the **Places to Stay map** *(☙ pp37–38).*
They usually provide fuelling facilities,
convenient water stands for drinking
water and electricity points, WCs,
showers and sometimes laundry
facilities, handling equipment and
repair facilities and a 24-hour guard.
France Stations Nautiques is an
association of coastal villages, tourist
sites and marinas offering first-rate
facilities for nautical sports.

- **France Stations Nautiques**
  17 r. Henri-Bocquillon, 75015 Paris.
  ✆01 44 05 96 55.
  www.france-nautisme.com.

For further information on
sailing, contact:

- **Fédération Française de Voile**
  17 r. Henri-Bocquillon, 75015 Paris.
  ✆01 40 60 37 00.
  www.ffvoile.net.

*☙ Foreigners who own or want to rent
a boat (with an engine of more than
6hp) in France must take a compulsory
test in sailing skills* (carte mer).

SKIN DIVING

The right conditions for deep-sea
diving are to be found between
Dieppe and Le Havre and between
Barfleur and Avranches on the
Cotentin coast.

- **Fédération Française d'Étude et
  de Sports sous-marins**
  24 quai de Rive-Neuve,
  13284 Marseille Cedex 07.
  ✆04 91 33 99 31.
  www.ffessm.fr.

SPAS

Normandy has several centres for **thalassotherapy and water cures**. In addition to the bracing climate and vivifying sea air, they rely on the curative virtues of the local waters, mud and algae:

Bagnoles-de-l'Orne

The Grande Source, **a hot spring** with slightly radioactive mineralised water, is said to provide relief for circulatory problems, especially in the legs, and for arthritis and rheumatism as well as problems of the endocrine glands. The season runs mid-Mar–early Nov.

- **Thermes de Bagnoles-de-l'Orne**
  r. du Prof.-Louvel, BP 33,
  61140 Bagnoles-de-l'Orne.
  ℘08 11 90 22 33.
  www.thermes-bagnoles.com.
- **Centre d'Animation et de Congrès de Bagnoles-de-l'Orne**
  1 r. du Prof.-Louvel, BP 27, 61140,
  Bagnoles-de-l'Orne.
  ℘02 33 30 72 70.
  www.bagnoles-de-lorne.com.

Deauville

- **Thalsasso-Deauville**
  3 r. de Sem, 14800 Deauville.
  ℘02 31 87 72 00.
  www.thalasso-deauville.com.

Granville
Le Normandy:

- **Centre de Rééducation et de Réadaptation Fonctionnelles en Milieu Marin**
  1 r. J.-Michelet, BP 619,
  50406 Granvile Cedex.
  ℘02 33 90 33 33.
  www.lenormandy.com.
- **Prévithal Institut de Thalassothérapie**
  3 r. J.-Michelet, BP 618,
  50 406 Granville Cedex.
  ℘02 33 90 31 10.
  www.previthal.com.

Luc-sur-Mer

- **Institut de Cure Marine**
  r. Guynemer, 14530 Luc-sur-Mer.

℘02 31 97 32 22.
www.thalasso-normandie.com.

Ouistreham

- **Thalazur Ouistreham - Normandie**
  av. du Cmdt-Keiffer,
  14150 Ouistreham.
  ℘02 31 96 40 40.
  www.thalazur.fr.

SWIMMING

The Norman beaches are of two types: **sandy** along the Côte Fleurie (Cabourg, Houlgate, Deauville, Trouville, Honfleur, etc.) and **shingle** (stony) along the Alabaster Coast (Étretat, Yport, Fécamp, St-Valéry-en-Caux, Varengeville, Dieppe, etc.). Guarded beaches have a system of flags to warn bathers of possible risks: **green** – safe bathing; **orange** – dangerous, be careful; **red** – bathing prohibited; **violet** – polluted water. If you want to know the water quality of any beach, check on: www.infosplage.com.

WINDSURFING

This sport, which is permitted on lakes and in sports and leisure centres, is subject to certain rules. Apply to local sailing clubs. Boards may be hired on all major beaches. www.ffvoile.net.

ACTIVITIES FOR KIDS

In this guide, sights of particular interest to children are indicated with a KIDS symbol (👥). Some attractions may offer discount fees for children.

SHOPPING

In France, the big stores and larger shops are open Mondays to Saturdays from 9am to 6.30 or 7.30pm. Smaller, individual shops may close during the lunch hour, almost universally so in smaller towns. Food shops – grocers, wine merchants and bakeries – are generally open from 7am to 6.30 or 7.30pm; some open on Sunday mornings. Many food shops close between noon and 2pm and on Mondays. Hypermarkets usually remain open non-stop until 9pm or later. People travelling to the USA cannot import plant products or fresh food, including fruit, cheeses and nuts. It is acceptable to carry tinned products or preserves.

Channel Islands

In Jersey, shops are open from 9am to 5pm, 5.30pm or 6pm, and are closed on Sunday and Thursday afternoon. On Guernsey, shops are open Monday to Saturday from 9am until 5.30pm.

TRADITIONAL MARKETS

All cities and nearly all towns have weekly markets, usually held in the morning. The following are only examples – there are literally hundreds. Check with tourist offices.

Calvados

Bayeux (r. St-Jean Wed, pl. St-Patrice Sat); **Honfleur** (Sat; organic produce Wed; antiques 2nd Sun of month; flowers Sat); **St-Pierre-sur-Dives** (Mon); **Trouville** (Wed and Sun).

Eure

Les Andelys (Sat); **Bernay** (Sat); **Évreux** (town centre Wed and Sat, la Madeleine Sun); **Lyons-la-Forêt** (Thu and weekends); **Le Neubourg** (Wed); **Pont-Audemer** (Mon and Fri); **Verneuil-sur-Avre** (Sat).

Manche

Coutances (Thu); **St-Hilaire-du-Harcoët** (Wed); **St-Vaast-la-Hogue** (Sat); **Valognes** (Fri).

Orne

L'Aigle (animal market at 7.30am Tue, followed by traditional market); **Bagnoles-sur-l'Orne** (Tue, Wed, Fri and Sat).

Seine-Maritime

Caudebec-en-Caux (Sat); **Dieppe** (Sat); **Étretat** (Thu); **Eu** (Fri); **Fécamp** (Sat); **Forges-les-Eaux** (Thu and Sat); **Harfleur** (Sun); **Le Havre** (Les Halles centrales Mon–Sat except holidays; antiques, cours de la République, Fri);

Vieux Rouen place St-Marc (Sun); **Yvetot** (Wed).

VALUE ADDED TAX

There is a **Value Added Tax** (VAT) in France of 19.6 percent on almost every purchase. VAT **refunds** are available to visitors from outside the EU only if purchases exceed €175on one day in one store; the VAT cannot be refunded for items shipped. The system works in large stores which cater to tourists, in luxury stores and other shops advertising Duty Free. Show your passport, and the store will complete a form which is to be stamped by a customs agent at the airport or at whatever point you are leaving the EU. You may have to show the agent the items purchased, so don't pack them in checked luggage. www.douane.gouv.fr.

Channel Islands

There is no VAT on the Channel Islands, which accounts for the profusion of very busy shops. The most popular purchases are alcohol, tobacco, perfume, cream caramels and the famous Jersey and Guernsey wool.

SIGHTSEEING
GUIDED TOURS

Many sights, such as châteaux, can be visited only on a guided tour. The departure time of the last tour of the morning or afternoon may be up to 1hr before the actual closing time. Most tours are conducted by French-speaking guides; some of the larger and more popular sights may offer guided tours in other languages. Enquire beforehand. Also available are notes, pamphlets or audioguides.

CHURCHES

Churches are usually closed from noon to 2pm. Visitors should refrain from walking about during services. Visitors to chapels are accompanied by the person who keeps the keys. A donation is welcome.

BOOKS
BATTLE OF NORMANDY

D-Day: the First 24 Hours
    Will Fowler (Spellmount, 2006)
The Germans in Normandy
    Richard Hargreaves, Pen & Sword,
    2006)
The Americans at Normandy,
The Americans at D-Day
    Two books by John C McManus
    (Forge, 2005)
British Armour in the Normandy
Campaign 1944
    John Buckley (Routledge, 2004)
The D-Day Landings
    Philip Warner (Pen & Sword, 2004)
Overlord-D-Day and the Battle of
Normandy, 1944
    Max Hastings (Pan, reissued, 2010)
A Traveller's Guide to D-Day
    Carl Shilleto, Mike Tolhurst
    (Weidenfeld & Nicolson, 2000)

CLAUDE MONET

Monet in Normandy
    Richard Brettell (Rizzoli, 2006)
Claude Monet
    Christoph Heinrich (Taschen,
    revised 2000)

CUISINE

Cuisine Grandmere: From Brittany,
Normandy, Picardy and Flanders
    Jenny Baker (Faber and Faber,
    1995)
The Cuisine of Normandy
    Princess Marie-Blanche de Broglie
    (Houghton-Mifflin 1984)

GARDENS

Gardens in Normandy
    Marie-Françoise Valéry
    (Flammarion, 2000)
The Magic of Monet's Garden
    Derek Fell
    (Firefly Books Ltd., 2007)

MONT-ST-MICHEL

Mont-Saint-Michel from A to Z
    Henry Decaens, Adrien Goetz,
    Gerard Guiller (Flammarion, 1997)
Tides of Mont-St-Michel
    Roger Vercel (1938, reissued by
    Kessinger Publishing, 2005)

NORMAN CONQUEST

The Norman Conquest: A New Introduction
    Richard Huscroft (Pearson, 2009)
1066: The Hidden History in the
Bayeux Tapestry
    Andrew Bridgeford (Walker, 2005)

FILMS

Mr. Hulot's Holiday (1953)
    Jacques Tati's misadventures on
    his Normandy holiday.
Dunkirk (1958)
    Sombre portrait of the Dunkirk
    evacuation (MGM/UA).
Jules and Jim (1961)
    François Truffaut's tale of two
    young men and a woman, filmed
    in Rouen.
The Umbrellas of Cherbourg (1964)
    With Catherine Deneuve: Jacques
    Demy's charming musical about
    love and loss in Normandy.
A Man and a Woman (1966)
    Cult Claude Lelouch film about
    falling in love again, in Deauville.
Tess (1979)
    Roman Polanski's gorgeous
    version of Thomas Hardy's novel
    was shot in the lush Norman
    countryside.
The Longest Day Fox Video (1962)
    Re-creation of the Normandy
    Landings.
Saving Private Ryan (1998)
    Steven Spielberg drama about the
    Battle of Normandy.
Band of Brothers (2001)
    TV drama (HBO) based on the
    Stephen Ambrose book.

Calendar of Events

Especially during summer months, towns and villages throughout Normandy hold fairs, festivals, commemorations of all sorts. You can plan an itinerary to take in these events, whose dates tend to shift from year to year. Consult www. normandie-tourisme.fr for exact dates, and ask at local tourist offices.

MARCH

Caen – Aspects of Contemporary Music. ✆ 02 31 27 14 14.

Deauville – Festival of Asian Film and Festival of Scientific Film.

APRIL

Caen – Easter Fair.

30 APRIL–1 MAY

Rouen – 24-hour motorboat races. www.rouenvalleedeseine.com.

APRIL–OCTOBER

Le Havre – International regattas.

SUNDAY PRECEDING ASH WEDNESDAY

Granville – Carnival. ✆ 02 33 91 30 03. www.ville-granville.fr.

1 MAY

Le Marais Vernier – Branding of cows. ✆ 02 32 57 61 62.

MAY

Cherbourg - Children's and comic book festival. ✆ 02 33 93 52 02.

Conches-en-Ouche – Meetings of area farmers (Les Comices Agricoles). ✆ 02 32 30 20 41.

Coutances – Jazz Festival Under the Apple Trees (Ascension week). ✆ 02 33 45 48 36. www.jazzsouslespommiers.com.

Deauville – Easter Festival, two weeks of classical music. ✆ 02 31 14 40 00.

Mont de Cerisy – Rhododendron Fair (end of month). ✆ 02 33 65 06 75.

Ste-Adresse – Dixie Days Jazz Festival. www.lehavretourisme.com.

Le Tréport – Nautical Sports Festival.

WHIT SUNDAY AND WHIT MONDAY (PENTECOST)

Bernay – Pilgrimage to Notre-Dame-de-Couture. ✆ 02 32 43 32 08. www.bernaytourisme.fr.

Honfleur – Seamen's Festival: Sunday: Blessing of sea; Monday: Seamen's Pilgrimage

La Perrière – Contemporary art market. ✆ 02 33 73 35 49.

MAY–DECEMBER

Montivilliers – *Les Concerts de l'Abbaye* Music Festival. ✆ 02 35 30 96 58.

International regattas, Le Havre

JUNE

Pays d'Auge – Heritage Days.
www.pays-auge.fr.

Cabourg – Cabourg Film Festival.
☎02 31 91 20 00. www.festival-cabourg.com.

Cherbourg - Festival des Rart'zilutes.
Music festival including street
concerts, events, sports.
☎02 33 93 52 02.

Deauville – 🐎 International Horse
Jumping Competitions.
☎02 31 14 40 00.

Deauville – ⚓ International
Sailing Week. ☎02 31 14 40 00

Évreux – Rock Music Festival.

Le Havre – Biennial Show of
Contemporary Art.

Ste-Mère-Église – Commemoration
of the D-Day Landings (6 June).
☎02 33 41 41 35.

Utah Beach – Commemoration of
the landings of 6 June 1944.
☎02 33 71 58 00.

JUNE–JULY

Blainville-Crevon – *Archéo-Jazz*,
festival of jazz and contemporary
music. www.archeojazz.com.

Caen – International Organ Festival.
☎02 31 30 46 86.

Mont-St-Michel – 🥾 Rando-Baie du
Mont-St-Michel (hike around the
bay). ☎02 33 89 64 00. ww.rando-baie-mont-saint-michel.fr.

Mortagne-au-Perche – *Les Musicales
de Mortagne*, festival of chamber
music. ☎02 33 81 60 00.

Rouen – Joan of Arc Festival,
performances in medieval dress.
www.rouenvalleedeseine.com .

JULY

Barneville-Carteret – ⚓ Jersey–
Carteret Sea Race.
☎02 33 04 90 58.

Bayeux – Medieval Festival.
☎02 31 51 28 28.

Le Bourg-Dun– Festival of Linens
and Needlework.

Dives-sur-Mer – *Festival de la
Marionnette* (Puppet Festival).
☎02 31 28 12 53.

Haras National du Pin – 🐎 Summer
performances. ☎02 33 36 68 68.

Le Haye-de-Routot – St-Clair bonfire
night (16 July).

Pontmain – 🚗 Blessing of cars and
motorcycles (2nd Sun of July).
☎02 43 05 07 26.

Rouen – *Les Terraces du Jeudi*,
concerts in front of bars and
cafés on Thursdays. www.
rouenvalleedeseine.com.

Rouen – ⚓ Armada of Tall Ships (every
4 years, next date 2013).

St-Christophe-le-Jajolet –
🚗 Motorists' Pilgrimage (last
Sun of July). ☎02 33 35 34 24.

St-Vaast-la-Hougue – Book fair.
☎02 33 23 19 32.

Le Tréport – ⚓ Festival of the Sea.

**LAST SUNDAY IN JULY OR
FIRST SUNDAY OF AUGUST**

Granville – Pardon of the
Corporations of the Sea:
Procession of guilds with their
banners; open-air mass and
torchlight procession.
☎02 33 91 30 03.

JULY–AUGUST

Bellême – Perche sound-and-light
show. ☎02 33 25 23 23.

Cherbourg – *Les Estivales*. Free
guided tours of the historic
district, Ravalet Chateau,
botanical gardens, Voeu Abbey.
☎02 33 93 52 02.

Dreux – *L'été sous les charmes*, world
music festival, free concerts.
☎02 37 38 87 00.
www.dreux.com.

La Mayenne region – *Les Nuits
de la Mayenne*: entertainment
organised around the region.
☎02 43 53 63 90.
www.nuitsdelamayenne.com.

EARLY AUGUST

Barfleur – ⚓ Regattas.
☎02 33 54 02 48.

Carrouges – 🏹 Festival of hunting
and fishing (1st weekend of
August). ☎02 33 80 66 33.

Crèvecoeur-en-Auges –
Les Mediévales (Medieval Festival)
(1st 2 weeks of August).
☎02 31 63 02 45.
www.chateau-de-crevecoeur.com.

Jobourg – *Foire aux moutons* (Sheep Fair) (1st Saturday of August). ✆02 33 10 00 40.

St-Lô – 🐎 Normandy Horse Show (around 15 August). ✆02 14 29 00 17. www.saint-lo.fr.

AUGUST

Barfleur – Antiques Show. ✆02 33 54 02 48.

Blangy-sur-Bresle – Glass Festival.

Deauville – 🐎 Sale of yearlings (3rd or 4th week of August). ✆02 31 14 40 00.

Deauville – 🐎 Grand Prix: Horse racing events and Polo Championship Cup. ✆02 31 14 40 00.

Deauville – *A Musical August*, a week of classical music. ✆02 31 14 40 00.

Dieppe – Biennial international kite festival (2nd–3rd weekend August, next in 2012). ✆02 32 90 04 95. www.dieppe-cerf-volant.org.

Houlgate – Festijazz (3rd weekend of August). www.jazzcaen.com.

Laval – *Face des Etoiles* summer festival. ✆02 43 49 19 55.

Île de Tatihou – *Les Traversées de Tatihou*: Music festival on the island, near St Vaast-la-Hougue (2nd or 3rd week of August, depending on tides). http://tatihou.manche.fr/festival-traversees-tatihou.asp.

FESTIVALS OF THE VIRGIN, ON OR ABOUT 15 AUGUST

Douvres-la-Délivrande – Feast Day of the Coronation of the Virgin: Procession of the Black Virgin (1st or 2nd Sat after 15 August). ✆02 31 36 24 24.

Lisieux – Procession to the Smiling Virgin. ✆02 31 48 55 08. www.therese-de-lisieux.com.

Pontmain – Pilgrimage to the Virgin. www.sanctuaire-pontmain.com. ✆02 43 05 07 26.

Pont d'Ouilly – The Pardon of St-Roche (Sun after 15 August). ✆02 31 69 80 46.

St-Cyr-la-Rosière – Festival of the Percheron Horse at the Priory of Ste-Gauburge. ✆02 33 73 48 06.

SEPTEMBER

Alençon, **Argentan**, **Bagnoles-de-l'Orne**, **Mortagne**, **Flers**, **Sées** – *Septembre musicale de l'Orne*. Weekend classical music concerts throughout the month. ✆02 33 26 99 99.

Deauville – American Film Festival (1st week of September). ✆02 31 14 40 00.

Haras National du Pin – 🐎 Competition for Percheron horses (last weekend of September). ✆02 33 36 68 68.

Lessay – *Foire de la Ste-Croix*: Holy Cross Fair, the largest and most typical fair in Normandy (2nd weekend of September). ✆02 33 76 58 80.

Lisieux – Feast of Ste-Thérèse (last weekend of September). ✆02 31 48 55 08.

SEPTEMBER–OCTOBER

Bellême – International Mushroom Festival. www.mycologiades.com.

Fécamp – ⛵Multicup 60' Catamaran sailing races, boat salon (4 or 5 days).

OCTOBER

Cherbourg, Foire de Cherbourg. Crafts presented around a theme that changes each year. Last weekend of October. ✆02 33 93 52 02.

Deauville – Equi'Days, Festival of Calvados horses and races.

Deauville – Paris–Deauville Rally, with classic cars.

Haras national du Pin – 🐎 Horse racing events; prestigious cross-country race and procession of carriages and stallions. ✆02 33 36 68 68.

Mont-St-Michel – Feast of the Archangel Michael: mass in the abbey church in the presence of the bishops of Bayeux and Coutances (1st Sunday of October). ✆02 33 60 14 05.

OCTOBER–NOVEMBER

Caen – Puces Caennaises: Fleamarket (last weekend of November) ✆02 31 29 99 99.

Les Flambarts, Dreux

© Patrick Forget/SAGAPHOTO.COM/Alamy

Calvados – 🐎 Equi' Days: Horse-riding events throughout the region. ℰ02 31 27 90 30.

Neufchâtel-en-Bray – International/ National Agricultural Show. Juried competitions, together with Feast of St Martin Fair. ℰ02 35 93 22 96.

Seine-Maritime and Eure départements – Several cities participate in autumn festivities in Normandy; music, theatre and dance. ℰ02 32 33 79 00.

DECEMBER

Sées – Turkey Fair. An event over a hundred years old. Breeders, juried events, sale of foie gras. ℰ02 33 28 74 79.

Dreux – *Les Flambarts* Carnival over three days. Parades, sailing of tiny lighted boats, Christmas fair, skating rink. Festivities celebrating light. ℰ02 37 38 87 00.

St-Hilaire-du Harcouët – Nativity Play (2nd fortnight of December) with over 40 actors, many live animals. ℰ02 33 90 80 09. www.creche-vivante.org.

Caen – Christmas fair. Skating rink, market, parades, storytelling, Christmas lighting. ℰ02 31 27 14 14.

GASTRONOMIC FAIRS

Every year a number of fairs and events are held throughout Normandy offering local specialities and special events. The following list offers a sample:

MARCH

International Black Blood Sausage Festival in **Mortagne-au-Perche** (3rd weekend of March). Sweet, savoury blood sausages, over 600 international competitors. ℰ02 33 85 11 18.

MAY AND JUNE

Festival of AOC and AOP Regional Products of Normandy in **Cambremer** (1st weekend of May). Major event put on by region. ℰ02 31 63 08 87.

Mussels Fair in **Le Tréport** (1st weekend in May or June). ℰ02 35 86 05 69.

Cherry Fair in **Vernon** (4 days over Whit' weekend/Pentecost) ℰ02 32 64 38 00.

JULY AND AUGUST

Cheese Fair in **Livarot** (1st weekend of August); many regional products too. ℰ02 31 63 47 39.

Carrot Festival in **Créances** (2nd Sat in August); competitions, regional products. ℰ02 33 46 30 18.

SEPTEMBER

Cheese Fair in **Neufchâtel-en-Bray** (3rd Sun of September); held during Heritage Days; farm market, crafts products, cheese recipe competition, parade of gastronomic brotherhoods. ℰ02 35 93 22 96.

OCTOBER–NOVEMBER

Cider festival in **Beuvron-en-Auge**, (All Saints' weekend); open-air market featuring apple and other products; cider press, tastings. ✆02 31 63 08 87.

Prawn Festival in **Honfleur** (1st weekend of October); concerts, workshops, kids' event, prawn-shelling competition. ✆02 31 89 23 30.

Foie gras market in **Le Neubourg** (1 Sat in October, in November, and in December). ✆02 32 35 17 33.

Festival of gastronomy in **Rouen** (1 weekend) in Old Market; cooking demonstrations, regional products. ✆02 32 08 32 40.

Apple Fair in **Vimoutiers** (mid-October). ✆02 33 39 80 60.

Surf and turf fair in **Cherbourg**, mid November. ✆02 33 93 52 02.

Herring Fairs in **Dieppe** (scallops too), **Fécamp, Le Tréport, Etretat** and **St-Valery-en-Caux**. ✆02 35 12 10 10.

THE CHANNEL ISLANDS

For **Jersey** tourism information: ✆+44 (0) 1534 44 88 00 and www.jersey.com.

For **Guernsey**: ✆+44 (0)1481 723552 and www.visitguernsey.com.

For **Herm**: ✆+44 (0) 1481 72 23 77 and www.herm-island.com.

For **Sark**: ✆+44 (0) 1481 83 23 45 and www.sark.info.

For **Alderney**: ✆+44 (0) 1481 822811 and www.visitalderney.com.

APRIL

Guernsey – Spring Floral Guernsey Festival Week.

Herm – Tuesday garden tours through end August.

Sark – Wildflower Fortnight. Guided tours.

MAY–JUNE

Guernsey & Jersey – Liberation Day (9 May) commemorating WWII liberation of the islands.

Guernsey - Healthspan Spring Walking Week; Photography Festival; Literary Festival (readings, talks, book fair).

Jersey – Spring Walking Week.

JUNE–JULY

Guernsey & Jersey – *Le Tour des Ports de la Manche* yacht race.

Guernsey – La Fete de Musique de Ville at St Peter Port (live music); Le Viaer Marché (food, entertainment, traditional Guernsey evening).

Jersey – Jersey in Bloom Festival (talks, open gardens, floral festival); *Bonne Nuit* Harbour Festival (water and beach events).

Sark – Folk festival (major music event); sheep-racing weekend.

AUGUST

Alderney – Carnival week.

Guernsey – North Show and Battle of Flowers.

Jersey – Samarès Manor Autumn Fair; Battle of Flowers.

Sark – Grand Autumn Show. Preserves, baked goods, produce.

SEPTEMBER

Guernsey & Jersey – Autumn Walking Week (guided walks); Channel Islands Festival of Arts and Crafts.

Guernsey (morning) & Jersey (afternoon) - International Air Display including commemorative Battle of Britain memorial flight; one of Europe's major free air displays.

OCTOBER

Guernsey – Floral Guernsey Autumn Festival.

Jersey – Standard Chartered Jersey Marathon (a run through St Helier and across the island); Autumn Cattle, Fruit, Flower and Vegetable Show.

OCTOBER–NOVEMBER

Guernsey & Jersey – Tennerfest, gastronomic festival with meals at reduced prices.

DECEMBER

Jersey – *La Fête de Noué* fair: moonlight walks, light displays, markets, parades, street theatre.

Know Before You Go

USEFUL WEBSITES

The following selected websites offer information in English and provide links to other useful sites.

www.normandy-tourism.org

This official site of the Normandy Tourist Board provides information about places to visit, maps, suggested itineraries as well as tips for those interested in sports, gastronomy, the travel industry, etc. There are also links to tourist offices, for booking hotels and lodging, transport and other services.

www.francetourism.com

This commercial site offers information about France generally, with a section on each region, including Normandy. Maps, information on tours, places of interest, hotel and transport bookings and lots of links.

www.franceguide.com

The site of the French Government Tourist Office offers information aimed at foreign visitors, with sites adapted for each country. It has a particularly good practical information section, and a list of facilities accessible to people with disabilities.

www.normandie.visite.org

This site is updated daily and provides weather news, schedules for festivals and other events, and tourist information as well as links to websites covering news, education, business, shopping, chat sites, e-cards, etc.

www.abmc.gov

The site of the American Battle Monuments Commission offers information on events at the Normandy American Cemetery and Memorial. There is a link to the World War II database giving the location of individual casualties buried in ABMC cemeteries.

www.info-france-usa.org

The French Embassy's website provides practical information (visa requirements, driving, transport, tipping), a link to the US Embassy website in Paris (www.amb-usa.fr), recent news stories, and links (consulates in the US, regions, cities, ministries, commercial sites).

www.ambafrance-ca.org

The Cultural Service of the French Embassy in Ottawa has a bright and varied site information about travel in France, France–Canada relations, links to consulates, and much more.

www.visiteurope.com

The European Travel Commission provides useful information on travelling in 30 European countries, and includes links to commercial booking services (such as vehicle hire), rail schedules, weather reports and more.

TOURIST OFFICES

For information, brochures, maps and assistance in planning a trip to France, you should apply to the French Tourist Office, represented by Atout France, in your own country.

FRENCH TOURIST OFFICES ABROAD

Australia – New Zealand
Sydney – Level 13, 25 Bligh St, Sydney.
℘61 (0)2 9231 5244.
http://au.franceguide.com.

Canada
Montreal – 1800 ave McGill College, Suite 1010, Montreal, Quebec H3A 3J6.
℘(514) 288-2026.
http://ca-en.franceguide.com.

Ireland
Dublin – 30 Upper Merrion Street Dublin 2.
℘(1) 560 235 235.
http://ie.franceguide.com.

South Africa
Johannesburg –

3rd floor Village Walk Office Tower cnr Maude and Rivonia, Sandton.
☎ 00 27 (0) 11 523 82 92.
http://za.franceguide.com.

United Kingdom
London – Lincoln House, 300 High Holborn, London WC1V 7JH.
☎09068 244 123 (60p/min).
http://uk.franceguide.com.

United States - New York
825 Third Avenue, 29th Floor, New York NY 10022.
☎514 288 1904.
http://us.franceguide.com.

REGIONAL TOURIST OFFICES

A plethora of maps, brochures and other information can be downloaded directly from the website for the Comité Régional de Tourisme de Normandie, the overseeing office of Normandy's individual departmental tourist offices, which can be contacted for more precise local information. All offices respond rapidly during opening hours if you address them by filling out the form found on their websites.

♦ **Comité Régional de Tourisme de Normandie**
14 r. Charles-Corbeau, 27000 Evreux.
☎02 32 33 79 00.
www.normandy-tourism.org.

Departmental Tourist Offices
♦ **Calvados**
8 r. Renoir, 14054 Caen Cedex 4.
☎02 31 27 90 30.
www.calvados-tourisme.com.
♦ **Eure**
Hôtel du Département
bd Georges Chauvin
BP 367, 27003 Evreux Cedex.
☎02 32 62 04 27.
www.eure-tourisme.fr
♦ **Manche**
Maison du Département
98 rte de Candol, CS 73108
50008 St-Lô Cedex.
☎02 33 05 98 70.
www.manchetourisme.com.

♦ **Mayenne**
84 av. Robert Buron, BP 0325, 53003 Laval.
☎02 43 53 18 18.
www.tourisme-mayenne.com.
♦ **Orne**
86 r. St-Blaise, BP 50, 61002 Alençon Cedex.
☎02 33 28 88 71.
www.ornetourisme.com.
♦ **Seine-Maritime**
6 r. Couronné, BP 60, 76420 Bihorel.
☎02 35 12 10 10.
www.seine-maritime-tourisme.com.

TOURIST INFORMATION CENTRES

Contact details for the local tourist office of each Principal Sight can be found in the green-coloured Orient Panels of the *Discovering Normandy* section of this guide.

INTERNATIONAL VISITORS
DOCUMENTS
Passport
Nationals of countries within the European Union entering France need only a national identity card or, in the case of the British, a passport. Nationals of other countries must be in possession of a valid national passport. In case of loss or theft, report to your embassy or consulate and the local police. You must carry your documents with you at all times; they can be checked anywhere.

Visa
No entry visa is required for Australian, Canadian, New Zealand and US citizens travelling as tourists and staying less than 90 days, except for students planning to study in France. If in doubt, apply to your local French Consulate.
US citizens should download *Know Before You Go* for free at www.pueblo. gsa.gov (click on travel publications). General passport information is available by phone toll-free from the Federal Information Center (item 5 on the automated menu), ☎800-688-9889.

EMBASSIES AND CONSULATES IN FRANCE

Australia	Embassy	4 rue Jean-Rey, 75015 Paris. ☎01 40 59 33 00. www.france.embassy.gov.au.
Canada	Embassy	37 avenue Montaigne, 75008 Paris. ☎01 44 43 29 00. www.international.gc.ca.
Eire	Embassy	4 rue Rude, 75016 Paris. ☎01 44 17 67 00. www.embassyofireland.fr.
New Zealand	Embassy	7 ter rue Léonard-de-Vinci, 75016 Paris. ☎01 45 00 24 11. www.nzembassy.com/france.
South Africa	Embassy	59 quai d'Orsay, 75007 Paris. ☎01 53 59 23 23. www.afriquesud.net.
UK	Embassy	35 rue du Faubourg St-Honoré, 75008 Paris. ☎01 44 51 31 00. http://ukinfrance.fco.gov.uk/en.
	Consulate	16 bis rue d'Anjou, 75008 Paris. ☎01 44 51 31 00.
	Consulate	353 boulevard du Président Wilson, 33073 Bordeaux. ☎05 57 22 21 10.
USA	Embassy	2 avenue Gabriel, 75008 Paris. ☎01 43 12 22 22. http://france.usembassy.gov.
	Consulate	2 rue St-Florentin, 75001 Paris. ☎01 43 12 22 22.

US passport forms can be downloaded from http://travel.state.gov.

CUSTOMS

In the UK, **HM Revenue & Customs** (www.hmrc.gov.uk) publishes *A Customs Guide for Travellers Entering the UK* (download only) on customs regulations and duty-free allowances. **US citizens** should view *Tips for Traveling Abroad* online *(http://travel.state.gov/travel/tips/tips_1232.html)* for general information on visa requirements, customs regulations, medical care, etc. There are no customs formalities when bringing caravans, pleasure boats and outboard motors into France for a stay of less than six months, but a boat's registration certificate should be kept on board.
Canadians can consult and download *I Declare* at www.canadaonline.about.com. For **Australians**, *Know Before You Go* is available at www.customs.gov.au. For **New Zealanders**, *Advice for Travellers* is at www.customs.govt.nz. After an absence of about a week, **Americans** can bring home, tax free,

US$800 worth of goods; **Canadians** CDN$750; **Australians** AUS$900 and **New Zealanders** NZ$700. People living in a Member State of the European Union are not restricted in regard to goods for private use, but the recommended allowances for alcohol and tobacco can be found at www.taxfreetravel.com/UK%20duty%20free%20allowances.
There are no customs formalities for holidaymakers bringing their cars or caravans into France for a stay of less than six months. No customs document is necessary for pleasure boats and outboard motors for a stay of less than six months but the registration certificate should be kept on board.

HEALTH

First aid and medical advice are available from chemists/drugstores *(pharmacie)* identified by the green cross sign. In every town, a *pharmacie* remains on duty at night, based on a revolving schedule. All prescription drugs must be clearly labelled; it is essential you carry the prescriptions.

You should take out comprehensive insurance coverage as recipients of medical treatment in French hospitals or clinics must pay. Nationals of non-EU countries should check with their insurance companies about policy limitations. **Americans and Canadians** can contact the International Association for Medical Assistance to Travelers: for the USA ℘(716)754-4883 or for Canada ℘(416) 652-0137 or ℘(519) 836-0102. www.iamat.org.

British and Irish citizens (and all EU citizens) should apply for a European Health Insurance Card (EHIC), which has replaced the E111. Everyone in the family must have one, even children. **UK subjects** can apply online to www.dh.gov.uk/travellers, or telephone ℘0845 606 2030, or pick up an application at a post office. **Irish citizens** may visit www.ehic.ie. UK subjects travelling to the **Channel Islands** should carry private health insurance, as National Health Service does not cover them.

ACCESSIBILITY

The sights described in this guide which are easily accessible to people of reduced mobility are indicated for the Sights in the *Admission times and charges* by the symbol ♿.
For a list of accessible sites, carrying the Tourisme et Handicap designation, go to www.franceguide.com. For Normandy, booklets in English describing disabled access can be downloaded from www.normandie-tourisme.fr. The principal French source for information on facilities is the **Association de Paralysés de France**, 17 bd Auguste-Blanqui, 75013 Paris, www.apf.asso.fr (in French only). The APF publishes a *Handiguide* which may be purchased on the website; it lists over 600 French accommodations offering access to persons with reduced mobility.
The **Michelin Guide France** and the **Michelin Camping Caravaning France**: Revised every year, these guides indicate where to find facilities accessible to the disabled.
The French railway (SNCF) gives information on travel at www.voyages-sncf.com, as does Air France at www.airfrance.fr.

THE CHANNEL ISLANDS
ENTRY REGULATIONS

Passports are not required for British subjects. The same requirements apply for other tourists as in France.

TRAVEL
By Air
There are flights to **Jersey**, **Guernsey** and **Alderney**:
Jersey, **Guernsey** and **Alderney** airports are served by British Airways, (www.britishairways.com), Flybe (www.flybe.com), Air Southwest (www.airsouthwest.com), BmiBaby (www.bmibaby.com), Jet2 (www.jet2.com), Blue Islands (www.blueislands.com) as well as Swiss (www.swiss.com) from Zurich and TwinJet (www.twinjet.com) from Paris.
Aurigny Air Services offers flights between Guernsey, Jersey and Alderney and several British airports as well as Dinard in France. www.aurigny.com.

By Sea
Fast catamaran ferries run to the Channel Islands from England (Poole, Weymouth and Portsmouth) and France (Granville, Diélette, Carteret, St-Malo). Contact www.condorferries.co.uk; www.hdferries.org; www.manche-iles-express.com.
Scheduled ferries run among the islands. Note that, for all ferry services, where they land and at what time depends on tides.

Getting There and Getting Around

BY AIR

The principal cities of Normandy are served out of St-Exupéry airport in Lyons.

Brit'Air (Air France) has flights to and from Caen, Rouen and Le Havre daily. Information and reservations: ℘0 820 820 820. www.airfrance.com or www.britair.com.

Twin Jet has flights connecting Paris/Orly and Cherbourg-Jersey. ℘0 892 707 737. www.twinjet.net. The regional airports are:

Aéroport de Caen-Carpiquet – ℘02 31 71 20 10. www.caen.aeroport.fr.

Aéroport de Cherbourg-Maupertus ℘02 33 88 57 60. www.cherbourg.aeroport.fr.

Aéroport Le Havre-Octeville – ℘02 35 54 65 00. www.havre.aeroport.fr.

Aéroport Rouen Vallée de Seine – ℘02 35 79 41 00. www.rouen.aeroport.fr.

BY SEA

There are numerous **cross-Channel passenger and car ferry services**, from the United Kingdom and Ireland.

- **P & O Ferries**, Channel House, Channel View Road, Dover, Kent CT17 9JT. ℘08705 980 333 (in the UK) or ℘0825 120 156 (in France) www.poferries.com. Service between Dover and Calais.

- **Norfolk Line**, Norfolk House, Eastern Docks, Dover, Kent CT16 1JA. ℘870 870 10 20 (in the UK) or ℘03 28 59 01 01 (in France). www.norfolkline.ferries.org. Service between Dover and Dunkerque.

- **Brittany Ferries**, Millbay Docks, Plymouth, Devon PL1 3EW. ℘0870 9 076 103 (in the UK) or ℘0825 828 828 (in France). www.brittany-ferries.co.uk.

Service between Portsmouth, Poole, Plymouth and Cork and ports in France and Spain.

- **Irish Ferries**, Ferryport, Alexandra Road, Dublin 1. ℘8705 17 17 17 (UK), ℘0818 300 400 (in N. Ireland), ℘0818 300 400 (ROI), ℘(01) 44 88 54 50 (France). www.irishferries.com. Service between Rosslare in Ireland and Cherbourg and Roscoff in France.

- **Seafrance Ferries Ltd**. Whitfield Court, Honeywood Close, Whitfield, Kent CT16 3PX. ℘0871 663 2546 (in the UK). www.seafrance.com. Service between Dover and Calais.

- **LD Lines**, Continental Ferry Port, Wharf Road, Portsmouth P02 8OW. ℘0844 576 8836 (in the UK) or **www.ldlines.co.uk**. Service between Dover and Boulogne.

BY RAIL

Eurostar runs via the Channel Tunnel between **London** (St Pancras International) and Paris in 2hr15min. The trip from **London** to Lille takes 1hr20min. At present, the only high-speed train serving Normandy connects **Marseilles** and **Le Havre** in 6hr30min.

Bookings and information: ℘0345 303 030 in the UK; ℘1-888-EUROSTAR in the USA or www.eurostar.com. Or contact the French national railways **www.voyages-sncf.com**. SNCF operates a **telephone information, reservation and prepayment service in English** from 8am to 7pm (French time). In France call ℘0892 33 35 39 (when calling from outside France, drop the initial 0 and add 33). Dial 42 as soon as the connection is made. The **Corail Intercités** network connects Paris with Norman cities: Rouen, Le Havre, Dieppe, Trouville, Dreux, L'Aigle, Beauvais and Le Tréport. Trains run several times daily. **Trains express régionaux (TER)** form an efficient local network, which also makes use of buses.

Eurailpass, Flexipass, Eurailpass Youth, EurailDrive Pass and

Saverpass may be purchased by residents of countries outside the EU. In the Western Hemisphere go to **www.raileurope.com**. Alternatively, in the **USA**, contact Rail Europe ✆800-622-8600. In **Canada**, contact ✆800-361-7245. **Australians**, call ✆1300 555 003, for **New Zealanders**, call ✆649 377 5415. **European residents** can buy an individual country pass if not a resident of the country where they plan to use it. In the **UK or Ireland**, contact Rail Europe ltd at www. raileurope.co.uk or ✆0870 848 848. Tickets bought in France must be validated *(composter)* by using the orange automatic date-stamping machines at the platform entrance. Failure to do so may result in a fine.

BY BUS

Each *département* in Normandy operates local and intercity bus services with inexpensive fares. Information is available, in French, from the website of each *département*. **Calvados**: www.cg14.fr; **Eure**: www.cg27.fr; **Manche**: http:// manche.fr; **Orne**: www.cg61.fr; **Seine-Maritime**: or www.seine-maritime.net/fr.
You can also consult local tourist offices once you arrive in Normandy.

DRIVING IN FRANCE
PLANNING YOUR ROUTE

Michelin **Local** maps give a close, detailed look at two or three *départements*, with maps of major towns. For Normandy, you will need **Local 310** (covering the *départements* of Mayenne, Orne, Sarthe), **303** (Calvados, Manche) and **304** (Eure, Seine-Maritime), and may also want the **Regional 513** (Normandy, including maps of Caen and Rouen) and **517** (Pays-de-la-Loire) maps, which list towns, show secondary roads and offer information for tourists.
The map of France 721 offers a view of all Normandy, with major arteries leading from your point of arrival.

The latest Michelin route-planning service is available on the internet, **www.ViaMichelin.com**. Travellers can calculate a precise route using such options as shortest route, route avoiding toll roads, GPS navigation, Michelin-recommended route and gain access to tourist information (hotels, restaurants, attractions). The roads are very busy during the holiday period (particularly weekends in July and August), and you should consider recommended secondary routes (signposted as *Bison Futé – itinéraires bis*). For information on traffic conditions, call ✆0 892 681 077 or visit **www.autoroutes.fr**.

DOCUMENTS

Travellers from other EU countries or North America can drive in France with a valid national, home-state or provincial **driving licence** for up to a year; you should have a French translation attached. An **international driving licence** is recommended, however. To procure one in the **USA**, contact the National Automobile Club ✆1-800-622-2136, www.nationalautoclub.com, or contact your local branch of the American Automobile Association or go online to www.aaa.com.
In Canada, contact www.caa.ca.
The Australian Automobile Association is at www.aaa.asn.au and the **New Zealand Automobile Association** is at www.aa.co.nz.
For the vehicle, you must have the registration *(carte grise)* and the insurance certificate *(carte verte)*.

INSURANCE

Certain motoring organisations (AAA, CAA, AA, RAC) offer accident insurance and breakdown service schemes for members. Check with your current insurance company in regard to coverage while abroad. If you plan to hire a car using your credit card, you may have liability insurance automatically (and thus save paying for optimum coverage).

ROAD REGULATIONS

The minimum driving age in France is 18. Traffic drives on the right. It is compulsory for all passengers, in front and back seats, to wear **seat belts**. Children under the age of 10 must travel on the back seat of the vehicle. In the case of a **breakdown** a red warning triangle or hazard warning lights are obligatory. In the absence of stop signs at intersections, as in roundabouts, cars must **yield to the right**. Vehicles must stop when the lights turn red at road junctions and may filter to the right only when indicated by an amber arrow. The regulations on **drinking and driving** (limited to 0.05 percent or 0.50g/l) and **speeding** are strictly enforced – usually by an on-the-spot fine and/or confiscation of the vehicle. From Spring 2012, all cars must carry a compulsory portable alcohol breathalyzer kit.

Speed Limits

Speed limits are 50kph (31mph) in towns and built-up areas; 90kph/56mph on ordinary roads; 110kph/68mph on dual carriageways and motorways without tolls; and 130kph/81mph on toll motorways (*autoroutes*). Check for variations.

Parking

In town there are zones where parking is either restricted or subject to a fee; tickets should be obtained from ticket machines (*horodateurs* – small change necessary) and displayed inside the windscreen on the driver's side; failure to display may result in a fine, or towing and impoundment. In some towns

where you find blue parking zones (*zone bleue*) marked by a blue line on the pavement or road and a 🅿 sign, a cardboard disc gives you 1hr30min (2hr30min over lunchtime) free. Discs are sold in supermarkets or gas stations (ask for a *disque de stationnement*) and are sometimes given away free.

Tolls

Most motorway sections are subject to a toll (*péage*). Pay by cash/credit card.

Fuel: Petrol/Gasoline

French service stations dispense *sans plomb* 98 (super unleaded 98), *sans plomb* 95, *diesel/gazole* (diesel) and GPL (LPG). Fuel in France is relatively expensive; is usually cheaper off the motorway, so check the hypermarkets.

CAR RENTAL

There are car rental agencies at airports, railway stations and in all large towns throughout France. Most European cars have manual gearboxes; automatic cars are available only if an advance reservation is made. Drivers must be over 21; between ages 21 and 25, drivers must pay an extra daily fee. Hiring a car in France is expensive: take advantage of fly-drive offers, or ask a travel agent.

MOTORHOME RENTAL

Several companies offer motorhome rental in France. Caravans are not allowed into the Channel Islands. See: www.motorhomesworldwide.com; www.ukandeuropetravel.com; www.car-rental-hire.co.uk; www.ideamerge.com.

RENTAL CARS – CENTRAL RESERVATION IN FRANCE		
Avis:	✆ 08 20 05 05 05	www.avis.fr
Europcar:	✆ 08 25 35 23 52	www.europcar.fr
Budget France:	✆ 08 00 10 00 01	www.budget.fr
Hertz France:	✆ 01 39 38 38 38	www.hertz.fr
SIXT- Eurorent:	✆ 01 40 65 01 00	www.sixt.fr
National-CITER:	✆ 01 45 22 88 40	www.citer.fr

Where to Stay and Eat

The *Michelin Green Guide* is pleased to offer a selection of accommodations and restaurants for Normandy. Turn to the **Addresses** sections within the individual Sights for descriptions and prices of typical places to stay **(Stay)** and to eat **(Eat)**. The Legend on the cover flap explains the symbols and abbreviations used in these sections. ☺*Please note: Coin ranges for the Channel Islands are derived from approximate conversions of the euro coin ranges in the same Legend into Pound Sterling (£).*

WHERE TO STAY
FINDING A HOTEL

Turn to the **Addresses** within individual sight listings for descriptions and prices of typical places to stay **(Stay)** with local flair. Use the **Places to Stay** map in the following pages to identify recommended places for overnight stops. It can be used in conjunction with the **Michelin Guide France** – with its well-known star-rating system – which lists an even greater selection of hotels and restaurants.

For further assistance, **La Fédération Loisirs Accueil** is a booking service that has offices in most French *départements*: 280 bd St-Germain, 75007 Paris. ☎01 44 11 10 44. http://www.loisirsaccueilfrance.com.

Relais et Châteaux provides information on booking in luxury hotels with character: 15 r. Galvani, 75017 Paris. ☎01 45 72 90 00. www.relaischateaux.com.

ECONOMY CHAIN HOTELS

If you need a place to stop en route, these can be useful, as they are inexpensive (€35–45 for a double room) and generally located near the main road. There may not be a restaurant; rooms are small, with a television and private bathroom. Rather than sort through hotels yourself, you can go to websites that cover several chains, where you can select your hotel and book online:

www.accorhotels.com covers some 1,400 hotels in france, including the Formule 1 chain, at about 35€, as well as Novotel, Mercure, Sofitel, etc.

www.activehotels.com covers a wide range of hotels and reviews. www.day-tripper.net covers reasonably priced hotels, by location, throughout France.

www.louvrehotels.com covers more expensive hotels (more than 60€) Campanile, Kyriad, and Première Class. Here are some modestly priced chains:

- **Akena**
  ☎01 69 84 85 17.
  www.hotels-akena.com.
- **B&B**
  ☎02 98 33 75 00.
  www.hotel-bb.com.
- **Etap Hôtel**
  ☎08 92 68 89 00.
  www.etaphotel.com.
- **Best Hôtel**
  ☎03 28 27 46 69.
  www.besthotel.fr.

RURAL ACCOMMODATION

The **Maison des Gîtes de France et du Tourisme Vert** is an information service on self-catering accommodation in the regions of France. *Gîtes* usually take the form of a cottage or apartment decorated in the local style where visitors can make themselves at home. The organisation also covers specialised gîtes for fishing, camping, hiking, etc.

Contact **Gîtes de France:** 59 r. St-Lazare, 75439 Paris Cedex 09. ☎01 49 70 75 75. www.gites-de-france-normandie.com. You can order five different brochures at no charge; two can be downloaded. In total, the association lists some 2,000 rural gîtes and more than 1,000 bed-and-breakfasts in Normandy.

The publication **Bienvenue à la Ferme** lists some 300 Norman farmers who offer accommodation of varying degrees of comfort on their farms, including meals: Service Agriculture et Tourisme, 9 av. George V, 75008 Paris,

Places to stay

- ● Seaside resort
- ● Spa

   Seaside resorts ⚓ and spas ⚕
   are classified according to the
   quality and range of facilities offered

- ● Short holiday
- ▭ Weekend destination
- — Overnight stop
- ⛵ Marina

Abbeville

⛵ ⚓ le Tréport

Eu

⚓ Varengeville

Vasterival

St-Valéry-en-Caux

DIEPPE

Veulettes-s-Mer

Ste-Marguerite-s-Mer

⚓ FÉCAMP

ÉTRETAT

FORGES-LES-EAUX

CAUDEBEC-EN-CAUX

Duclair

⚓ LE HAVRE

Parc naturel

régional des Boucles

de la Seine normande

ROUEN

Lyons-la-Forêt

⚓⚓⚓ ⛵

DEAUVILLE

le Bec-Hellouin

St-Pierre-du-Vauvray

les Andelys

LISIEUX

Brionne

Orbec

Évreux

Conches-en-Ouche

Ivry-la-Bataille

Normandie-Maine

Parc naturel

régional

Chartres

⚓ Alençon

du Perche

Fresnay-s-Sarthe

Châteaudun

LE MANS

ORLÉANS

Rivers and roads labelled: A 16, D 925, Bresle, A 28, Béthune, N 27, D 915, N 29, D 926, A 29, A 151, A 28, Andelle, D 915, A 131, N 31, A 13, N 14, SEINE, Epte, A 13, N 13, N 13, N 154, A 13, Touques, N 138, Risle, Iton, Avre, Eure, N 12, N 26, N 12, N 154, A 11, Dives, Eure, N 10, A 10, N 154, D 955, Huisne, Loir, Sarthe, A 11, D 955, Loir, A 81, A 28, A 11, N 157, N 10, N 157, A 10

℘01 53 57 11 44. You can order the free book or download it at www.bienvenue-a-la-ferme.com.

For hikers, skiers, climbers, kayakers, bicyclists and others seeking rustic accommodation off the beaten track, consult www.gites-refuges.com. The website owners also publish a down-loadable guide: *Gîtes d'Étape, Refuges* by A and S Mouraret (scroll down homepage; €5). The **Fédération Française des Stations Vertes de Vacances** (*BP 71698, 21016 Dijon Cedex. ℘03 80 54 10 50, www.stationsvertes.com*) lists family-orientated accommodation, leisure facilities and natural attractions in rural locations through-out France, including Normandy.

BED-AND-BREAKFAST

Gîtes de France publishes a booklet Tous nos Gîtes en Normandie (20€) updated yearly, which lists establish-ments offering a room and breakfast at a reasonable price. Buy online at http://librairie.gites-de-france.fr.

CAMPING

There are many officially graded sites with varying standards of facilities throughout the region; the **Michelin Camping & Caravanning France** guide lists a selection of the best campsites, visited regularly by our inspectors. Tourist offices and their websites also provide lists of camp-sites.

VACATION RENTAL PROPERTIES

La Fédération National Clévacances offers a list of more than 1,000 rental properties and rooms in Normandy: 54 bd de l'Embouchure, BP 52166, 31022 Toulouse Cedex. ℘05 61 13 55 66. www.clevacances.com.

YOUTH HOSTELS

Youth hostels (*auberges de jeunesse*) offer spartan but inexpensive and sometimes convivial accommodation. You do not have to be a youth to stay in a hostel. **Ligue Française pour les Auberges de Jeunesse** (*67 r. Vergni-aud, Bâtiment K, 75013 Paris. ℘01 44 16 78 78. www.auberges-de-jeunesse.com*). Membership in the Ligue (LFAJ), which issues a membership card, is available for an annual fee of €11 for those under age 26, and €16 for those older. **Fédération Unie des Auberges de la Jeunesse** (*27 r. Pajol, 75018 Paris. ℘01 44 89 87 27. www.fuaj.org*). The **Fuaj** card costs 11€ a year (under age 26), and €16 for those older and €23 for families with children under 14. You will find affiliated hostels in Bayeux, Caen, Cherbourg, Dieppe, Eu, Genêts, Granville, Pontorson and Vernon.

To obtain an International Youth Hos-tel Federation card, contact the IYHF in your own country: **USA** ℘202-783-6161, www.hiusa.org; **UK** ℘1707-324-170, www.hihostels.com; **Canada** ℘613-237-7884, www.hihostels.ca; **Australia** ℘61-2-9565-1669, www.hihostels.com. You can book through www.hihostels.com.

WHERE TO EAT

A selection of places to eat in the different locations covered in this guide can be found in the **Addresses** appearing in the section entitled *Discovering Normandy*.

Use the **Michelin Guide France**, with its famous star-rating system and hundreds of establishments all over France, for a greater choice.

In the countryside, restaurants usually serve lunch between noon and 2pm and dinner between 7.30pm and 10pm. It is not always easy to find an establishment open between lunch and dinner, as "round-the-clock" restaurants are still scarce in the prov-inces. However, a hungry traveller can usually get a sandwich in a cafe, and ordinary hot dishes may be available in a brasserie.

Many restaurants participate in the **Assiette de Pays** programme, which promotes local specialities at 6–18€ for a single dish and drink; participants post the logo in their windows, and you can get a list at www.normandie-pays.com, under *Assiette de Pays*.

Useful Words and Phrases

Commonly Useful Words

	Translation
Goodbye	Au revoir
Hello/Good Morning	Bonjour
Excuse Me	Excusez-moi, Pardon
Thank You	Merci
Yes/no	Oui/non
Please	S'il vous plaît

Sights

	Translation
Abbaye	Abbey
Beffroi	Belfry
Chapelle	Chapel
Cimetière	Cemetery
Cloître	Cloisters
Cour	Courtyard
Couvent	Convent
Écluse	Lock (Canal)
Église	Church
Gothique	Gothic
Halle	Covered market
Jardin	Garden
Mairie	Town Hall
Maison	House
Marché	Market
Monastère	Monastery
Moulin	Windmill
Musée	Museum
Place	Square
Pont	Bridge
Port	Port/harbour
Quai	Quay
Remparts	Ramparts
Romain	Roman
Roman	Romanesque
Tour	Tower

Natural Sites

	Translation
Barrage	Dam
Belvédère	Viewpoint
Cascade	Waterfall
Corniche	Ledge
Côte	Coast, hillside
Étang	Pond
Falaise	Cliff
Forêt	Forest
Grotte	Cave
Lac	Lake
Marais	Marsh
Plage	Beach
Rivière	River
Ruisseau	Stream
Signal	Beacon
Source	Spring
Vallée	Valley

On the Road

	Translation
Car Park	Parking
Diesel	Diesel/Gazole
Driving Licence	Permis de conduire
East	Est
Garage (for repairs)	Garage
Left	Gauche
Motorway/highway	Autoroute
North	Nord
Parking Meter	Horodateur
Petrol/Gas	Essence
Right	Droite
Roundabout	Rond-point
South	Sud
Toll	Péage
Traffic lights	Feu tricolore
Tyre	Pneu
Unleaded	Sans plomb
West	Ouest

Time

	Translation
Today	Aujourd'hui
Tomorrow	Demain
Yesterday	Hier
Week	Semaine
Monday	Lundi
Tuesday	Mardi
Wednesday	Mercredi
Thursday	Jeudi
Friday	Vendredi
Saturday	Samedi
Sunday	Dimanche

Numbers

	Translation
0	Zéro
1	Un
2	Deux
3	Trois
4	Quatre
5	Cinq
6	Six
7	Sept
8	Huit

9	Neuf
10	Dix
11	Onze
20	Vingt
50	Cinquante
60	Soixante
100	Cent
1,000	Mille

Shopping

	Translation
Bakery	Boulangerie
Bank	Banque
Butcher Shop	Boucherie
Chemist's/drugstore	Pharmacie
Closed	Fermé
Cough mixture	Sirop pour la toux
Entrance	Entrée
Exit	Sortie
Fishmonger's	Poissonnerie
Grand	Big
Grocer's	Épicerie
Newsagent/bookshop	Librairie
Open	Ouvert
Painkiller	Analgésique
Plaster (Band-Aid)	Sparadrap
Post office	Bureau de poste
Pound (Half Kilo)	Livre
Pull	Tirer
Push	Pousser
Shop	Magasin
Stamps	Timbres

Food And Drink

	Translation
Beef	Bœuf
Beer	Bière
Butter	Beurre
Bread	Pain
Breakfast	Petit-déjeuner
Cheese	Fromage
Chicken	Poulet
Dessert	Dessert
Dinner	Dîner
Duck	Canard
Fish	Poisson
Fork	Fourchette
Fruit	Fruits
Glass	Verre
Ham	Jambon
Ice cream	Glace
Jug of water	Carafe d'eau
Knife	Couteau
Lamb	Agneau

Lunch	Déjeuner
Meat	Viande
Mineral water	Eau minérale
Mixed salad	Salade composée
Mussels	Moules
Orange juice	Jus d'orange
Oysters	Huîtres
Plate	Assiette
Pork	Porc
Red wine	Vin rouge
Salt	Sel
Sparkling water	Eau gazeuse
Spoon	Cuillère
Sugar	Sucre
Vegetables	Légumes
White Wine	Vin blanc

Personal Documents and Travel

	Translation
Airport	Aéroport
Credit card	Carte de crédit
Customs	Douane
Passport	Passeport
Platform	Voie
Railway station	Gare
Suitcase	Valise
Train/plane ticket	Billet de train/ d'avion
Wallet	Portefeuille

Clothing

	Translation
Coat	Manteau
Dress	Robe
Jumper	Pull
Raincoat	Imperméable
Shirt/blouse	Chemise
Shoes	Chaussures
Trousers	Pantalon

USEFUL PHRASES

Do you speak English?
Parlez-vous anglais?
I don't understand
Je ne comprends pas
Talk slowly, please Parlez lente-
ment, s'il-vous plaît
Where is...? Où est...?
When does the ... leave?
A quelle heure part...?
When does the ... arrive?
A quelle heure arrive...?
When does the museum open?
A quelle heure ouvre le musée?

How much does it cost?
Ça coûte combien?
**Where is the nearest petrol/
gas station?** Où se trouve la station
d'essence la plus proche?
**Where can I change traveller's
cheques?** Où puis-je changer un
traveller's chèque?

Where are the toilets?
Où se trouve les toilettes?
Do you accept credit cards?
Acceptez-vous les cartes de crédit?
**I have an allergy to nuts/dairy
products** J'ai une allergie aux fruits
à coque et à larachide/aux
produits laitières

Basic Information

BUSINESS HOURS

Offices and other businesses are open
Mon–Fri, 9am–noon, 2–6pm. Many
also open Saturday mornings. Town
and village shops are generally open
Tue–Fri; there are local variations.
Midday breaks may be much longer
in the south. However, in cities, tourist
centres or resorts, businesses may
keep longer hours or stay open all day,
seven days a week, especially if they
primarily serve the tourist market.

ELECTRICITY

The electric current is 220 volts/50 Hz.
Circular two-pin plugs are the rule.
Adapters should be bought before you
leave home; they are on sale in most
airports.

EMERGENCIES

Police (Gendarme) 17
Fire (Pompiers) 18
Ambulance (SAMU) 15
First aid, medical advice and chemists'
night-service rotas are available from
chemists/drugstores (*pharmacie*,
identified by a green cross sign).
American Express offers its
cardholders a service, "Global Assist",
for any medical, legal or personal
emergency: ℘01 47 77 70 00.

MAIL/POST/INTERNET

Look for the bright yellow *La Poste*
signs. Main post offices are generally
open Mon–Fri 9am–7pm, Sat 9am–
noon. Smaller branches generally
open 9am–noon, 2–4pm weekdays.

There are often automatic tellers
(*guichets automatiques*) inside which
allow you to weigh packages and
buy postage. You may also find that
you can use a Minitel, change money,
make copies, send faxes and make
phone calls in a post office. To mail
a letter from the street look for the
bright yellow postboxes. Stamps are
also sold in newsagents and cafés that
sell cigarettes (*tabac*). www.laposte.fr.
Wifi is widely available in cities such as
Rouen; check with your hotel if it has
Wifi access (there may be a charge.)

MONEY
CURRENCY

There are no restrictions on the
amount of currency visitors can take
into France. Visitors wishing to export
currency in foreign banknotes in
excess of the given allocation from
France should complete a currency
declaration form on arrival.
Coins and notes – The unit of
currency is the **euro** (€). One euro
is divided into 100 cents or *centimes
d'euro*. Old franc notes could still be
exchanged by the Banque de France
until early 2012.
In the Channel Islands, legal tender
is the **Pound Sterling** (£). The local
currency issued by the banks of Jersey
and Guernsey is not legal tender
outside the islands. All British clearing
banks have branches in the Channel
Islands.

BANKS AND CURRENCY EXCHANGE

Banks are generally open Mon–Fri
9am–5.30pm. Some branches are
open for limited transactions on

Saturday. Banks limit opening hours on the day before a bank holiday. A passport or other ID may be necessary when cashing cheques (traveller's or ordinary) in banks. Commission charges vary and hotels usually charge considerably more than banks for cashing cheques, especially for non-residents.

By far the most convenient way of obtaining French currency is the **24-hr cash dispenser** or ATM (*distributeur automatique de billets* in French), found outside many banks and post offices and easily recognisable by the CB (Carte Bleue) logo. Most accept international credit cards (don't forget your PIN) and almost all also give instructions in English. Note that American Express cards can be used only in dispensers operated by the Crédit Lyonnais bank or by American Express. Foreign currency can also be exchanged in major banks, post offices, hotels or private exchange offices found in main cities and near popular tourist attractions.

CREDIT CARDS

Major credit and debit cards (Visa, MasterCard, Eurocard, Maestro) are widely accepted in shops, hotels, restaurants and petrol stations. Pay-at-the-pump automatic petrol stations accept most cards (including Maestro debit cards). If your card is lost or stolen call the appropriate 24-hr hotlines: **American Express:** *℘*01 47 77 72 00. **Visa:** *℘*08 36 69 08 80. **MasterCard:** *℘*08 00 90 13 87.

You must report any loss or theft of credit cards or traveller's cheques to the local police who will issue you with a certificate (useful proof to show the issuing company).

PUBLIC HOLIDAYS

There are 11 public holidays in France. In addition, there are other religious and national festivals days, and a number of local saints' days, etc. On all these days, museums and other monuments may be closed or may vary their hours of admission.

PUBLIC HOLIDAYS	
1 January	New Year's Day (*Jour de l'An*)
Mon after Easter Sun	Easter Monday (*Pâques*)
1 May	Labour Day
8 May	VE Day
Thu 40 days after Easter	Ascension Day (*Ascension catholique*)
7th Sun after Easter	Whit Monday (*Pentecôte*)
14 July	Fête National France's National Day (or Bastille Day)
15 August	Assumption (*Assomption*)
1 November	All Saints' Day (*Toussaint*)
11 November	Armistice Day
25 December	Christmas Day (*Noël*)

SCHOOL HOLIDAYS

French schools close for holidays five times a year. In these periods, all tourist sites and attractions, hotels, restaurants and roads are busier than usual. These school holidays are one week at the end of October, two weeks at Christmas, two weeks in February, two weeks in spring, and the whole of July and August.

SMOKING REGULATIONS

In February 2007, France banned smoking in public places such as offices, universities and railway stations. The law became effective for restaurants, cafés, bars, nightclubs and casinos in January 2008.

TELEPHONES

The telephone system in France is still operated largely by the former state monopoly France Télécom. They offer an English-language enquiries service on *℘*0800 364 775 (within France) or *℘*00 33 1 55 78 60 56 (outside France). The French **ringing tone** is a series of long tones.

To use a **public phone** you need to buy a prepaid phone card (*télécarte*). Some telephone booths accept credit cards (Visa, MasterCard/Eurocard). *Télécartes* (50 or 120 units) can be bought in post offices, cafés that sell cigarettes *(tabac)* and newsagents, and can be used to make calls in France and abroad. Calls can be received at phone boxes where the blue bell sign is shown.

MOBILE/CELL PHONES

While in France, all visitors from other European countries should be able to use their mobile phone just as normal. Visitors from some other countries, notably the USA, need to ensure before departure that their phone and service contract are compatible with the European system (GSM).

All the charges are given in the 'welcome' message you will receive on using your phone for the first time in France. The three main mobile phone operators in France are SFR, Orange and Bouygues.

If you do not have your mobile phone with you, or you discovered it would not be compatible with the European system, depending on the length of your visit and on how often you plan on using the phone, it may be wise to consider buying or hiring one with a coverage plan that fits your needs. There are a variety of options you can choose from, making it less expensive than you might imagine.

Bouygues www.bouyguestelecom.fr.
Orange www.orange.fr.
SFR www.sfr.fr.

NATIONAL CALLS

French telephone numbers have ten digits. Numbers begin with 01 in Paris and the Paris region; 02 in northwest France; 03 in northeast France; 04 in southeast France and Corsica; 05 in southwest France. However, all ten numbers must be dialled even in the local region.

INTERNATIONAL CALLS

To call France from abroad, dial the country code 33, omit the initial zero of the French number, and dial the remaining nine-digit number. When calling abroad from France dial 00, followed by the country code, followed by the local area code (usually without any initial zero), and the number of your correspondent.

To use the personal calling card of a telephone company, follow the instructions on the card, dialling the access code for the country you are in. e.g.:

AT&T ✆0800 99 0011.
BT ✆0800 99 0244.
MCI/Verizon ✆0800 99 0019.
Sprint ✆0800 99 0087.
Canada Direct ✆0800 99 0016.

Cheap rates with 50 percent extra time are available at various times to the UK, Canada, Australia and the USA.

Toll-free numbers in France begin with 0800.

TIME

WHEN IT IS **NOON IN FRANCE**, IT IS	
3am	in Los Angeles
6am	in New York
11am	in Dublin
11am	in London
7pm	in Perth
9pm	in Sydney
11pm	in Auckland

TIPPING

Under French law, any service charge is included in the prices displayed for meals and accommodation. Any additional tipping in restaurants and hotels is at the visitor's discretion. However, in bars and cafés it is not unusual to leave any small change that remains after paying the bill, but this generally should not be more than 5 percent. Taxi drivers do not have to be tipped, but it's usual to give a small amount, not more than 10 percent. Attendants at public toilets should be given a few cents. Tour guides and drivers should be tipped according to the amount of service given: from 2 to 5 euros.

Normandy Today

21ST CENTURY

Normandy today takes pride in its agricultural and fishing traditions as one of the most rural regions of France, while adapting to the wider European economy as a major centre for maritime trade; technology-based industries are also coming to the fore. Today, Basse-Normandie (Lower Normandy) markets its milk, cider and Camembert cheese around the world. Haute-Normandie (Upper Normandy) has continued development as a centre for modern industry, although parts remain quite rural.

POPULATION

Although Lower Normandy (population 1.457 million) remains rural in terms of economy, some 65 percent of the population lives in and around the urban centres of Alençon, Caen and Cherbourg; in the countryside, demographic decline is a worry, as young people leave. Seaside resorts, on the other hand, have attracted new inhabitants. Upper Normandy (population 1.811 million), with its industrial and service employment and proximity to Paris, has a more evenly distributed population. Normandy has a fairly young population, with about 25 percent under the age of 20. Life expectancy for men is 75 years, and for women 82 years.

LIFESTYLE

Normandy immediately conjures images of a leisured life along broad beaches, or among verdant pastures and dew-drenched orchards. Curiously, the fact that most inhabitants live in urban areas has left the countryside bucolic.

In addition, quite a few of those pretty half-timbered houses and quaint seaside villas, as well as the many flats in buildings along the coast, belong to Parisians who drive up only on holidays, so roads are rarely crowded during the week. Despite this holiday atmosphere, the locals are famously hard working.

RELIGION

Normandy's rich heritage of churches and abbeys dates, with very few exceptions, to older times. Today, religion plays a far smaller part in daily life. Some 75 percent of Normandy residents profess Roman Catholicism, with a light dusting (1–2 percent) of Protestants and Muslims (1–3 percent), the latter living in urban areas of Upper Normandy. A quarter of inhabitants profess no religion, about the French average. Churches fill up for traditional festivals, but not for Sunday mass. Yet the buildings, which belong to the French state, are carefully maintained. Catholic tradition remains strong.

FOOD

Local Specialities

According to Norman tradition one should eat duck in Rouen, tripe in Caen and La Ferté-Macé, leg of lamb from the salt meadows of Mont-St-Michel Bay and an omelette in Mont-St-Michel; one should also taste Dieppe sole, Duclair duckling, Auge Valley chicken garnished with tiny onions, Vire chitterlings *(andouillette)*, black pudding from Mortagne-au-Perche and white pudding from Avranches. Among the tasty meat dishes, try the *côtes de veau vallée d'Auge*, which are veal cutlets fried in butter and flambéed in Calvados then braised in cider and fresh cream.

As for seafood, there are shrimps and cockles from Honfleur, mussels from Villerville and Isigny, lobsters from La Hague and Barfleur, and oysters, Atlantic crabs, spider crabs, winkles and whelks from Courseulles and St-Vaast. Seafood may be accompanied by rye bread, salted butter and a glass of dry cider.

Fish – sole, turbot and mackerel to mention only a few – is often served with a delicious sauce.

Local pastries, all made with butter, include apple turnovers *(chaussons aux pommes)*, flat cakes baked in the oven *(falues* or *fouaces)*, biscuits *(galettes)*, shortbread *(sablés)* and buns *(brioches)*. *Douillons* are pears hollowed out and filled with butter, wrapped in pastry and baked.

Cream and Normandy Sauce

Cream, the mainstay of the Normandy kitchen, is at its best in the so-called Normandy Sauce *(sauce normande)*, which elsewhere is just a plain white sauce, but here both looks and tastes quite different.

Cheese

If cream is the queen of Normandy cooking, cheese is the king of all fare. **Pont-l'Évêque** has reigned since the 13C; **Livarot** is quoted in texts of the same period; the world-renowned **Camembert** probably dates to the 17C, at least.

The Normandy cheeseboard also includes fresh cheese from the Pays de Bray – the **bondons**, *demi-sel* or double cream. Before sweeping France, the **petit-suisse** was a much appreciated farmhouse cheese. **Neufchâtel** cheese can be eaten within 12 days of being made, although a mature Neufchâtel takes up to three months.

CIDER

Apple cider has been made locally since the Middle Ages, and it is still possible to find a farmhouse brew distilled in the traditional way.

The apples are gathered in huge baskets then stored for a short while before being emptied into a circular granite trough, where they are crushed by a round wooden millstone pulled by a horse. The crushed apples *(marc)* are transferred to the press, where they are laid between layers of rye straw and then pressed. The rye straw is then extracted and the apple pulp is put to soak in a vat before being pressed a second time to produce a weaker brew which is kept for use on the farm.

Whether it is *brut* (dry, strongly flavoured with apple with an alcohol content of 4–5 percent), *demi-sec* or *doux* (made artificially sweet by stalling the fermentation process when the alcohol content reaches 2.5–3 percent), cider is the perfect accompaniment for pancakes or apple desserts. It should always be served chilled.

Calvados

Calvados, or *calva* as it is better known, is a cider brandy made from a mash of apples fermented with yeast; it is distilled twice and matured in oak for six to ten years. The tradition of the *trou normand* (Norman hole) is still observed; during a heavy meal a small glass of Calvados is swallowed at one go to help the digestion. Restaurants often serve an apple and Calvados sorbet instead. Calvados is usually drunk after coffee; for just a taste, eat a sugar lump dipped in Calvados. A great many distilleries and storehouses are open to the public.

Perry

Perry *(poiré)* is similar to cider but is made from pears and usually comes from the areas around Mortain and Domfront.

Pommeau

This alcoholic beverage is made by mixing two-thirds of apple juice with one-third of Calvados and features an alcohol content of 16–18 percent. The ageing process is carried out in oak casks for a period of 18 months. It can be drunk chilled as an apéritif, or at room temperature to accompany oysters, foie gras, melon or apple pie. It is also popular for cooking with.

ECONOMY

Normandy's two regions present very different economic profiles. Upper Normandy, which stretches along the Seine river estuary, has a large industrial sector, with Renault car manufacturing plants at Elbeuf and Le Havre, oil refineries, petrochemical plants, a big construction industry and many light industries. The principal import is crude oil; principal exports are refined petroleum and petrochemical products, and cars and car parts. The ports of Le Havre and Rouen are among France's biggest.

In Lower Normandy, three-quarters of the land is agricultural, by far the highest proportion in all France, much of it devoted to dairy cows. Industry occupies only 20 percent of the workforce, and milk processing is the biggest industry. Many people are employed in small businesses and tourism. Norman farms produce grain (wheat, maize, barley), oils (linseed, rape), several sorts of fruit, animal feed, sugar beet and potatoes. Calvados and Manche produce 12 percent of the French fish catch, much of it shellfish, and nearly all of it sold dockside to wholesellers.

Lower Normandy's agricultural sector sheltered its economy during the 2008–2009 recession. Upper Normandy was hit hardest, although the combination of low fuel prices and good grain harvests kept ports humming, while French holidaymakers choosing to stay at home supported the Norman tourist industry.

GOVERNMENT

The area covered by this book corresponds to the former province of Normandy, divided in 1789 into five *départements*, with remaining bits absorbed by the départements of Eure-et-Loire and Mayenne. Eure and Seine-Maritime make up the region of Upper Normandy, while Calvados, Manche and Orne make up Lower Normandy.

There are 26 **regions** in France (22 within French borders, four overseas), governed by elected councils. The regions are composed of **départements** (100 in all of France), each of which is divided into **communes**, governed by municipal councils and mayors. **Cantons** exist only to elect members to the departmental council.

A large *commune*, such as Le Havre, will include several *cantons*. In a rural area, there may be several *communes* in a *canton*. In recent years, the regions have gained more authority over the *départements*. You can tell where people are from by reading the licence plates on their cars: each *département* has its own number.

History

TIMELINE
ROMAN PERIOD

58-51BC	Roman conquest. New towns appear: Rotomagus (Rouen), Caracotinum (Harfleur), Noviomagus (Lisieux), Juliobona (Lillebonne), Mediolanum (Évreux).
56BC	The Unelli crushed by Sabinius in the Mont Castre area.
1C	Growth of main settlements (Coutances, Rouen, Évreux, etc.).
2C	Nordic (Saxon and Germanic) invasions of the Bessin region. Conversion to Christianity.
260	Bishopric of Rouen founded by St-Nicaise.
284 and 364	Nordic invasions.

FRANKISH DOMINATION

497	Rouen and Évreux occupied by Clovis.
511	Neustria or the Western Kingdom inherited by Clothaire, Clovis's son.
6C	The first monasteries founded.
7C	Monasteries flourish: St-Wandrille, Jumièges.
709	Mont Tombe consecrated to the cult of St Michael by Aubert, Bishop of Avranches.

VIKING INVASIONS

	The Vikings or Norsemen who sailed from Scandinavia harassed western Europe, parts of Africa and even headed into the Mediterranean.
800	Channel coast invaded by Vikings.
820	Seine Valley laid waste by Vikings.
836	Christians persecuted in the Cotentin region.

858	Bayeux devastated by Vikings.
875	Further persecution in the west.
885	Paris besieged by Vikings.
911	Treaty of St-Clair-sur-Epte: Rollo becomes the first Duke of Normandy.

THE INDEPENDENT DUKEDOM

	Under William Longsword the dukedom takes on its final form with the unification of the Avranchin and the Cotentin.
10-11C	Consolidation of ducal powers. Restoration of the abbeys.
1027	Birth of William, the future conqueror of England, at Falaise.
1066	Invasion of England by William. King of France threatened by his vassal, the Duke of Normandy, now also King of England.
1087	Death of William the Conqueror in Rouen.
1087-1135	William's heirs in dispute; ducal authority restored by Henry Beauclerk who becomes King of England as Henry I (1100–35) after his brother William Rufus.
1120	The wreck of the White Ship off Barfleur Point with the loss of Henry I's heir, William Atheling, and 300 members of the Anglo-Norman nobility.
1152	Marriage of Henry II Plantagenet, to Eleanor of Aquitaine, whose dowry included all of southwest France.
1154-89	Henry II of England.
1195	Château-Gaillard built by Richard Lionheart.
1202	Loss of Norman possessions by John Lackland, King of England.
1204	Normandy united to the French crown.

FRENCH DUKEDOM TO THE PROVINCE OF NORMANDY

1315	Granting of the Norman Charter, symbol of provincial status, which remained in being until the French Revolution.
1346	Normandy invaded by Edward III of England.
1364-84	The Battle of Cocherel marks the start of Du Guesclin's campaigns.
1417	Normandy invaded by Henry V of England.
1424	English repulsed by Louis d'Estouteville, defender of Mont-St-Michel.
1431	Trial and burning of Joan of Arc at Rouen.
1437	Founding of Caen University.
1450	Normandy recovered by the French crown after the victory at Formigny and the recapture of Cherbourg.
1469	Charles of France, last Duke of Normandy, is dispossessed of his dukedom.
1514	The Rouen Exchequer becomes the Parliament of Normandy.
1517	Founding of Le Havre.
1542	Rouen created as a self-governing city for treasury purposes.
1589	Henri of Navarre victorious at Arques and the following year at Ivry-la-Bataille.
1625	Alençon also created as a treasury district.
1639-40	Revolt of the Barefoot Peasants provoked by the introduction of the salt tax (gabelle).
1692	Naval battle of La Hougue.
1771-75	Suppression of the Parliament at Rouen.

LATE 18C TO TODAY

1789	The Caen Revolt.
1793	The Girondins' attempted uprising; siege of Granville.
1795-1800	Insurrection of Norman royalists, the Chouans.

1843 Inauguration of the Paris-Caen railway.

1870-71 Franco-Prussian War; occupation of Haute-Normandie and Le Mans.

June 1940 Bresle Front breached.

August 1942 Dieppe Commando raid by Canadian and British troops.

June 1944 Allied landing on the Calvados coast. Battle of Normandy.

1954 René Coty, born in Le Havre, is elected President of the Republic.

1959 Inauguration of the Tancarville Bridge.

1967 Commissioning of the Atomic Centre at La Hague.

1971 Launch of the *Redoutable*, the first French nuclear submarine, at Cherbourg.

1974 Creation of the Brotonne Regional Nature Park.

1975 Creation of the Normandie-Maine Regional Nature Park.

1977 Completion of the Normandy motorway (A13).

1983-84 Start-up of Paluel Nuclear Power Station. Start-up of Flamanville Nuclear Power Station.

1987 Commemoration of the 900th anniversary of William the Conqueror's death.

1991 Inauguration of France's 27th regional nature park in the Cotentin and Bessin area.

6 June 1994 50th anniversary of the Battle of Normandy.

January 1995 Inauguration of the Pont de Normandie.

1997 A violent controversy breaks out between Greenpeace environmentalists and COGEMA over nuclear waste dumped near La Hague.

1999 Tall Ships Armada of the Century on the Seine, from Rouen to Le Havre.

1999 Violent windstorms in December uproot innumerable trees and damage buildings.

2000 Wreck of the *Evoli Sun*, an Italian ship loaded with chemicals, off Cap de la Hague.

2004 Sixtieth anniversary of the Normandy landings attended, for the first time, by leaders of Germany and Russia.

2005 The centre of Le Havre is named a UNESCO World Heritage Site.

2006 Port 2000 at Le Havre opened.

2009 65th anniversary of D-Day; the French president approves study to build the a Normandy high-speed train line between Paris and Le Havre, and between Paris, Caen and Cherbourg.

2011 Celebration of Normandy's 11th century.

2013 Tall Ships Armada at Rouen.

NORMANS THROUGHOUT HISTORY

The story of the Norsemen, or Vikings, who settled in the Frankish kingdom and from there set out on expeditions of conquest to southern Italy and Sicily as well as to England, Wales, Scotland and Ireland, has inspired many tall tales and cinematic extravaganzas.

In the 8C, pagan barbarians from Denmark, Norway and Iceland began their plunder of coastal settlements in Europe and by the 9C they had established a permanent foothold in the region that is now Normandy.

In the year 911, **Charles III (The Simple)** signed the treaty of **St-Clair-sur-Epte** with the Viking chief **Rollo**. According to Dudon de St-Quentin, the first historian of Normandy, the Viking simply placed his hands between those of the French king to ratify the agreement creating the dukedom of Normandy: no written treaty was ever drafted.

The Norsemen continued to expand their holdings until well into the 11C,

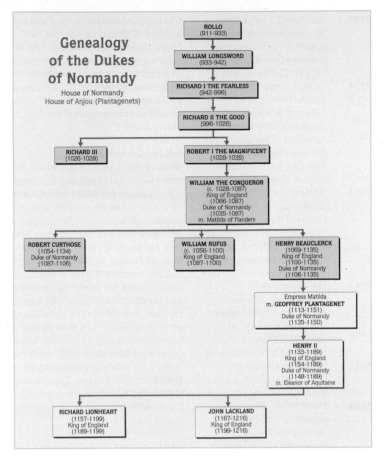

Genealogy of the Dukes of Normandy

House of Normandy
House of Anjou (Plantagenets)

ROLLO
(911-933)

WILLIAM LONGSWORD
(933-942)

RICHARD I THE FEARLESS
(942-996)

RICHARD II THE GOOD
(996-1026)

RICHARD III
(1026-1028)

ROBERT I THE MAGNIFICENT
(1028-1035)

WILLIAM THE CONQUEROR
(c. 1028-1087)
King of England
(1066-1087)
Duke of Normandy
(1035-1087)
m. Matilda of Flanders

ROBERT CURTHOSE
(1054-1134)
Duke of Normandy
(1087-1106)

WILLIAM RUFUS
(c. 1056-1100)
King of England
(1087-1100)

HENRY BEAUCLERCK
(1069-1135)
King of England
(1100-1135)
Duke of Normandy
(1106-1135)

Empress Matilda
m. **GEOFFREY PLANTAGENET**
(1113-1151)
Duke of Normandy
(1135-1150)

HENRY II
(1133-1189)
King of England
(1154-1189)
Duke of Normandy
(1148-1189)
m. Eleanor of Aquitaine

RICHARD LIONHEART
(1157-1199)
King of England
(1189-1199)

JOHN LACKLAND
(1167-1216)
King of England
(1199-1216)

ruling through a succession of ruthless dukes and counts.

Eventually, the Norse converted to Christianity and adopted the French language, but retained a reputation for recklessness, love of combat, cunning and outrageous treachery. At the same time, wherever they went, they showed a remarkable capacity for adapting to local customs. William, Duke of Normandy, became King of England in a coup known as the **Norman Conquest** (1066), while the Norman kingdom of Sicily was founded by the descendants of Tancrède de Hauteville. Norman rulers were among the most powerful and successful of their time, and established enduring political institutions.

In Normandy, the Normans quickly adopted the precepts of feudalism,

became masters of cavalry warfare and fostered the cult of knighthood. Eventually, their reputation for fierceness and brutality was softened by religion, marked by pilgrimages to Rome and the Holy Land. In England, their rule made the kingdom safer from foreign invasion and brought discipline to church organisations.

Later still, explorers continued to embark from Normandy in search of new lands:

1402   Jean de Béthencourt, of the Caux region, becomes King of the Canary Islands, but cedes his realm to the King of Castile.

1503   Paulmier de Gonneville, gentleman of Honfleur, reaches Brazil in the Espoir.

1506	Jean Denis, a sailor from Honfleur, explores the mouth of the St Lawrence, preparing the way for Jacques Cartier.
1524	Leaving Dieppe in the caravel *La Dauphine*, Giovanni da Verrazano, a native of Florence and navigator to François I, discovers the site of New York City, which he names Land of Angoulême.
1555	Admiral Nicolas Durand de Villegaignon sets up a colony of Huguenots from Le Havre on an island in the bay of Rio de Janeiro, but they are driven away by the Portuguese.
1563	Led by René de la Laudonnière, colonies of Protestants from Le Havre and Dieppe found Fort Caroline in Florida but are massacred by the Spaniards.
1608	Samuel de Champlain, Dieppe shipbuilder, leaves Honfleur to found Quebec.
1635	Pierre Belain of Esnambuc claims Martinique in the name of the King of France; the colonisation of Guadeloupe follows soon after.
1682	Cavalier de La Salle of Rouen, after reconnoitring the site of Chicago, sails down the Mississippi river and takes possession of Louisiana.

WILLIAM THE CONQUEROR

William was the son of Robert the Magnificent and his concubine Herleva (The Beautiful Arlette), from the town of Falaise. A descendant of the great Viking chief Rollo, he was first known as William the Bastard.

In 1035, when his father died on his way back from the Holy Land, William, then eight years old, became the seventh Duke of Normandy. His tutors instructed him in the rudiments of Latin and the fine points of military strategy, and also instilled in him a deep religious faith. Later, three of his guardians and his tutor were assassinated by parties who objected to the Bastard's succession. In 1046, barely 20 years old, he confounded yet another plot to undo him, and wisely sought out the support of the King of France, Henri I.

For the Love of Matilda

William built castles (Falaise – his birthplace – and Cherbourg) and towns (Saint-James), expanded Saint-Lô and Carentan, created the city of Caen, and negotiated peace with his enemies. Between 1054 and 1060, William held fast against the allied forces of the King of France, Guillaume d'Arques and the Geoffrey Martell of Anjou. He consolidated his power by marrying Matilda, daughter of Baldwin V, Count of Flanders. Mindful of all he had suffered as an illegitimate son, William was a faithful and trusting husband. When called away from Normandy, he left the realm in his wife's able hands. Tradition attributes the **Bayeux Tapestry** to Matilda, but it is unlikely that she busied herself with embroidery when William was abroad.

The Conquest

Edward the Confessor, King of England, had recognised William as his heir, but in January 1066 news arrived that **Harold** had claimed the English throne. The duke appealed to the Pope and Harold was excommunicated.

Within seven months, William was master of England. On 12 September 1066, protected by the Pope's ensign, about 12,000 knights and soldiers embarked upon 696 ships followed by smaller boats and skiffs bringing the total number of vessels to 3,000. On 28 September, at low tide, the Normans landed at Pevensey, Sussex. William, the last to disembark, stumbled and fell full length. The superstitious Normans were alarmed, but William laughed and, according to the records, retorted: "My Lords, by the glory of God have I seized this land with my own two hands. As long as it exists it is ours alone."

The Normans occupied Hastings. Harold, who had been busy fighting other attackers, rushed to the scene and pitched camp on a hill. On 14 October, William launched an assault, and after a terrible struggle the Normans were victorious; Harold died in combat. The history of the invasion is recounted in the Bayeux Tapestry, which shows fascinating details of combat dress and equipment.

While remaining Duke of Normandy, William was crowned King of England on Christmas Day, 1066, at Westminster Abbey, London. He suppressed revolts, brought to heel the corrupt aristocracy, encouraged noble Norman families to settle in England, and overcame the Pope's opposition to his control over church affairs. Norman art flourished in England, as the cathedrals at Canterbury, Winchester and Durham show.

Ruling 52 years in Normandy and 21 years in England, William maintained a large measure of peace and justice in his realm. He died on 9 September 1087 near Rouen and was buried at St-Étienne Church in Caen, as he had requested.

MONASTICISM IN NORMANDY

Normandy, like Champagne and Burgundy, was a centre of monasticism during the religious revival that swept the 11C, as the many abbeys attest.

Under **Benedictine Rule**, which gradually supplanted other religious rules, nuns and monks made vows of obedience, poverty and chastity. They practised fasting, silence and abstinence.

The monks' working day was taken up by divine office (prayers scheduled throughout the day), holy reading and, to a greater extent, manual labour, such as baking bread, weaving cloth for the monastic habits, carrying firewood, sweeping, serving meals, preparing the sacristy, growing vegetables, etc.

Throughout the Middle Ages monasticism played a vital role in society, securing the propagation of Christianity, promoting the authority of the Pope and contributing to the conservation and transmission of learning.

MEDIEVAL MONASTERIES

The monastic buildings surrounded the cloisters as detailed below.

Cloisters – Generally, four galleries corresponding to the compass points surrounded a central courtyard, often laid out as a medicinal herb garden.

Abbey Church – The abbey church was characterised by an extremely long nave; the monks spent long hours in church for mass and other religious offices. In Cistercian churches, a rood screen placed near the high altar separated the monks' choir from that of the lay brothers.

Sacristy – The room in which ecclesiastical garments and altar vessels were stored and in which the priest would don his robes before leading the service.

Chapter House – Used for daily monastic activities, including prayers before the day's work and the reading of a chapter taken from the monastic rule.

Calefactory – The only heated room in the monastery, accessible to all the monks under certain conditions.

Scriptorium – A room reserved for the copying out of manuscripts.

Refectory – A large bare room, endowed with surprisingly good acoustics. During meals, the reader in the elevated pulpit would recite passages from the Bible.

Dormitories – There were generally two: one for the monks above the chapter house and one for the lay brothers above the cellars. In the Cistercian order seven hours were allowed for rest. The monks slept fully dressed in a communal dormitory.

Outbuildings – These included the barns and the porter's lodge, often a grand building with a huge gateway to allow the passage of both carriages and people on foot. The porter's lodge had living quarters on the first floor, where alms were distributed and justice was dispensed to the population.

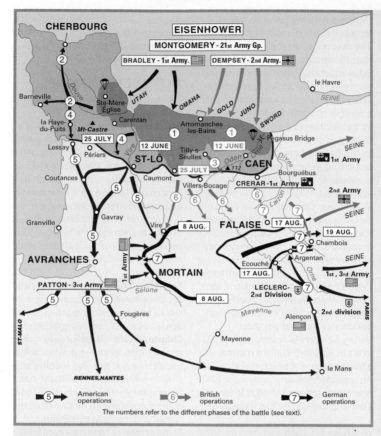

The numbers refer to the different phases of the battle (see text).

THE BATTLE OF NORMANDY

On 6 June 1944, the coast of Normandy was the setting for yet another crucial invasion which would, in its own turn, change the course of history.

From the autumn of 1941, the British authorities had envisaged a landing on the continent of Europe, but it was only after the entry of the United States that offensive action on such a scale could be seriously considered. The COSSAC plan, approved at the Churchill-Roosevelt meetings in Washington and Quebec in May and August 1943, foresaw the landing of invasion troops along the Calvados coast, which was defended by the German 7th Army. This sector was preferred to the Pas-de-Calais (15th German Army) because it meant that the Germans' lines of communication would be more vulnerable: Lower Normandy would be isolated if the bridges over the Seine and Loire were destroyed. It was also known that the enemy was preoccupied by the defence of the Pas-de-Calais.

Preparation

The building of artificial ports – a lesson learned as a result of the costly Dieppe commando raid of 1942 – and the construction of landing craft was carried out with other training in the winter of 1943–44. On 24 December 1943, General Eisenhower was named Chief of the Allied Expeditionary Force and General Montgomery made responsible for tactical coordination of all land forces (21st Army Group) for **Operation Overlord**.

Air raids to paralyse the French railway system began on 6 March 1944. During the spring of 1944 Field Marshal Rommel had the beaches and their approaches covered with obstacles. It became urgent to find a means of destroying these obstacles by using tanks as bulldozers or sending frogmen to dispose of them.

First Week of the Landing
Circled numbers refer to the map.
① Originally D-Day had been planned for 5 June but it was postponed for 24 hours owing to bad weather.
At dawn on D-Day, 6 June 1944, British and Commonwealth ground forces established beachheads at **Sword**, **Juno** and **Gold** and rapidly linked up with the airborne troops dropped to their east. The Americans, landing on **Omaha Beach**, joined up with their airborne flank only after the capture of Carentan on 12 June.

Layout of the Bridgehead
Advances were substantial but of unequal depth: the Americans threatened Caumont on 13 June; the British and Canadians were held up by very fierce fighting 6km/3.7mi north of Caen in the Tilly-sur-Seulles sector on 7 June and broke through only on the 20th – the village changed hands some 20 times. The Caen sector, as Montgomery had foreseen, became the principal hinge of the whole front.

Isolation of the Cotentin Peninsula and the Capture of Cherbourg
② The Americans attacked across the Cotentin Peninsula on 13 June and secured it, capturing Barneville on 18 June. Turning north they attacked Cherbourg, which fell on 26 June – a victory in the battle to ensure supply lines.

Battle of the Odon and Capture of Caen
③ On 26 June, a hard battle, which was to last a month, began for a crossing over the Odon upstream from Caen and the taking of Hill 112. Montgomery decided to outflank Caen

to the southwest. The city of Caen on the left bank was attacked in force from the west and northeast and fell on 9 July.

Breakthrough Preparation
In early July, General Montgomery laid out his breakthrough strategy: "Keep the greatest possible number of the enemy divisions on our eastern flank, between Caen and Villers-Bocage, and pivot the western flank of the Army Group towards the southeast in a vast sweeping movement in order to threaten the line of retreat of the German division."

War of the Hedgerows
For the American soldiers of 1944, the Cotentin campaign – the advance to Cherbourg and the Battle of St-Lô – was simply "the war of the hedgerows".
Leafy hedges and sunken lanes such as those that divide the Normandy countryside came as an unpleasant surprise for the attackers, but for defensive warfare or guerrilla tactics the terrain offered unending opportunities.
Modern arms were not much help: four-inch shells scarcely shook the tree-covered embankments, which constituted natural anti-tank barriers; only the foot soldier could fight successfully in this hell of hedges. The effort of fighting against an invisible enemy was exhausting; every field and orchard crossed was a victory in itself; progress was slow and was often estimated by the number of hedges passed. So that the tanks could operate with a maximum of efficiency, an American sergeant devised a system whereby a sharp steel device, not unlike a ploughshare, was attached to the front of each tank.

The Battle for St-Lô
④ On 3 July, the American 8th Corps launched its offensive, in the face of fierce German resistance, towards the road centre of St-Lô, thus assuring more favourable positions for the large-scale operations to come. Fighting was fierce for La Haye-du-

Puits and Mount Castre. St-Lô fell on 19 July and the Americans entrenched their position behind the Lessay–Périers–St-Lô stretch of road. Progress at this time was slow in the Caen sector. A breakthrough was attempted towards the southwest of the town but was halted in the Bourguébus sector on 19 July. For one interminable week, from 19 to 25 July, bad weather suspended operations on all fronts.

The Breakthrough (Operation Cobra)

⑤ At midday on 25 July, following intense aerial bombardment, the 7th corps attacked west of St-Lô, the 8th between Périers and Lessay.

By 28 July, Allied armour was driving down the main roads, carrying out vast encircling movements. Coutances fell on 28 July, Granville and Avranches on 31 July. On 1 August, General Patton, taking command of the 3rd Army, hurled it into the lightning war. The 8th Corps burst west into Brittany (Rennes fell on 4 August and Nantes on 12 August), while the 15th Corps and the French 2nd Armoured Division under General Leclerc moved east towards Laval and Le Mans (9 August).

The Thrust South of Caen

⑥ Backing up these operations, Montgomery, with the 1st Canadian Army (General Crerar), moved up to the Caen-Falaise road at the eastern end of the front; the British divisions, pushing southeast from Caumont and Villers-Bocage (5 August), overwhelmed the last defences on the west bank of the Orne.

Battle of the Falaise-Mortain Pocket

⑦ When the German 7th Army was threatened by the American 15th Corps to their rear and the British to the north, Hitler organised a counter-offensive to cut off the 3rd Army from its supply bases by taking control of the Avranches bottleneck. The German 7th Army began its westerly counter attack on 6–7 August in the Mortain region. The Allied air forces crushed the move at daybreak. After a week of bitter fighting the Germans retreated east (12 August). During this time the French 2nd Division moved northwards from Le Mans, took Alençon on 12 August and on 13 August breached the Paris-Granville road at Écouché. The Canadians, halted between the 9 and 14 August at the River Laison, entered Falaise on 17 August, thus forming the northern arm of the pincer movement. Meeting with the Americans at Chambois (19 August), they cornered the German 7th Army and forced its surrender at Tournai-sur-Dives. By the night of 21 August the Battle of Normandy was over – it had cost the Germans 640,000 men, killed, wounded or taken prisoner.

Reconstruction

The Scale of Devastation

Normandy, like Britain and unlike many other French and European territories, is not on any European invasion route and so had remained unscathed since the Wars of Religion; towns had scarcely altered since the 16C. The German invasion of 1940 and the air raids and army operations of 1944 caused widespread devastation and nearly all the great towns suffered – Rouen, Le Havre, Caen, Lisieux. Of the 3,400 Norman *communes*, 586 have been rebuilt to modern standards.

Town Planning and Reconstruction

Modern town planning has altered what were narrow winding main streets into wide straight thoroughfares to accommodate increased traffic, while providing for public gardens, parks and car parks. Houses, flats and offices have been built and an effort has been made to restore individual character to towns and villages; limestone is used for buildings on the Norman sedimentary plain and plateaux, while sandstone, granite and brick are used in the woodland regions. Many historic monuments were damaged but most have been restored and are enhanced by improved settings.

Montgomery explaining troops' dispositions and battle movements to the King

© UPPA/Photoshot

Commanders in the Battle of Normandy

General Dwight Eisenhower (1890–1969) was the Supreme Allied Commander for Overlord. He was present when the German capitulation was signed in Berlin on 8 May 1945. Eisenhower was then to become US president from 1953 to 1961.

General George Patton (1885–1945) commanded the 3rd American Army. After the Avranches breakthrough his units swept across Brittany, the Paris basin, participated in the defence of Bastogne in the Battle of the Bulge, then went as far as Bohemia.

General Omar Bradley (1893–1981) commanded the American assault forces during the landing operation. He then led his troops from Brittany across Europe in the Advance to the Elbe.

General Bernard Montgomery (1887–1976) commanded the land forces for the Allied landing operation. Montgomery then led the northern wing of the 21st Army Group through the Netherlands and Denmark in the Drive to the Baltic.

General Philippe de Hauteclocque (1902–47), known as **Leclerc**, commanded the 2nd Armoured Division of Free French Forces. He landed at Utah Beach on 1 August and took the 2nd Armoured Division from Cotentin to Colmar, liberating Paris on the way.

Field Marshal Erwin Rommel (1891–1944) was overall commander of German forces along the North Sea and Atlantic coasts and chief of the armies of the B group. Wounded on 17 June, suspected of having taken part in a plot against Hitler, he committed suicide on 14 October 1944.

Art and Culture

The Norse, a people long considered barbaric, were in fact masters of wood-carving and metalworking, as their sophisticated domestic implements and fine jewellery testify. Over the centuries, their descendants produced the great Norman and Gothic religious architecture of the 11C to 13C, and later proved great innovators in the decorative arts, music (Saint-Saëns, Honegger, Satie), literature (Corneille, de Toqueville, de Maupassant, Flaubert, Maurois), painting (the 19C Impressionists) and, most recently, the cinema.

ARCHITECTURE
NORMAN BUILDING MATERIALS

Rouen and the towns of the Seine are built with chalky limestone from the valley sides. A similar affinity exists between the local materials and the buildings in the Caux region, where pebbles are set in flowing mortar. Clay, in cheap and plentiful local supply, was used for the cob of the timber-framed thatched cottages and for making bricks, which were often ingeniously set to make decorative patterns.

ROMANESQUE (11C–EARLY 12C)

The Benedictines and Romanesque Design

In the 11C, immediately after the period of Viking invasions, the Benedictines returned to their task of clearing the land and constructing churches and other monastic buildings. These architect monks retained the robust building methods employed by the Carolingians and then embellished their constructions with the Oriental dome or the barrel vault used by the Romans for bridges and commemorative arches. This new architectural style, created by the Benedictines, was named Romanesque by Arcisse de Caumont, an archaeologist from Normandy, who in 1840 outlined the theory of regional schools of architecture. Despite its apparent simplicity Romanesque architecture is wonderfully diverse. In England the style is known as Norman.

The Norman School and Its Abbey Churches

The Benedictines, supported by the dukes of Normandy, played an immensely important part in the whole life of the province; only their work as architects and creators of the Norman School is described below.

The first religious buildings of importance in Normandy were the churches of the rich abbeys. Early monastic buildings may have disappeared or been altered, particularly after the Reform of St Maur, but examples of the Benedictine flowering have survived – the ruins of Jumièges Abbey and the churches on Mont-St-Michel, in Cerisy-la-Forêt, St-Martin-de-Boscherville as well as Église St-Étienne and Église de la Trinité in Caen.

The **Norman School** is characterised by pure lines, bold proportions, sober decoration and beautiful ashlared stonework. The style spread to England after the Norman Conquest. Durham Cathedral provides the first official example of quadripartite vaulting, erected at the beginning of the 12C. The Norman style is to be seen in Westminster Abbey, which was rebuilt by Edward the Confessor, in the two west towers and the square crossing tower of Canterbury Cathedral and in the cathedrals of Southwell, Winchester and Ely in England.

Norman architecture also appeared in Sicily in the 11C in the wake of noble Norman adventurers; in France it paved the way for the Gothic style.

The abbey churches are characterised by two towers on either side of the west front, giving the west face an H-like appearance, and a square lantern tower above the transept crossing, which also served to increase the light inside.

The towers, bare or decorated only with blind arcades below, get lighter with multiple pierced bays the higher they rise (in the 13C many were crowned by spires quartered by pinnacles).

ABC of architecture

Religious Architecture

ROUEN – Ground plan of the Cathédrale Notre-Dame (12-15C)

Lady chapel: in churches that are not dedicated to the Virgin, this chapel is often consecrated to Our Lady.

Ambulatory: semicircular or polygonal aisle enclosing the apse, originally used for processional purposes in pilgrimage churches

Arms of the transept: sometimes projecting

Bay: transverse section of the nave between two pairs of pillars

Radiating chapel

High altar

Apsidal chapel

Transept crossing

Side aisles, sometimes double

Narthex: enclosed vestibule stretching across the entrance to the church

East end

Chancel

Nave

ROUEN – Cross-section of the Cathédrale Notre-Dame (12-15C)

Attic or roof space

Pinnacle

Semicircular vault

Flying buttress

Clerestory windows

Pier of a flying buttress

Capital

Buttress supporting the base of the wall

Nave

Side chapel

Side aisle

CAUDEBEC-EN-CAUX
Vaulting in the Lady Chapel of the Église Notre-Dame (14C)

Keystone

Quarter or cell

Lierne: subordinate rib connecting two main ribs in Gothic vaulting

Tierceron: intermediate rib inserted between the transverse and diagonal ribs

Pendant: characteristic of Late Gothic

R. Corbel

61

CAUDEBEC-en-CAUX – Église Notre-Dame (14C)

Tiered octogonal spire ornamented with 3 *fleurs-de-lis* crowns known as the *"Caudebec tiara"*

Openwork balustrade: in the Middle Ages two cantors would stand here and sing the introit on Ascension Day

Finial

Spire

Pinnacle: small conical termination crowning spires or buttresses, often ornamented with crockets

Processional gallery

Pavillon roof

Central nave

Louver board

Bell tower

Side porch

R. Corbel

Window tracery: the interlacing ribs here represent flames, which explains why the term Flamboyant was applied to Late Gothic architecture in France

Abutment of pilaster

East end: the cuter façade of the choir (the inside extremity is called the apse)

ROUEN – Portail des Librairies, Cathédrale Notre-Dame (1482)

Semicircular arching

Large rose window

Gable: triangular ornamental feature surmounting doors and windows (here pictured with carved openwork rose windows)

Openwork bay with a slender balustrade

Crockets

Quatrefolls

Tympanum, historiated in parts

Arching, covings (with string courses, mouldings, carvings or adorned with statues) surmounting a doorway or window, collectively referred to as the archivolt

Lintel

Pier (often adorned with a statue)

Arch shafts: vertical columns supporting the arching over a doorway

Base

R. Corbel

ROUEN – Chancel and Transept Crossing in the Abbatiale St-Ouen (14C)

Main arcade

Clerestory windows

Arcature with mouldings

Tracery: ornamental stone ribwork in the upper part of a window

Sculpted spandrel: triangular area comprised between an arch and its framing

Equilateral arch

Mullion: vertical shaft dividing a window into two or several lights

Triforium

Diagonal rib

Compound pier

CAUDEBEC-EN-CAUX – Grand Organ in the Église Notre-Dame (1541-1542)

Towers: they can be polygonal or circular

Great organ case containing the pipes

Façade: large pipes forming the organ front

Flat: vertical row of pipes

Stop: a set of pipes

Foundation supporting the weight of the pipes

Choir organ: small organ with one keyboard located behind the organist

Small organ case containing the choir organ (the organ case here is waisted with the upper part protruding)

Organ loft

R. Corbel

ÉVREUX – Stained glass (early 14C) in the Cathédrale Notre-Dame

The main function of stained glass is to provide a translucent framing for church windows and to regulate the intensity of the light inside the building. "The stained-glass windows in the chancel of Évreux Cathedral are the finest examples of 14C work. They are pure in the extreme, artfully combining light yellows and limpid blues with transparent reds and silvery whites... They are in perfect harmony with the radiant chancel, suffused with dazzling day light", remarked Emile Mâle

Glass edging surrounding the finished panes

French T-bar armature: iron band used between panels to fix them onto the saddle-bar

Ferramenta: iron framework that provides a fixing for the panels within the window

Internal lead: strip of lead used to fit together the pieces of glass in the panel

Silver stain: pigment made of silver nitrate mixed with ochre that produces a lovely yellow after firing in the kiln

Grisaille: pigment made with iron oxide producing a variety of greys and blacks after firing in the kiln

Saddle-bars: iron shafts embedded in the masonry of windows to support the panels

R. Corbel

ÉCOUIS – Stalls in the chancel of the Collégiale Notre-Dame (14C)

High back

Elbow rest

Cheek: narrow upright face forming the end of a row of stalls

Separation between two stalls

Misericord: ledge projecting from the underside of a hinged seat which, when the seat is raised, provides support to worshippers or choir singers out of mercy (per misericordiam). 15C and 16C stalls were often sculpted with amusing grotesques or bizarre creatures called "**drolleries**"

R. Corbel/MICHELIN

Rural Architecture

Thatched Cottage at LYONS-LA-FORÊT

Chimney: its weight is essential for the foundations and overall stability of the house

Chimney stack: piece of masonry enclosing the flue

Angle post

Roofing: first the roof is covered with straw or reed thatching. Then a firmly-packed layer of clay is placed along the rooftop and planted with iris bulbs whose roots maintain the thatching in place, cultivating a certain dampness

Thatching: formerly made with straw, it now tends to be made with reed

Lintel

R. Corbel

Small post   **Dwarf stud**

Stone foundations

Cob: building material consisting of sand, clay and chopped straw, sometimes mixed with horsehair and cows' hair.

Foundation sill: long horizontal timber placed nearest the ground and used to distribute concentrated loads

Military Architecture

Château d'HARCOURT (13C)

Although it has suffered from the ravages of time and history, the **Château d'Harcourt** remains a perfect example of medieval defensive architecture.

Battered wall: a wall or rampart is said to be battered when it recedes as it rises, forming a slant

Pepperpot turret

Gatehouse with its **twin towers**

Inner bailey: unlike the outer bailey, this was contained within the lord's residence.

Inner moat

Counterscarp: outer side of a ditch

Escarp: inner side of a ditch

R. Corbel

Bridge

Garrison quarters

Arrow silt: loophole through which archers shot their arrows, converted here to receive artillery cannons in the 14C

Outer moat

Flanking Towers: they facilitated the firing of weapons along the outer face of the walls

Curtain wall: enclosing rampart connecting two bastions or towers

Outer bailey: courtyard lying outside the castle perimeter but protected by its ramparts: it was used to accommodate the quartermasters' lodgings and to receive the population in the event of a siege

Seaside Architecture

DEAUVILLE – Villa Strassburger (early 20C)

This villa is a pastiche of the half-timbered mansions typical of the area. Its genuine Norman characteristics are combined with those from Alsace and some other French regions, complemented by a few eccentric touches prompted by the imagination of architect **G. Pichereau**: asymmetrical rooftops, profusion of skylights and dormer windows, projecting eaves.

Inclined dormer window: provides light to the space contained under the roof

Saddleback roof

Overhanging shreadhead

Chimney cap: cornice forming the crowning termination of a chimney

Clipped gable: gable with several slopes cut across by a shreadhead

Rooftop finial: ornamental device in metal or ceramics

Pavillon roof with four slopes

Corbelled upper floor

Tie beam: main horizontal timber

Dormer window

Window with surbased arch

Superimposed eaves

Balustrade: parapet formed by a row of balusters

Stacked bond: a bond in masonry in which the bricks form a chequered pattern

Wind-brace

R. Corbel

Civil Engineering

The Pont de NORMANDIE (1988-1994)

Radio relay aerial

Tower head

Staying cables, each consisting of fifty sheathed steel strands

Anti-vibration rods

Pylon struts

Upper brace

Lower brace

Aerodynamic vehicle deck

Piers

Badplates

Entrance providing access inside the pylon

R. Corbel

Charming country churches are often surmounted by Romanesque belfries, which are crowned with a saddleback roof or a four-sided squat wood or stone pyramid, the forerunner of the Gothic spire.

The interior light and size of Norman abbeys is very striking. The naves are wide with an elevation consisting of two series of openings above great semicircular arches – an amazingly bold concept for a Romanesque construction. The Norman monks eschewed the heavy barrel vault in favour of a beamed roof spanning the nave and galleries, reserving groined stone vaulting (the crossing of two semicircular arches) for the aisles. The vast galleries on the first level open onto the wide bays of the nave and repeat the design of the aisles. At clerestory level a gallery or passage in the thickness of the wall circles the church. A dome over the transept crossing supports a magnificent lantern tower which lets in the daylight through tall windows.

Norman Decoration

The abbey churches, like all others of Romanesque design, were illuminated on a considerable scale with gilding and bright colours as were the manuscripts of the time. The main themes were those of Byzantine iconography.

Norman sculptural decoration is essentially geometric; different motifs stand out, of which the most common is the key or fret pattern (straight lines meeting at right angles to form crenellated or rectangular designs). The decorative motifs are sometimes accompanied by mouldings, human heads or animal masks emphasising recessed arches, archivolts, cornices and mouldings. Sometimes the monks executed in low-relief motifs copied from cloth, ivories or metalwork brought back from the Orient; this is the origin of the cornerstones in the great arcade in Bayeux.

Capitals are rare and, where they exist, they are carved with gadroons or stylised foliage.

GOTHIC (12C–15C)

The style, conceived in Île-de-France, apart from quadripartite or rib vaulting, which originated in Norman England, was known as French work or French style until the 16C when the Italians of the Renaissance, who were resistant to the Parisian trend, scornfully dubbed it Gothic. The name survived. The French copied the H-shaped façades and great galleries of the Norman abbeys (the west front of Notre-Dame in Paris is based on that of the Église de la Trinité in Caen and its galleries on those of the Église St-Étienne).

The Cathedrals

Gothic is an ideal artistic style for cathedrals, as it symbolises the religious fervour of the people and the growing prosperity of the towns. In an all-embracing enthusiasm, a whole city would participate in the construction of the house of God. Under the enlightened guidance of bishops and master builders, all the guilds contributed to the cathedral's embellishment: stained-glass makers, painters, wood and stone carvers went to work. The doors became the illustrated pages of history.

Gothic Architecture in Normandy

Gradually the national Gothic style percolated into Normandy before the province was seized by Philippe Auguste in 1204.

In the 13C, the Gothic and traditional Norman styles merged. The best example of this fusion is Coutances Cathedral, where the pure proportions and the lofty austerity of the Norman style combine with Gothic sophistication as in the lantern tower. This was also the period of the superb belfries of the Caen and Bessin plains, typified by their tall stone spires, often pierced to offer less resistance to the wind, and quartered with pinnacles.

The magnificent Merveille buildings of Mont-St-Michel give an idea of total Norman Gothic ornamentation. Sobriety provides the foundation over which foliated sculpture reigns supreme;

plants of every variety decorate the round capitals, cover the cornerstones and garland the friezes. The three- and four-leafed clover in relief or hollowed out is a frequent motif but statuary is rare. Lisieux Cathedral and the Tour St-Romain of Rouen Cathedral show the degree of French Gothic influence in Normandy by the end of the 12C.

The Flamboyant Style

By the 14C, the period of great cathedral building had come to an end. The Hundred Years War (1337–1453) killed architectural inspiration; bits were added, buildings were touched up, but little was created. When the war was over a taste for virtuosity alone remained – and the Flamboyant style was born. Rouen is the true capital of the Flamboyant, which was particularly widespread in Haute-Normandie.

In this new style, the tracery of bays and rose windows resembles wavering flames – the derivation of the term Flamboyant. The Flamboyant style produced such single masterpieces as the Église St-Maclou in Rouen, the Tour de Beurre of Rouen Cathedral, the belfries of Notre-Dame in Caudebec and La Madeleine in Verneuil-sur-Avre. Civil architecture developed in importance and passed from Flamboyant to Renaissance – a change symbolised in the gables, pinnacles and balustrades of the Palais de Justice in Rouen.

Feudal Architecture

In medieval Normandy permission to build a castle was granted to the barons by the ruling duke, who, prudent as well as powerful, reserved the right to billet his own garrison inside and forbade all private wars. Over the years the building of castles along the duchy's frontiers was encouraged – Richard Lionheart secured the Seine with the most formidable fortress of the period, Château-Gaillard.

Originally only the austere keeps were inhabited, but from the 14C a courtyard and more pleasing quarters were constructed within the fortifications. This evolution can be seen in the castles at Alençon, and Dieppe and some of the Perche manor houses.

A taste for comfort and adornment appeared in civil architecture; wealthy merchants and burgesses built tall houses where wide eaves protected half-timbered upper storeys that overhung stone-walled ground floors. The results were as capricious as they were picturesque: corner posts, corbels and beams were decorated with lively and fantastic carvings.

THE RENAISSANCE (16C)

Georges I d'Amboise, Archbishop of Rouen and patron of the arts, introduced Italian taste and usage to Normandy. The new motifs – arabesques, foliated scrollwork, medallions, shells, urns, etc. – were combined with Flamboyant art. Among the outstanding works of this period is the chevet of the Église St-Pierre in Caen, a masterpiece of exuberance.

Castles, Manor Houses and Old Mansions

The Renaissance style reached its fullest grace in domestic architecture. At first, older buildings were ornamented in the current taste or a new and delicately decorated wing was added (Château d'O and the château at Fontaine-Henry); fortifications were replaced by parks and gardens.

The Classicism rediscovered by humanists took hold so that architects aimed for correct proportion and the imposition of the three Classical Orders of Antiquity.

Imperceptibly the search for symmetry and correctness produced aridity; fantasy was stifled by pomposity.

In Normandy, the Gothic spirit survived, appearing most successfully in small manor houses and innumerable country houses with sham feudal moats, turrets and battlements incorporated in either half timbering or stone and brick.

Norman towns contain many large stone Renaissance mansions. The outer façade is always plain and one must enter the courtyard to see the architectural design and the rich decoration (Hôtel d'Escoville, Caen; Hôtel de Bourgtheroulde, Rouen).

In the 16C, decoration became richer and less impulsive but the half-timbered construction technique remained the same. Many of these old houses have been carefully restored and there are good examples to be found in Alençon, Bayeux, Bernay, Caen, Domfront, Honfleur, Pont-Audemer, Verneuil-sur-Avre and Rouen.

CLASSICAL (17C–18C)

In this period, French architectural style, now a single concept and no longer an amalgam of individual techniques, imposed its rationalism on many countries beyond its borders.

Louis XIII and the "Jesuit Style"

The reign of Henri IV marked an artistic rebirth. An economical method of construction was adopted in which bricks played an important part: it was a time of beautiful châteaux with plain rose and white façades and steep grey-blue slate roofs.

The first decades of the 17C coincided with the Counter-Reformation. The Jesuits built many colleges and chapels – cold and formal edifices, their façades characterised by superimposed columns, a pediment and upturned consoles or small pavilions joining the front of the main building to the sides.

The Grand Siècle in Normandy

The symmetrical façades of the Classical style demanded space for their appreciation as in the châteaux at Cany, Beaumesnil, Balleroy and elsewhere. The Benedictine abbeys, which had adopted the **Maurist Reform** (the Benedictine Congregation of St Maur was founded in 1621), rediscovered their former inspiration. At the beginning of the 18C, the monastery buildings of the Abbaye-aux-Hommes in Caen and at Le Bec-Hellouin were remodelled by a brother architect and sculptor, **Guillaume de la Tremblaye**. The original plan was conserved but the design and decoration were given an austere nobility.

The urban scene was transformed by the construction of magnificent bishops' palaces, town halls with wide façades and large private houses.

CONTEMPORARY (19C–20C)

Following the extensive destruction caused by World War II many towns and villages in Normandy were rebuilt in the mid-20C in accordance with the precepts of modern town planning. A good example of successful reconstruction is Aunay-sur-Odon, with its large and imposing church.

Auguste Perret (1874–1954), the architect who pioneered the use of reinforced concrete construction, was appointed Chief Architect for the reconstruction of Le Havre; his works include the modern district of Le Havre and the Église St-Joseph. His work makes use of textured concrete and is designed to take the best advantage of natural light. Normandy is a region of innovation as well; in Le Havre, note the **Espace Oscar-Niemeyer**, named after the Brazilian architect, as an example. Two surprising white structures evoke a volcano, and stand out in contrast to the buildings designed by Perret. The Musée des Beaux-Arts André-Malraux, also in Le Havre, resembles a glass ship at anchor. In Rouen, the renovation of place du Vieux-Marché in the 1970s included the construction of the Église Ste-Jeanne-d'Arc, based on a design by Louis Arretche. The roof of the church is in the shape of a boat hull (upside down).

Three of Normandy's bridges are also noteworthy examples of modern architecture: the **Tancarville bridge** was inaugurated in 1959, the **Brotonne bridge** in 1977, and the colossal **Pont de Normandie**, spanning the Seine estuary, opened in 1995. The most recent bridge is not only a boon to travellers, it is also a work of art and a technological feat, a milestone of civil engineering. It is a cable-stayed bridge, more elegant and cheaper to build than a suspension bridge, made of steel and concrete, able to withstand winds of 440kph/274mph. More recently, Michel

Virlogeux again constructed a bridge, Rouen's sixth, known as the Gustave Flaubert bridge (⚓ *See p99*).

POPULAR ARCHITECTURE

Normandy is often associated with **half-timbered** houses. The basic box frame is essentially composed of horizontal and vertical beams, but there are very often different local methods of construction. Footings or a base of some solid material is laid to prevent damp from rising.

A wooden sill or horizontal beam is laid along this base to ensure the correct spacing of the upright posts or studs. It is divided into as many sections as there are intervals between the vertical posts. The upper horizontal beam, sometimes known as a summer or bressumer, consists of a single beam. Along the gable ends it is known as a tie-beam. Bricks are often ingeniously used to make attractive patterns between the timbers.

Roofing materials such as thatch, which is so vulnerable to fire, and shingles of sweet chestnut, are becoming increasingly rare. The schist slabs of the Cotentin are a typical part of the landscape. The slate which has been used since the 18C for houses and outbuildings alike has a silver tinge.

A watertight roof depends on the correct hanging of the slates. The appearance of the villages is conditioned by the local materials used and the trades of the various villagers. One well-known building material, **Caen stone**, is quarried from the Jurassic deposits. It can be either friable or durable and varies in colour through grey and off-white to its more characteristic light creamy colour. The ashlar blocks are divided into two groups, one with the grain running vertically for façades, corner stones and gables and the second with a horizontal grain for courses and cornices.

Farms

In the open landscape of the **Caen plain** the typical courtyard farms are surrounded by high walls. A gateway gives access to the courtyard with the one- or two-storeyed farmhouse at the far end. The smaller crofts usually consist of two buildings, one long house for the living quarters and cowshed or barn and another for the stable or byre.

The farm buildings of the **Bessin** stand round a large courtyard that has two entrances, side by side, one for wheeled vehicles and a second for people. The house stands at the far end with the service and outbuildings to the right and left. There is usually a well in the middle. Built of limestone or Jurassic marls, the house has a pristine appearance. The windows are tall and wide; the roofing is either tiles or slates.

The small flat-tiled houses in the **Argentan** area have symmetrical façades. The buildings are usually a harmonious mixture of schist, brick (chimneys and window surrounds) and limestone (the walls). Some are surrounded by walls or a screen of vegetation. Large barns are frequently adjoined by sheds.

Brick and small laminated schist tiles predominate in the **Sées** countryside. Sometimes the buildings fit snugly one against the other, creating a jumble of roofs of varying pitch.

The farms in the region of **Alençon** are built around an open courtyard. The infinitely varied architecture reflects the wide range of rocks: granite, schist, flint, clay and kaolin.

The most common house type in the **Falaise** countryside is akin to those found in the Caen region. The walled courtyard predominates. The brick chimney replaces the rubblework one and tiles are used for roofs in the area bordering the Auge region.

The houses in the **Suisse Normande** are built of schist known as Pont-de-la-Mousse slate quarried near Thury-Harcourt and the settlements often have the rugged appearance of mountain villages. In the Orne Valley the houses huddle closely together on the flats whereas those on the slopes are scattered, even isolated.

The farm courtyard in the **Vire** *bocage* is often planted with apple and pear trees. On either side of the farmhouse are the barns, cattle sheds and outbuildings for

Dovecotes of Normandy

Manoir de Caudemonde

Château de Crèvecoeur-en-Auge

Manoir d'Auffray, Oherville

Dovecote in the hamlet of Petit Veauville, Héricourt-en-Caux

Château de Betteville

M. Dewynter/MICHELIN

the cider press. Brown or red schist is the main building stone.

Seaside Architecture

In the 19C, the coast became a popular destination and bathing in the sea a novel pastime. Wealthy patrons ordered quirky houses for their holiday pleasures. Sometimes they were built in or near existing fishing villages, and in other places whole resort communities sprang up. Many of these villas are still standing along the coast at Cabourg, Houlgate, Villers, Deauville, Trouville, Villerville, Ste-Adresse, Étretat, Dieppe, Le Tréport, Mers-les-Bains, etc. Generally, they are remarkable for their multicoloured façades, busy with balconies, bow windows, railings, gables and other decorative elements.

A profusion of skylights, projecting eaves and rooftop finials adds to the exuberance. Other models are more reserved and even stately, recalling the Renaissance style. Some are more modestly termed chalets, and are said to be in the Swiss, Spanish or Persian style, depending on their features.

NORMAN DOVECOTES

The practice of keeping pigeons, formerly known as doves, dates back to the earliest civilisations. Although domestication is believed to have originated around 4,500 BC, the practice became widespread some 2,000 years later, in ancient Egypt, where pigeon was appreciated for its succulent flesh, a fact evidenced by the many frescoes of feasts and banquets.

THE CARRIER PIGEON

The carrier pigeon is mostly known for its military role in times of war. News of the conquest of Gaul by Julius Caesar was relayed to the capital by means of pigeons, as was Napoleon's defeat at Waterloo. During the Siege of Paris in 1870, 400 birds helped defend the city by carrying tiny strips of film attached to their claws.

More recently, during World War I, English troops entrusted some 10,000 messages to their feathered friends.

Several warrior birds became legendary figures and some were even awarded a military decoration: The Mocker, Lord Adelaide, Burma Queen, etc. The cities of Brussels and Lille have erected memorials to these worthy messengers.

THE HOMING PIGEON

In the early 19C, a new sport appeared in Belgium – pigeon racing, in which birds are trained to return to their home loft after being released in the wild. The first long-distance race (160km/99.4mi) was held in 1818 and the sport gradually gained prominence in Great Britain, France and the United States. Today, many French villages have their own Pigeon-Fanciers Club (Société Colombophile) and organise races regularly.

FOR THE BIRDS

A familiar sight in Normandy, especially in the Pays de Caux, is the dovecote (colombier). Norman dovecotes are square, polygonal or round; the last type is the most common. The door is at ground level, usually rectangular but sometimes rounded at the top and often surmounted by the arms of the owner. The projecting ledge halfway up (larmier) is designed to prevent the entry of rodents. There are openings for the pigeons all round. The roofs, conical on circular dovecotes and faceted on square or polygonal dovecotes, are often covered with slates. The lead finial may be in the shape of a pigeon or a weathervane.

The interior is lined with pigeon-holes (boulins) – one hole for each pair of pigeons – and the number varies according to the wealth of the owner. They are reached by a ladder fixed to an arm attached to a central post which pivots on a hard stone. In some dovecotes only the upper part is intended for pigeons; the lower part may be used as a hen house or a sheep pen. When the two parts are separated by a wooden floor, the door to the upper part is above the stone rat ledge and reached by an external detachable ladder.

There are two kinds of dovecote. The standard or classic type is built of ashlar stone (not common), in an attractive contrast to black flint and white stone (north and northeast of Le Havre), in brick, black flint and ashlar stone (brick tended to replace black flint after the 17C), or in brick and stone (fairly common). The type of dovecote called secondary includes buildings in light coloured flint (a similar shade to ashlar stone), in flint and stone, or in flint, brick and stone.

The first known laws on pigeon breeding were instituted in the Middle Ages. In Normandy, the owners of fiefs were the only ones entitled to build dovecotes. This right, known as the *droit de colombier*, was abolished on 4 August 1789 and very few new dovecotes were built after the French Revolution.

A total of 535 were officially registered in the Seine-Maritime in the early 20C. However, many have been abandoned and are now in a state of neglect. The French government and local authorities have recently taken measures to finance the restoration of these charming buildings, which are an essential part of Normandy's rural heritage.

DECORATIVE ARTS
CERAMICS AND POTTERY

The glazed pavement in the chapter house of St-Pierre-sur-Dives (13C) demonstrates the long tradition of ceramic art in Normandy. In the mid-16C, Masséot Abaquesne was making decorated tiles, which were greatly prized in Rouen, whereas potteries in Le Pré-d'Auge and Manerbe (near Lisieux) were producing "earthenware more beautiful than is made elsewhere". In 1644, **Rouen faïence** made its name with blue decoration on a white ground and white on blue.

By the end of the century production had increased so that when the royal plate was melted down to replenish the Treasury, "the Court changed to chinaware in a week" (Saint-Simon). The so-called radiant style is reminiscent of the wrought-iron work and embroidery for which the town was well known. The

desire for novelty brought in the vogue for chinoiserie. In the middle of the 18C came the Rococo style with its quiver decoration and the famous Rouen cornucopia, a horn of plenty overflowing with flowers, birds and insects. This industry was ruined by the 1786 trade treaty, which allowed the import of English chinaware into France.

NORMAN FURNITURE

Sideboards, longcase clocks and wardrobes – the three most characteristic and traditional pieces of furniture in Normandy – are valued for their elegance, solidity and generous proportions.

The wardrobe, which gradually replaced the medieval chest, first appeared in the 13C; by the beginning of the 17C, the sideboard was already in existence and in the 18C longcase clocks became widespread. The golden age of furniture making in Normandy produced well-proportioned and delicately carved sideboards or kitchen dressers; coffin clocks (broader at the top than at the bottom); longcase clocks characterised by carved baskets of fruit and flowers round the clockface; tall pendulum clocks, with delicately chased dials in gilt bronze, copper, pewter or enamel; majestic oak wardrobes, ornamented with finely worked fittings, in brass or other metals, or with medallions, surmounted with carved cornices of doves, birds' nests, ears of corn, flowers and fruit or Cupid's quiver, etc.

The wardrobe was often part of a young woman's dowry and contained her trousseau; its transfer from her parents' house to her new home was the occasion for traditional celebrations.

PAINTING

Painting took first place among the arts in 19C France. Landscape totally eclipsed historical and stylised painting and Normandy was to become the cradle of Impressionism.

THE OPEN AIR

While the Romantics were discovering inland Normandy, Eugène Isabey, a lover of seascapes, began to work on the still deserted coast. **Richard Bonington** (1801–28), an English painter who went to France as a boy, trained there, and, in his watercolours, captured the atmosphere of the beaches.

In the second half of the 19C artistic activity was concentrated on **Eugène Boudin** (1824–98) round the Côte de Grâce. This painter from Honfleur, named King of the Skies by Corot, encouraged a young 15-year-old from Le Havre, **Claude Monet**, to drop caricature for the joys of real painting and urged his Parisian friends to come and stay in his St-Siméon farmstead.

IMPRESSIONISM

The younger painters, nevertheless, were to outstrip their elders in their search for pictorial light. They wanted to portray the vibration of light, hazes, the trembling of reflections and shadows, the depth and tenderness of the sky, the fading of colours in full sunlight. They – Monet, Sisley, Bazille and their Paris friends, Renoir, Pissarro, Cézanne and Guillaumin especially – were about to form the Impressionist School, which gave France a front rank in the history of painting.

From 1862 to 1869, the Impressionists remained faithful to the Normandy coast and the Seine estuary. After the Franco-Prussian War they returned only occasionally – although it was in Normandy, at Giverny, that Claude Monet set up house in 1881 and remained until he died in 1926.

Impressionism, in its turn, gave birth to a new school, **Pointillism**, which divided the tints with little touches of colour, applying the principle of the division of white light into seven basic colours, to get ever closer to a luminous effect. Seurat and Signac, the pioneers of this method, also came to Normandy to study its landscapes.

In the early 20C, **Fauvism** was born as a reaction against Impressionism and neo-Impressionism. These brightly coloured linear compositions exploded on the canvas.

For half a century, therefore, the Côte de Grâce, the Pays de Caux, Deauville, Trouville and Rouen were the sources of inspiration of a multitude of paintings.

A PLEIAD OF PAINTERS

Numerous artists still came to Normandy in the first half of the 20C, notably Valloton and Gernez (the latter died in Honfleur); Marquet, who had worked in Gustave Moreau's studio in Paris; Othon Friesz, who particularly enjoyed Honfleur, which he portrayed in its many aspects; and Van Dongen, painter of the worldly and the elegant and a frequent guest at Deauville.

Marquet, Friesz and Van Dongen were strongly influenced by Fauvism, whereas **Raoul Dufy**, a native of Le Havre, soon overthrew accepted convention to associate line drawing and richness of colour in compositions which were full of movement.

LITERATURE

Literature and architecture both sprang from the monasteries. It is therefore hardly surprising that Normandy and its abbeys became rich in literary activity from the 13C. Monks and clergymen with a sound knowledge of history and legend, together with travellers and pilgrims, provided the poets with the inspiration needed to create the Christian epics known as the *chansons de geste*.

Such verse appeared chronologically after the early hagiographic literature (lives of saints) but remains one of the first examples of the use of French as a literary mode of expression. In the 12C, the Anglo-Norman **Robert Wace**, who was born in Jersey but brought up in Caen, wrote two notable verse chronicles. *Le Roman du Rou* (1160–74) was commissioned by Henry II of England and is a history of the dukes of Normandy.

17C

Pierre Corneille (1606–84) is often called the father of French Classical tragedy. His main works are known together as the classical tetralogy: *Le Cid* (1637), *Horace* (1640), *Cinna* (1641) and *Polyeucte* (1643).

The dramatist enjoyed a happy life with his extended family in Rouen (he married and had seven children; his brother married his wife's sister and their households were very close), and despite occasional brushes with the authorities, his plays were generally well received. Balzac praised him, Molière acknowledged him as his master and the foremost of dramatists, Racine lauded his talent for versification. From the 20C viewpoint, it is clear that Corneille also had a great impact on the rise of comedy, and in the development of drama in general, in particular in regard to his ability to depict personal and moral forces in conflict.

18C

Born in Le Havre, **Bernardin de St-Pierre** (1737–1814) travelled the world to fulfil his dreams, and spent part of his life on the Indian Ocean island of Mauritius. In Paris, he became the disciple of the Romantic philosopher Jean-Jacques Rousseau. His best-known works are *Paul and Virginie* (1787) and *Studies of Nature* (1784).

19C

The founder of Norman regionalism is **Barbey d'Aurevilly** (1808–99), a nobleman from Cotentin, who was born in St-Sauveur-le-Vicomte. In a warm and bright style, illuminated with brilliant imagery and original phrases, he sought, like the Impressionists, to convey the atmosphere, the quality, the uniqueness of his region. Valognes, the town where he spent most of his adolescence, is mentioned in several of his works (*Ce qui ne meurt pas*, *Chevalier des Touches* and *Les Diaboliques*).

Although born in Paris, **Charles Alexis de Tocqueville** (1805–59) was from an old Norman family. It was during stays at the ancestral home, the Château de Tocqueville, not far from Cherbourg, that he wrote many of the works which were to bring him fame. This political scientist, politician and historian is best-

known for his timeless classic *Democracy in America.*

Gustave Flaubert (1821–80), a prime mover of the Realist School of French literature, considered art as a means to knowledge. His masterful *Madame Bovary* (1857), a portrait of bourgeois life in the provinces, took him five years to complete. The French government sought to block its publication and have the author condemned for immorality – he narrowly escaped conviction.

Flaubert greatly influenced **Guy de Maupassant** (1850–93), a family friend born in Dieppe who regarded himself as the older author's apprentice. Maupassant's work is thoroughly realistic, the language lucidly pure and the imagery sharp and precise. The author wrote best-selling novels (*Une Vie*, *Bel-Ami*, *Pierre et Jean*), but his greatest achievement lies in his short stories; many of these works are considered among the finest in French literature. Today, he is one of the most widely read French authors in English-speaking countries.

Octave Mirbeau (1848–1917), from Trévières near Bayeux, was an active participant in the literary and political quarrels of his time, speaking out in defence of anarchist ideas. As a novelist, he was fiercely critical of the social conditions of the time.

Detail of On the Beach *(1880) by Eugène Boudin*

©Imagestate/Tips Images

20C

Maurice Leblanc (1864–1941), born in Rouen, created the gentleman burgler Arsène Lupin. A museum in Étretat is devoted to this still-popular author.

André Maurois (1865–1967), born Émile Herzog in Elbeuf, is known for his war memoires, novels, biographies of literary figures such as Disraeli, Shelley, Victor Hugo, Balzac and Proust, and historical works (*History of England*, 1937, *History of the United States*, 1943).

Alain (1868–1951), made a name for himself by his columns in a Rouen newspaper. A professor of philosophy and author of many essays, he revolted against all forms of tyranny. His works *Remarks on Happiness* (1928) and *Remarks on Education* (1932) are noteworthy.

Jean de la Varende (1887–1959), from the Ouche region, evokes in his novels the Normandy of yesteryear. His work *Par Monts et Merveilles de Normandie* is a description of all he saw and admired in the region.

André Breton (1896–1966), from Tinchebray in the Orne, was a poet, essayist and "Pope" of the Surrealist movement. His work, including *Nadja* (1928), *L'Amour Fou* (1937) and two Surrealist manifestos, stirred up, as intended, intense controversy.

Armand Salacrou (1899–1989), born in Rouen, called his dramatic works a "meditation on the human condition". He experimented with different dramatic styles. Two of his popular successes were *Un homme comme les autres* (1926) and *Boulevard Durand* (1961).

Raymond Queneau (1903–76) was born in Le Havre and achieved distinction as the director of the prestigious *Encyclopédie de la Pléiade*, a scholarly edition of past and present authors.

As the author of many poems, novels and plays, Queneau stands out for his quirky style and verbal juggling, revealing the absurdity that underlies our everyday world. One of his best-loved works, *Zazie dans le métro* (1959), was made into a charming film.

MUSIC

Composer of operas and comic operas, **François-Adrien Boieldieu** (1775–1834) was born in Rouen. His work *The Caliph of Baghdad* (1800) earned him a glowing reputation throughout Europe. From 1803 to 1810, he was Director of Music at the Imperial Opera of St Petersburg. His talent was universally recognised with his masterpiece *La Dame Blanche* in 1825. **Camille Saint-Saëns** (1835–1921) was born in Paris, but his father was from Normandy. A brilliant pianist, he composed symphonies, operas, concertos and religious works. He is best known for the *Danse Macabre* (1875) and *Samson et Dalila* (1877).

Arthur Honegger (1892–1955) was born in Le Havre, of Swiss origin. At first he composed melodies to poems by Cocteau, Apollinaire and Paul Fort, then *Pacific 231* (1923) and *King David* (1924). *Joan at the Stake* (1935) and *The Dance of the Dead* (1938) have texts by Paul Claudel.

Born in Honfleur, **Erik Satie** (1866–1925) began as a pianist in the cabarets of Montmartre (The Black Cat), where he met Debussy. Sarcasm and irony permeate his works, his greatest being the symphonic drama *Socrates* (1918) for voice and orchestra based on texts by Plato. Satie exerted an undeniable influence both on his time and on musicians such as Ravel, Debussy and Stravinsky.

CINEMA

One of France's early great directors, **Georges Méliès** (1861-1938) first worked here, and the trend has continued since with names like Malle, Renoir, Truffaut, Chabrol, Lelouch.

Home to the prestigious American Film Festival, in Deauville, Normandy is inextricably linked to the world of cinema.

Nature

Normandy is not a homogeneous geographical unit, rather it is an old province, formerly a dukedom, embracing two large areas with different geological structures, which become progressively younger from west to east. The sandstone, granite and Precambrian schists of the Armorican Massif in the west give way to strata of clay, limestone and chalk dating from the Triassic (beginning 254 million years ago) to the Tertiary (beginning 65 million years ago) periods, which belong to the geological formation of the Paris basin. Normandy can therefore be conveniently divided into two quite distinct regions: Haute-Normandie, which lies northwest of the Paris basin, and Basse-Normandie, which resembles its neighbour Brittany and consists of an eroded foundation of ancient rocks. The administrative region of Haute-Normandie is made up of the Eure (27) and Seine-Maritime (76) *départements*; Basse-Normandie includes the Calvados (14), Manche (50) and Orne (61) *départements*.

REGIONS OF NORMANDY

The inland areas can be divided into two types of regions, **open country** and **woodland**. In the strictest sense, the open country *(campagne)* consists of dry, windswept plains and cultivated fields. The woodland *(bocage)* is typical of the Armorican Massif, although to the east it spills over into the Maine, the Perche and the Auge regions. Typical of the countryside, and sometimes confusing for casual ramblers, a network of dense hedges grows on earthen banks, enclosing fields and meadows and forming a sort of labyrinth.

The people living on the farms and hamlets scattered along the sunken roads have for a long time lived in relative isolation. Lastly, the different parts of the **coast** of Normandy also have distinctive characteristics.

OPEN COUNTRY

The **Pays de Caux** is a vast limestone plateau, stretching from Le Havre to Dieppe, covered with fertile silt, ending along the coast in cliffs famous for their hanging valleys *(valleuses)* and bordered to the south by the Seine Valley. The area produces wheat and industrial crops such as flax, sugar beet and rape. Cattle here are raised for meat.

Bordered by the valleys of the Epte and the Andelle, the **Vexin normand** is covered by a particularly thick layer of alluvial soil which favours the intensive cultivation of wheat and sugar beet.

The **Plaine du Neubourg** and the **Évreux-St-André** district present a flat landscape of open fields, similar to the area known as **Caen-Falaise**. The fertility of the soil in these areas favours large-scale arable farming coupled with cattle-breeding for the production of meat. Vegetables are grown around Caen.

The **Argentan-Sées-Alençon** country, north of the Sarthe Valley and the Alpes Mancelles, is composed of small chalk regions where horses and cattle graze in the open orchards.

TRANSITIONAL REGIONS

The **Roumois** and **Lieuvin** plains, marked by hedges and apple orchards, are separated by the Risle Valley. The **Pays d'Ouche** is more densely forested, whereas the rolling hills of the **Perche normand**, a famous horse-breeding district, form a transition between the Paris basin and the Armorican Massif.

WOODLANDS

The Norman part of the **Pays de Bray** is a vast clay depression, known as the buttonhole, bordered by two limestone heights. It is stock-raising country and has increased its production of meat; it also specialises in fresh dairy produce such as yoghurts and *petits-suisses*.

The **Pays d'Auge**, which contains the river valleys of the Touques and the Dives, differs from the other regions in that the chalk strata have been deeply fissured by streams. High local humidity promotes the growth of grassland and

Quaternary Era		Alluvial deposits
Tertiary Era		Sedimentary deposits
Secondary Era	{	Cretaceous limestone
		Jurassic limestone
Primary Era	{	Granite
		Metamorphic rocks

hedges. Apples are turned into cider and Calvados, and milk into Camembert. Horse breeding is also a tradition near the coast and the Perche region.

The **Bessin**, with Bayeux as its capital, lies to the east of the Armorican Massif. Breeding of saddle-horses and trotters is a long tradition, while famed local dairy produce carries the name Isigny.

South of the Bessin is the **Bocage normand**, where meadows, sometimes planted with apple or pear trees, are enclosed by hedges. Dairy farming is still the main activity. In addition to the traditional Normandy cream and butter, farmers produce sterilised milk with a long shelf life and which needs no refrigeration (UHT milk) and a great variety of low-fat dairy produce.

The remote peninsula of **Cotentin**, which lies between the Vire estuary and Mont-St-Michel Bay, is part of the Armorican Massif. The peninsula itself is divided from the Bocage normand by a sedimentary depression, which is flooded at certain times of the year; there are three distinct areas within the peninsula: the Cotentin Pass, the Val de Saire and Cap de la Hague.

The region is still largely devoted to stock raising except along the coast where vegetables are grown, as they are in nearby Brittany.

THE COAST

The coast of Normandy from the River Bresle west to the River Couesnon is as varied as its hinterland. Erosion by the sea has transferred material from rocky projections and deposited it in sheltered coves. The sea has brought shingle (stones) to the bays and ports of the Pays de Caux and mud to the Seine estuary; it has silted in more than one port (Lillebonne was a sea port in Gallo-Roman times).

The Pays de Caux meets the sea in what is known as the **Côte d'Albâtre** (Alabaster Coast), a line of high limestone cliffs, like the White Cliffs of Dover, penetrated by shingle-bottomed (stony) inlets. The sea beating at the foot of the cliffs has eroded the cliff face, forming hanging valleys where streams once flowed.

The **Côte Fleurie** offers miles of fine sand beaches where the sea may withdraw more than a mile at low tide; it also enjoys a high level of sunshine. The Calvados coast is composed of the low Bessin cliffs, interspersed with sand dunes and salt marshes (Caen area).

To the west are the sand or sand and shingle (stony) beaches of the bracing **Côte de Nacre** (Mother-of-Pearl Coast). The Cotentin Peninsula resembles Cornwall and Brittany with its rocky inlets, although sand dunes and beaches stretch along the coast where the continental rock base does not reach the shore. Mont-St-Michel Bay is known for its vast sands and mud flats from which the sea seems to withdraw completely at times.

The **lighthouses** along the Normandy coast, which guide navigators in the Channel, also make good vantage points. The Norman engineer **Augustin Fresnel** (1788–1827) replaced the conventional parabolic reflector with compound lenses, which led to great progress in the length of beam projected out to sea. At night, in the more difficult sectors, several lighthouses can be seen at once, each with its own peculiarities: fixed, revolving or intermittent beam.

HORSES: THE PRIDE OF NORMANDY

More than 70 percent of all French thoroughbreds and trotters are bred in Basse-Normandie as well as the most powerful draught horses (Percherons) and some of the best carriage-horses (cobs).

Thoroughbreds are the fastest and the most refined horses, but their racing career does not exceed three years. The sale of yearlings at the end of August in Deauville attracts international racing stable owners. The sale of brood mares and foals is held in late November.

French trotters were developed from Normandy mares and Norfolk-roadster trotters.

French saddle-horses, a term which first appeared in 1958, encompasses almost all French competition horses, particularly for show jumping.

Whether chestnut or bay, the **Norman cob** is strong, compact, likeable, full of energy and has a pleasant way of trotting. Cobs can work in the fields or be harnessed to a carriage.

Percherons, dappled grey or black, are the most sought-after heavy draught horses in the world; the race was developed from cobs and Arabs, some say as far back as the Crusades.

Finally, one can not ignore the **Cotentin donkey**, recognised by the national stud in 1997, which has a soft grey coat, with a cross of St Andrew on its back. These gentle beasts now carry tourists on treks across the Cotentin.

NATIONAL STUD FARMS

As one of the oldest French institutions – the first was founded by Colbert in 1665 – the system of 23 national stud farms works in close collaboration with the Institut National de la Recherche Agronomique to improve breeding techniques. The system also supervises all equestrian activities, horse racing and betting in France.

Normandy has the two of the most beautiful and remarkable stud farms in France: the early 18C Le Pin stud farm is virtually a monument to the horse; while the St-Lô stud farm provides 20 percent of France's production.

Mont-St-Michel
© Vasilyev Dmitry/Fotolia.com

ROUEN *and the Boucles de la Seine*

The region surrounding Rouen is remarkable for being crisscrossed by one of the most beautiful rivers in the world: the Seine. Its meanderings water the land, making for green, lush scenery with that gentle charm typical of the Norman landscape. The inhabitants love this countryside as much as they do their beautiful city of Rouen, and they enjoy life here to the hilt. So whether you love the outdoor life, the arts, sports or architecture, you will find your stay here fulfilling – and convivial.

Highlights

The Seine

This river is an integral part of the Rouen landscape. Dividing the Norman capital into two distinct banks, it is also a material link between a great many towns and villages in the surrounding region. Lovely, multifaceted, the Seine offers delight to pleasure-craft enthusiasts and nature-lovers alike. Its economic and industrial impact cannot be overlooked, however; for centuries it has marked the region's history and relief, its quays, towpaths and ports providing tangible proof of its importance for the inhabitants of Rouen and its region.

A place in history

The history of Rouen and its region cannot be evoked without Jeanne d'Arc. She is everywhere here, from the vestiges of the Philippe-Auguste's castle where she was imprisoned and judged, to the museum devoted to her life, a few steps from the square where she was burned alive on 30 May 1431.

Yet Rouen is this and much more. From when the Vikings first sailed up the Seine to the brilliance of the city's golden age in 16C to 18C, from its period of economic and social crisis in the early 19C to its phenomenal industrial rise, from emerging from the destruction

Beech grove in the Brotonne Forest, Parc naturel régional des Boucles de la Seine

© Gérard Labriet/Photononstop

Abbaye de St-Wandrille

of World War II to the modern Rouen assuming leadership for its region, the city remains a stage on which history plays and leaves its trace.

Remarkable architecture

Rouen owes its fame in great part to the wealth of its architectural heritage, museums and monuments where culture is often combined with a remarkable setting, from St Wandrille Abbey to Elbeuf's circus-theatre. Over 200 sites await you, not only religious and civil buildings, but museums, sites related to Impressionist history, and the lively streets and squares of Elbeuf, Louviers, Caudebec-en-Caux and, of course, Rouen.

The cradle of Impressionism and Post-Impressionism

It was Rouen architecture that became a major element in the history of art. It was here that from 1892-1893 Monet painted the series of 30 paintings of Rouen Cathedral, seen in different lights and from three different viewpoints. His work enthused and influenced celebrated artists such as Renoir, Cézanne, Pissaro and Degas, launching an entire art movement that would change the way both artists and art-lovers see the world around them. In a word: Impressionism.

But it did not stop there. While the Impressionist movement was taking the rest of the world by storm, Rouen went on to become the cradle of the post-Impressionist movement, known today as the Rouen School, including artists such as Lebourg, Fréchon, Delattre or Pinchon, who expressed their deep attachment to their native land by capturing the changing, misty quality of the landscapes on the Seine's banks. Many of the masterpieces that left their trace on art history can be seen today in the fabulous collection at Rouen's Musée de Beaux Arts, while modern ones are in the making here.

Verdant landscapes and outdoor life

Throughout the year you can experience the quiet beauty of the Seine Valley's many parks and gardens. The Parc Naturel Régional des Boucles de la Seine Normandie is a place of calm for nature-lovers, but also an outdoor education for families, with its numerous flora and fauna. There are a great many itineraries to take you on a voyage of discovery of the region's marshlands, coastal river, forests and meadows, while sports such as kayaking, canoeing, trekking, cycling and especially horse riding are appreciated and flourish here for visiting enthusiasts to enjoy.

ROUEN AND LES BOUCLES DE LA SEINE

Gourmet treats

Between gourmet pleasures and Rouen regional traditions, food-lovers will be delighted with what is to be found here. The apple reigns, and from apple juice, to cider, from Calvados to pommeau and beer, Rouen and the Seine Valley have a great many beverages of renown – and a few surprises in store as well. Yet chocolates, sweets and biscuits await you here too, made with the fresh Normandy cream and butter that makes them a unique taste experience.

Food is taken seriously here, but Norman conviviality has to be there too. Therefore, visitors will enjoy not only the pleasure of dining in fine restaurants and charming bistros, and shopping for local products at open-air markets; they will also have the fun of gastronomic fairs like the October Fête du Ventre in Rouen.

Try Rouen specialities such as Larmes de Jeanne d'Arc, Cadran du Gros Horloge,

Pavé du Vieux Marché, the 100 clochés, caramel apples or sable biscuits, but save room for dinner – something à la crème, of course!

Craftsmanship

Rouen is the biggest and most important centre for ceramics in France, its know-how having had considerable influence on French faïence. Production began here in the 16C with apothecary pots, but it was in the 17C that the famous blue decoration inspired by both Italian and Chinese patterns began to develop. At its high point, Rouen had as many as 22 ceramics works.

The history of Rouen and the Seine Valley, however, is inextricably linked to that of cloth making, Norman drapers providing 60 percent of French production. In eastern Rouen, it is difficult to miss the close link between the city.

Rouen★★★

Rouen, capital of Upper Normandy, has undergone a remarkable campaign of restoration that has given new life to the old city's network of narrow, winding streets lined with magnificent half-timbered houses. In addition, Rouen is a city of first-rate museums – the Musée de Beaux-Arts alone is worth the trip – and possesses one of the most sumptuous Gothic cathedrals in France. Rouen sits in a lovely valley surrounded by high hills, from which there are extensive views over the city and the Seine.

A BIT OF HISTORY

Rollo the Forerunner – After the Treaty of St-Clair-sur-Epte in the year 911, Rollo, the Viking chief and first Duke of Normandy, was baptised at Rouen, the capital of the new duchy, and took the name Robert. He proved to be a far-sighted planner: he narrowed and deepened the river bed, built up unused marshlands, linked the downstream islands to the mainland and reinforced the banks with quays.

His works lasted until the 19C, unrivalled for their efficiency.

Goddons – Rouen was hard hit during the Hundred Years' War: in 1418, Henry V of England besieged the town, which was starved into capitulation after six months. Revolts and plots followed against the Goddons – the nickname for the English derived from their common blasphemous phrase, "God damn". Hope was reborn by the exploits of Joan of Arc and the coronation of Charles VII, then Joan was taken prisoner at Compiègne by the Burgundians. The English threatened the Duke of Burgundy with economic sanctions and through the mediation of Pierre Cauchon, Bishop of Beauvais, Joan was handed over to the English. On Christmas Day 1430, she was imprisoned in the Tower of the Fields in the castle built in the 13C by Philippe Auguste. A strong military presence under Lord Warwick deterred any uprisings.

▶ **Population:** 107,904.

Michelin Map: 304: G-5.

Info: 25 pl.de la Cathédrale. ℘02 32 08 32 40. www.rouentourisme.com.

Location: Some 130km/ 81mi NW of Paris, Rouen spreads out along both banks of the Seine.

Parking: Car parks are found on: place du Général-de-Gaulle (Hôtel de Ville), Square Verdrel, Palais, Vieux-Marché, La Pucelle, Charrettes, la Bourse (rue du Général-Leclerc), la Haute-Vielle-Tour, St-Marc, 39e RI and St-Vivien. There are free car parks on the lower quays of the left bank and at Boulingrin, near the train station.

Don't Miss: The Gothic splendour of the cathedral and of the churches of St-Maclou and St-Ouen; the lovely half-timbered houses of Old Rouen; the Musée des Beaux-Arts.

Timing: Spend at least one day here: the morning exploring the old streets, reserving the afternoon for museums. A ticket for 5.35€ gives entry to three major museums: Beaux-Arts, Céramique and Le Secq des Tournelles. Purchase at participating museums.

Kids: Musée Flaubert; Musée d'Histoire de la Médecine; Musée Maritime, Fluvial and Portuaire.

Golden Century – The period between the French reconquest (1449) and the Wars of Religion (1562–98) was a golden century for Normandy and particularly for the city of Rouen. Local dignitaries built sumptuous stone mansions and carved woodwork adorned the façade

Joan of Arc

Trial of Joan of Arc – Bishop Cauchon promised a fair trial and opened the first session on 21 February 1431. An amazing dialogue began between Joan and her judges: the Maid replied to all the tricks and subtleties of the churchmen and lawyers. On 24 May, in the cemetery of the Abbey of St-Ouen, tied to a scaffold, Joan was pressed to recant; she finally gave in, was granted her life but condemned to life imprisonment. The English were furious and threatened the judges; Cauchon replied, "We will get her yet." On Trinity Sunday the guards took away Joan's women's clothes which she had promised to wear, and gave her men's clothing instead. At noon "for the necessities of the body, she was constrained to go out and indulge in the said habit". She was thus said to have broken her promise and was condemned to the stake. On 30 May she was burned alive in place du Vieux-Marché. In 1449 Charles VII entered Rouen; in 1456 Joan was rehabilitated and in 1920 she was canonised and made **Patron Saint of France**.

of burgesses' houses.

Rouen merchants in cooperation with Dieppe navigators traded along all the main maritime routes.

Industrial Upsurge – Industrialisation, launched by textile manufacturing, called for changes in the port: in the 19C docks were constructed, the railway was built; the old city on the right bank spread to the tributary valleys and hillsides.

Modern City – Industrial expansion accelerated at the beginning of the 20C. During World War II, the old districts close to the Seine and the industrial zone on the south bank were destroyed. On the right (N) bank, a series of arching boulevards define the city centre, its old residential districts and historic centre. On the left (S) bank are administrative offices, the Préfecture, modern residential and business districts, and the industrial zone.

Lacroix Island, formerly industrial, has become residential with parks and open spaces.

Port – *Bd Émile-Duchemin, Hangar 13 (on the road to Le Havre from the Pont Guillaume-le-Conquérant)* Rouen is France's fifth-busiest port after Marseilles, Le Havre, Dunkerque and Nantes-St-Nazaire, and the third-biggest river port. Its location between Paris and the sea is a great advantage.

Owing to improved maritime access, modernisation of port equipment and facilities, and the building of silos and new terminals, the growth of the port has been constant. It now stretches from Rouen to Tancarville on the right bank of the Seine and from Rouen to Honfleur on the left bank.

Houses in Old Rouen

© John Frumm/hemis.fr

CATHÉDRALE NOTRE-DAME★★★

Allow 1hr30min

♿*Tactile map and brochures in braille available.* 🕐*Open daily except Mon morning.* 👥*Guided tour (1hr30min) including the baptistry, the Chapel of the Virgin and the crypt, usually closed to the public, Sat–Sun at 2.30pm (daily during school holidays).* 🕐*Closed 1 Jan, 1 May, 8 May, 11 Nov.* 🎟*No charge.* 📞*02 35 71 71 60.*

The cathedral of Rouen is one of the most beautiful examples of French Gothic architecture. Construction began in the 12C, but after a devastating fire in 1200, the building was reconstructed in the 13C. The cathedral took on its final appearance in the 15C under the master builder Guillaume Pontifs and in the 16C under Roulland le Roux. In the 19C it was crowned with the present cast-iron spire. Badly damaged during World War II, the cathedral is open but the enormous restoration work started over 50 years ago continues.

The attraction of Rouen Cathedral lies in its infinite variety, including an immense façade bristling with openwork pinnacles and framed by two totally different towers: the Tour St-Romain on the left and the Tour de Beurre on the right.

West front

This imposing façade was used in a series of paintings by Monet to study the effects of lighting at different times of the day on the same subject. Dating from the 12C, the **Portail St-Jean** *(left)* and the **Portail St-Étienne** *(right)* doorways each have a delicately carved semicircular arch crowned by a small colonnade. The two tympana are 13C. The lattice-work window gallery (1370–1420) above the two portals is in the Flamboyant style; the niches decorated with statues and topped by openwork gables are 14C and 15C.

The **central doorway** (early 16C) is flanked by two powerful pyramid buttresses decorated with statues of the Prophets and Apostles. The tympanum is decorated with a Tree of Jesse, destroyed by the Huguenots and restored in 1626.

The **Tour St-Romain**, to the left, is the oldest tower (12C), and in the Early Gothic style. The sumptuous **Tour de Beurre** (Butter Tower) was thus named in the 17C when it was believed that it had been paid for by dispensations granted to those did not fast during Lent. It never received a spire but was surmounted by an octagonal crown. Inside is a carillon of 56 bells.

South side – The **central lantern tower** with its spire is the tallest in France (151m/495.5ft) and the glory of Rouen. It was started in the 13C and was raised in the 16C. The present spire, in cast iron, replaced in 1876 the wooden spire covered in gilded lead, which dated from 1544. The **Portail de la Calende** (Calende doorway), which opens between two 13C square towers, is a 14C masterpiece.

North side – On skirting the **Cour d'Albane** (Albane Court), closed to the east by the cloister gallery, one can see the north side, the lantern tower and spire and the upper section of the Booksellers' transept.

A little further on the **Cour des Libraires** (Booksellers' Court) is closed by a magnificent stone gateway in the Flamboyant style. At the end of the court is the **Portail des Libraires** (Booksellers' Doorway) (©see Introduction: Religious architecture, p62), which opens on to the north side aisle.

The tympanum (late-13C) is decorated by a Last Judgement depicted in terrifying detail.

Interior

Nave – In the early Gothic style, the nave is made up of 11 bays four storeys high. Dominating the transept crossing is the **lantern tower** rising with incredible boldness 51m/167.3ft on enormous piles which sweep upwards.

Transept – In the north arm is the famous Escalier de la Librairie (Booksellers' Stairway); from a charming little balcony rise the two flights of the staircase (the first is 15C, the second 18C).

Chancel – The choir of finest 13C style is the most noble part of the cathedral on account of its simple lines and the lightness of its construction. The high altar is made of a marble slab from the Valle d'Aosta, and dominated by a Christ in gilded lead (18C). Opening off the south arm is the apsidal chapel dedicated to Joan of Arc and embellished with modern stained-glass windows by Max Ingrand.

Crypt, Ambulatory, Lady Chapel (&♿ Guided tours 1hr30min) – The 11C ring-shaped crypt preserves its altar and its curb stone well (5m/16.4ft deep). The heart of Charles V is preserved in a coffer embedded in the east wall.

The ambulatory (access south arm – exit north), which is made up of three apsidal chapels, holds the recumbent

South doorway of Cathédrale Notre-Dame

S. Sauvignier/MICHELIN

figures of Rollo, Richard Lionheart (late 13C), Henry (second son of Henry II of England) the Young King (13C), and William Longsword, Duke of Normandy and son of Rollo (14C). Also shown are five 13C **stained-glass windows**★, the bottom one of which, depicting St Julian the Hospitaller, was presented by the Fishmongers' Guild and inspired Flaubert to write a tale.

The Lady Chapel (14C) contains two admirable 16C tombs. To the right, the **tomb of the Cardinals of Amboise**★★ of the Early Renaissance (1515–25) was carved after drawings by Roulland le Roux. The two cardinals – Georges d'Amboise (left), minister under Louis XII and Archbishop of Rouen, and his nephew, also Georges (right) – are shown kneeling.

On the left, stuck on the recess of the Gothic tomb of Pierre de Brézé (15C) is the **tomb of Louis de Brézé**★, Seneschal of Normandy and husband of Diane de Poitiers, who became the mistress of Henri II after her husband's death. It was built between 1535 and 1544.

The chapel also houses 14C stained-glass windows representing the Archbishop of Rouen and a fine picture by Philippe de Champaigne, The Adoration of the Shepherds, framed in a rich altarpiece of 1643.

🛶 WALKING TOURS

OLD ROUEN★★★
Allow about 30min.

▶ *Depart from place de la Cathédrale.*

Place de la Cathédrale
Opposite the cathedral on the corner of rue du Petit-Salut stands the former **Bureau des Finances** (House of the Exchequer – tourist office), an elegant Renaissance building (1510).

Rue Saint-Romain★★
One of Rouen's most fascinating streets with its beautiful 15C–18C half-timbered houses and at the end the spire of the Église St-Maclou. Note no 74, a Gothic house with 15C bay windows.

Archevêché
⚲*Closed for tours.*
Next to the Booksellers' Court stands the 15C Archbishop's Palace (altered in the 18C). A gable pierced by the remains of a window is all that is left of the chapel where the trial of Joan of Arc ended on 29 May 1431, and where her rehabilitation was proclaimed in 1456. Cross rue de la République to reach **place Barthélemy** bordered with picturesque half-timbered houses where St Maclou's Church stands.

Église St-Maclou★★
3 r. du Gén.-Sarrail. ◷*Open Apr–Oct Mon and Fri–Sun 10am–noon, 2–6pm; Nov–Mar to 5.30pm.* ◷*Closed 1 Jan, 25 Dec.* ☏*02 35 71 28 09.*
This beautiful church of Gothic-Flamboyant style, built between 1437 and 1517, is remarkable for its homogeneity, despite being finished during the heyday of the Renaissance. Only the spire of the belfry is modern. The west façade, the finest part of this building, is preceded by a large five-panelled porch set like a fan. Two of the three doorways, the central one and that on the left, are celebrated for their Renaissance **panels**★★.
These panels are divided into two parts: the leaf of the door has charming little bronze heads of lions and other animals and designs in semi-relief of pagan inspiration, whereas the upper panel, which is a little heavy, has a carved medallion. The medallions on the central door represent the Circumcision on the left and the Baptism of Christ on the right; the upper part of the door represents on the left God the Father before the Creation; on the right, God the Father after the Creation.
The Font Door on the left has only one panel. The medallion represents the Good Shepherd entering the pasture after he has expelled the thieves.
Inside, the **organ case**★ (1521) has remarkable Renaissance woodwork. The **spiral stairs**★ (1517), magnificently carved, are from the choir screen.

Rue Martainville★
The street has kept some marvellous 15C–18C half-timbered houses. On the northwest corner of St Maclou's Church is a lovely Renaissance fountain.

Aître St-Maclou★★
184–186 r. Martainville.
This 16C ensemble is one of the last examples of a medieval plague cemetery. The half-timbered buildings which surround the yard were built from 1526 to 1533; the south side was built in 1640 and never served as a charnel house.
The ground floor of these buildings is made up of galleries which were once open – as in a cloister. On the column shafts (formerly door frames) are carved figures (damaged) portraying the Dance of Death.
Above the ground floor, the attic was used as a charnel house until the 18C. These buildings now house the School of Fine Arts (École des Beaux-Arts).

▶ *Return to the west end of St-Maclou and turn right.*

Rue Damiette★
The street is lined by half-timbered houses and offers a nice vista of the central tower of St Ouen's Church. Note on the right the picturesque blind alley of the Hauts-Mariages.

St Romain and the Gargoyle

In the 7C, St Romain was the Bishop of Rouen, and at the time, a terrible monster known as the Gargoyle was terrorising the city. To rid Rouen of this horrible beast, St Romain needed help. A man who had been condemned to death was the only person brave enough to come forward. Together they set out to confront the dragon. The bishop managed to wrap his stole around the dragon's neck and they led the beast back into town, where it was killed. The courageous prisoner was freed. From the 12C and until the Revolution, one prisoner was chosen by the canons of the church every year to present the reliquary holding the holy remains of St Romain to the crowd from the top of the Haute-Vieille Tower. In return, he would be freed. Nowadays, the legendary event is recalled in the annual fun fair held in the month of October.

In place du Lieutenant-Aubert bear left onto rue d'Amiens to the 17C **Hôtel d'Étancourt** and admire its façade embellished with large statues.

▷ *Return to place du Lieutenant-Aubert; turn left onto rue des Boucheries-St-Ouen; turn right onto rue Eau-de-Robec.*

Rue Eau-de-Robec

In this street, lined with old houses boasting recently restored timber framing, flows a little stream, spanned by a series of footbridges. Several of these tall buildings have workshop-attics, where drapers would leave their skeins of cotton and sheets of fabric out to dry.

Musée national de l'Éducation★

185 r. Eau-de-Robec. ♿ ⏱*Open Mon and Wed–Fri 10am–12.30pm, 1.30–6pm, Sat–Sun 2–6pm; school holidays Wed–Mon 2–6pm.* ⏱*Closed public holidays.* ✆€3 (children no charge). ✆02 35 07 66 61. www.inrp.fr/musee.

The National Museum of Education is housed in a handsome 15C residence known as the **Maison des Quatre Fils Aymon**★. It was once a notorious trysting spot referred to as the House of Marriages on account of the many casual encounters that took place there.

The museum evokes school life from the 16C up to the present day. A 19C classroom has been reconstituted.

On the corner of rue du Ruissel, note the **Pavillon des Vertus**, a fine 16C mansion decorated with statues of women symbolising the cardinal virtues.

▷ *Return to rue des Boucheries-St-Ouen.*

Abbatiale Saint-Ouen★★

pl. du Gén-de-Gaulle. ⏱*Open Apr–Oct Tue–Sun 10am–noon, 2–5.30pm.* ⏱*Closed 1 Jan, 25 Dec.* ✆02 35 71 85 65.

Remarkable for its proportions and the purity of its lines, this former abbey church is one of the jewels of High Gothic architecture. The construction, which began in 1318 and slackened during the Hundred Years War, was completed in the 16C.

Exterior – On the south side is the beautiful door named after the wax candle merchants *(ciriers)* who held their market here. The **east end**★★ is beautiful, with flying buttresses and pinnacles and individually roofed radiating chapels. At the transept crossing, the square **central tower**★, flanked by small towers, rises two tiers before ending in a ducal coronet.

The **Porche des Marmousets**, which occupies the lower level, is unusual: its arching leans to one side and appears to end in mid-air, resting not on colonnades but on two false keystones.

Interior – The **nave** (👁*see illustration in INTRODUCTION*), of a light construction, demonstrates elegance and harmonious proportions. Such perfection could be explained by the golden mean, which in this particular case would be a ratio of 1 to 3: the piers are each separated by

11m/36ft and the vaults reach a height of 33m/108.3ft.

This slender structure is further enhanced by the warm, radiant light that filters through the large **stained-glass windows**★★. The oldest ones date from before 1339 and are still embedded in the chapels surrounding the chancel. The 16C clerestory windows in the nave are devoted to the Patriarch (north) and to the Apostles (south). The two 15C rose windows in the transept arms illustrate the Celestial Court (north) and a Tree of Jesse (south). The modern Crucifixion adorning the axial bay is by Max Ingrand (1960). The big rosette to the west is the work of Guy le Chevalier (1992).

The chancel is closed off by gilded **grilles**★★ (1747) executed by Nicolas Flambart.

▷ *Follow rue de l'Hôpital.*

At the corner of rue des Carmes stands the attractive Gothic Crosse fountain (restored), and further on at the corner of rue Beauvoisine and rue Ganterie is a handsome half-timbered house.

▷ *Turn right onto rue Beauvoisine, which crosses rue Jean Lecanuet, one of Rouen's most commercial streets.*

In rue Beauvoisine note **no 55**, a carved half-timbered house with courtyard: **no 57** is a Renaissance house. Turn left onto rue Belfroy, bordered at the beginning by 15C–16C half-timbered houses, to reach place St-Godard.

Église Saint-Godard★

r. Jacques-Villon. ◖*Open 1st and 3rd Sat of month and eves of religious holidays 3–7pm.*

This late-15C church contains wonderful **stained-glass windows**★, in particular a 16C one on the right side showing the Tree of Jesse. The window of the Virgin, is made up of six 16C panels.

▷ *Follow rueJacques-Villon.*

Musée Le Secq des Tournelles★★

r. Jacques-Villon. ◖*Open Wed–Mon 10am–1pm, 2–6pm (last entry 40min before closing).* ◖*Closed public holidays.* ◌*€2.30.* ✆*02 35 88 42 92.* *www.rouen-musees.com.*

The Wrought Ironwork Museum is housed in old Église St-Laurent, a fine Flamboyant building, and is exceptionally rich (3C–20C).

The nave and transept contain large items, such as balconies, signs, railings, etc., and in the display cabinets, locks, door knockers and keys. Note their evolution from Gallo-Roman times.

The north aisle includes displays of locks, belts and buckles from the 15C to 19C.

The south aisle exhibits a large variety of domestic utensils and tools.

The north gallery on the first floor is devoted to accessories such as jewels, clasps, combs and smoking requisites. A rare 16C–19C collection of professional tools is housed in the south gallery.

▷ *Turn back, cross place Restout and head along the edge of square Verdrel to the corner with rue Faucon.*

Musée de la Céramique★★

1 r. Faucon or 94 r. Jeanne-d'Arc. ◖*Open Wed–Mon 10am–1pm, 2–6pm (last entry 40min before closing).* ◖*Closed public holidays.* ◌*€2.30.* ✆*02 35 07 31 74.* *www.rouen-musees.com.*

The 17C Hôtel d'Hocqueville houses the Ceramics Museum, which presents an outstanding collection of 16C to 18C Rouen faïence.

The work of Masséot Abaquesne, Rouen's first faïence maker, who plied his trade around 1550, is represented by paving flags and portrait vases.

After a lull, production resumed with Louis Poterat (1644–1725), whose workshop produced dishes and tiles enhanced with a blue and white décor. The colour red made its first appearance around 1670.

Faïence was to enjoy a surge of popularity in the early 18C. Decors

Detail of View of Rouen (1892) by Claude Monet, Musée des Beaux-Arts de Rouen

Catherine Lancien et Carole Loisel/Musée des Beaux-Arts de Rouen

featuring five colours (starch or yellow ochre ground) appeared. In the room devoted to polychrome decoration, note the **celestial globe** by Pierre Chapelle, a masterpiece of faïence making. After 1721, motifs became more varied. Subsequently, around the mid-18C, the Rococo style came into fashion, embellished with varied floral motifs.

▶ *Walk around square Verdrel until you get to the corner with rue Jean-Lecanuet.*

Musée des Beaux-Arts★★★

espl. Marcel-Duchamp. A plan handed out at the entrance shows the layout of the museum. For a chronological visit, start with the south wing, to the right of the reception area. &⊙*Open Wed–Mon 10am–6pm (south wing closed 1–2pm) (last entry 1hr before closing).* ⊙*Closed public holidays.* ⊚€5. ℘02 35 71 28 40. www.rouen-musees.com. The 19C Museum of Fine Arts, restored between 1989 and 1994, has recovered its original harmonious proportions and gained modern exhibition areas.

15C–17C Painting – One of the most striking canvases is an oil painting on wood, *The Virgin among the Virgins*, by Gérard David (c. 1460–1523), one of the masterpieces of Flemish Primitive painting. Besides the Italian Primitives, you can admire works by Guerchin, Giordano, Bronzino and especially Veronese *(St Barnabus Healing the Sick)* and Caravaggio *(The Flagellation of Christ)*. Spanish masters include Velásquez and Ribera; Dutch art is represented by Martin de Vos, Van de Velde, N Berchem and Rubens *(The Adoration of the Shepherds)*. French painters include François Clouet *(Diane Bathing)*, Louis de Boullogne *(Ceres or Summer)*, Poussin *(Venus Arming Aeneas* and *The Storm)*, Simon Vouet and Jouvenet.

18C Painting *(second floor of the south wing)* – The most noteworthy painters are Lancret *(The Bathers)*, Fragonard *(The Washerwomen)*, Van Loo *(Virgin with Child)* and Traversi *(The Music Lesson)*.

19C Painting – This section is the highlight of the museum, in terms of both its size and the high standard of its collection. Europe's main artistic movements are represented – Neoclassicism, Impressionism or Symbolism – as well as great masters: Ingres, Monet, David, Géricault, Degas, Caillebotte, Corot, Chassériau, Millet, Moreau, Sisley, Renoir and many others.

In the Salle du Jubé (Rood Screen Room), Romanticism is represented by five sculptures by David d'Angers along with *Justice of Trajan* by Delacroix and *Les Énervés de Jumièges*, a hyper-realist painting by Vital-Luminais.

20C Painting – More recent painters' works exhibited include Modigliani, Dufy *(The Seine River)*, the Duchamps brothers, Dubuffet, Nemours and others.

▶ *On leaving take allée Eugène-Delacroix, then rue Ganterie on the left.*

Rue Ganterie★ is a charming street lined with old half-timbered houses.

ROUEN

0 ——— 100 m
0 ——— 100 yds

WHERE TO STAY

WHERE TO EAT

In the other direction, towards place Cauchois, this street is **rue des Bons-Enfants**, where several 15C houses still stand; on no 22, notice the sculpted figures.

> ◗ *Take rue des Carmes to the right, then turn right again on rue aux Juifs, which runs alongside the Palais de Justice.*

Palais de Justice★★

This splendid 15C and early 16C Renaissance building was built to house the Exchequer of Normandy (law courts). Renovated in the 19C, it was badly damaged in August 1944.

The **main court** – excavations have revealed a 12C Jewish place of worship – is flanked by two wings, the **façade**★★ (1508–26) of which is exquisite.

The decoration of the façade, is typical of the Renaissance: the base is quite plain but the ornamentation increases on each floor so that the roof line is a forest of chiselled stone with pinnacles, turrets, gables and flying buttresses.

The left-wing stone staircase leads to the **Salle des Procureurs** (Prosecutors' Room). This large room has a splendid modern panelled ceiling.

Place du Vieux-Marché★

In the Middle Ages the square was the scene of public mockery and executions. On the north, the foundations of the pillories have been excavated, and on the South, an outline marks the tribune from where the judges of **Joan of Arc** watched her execution. A cross has been erected at the spot where she was burned at the stake on 30 May 1431.

Église Ste-Jeanne-d'Arc – *pl. du Vieux-Marché.* ◷*Open Apr–Oct Mon–Thu and Sat 10am–noon, 2–6pm, Fri and Sun 2–6pm; Nov–Mar to 5.30pm.* ℘*02 32 08 32 40.*

Completed in 1979, the church is shaped like an upturned ship. Inside are 13 panels of superb **Renaissance stained glass**★★ (16C) from St Vincent's Church, which was destroyed in 1944. This unique ensemble depicts the Childhood of Christ, the Passion, the Crucifixion, the Resurrection, and the lives of St Anne, St Peter and St Anthony of Padua in a variety of rich colours.

Musée Jeanne-d'Arc – *33 pl. du Vieux-Marché.* ◷ *Open mid-Apr–mid-Sept 9.30am–7pm; rest of year 10am–noon, 2–6.30pm.* ◷*Closed 1 Jan, 25 Dec.* ☞€5. ℘*02 35 88 02 70. www.jeanne-darc.com.* Exhibits include a wax museum and a vaulted cellar with a model of the castle where Joan of Arc was imprisoned.

Rue du Gros-Horloge★★

Connecting place du Vieux-Marché to the cathedral is the abbreviated rue du Gros, a busy commercial street during the Middle Ages and the seat of local government from the 13C to the 18C. With its large cobblestones and attractive 15C–17C half-timbered houses, rue du Gros-Horloge is nowadays one of the city centre's major tourist attractions.

Gros-Horloge *Apr–Oct Tue–Sun 10am–1pm, 2–7pm; Nov–Mar Tue–Sun 2–6pm;* ◷*Closed 1 Jan, 25 Dec;* ☞€6; ℘*02 32 08 01 90).*

The most popular monument in Rouen. The clock, formerly placed in the belfry, was moved to its present location in 1527 when the arch was specially constructed to receive it. In addition to the single hand which gives the hours, there is the central section telling the phases of the moon and the lower inset indicating the weeks.

The small tower is topped by a dome added in the 18C to replace the one removed by Charles VI in 1382 to punish the citizens of Rouen, who had organised a tax revolt, known as La Harelle.

Within there is a spiral staircase (1457). Inside are the two bells (13C) which gave the signal for the Harelle uprising: on the right the Rouvel (not operated since 1903); on the left, the Cache-Ribaud, which sounds the curfew every night at 9pm. From the top of the belfry there is a majestic **vista**★★ of the city, its port and the surrounding countryside.

Next to the belfry is the Renaissance loggia, where the Great Clock keeper used to stand, as well as a beautiful 18C fountain.

On the corner of rue du Gros-Horloge

and rue Thouret stands the old town hall (1607).

▶ *Rue du Gros-Horloge leads back to place de la Cathédrale.*

After this long walk around town, you will want to relax in one of the outdoor cafés set up around the square.

▶ *From place de la Calende, rue de l'Épicerie leads to the Fierté St-Romain and the Halle aux Toiles.*

Fierté St-Romain

This charming Renaissance building is crowned by a stone lantern that used to contain the relics of St Romanus.
The building adjoins the **Halle aux Toiles** (Linen Hall), with exhibit, conference and banquet rooms.

OTHER SIGHTS
Hôtel de Bourgtheroulde

15 pl. de la Pucelle, behind the place du Vieux-Marché. This magnificent building recently became home to a 4-star hotel, Le Camp du Drap d'or. Visits remain possible, by appointment only:
℘02 35 14 50 50.

This famous early 16C mansion (pronounced Boortrood), inspired both by Gothic and early Renaissance styles, was built by Guillaume le Roux, Lord Bourgtheroulde. Stand back a little to look at the façade and then enter the inner court.
The end building is pure Flamboyant, with a hexagonal staircase tower. The left gallery is entirely Renaissance with six wide basket-handle arches. It is surrounded by friezes: the upper one, disfigured, shows the Triumphs of Petrarch, the lower, the famous meeting of Henry VIII and François II on the Field of the Cloth of Gold (1520).

Musée Pierre Corneille

4 r. de la Pie. Jul–Aug Wed–Sun and public holidays 2–6pm; Sept–Jun Sat–Sun and public holidays 2–6pm (last entry 30min before closing). ◐*Closed 1 Jan, 25 Dec.* ⊘*No charge.*
℘02 35 71 28 82.

The French playwright **Pierre Corneille** (1606–84) was born and lived here for 56 years. Considered the father of French Classical tragedy he wrote, among others, *Mélite* (1629; first performed in Rouen), *Le Cid*, *Horace* and *Cinna*.

♟♟ Musée Flaubert et d'Histoire de la Médecine

51 r. de Lecat. ◐*Open Tue 10am–6pm, Wed–Sat 10am–noon, 2–6pm, ticket office closes at 5.30pm.* ◐*Closed public holidays. No admission.* ℘*02 35 15 59 95. www.chu-rouen.fr/museeflaubert.*
The Hôtel-Dieu (17C–18C) has a Classical façade. This museum devoted to the history of medicine is set in the home where **Gustave Flaubert** (1821–80) was born. His father worked as a surgeon. Souvenirs of Flaubert are on display.

Musée des Antiquités de la Seine-Maritime★★

198 r. Beauvoisine. ♿◐*Open Wed–Mon 10am–12.15pm, 1.30–5.30pm, Sun and holidays 2–6pm.* ⊘€*3.*
℘02 35 98 55 10.
A 17C convent houses this museum which displays objects from prehistory to the 19C. From the Middle Ages and the Renaissance are items including stunning religious gold and silver plate (12C Valasse Cross), 12C–13C **enamels**★, 5C–16C **ivories**★ (a 14C seated Virgin) as well as a collection of arms and Moorish and Italian majolica. In a long gallery are Gothic and Renaissance **carved façades**★ from half-timbered houses in old Rouen. A separate gallery contains the 15C **Winged Deer tapestry**★★ and Renaissance furnishings.
The **Gallo-Roman collection**★, famed for its bronzes and glassware, includes the **Lillebonne mosaic**★★ (4C, restored 19C), the largest signed and illuminated Roman mosaic in France.
Near the museum gardens stands the large **Fontaine Ste-Marie** by Falguière.

Église St-Patrice

Corner r. St-Patrice and r. de l'Abbé-Cochet. ◐*Call for hours.*
℘02 35 71 85 65.
This Gothic church is remarkable for

Rouen Faïence

The word ceramics covers all aspects of terracotta (baked clay), whereas faïence is a type of ceramic made of compound clay covered with a tin-based enamel. White in colour, faïence can be decorated. Two types of earth went into the making of Rouen faïence: St-Aubin (from the Boos Plateau), clayey and bright red, and earth from Quatre-Mares (between Sotteville and St-Étienne-du-Rouvray), a light, sandy alluvial soil. Mixed in the right proportions, the result was ground, washed, dried, powdered, sifted and placed in decantation containers. When sufficiently consistent, the mixture was placed near an oven to finish the evaporation process, and then trodden to extract fermentation gases. Sand was then added to form a ceramic compound. Finally there were the different processes of shaping, casting, glazing, painting and curing.

its **stained-glass windows**★ made between 1538 and 1625. The windows on the north side of the chancel depict the Triumph of Christ; in the adjoining chapels are St Faron, St Fiacre, St Louis and St Eustache, and an Annunciation in Italian Renaissance style as well as a Nativity scene. In the north aisle are the stories of St Barbara and St Patrick and Job. An 18C gilt baldaquin crowns the altar.

Tour Jeanne-d'Arc

r. du Donjon. ⏰*Open Apr–Sept Mon and Wed–Sat 10am–12.30pm, 2–6pm, holidays 2–6.30pm; rest of year, Mon and Wed–Sat 10am–12.30pm, 2–5pm, holidays 2–5.30pm.* ∞€1.50 ☎02 35 88 02 70.

This is the former keep in Philippe Auguste's 13C castle, where Joan was tortured on 9 May 1431. The second floor is devoted to the life of Joan of Arc.

Église St-Romain

r. de la Rouchefoucauld. ⏰*Call for hours.* ☎02 35 71 42 64. The former 17C Carmelite chapel, restored in the 19C and again in 1969, contains interesting Renaissance **stained glass**.

Muséum d'Histoire naturelle

198 r. Beauvoisine. ⏰*Open 2–5.30pm.* ∞*3€.* ☎ 02 35 71 41 50. www.rouen.fr. &. The reopening of the museum in 2007 allowed the public to rediscover the 400,000 or so objects that made it renowned. In a 17C former convent,

this museum is halfway between a cabinet of curiosities and a futuristic laboratory! Ornithology, ethnography, botany: the collections showcase the history of science (notice especially the dioramas). Nevertheless, the collections are turned to the future; it is difficult to visit without thinking about biodiversity, respect for the ecosystem and management of natural resources.

Close to the museum gardens and overlooking rue Louis-Ricard, the monumental **Ste-Marie fountain** (C1), sculpted by Falguière, hides a water tower. The **lycée Corneille**, a school a step away *(rue Joyeuse)*, is in a former Jesuit school (17C–18C) frequented by Corneille and Cavelier de La Salle. Corot, Flaubert, Maupassant, Maurois studied there and the philosopher Alain taught there.

Musée maritime, fluvial et portuaire

Quai E.-Duchemin, Hangar n° 13. &⏰*Open Mon and Wed–Fri, 10am–12.30pm, 2–6pm, Sat–Sun and holidays 2–6pm;* •guided tours possible (2hr, by appointment 15 days prior). ⏰*Closed 1 Jan, 1 Mar, 25 Dec. €4.50(-6 years old, free).* ☎0 32 10 15 51. www.musee-maritime-rouen.asso.fr.

Special documentation makes this maritime, river and port museum very accessible to children.

In an old hangar in Rouen's port, this museum presents the history of the city's river activity, with photos and informative panels as support. It addresses first all professions tied to the sector. Both voters and mechanics are exhibited as well as models, with a look back at certain legendary ships such as *La Combattante*. Temporary exhibitions and conferences.

Right bank quay

There is an esplanade on the right bank quays from the Croisière terminal to pont Corneille (B2), going by the quai du Havre (A2) and the quai de la Bourse (B2). A path gives access on foot, bicycle or skates to the old hangars are stored in the 19C.

In Hangar 2, **Espace H2O** (*quai de Bois-Guilbert, Espace des arégraphes.* ⏱*Open Mar–Aug 9am–6.30pm, Sat–Sun 2.30–6.30pm, Sept–Feb 9am–5.30pm, Sat–Sun 2.30–5.30pm. Closed Mon, 1 May, 25 Dec, 1 Jan.* ✎€3 (under-7 year-olds free); ⏱No admission 1st Sun and 3rd Wed of month. ✆02 35 52 95 29; www.la-crea.fr*) is dedicated to eco-sciences and sustainable development. The space was created for children (from age 7) and adults. There are three levels of exhibition rooms, and ordered for him and workshops. The ground floor has interactive temporary exhibitions.

Pont Gustave-Flaubert

Constructed upstream of the five current bridges, the Gustave Flaubert is a transporter bridge and the sixth to cross the Seine. The designers include Michel Virlogeux, who designed the Normandy bridge and Millau viaduct. Inaugurated in 2008 at the time of the Armada, the Flaubert bridge is the longest of its type in Europe (670m/2,197ft). Its horizontal deck raises in 12 minutes, to allow passage of cruise ships and yachts returning periodically to Rouen for the Armada.

EXCURSIONS
Jardin des Plantes★

▷ *2.5km/1.5mi. Leave Rouen by avenue de Bretagne, or take bus route no 7 and get off at Dufay or Jardin des Plantes. 114 av. des Martyrs-de-la-Résistance.*

♿⏱*Open daily 8am–7.45pm in summer, 8.30am–5.15pm in winter. Greenhouses open 9–11am, 1.30–4.30pm.* ✎*No charge.* ✆*02 32 18 21 30.* This beautiful 10ha/25-acre park, originally designed in the 17C, contains around 3,000 plant species inside the conservatories and **tropical hothouses** and a further 5,000 out in the open air. A star attractions is the **Victoria Regia**, a giant water lily from the Amazon, whose large, flat leaves can reach a diameter of 1m/3.3ft in summer. Its flowers bloom, change colour and die the same day.

Centre Universitaire

▷ *5km/3mi. Leave Rouen by rue Chasselièvre NW.*

From the road, which ends on the Mont-aux-Malades plateau where the university lies, there is a good **panorama**★★ of the city, the port and the curve in the river.

Cimetière monumental

▷ *2 km/1.2mi northwest of centre. Leave from place Beauvoisine (C1) and reach place du Boulingrain by bd de l'Yser. Take avenue Georges-Métayer on left by the Saint-Hilaire exit.*

The "Père Lachaise" of Rouen, this monumental cemetery is worth going out of your way for, with various architectural styles for the tombs of well-known figures dear to Rouen inhabitants: Gustave Flaubert (1821–1880), François-Adrien Boieldieu (1775–1834), the city's mayors and politicians and major industrialists. Superb panoramic view of Rouen.

Manoir Pierre-Corneille

▷ *In Petit-Couronne, 8km/5mi. From Rouen take avenue de Bretagne, on the map; turn right by the first houses of Petit-Couronne onto rue Pierre-Corneille.* 🅿*Leave the car before no 502.* ♿⏱*Open Apr–Sept Wed–Sat and public holidays 10am–12.30pm, 2–6pm, Oct–Mar Wed–Sat and public holidays 10am–12.30pm, 2–5.30pm, Sun 2–5.30pm.* ⏱*Closed 1 Jan, 1 May, 11 Nov, 25 Dec.* ✎€3. ✆*02 35 68 13 89.* The Norman "house in the fields" was bought in 1608 by the poet's father, who died in 1639, leaving it to Corneille. The museum evokes the writer's family life with 17C furniture.

Musée industriel de la Corderie Vallois

◑ 8km/5mi NW. Leave Rouen by quai Gaston-Boulet and proceed towards Dieppe; follow N 27 until you reach Notre-Dame-de-Bondeville.
&⚲☛ Guided tour (1hr20min) daily from 2pm. Open 1.30–6pm. ◷ Closed 1 Jan, 1 May, 1 and 11 Nov, 25 Dec.
⚄ €3. (-18 years old free)
𝄢 02 35 74 35 35.
Recently restored, this old factory has retained 19C rope-making machinery in working order. A huge paddle wheel drives the whole complex mechanism.

Forêt Verte

◑ 23km/14.3mi – Allow about 1hr. Leave Rouen by rue Bouquet.
The road passes through the forest, a favourite spot with the Rouennais.

Barentin

◑ 17km/10.5mi NW. Leave Rouen by A 15 or N 15.
Entering Barentin from Mesnil-Roux you see a 13.5/44.3ft polystyrene Statue of Liberty, made for a film. The town boasts works by Rodin, Janniot, Bourdelle and Gromaire. On place de la Libération is a 17C fountain by Coustou.
The brick railway viaduct, 505m/1,657ft long, which carries the Paris–Le Havre railway line across the Austreberthe Valley, stands in Barentin.
The 19C **church** (◷ Open Mon–Tue and

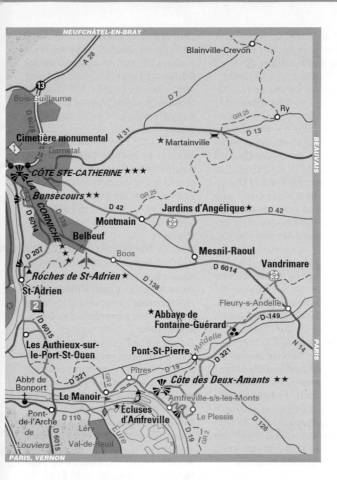

NEUFCHÂTEL-EN-BRAY

Blainville-Crevon

Bois-Guillaume

Cimetière monumental

Darnetal

★ Martainville

Ry

BEAUVAIS

CÔTE STE-CATHERINE ★★★

Bonsecours ★★

LA CORNICHE

Jardins d'Angélique ★

Montmain

Belbeuf

Boos

Mesnil-Raoul

Vandrimare

Rôches de St-Adrien ★

St-Adrien

Fleury-s-Andelle

★ Abbaye de
Fontaine-Guérard

PARIS

Les Authieux-sur-
le-Port-St-Ouen

Pont-St-Pierre

Pitres

Abb. de
Bonport

Le Manoir

Côte des Deux-Amants ★★

Amfreville-s/s-les-Monts

★ Écluses
d'Amfreville

Pont-
de-l'Arche
de

Léry

Le Plessis

Louviers

Val-de-Reuil

PARIS, VERNON

Thu–Sat 9.30am–5pm. ◑*Closed public
holidays;* ✆*02 35 91 21 35)* has modern
windows depicting the lives of St Martin,
St Helier and St Austreberthe.

🚗 DRIVING TOURS

1 LA BOUCLE DE ROUMARE
*Itinerary on map above. 50 km/31mi.
4hr30min.*

▶ *Motorway south from Pont Guillaume
le Conquerant, then N 138 for Caen, Orival
exit by RD 938. At Orival take D 64 for La
Bouille. Turn left right after going under
motorway bridge.*

The tour begins with the **Château
de Robert-le-Diable** (◑*Nov–Mar*

10am–4.30pm; Apr–Oct 10am–6.30pm
– only wall-walk open), which was
Robert-the-Devil's 11C Seine fortress.
From the château, take the D 64 north
to **Moulineaux**, which has a 13C
church with attractive **stained-glass
windows**★.
From Moulineaux you must backtrack
on the D 64 to **La Bouille**, Hector Malot's
pretty birthplace. From here you can
take a ferry across the Seine to **Sahurs**,
where you catch sight of the 16C Mar-
beauf Chapel *(closed to public)*. Nearby
are the ▰▰**Fôret de Roumare - Parc
animalier** *(26ha/64 acres. Brochure at
tourist offices)* and **Eglise de Sahurs**,
which enjoys a pretty view.
Take the D 67 north along the Seine to
St-Pierre de Manneville and the grand
residence and park of **Manoir de Vil-**

lers (*☎02 35 32 07 02; ⊙Open May–Sept park open Sat–Wed; Apr, Oct Sat 2.30–5.30pm, Sun, hols 3–6.30pm. ⊙Closed Nov–Mar. ⊛€7 manor, park; €5 park*).

In **Quevillon** is the sumptuous 17C château de la Rivière-Bourdet (⊙closed to public). Further along the D 67 is **St-Martin-de-Boscherville** ★★. The **Abbaye St-Georges** ★★ (⊙Open daily Apr–Oct 9am–6.30pm; Nov–Mar 2–6pm. ⊙Closed 1 Jan, 25 Dec. ⊛€4.50/5.50; ☎02 35 32 10 82) was founded by William of Tancarville in 1144 and built where a collegiate church once stood. Concerts are often organised here (contact the tourist office). The chapter house dates from the 12C, surmounted by a 17C structure. The conventual outbuilding, built in 1690 and partly demolished by the Revolution, was restored in 1994; the chapelle des Chambellans was built in 13C for Chambellans of Tancarville. The formal French **park** was restored in the 17C style.

Leaving St-Martin-de-Boscherville, take the D 982 to **Duclair**, where two trekking paths leave from the tourist office (227 av. du Prés.-Coty). Duclair also has a 12–15C church, the **Église Saint-Denis**, as well as the formal English-style **château du Taillis park** (☎02 35 37 95 46. ♿. ⊙Open May–mid-Oct Wed–Sun 2–5pm. ⊙Closed Nov–mid-Apr. ⊛€1) and a good World War II museum.

② TOWARDS THE VEXIN

Itinerary on map pp100–1. 110km/34mi, 4hr30min. From place St-Paul in Rouen (C2) take r. Henri-Rivière, then r. du Mont-Gargan; right on r. Annie-de-Pène.

The winding road of the **Côte Ste-Catherine** ★★★ has a **panoramic view** of the river, Rouen and its surrounding area. Follow the D 95 and then the route marked on the map to get to **Bonsecours** ★★ and its neo-Gothic basilica (1840), which has magnificent **panoramic views** ★★, as does the cemetery.

Head towards Mesnil-Esnard on D 6014; continue 3km/1mi, then turn right on D7 to park right in front of the 18C château of **Belbeuf**. Belbeuf's pretty church is worth a look while you are here.

Leaving Belbeuf, follow the D 7 then N15 for St Adrien. **Roches de St-Adrien** ★ includes the two 🚶‍♂️**Coteau de St-Adrien** walking routes (info at tourist office) to a rocky spur. The chapelle St-Adrien (by foot ⊙Tue and Sat 10am–noon, 2–5pm) is a 13C partly troglodytic chapel

Follow the N15 then signs to **Les Authieux-sur-le-Port-St-Ouen**, which is notable for the Renaissance window of its church (contact the mairie at ☎02 35 23 35 35). From here, take the D13, N15, D 321, then D508 to get to **Le Manoir**, which has a fine glass-brick modern church.

From Le Manoir take the D508, D20 and D19, then turn right for Amfreville-sous-les-Monts, where the **Côte des Deux-Amants** ★★ coastal road begins. There is a magnificent view of the Seine and Eure; the **panorama des Deux-Amants** ★★.

Return via Le Plessis and Amfreville-sous-les-Monts to get to the locks, dam and fishery with observation room at the **Écluses d'Amfreville** ★ (☎02 32 59 08 44. ⊙Open Sat–Sun, hols 2–6.30pm; €4) and the musée de la Batellerie.

Moving on, follow the D20 south, then the D508 north to **Pont-St-Pierre** and its 11–12C church with **sculpted wood** ★. At the 12C **Abbaye de Fontaine-Guérad** ★ (☎02 32 49 03 82. ♿. ⊙Open Jul–Aug Tue–Sun 10.30am–6.30pm; Sept–Jun 2–6pm) there is an interesting chapter room and dormitory.

Follow D149 and D505 to **Vandrimare**, which has a chateau, park and gardens (☎02 32 49 03 57. ⊙Open mid-Apr–mid-Oct Fri–Sun, hols 2.30–7pm; closed 1st wkd Jul and Aug), then take the D6014 and follow signs to Le Mesnil-Raoul for the **Le Mesnil-Raoul mechanical music museum** (☎02 35 82 42 42. ⊙Open May–Sept Wed–Mon 2–6pm, Oct–Mar by appt).

Finally, the tour ends further along the D42, en-route to see the 2,000 varieties of rose on display in the gardens at **Montmain - Jardins d'Angélique** (☎02 35 79 08 12. ⊙Jul–Oct Wed–Mon 10am–7pm; May–Jun 10am–7pm; closed Nov–Apr).

Clères★

One of Normandy's greatest attractions is the animal park at the château of Clères. The original castle, now in ruins, was built in the 11C. The present château consists of a 19C western wing in the neo-Gothic style, and an eastern wing dating from the 15C, which was remodelled towards 1505. In the market square stands the wooden structure and slate roof of an 18C covered market.

SIGHT

▲▲ Parc Zoologique de Clères-Jean-Delacour★

&▲🕐*Open daily Apr–Sept 10am–7pm; Mar and Oct 10am–6.30pm; Feb and Nov 1.30–5pm.* ☞*€6 (-18 years old €4, 13 free).* ✆*02 35 33 23 08. www.parcdecleres.net.* ✍*The best time to visit is before end Jun.*

In an exceptional natural setting, the park of Clères provides a wonderful opportunity to see the birds and mammals collected by the botanist and ornithologist **Jean Delacour** (1890–1985). In the garden are pink flamingos, ducks and exotic geese. Antelope, kangaroos, gibbons, cranes, peacocks and deer roam in partial liberty. Indoor and outdoor aviaries are reserved for lesser-known birds, some endangered species: around 2,000 birds. In the former main room of the château, a gallery houses rare exotic birds.

EXCURSIONS

▲▲ Parc du Bocasse

▶ *2km/1mi W by D 6.* ✆*02 35 33 22 25. www.parcdubocasse.fr.* &. *Jul–Aug 10am–6.30pm (last entry 1 hour before closing); Apr–Jun and Sept see website or contact for details.* ☞*€13 .*

With 30 attractions including mini golf and plenty of head-spinning fairgound rides, this place will keep children (and adults accompanying them) amused for hours. You can bring a picnic.

▶ **Population:** 1,303.
👌 **Michelin Map:** 304: G-4.
🄸 **Info:** 59 av. du Parc. ✆02 35 33 38 64. www.ot-cleres.fr.
▶ **Location:** Clères is 30km/18.5mi N of Rouen, following A 150, A 151 and D 6, or about 50km/31mi S of Dieppe by N 27 and D 6.
👁 **Don't Miss:** The rare birds in the aviary at Clères.
🕐 **Timing:** Give yourself a good 2hr to tour the zoo.
▲▲ **Kids:** After the Clères zoo, visit the amusement park at Bocasse.

Parc Zoologique de Clères-Jean-Delacour

© Thomas Pozzo Di Borgo/Dreamstime.com

Montville

▶ *6km/4mi S on the D 155.*

The ▲▲**Musée des Sapeurs-Pompiers de France** (✆*02 35 33 13 51.* &. 🕐*Open Apr–Oct Mon–Fri 9am–12.30pm, 2–6pm, Sat–Sun 2–6pm; Nov–Mar Mon–Fri 9am–12.30pm, 2–5pm, Sat–Sun 2–5pm.* 🕐*Closed Christmas school hol, 1 Jan, 1 May, 1 and 11 Nov, 25 Dec.*☞*€4 (children €1.50)* has a fine collection of red fire engines, banners and uniforms, tall ladders and gleaming helmets. The museum retraces the glorious history of the French fire brigades.

Louviers★

Badly damaged in 1940, Louviers has been carefully reconstructed, sparing the remaining old houses and delightful avenues along the River Eure. The old town north of Notre-Dame Church has pretty half-timbered houses, such as in rue Tatin, rue du Quai and rue Pierre Mendès-France. Louviers remains an industrial centre, especially in the north of the town.

WALKING TOUR

From the Notre-Dame Church in the town centre, take rue de la Poste, which crosses both branches of the Eure river.

Ancien couvent des Pénitents

Allow 30min.
All that remains of this Franciscan convent, built in 1646 on a tributary of the Eure, is the inhabited main building together with three small arcaded galleries belonging to the cloister. The western gallery is in a ruinous state and overlooks a square with lawn and trees. Rue de la Trinité *(on the left)* leads into the former manufacturing district and to **rue Terneaux**, where the buildings have large attics once used for drying out dyed fabrics.

Take the short rue Polhomet to the right, then turn right again on rue du Quai. Pretty half-timbered houses line the street. Rue au Coq, on the left, leads to the museum; rue Pierre-Mendès-France takes you back to the east end of Notre Dame Church.

▶ **Population:** 18,785.

Michelin Map: 304: H-6.

Info: 10 rue du Maréchal-Foch. ℰ02 32 40 04 41. www.tourisme-seine-eure.com.

Location: Louviers is 32km/20mi S of Rouen and 103km/64mi NW of Paris via A 13.

Don't Miss: The Flamboyant Notre-Dame Church and Acquigny park.

Timing: You will need 1hr30min to see the town.

Musée municipal

Open Wed–Mon 2–6pm. Closed 1 Jan, 1 May, 25 Dec. No charge.
ℰ02 32 09 58 55. www.ville-louviers.fr.
The museum hosts temporary exhibitions of faïence, furniture and painting. One room is devoted to the clothing industry.

Maison du Fou du Roy

10 r. du Maréchal-Foch.
This half-timbered house in the main street is also the tourist office. It once belonged to Guillaume Marchand, an apothecary, who became Henri IV's jester (Fou du Roy) after the previous incumbent was killed in battle.

Église Notre-Dame

Major restorations until 2012. To visit call ℰ02 32 40 04 41 (tourist office).
Built in the 13C, this church received its famous Flamboyant exterior in the

---

Normandy's Literary Ghosts

Many of Normandy's towns, villages, manor houses, coastal and rural scenes were described often under a fictional name by one of the region's celebrated writers.
Cabourg – the Balbec in Marcel Proust's *À la recherche du temps perdu*.
Ry – the Yonville-l'Abbaye of Gustave Flaubert's *Madame Bovary* (1857).
Le Havre – Guy de Maupassant's *Pierre et Jean* (1888).
Inland from Yport – Maupassant's *Une Vie* (1883).
The Cotentin – Barbey d'Aurevilly's (the Walter Scott of the region) *Le Chevalier des Touches*, *Une vieille maîtresse* and *L'Ensorcelée*.

Église Notre-Dame

© Marek Slusarczyk/Fotolia.com

late 15C. Outside, the **porch**★ is stone lacework, but it is especially the south side that shows great Gothic virtuosity. Several Interesting **artworks**★ inside.

🚗 DRIVING TOURS

Between the Seine and the Eure
3km/32mi. Allow 2hr.

▶ *Leave Louviers south on D 71, then left on D 82.*

Acquigny French Gardens
℘02 32 50 23 31. www.chateau-acquigny.com. ♿Open daily Jul–Aug 2–7pm; Apr–Jun and Sept–Oct wkds and public holidays 2–6pm. ⬤€7.
The formal **French gardens**, lying at the confluence of the River Eure and River Iton, still have long avenues and orangery. Waterfalls, artificial streams and recall the Romantic period.

▶ *Cross the Eure to reach the D 164. From the bridge over the river, preview of the late 16C château. Take the D 164 north, then turn righte onto the D 6155. At Heudebouville, head northwest to Vironvay on the D 6015.*

Vironvay
The isolated church overlooks the Seine Valley. The **view**★ on approaching extends over the river spanned by the bridge at St-Pierre-du-Vauvray and, further east, the ruins of Château-Gaillard.

▶ *Take the D 6015. At Vaudreuil, turn right onto the D 77. Before Les Damps, follow the sign on the right indicating "Base de loisirs de Léry-Poses".*

👥 Réserve ornithologique de la Grande Noë
D3 ℘02 31 43 52 56. www.gonm.org.
Guided tours of the ornithological reserve in summer; a great many species of migrating birds make a stop here, taking advantage of the wide diversity of environments for refuge.

Pont-de-l'Arche
▶ *11km/7mi E by D 321 along the south bank of the Seine.*
The small town, named after the first bridge to be built over the lower Seine, is pleasantly set in a valley. On the south side is Bord Forest.
The **Église Notre-Dame-des-Arts** exhibits the Flamboyant Gothic style in the doorway and the ornate south side. The interior is lit by 16C and 17C windows. The Louis XIII altarpiece shows the Resurrection by CLF Le Tourneur (1751–1817).

Elbeuf

Elbeuf was once a major cloth-making centre, but the 15C industry begun here declined; today there is manufacturing of chemicals, electrical goods, machinery, metallurgy and automobiles.

⚡ WALKING TOUR

OLD TOWN

◑ *Allow 1 hour. Leave your car in the car park opposite the hôtel de ville.*

All that is Viking about Elbeuf now is its name - the Scandinavian suffixes *bo* or *bou* gave *beuf* (from *budh*: "temporary shelter"). The itinerary therefore concentrates more on the town's cloth-making past.

◑ *Take rue Henry.*

Église St-Jean-Baptiste

pl. St-Jean. ⏱*Open Mon–Fri 9am–1.30pm.* ⚬*Choir closed for repairs.*
Gothic church, Classical ornamentation and furnishings, 16C stained glass. The oldest and best preserved is in the 1st, 3rd, 4th and 5th north aisle windows and the first south aisle window.
Across from the church, **place St-Jean** and the Puchot district are at the heart of the old town.

18C house in the Old Town

G. Targat/MICHELIN

▶ **Population:** 17,277.
♿ **Michelin Map:** 304: G-6.
▤ **Info:** 28 rue Henry. ☏02 35 77 03 78. www.tourisme-elbeuf.org.
◐ **Location:** Elbeuf is 20km/12.4mi north of rouen or 14km/8.5mi south of Louviers).
◉ **Don't Miss:** The old cloth-making neighbourhoods; a River Oison excursion.
◑ **Timing:** Attractions are more likely to be open in afternoons.

◑ *Turn left on rue Guyemer.*

At **no 72** rue Guyemer, the large 18C building was the **manufactory of Grandin de L'Epervier.** At **no 63** was the **Godet manufactory**; an 18C workshop and a old mill (19C) surround the courtyard remains. Note the ostentatious roof on the Maison 1740 in the same street.

◑ *Straight along rue R.-Poulain, first right to place de la République.*

From **place de la République** note the old 19C smokestack; the **Clarenson factory** replaced the Petou manufactory before closing in 1961. The beautiful 18C structure, under restoration, is best seen from the back.

◑ *rue aux Bœufs; cross rue Boucher-de-Perthes. Go through the gardens to St-Étienne Church.*

Église St-Étienne

r. de la République. ⏱*Open May–Oct Sat 10.30am–1pm.*
Flamboyant church with 16C stained glass. Note the Crucifixion on the apse's top right window, the north aisle Life of the Virgin and Tree of Jesse near the Lady Chapel. St Roch is in the south aisle chapel, and a panel shows drapers in work clothes. Carved Louis XV-style rood beam, 13C recumbent Christ; St Stephen and St John flank the chancel.

Musée intercommunal d'Elbeuf A2

Cours Gambetta. ♿⏰*Open Tue–Sun, 2–6pm.* ☏*02 32 96 30 40.* *www.la-crea.fr.* ✎*No charge.*
This new museum is in the **former Blin & Blin textile factories**. The theme of the Seine links the three collections of Elbeuf's natural history, archaeology and industrial heritage. Temporary exhibitions.

Circus-Theatre B1

2 rue Henry. www.cirquetheatre-elbeuf.com. ☏*02 32 13 19 83.*
✎*Guided tours only by appointment.*
Recently restored octagonal building, a remaining examples of 19C circus architecture.

▶ *Return by r. Augustin Henry to get to place A. Briand.*

EXCURSIONS

Saint-Ouen-de-Pontcheuil

▶ *8km/5mi S via D 840. Moulin Amour* ♿⏰*Open 11 Jul–24 Aug Tue–Sat 2.30–6.30pm; 25 Apr–10 Jul and 25 Aug–3 Oct Sun and public holidays 2.30–6.30pm.* ✎€4. ☏*02 32 35 80 27.* *www.moulinamour.com.*
The **Moulin Amour**, the last official water mill along the River Oison's banks, operates only in demonstrations.

Les Roches d'Orival ★

♿*See HONFLEUR, p182.*

Château de Robert le Diable★

Musée des Vikings. ⚷*Closed to visitors.* The castle overlooks the Seine Valley. Robert the Devil is vaguely on Robert the Magnificent, William the Conqueror's father. Destroyed in 1204, Philippe Auguste rebuilt it before the French again destroyed it in the 15C to prevent it from falling to the English.

Abbaye de Jumièges★★★

Jumièges is one of the most impressive ruins in France, occupying a splendid site on the Lower Seine. The history, galleries, south aisle, the nave roof, the transept crossing, the chancel apse and the roofless cloisters are described below.

A BIT OF HISTORY

Jumièges Almshouse – In the 10C Duke William Longsword rebuilt Jumièges on the ruins of the 7C abbey destroyed by the Vikings. The new Benedictine abbey soon became known as the Jumièges Almshouse as well as a centre of learning. The abbey church was consecrated in 1067 in the presence of William the Conqueror.

The last monks dispersed at the Revolution, and in 1793 the abbey was bought by a timber merchant who intended to turn it into a stone quarry

Abbaye de Jumièges

© Ghorg/Fotolia.com

- ⚜ **Michelin Map:** 304: E-5.
- ℹ **Info:** Rue Guillaume-le-Conquérant. ✆02 35 37 28 97. www.jumieges infotourisme.com and www.jumieges.fr.
  ♿🕐Open daily Jul–Aug 10am–12.30pm, 2–6pm; Apr–Jun and Sept Mon, Tue 2.30–6pm, Wed 10am–noon, Thu–Sun and hols 10am–noon, 2.30–6pm; rest of the year: Tue–Sat 10am–12.30pm, 2–5.30pm. 🕐Closed Sat afternoon (Nov–Feb), 1 May, 1, 11 Nov, 25 Dec. ✆02 35 37 24 02.
- ▶ **Location:** Jumièges is located on a graceful meander of the Seine, between the villages of Duclair and Trait, 28km/17.4mi W of Rouen.
- 😊 **Don't Miss:** Not far from Jumièges, in Mesnils sous Jumièges *(5km/3mi SE via the D 65)* sits the 13C manor where the lovely and astute Agnès Sorel, mistress of Charles VII, died in 1450.
- 🕐 **Timing:** You may wish to spend time admiring the view and strolling near the Seine.
- 😊 **Advice:** Jumièges is a ruin and exposed to the elements: dress for the weather.

and used explosives to bring down the church lantern. A new proprietor in 1852 set about saving the ruins, which now belong to the nation. Many consider these to be the most beautiful ruins in France.

THE ABBEY★★★
Église Notre-Dame

The projecting porch is flanked by twin towers (43m/141ft high),whose spires were visible until 1830.

The entire nave (27m/88.6ft high)

ABBAYE DE JUMIÈGES

still stands, together with part of the transept and the chancel. At the west end there is a deep gallery overlooking the nave, which is articulated by strong square pillars, quartered by columns, alternating with more slender clusters of columns; the aisles are covered by rib vaulting. Most of the transept was demolished in the 19C. Only the west side of the lantern has survived, resting on an arch which is impressive for its height and reach. A slim, pepper-pot turret is attached to the NW corner.

Passage Charles-VII – The passage leading to St Peter's Church was named for the visit of King Charles VII (1403–1461) to Jumièges.

Église St-Pierre – The porch and first bays of the nave are Norman Carolingian (oculi and twinned arcades) the remaining ruins date from the 13C and 14C. The arched entrance porch is flanked by two small doors with stairs to the gallery towers behind. The first two bays of the nave are a rare example of 10C Norman architecture.

Chapter house – Between the abbey

and St Peter's, the 12C chapter house opens off the cloisters. The square body and apse were covered with some of the earliest ogival vaulting known to have existed.

Cloisters – In the middle of the cloisters grows an ancient yew tree. The four galleries once consisted of 26 bays. The refectory was on the south side.

Storeroom – The great cellar dates to the late 12C.

Gardens – Beyond a fence, a 17C set of steps leads to a broad terrace and the gardens.

Abbot's Lodging – Beyond the lawn rises the former abbot's lodging, a majestic 17C rectangular building.

Église paroissiale St-Valentin

⏰*Open Jul–Aug Wed–Mon 2–6pm.*
☎*02 35 37 28 97.*

The parish church, which dominates the village, has an 11C–12C nave and a 16C chancel and ambulatory; inside, altarpieces and 15C–16C stained-glass windows in ambulatory chapels escaped pillaging in the Revolution.

Parc naturel régional des Boucles de la Seine★★

The Brotonne Forest was made readily accessible by the creation of the Parc naturel régional des Boucles de la Seine in 1974 and the construction of the Brotonne Bridge in 1977. La Haye-de-Routot is part of the Écomusée de la Basse-Seine (regional open-air museum), which preserves ancient crafts.

DRIVING TOUR

FORÊT DE BROTONNE
80km/50mi. About 3hr.

▶ *Leave Notre-Dame-de-Bliquetuit on D 913/D 313 S.*

Some say that the Breto Forest is named after St-Condède, a Breton hermit to whom the Merovingian King Theodoric II gave part of the forest of Arelaune; others say it went to a certain *Burton*. No matter, the **forest roads** (D 40 and D 131) offer beautiful views between the beaches, oaks and firs.

Notre-Dame-de-Bliquetuit
Nearby, the Parc naturel des Boucles de la Seine normande is headquartered in old farm buildings at the **Maison du Parc**. Discover a conservatory orchard, laid hedge and duck pond while learning about tree species. Two walking routes (8 to 12 km) depart from here.

The " Chêne à la cuve "
100m/yd from the D 313, at milestone 11, to the right of the road. Four oak trunks from the same roots form a natural bowl 7 m across. From here, continue on D 313. After the forest, take the D 90 (right).

Moulin de Hauville
Open May–Sept on differing days.
02 32 56 57 32. €2.

Michelin Map:
304: D-5 to E-5.

Info:
Maison du Parc, 76940 Notre-Dame-de-Bliquetuit. 02 35 37 23 16. www.pnr-seine-normande.com.

Location:
The park extends on either side of the Seine below Rouen. Bridges at Tancarville and Brotonne as well as ferries pass from one bank to the other.

Don't Miss:
The many marked paths in the forest, as well as Vieux-Port and its surroundings.

Timing:
Find lodging outside the park, near Pont-Audemer, and pack a lunch.

This 13C grain mill belonged to the Abbey of Jumièges (*see Abbaye de Jumièges, p108*). Oak roof beams with reed thatching; works visible in stone tower. Small museum in miller's house.

▶ *At Hauville head west for La Haye-Aubrée; take D 686 (right).*

La Haye-de-Routot
Two colossal 1,000-year-old **yews**★ – one contains a chapel, the other an oratory – are next to the cemetery surrounding the small **church** (Sun 2pm–6pm).
The wood-burning **bread oven** (02 32 57 35 74; Jul–Aug 2–6.30pm; Mar–Jun and Sept–Nov Sun and holidays 2–6pm. Closed 1 Jan, 8 May, Mon of Pentecost, 11 Nov, 25 Dec. €2, Sun free for under-16s; breadmaking demonstration and tour of Clog Museum, €3.70) is an 18C structure, demonstrating breadmaking of yore. Exhibition of bakers' tools and fantasy breads.
The **clog museum** (02 32 57 35 74; Jul–Aug 2–6pm; Mar–Jun and Sept–Nov Sun 2–6pm; guided tour possible. Closed 1 Jan, 8 May, Mon of Pentecost, 1 and 11 Nov, 25 Dec. €2) is in a traditional 17C Roumois house; it presents early tools and techniques.

PARC NATUREL RÉGIONAL DES BOUCLES DE LA SEINE NORMANDE

Park border	**M** Museum or exhibition	Bicycle rental	ℹ Information centre
_GR_ Main trails	◊ Outdoor activity area	**F** Ferry	

▷ *Take the D 40 into the forest. At the D 686 intersection turn left, then right on D 90 to Bourneville, then northwest on D 89 for Quillebeuf. At Trouville-la-Haule, turn right on D 95.*

Vieux-Port★

Charming thatched-roofed village nestles in the greenery alongside the Seine. Two itineraries lead from the esplanade alongside the Seine, the **Parcours historique Portut tutus**" and "**Chemin des sources bleues**".
The first (*2km/1mi*) is about the village's origins, the second (*7.8km/5mi*) reveals beautiful thatched houses in hedged farmland alongside the Seine. A mountain bike itinerary (*22 km/13mi*) also leaves from Vieux-Port.

▷ *Continue on the D 95 and go through Aiaier.*

Aizier

The stone belltower of the 12C Romanesque church looks very archaic.
Near the church a stone slab covers the remains of a covered alley (2,000 BC).

▷ *Continue to Vatteville-la-Rue by the D 95, then the D 65.*

Vatteville-la-Rue

In the church's Renaissance nave the walls have an armorial band of black, a trace of a lord's funeral. There is 16C stained-glass in the Flamboyant chapel. Three trekking paths depart from the church to the village centre (5km/3mi), the Seine (10km/6mi) or the forest (17km/10mi).

▷ *St-Nicolas-de-Bliquetuit.*

Beautiful enclosed gardens and quaint half-timbered houses. A trekking path (*5.5km/3mi or 7km/4mi*) leaves from the ferry slipway, heading for the Barre-y-Va meadows (*see p114*).

▷ *From the village, head for the **Pont de Brotonne★**; the bridge, which spans the Seine above Caudebec-en-Caux, was opened in 1977.*

Caudebec-en-Caux★

Caudebec settles around the Seine where the Ste-Gertrude Valley runs into the river. The Brotonne Bridge leads directly to the forest of the same name. A fire in 1940 destroyed most of the old buildings, but the fine Church of Our Lady was virtually undamaged and three old houses to the left of the church give some idea of what Caudebec must once have looked like.

A BIT OF HISTORY

A Short-Lived Prestigious Past – The name Caudebec first appears in the 11C on a charter granted to the monks of St-Wandrille Abbey. In the 12C the town was fortified to resist the English who were nevertheless victorious in 1419. After submitting to Henri IV in 1592, during the Wars of Religion, it became a flourishing glove- and hat-making centre. The Revocation of the Edict of Nantes in 1685, which revived the persecution of Protestants, put an end to this period of prosperity.

◆ WALKING TOUR

2km/1mi. About 1hr starting from the tourist office. From place du Général de Gaulle, take rue de la Vicomté.

The Sentier de la Gribane (signposted and dotted with explanatory panels) provides an interesting itinerary for visiting the city. The promenades of La Vignette and Mont-Calidu offer lovely vistas of the town. On the right , the old prison is set in the 14C ramparts.

▷ *Continue along rue Thomas-Basin.*

Maison des Templiers

1 r. Thomas-Basin. ○*Open early Apr–4 Oct, Wed–Fri and Sun 2.30–6.30pm.* ○*Closed 25 Dec.* ◈*€4.* ℘*02 35 96 95 91.* The Templars' House is a precious specimen of 13C civil architecture which has retained its two original gable walls.

▷ **Population:** 2,336.
◉ **Michelin Map:** 304: E-4.
🗓 **Info:** place du Général-de-Gaulle. ℘02 32 70 46 32. www.tourismecauxseine.com.
▷ **Location:** Midway between Rouen (48km/30mi E) and Le Havre (52km/32.5mi W), Caudebec is on the banks of the Seine.
🅿 **Parking:** Public lots are located on place du Marché (except Saturday mornings), place Henri-IV and place d'Armes.
◉ **Don't Miss:** The Flamboyant architecture of Notre-Dame church, and the pretty town of Villequier.
◷ **Timing:** You need a day at Caudebec.

▷ *Follow cours de la Ste-Gertrude.*

You walk by two towers: **Tour des Fascines** and **Tour d'Harfleur**.

▷ *Take rue du Havre, on the left, and then left again on rue Planquette.*

Église Notre-Dame★

30min. Place du Parvis.

This fine Flamboyant edifice (◉ *see illustration in Introduction: Religious architecture, p62*) which Henri IV described as "the most beautiful chapel in the kingdom" was built between 1425 and 1539.

Exterior – The belfry (53m/174ft high) adjoining the south wall has a delicately worked upper part surmounted by a stone crown spire.

The west face is pierced by three beautiful Flamboyant **doorways** – the larger of the two is said to portray 333 different characters – and by a remarkable rose window surrounded by small statues.

Interior – There is no transept. The triforium and tracery are the most characteristically Flamboyant features.

The 17C **font** *(left)* is decorated with

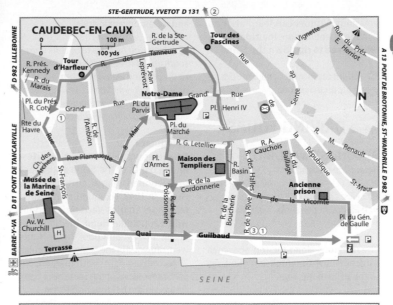

CAUDEBEC-EN-CAUX

WHERE TO STAY	WHERE TO EAT
Marine (Normotel la).. ①	Cheval blanc (Le)... ①
Normandie (Hôtel le).. ③	Rendez-Vous des Chasseurs (Au)..................... ②

intricately carved panels. The **great organ**★ (early 16C – ⌚*see illustration in Introduction: Religious architecture, p63*) was restored in 1972; it has 3,345 pipes of *repoussé* pewter.

Chapelle du St-Sépulcre – The chapel inspired Fragonard to sketch it. Beneath the 16C baldaquin a recumbent Christ, carved in incredible detail, faces some very large stone statues – all from Jumièges Abbey. The Pietà between the windows is 15C.

Chapelle de la Vierge – The Lady Chapel is famous for its **keystone**★, a 7t monolith supported only by the dependent arching and forming a 4.3m/13ft pendentive. The architect of this feat, Guillaume Le Tellier, lies buried in the chapel and is commemorated in a plaque beneath the right window.

▶ *Head for place du Marché, on the right side of the church, and take rue de la Poissonnerie; it overlooks the quays, where you reach them on the right. Continue toward avenue Winston Churchill.*

Musée de la Marine de Seine

av. Winston-Churchill. ⏱*Open Apr–Sept 2–6.30pm; Oct–Mar 2–5.30pm.* ⏱*Closed 1 Jan, 25 Dec.* ✆€4. *☎02 35 95 90 13.*
The museum is devoted to the history of navigation along the River Seine: ports, commercial exchanges, shipbuilding,

Caudebec-en-Caux and the Pont de Brotonne
© Gilles Rigoulet/hemis.fr

crossings. Visitors can learn about a bygone phenomenon, the **tidal bore, which used to rip down the Seine**.

▷ *Return to place du Général de Gaulle along the quai Guilbaud.*

🚗 DRIVING TOURS

AROUND ST-WANDRILLE
Round-trip of 8km/5mi.

▷ *Leave Caudebec by rue St-Clair and follow chemin de Rétival keeping to the right.*

The road runs along the top of a small escarpment with tantalising glimpses of the bend in the river.

▷ *At the bottom of a steep descent take D 37 on the left.*

The road goes up a delightful little **valley**★ with thatched farmhouses scattered here and there.

▷ *Before Rançon, turn right on D 33 to St-Wandrille.*

Abbaye de St-Wandrille★
See Abbaye de St-Wandrille, p115.

▷ *Take D 22 and D 982 back to Caudebec.*

Latham-47 Monument
This commemorates the polar explorer **Roald Amundsen** and his companions, who disappeared in the Arctic in 1928.

▷ *Take D 22, than D 982 to return to Caudebec.*

AROUND BARRE-Y-VA
Round-trip of 21km/13mi. Allow 1hr.

▷ *Leave Caudebec to the north on the Yvetot road and turn left onto D 40.*

Ste-Gertrude
The small **church** stands in attractive surroundings. It was consecrated in 1519

and is Flamboyant in style.

▷ *Head west on D 40, then D 30. Turn south on D 440 towards Anquetierville. At the junction with D 982 turn left, then at St-Arnoult right onto D 440. Turn right onto D 281 and almost immediately left down a steep hill to Villequier.*

Villequier★
Villequier occupies a beautiful **site**★ on the banks of the Seine at the foot of a wooded height crowned by a castle. In 1843, six months after their marriage, Charles Vacquerie and his wife, Léopoldine Hugo, the daughter of the novelist and poet Victor Hugo, were drowned in the Seine at Villequier. 🚶Walking paths with magnificent panoramic views of the Seine have been created in the neighboring forest.
When you leave the town, on the D 81 heading west, there is a bicycle route 12km/7mi long, waiting to be enjoyed by foot, by bicycle or on in-line skates. It follows the towing path as far as Petiville.

Musée Victor-Hugo – Maison Vacquerie★ - *Access through the rue Ernst-Binet.* & ⓒ*Open Apr–Sept Wed–Sat and holidays 10am–12.30pm, 2–6pm, Sun 2–6pm; Oct–Mar Mon, Wed–Sat and holidays 10am–12.30pm, 2–5.30pm, Sun 2–5.30pm.* ⓞ*Closed certain holidays, telephone* ℘*02 35 56 78 31 for information.* ⊜€3.
A house once owned by the Vacquerie family, rich boat builders from Le Havre.

▷ *Take D 81 back to Caudebec.*

Barre-y-Va
This tiny hamlet is named after the tidal wave or bore *(barre)* which used to swell upstream along the Seine. There is an oratory and a small **chapel** perpetuating the memory of pilgrimages; there are also votive offerings that sailors of the Seine have used to express their gratitude and thanks for their safe return.

▷ *Return to Caudebec via D 81.*

Abbaye de St-Wandrille★

St-Wandrille Abbey, like Le Bec-Hellouin, is a moving testimony to the continuity of the Benedictine Order in Normandy. Today, the monks earn their living mainly from the manufacture of furniture polish and household products.

A BIT OF HISTORY

God's Athlete (7C) – King Dagobert's court was celebrating the marriage of Count Wandrille, who seemed destined for a brilliant career, when, to general surprise, the bride entered a convent and Wandrille joined a group of hermits. The king ordered Wandrille to return to court but, enlightened by a miracle, accepted the choice. Wandrille's saintliness and magnificent physique earned him the nickname of God's Athlete.

Valley of the Saints (7C–9C) – In 649, Wandrille founded Fontanelle monastery, "where saints flourish like rose trees in a greenhouse".

Benedictine Continuity – In the 10C, monks began to rebuild the abbey, destroyed by Vikings. It survived the Wars of Religion, but the Revolution scattered the monks and the buildings fell into ruin. In 1931, the Benedictines returned permanently.

Abbaye★

Allow 45min.
The entrance to the abbey is through a 15C door surmounted by a symbolic pelican. The porter's lodge and its twin are 18C. The imposing 18C Porte de Jarente leads to the main courtyard, accessible on guided tours only. The only parts of the abbey church still standing are the tall columns.

Cloisters★

Abbaye de Fontenelle, 2 r. St-Jacques.
🕙*10.30am–12.30pm, 2.30pm–5pm.*
👣*Guided tours possible (1hr).* ⚬€4.
📞*02 35 96 23 11. www.st-wandrille.com.*
The 14C south gallery *(only one open to the public)*, parallel with the nave, was

▶ **Population:** 1,179.
👆 **Michelin Map:** 304: E-4.
ℹ **Info:** 15 rue des Caiettes, 76490 Saint-Wandrille-Rançon. 📞02 35 96 10 89. www.saint-wandrille-rançon.fr.
▶ **Location:** The village and abbey lie on D 982, 4km/2.5mi E of Caudebec and 51km/32mi W of Rouen.
👁 **Don't Miss:** The cloister, the only part of the abbey still intact.
🕐 **Timing:** Visit on Sunday morning or, on other days, in the afternoon.

linked to it by a door surmounted by a now mutilated tympanum illustrating the Coronation of the Virgin. A niche in the 13C church wall contains the graceful 14C statue of Our Lady of Fontenelle.

Èglise

Abbaye de Fontenelle, 2 r. St-Jacques.
🕙*Mass in Gregorian chant at Abbaye de St-Wandrille: 9.45am, Sun and holidays 10am, Vespers 5.30pm, Thu 6.45pm, Sun and holidays 5pm. No visits during services.* 📞*02 35 96 23 11.*
The church is an old 13C tithe barn, the Canteloup Barn, which was transported in 1969 from La Neuville-du-Bosc in the Eure and re-erected at St-Wandrille.

Chapelle St-Saturnin

🔒*Closed to the public. By car, follow the signs;* 👣*on foot about 45min there and back. Leave the abbey and take the path downhill (right); note the 16C Entombment in a niche. Skirt the wall for 150m/164yd; go around a field and take the path beside the abbey wall.*
This small 10C oratory was probably built on Merovingian foundations. The façade was remodelled in the 16C.

Lillebonne

The small industrial town of Lillebonne was once a Roman military camp named Juliobona, after Julius Caesar. With the arrival of several textile factories towards the end of the 19C, the Lillebonne-Bolbec valley came to be known as the Golden Valley.

SIGHTS

Théâtre-Amphithéâtre romain

☛*Under renovation for an undetermined length of time.*
☛*Guided tours by reservation. Enquiries:* ℘*02 35 15 69 11.*
From place de l'Hôtel-de-Ville it is possible to see the general layout of this Roman amphitheatre, built in the 1C and 2C. The central arena follows the usual plan of amphitheatres in north-west Gaul, where all kinds of spectacles were held (mythological scenes, gladiator fights, performing animals, hunts with small game). The crowd watched on from the **cave**★, a series of stands probably made of wood.

Château

Access by 46 r. Césarine.
℘*02 35 38 08 45.* ☚*No charge; contact tourist office for visiting hours.*
Little remains of the fortress (rebuilt in the 12C and 13C), where William the Conqueror assembled his barons before invading England: one wall of an octagonal tower and, on the left, a round three-storey keep.

Église Notre-Dame

rue Sadi-Carnot.
This 16C church has a sweeping spire (55m/181ft) rising above a square tower. Inside, a stained-glass window tells the story of John the Baptist. The stalls were originally from the Abbaye du Valasse.

Musée gallo-romain

pl Félix-Faure. ◷*Open May–Oct 10am-12pm and 2–6pm, Nov–Apr Wed–Mon 2–6pm.* ◷*Closed 1 Jan and 25 Dec.* ☚*€1.65, €2.30 combined admission with Mesnil-sous-Lillebonne*

church-museum (in season) (under-12s free). ℘*02 32 84 02 07.*
Permanent exhibition on ground floor on the town in the Gallo-Roman period, with local archaeological collections: incineration tomb, pottery, 1C–3C ironwork. First floor: folk arts and traditions including tools and instruments, art objects, furniture is and documents referring to history of Lillebonne and Normandy. Very pretty view from garden of medieval castle's ruins and curtain wall.

EXCURSIONS

👥 L'Abbaye du Valasse at Le Parc Eana

▶ *6km/3.7mi NW by D 173; turn left at Le Becquet.*
Since 2009, the site has operated as a **leisure park**, with access to the abbey, gardens and park. The foundation of the abbey resulted from two vows; the first one was made by Waleran de Meulan for having escaped from a shipwreck, and one made by Empress Matilda, William the Conqueror's granddaughter. In her case it was for having survived the difficult struggle she undertook for the throne of England against her cousin Stephen of Blois.
The abbey, consecrated in 1181, prospered until the 14C, when the Hundred Years' War and the Wars of Religion

---

Population: 9,651.
Michelin Map: 304: D-4.
Info: rue Victor-Hugo. ℘02 35 38 08 45.
Location: Lillebone is 67km/41.6mi W of Rouen and 37km/23mi E of Le Havre via D 982.
Don't Miss: The Roman theatre and artefacts at the museum.
Timing: Although some sights are closed for renovation, you can admire them from the outside while enjoying their surroundings.

brought ruin. The building was sold at the Revolution, converted into a château, then sold to a dairy; in 1984 it was bought by the municipality of Gruchet-le-Valasse.

The main façade is an elegant 18C composition with two return wings. The central pediment bears the arms of Empress Matilda: three Norman leopards (from William the Conqueror) and an eagle (from her husband, the German Emperor Henry V).

Le Mesnil-sous-Lillebonne

◉ *2km/1mi S.* ◷*Church open Jun– Sept 2–6pm; rest of the year, by appointment* ✏*€1.50; €2.15 for ticket combining admission to the Musée municipal de Lillebonne.* ✆*02 32 84 02 07.*
The extremely ancient parish **church** has recently been restored. It presents a display of religious art and a collection of fossils and minerals.

Notre-Dame de Gravenchon B1

Interesting modern church, with St George and the Dragon on the façade in lead and brass. Abstract stained glass by Max Ingrand.

Château d'Etelan

◉ *15km/9mi by the D 51 and, at Norville, take the D 281 on the right to St-Maurice-d'Etelan.* ◷*Open mid-Jun to end Sept Thu–Tue 11am–1pm (only park and chapel) and 2.30–6.30pm; park, chapel, château, exhibition (last admission 1 hour before closing).* ✏*€3 morning, €5 afternoon.* ✆*02 35 39 91 27. www. chateau-etelan.fr.*
Built in 1494 on the site of a former fortress, this Flamboyant château overlooks the valley. An elegant stairway tower lit by nine bays announces "the first Norman Renaissance". In the restored chapel, interesting 16C murals and beautiful carved wood panels. Some rooms are furnished and inhabited, while others are for exhibitions and concerts.

View from chateau terrace: marshlands of St-Maurice-d'Etelan and Norville, Brotonne Forest, as well as unexpected show of boats sailing up and down the Seine.

Take a stroll in the former vegetable garden, recently restructured; beautiful collection of squashes and melons, as well as herbs. There is also a "vine terrace" in a pergola nearby.

Tancarville

◉ *9km/5.5mi southwest.*
Standing on the chalky protrusion of cliffs before the estuary spreads out, the castle overlooks the Seine's right bank; it is also from here that the suspended bridge springs over the river.

Feudal castle - ✆*02 35 96 00 21;* ◷*visits by appointment (7 days prior);* ✏*€3.*
This was part of the overall strategy controlling the Seine estuary. In the 11C, William the Conqueror granted privileges in the person of Raoul de Tancarville, his advisor. The oldest parts date to the 10C; only the Tour de l'Aigle (15C), shaped like a spur, remains intact. Of square residential tower (12C) rise on the other side of the terrorists. Two round towers flank the small entrance castle. Ruins of the main building remain in the courtyard, opened by three pointed arches. A restaurant is in the rebuilt side, looking over the valley.

Road bridge★ *Toll.* Until 1959, when the bridge was inaugurated, ferries ran between the two banks. Today two 125m/414ft pylons support the suspended deck at 48m/157ft.
1,400m/4,592ft long, it has 960m/3,148ft of metal bays. It offers a **view★** of the Seine estuary (*leave the car at the end of the bridge*): in the foreground, the Tancarville canal, and more downstream, the Pont de Normandie.

Sentier du Vivier 🥾 *From Place de Tancarville-Bas. Way marked to the right, behind the bakery.* This path, part of the regional nature park, takes you on a 12-part stroll along the river of the same name, to a source.

Saint-Jean-d'Abbetot

◉ *16km/10mi west, going through Tancarville and heading for St-Romain-de-Colbosc. Go for 4km/2.5mi on the D 39 and turn left for the D 112.*
In the 11C **church** crypt there are remarkable 12C, 13C and 16C **frescoes★**.

Pont-Audemer★

This quaint town of 16C houses is sometimes called the Venice of Normandy, its canals once serving a prosperous tanning trade.

 WALKING TOUR

OLD TOWN

Allow 45min. Start from place du Général de Gaulle. Take rue des Carmes, then rue de la République on left. 100m/yds, then left again into Impasse de l'Epée; come out, turn left into parallel Impasse St-Ouen alongside Église St-Ouen.

Église St-Ouen – 11C–16C. Renaissance **stained-glass★** in side chapels.

▶ *Take rue Thiers to the left.*

Pretty view from **Risle River bridge**.

▶ *From place Victor-Hugo, go to Place Louis-Gillain, right, and into rue des Cordeliers.*

A turreted, half-timbered house with a stone ground floor, rises on the corner of rue des Cordeliers.

▶ **Population:** 9,058.
▶ **Michelin Map:** 304: D-5.
▶ **Info:** place Maubert. ℰ02 32 41 08 21. www.ville-pont-audemer.fr.
▶ **Location:** 24km/15mi E of Honfleur and 58km/36mi W of Rouen.
▶ **Parking:** Car park on place Général de Gaulle.
▶ **Don't Miss:** Compass cards painted on the ground, let you explore the town at your own pace.

▶ *Take rue Thiers to the left.*

Note the sculpted doorways (*nos 8, 16, 18, 20 and 27 bis*). **Rue Place-de-la-Ville** (*right*) crosses a small bridge into rue de la République, at St-Ouen.

▶ *Go up rue de la République and take the first passage right, after rue des Carmes.*

Cour Canal has lovely half-timbered houses.

🚗 DRIVING TOUR

The Risle Valley

Pont-Audemer to Montfort-sur-Risle.
50km/32mi – about 1hr30min.

Corneville-sur-Risle B2

The 12-bell **chimes** in the Hôtel Les Cloches were made following the incredible success of an 1877 operetta by Robert Planquette, *The Bells of Corneville*. Information at 📞*02 32 41 08 21.*

Appeville-Annebault B2

In the 16C the Admiral d'Annebault, Normandy's governor, conceived the plan to make Risle navigation possible; he also had built the large church while preserving its 14C chancel. Note the keystones and beautiful staffs of the charitable brotherhoods.

Montfort-sur-Risle B2

This charming municipality is next to the Montfort Forest hills and dales, and enjoys a river. A club offers Risle canoeing and kayaking (*a day or half-day, with or without guide*), a relaxing moment with verdant scenery.
Castle – *By car from town centre; take rue de l'Ecu, follow signs; reached on foot, 231 steps behind the church – guided tour, information at 📞02 32 56 35 76.* Only ruins remain of the 11C castle, still extending over 4.5ha/11acres. An itinerary helps envision the original fortress the English dismantled. Vegetation invades the pretty setting; wonderful view of Montfort and the Risle Valley.
🚶 **"Les Catellers"** – *Leave Montfort-sur-Risle by D 91 east; about 1.5 km/1mi into the forest you reach Beuvron roundabout, take Chemin de la Mare Votret (head for "Les Catellers").* A 2.7km/1.5mi path signposted with black leaves on white teaches about Montfort state forest trees. *Brochure from Montfort-sur-Lisle tourist office.*

▷ *Cross the Risle by the D 47, then Pont-Audemer by the D 39.*

The Risle Estuary

Take D 675 to Toutainville exit, turn right into the D 312.

Saint-Sulpice-de-Grimbouville A2

Medieval House – 📞*02 32 41 44 89.* *www.normandie-accueil.fr.* ♿.
Lovely corbelled-out gatehouse (*timberwork*). Also: 15C thatched cottage, 19C building, two old washhouses (perhaps paleo-Christian baptistry); dolmen.
🚶 **"Le sentier de l'Anguille"** – *Starts at the mairie – 4.2 km/2.5mi, blue waymarking. Brochure in region's tourist offices. 👢Wear boots.*
An educational walk to the Risle coastal river marshlands, to learn about sources and biodiversity.

🚶 **"Le sentier de la Risle maritime"** – *Starts at the mairie – 12.5km/7.5mi. Brochure in region's tourist offices.* Signposted walk through peat marshes by an old towpath; pretty, typically Norman houses.

▷ *Continue on the D 312 to Foulbec*

FOULBEC A2

"**Le sentier de la Brûlette**" – *Starts at Place de la Maison-du-Village – 8km/5mi. Brochure in the region's tourist offices.* Signposted walk with nice panorama of Brûlette coastline; walk in woods.

▶ *Continue on the D 312 until Conteville.*

Conteville A2

"**Le sentier des hameaux et du Marais**" – *Starts at the church – 12.5 km/7.5mi. Brochure in the region's tourist offices.* Pretty, signposted, for discovering the Risle coastal river marshland while overlooking the valley.

▶ *D 312 to Berville-sur-Mer.*

Berville-sur-Mer A2

"**Le sentier à fl'Eure de l'eau**" – Footpath 2.3 km/1.5mi long, organised to permit discovery of the village's history and the estuary's aquatic environments.
"**Le sentier des Voiles de la liberté**" – *Leaves from the esplanade - 13km/8mi or 18km/11mi. Brochure in the region's tourist offices.*
Pretty walk and panoramic views of estuary, goes through forest.

▶ *West to Pont-Audemer by the D 180, heading for La-Rivière-St-Sauveur.*

The Vernier Marshlands

▶ *55km/34mi, 1hr30min. Leave Pont-Audemer heading north on the D 810.*
Perhaps you'll meet the "marshlands clown", a spaniel so called because he loves hunting in the marshlands.

Ste-Opportune-la-Mare

Follow the signs *Panorama de la Grande Mare* to viewpoint over Great Marsh and beyond to the reclaimed Marshland.

▶ *To drive here, take a little road in Ste-Opportune to the Vernier marshland, turn left*

Réserve naturelle des Mannevilles

Guided tours (3hr) from Ste-Opportune-la-Mare. Jul–Aug, Sun 2–5pm. €3. Information, reservations: 02 32 37 23 16. Wear boots.
Flora and fauna of the marshlands, visit with Camargue horses , Scottish highland cattle.

▶ *D 810 to the Seine, then D 87.*

Quillebeuf-sur-Seine

Until the 19C captains waited here for high tide, to sail its dangerous channel. Today, the old port is has many oil refineries and petrochemical installations in Port Jérôme. The town still feels authentic, and has an excellent view of Port Jérôme from the lighthouse. Église Notre-Dame-de-Bon-Port has a fine but incomplete Romanesque tower.

Pointe de Quillebeuf – This is the tip of a promontory separating the Vernier marshland meander from that of Vieux-Port. Small lighthouse, good view of river, Port-Jérôme, Shea's andTancarville bridge.

Two mountain bike itineraries (*13km/8mi and 32km/20mi*) starting from lighthouse at the end of the quay.

Église Notre-Dame-du-Bon-Port - Incomplete but lovely Romanesque tower; 12C portal. Purely Romanesque nave with archaic capitals, 16C chancel. Boat models and sailors' graffiti recall port's role in Seine navigation.

▶ *Take the D 103 across marshland, to Pointe de la Roque.*

Pointe de la Roque★

From lighthouse, **panorama** of Seine estuary to Cap de la Hève, Côte de Grâce. Tancarville cliffs and bridge to the right.

ADDRESSES

🛏 STAY

ROUEN

🛏 **Hôtel Andersen** – *4 r. Pouchet.* 📞*02 35 71 88 51. www.hotelandersen.com. 14 rooms.* 🚇*€7.80.* Pleasantly quiet and refined. Remarkable welcome. A little street noise on weekends.

🛏 **Youth Hostel** – *Le Robec, 3 r. du Tour, route de Darnétal.* 📞*02 35 08 18 50. www.fuaj.org. 7am–12pm, 5–10pm, weekends and holidays 6pm–10pm – reservation 48 hours prior. 108 beds.* 🚇 In old Auvray dyers installations, typically 18C architecture. At Robec River, home, charming, Simple, functional rooms.

🛏 **Chambre d'hôte La Muette** – *1057 r. des Bosquets, 76230 Isneauville, 10km/6mi NE.* 📞*02 35 60 57 69. www.charmance-lamuette. com. Closed mid-Dec–mid-Mar. 5 rooms.* 🚻🚇. Spacious, cosy, themed rooms in stunning 18C Norman building. Breakfast room overlooking the park.

🛏 **Hôtel des Carmes** – *33 pl. des Carmes.* 📞*02 35 71 92 31. www.hoteldescarmes.com. 12 rooms.* 🚇. Not far from the cathedral. Delightful, artistic reception; clutter-free bedrooms. Value for money.

🛏 **Hôtel Le Cardinal** – *1 pl. de la Cathédrale.* 📞*02 35 70 24 42. www.cardinal-hotel.fr. Closed 18 Dec–14 Jan. 20 rooms.* 🚇*€8.* Near Notre Dame Cathedral, family hotel with distinctive red façade; moderate-sized rooms, modern furnishings. Summer breakfasts on terrace.

🛏 **Hôtel Le Vieux Carré** – *34 r. Ganterie.* 📞*02 35 71 67 70. www vieux-carre.fr. 13 rooms.* 🚇*7€.* Charming, half-timbered property (1715), modern rooms.

🛏 **Le Versan** – *3 r. Jean-Lecanuet.* 📞*02 35 07 77 07. www.rouen-hotel-versan. Four rooms.* 🚇*€9.* Practical, on boulevard near hôtel de ville. Functional, renovated rooms, efficient soundproofing.

🛏–🛏🛏 **Hôtel de la Cathédrale** – *12 r. St-Romain.* 📞*02 35 71 57 95. www.hotel-de-la-cathedrale.fr. 26 rooms.* 🚇*€8.50.* Beautiful 17C building in a pretty, pedestrian street near cathedral. Rooms comfy, atmosphere delightful. Lovely patio.

🛏🛏🛏 **Hôtel La Bertelière** – *1641 av. Mesnil-Grémichon, 76160 Saint-Martin-du-Vivier.* 📞*02 35 60 44 00. www.laberteliere. fr. Open all year. 44 rooms.* 🚇*€17.Restaurant*

🛏–🛏🛏🛏. Comfy rooms on Rouen heights, wide salons open on gardens. 10 min from downtown Rouen, near A 28. Nice welcome, rooms with access for disabled.

🛏🛏🛏 **Hôtel Dandy** – *93 bis. r. Cauchoise.* 📞*02 35 07 32 00. www.hotels-rouen.net. Closed 26 Dec–2 Jan. 18 rooms.* 🚇*€11.* Near Place du Vieux-Marché; tearoom, charming bar. Rooms refined, pretty breakfast room.

🛏🛏🛏 **Hôtel de Dieppe** – *pl. Bernard Tissot (oppoite train station).* 📞*02 35 71 96 00. www. hotel-dieppe.fr. 41 rooms.* 🚇*€11.* Run by the same family since 1880. Neat rooms each with own décor. Rouen duck is restaurant speciality.

🛏🛏🛏🛏 **Hôtel du Camp du Drap d'or – Hôtel de Bourgtheroulde** – *5 pl. de la Pucelle.* 📞*02 35 14 50 50. www. hotelsparouen.com. 78 rooms.* 🚇*€18.* Pleasant, contemporary rooms. Spacious, light. Marble bathrooms, steam bath, sauna, brasserie, upscale restaurant l'Aumale. Prestigious address

ELBEUF

🛏🛏🛏🛏 **Le Manoir des Saules** – *2km/1mi south, 2 pl. St-Martin, 27370 Saussaye.* 📞*02 35 87 25 65. www.manoirdessaules.com. Closed 3 weeks in Nov, 21 Feb–9 Mar, Sun evening Sept–Apr, Mon and Tue.* 🚻 *9 rooms.* 🚇*€22. Restaurant* 🛏🛏🛏🛏. Charming welcome in authentic Norman manor with garden. Half-timbering, turrets; beautiful furniture in rooms. Unique dining rooms, up-to-date cuisine with local ingredients. Beautiful cellars.

CAUDEBEC-EN-CAUX

🛏🛏 **Hôtel Le Normandie** – *Quai Guilbaud.* 📞*02 35 96 25 11. www.le-normandie.fr. 15 rooms.* 🅿️*7.50€. Restaurant*🛏🛏. On road along Seine, small, simple hotel. Some rooms wth balconies. Traditional Norman cuisine.

🛏🛏 **Normotel La Marine** – *18 quai Guilbaud.* 📞*02 35 96 20 11. www.normotel-lamarine.fr. 31 rooms.* 🅿️🚇. *Restaurant*🛏🛏. On the quai along the Seine, best rooms have balconies over river. Traditional cuisine. Terrace on water.

PONT AUDEMER

🛏 **Camping Les Etangs Risles-Seine** – *19 route des Etangs.* 📞*02 32 42 46 65. 61 pitches.* Spend one or several nights in protected natural site next to Pont Audemer ponds. Hedges edge pitches for complete privacy.

Chambre d'hôte La Venise Normande – *9 r. Sadit-Carnot.* *02 32 56 82 53 or* *06 87 76 49 63. www.venisenormande. com. 3 rooms* . A former 17C–18C butcher's converted into charming B&B.

Chambre d'hôte Le Prieuré des Fontaines – *rte de Lisieux, 27500 Les Préaux, 5km/3mi SE by D 139.* *02 32 56 07 78. www. prieure-des-fontaines.fr.* . This restored 17C building has spacious, comfortable rooms.

EAT

ROUEN

Le Bistrot de Panurge – *91 r. Ecuyères.* *02 35 15 97 02. Closed Sat noon and Sun -* . A traditional address. Roast lamb with *flageolet* beans is house speciality.

Les Maraîchers – *37 pl. du Vieux-Marché.* *02 35 71 57 73. www.les-maraichers.fr.* Parisian style in half-timbered house. Improvised cuisine. Norman-style second dining room on ground floor.

Pascaline – *5 r. de la Poterne.* *02 35 89 67 44. www.pascaline.fr. Reservations advised.* Nice restaurant with bistro façade. Brasserie décor, handsome wood counters, long seats, yellow walls. Good fixed-price menus. Book ahead – often full.

La Marmite – *3 r.de Florence.* *02 35 71 75 55. http://lamarmiterouen. unblog.fr.* Near place du Vieux-Marché. Delicately flavoured cuisine, fresh products, attentively prepared. Dining room freshly renovated.

La Toque d'Or – *11 pl. du Vieux-Marché.* *02 35 71 46 29. www.toquedor.fr.* Well-placed, pretty half-timbered house with two restaurants. Ground floor: elegant, with refined fare; upstairs, more casual and served faster; grilled meats.

Le Bistrot du Siècle – *75 r. Jules Ferry, 76480 Duclair, 20km/12.4mi NW.* *02 35 37 62 36. Closed 25 Dec–1 Jan, Sun and Mon.* Little bistro with fine local reputation. Convivial two dining rooms: one with old poster, other on veranda.Flame-grilled meats, a few dishes from Reunion Island.

Le 37 – *37 r. St-Étienne-des-Tonneliers.* *02 35 70 56 65. Closed Sun, Mon, 11–19 Apr and 1–25 Aug.* Trendy bistro, casual, chef at the piano! Up-to-date cuisine, daily specials.

Les P'tits Parapluies – *pl. Rougemare.* *02 35 88 55 26. Closed 3–19 Aug, 2–8 Jan, Sat lunch, Sun eve, Mon.* 16C former umbrella factory (hence the name). Pleasant, modern, yet with period beams.

Reverbère – *5 pl. de la République.* *02 35 07 03 14. Closed 28 Apr–4 May, 28 Jul– 17 Aug, Sun, public holidays.* A discreet glass front on small square, near river. Modern dining room, small, low-key lounge, wooden staircase to a rustic lounge.

L'écaille – *26 rampe Cauchoise.* *02 35 70 95 52. www.restaurant-lecaille.fr.* Seafaring restaurant with blue-green décor, modern paintings, up-to-date fish dishes.

La Couronne – *31 pl. du Vieux-Marché.* *02 35 71 40 90. www.lacouronne. com.fr.* Superbly preserved, 1345 home is France's most beautiful inn. Rustic setting, flower-decked terrace in summer.

Gill – *9 quai de la Bourse.* *02 35 71 16 14. www.gill.fr. Closed 4–20 Apr, 1–25 Aug, Sun.* On the Seine, elegant, comfortable, simple dining room. Inventive cuisine, Norman ingredients.

ELBEUF

Helpful Hint – In the autumn Elbeuf's leeks (called "Monstrueux d'Elbeuf", in fact an older variety of leek) stand soldier-like in the alluvial planes of the Seine and the Eure. Norman chefs don't miss the chance to showcase this.

Le Baillage – *1.5 km, 62 route Pont-de-l'Arche, 76410 Freneuse.* *02 35 87 57 37. Closed Sun evening, Mon and Wed evening.* Beautiful, bourgeois house and country restaurant with pretty terrace and veranda. Traditional cuisine, fish specialities.

La Pomme – *44 r. Eure, 72340 Les Damps, Pont de l'Arche, 11km/7mi E of Elbeuf via D 921 and D 321.* *02 35 23 00 46. www. laubergedelapomme.com. Closed 9–25 Aug.* A pretty Norman cottage on the banks of the Eure with a pleasant dining room.

CAUDEBEC-EN-CAUX

Au Rendez-Vous des Chasseurs – *Hameau de Sainte-Gertrude, 76490 Maulévrier Ste-Gertrude, 3.4km/2mi.* *02 35 96 20 30. Closed Sun eve and Mon.* Beautiful half-timbered building with pretty garden terrace, smart décor and traditional, regional cuisine.

Le Cheval Blanc – *4 pl. R.-Coty.* *02 35 96 21 66. www.le-cheval-blanc.fr. Closed 25 Dec–3 Jan, Sat, Sun evening and Fri.* Clean and bright rooms, satisfactory soundproofing in this downtown hotel. The owner-chef offers country cuisine. Flower-decked terrace.

PONT-AUDEMER

⊖⊜ **Auberge du Cochon d'Or** –
27210 Beuzeville, 14km/8.7mi W via D 675.
℘02 32 57 70 46. www.le-cochon-dor.fr.
Locals appreciate the changing menus.

⊖⊜ **Erawan** – *4 r. de la Seule. ℘02 32 41*
12 03. Closed Aug, Sun and Wed. Thai menu
and Norman setting; a surprising, charming
contrast next to Risle River.

⊖⊜⊜ **Le Petit Coq aux Champs** –
La Pommeraie Sud, 27500 Campigny, 6km/
3.7mi S via D 810 and D 29. ℘02 32 41 04 19.
www.lepetitcoqauxchamps.fr. Closed 2–29
Jan. Reservations required. This beautiful
thatched cottage houses a restaurant and
12 guest rooms.

☽ NIGHTLIFE

ROUEN

Famed as where Joan of Arc met her end,
place du Vieux-Marché is today a lively
nightspot; lots of bars and restaurants,
many with terraces. Check *The Viking*, a free
information brochure distributed locally.
Bar de la Crosse – *53 r. de l'Hôpital.*
℘02 35 70 16 68. Closed Sun, 1st half Aug,
public holidays. This small bar has gained
its popularity from the relaxed and friendly
atmosphere you find here.
Le Bateau Ivre – *17 r. des Sapins.*
℘02 35 70 09 05. http://bateauivre.rouen.free.
fr. Closed Sun–Mon, Aug. Ever on the lookout
for new talent, this bar has been livening
up Rouen nightlife for the past 20 years.
Concerts Fridays and Saturdays, ballads and
poetry Thursdays, café-theatre or French
songs Tuesday evenings.
Taverne St-Amand – *11 r. St-Amand.*
℘02 35 88 51 34. Closed Sun and 3 weeks in
Aug. Set up as a restaurant-bar for 32 years,
this 17C house has welcomed painters,
writers, actors and other artistic habitués.

☻ PERFORMING ARTS

ROUEN

Théâtre de l'Écharde – *16 r. Flahaut.*
℘02 35 15 33 05. Tickets also sold at theatre
before performance. Theatre with 100 seats
with shows for young theatre-goers.
Théâtre des Arts – *7 r. du Dr-Rambert, Vieux-*
Marché. ℘02 35 71 41 36. www.operaderouen.
com. A whole host of concerts, plays and
operas shown.
Théâtre des Deux Rives – *48 r. Louis Ricard.*
℘02 35 70 22 82. www.cdr2rives.com. Classical
and modern theatre, with an emphasis on
living playwrights.

☒ SHOPPING

ROUEN

Faïencerie Augy-Carpentier – *26 r.*
St-Romain. ℘02 35 88 77 47. www.fayencerie-
augy.com. Closed Sun–Mon. Tour of the
workshop by appointment. The last hand-
made and hand-decorated earthenware
workshop in Rouen offers copies of many
traditional motifs from blue monochrome
to multicoloured
Chocolatier Auzou – *163 r. du Gros-Horloge.*
℘02 35 70 59 31. www.auzou-chocolat.fr.
Closed Sun Jul–Aug, 1 Jan, 1 May. Located
in a half-timbered house, this renowned
chocolatier will tempt you with *les Larmes*
de Jeanne d'Arc (Joan of Arc's Tears: lightly
roasted almonds covered with nougatine
and chocolate) or *l'Agneau Rouennais* (a sort
of sponge cake) and candied apples.
Hardy – *22 pl. du Vieux-Marché. ℘02 35*
71 81 55. Closed Sun. This delicatessen
occupies a suberb half-timbered house
on one of the liveliest squares in Rouen.
Specialities include sheep's foot à la
rouennaise, *andouilles* with hot peppers
and Caen tripe cooked in Calvados and
cider. In the afternoons, you can eat in the
establishment's restaurant.

ANTIQUES MARKET
Place St-Marc Sun 8am–1.30pm
TRADITIONAL MARKETS –
Place St-Marc– Tue and Fri–Sun.
Place des Emmurées – Tue and Sat.
Place du Vieux-Marché – Tue–Sun.

☆ LEISURE

ROUEN

The tourist office distributes two useful
brochures: *L'Agenda rouennais* (3-weekly)
and the *Rouen magazine* (bi-monthly).
Audio-guided Tours in 6 languages are
available, along with **horse-and-carriage**
tours, **group tours** and **little train tours**
through the city.

CULTURAL EVENTS

ROUEN

Evening light shows – *℘02 32 08 32 40*
(Rouen tourist office). Open early Jun–late Sept
from about 10pm. A dozen cathedral pictures
inspired by Monet are projected onto the
façade of Rouen Cathedral, creating strange
forms and colours.

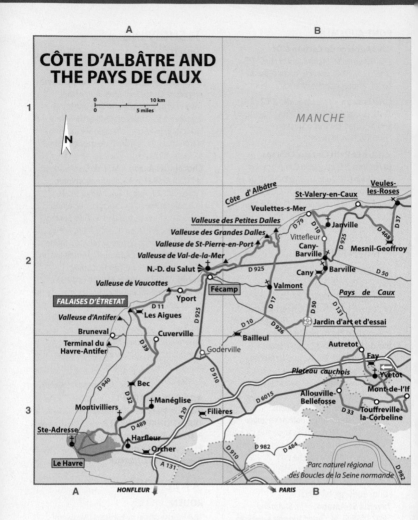

CÔTE D'ALBÂTRE AND THE PAYS DE CAUX

The Pays de Caux, lying between Rouen and Le Havre, has a charming, intimate feel to it, ideal for a family excursion, a romantic getaway or simply getting a break. The Seine meanders through a lovely, forested landscape dotted with small villages on its way to the sea: ideal for exploring on a bicycle, on horseback or by foot. In sharp contrast is the land that will appeal to more intrepid walkers, the Alabaster Coast with its cliff views and the sight of the endless sea and sky.

Highlights

1 **Maison de l'Armateur** (p130)
2 **Etretat** cliff walks (p133)
3 **Palais Bénédictine** (p135)
4 **Alabaster Coast** drive (p138)
5 **Dieppe castle-museum** (p147)

The Pays de Caux is a mosaic ranging from city to river, while the Alabaster Coast has the pure, wild beauty of the sea crashing against chalky cliffs.

Le Havre, a deep-water port at the mouth of the Seine, suffered grievously during World War II; from ruins, it is today a model of city planning. Dieppe, an old fishing port, hideout of privateers

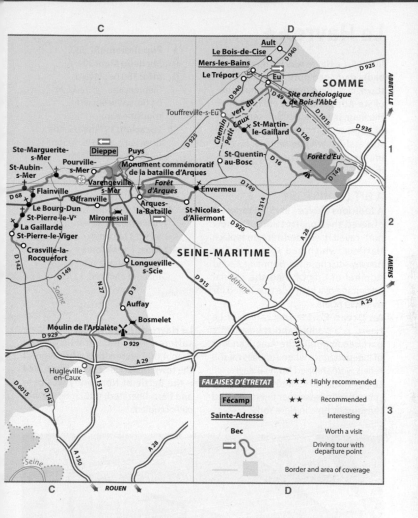

and a redoubt against the English, has both a sturdy castle and lovely beaches, and is France's oldest seaside resort. The city suffered in the 1942 Dieppe Raid but still has its attractive old quarter.

At the charming seaside resort of Varengeville-sur-Mer visitors may enjoy the intimate feel of an English-style garden before their nature walk. Eu's collegiate church and château offer architectural heritage, while the pretty little port of Le Tréport takes pride in its church and calvary. Walks along the cliffs at Étretat are absolutely not to be missed, giving breathtaking views over the beaches and headlands. Hikers will want to explore its famous *valleuses* (valleys giv-

ing access to the sea) as well. Fécamp, from which intrepid fishermen sailed to Newfoundland for cod, has a magnificant ducal church and a 19C Benedictine palace, where the well-known liqueur is made.

The region around the seaside resorts of Veules-les-Roses, St-Valéry-en-Caux and Veulettes-sur-Mer offers driving itineraries taking in pretty little villages and stately châteaux, ancient churches and hedged farmland, and even a chance to learn how linen is made.

Last, a visit to the Caux Plateau will include not only the oldest oak in all of France, but also manors and a church with stained glass by Max Ingrand.

Le Havre★★

In 1945, Le Havre was Europe's most badly damaged port; today the town, including the residential area of Ste-Adresse and the old port of Harfleur, is a remarkable example of large-scale reconstruction and successful town planning. Le Havre's university is new, it opened here in 1986.

A BIT OF HISTORY

A Judicious Choice – In 1517, **François I** ordered the construction of a new port, called Havre-de-Grâce, to replace Harfleur, which had silted up. The marshy site chosen by Bonnivet, Grand Admiral of France, had the crucial advantage of a high tide that lasted for over two hours.

An Ocean Port – The career of Le Havre as a trading and transatlantic port began during the American War of Independence when supplies for the rebels were shipped from Le Havre.
Le Havre bustled in the 19C when great transatlantic passenger liners reduced the journey time in New York.

▶ **Population:** 182,580.
🕐 **Michelin Map:** 304: A-5.
Info: 186 boulevard Clemenceau. ✆02 32 74 04 04. www.lehavre tourisme.com.
▶ **Location:** 197km/122.4mi from Paris and 90km/56mi from Rouen. Car ferries operate to England and the Republic of Ireland.
🕐 **Timing:** The best time to visit is Wednesday or weekends, when all sites are open.
Kids: The Malraux museum has a tour map for children.

Le Havre during the War – Le Havre suffered 146 raids, in which more than 4,000 were killed. The siege of the town began on 2 September 1944 – the Battle of Normandy was over and Paris liberated, but Le Havre was still occupied.

Musée des Beaux-Arts André-Malraux

© Leroy Arthur/age fotostock

Allied air raids went on ceaselessly for eight days from 5 September; the Germans were determined to blow up any port installations still in existence. On 13 September 1944, Le Havre was liberated. It took two years to clear the destruction and reconstruction began only in 1946.

WALKING TOUR

THE MODERN TOWN★

The old town was virtually wiped out in 1944. A new town was planned by **Auguste Perret** (1875–1954), the pioneer of reinforced concrete construction, who achieved remarkable architectural unity. *See map, p128.*

Bassin du Commerce and Espace Oscar-Niemeyer

The commercial dock is the focal point of the new district accessible by an elegant footbridge, designed by the architects Gillet and Du Pasquier.

At the west end, facing the war memorial, is the **Espace Oscar-Niemeyer** complex on place Gambetta. The main pavilion (Grand Volcan) has a large theatre, a cinema and exhibition rooms.

Appartement-témoin Auguste-Perret★

Open Wed and Sat–Sun, 2pm, 3pm, 4pm and 5pm – guided tour (40min).
Closed 1 Jan, 25 Dec. €3 (-26 years old free), no charge 1st Sat of month.
02 32 74 04 04.

A beautiful recreation of the model apartment Auguste Perret first presented at the 1947 World Exhibition, then again two years later to Le Havre, which was to be rebuilt.

The tour gives a good idea of the architect's vision, which called for well thought-out, flexible space.

The clean-lined, functional furniture by designers such as René Gabriel, Marcel Gascoin or André Beaudoin, as well as the many day-to-day objects, create a lively environment, while giving a glimpse of post-war social changes.

Place de l'Hôtel-de-Ville★

The square, which was designed by Auguste Perret, is bordered by three-storey buildings, punctuated by taller ten-storey blocks.

The open space is laid out with fountains, lawns, arbours and yew hedges. The **hôtel de ville**, an austere building, is distinguished by a great tower (72m/236ft high) in concrete.

> *Leave the square E and walk along Avenue Foch.*

Avenue Foch★

The central roadway is bordered by lawns shaded by trees; the Porte Océane marks the west end of the street on the seafront.

North dyke and the beach★

The north breakwater that serves to reinforce the jetty, encloses the marina. The Le Havre and Ste-Adresse Beach stretches from the North Breakwater to the Hève Cape.

There are views of the Seine estuary from the dyke walk (*boulevard Clemenceau*). Note the turn-of-the century **villas** spared the 1944 bombings, especially the exquisite Villa Maritime at no. 66. Summer restaurants and greenery are found along the pleasant 4km/2mi walk. In season some 600 beach huts dot the beach; they were authorised in 1910 for a sense of propriety and to protect visitors from the chill.

> *When you reach the "Porte Océane", head S along bd Clemenceau, which runs alongside anse des Régates and anse de Joinville. Turn left down rue Frédérick Lemaître where you have a pretty view of the pleasure port.*

Église St-Joseph★★

Bd François 1er.

This sober **church** typical of Auguste Perret's style was built of concrete between 1951 and 1957. It is surmounted by an octagonal lantern-belfry (109m/357.6ft high). The **interior**★★ is monumental and impressive.

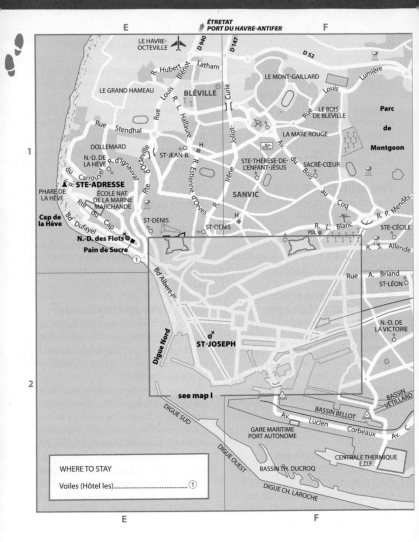

ÉTRETAT
PORT DU HAVRE-ANTIFER

WHERE TO STAY

Voiles (Hôtel les).......................... ①

Return to bd Clemenceau. Follow it to the museum.

Musée des Beaux-Arts André-Malraux★★

2 bd Clemenceau. ⚓⏰Open Wed–Fri and Mon 11am–6pm, Sat–Sun 11am–7pm. Closed 1 Jan, 1 May, 14 Jul, 11 Nov, 25 Dec. ⚲€5 (no charge 1st Sat of month or for under-26 years old).
✆02 35 19 62 62. www.lehavre.fr.
The glass and metal building looks out to the sea through a monumental concrete sculpture known locally as Le Signal. The roof, designed to provide the best possible light to the galleries inside, consists of six sheets of glass covered by an aluminium sun blind. The museum presents a fine **collection★** of works by **Raoul Dufy** (1877–1953), who was born in Le Havre, and **Eugène Boudin** (1824–98), a native of Honfleur.

Sémaphore

The view from the end of the pier embraces the harbour entrance and the long southern breakwater protecting the outer harbour.

LE HAVRE
Map II

Continue along the seafront and take quai Southampton up to Maison de l'Armateur.

Maison de l'Armateur★★

3 quai de l'Île. Open Mon, Fri, Sat–Sun and holidays 11am–6pm, Wed 2–6pm. Guided tour available (1hr). Closed Thu, 1 Jan, 1 and 8 May, 14 Jul, 11 Nov and 25 Dec. €3 (-26 no charge). 02 35 19 09 85. www.musees-haute-normandie.fr.

This late 18C house is a rare survivor of the 1945 bombings. Built for the personal use of the city's architect and foun-

tain-builder, M. Thibault, a shipowner bought it in the early 19C – hence its name (the "shipowner's house"). Five circular levels embellished with carved wood fit around a remarkable octagonal light well. All the rooms have been recreated to showcase the aesthetics of the elite: stables, bedrooms, trade office, cabinets of curiosities and an observation room.

Take rue du Général-Faidherbe on the left, then the Notre-Dame Bridge. Take the quay Videcoq on the right, then head up rue des Drapiers on the left. Just *before getting to the cathedral you will see the museum of natural history on the right.*

Muséum d'histoire naturelle

place du Vieux-Marché. 🕐*Open Tue–Wed and Fri–Sun 9.30am–noon, 2–6pm, Thu 2–6pm.* 🕐*Closed 1 Jan, 1 and 8 May, 14 Jul, 25 Dec.* ✏*No charge.* ☎*02 35 41 37 28. http://museum.ville-lehavre.fr.*
The Natural History Museum is housed in the old 18C law courts. One of the rooms displays works by the naturalist painter **Charles-Alexandre Lesueur** (1778–1846).

Cathédrale Notre-Dame

Rue de Paris.
Built between 1575 and 1630, the cathedral is a combination of Gothic and Renaissance styles and bristles with buttresses decorated with gargoyles. The organ (1637) was presented by Richelieu and bears his arms.

▷ *Rue de Paris takes you to place du Général-de-Gaulle.*

ADDITIONAL SIGHTS
Quartier de l'Eure

The 19C **Vauban docks** were recently redone to offer a large commercial gallery with the major names in culture, fashion and leisure.
There is a nice walk beyond the Paul-Vatine Basin with its surprising moveable bridge. The **Bellot Esplanade** and canal gardens will be part of a 9ha/22 acre city park that strollers, skaters and cyclists may enjoy.
Les Bains des Docks – *quai de la Réunion.* ☎*02 32 79 29 55. www.vert-marine. com.* This development won the architectural award, the Pritzker Prize, in 2008, bringing prestige to one of Le Havre's major installations. Inspired by Roman thermal baths, this nautical complex of 5,000sq m/5,980sq yd plays on light, lines, openings and volumes. The noon sun accentuates the sense of calm and well-being that pervades the space. Numerous basins, for various

ages and various users. Balneotherapy, cardiotherapy spaces, fitness rooms, Olympic pools and areas just to have fun.

The Port★★

To visit the port contact the tourist office. For futher information, www.havre.port.fr.
Le Havre is a deep-water port situated in the Seine estuary; it ranks first among French ports for exports and container traffic, and fourth in Europe for total traffic. Le Havre also has frequent car-ferry links with Great Britain (Le Havre–Portsmouth) and Ireland (Le Havre–Rosslare, Le Havre–Cork). Each year 7,000 merchant ships dock in Le Havre, including 2,250 container ships.

EXCURSIONS
Sainte-Adresse★

▷ *Plan II E. Allow 1hr.*
This a pleasant district extends from the edge of Le Havre towards the Hève Cape and consists of a seaside resort and the old town of Ste-Adresse.
Boulevard Albert-1er runs alongside the beach to place Clemenceau and the statue of Albert I, King of the Belgians from 1909 to 1934.

▷ *Follow the signs for Pain de Sucre and Notre-Dame-des-Flots.*

After a few bends in the road you arrive at the **Pain de Sucre**. A little higher up on the right the **Chapelle Notre-Dame-des-Flots** contains sailors' votive offerings.

▷ *Turn left onto route du Cap.*

The road passes in front of the École Nationale de la Marine Marchande (Merchant Navy College).

Cap de la Hève

Continue to the lighthouse.
🔲 *Allow 15min on foot there and back.*
This rocky site overlooks the mouth of the Seine. Boulevard du Président-Félix-Faure, to the right and facing the ocean, offers an extensive **view**★.

Port of Le Havre

© Hervé Hughes/hemis.fr

▷ *Return to place Clemenceau.*

Harfleur
Église St-Martin
▷ *Access by rue Aristide-Briand and rue de Verdun following the direction of Rouen.*
The 15C belltower (83m/272.4ft) of the Église St-Martin is famous in the Caux region. Take rue des 104 and rue Gambetta, right, to the **bridge** over the Lézarde from which there is a good view.

Montivilliers
▷ *8km/4mi. Leave Le Havre by the D 489.*
Following over 20 years of works, the abbey St Philibert, founded in the 7C, now stages the historical retrospective **"Cœur d'Abbayes★"** ⟳ ⓞ*Open Apr–Sep 10am–7pm Sat–Sun and holidays 2–7pm; Oct–Mar Tue–Fri 10am–5pm, Sat–Sun 2–6pm.* ⓞ*Closed 1 Jan and 25 Dec.* ⊛€5. ℰ*02 35 30 96 66; www.ville-montivilliers.fr.*
Église St-Sauveur★ – Walk round on the left to see the transept's 11C lantern tower. The Romaneque tower's spire was redone in the 19C. Two naves: the larger, Romanesque, has a carved oak pulpit;

the Gothic side nave was added in the 16C. Flamboyant organ-loft behind the belltower.
Aître de Brisegaret – *Reached by route de Fécamp (left before monumental mason's).* Only a 16C wood-vaulted gallery remains of this old ossuary. Pillars with skeletons, faces, shields, etc.

Château de Filières
▷ *20km/12.4mi NE via N15; D 31 left after St-Romain, then D 80 to the right.*
⟿*Guided tours (30min) Jul–Aug daily 2–6pm; May–Jun and Sept Sun 2–6pm.* ⊛€6. ℰ*02 35 20 53 30.*
The château, in a fine park, is in white Caen stone after designs by Victor Louis. The late 16C wing is to the left, and the 18C central pavilion has a Classical façade and the Mirville family arms. Ancestors of today's owners, they built the château.
In the park, west of the château, are seven rows of magnificent beech trees, known as the **Cathedral**★ because their branches meet overhead to form a living vault.

Falaises d'Étretat★★★

The elegant resort of Étretat is renowned for its magnificent setting. The grandeur of the high cliffs and crashing waves has inspired many writers, artists and film directors. Maurice Leblanc described the Aiguille Creuse through his famous character, Arsène Lupin. Maupassant spent his childhood here, "leading the life of a wild foal". Other famous habitués included Alexandre Dumas, André Gide, Victor Hugo, Gustave Courbet, Jacques Offenbach and Claude Monet.

▶ **Population:** 1,531.

Michelin Map: 304: B-3.

Info: Place Maurice-Guillard. ℰ02 35 27 05 21. www.etretat.net.

Location: This seaside resort is located 47km/29.2mi N of Honfleur, 90km/56mi NW of Rouen and 219km/136mi from Paris.

P Parking: place du Général-de-Gaulle (fee). Free car parks: the Grand Val (rue Guy de Maupasssant, 300m/328yd from the centre), the route du Havre to the S and near the former train station to the N.

Don't Miss: Panoramic view from the cliffs of Aval and Amont.

Kids: The Tourist Train between Étretat and Les Loges.

ÉTRETAT

Étretat's setting is a magnificent landscape that is unforgettable no matter the season in which it is seen. With a **dyke-walkway** running along its edge, the pebbled **beach** is framed by the famous white-chalk **cliffs.** The view is so spectacular it is almost hard to believe it is real: to the right, the Amont Cliff with the little chapel of Notre-Dame-de-la-Garde and the monument to the lost aviators Nungesser and Coli; to the left, the Aval Cliff with its natural monumental arch, the Porte d'Aval. The Aiguille, 71m/232ft high, stands a little further off, a lonely needle of rock among the waves.

The quaint thatched *caloges,* former fishing boats converted to store fishermen's equipment, have disappeared – three recreated *caloges* stand there today.

Halles – This wooden covered market in place du Maréchal-Foch is a reconstruction.

Église Notre-Dame – *rue Notre-Dame at corner of rue Nungesser et Coli* – This church has a Romanesque doorway with a 19C tympanum. The rest of the building is 12C. Go to the transept crossing to admire the 13C lantern turret.

Le Clos Arsène Lupin★ – *15 r. Guy-de-Maupassant.* ○*Open Apr–Sept daily 10am–5.45pm; Oct–mid-Nov and mid-Dec–Mar Fri–Sun and school holidays* 11am–4.45pm. Audioguided tours (45min). ○*Closed 1 Jan, 25 Dec.* €6.75. ℰ02 35 10 59 53. www.arsene-lupin.com. Arsène Lupin is a gentleman burglar; a character created by author Maurice Leblanc. The museum, in a vast Norman family home, mingles mementos of the two.

CLIFF WALKS

Falaise d'Aval★★★

Allow 1hr on foot there and back. From the west end of the promenade climb the steps (180 steps, handrail) to the path which scales the cliff face. Walk along the edge of the cliff as far as the ridge of Porte d'Aval. Magnificent view: the massive Manneporte arch (left), the Aiguille opposite and Amont Cliff on the bay's far side.

Falaise d'Amont★★

Allow 1hr on foot there and back. From the east end of the promenade take the steps cut into the chalk cliffs and the path to the clifftop.

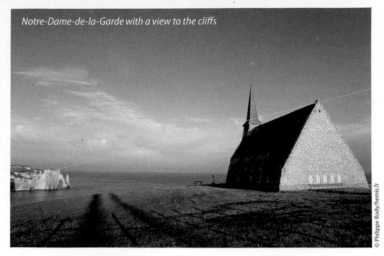
Notre-Dame-de-la-Garde with a view to the cliffs

© Philippe Body/hemis.fr

Access by car: take D 11 Fécamp par la Côte; just before the sign indicating the end of the built-up area, turn sharp left onto a steep and narrow uphill road. Park near the monument.

From **Notre-Dame-de-la-Garde** there is a magnificent **view**★ of Étretat and its surroundings, with the long shingle beach from Aval arch to Aiguille. Behind the chapel an immense spire points skyward, memorial to Nungesser and Coli. These French aviators made the first attempt to fly the Atlantic on 8 May 1927, their craft, Oiseau Blanc, was last seen here.

Château des Aygues – D 940,

Etretat exit to Fécamp.www. chateaulesaygues.com. ℘02 35 28 92 77. Jul–Sept Wed–Mon 2–6pm. €6 (children over 7, €5). Guided tour.

Built in 1866, this was the summer residence of the queens of Spain, Maria Cristina of Bourbon and Isabella II. It welcomed famous guests such as Jacques Offenbach and Alexandre Dumas. A beautiful collection of Chinese ceramics and porcelains pay homage to Isabella II.

EXCURSIONS
Terminal du Havre-Antifer

◗ 15km/9mi S. Leave Étretat on avenue George-V, D 940. The cliffs can collapse without warning. Do not walk directly beneath them; beware of tides

Valleuse d'Antifer – From Tilleul take rue de Mer, across from the church portal; take rue d'Antifer, right, which takes you to a car park; take the pretty path down through woods and meadows for about 20min.

This cliff hollow (valleuse) is an effort to reach, but worth it. You may not be alone when you reach the beautiful, famous view! Two local conservation associations protect the valleuse and offer summer nature walks. Contact Étretat tourist office.

Bruneval – Return to the D 940 and 800m/875yd after Le Tilleul, take the D 111 towards La Poterie-Cap-d'Antifer. An Allied raid on the night of 27–28 February 1942 was aimed at the German radar installation near the beach. Three British parachutist detachments destroyed the position, re-embarking almost without loss.

Terminal du Havre-Antifer – Between Bruneval and St-Jouin, the road leads through pretty countryside to the oil terminal.

Le Havre-Antifer port was created in 1976 to receive oil tankers too big for the facilities at Le Havre. On the way back to St-Jouin, a narrow road on the right (signalled Port du Havre/Antifer/Belvédère), leads to a belvedere with a fine **view**.

Fécamp★★

Fécamp is a fishing port as well as a centre for pleasure boats. The town is also the home of Benedictine liqueur – a link with its monastic past. Guy de Maupassant was one frequent visitor to the town, which features in several of his works.

A BIT OF HISTORY

As early as the 7C there was a monastery in Fécamp with a relic of the Precious Blood. Richard II, Duke of Normandy from 996–1027, established a Benedictine community here. Before the rise of Mont-St-Michel, this was the foremost place of pilgrimage in Normandy.

TOWN

Until 1863, **Guy de Maupassant** often came to his maternal grandmother's home in Fécamp. *La Maison Tellier* and various episodes in his tales are situated in this port town; little remains of that time, aside from the abbey church of La Trinité at place des Halettes. Fécamp's heart is however forever in its port. The *"Bout menteux"* (Liars' Corner), between quays Vicomté and Bérigny, a former sea dog lair, is just as lively today as it was in the past. The beach stretches from the channel entrance to the casino. As for the Gayant causeway crossing the inner harbour (moveable bridge), it connects with the north cliff and Côte de la Vierge; the Notre-Dame-de-Salut chapel can be made out against the horizon *(see Excursions)*.

The Port

The Freycinet handles commercial traffic. Verdun Quay receives vessels loaded with gravel, sand for glass-making, salt from the Salins du Midi and logged or sawn wood.

Abbatiale de la Trinité★
pl. des Ducs Richards.
The abbey church built by Richard II was struck by lightning and burned down. The subsequent building (12C–13C) was modified several times between the 15C and 18C.

▶ **Population:** 19,424.
◔ **Michelin Map:** 304: C-3. Local map, *◔see Pays de Caux, p124.*
▯ **Info:** Quai Sadi-Carnot. ℘02 35 28 51 01. www.fecamptourisme.com.
▷ **Location:** Fécamp is 43km/ 26.7mi NE of Le Havre and 72km/44.7mi NW of Rouen.
◔ **Don't Miss:** The rich collections of the Benedictine palace, the abbey of La Trinité and the superb view from Cap Fagnet and Valmont Abbey.
◔ **Timing:** Fécamp and its surroundings will take up a day.
▲▲ **Kids:** The museum of Terre-Neuvas et de la Pêche.

Exterior – The cathedral is one of the longest (127m/417ft) in France. The Classical façade does not accord with the rest of the building and the nave walls are austere. Skirt the south porch: the tympanum above the door is a good example of Norman Gothic decoration. Above the transept crossing rises the square lantern tower (65m/213.3ft high), designed in the typical Norman style.
Interior – The south transept contains a beautiful late 15C **Dormition of the Virgin**★. On the right of the the altar is the Angel's Footprint. In 943, when the reconstructed church was being consecrated, it is said that an angel appeared and left his footprint on the stone.
The chancel's dimensions make it magnificent. The stalls, baldaquin and high altar are all good 18C works by the Rouen artist De France. A Renaissance altar stands behind the high altar. In the centre of the sanctuary is an ancient shrine adorned with low-relief sculptures dating from the 12C. The chapels off the chancel aisles and radiating chapels were embellished with wonderful **carved screens**★ in the 16C. In the fourth chapel, on the right, is the **tomb**★ of Abbot Thomas of St-Benoît,

who died in 1307; the tomb is decorated with scenes from the abbey's history on its base.

The 15C **Lady Chapel**★forms a separate group in the Flamboyant style. The wood medallions are 18C; the windows are 13C, 14C and 16C. Facing the chapel is the white-marble **tabernacle**★ of the Precious Blood. The 17C tomb in the chapel of the Sacred Heart belongs to **Guglielmo da Volpiano**, first abbot of Fécamp, who died in 1031.

Palais Bénédictine★★

110 r. Alexandre-le-Grand.
⊙*Open early Feb to 1 Apr and mid-Oct to end Dec 10.30am–11.45am, 2–5pm; from 2 Apr–mid-Oct 10am–noon, 2–5.30pm.* ⊙*Closed 1 May and 25 Dec.* ☞€7. ☏02 35 10 26 10.

The building, designed by Camille Albert in the late 19C, is a mixture of neo-Gothic and neo-Renaissance styles. The **museum** displays a large collection of objets d'art: silver and gold work, ivories, Nottingham alabasters (late 15C), wrought-iron work, statues and many manuscripts.

The Gothic Room is covered by a fine pitched roof made of oak and chestnut, shaped as the upturned hull of a ship; it houses the library: 15C Books of the Hours with fine **illuminations**, numerous **ivories**, a collection of **oil lamps** dating from the early days of Christianity and a Dormition of the Virgin, a painted low-relief wooden carving of the German School.

The Alexander Le Grand Room, named after the Fécamp merchant who first marketed the Benedictine liqueur in 1863, displays objects and documents relating to its history.

Musée des Terre-Neuvas et de la Pêche★

27 bd Albert I. ⚐⊙*Open Jul–Aug daily 10am–6.30pm; Sept–Jun Wed–Mon 10am–noon, 2–5.30pm.* ⊙*Closed 1 Jan, 1 May, 25 Dec.* ☞€3. ☏02 35 28 31 99.

The Newfoundland and Fishing Museum evokes memories of the Fécamp fishing industry. The lower gallery explores the great adventure of the cod fishermen on the Newfoundland banks in the days of the sailing ship and the dory, a flat-bottomed craft rising at bow and stern. One room is devoted to shipbuilding, featuring a model of the Belle Poule, the naval training ship built in Fécamp

Deep-Sea Fishing, an Old Tradition

The herrings of Fécamp have been renowned since the Middle Ages. During the Renaissance ships sailed from Fécamp to Newfoundland to fish for cod. Fishing techniques did not change much for nearly 400 years: the fish was caught with a ground line by two men aboard a 5m/5.5yd-long flat-bottomed boat called a doris. The fish was then gutted, cleaned, boned, salted and stored in the hold; this was called fishing for green cod. Fishing for dried cod meant fishermen had to settle during the season on the coast of Newfoundland, where they would build drying racks for their catch. During the 1970s, 15 huge trawlers with a crew of 900 men salted and froze 21,000t of cod in the icy waters of the North Atlantic. Today, pleasure boats have replaced trawlers, but until recently one could still meet old fishermen recalling their memories at the Bout Menteux (Liars' Corner, situated between quai Vicomté and quai Bérigny).

in 1931. Exhibits trace the development of fishing methods and types of craft. The outdoor terrace provides a magnificent **view**★ of the sea.

EXCURSIONS
Cap Fagnet
◗ *On the cliff north of Fécamp's port.*
The cape has been home to five wind turbines since 2005. The place is worth a visit for the pretty little 11C **Notre-Dame-du-Salut** chapel built to protect sailors (votive offerings). A magnificent panoramic view may be found here.
Hollows (valleuses). Respect safety measures! Watch children and avoid clifftops; rare landslides do happen.

Vaucottes
◗ *9km/5mi SW of Fécamp, from Yport or Vattetot (12 km/7mi SW of Fécamp via D 940 and D 11) by a pretty road from Les Hogues or from Yport by a beautiful coast road.* This *valleuse* belongs to Vattetot-sur-Mer, its church steeple is a sailors' seamark. The site is restricted, with a path down to sea to pretty, early-20C villas.

Val-de-la-Mer
◗ *At Senneville-sur-Fécamp (5km/3mi NE by D 925), take r. du Val-de-Mer, after church on left.* These impressive cliffs are especially favoured by birdwatchers. There are stairs, but you may prefer to enjoy the view from top of the steps because of the risk of frequent cliffslides.

St-Pierre-en-Port
◗ *13km/8mi NE from Fécamp by D 925*

and D 79. This old port at end of a *valleuse* today has pretty, familial beach and a magnificent view.

Les Grandes Dalles
◗ *Just NE of St-Pierre-en-Port.* This early fishing village is set in a cliff hollow and is easily reached. There is a children's tuberculosis sanatorium and a little pebbled beach with a superb view.

Les Petites Dalles★
◗ *NE of St-Pierre-en-Port, 1.5k/1mi from Sassetot-le-Mauconduit.*
Late 19C homes combine with a delightful setting and a magnificent sea view, enjoyed by some leading lights of history including Monet, Pissarro, Delacroix and, **Sissi**, Empress of Austria. Almost carried off by the currents, Sissi granted her rescuer a gold watch. In 1940 **Rommel** and his men forced through here to separate the French and English troops. They celebrated afterwards with a swim. The Petites Dalles **cavern** (guided tour (1hr) Jul–Sept by appt with tourist office, 75 r. Joseph-Heuzé; 02 35 27 87 98) was discovered in 1966. It eroded itself into existence about 800,000 years ago.
A **walking route** *(3h30min RT, take southern coastal path (GR 21) from small car park over the beach; picnic areas on path, among pastures and cliffs)* links Les Petites Dalles, Les Grandes Dalles, St-Pierre-en-Port and Sassetot-le-Mauconduit in a ring. There are beautiful panoramic views of the sea, the *valleuses*, and the Château de Sassetot park. The trip down to Les Petites Dalles

from Sassetot, through a forest and to a chapel in a hamlet, is magical.

Château de Bailleul
▶ *10km/6mi SE by D 73.*
This elegant 16C château *(o━ closed to the public)* consists of a central square building flanked by four pavilions. The medieval side façades are almost blind. A chapel stands in the wooded park.

Valmont
▶ *11km/7mi E via D 150.*
Located in the very heart of the Pays de Caux and dominated by a castle built on a rocky spur, the village of Valmont is known for the ruins of its Benedictine abbey.
Abbey★ – ௸⊙*Church open Wed–Mon 3–5pm; guided tour possible (30min, request 2wks prior).* ⊙*Closed 1 Jan, Easter Sun, Pentecost Sun, 1 Nov, 25 Dec.*⊚*€3.*

℘*02 35 27 34 92. http://abbayevalmont. free.fr* Founded in the 12C, the Benedictine abbey of Valmont was rebuilt in the 14C following a fire and was radically altered in the 16C. After the Revolution the abbey became a private residence The **Chapelle de la Vierge★**, or Six o'Clock Chapel (the monks celebrated Mass at this time every day), which has remained intact among the ruins, has an overall effect of great grace. Above the altar is a tiny room which has exquisite decorations and also a picture of the Annunciation attributed to Germain Pilon.
Château – o━ *Closed to the public –* Property of the Estoutevilles, lords of Valmont, this former military fortress preserves a Romanesque keep flanked by a Louis XI wing, crowned by a covered watch-path, and a Renaissance wing.

Pays de Caux★

The Caux is mainly known for its impressive coastline. Visitors delight in the natural beauty of the area, returning each year to the vast beaches below the splendid chalk cliffs. The surrounding countryside offers a swathe of remarkable churches, castles and manor houses.

GEOLOGY
Côte d'Albâtre – Along the Alabaster Coast the chalk cliffs, with alternate strata of flint and yellow marl, are worn away ceaselessly by the action of the tides and the weather.
The Étretat needle rocks and underwater shelves 1.6km/1mi from the shore indicate the former coastline. At the particularly exposed point of **Cap de la Hève**, erosion carves away 2m/6.5ft a year; the water is milky with chalk, and flints are pounded endlessly upon the beaches. The hollows *(valleuses)* cut into every clifftop as far as the eye can see are dry former river valleys, truncated by the retreating coastline. Some rivers were powerful enough to carve valleys

- ௸ **Michelin Map:** 512 folds 7-10, 19-22.
- ▣ **Info:** Several villages have their own tourist offices. Those of Dieppe, Étretat, Le Havre and Caudebec-en-Caux also serve the Caux region.
- ▶ **Location:** The Pays de Caux is bounded on the S by the Seine Valley, on the W and N by the Alabaster Coast and on the E along a line extending between Dieppe and Rouen.
- ⊕ **Don't Miss:** The resorts and little villages of the Alabaster Coast, as well as the charming villages of the interior and the Parc des Boucles de la Seine.
- ⊙ **Timing:** You will need several days to tour this region.
- ♟ **Kids:** The outdoor centre on Lac de Caniel offers sports and games.

right down to the coastline, and that is where ports and resorts have appeared.
Caux Farmsteads – The farms appear as green oases surrounded by 2m/6.5ft-high windbreaks topped by a double row of oaks, beeches or elms.

The **farmstead** comprises a meadow planted with apple trees in which stand the half-timbered farm buildings. The entrance is often through a monumental gateway. In spring, cattle and horses are tethered to a post *(tière)* and each animal marks out its territory in the form of a perfect circle. Milk production is the chief source of income.

DRIVING TOURS

1 CÔTE D'ALBÂTRE★

From Dieppe to Étretat, 77km/48mi.
Allow about 2hr30min.

▷ *Leave Dieppe by D 75 (see Dieppe).*

Glimpses of the sea and cliffs and pleasant views of resorts are the main features of this drive, which is at its best in the morning.

Pourville-sur-Mer

This seaside resort, pleasantly situated near jagged cliffs, has risen from the ruins of the Dieppe commando raid of 19 August 1942; the Cameron Highlanders and a Canadian Regiment, the South Saskatchewan, landed to the sound of bagpipes and inflicted severe damage on the enemy. Under cover of the Navy and sacrificing their rearguard, they re-embarked early in the afternoon. A commemorative stele of pink marble stands on the seafront.

▷ *Continue west on D 75 through*
Varengeville-sur-Mer *(see Varengeville-sur-Mer).*

Ste-Marguerite-sur-Mer

The 12C church, which has no transept, was considerably remodelled in the 16C. Inside, four of the original **arches**★ remain on the north side; those on the south date from 1528. The high

altar dates from 1160 and is one of the very few remaining of this period.

Saint-Aubin

The pretty 16C **church** still betrays numerous traces of the Romanesque period, such as the portal and the tower in flint. The **town**, standing at its post at the mouth of the Dun River, is a sort of entranceway to the pretty **valley** of the same name, 10–12km/6–7mi long and on the list of Seine-Maritime's beautiful sites. It is also know as the "linen valley" owing to the chateaux, manors, farms and thatched homes of drapers that are all part of the region's rich architectural heritage. *The valley offers numerous options for excursions by foot or bicycle. Contact the Bourg-Dun tourist office (see below). Bicycles can be rented there.*

▷ *Take the D 237 on the left.*

Flainville

Halfway between St-Aubin-sur-Mer and the Bourg-Dun, on the left.
Beautiful Renaissance frescoes can be found inside the 16C **chapel of St Julien**. The recently restored **bread oven**, presents all the bakers' tools of yesteryear.

▷ *Take the D 237 south.*

Le Bourg-Dun

Notre-Dame-du-Salut is a vast composite church, remarkable for its **tower**★, built on a massive square 13C base. The hatchet-shaped roof is 17C. A Renaissance door opens into the south aisle. Beneath Flamboyant vaulting in the south transept are a Renaissance bay and piscina; three arches in the chancel open into the beautiful south aisle, added in the 14C. The font in the north aisle is Renaissance.

▷ *Continuez sur la D 237.*

Saint-Pierre-le-Vieux

The 12C and 13C **church** has its Romanesque-style belltower and Gothic and Neo-Gothic elements from the 14C and 16C. Note the **dial** at the foot of the church; the road-mender used it in the past to show which direction he had gone to work in.

○ *Continue on the D 237.*

La Gaillarde

The pretty **St Margaret's chapel** is remarkable for the finesse of its sculpted Romanesque porch, especially the heads forming the column capitals. There is an old bread oven in the centre of the village.

○ *Continue on the D 237.*

Saint-Pierre-le-Viger

Two Friday afternoons a month you can visit the "**Terre de lin**" factory (*on request, 15 days prior, guided tour on Fri at 2pm and 4pm; information at the Plateau de Caux maritime tourist office; www.terredelin.com. ☎02 35 84 19 55. ☜€3, -18 years €1*), one of France's largest linen-making cooperatives. Here you can learn about the various stages required to convert the plant into a textile fibre. There is a pretty limestone **manor** alongside the Dun, dating 16C and 17C.

○ *Take the D 142 S then the D 108 on the left.*

▲▲ Crasville-la-Rocquefort

The **St-Cosme** farm (*ride drawn by team of horses, on prior request,* ⏰2.30–6.30pm; visit to the farm and goat cheese dairy 5–7pm. ☜€3 (-12 years old, €2), ride with team of horses €6 (-12 years €4). ☎02 35 97 41 76 or 06 22 60 37 64 *)* is in an enclosure, surrounded by a windbreak of beeches and fields of wheat, beets and flax. The family organises farm visits in a warm and friendly atmosphere, a chance to discover the goat cheese dairy, the pigs, turkeys, cows and rabbits. A film presents the farm's production activities, including cheese-making and flax treatment. Kids will enjoy the horse and cart rides on offer *(book ahead)*. A variety of cheeses are on sale here, including the house creation and speciality, the galet d'Albâtre.

○ *Return to St-Aubin and head left on the D 68.*

Veules-les-Roses★

The seaside resort, sheltered in a small valley, has pretty surroundings, notably windmills and picturesque villas dating from the 19C, when the town attracted fashionable Parisians. **St-Martin**, in the town itself, is a 16C–17C church with a 13C lantern. A timber-framed roof covers the nave and aisles. Inside are five 16C twisted limestone columns and ancient statues.

🚶 A walking route takes you past mills, villas and homes built of brick and flint. Some spots are very pretty, especially near the watering trough where watercress is grown (*27 r. Victor-Hugo. ☎02.35.97.64.11. www.veules-les-roses.fr*).

Veules-les-Roses on a winter morning

I. Lainey/MICHELIN

▶ *Turn left onto D 37.*

Église de Blosseville

The church, surmounted by a 12C belfry, possesses beautiful Renaissance stained-glass windows and some old statues.

▶ *Continue towards Ermenouville on D 37.*

Château du Mesnil-Geoffroy

Ermenouville. ☞Guided tours (45min) May–Sept Wed–Sun 2.30–6pm. ⏱Closed 1 May. ✐€6. ✆02 35 57 12 77. www.chateau-mesnil-geoffroy.com. Guest rooms available (☺☺☺).

Surrounded by a 9ha/22.2-acre formal French park with a famous rose garden (2,500 species), this 17C and 18C château is an interesting testimony to the gentle art of living under Louis XV.

▶ *On leaving the château, turn right on the D 70.*

Mesnil-Durdent

Make sure you visit this charming village and its wild garden, the **Jardin communal d'Amouhoques**, an irregular plot of land with many paths and embankments, planted with all manner of herbs carrying quaint, old-fashioned names.

▶ *Take the D 468 until you reach St-Valery-en-Caux.*

Port of St-Valery-en-Caux

G. Targat/MICHELIN

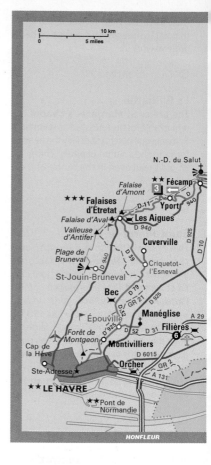

Saint-Valery-en-Caux★

St-Valery is both a popular seaside resort, with a promenade overlooking the long shingle beach, and a fishing and coastal trading port.

The **Falaise d'Aval**★ (West Headland) *(access on foot via sentier des Douaniers and steps)* is crowned by a monument commemorating the battles of June 1940 (51st Highland Division and the French 2nd Cavalry Division).

The view embraces the Ailly lighthouse and, on a clear day, Dieppe. The **Maison d'Henri IV** *(quai du Havre)* is a beautiful Renaissance house with carved beams. On the **Falaise d'Amont** (East Headland) *(access by steps)* stands the 51st Highland Division Monument overlooking the town, harbour and beach. The more modern monument nearby was

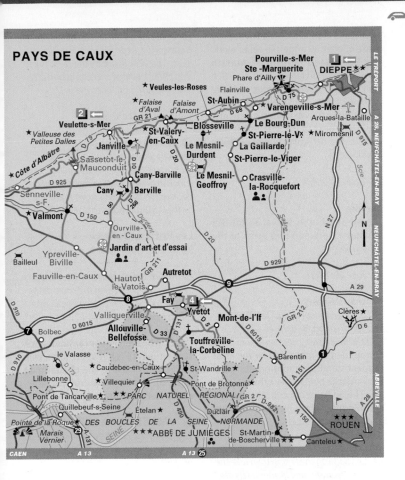

erected in memory of Coste and Bel-lonte, who in 1930 made the first flight from Paris to New York.

🚶 The area around St-Valery-en-Caux offers many pleasant walks *(tourist office, Maison Henri IV. ℰ02 35 97 00 63).*

Veulettes-sur-Mer

The 11C and 13C church stands halfway up a hill overlooking the seaside resort, which has a 2.5km/1.5mi beach.

The finest **panorama**★★ is between Senneville *(narrow road)* and Fécamp, near the **Chapelle Notre-Dame-du-Salut** (sailors' pilgrimage). The cliffs to the west of Fécamp stretch as far as Étretat.

② VALLÉE DE LA DURDENT

52km/32mi. Allow 3hr. Leave Veulettes on the D10 south. At Paluel take the D68 left.

La Durdent wends its way to lazily spill out at Veulettes-sur-Mer, having worn a wide green valley through the open spaces of the Caux plateau.

Chapelle de Janville

This pilgrimage church has an attractive wrought-iron grille in the chancel.

▷ *Return to Paluel. Turn left onto D 10.*

Cany-Barville

◦ *Guided tours on request from tourist office. ℰ02 35 57 17 70.*

The **church** on the west bank, rebuilt in the 16C, has a 13C belfry. On the high altar (18C) stands a Christ in Majesty made of over 80 angels in relief work. The **Ecomusée Moulin St-Martin** (*1, rue de l'Abreuvoir.* ○*Open Apr–Oct, daily by appt;* ○*guided tour;* ○*€4 (-12 years no charge.* ℘*02 35 97 59 71. www. cany-barville.fr*) is in the old mechanics workshop next to the 15C wheat mill. It contains a rich collection of old tools and objects.

▷ *Take the D 268.*

Barville
The small church has a delightful **setting**★ between two arms of the River Durdent.

▷ *Take the D 131.*

Château de Cany
○*Guided tours (45min) Jul–Aug Sat– Thu 10am–noon, 3–6pm.* ○*€7.* ℘*02 35 97 87 36.*
Surrounded by moats fed by the River Durdent stands an imposing stone and brick château built in 1640, the Louis XIII era. The apartments contain fine 17C and 18C furnishings. In the basement, a kitchen contains utensils, crockery and costumed figures.

▷ *Continue on the D 268, then take the D 131 on the right, and immediately after the D 50 on the left. Go past Ourville- en-Caux. When you get to Normanville, leave the village on your right and go a little further, following the signs indicating the garden on the right.*

♣♣Jardin d'Art et d'Essai★
○ *D 50, rte de Fauville, Normanville.* ○○*Open Jun–Aug, Thu–Tue 2.30pm–nightfall ; rest of the year, contact number below for information.* ○*Closed 1 Jan and 25 Dec.* ○*€6 (-14 years old €3, -7 years old no charge).* ℘*02 35 29 62 39. http://aisthesie.free.fr.*
An organic garden of unusual plants, superb trees, meandering waters and beautiful bamboo. A walk that will wake all five of your senses!

▷ *Continue on the D 33 after leaving Normanville; head for Sorquainville and get to Ypreville-Biville by the D 75. Take the D 926 heading for Fécamp and after 2km/1mi turn right onto the D 17.*

Valmont (○*See Valmont*).

▷ *Continue north on the D 17 to head for Thérouldeville, then Sassetot-le- Mauconduit. In crossing the village, take a look to the left to admire the Château de Sassetot, then head town to the sea by the D 5 until you reach Petites Dalles.*

Les Petites Dalles★
(○*See Les Petites Dalles*).

▷ *Return to Sassetot-le-Mauconduit and take the D 79 along the coast in the direction of Senneville. Head along the cliff to reach Fécamp.*

The most beautiful **panoramic view**★★ of the itinerary is between Senneville and Fécamp, close to the **chapelle de N.-D.-du-Salut** (sailors' pilgrimage), where there is a viewpoint.

③ VALLÉE DE LA LÉZARDE
33km/21mi. Allow 1hr.

▷ *Leave Fécamp on the D940.*

Yport
Yport, a seaside resort tucked away in a valley, had a fishing fleet until 1970.

Étretat★★★ ○*See Falaises d'Étretat.*

▷ *Leave Étretat by D 39. At Criquetot- l'Esneval turn left onto D 239.*

Cuverville
The writer **André Gide** (1859–1951) is buried in the small cemetery, under a simple gravestone at the fromt of the church. The author of the *Nourritures terrestres* spent long periods at Cuver- ville on the property of his cousins, the Rondeaux.

▷ *The road descends into the pleasant Lézarde Valley.*

Château du Bec
⚬━ *Closed for visits.*
The 12C–16C castle has an enchanting setting of trees and still waters.

▷ *In Épouville turn left onto D 925 and then right onto D 52.*

Manéglise
The small church is a graceful example of Romanesque architecture.

▷ *Return to Épouville; continue south.*

Montivilliers
An 11C lantern tower above the transept crossing and a Romanesque belfry surmounted by a spire (restored in the 19C) identify the **Église St-Sauveur**★.

▷ *The road leaves the Vallée de la Lézarde via Rouelles, just outside Le Havre. The road skirts the edge of Montgeon Forest, and leads to the Jenner tunnel, which leads to the town centre.*

4 PLATEAU CAUCHOIS★

Round trip starting from Yvetot. 50km/32mi. Allow 1hr30.

Yvetot
The town, made famous in a song as the capital of an imaginary kingdom, is in fact a large market town on the Caux plateau. The **Église St-Pierre** (🕐*Open Mon–Sat 8.30am–7pm, Sun and holidays 8.30am–noon; audio guides available at tourist office*), built in 1956, contains remarkably large **stained-glass windows**★★ by Max Ingrand, which produce a dazzling effect; other windows show founders of religious orders, saints of the Rouen diocese and the saints of France. The Lady Chapel *(behind the altar)* windows depict episodes in the life of the Virgin.

▷ *Leave Yvetot by heading for Ste-Marie-des-Champs (D 37). After the Yvetot exit, turn left at the roundabout. Take rue du Vieux-Ste-Marie to the Manoir de Fay.*

Manoir de Fay
This pretty 17C manor (*not open to the public*), in brick with pale stone wall ties and toothing, apparently once welcomed the uncle of French literary luminary Pierre Corneille. Undergoing restoration, the property has an immense orchard and walled vegetable garden which is pleasant for a wander. A great deal of charm.

▷ *Continue on rue du Vieux-Ste-Marie then take route de La-Linerie on the left to get to D 131 on the right, to be taken to Autretot.*

Autretot
A pretty village typical of the Caux region, which prides itself on its flowers – close to 20,000 are planted every year to brighten the centre of Autretot.

▷ *On leaving Autretot, just before the water tower, take the D 110 on the left and follow it to Allouville-Bellefosse; you will pass through Veraval, Hautot-le-Vatois, Écretteville-lès-Baons and Valliquerville.*

Allouville-Bellefosse
The village is known for the **oak tree** *(chêne)* which grows in front of the church; it is believed to be more than 1,300 years old, one of the oldest in France and the most famous tree in Normandy.

Touffreville-la-Corbeline
Touffreville has an 18C church with 12C belltower. The tomb here is of the Bossières brothers, explorers of southern climes. Moving on from here, you find pretty farms along the roadside.

▷ *Continue on the D 104, then take successively the D 89 on the left, the D5 on the right and then D 304 on the left to Mont-de-l'If.*

Mont-de-l'If
There are two manors in this village; church with 11C vestiges.

▷ *Take the D 304 then the D 5 to return to Yvetot.*

Varengeville-sur-Mer★

The resort consists of a series of hamlets in a charming landscape of hedges and half-timbered houses. The church stands on an attractive site★ overlooking the sea.
The stained-glass window in the south aisle depicting the Tree of Jesse is by 20C abstract artist Georges Braque, who is buried in the graveyard.

SIGHTS
Église
The church site★ overlooks the sea. The tombs of artist **Georges Braque** (1882–1963) and musician and composer **Albert Roussell** (1869–1937) are found here. Braque's stained-glass Tree of Jesse is in the south nave.

▲▲ "Les Bruyères" nature walk
1hr. Take route de l'Aumône across from the mairie and follow bois des Communes
This 500m/546yd long path is way-marked with panels explaining the geology, flora and fauna of the Bois des Communes moors.

Parc floral du Bois des Moutiers★
Open mid-Mar–mid-Nov daily 10am–noon, 2–6pm, public holidays 10am–7pm. €8. 02 35 85 10 02.
In a valley facing the sea is a lovely English-style garden (9ha/22 acres). The **house** (1898) was designed by the renowned English architect Sir Edwin Luytens and the **garden** by his frequent collaborator, Gertrude Jekyll.

Chapelle St-Dominique
On the outskirts of Varengeville, on the left side of the road to Dieppe.
Open Jun–mid-Sept daily 9am–5.30pm. 02 35 85 12 14.
There is more **stained glass** by Braque as well as a painting by 20C artist Maurice Denis.

▶ **Population:** 1,071.
Michelin Map: 304: F-2.
Info: 6 place du Village, 76740 Le-Bourg-Dun. 02 35 97 63 05.
Location: The pretty coastal road D 75 leads to Varengeville, which is 4km/2.5mi W of Dieppe, between Pourville-sur-Mer and Vasterival.
Don't Miss: The beautiful view from the church; the garden at the Bois des Moutiers, designed by Gertrude Jekyll.
Timing: Take 1hr to see the garden.

EXCURSIONS
Phare d'Ailly★
1km/0.6mi on D 75A off D 75.
Guided tour (15min), call 1 wk prior, mid-Apr–mid-Sept Mon–Fri 10am–noon, 2–4.30pm. 02 35 85 11 19.
A modern lighthouse has replaced the two older ones (18C–19C), lost in 1944.

Manoir d'Ango
Follow the signs from D 75 onto a little road, and turn right a bit further on a drive to car park. Open Apr–Oct 10am–12.30pm, 2–6pm; rest of year, call for info 02 35 04 19 94. €5.
This was the lovely Renaissance home of **Jean Ango**, the great 16C navigator, fleet-owner, governor of Dieppe and naval adviser to François I.
With a large inner courtyard, it also has an Italian-style **loggia**. Typically Renaissance, there are many sculpted ornaments forming foliage, seashells and medallions.

Valleuses
In the direction of the Ailly lighthouse.
The very beautiful Petit-Ailly and Vasterival are among the most typical of these hanging valleys. Garden-lovers will enjoy the Jardins du Vaserival (02 35 85 12 05).

Dieppe★★

Dieppe is home to Paris's closest beach and is thus France's oldest seaside resort. The harbour is modern but many old corners and alleys remain, along with churches, a castle and a museum. In the square du Canada stands a monument commemorating the men of Dieppe who explored Canada in the 16C, 17C and 18C, a reminder of more than 350 years of common history. A plaque recalls the Commando Raid in 1942.

A BIT OF HISTORY

Jean Ango and the Privateers' War (16C) – When the Portuguese decided to treat any vessel found off the African coast as a pirate ship, François I riposted by issuing letters of marque. The seamen of Dieppe took the lead. **Jean Ango**, shipbuilder and naval adviser to François I, produced a fleet of privateers, "which would make a king tremble". Among his captains was **Verrazano** from Florence who discovered the site of New York (1524). Within a few years Ango's ships had captured over 300 Portuguese vessels. Fearing ruin, the King of Portugal forced Ango to give up his letter of marque. The captain built himself a splendid mansion in Dieppe and a country residence in Varengeville. In 1535, he was appointed Governor of Dieppe. In 1551, he was buried in a chapel of St James' Church.

Dieppe Spa – According to the chronicler Pierre de l'Estoile, in 1578 Henri III, who was suffering from scabies (a skin disease), was advised by his doctors to bathe in the sea at Dieppe.

Later Madame de Sévigné mentioned in her letters that some of the court ladies went to Dieppe. She wrote of one of them, "The sea received her bare naked and thus was made proud; I mean to say the sea was proud, for the lady was greatly embarrassed."

Throughout the 19C the baths and casinos of Dieppe attracted extravagant people showing off their fine clothes, as well as celebrities such as King Louis-Philippe, Napoleon III, Eugène Delacroix, Camille Saint-Saëns, Alexandre Dumas and Oscar Wilde.

Canadian Commando Raid in 1942 – On 19 August 1942, Operation Jubilee was launched; it was the first Allied reconnaissance expedition on Europe's coast. Dieppe was the primary objective. Seven thousand men, mostly Canadians, landed at eight points between Berneval and Ste-Marguerite, but the Churchill tanks floundered hopelessly on the beach under intense fire. Five thousand men were killed or taken prisoner; the Allies learned from this raid that German

▶ **Population:** 33,618.

◔ **Michelin Map:** 304: G-2 – Local map, ◔ see Pays de Caux, p124.

▯ **Info:** Pont Jean-Ango. ℘02 32 14 40 60. www.dieppetourisme.fr.

◔ **Location:** Dieppe is 65km/40.5mi N of Rouen and 108km/67.5mi from Le Havre. The city is cut in two by the River Béthune, with the picturesque old districts on the right bank and the commercial and government buildings on the left bank around the Grande-Rue and the rue de la Barre.

▣ **Parking:** Look for free parking along the seafront (bd de Verdun), along the quai de Bérigny (cultural centre) and behind the train station. The car park opposite the town hall (Mairie) on Maréchal-Joffre is paying.

◔ **Don't Miss:** The 18C buildings along rue de la Barre and the wonderful view of the city from the château museum.

◔ **Timing:** You need a day to see Dieppe, and half a day to tour the Forest of Eawy.

NEWHAVEN

ROUEN, PARIS LE TRÉPORT, ABBEVILLE

CAR-FERRY

DIEPPE

0   300 m
0   300 yds

N

LA MANCHE

N.-D.-de-Bon-Secours

EU, LE TRÉPORT

Cité de la Mer

Bout-du-Quai

Le Pollet

Av. Gén. Leclerc

D 925

Port de Plaisance

TOUR AUX CRABES

Porte des Tourelles

R. du Haut Pas

Place Nationale Saint-Jacques

CASINO

ST-RÉMY

Pont Colbert

Gde Rue du Pollet

N.-D. DES GRÈVES

Mémorial du 19 août 1942

Pl. du Puits-Salé

R. St-Jacques

R. de la Bonne Nouvelle

NEUCHÂTEL-EN-BRAY D 1 ST-NICOLAS D'ALIERMONT

Château-musée

R. V. Hugo

Port de Pêche

Port

Ch. de la Citadelle

R. C. Groulard   Bd   Général   de   Gaulle

R. Desmarets

CENTRE CULTUREL J. RENOIR

Commerce

POURVILLE-SUR-MER FÉCAMP PAR LA CÔTE

R. Toustain

R. de Blainville   Bd   G.   Clemenceau

POL

H

VEULES-LES-ROSES VARENGEVILLE-S-M.

R. du Fg de la Barre

R. des Fontaines

Montigny

Avenue

Rue   de   la   République

Rue   Jean   Ribault

Gambetta

Dijon

Thiers

LE HAVRE D 925   CHÂTEAU DE MIROMESNIL

D 927 ROUEN D 915 PARIS

ST-JEAN-D'ALIERMONT

ROUEN D 154E ARQUES-LA-BATAILLE

LE HAVRE, PARIS D 925 LE TRÉPORT

WHERE TO STAY	
Aguado	①
Capucins (Villa des)	③
Europe (Hôtel de l')	⑥
Grand Duquesne (Hôtel au)	⑨
Présidence (Hôtel)	⑭
Villa Florida (Chambre d'hôte la)	⑯

WHERE TO EAT	
Bistro du Pollet (Le)	①
Colombier (Le)	③
Marmite dieppoise (La)	⑥
New-Haven (Le)	⑨
Régates (Les)	⑪
Sully (Le)	⑫
Trou Normand (Au)	⑭
Voiles d'Or (Les)	⑯

defences were concentrated round the ports and, as naval losses were small, that amphibious operations on a larger scale might be successful; the Germans, however, concluded that future Allied attacks would be directed particularly at the ports.

They were wrong; the Allies developed artificial ports, the famous Mulberries, which they towed across the Channel for the Normandy Landings, avoiding highly defended ports.

WALKING TOURS

DOWNTOWN AND THE BEACH

About 1hr30min from the parking spot at place Nationale, near St-Jacques.

Place Nationale

In the centre of the circle stands a statue of Abraham Duquesne (1610–88), famous for defeating the Dutch navy and for hunting down and disarming pirate ships in the Mediterranean. Two of the buildings on place Nationale (nos **18** and **24**) date from the early 18C.

Église St-Jacques★

pl. St-Jacques.

Begin by going round the outside of the church, which has been considerably rebuilt over the centuries. Over the 14C central doorway is a fine rose window; the façade tower is 15C; the east end and radiating chapels are 16C; the unrenovated south transept, on the other hand, is a good example of early Gothic.

Interior – The well-proportioned nave, which is 13C, was ornamented in the 14C with a triforium and given tall windows a century later. The first chapel in the south aisle, the Chapel of the Holy Sepulchre, is 15C. The transept, the oldest part of the church, supports the dome, which was rebuilt in the 18C. A fine 17C wooden statue of St James stands above the high altar. The Sacred Heart Chapel on the right facing the high altar has original Flamboyant vaulting; the centre chapel is known for carved organ consoles (1635). Left, above the sacristy door, is a frieze of Brazilian Indians that recalls the voyages of Dieppe explorers.

Grand-Rue

Many of the houses in white brick date from the reconstruction of Dieppe after the British naval bombardment of 1694. No **21** (now the Globe Café) was once the home of the dreaded pirate Balidar, terror of the English Channel. In the courtyard of no **77**, there is a fountain dating from 1631. At no **186**, an apothecary's old sign on the first floor illustrates three elements of nature: an obelisk (mineral), a palm (vegetable) and a sun (fire).

Place du Puits-Salé

At the junction of six roads, this is the liveliest quarter of Dieppe. The name recalls an old salt-water well (the current well is purely decorative). The large white façade of the early 18C Café des Tribunaux has a clock from 1709.

Rue de la Barre

The pharmacy at no 4 was founded in 1683. Voltaire lodged here when he returned from exile in England, at

Port of Dieppe

© Joséphine Tricard/Iconotec / Photononstop

the home of his friend the apothecary **Jacques Féret**. The houses here are once again early 18C, with period balconies (nos **40**, **42**, **44**). The Protestant church at no **69** was once the chapel of a Carmelite convent (1645).

Château-musée★

From the east end of **boulevard de la Mer**, there is a magnificent **view★** of the city and the beach. Dieppe Castle was built round a massive circular tower which formed part of the earlier, 14C, town fortifications. Note the 17C curtain walls linking the castle to the square St-Rémy Tower. Formerly belonging to the governors of the town, it now houses the Municipal Museum.

Museum★ – *Within château.* ◷*Open Jun–Sept daily 10am–noon, 2–6pm; Oct–May 10am–noon, 2–5pm (Sun 6pm (last entry 30min before closing).* ◷*Closed 1 Jan, 1 May, 25 Dec.* ✆€5.10. ✆02 35 06 61 99. The collections centre on two themes: the navy and ivory. At the entrance is a display of ship models, maps and navigational tools. On the first floor, several rooms are devoted to Dutch painting and furniture – many seascapes and still-life pictures of fish (Pieter Boel, 17C) – as well as to 19C and 20C French and international painting: Isabey, Noël, Boudin, Renoir, Pissarro, Mebourg, Sisley, Jacques-Émile Blanche and Walter Sickert. There is an important collection of Pre-Columbian (Peruvian) pottery. On the first floor is an incomparable collection of **Dieppe ivories★**.

The craftsmanship is meticulous: model ships and navigational instruments, as well as religious items and secular pieces (toilet articles, sewing requisites, fans, snuff boxes, etc.).

A small workshop has been reconstituted to show the tools of local craftsmen who carved ivory imported from Africa and the Orient. In the 17C, there were 350 ivory carvers in the town.

Mémorial du 19 août 1942

A monument in the **square du Canada** recalls the 350 years of history uniting Dieppe and Canada, starting with the 17C colonists who left for Québec and continuing through the raid of 19 August 1942. In the summer, you can enter the château-museum from the square.

Boulevard de Verdun leads to the beach through the monumental gate **Les Tourelles**, the only survivor of five gates (15C) in the old fortifications. Continue along quai du Hâble in the neighbourhood known as **le Bout du Quai**. The little streets off place du Moulin-à-Vent have traditionally been home to local fishermen. The **Maritime Museum** (Estran-Cité de la Mer Museum, see below) is on the north side. Just before the corner of rue de la Rade and quai du Hâble, are the vestiges of a 14C tower (Tour aux Crabes). Follow quai Henri IV along the marina.

Estran-Cité de la Mer★

37 r. de l'Asile-Thomas. &♿🕐*Open daily 9am–noon, 2–6pm.* 🕐*Closed 1 Jan, 25 Dec.* ⊚€6. 📞02 35 06 93 20. http//:.estrancitedelamer.free.fr.

Situated at the heart of an old fishermen's district, this museum is devoted to maritime industry and to the ecosystem of the eastern Channel.

THE PORT, LE POLLET AND THE CLIFF

🚶 *2hr, starting from the tourist office. Go up the cliff from the fishermen's neighbourhood, Le Pollet, for a view.*

Avant-Port

Tall, dark stone buildings surround the basin where the Newhaven–Dieppe ships used to moor.

A yachting marina designed to accommodate up to 400 boats was recently built following the 1994 transfer of the car ferry terminal onto the new outer port. To reach the terminal on foot, cross two bridges, Pont d'Ango and Pont Colbert, built in 1889 from designs by Gustave Eiffel. They lead to the Pollet district. Follow along the base of the cliffs, where you can see *gobes*, former cliff dwellings, now walled up.

▷ *Go back to the Colbert Bridge and take ruelle des Grèves (next to a butcher's shop). From rue Guerrier, take rue du Petit-Fort, which ends in a stairway to the top of the cliffs.*

Le Pollet and Cliff

There is a very old street leading off rue Guerrier, rue Quiquengrogne; the strange name was a rallying cry of pirates on the Channel in the 15C. Next to no 3 rue du Petit-Fort, a tiny fisherman's cottage, its roof caved in, predates the 1694 bombardment of Dieppe by the English. On top of the cliff stands the **Chapelle Notre-Dame de Bon-Secours**, built in 1876. The military light signal is operational 24hr. Step away from the mast for an extensive **view**★ of the city and harbour.

Port de pêche (bassin Duquesne)

Dieppe has a large fishing fleet which goes out to sea on shortish expeditions (one to five days), bringing back fish and seafood for auction. The early-morning fish market is a colourful sight. Dieppe is France's leading source of scallops (*coquilles St-Jacques*), as well as of sole and other fine fish.

Port de commerce (arrière-port)

The fruit trade continues to be very important at this port, with deliveries of Ivory Coast bananas, pineapples and mangoes, and Morocco citrus fruits, potatoes and spring vegetables. Oils, cereals, crabs, and wood also count among the imports here.

You can buy fish and shellfish from the fishermen stalls in front of the tourist office. *Tue–Sat, mornings.*

DRIVING TOUR

Le Long de la Scie

55km/34mi circuit. Allow 3hr.

Leave Dieppe on the D 915, then take the D 927 for St-Aubin-sur-Scie and turn left to Sauqueville to see the **Château de Miromesnil**★ (♿ ⏱ *Open Apr–Oct 2–6pm; visit vegetable garden and park Jul–Aug 10am–1pm;* ⚬ *château by guided tour (1hr) only;* ⚬ *€7.50, €5 garden and park.* ✆ *02 35 85 02 80. www. chateaumiromesnil.com),* where Guy de

Maupassant was born. The château has a monumental Louis XIII façade. The south front is in the Henri IV style, in brick with stone trim. Note the 16C chapel, part of an earlier château. Rich interior decoration from 1780. The flowery gardens and **vegetable plots**★ are surrounded by brick walls supporting espaliered fruit trees. The 16C **chapel**, richly decorated inside, is all that remains of the fortress destroyed in 1589.

Take the D 3 at Sauqueville, then head south to **Auffray** via Longueville-sur-Scie. At Auffay you can see the famous **bell-strikers** in the imposing late 11C collegiate church. Also, enjoy the 120km/74mi of marked footpaths around Auffay. Ask at the tourist office for more details.

Arques-la-Bataille

Arques lies under a massive medieval fortress where the future Henri IV won a celebrated battle. A nearby château, Miromesnil, was the birthplace of writer Guy de Maupassant.

A BIT OF HISTORY

When **Henri IV** (1553–1610) was still a king without a kingdom, he possessed the formidable fortress of Arques, where he dug in, with 7,000 men, to await 30,000 soldiers under the Duke of Mayenne. The battle fell on 21 September 1589. A fog delayed artillery but finally Henri's cannon thundered into the besiegers. Mayenne had to beat a hasty retreat.

SIGHTS

Château

Allow 30min. From place Desceliers, where the town hall (Mairie) is located, take the second road to the right, uphill to the castle entrance, about 45min; the road is very narrow, steep and winding. ⚬ *Closed for safety reasons.* ⚬ *Château grounds, no charge.*
The 12C keep occupies the highest

▶ **Population:** 2,468.
◔ **Michelin Map:** 304: G-2.
◗ **Location:** Arques is 8km/5mi SE of Dieppe, near the confluence of the rivers Varenne and Béthune. The Forest of Arques lies to the NE.
◉ **Don't Miss:**
The medieval fortress offers a magnificent view of the countryside; the gardens of Miromesnil are splendid.
⏱ **Timing:** You can visit only the exterior of the fortress, which takes 30min. Plan at least 1hr30min for the Miromesnil château.
⚬ **Kids:** Cool off the kids at the waterpark.

point, with the earliest part from 1038–1043. In 1053, William the Conqueror attacked and Henri I rebuilt in 1123; the 14C brought two new towers. Vital in the late 16C wars of religion, Protestant forces under the future Henri IV repelled the Catholic League in 1589. On the last of the triple doors to the castle, a carved low relief depicts Henri IV at the Battle of Arques. Follow the old sentry path along the moat to enjoy a view of the Arques Valley.

Église Notre-Dame-de-l'Assomption
Rue des Bourguignons.
Rebuilt around 1515, the church belfry is 17C. The nave with wood cradle vaulting and apse windows are 16C. A chapel right of the chancel has a small bust of Henri IV. 15C *Pietà* in south chapel.

Varenne Plein Air ⛷
Base de Loisir, 76510 St-Aubin-le-Cauf.
🕐*Open 9am–noon, 1.30–5.30pm.*
📞*02 35 85 69 05.*
www.varennepleinair.fr.
On the edge of a lake near Arques, this recreational centre offers facilities for water sports.

🚗 DRIVING TOUR

LA FORET D'ARQUES
30km/18mi circuit. Allow 1hr.

▷ *Leave Arques heading E on the D 56.*

This beech forest tops a spur surrounded by the Eaulne and Béthune, which join at its feet to form the Arques. The D 56 crosses the river of the forest while running along an old Roman way.

Saint-Nicolas-d'Aliermont
Like the other villages stretching along the D 56 on the narrow Aliermont plateau, this town is an example of a "street village", typical of 12C and 13C colonisation developing along travel routes.
Musée de l'Horlogerie★ –
48 r. Édouard-Cannevel. 🕐*Open early Jun–end Sept daily Tue–Sun, 10am–noon, 2–6pm; Oct–Dec and mid Feb–end May Wed–Sun 2.30–6pm.* 🕐*Closed Jan–mid-Feb and hols.* 💰*€3.50 (14–18 years old, €1.50).* 📞 *02 35 04 53 98.*
www.musee-horlogerie-aliermont.fr.
At the heart of the watchmaking and clockmaking industry for close to three centuries, Saint-Nicolas-d'Aliermont reopened its museum in 2007. The col-

lections, presented chronologically, highlight local history and the evolution of techniques. A workshop in the museum lets you watch a watchmaker conducting his precise work.

▷ *On leaving St-Nicolas, turn left onto the D 149.*

Envermeu
The **church** in this village, in the Gothic style with Renaissance motifs, remains unfinished. Note the barley-sugar columns, carved wood pulpit, canopy, majestic **chancel★** and apse.

▷ *From Envermeu, take the D 920, to the west, then the D 54 taking you to Martin-Église.*

The village of **Martin-Église**, at the forest's edge, is known for trout fishing.

▷ *Take the D 1 to Arques.*

Immediately after a beautiful wooden house (hotel) and a bridge over the Eaulne, take a narrow road on the left. 600m/0.5mi further, before a house, turn right into the forest road of **Bivouac**, which remains very close to the forest edge; you will have some beautiful glimpses of the Arques valley.

Monument commémoratif de la bataille d'Arques
🚶*15min return. Leave the car in the curve on the left (grassy lot on the right).* You will see a path to the obelisk, which was raised during the Restoration, commemorating Henri IV's victory here. Arques-la-Bataille and its castle can be seen on the valley's other side. The road then heads deep into the forest.

▷ *After the Henri IV roundabout, after going straight, turn right into the Sully forest road.*

The road crosses another part of the forest. The D 56, right, leads to Arques.

Eu★

Eu is a small town on the River Bresle, set between the sea and the forest from which it takes its name. The town centres around its beautiful 11C collegiate church. It was in Eu that the two Anguier brothers, François (1604–69) and Michel (1612–86), were born: these Baroque sculptors contributed to the building of the Louvre and the Val de Grâce in Paris.

SIGHTS
Collégiale Notre-Dame et St-Laurent★

pl. Guillaume-le-Conquérant. ⊙*Open daily Apr–Oct 9.30am– 12.30pm, 2–6pm; Nov–Mar 9am–noon, 2–5pm .* ⊙*Closed 1 Jan, Sun and hol mornings.* ⊕*No charge.* ✆*02 35 86 19 34.*

The collegiate church was erected in the 12C and 13C in the Gothic style. In the 15C the apse was remodelled and in the 19C Viollet-le-Duc, the architect and restoration specialist, undertook a general restoration of the building. The church is dedicated to the Virgin Mary and St Lawrence O'Toole, Primate of Ireland who died in Eu in 1180.

The **interior** is striking for its size and harmonious proportions. Beneath a Flamboyant canopy in the second ambulatory chapel on the right, the Chapel of the Holy Sepulchre, is a

- ▶ **Population:** 7,571.
- 🚗 **Michelin Map:** 304: i-1.
- ℹ **Info:** Place Guillaume-le-Conquérant. ✆02 35 86 04 68. www.ville-eu.fr.
- ⟩ **Location:** Eu is 4km/2.5mi E of Le Tréport by D 1915 and 34kim/21mi NE of Dieppe by D 925.
- 🅿 **Parking:** There is parking on the square between the château and the church.
- ⊘ **Don't Miss:** The château and its museum; the historic centre of town for its lively pedestrian streets.
- 🕐 **Timing:** Spend the morning seeing the city, then head towards the pretty forest of Eu.
- 👪 **Kids:** Take them to the archaeological site at Bois-Abbé and the Glass-Making Museum.

15C **Entombment**★; opposite is a magnificent head of Christ in Sorrow, also 15C.

Crypt

The crypt, which is beneath the chancel, was restored in 1828 by the Duke of Orléans, who reigned as King Louis-Philippe from 1830 to 1848. The 12–13C recumbent statue of St Lawrence

Château d'Eu

© Alonbou/Fotolia.com

O'Toole is believed to be one of the oldest in France.

Château★

Nothing remains of the original castle where William the Conqueror married Matilda of Flanders in 1050. It was destroyed in 1475 on the orders of Louis XI. The present château, a huge brick and stone building begun by Henri of Guise and Catherine de Clèves in 1578, has been restored several times since. It passed to the Orléans family and became one of the favourite residences of Louis-Philippe, who received Queen Victoria there twice. Viollet-le-Duc was commissioned to redecorate it between 1874 and 1879 for the Count of Paris, grandson of the king. The château, which now belongs to the town of Eu, is occupied by the town hall and the communal archives, and houses the **Louis-Philippe Museum**.

Musée Louis-Philippe

♿ ⊙ *Open mid-Mar–early Nov Wed– Thu and Sat–Mon 10am–noon, 2–6pm, Fri 2–6pm (last entry 1hr before closing).* ☞ *€4.* ☎ *02 35 86 44 00.*

On the ground floor visitors are shown the grand staircase and the Duchesse d'Orléans' suite, redecorated by Viollet-le-Duc in 1875, as well as the two salons and the bedroom where Queen Victoria and Prince Albert slept in 1843 and 1845, embellished with a superb inlaid parquet floor made under Louis-Philippe.

In the restored portico overlooking the garden, note the dazzling **wall of light** conceived by Viollet-le-Duc and master-glazier Oudinot.

On the first floor you can visit the 19C bathroom, the gold bedroom with its pretty green and gilt wainscoting bearing the monogram of the Grande Demoiselle (Princesse Anne Marie Louise d'Orléans, 1627–1693, who once lived here), the Louis-Philippe **dining hall** with its lovely 17C coffered ceiling, the Black Salon, with its strange pink and black colour scheme, and the vast **Galerie des Guise**, currently being renovated to house 145 family paintings

purchased in 2000. The gallery contains 10,000 volumes, including books from Eu's Jesuit College and those belonging to the last Comte d'Eu.

The south wing of the first floor, which once housed the private suites of Louis-Philippe and Marie-Amélie, is being restored to its former glory.

The Park

Most of the trees are beeches, one of which, known as the Guisarda, was planted in 1585.

Chapelle du Collège★

The Jesuit college now bears the name of the 17C Anguier brothers, who studied here. The chapel was commissioned in 1624 by Catherine de Clèves, widow of Henri de Guise, to whom she brought the County of Eu as a dowry in 1570.

The Louis XIII **façade**★ is quite remarkable. The beautifully restored brick and stone masonry lends both warmth and harmony to the whole ensemble.

♟ Musée des Traditions Verrières

r. Semichon, follow the signs from the Salle Audiard. ♿ ⊙ *Open Jul–mid-Sept Tue, Wed, Sat–Sun and public holidays 2.30–6pm; Apr–Jun and mid-Sept–Oct Tue, Sat–Sun and public holidays 2.30– 6pm.* ☞ *€3 (under 12 years free).* ☎ *02 35 86 04 68.*

The former stables of the Bresle cavalry house this museum devoted to glass-making techniques.

The Forêt d'Eu

This beech wood covers three isolated massifs with beautiful beech glades: St Martin's Priory Chapel (pretty doorway); **St Catherine's Viewpoint** (a 45min walk leads up to a view of the Yères Valley); **La Bonne Entente** (an oak and a beech growing intertwined); **St-Martin-le-Gaillard** (13C **church**).

The interior has cornices carved with humorous human figures; 18C Virgin and Child. Note that that Baby Jesus is receiving a fig.

Le Tréport

Set at the mouth of the Bresle near the border with Picardy, Le Tréport is a small fishing port and seaside resort, popular for its close proximity to Paris. During the summer lively crowds throng the harbourside as the town hosts a fair. The long shingle beach, backed by tall cliffs, is packed with visitors on weekends. Mers-les-Bains, on the right bank of the Bresle, is less commercial than Le Tréport and has many devotees, as has Ault, a beach further north.

▶ **Population:** 5,698.

Michelin Map: 304: I-1.

Info: Quai Sadi-Carnot. 02 35 86 05 69. www.ville-le-treport.fr.

Location: Le Tréport is 93km/57.8mi from Rouen and 30km/18.5mi NE of Dieppe by D 925, on the border of Picardy.

Don't Miss: The view from the Calvaire des Terrasses.

Timing: Spend the morning in Le Tréport, then see the pretty resort of Mers-les-Bains.

SIGHTS

Calvaire des Terrasses★

Allow 30min round-trip on foot. Access by car via rue de Paris, rue St-Michel and boulevard du Calvaire.
A flight of stairs *(378 steps)* leads up from the town hall to the Calvary on the clifftop. From the terrace, there is a **view**★ over the town, extending north beyond the Caux cliffs to Hourdel Point, the Somme estuary and inland, along the Lower Bresle Valley to Eu and the lower town's slate roofs, beach and harbour.

Église St-Jacques

The church, which stands halfway up the hill, dates from the latter half of the 16C, but was extensively restored in the 19C. The modern porch shelters a Renaissance doorway. Inside, at the far end of the church, stands a fine statue of the Virgin of Tréport. The chapel of Notre-Dame-de-la-Pitié (Our Lady of Mercy) holds a 16C *Piéta*. A low relief over the altar shows a Virgin surrounded by Biblical emblems.

ADDRESSES

🏠 STAY

LE HAVRE

Hôtel Marly – *121 r. de Paris. 02 35 41 72 48. www.hotellemarly.com. 37 rooms. €12.50.* On the boulevard

leading to the port, this hotel's rooms are rather large and functional. A good address to combine business and tourism.

Hôtel Richelieu – *132 r. de Paris. 02 35 42 38 71.www.hotel-lerichelieu-76.com. 19 rooms. €7.20.* Simple hotel in a busy street, edged with a great many shops. Completely renovated rooms and a variety of furnishings.

Hôtel Terminus – *23 cours de la République. 02 35 25 42 48. www.grand-hotel-terminus.fr. Closed 22 Dec–1 Jan. 42 rooms. €8.50. Restaurant .*
In the centre of Le Havre, across from the train station, this address has up-to-date, functional rooms. The discreet lounge-bar has a billiard table.

Art Hôtel – *147 r. Louis-Brindeau. 02 35 22 69 44. www.art-hotel.fr. Closed 25 Dec–1 Jan. 31 rooms. €13 .* Across from the Oscar-Niemeyer space, this 1950s building (classified façade) gives pride of place to modern architecture and art: luminous rooms with clean lines; exhibitions.

Hôtel Novotel – *20 cours Lafayette. 02 35 19 23 23. www.novotel.com. 134 rooms. €14. Restaurant €23/29 .* Contemporary architecture close to the station, sitting on the banks of the Vauban basin. Comfortable rooms corresponding to the "Novation" concept. Trendy seasonal cuisine served in a dining room with windows opening on for garden. Summer outdoor dining.

ÉTRETAT

Chambre d'hôte M. et Mme Delahais – *54 r. du Prés.-René-Coty, 76790 Le Tilleul, 3km/2mi S of Étretat via D 940. 02 35 27 16 39. 4 rooms.*
Basic comfort, a very considerate reception, quiet ambience and, above all, highly attractive prices for a room just 3min from Étretat by car!

Hôtel La Résidence – *4 bd René-Coty, BP 24. 02 35 27 02 87. 15 rooms.*
This downtown mansion was built in the 14C. Pleasant rooms with amusing, eclectic furniture. Cycle hire.

FECAMP

Chambre d'hôte Mireille Le Thuillier –*37 Le Val de la Mer, 76400 Senneville-sur-Fécamp, 5km/3mi E of Fécamp, dir. Dieppe, then secondary road. 02 35 28 41 93. www.val-de-la-mer.com. Closed 20 Aug–20 Sept. 3 rooms.* This charming Norman house, which has ancient look to it, is named for the little road that runs past it, leading to the sea. Guest rooms are decorated with exquisite taste. The biggest, sun-filled room is on the ground floor.

Hôtel de la Plage – *87 r. de la Plage. 02 35 29 76 51. www.hoteldelaplage-fecamp.com. 22 rooms.* Situated close to the waterfront, this very simple family hotel is a modest stopover. Rooms are spic-and-span and the breakfast room is picturesque with its marine décor and counter shaped like a ship's hull.

PAYS DE CAUX

Chambre d'hôte Le Château de Grosfy – *61 r. du Calvaire, 76570 Hugleville-en-Caux. 02 35 92 63 60. www.chateaudegrosfy.com. 4 rooms.* A lovely alley of lime trees leads to this 18C–19C family home, formerly a hunting lodge. Both rustic and reproduction antique furniture in the large, peaceful guest rooms. Billiards, library, board games and kitchen available. Large park with a little wood.

Chambre d'hôte Château de Mesnil Geoffroy – *76740 Ermenouville, 12 km/7.5mi S of St-Valery-en-Caux via D 20 and D 108. 02 35 57 12 77. www.chateau-mesnil-geoffroy.com. 5 rooms.* A 17C–18C château, ranked as an historic monument, surrounded by a park with a superb rose garden. Guest rooms are refined and furnished with antique family furniture and art objects. Pleasant welcome by true princes, fortunate proprietors of this remarkable site.

Chambre d'hôte Mme Genty – *5 rte de Quiberville, Hameau de Ramouville, 76740 St-Aubin-sur-Mer, 4km/2.5mi N of Bourg-Dun, then dir. Quiberville. 02 35 83 47 05. www.fermettederamouville.com. 5 rooms.* Skilful restoration work has revived the ancient appeal of this typical late 18C farm. Bedrooms are decorated in the country spirit. In the morning, the scent of warm bread will draw you towards the breakfast room.

DIEPPE

Aguado – *3 bd Verdun. 02 35 84 27 00. 56 rooms. €10.* The building is on a street leading to the seafront. The rooms on the promenade side or overlooking the town and harbour have efficient soundproofing.

Chambre d'hôte La Villa Florida – *24 ch. du Golf. 02 35 84 40 37. www.lavillaflorida.com. 4 rooms.* This hotel's rooms are modern and stylish; each with a terrace. Generous breakfasts.

Hôtel au Grand Duquesne – *15 pl. St-Jacques. 02 32 14 61 10. http://augrandduquesne.free.fr. 12 rooms. Restaurant.* While the guest rooms are somewhat spartan, the restaurant is remarkable. Vegetarian menu, along with traditional dishes.

Mercure Dieppe La Présidence – *1 bd de Verdun. 02 35 84 31 31. www.hotel-la-presidence.com. 81 rooms and 4 suites. €14. Restaurant.* This luxury hotel's rooms were entirely renovated in 2008. Ideally located near the beach, breakfast in bed is available from 6.30am–noon. Pleasant bar and lounge area.

Villa des Capucins – *11 r. des Capucins. 02 35 82 16 52. www.villa-des-capucins.fr. 2 rooms and 2 suites.* In the old Pollet quarter, this villa is set in splendid surroundings. Pretty rooms.

Hôtel de l'Europe – *63 bd de Verdun. 02 32 90 19 19. www.hotel dieppe.com. 60 rooms. €9.* A bland façade belies an interior with touch of class. Rooms are tidy and of a good size.

EU

Chambre d'hôte Manoir de Beaumont – *rte de Beaumont, 2km/1mi E via D 49, dir. Forêt d'Eu. 02 35 50 91 91. www.demarquet.com. 4 rooms.* This former hunting lodge of the Château d'Eu overlooks the valley. From your comfortable room, you'll savour the tranquillity of the park, the charm of the house and, above all, the first-class welcome.

⊜⊜ **Hôtel restaurant Maine** – *20 pl. de la Gare.* ℘*02 35 86 16 64. www.hotel-maine. com. 19 rooms.* ⌷. *Restaurant*⊜. Built in 1897, this bourgeois house has an old-fashioned appeal. Rooms generally plainly fitted out, but with small touches from the past. Belle Epoque dining room.

VARENGEVILLE-SUR-MER

⊜⊜ **Chambre d'hôte Les Catamurons** – *Route de l'Église.* ℘ *02 35 85 14 34 or* ℘*06 80 71 51 82. www.catamurons.com. 2 rooms.* ⌷. A pretty brick farmhouse repainted white and covered with climbing plants. The low ceilings give the place a charming air. The lower room gives onto the garden and smells pleasantly of the country. Comes with a kitchenette.

TRÉPORT

⊜⊜ **Golf Hôtel** – *102 rte de Dieppe.* ℘ *02 27 28 01 52. www.treport-hotels.com. Closed 17–26 Dec. Reservations advised wkds. 10 rooms.* ⌷*8.* ⊡ At the entrance to the campsite, turn left. An alley of trees takes you to this beautiful half-timbered 19C house. The rooms, non-smoking, are all different and well-equipped. Pleasant welcome. A small charming hotel at a reasonable price.

⅋ EAT

LE HAVRE

⊜ **Le Bistrot des Halles** – *7 pl. des Halles Centrales.* ℘ *02 35 22 50 52. Closed Sun evening.* Dining room covered with enamel advertising signs and old posters, where stylish waitresses officiate. Generous portions of meat.

⊜⊜ **La Petite Auberge** – *32 r. Ste-Adresse.* ℘ *02 35 46 27 32. Closed Wed noon, Sun evening, Mon.* In this small inn, formerly a way station, tasty country cuisine is to be had at good prices. Cared-for Norman façade.

⊜⊜ **La Taverne Paillette** – *22 r. Georges-Braque.* ℘ *02 35 41 31 50. Non-stop service from noon to midnight.* Authentic brasserie setting for this Le Havre institution; choose between traditional dishes such as sauerkraut or *cassoulet*, seafood platters and fish recipes.

⊜⊜ **Le Wilson** – *98 r. Prés.-Wilson.* ℘ *02 35 41 18 28. Closed Sun evening, Tue evening, Wednesday and 20 Jun–7 Jul.* Warm and simple bistro décor, convivial atmosphere and charming welcome characterise this small restaurant on a little square, in a busy commercial sector. In fine weather, enjoy the outdoor dining and animated surroundings. Traditional cuisine.

ETRETAT

⊜ **Lann Bihoué** – *45 r. Notre-Dame.* ℘ *02 35 27 04 65. www.lannbihoue.com. Closed Dec, Tue except during school holidays and Wed.* To make a change from Norman cuisine, try this crêperie near the town centre. Besides the classic Breton crêpes, there's a speciality with Guémémé sausages and caramelised apples. Friendly service.

⊜⊜ **Le Clos Lupin** – *37 r. Alphonse-Karr.* ℘ *02 35 29 67 53. www.le-clos-lupin.fr. Open Fri noon to Sun noon, and holidays. Reservations required.* Behind the stylish painted façade and lace trimmings, you'll find a long dining room in the heart of town. The menu features classic fare at decidedly reasonable prices.

⊜⊜⊜ **Le Galion** – *bd René-Coty.* ℘ *02 35 29 48 74. Closed 13 Dec–20 Jan, Tue–Wed except school holidays.* Situated in the town centre, this house, built with materials taken from an old Lisieux residence, has a noteworthy 14C ceiling of carved beams. Good cuisine and competitive prices.

FECAMP

⊜⊜ **Chez Nounoute** – *3 pl. Nicholas-Selle.* ℘*02 35 29 38 08. Closed Tue evening, Wed from Sept–Feb. Reservations advised.* Occasionally one likes to find an unusual place, managed by a rather special but friendly owner. Here you find seafood choucroute and fresh fish wonderfully cooked.

⊜⊜ **Le Maritime** – *2 pl. Nicolas-Selle.* ℘*02 35 28 21 71. www.le-maritime.com. Reservations advised.* This restaurant situated in the marina displays navigational instruments and wood panelling for a maritime décor. The menu offers seafood, as well as meat for famished buccaneers.

⊜⊜ **Le Vicomté** – *4 r. du Prés.-René-Coty.* ℘*02 35 28 47 63. Closed 5-11 Apr, 16-31 Aug, 20 Dec–3 Jan, Wed eve, Sun, holidays.* Near the great Benedictine palace, where a celebrated liqueur is produced, this small bistro is decorated with old engravings. The chef uses ingredients sourced from local markets to make delicious dishes.

🍲–🍲🍲 **Auberge de la Rouge** – rte du Havre, St-Léonard. ℘02 35 28 07 59. www.auberge-rouge.com. Closed Sun evening and Mon. ⊆€8. The restaurant in this hotel is just 5min from Fécamp. There is a charming garden and the traditional menu is highly praised.

PAYS DE CAUX

🍲 **La Boussole** –1 r. Max-Lerclec, 76460 St-Valery-en-Caux. ℘02 35 57 16 28. Closed Nov–Feb, Mon–Tue in Jan. Prettily set in a navy blue half-timbered house, this restaurant opposite the port is entirely devoted to seafood. Two cosy rooms with bistro chairs and wooden tables. Shellfish platters in summer and many fish specialities. Piano music in the evening.

🍲🍲 **Le Belvédère** – 76280 St-Jouin-Bruneval, 10km/6mi S of Étretat via D 940 then D 111. ℘02 35 20 13 76. www.restaurant-lebelvedere.com. Closed 10 Jan–9 Feb, Wed eve, Thu. A curious blue building perched upon the cliffs of the Pays de Caux. The comfortable dining room, nicely renovated, offers an exceptional view of the sea. Enjoy fish, mussels and other shellfish while gazing over the deep blue sea.

VARENGEVILLE-SUR-MER

🍲🍲 **La Maison des Jules** – Pl. des Canadiens. ℘02 35 84 28 97. Jul–Sep daily 10am–7pm, closed Tue ; rest of year 10am–7pm, closed Tue-Wed. A former butcher's is converted into a tea room, wine bar and gallery. A warm décor with stove, club chairs and exposed beams. In summer, small terrace set up outdoors. Platters of fresh food, oysters, quiches, pastries, etc.

ⵎ/ EAT

DIEPPE

🍲 **Au Trou Normand** – 76550 Pourville-sur-Mer, km-3mi W of Dieppe via the D 75. ℘02 35 84 59 84. Closed 23 Aug–7 Sept, 23 Dec–15 Jan, Wed and Sun evening. This inn overlooks the beach on which the Canadians disembarked in 1942 as part of the "Jubilee" operation. On the menu: surf and turf.

🍲 **La Marmite dieppoise** – 8 r. St-Jean. ℘02 35 84 24 26. Closed 20 Jun–3 Jul, 21 Nov–4 Dec, 8–16 Feb, Sun evening, Thu evening off-season and Mon. This small restaurant is well-known to the Dieppe regulars. Seafood and Dieppe *marmite*, the house speciality.

🍲 **Le Bistrot de Pollet** – 23 r. Tête-de-Bœuf. ℘02 35 84 68 57. Closed 26 Apr–3 May, 23–31 Aug, 1–11 Jan, Sun and Mon; only by reservation. A nice little ocean bistro with a convivial atmosphere on the Pollet harbour island. The cuisine varies with the market offerings, seasons and local fishing.

🍲 **Le Colombier** – R. Loucheur - 76550 Offranville, 6km/3mi SW of Dieppe. ℘02 35 85 48 50. Closed 21 Feb–11 Mar, 18 Oct–5 Nov, Tue evening off-season, Sun evening and Wed. This venerable Norman house (1509) is the dowager of the town. Yellow walls, restored beams, beautiful early fireplace and old roasting-spit in the dining room. Contemporary cuisine.

🍲 **Le New-Haven** – 53 quai Henri-IV, facing the pleasure port. www.restaurantdieppe.fr - ℘02 35 84 89 72. Closed Tue evening and Wed except Jul–Aug. A nice and simple restaurant: renovated dining room and veranda windows opening on to the pleasure port. The chef carefully selects his ingredients and makes traditional cuisine in generous servings.

🍲 **Le Sully** – 97 quai Henri-IV. ℘02 35 84 23 13. Closed mid-Jan–mid-Feb, Tue evening and Wed. Reservations advised on the wkd. A family restaurant with three different dining rooms: the first in the "retro" style with its port-side veranda; the second contemporary, the last rustic, embellished with stonework and exposed beams and a collection of copper pieces. Seafood has pride of place on the menu.

🍲 **Les Régates** – 30 r. du Casino - 76550 Pourville-sur-Mer, 5 km/3mi W of Dieppe by the D 75. ℘02 35 84 11 33. Don't miss this little place to taste mussels and chips and salads, with a view of the sea. Stop here for a before-dinner drink at sunset, surrounded by the many Dieppe regulars for whom this is a tradition.

🍲 **Les Voiles d'Or** – 2 chemin de la Falaise. ℘02 35 84 16 84. www.lesvoilesdor.fr. Closed 16 Nov–1 Dec, Sun evening, Mon–Tue. Reservations advised. Restaurant offering up-to-date cuisine, perched on a Pollet cliff; near the chapelle Notre-Dame-de-Bon-Secours and the lighthouse. Warm, colourful interior, designer furniture.

Port of Fécamp

© J-C &D. Pratt/Photononstop

TRÉPORT

Le Saint-Louis – *43 quai François-ler.* *02 35 86 20 70. Closed 15 Nov–18 Dec. Weekday menu.* Fish and seafood restaurant offering a view of the fishing port. Brasserie style décor, with moleskin-upholstered benches and cosy booths under a colourful glass roof. Covered veranda out front.

CAFÉS

LE HAVRE

Le Clapoutis – *Sente Alphonse-Karr, 76310 Ste-Adresse . *02 35 49 09 17. 10am–2am.* This establishment overlooks the sea. On the terrace in summer, large glass windows in winter. Seafood and fish on the menu. Café-tea room.

SHOPPING

LE HAVRE

Les Gobelins – *R. du Prés.-Wilson. Mon, Wed and Fri 7.30am–1.30pm.* Modest market right in the centre of town, on a big avenue next to the *mairie*. Numerous sellers of spring vegetables, butchers, specialised pork butchers and fishmongers offering products of excellent quality.

Les Halles Centrales – *Close Sun and holidays.* Stalls well-maintained, often by the best sellers in town. About 30 food stands.

LEISURE

ETRETAT

Étretat Tourist Train – Vélorail. At the train station. *6km/3.7mi east of Étretat via D 940, 76790 Les Loges. *02 35 29 49 61. www.lafrancevuedurail.fr/ttepac. Apr–Oct wkd, departure from Les Loges 10.30am–6.55pm and from Étretat from 11.15am–7.30pm (about 6 departures daily,

schedule varies by month). RT €4.50, 4–14 years old:RT €2.25. Closed Nov–Mar.* Across the green countryside between Étretat and Les Loges. You can also pedal the *vélorail* (a sort of bicycle on train tracks) from Loges.

FECAMP

Tourisme et loisirs maritimes – *15 r. Vicomte. *02 35 28 99 53 or t06 16 80 24 10. tlm76@wanadoo.fr. Aug excursions Fécamp–Etretat; Sept–Jul: tour of Le Havre port – sea excursion and port tour: €13.50 (children €9.50).* A variety of excursions on boats along the Norman coast are proposed, including fishing expeditions, both from Fécamp and from Le Havre.

The tourist office has suggestions for bicycle excursions and hikes in the area.

PAYS DE CAUX

Parc de Loisirs - lac de Caniel – *R. du Dessous-des-Bois between St-Valery-en-Caux and Fécamp, 6450 Vittefleur. *02 35 97 40 55. www.lacdecaniel.com. Closed 29 Sept–21 Mar.* A great many water sports: water skiing, boating, canoeing, kayaking, summer sledding, pedal boats, boats with lifeguards (Jul–Aug). Playing field, bowling, mini golf, billiards and restaurant area.

EU

Cycles Joostens – *1 r. Charles Morin. *02 35 86 22 24. Closed 2 weeks in Feb and Aug. Bike rentals.* Tourist offices has maps for some marked trails. If you dislike dirt paths, head for the Bois de Cise (before Ault and N of Mers), where the trails are paved and lead you to a little-frequented beach. The Hyères valley circuit (50km/31mi), starting from the beach at Mesnil-Val, passes through lovely countryside but you need to be in shape. There's an alternative, more relaxed circuit of only 25km/15.5mi.

The Vexin Normand has a rich history closely tied with that of Normandy itself. Richard the Lion Heart and Philippe Auguste shaped history here as they fought to possess these lands between the Duchy of Normandie (the Vexin Normand) and the Kingdom of France (the Vexin Français). The Pays de Bray is a place of beautiful, greatly varied landscapes, the irregularity of clay-rich soil and erosion explain this diversity which even created the remarkable geological event known as the "buttonhole". It is therefore not surprising to find here a long tradition of pottery, ceramics and brick and tile craftsmanship.

Highlights

1 William II's 11C château fort at **Gisors** (p160)

2 A drive through the **Vexin Normand** (p163)

3 Monet's atmospheric gardens at **Giverny** (p164)

4 Richard the Lionheart's stronghold, **Château Gaillard** (p165)

5 A visit to **Eawy Forest** (p177)

The Vexin Normand

This is the countryside that inspired painters Poussin, Pissarro, Monet, and Picasso, and writers Michelet and Flaubert, an artistic heritage continuing today with everything from mosaic to glass being worked here.

Yet the Vexin Normand remains rural, with majestic fortresses, châteaux and abbeys rising alongside charming little villages and country churches. The history of the region, however, can be understood at sites such as Les Andelys and especially the Château Gaillard, which today is a silent witness to the struggle between Richard the Lion Heart and Philippe Auguste to control the Seine and the route to Rouen.

But for nature lovers today the Vexin Normand, surrounded by the Lyons Forest, the Seine, the Andelle and the Epte, is a real haven of peace for exploration by foot, bicycle or on horseback – or to enjoy with a fishing rod in hand.

The Pays de Bray

To the east of the Seine-Maritime region, the Pays de Bray consists of green meadows and hedged farm land. Above all a region for lovers of the great outdoors, it is here that lies the magnificent Eawy Forest, which together with Lyons is the most beautiful beech forest in Normandy.

Forêt d'Eawy near St-Saëns

© Christian Heeb/hemis.fr

VEXIN NORMAND AND THE PAYS DE BRAY

ABBEVILLE

8 km
4 miles

N

SOMME

AMIENS

Foucarmont

D 77
Bures-en-Bray
Mesnières-en-Bray
Les V1 du Val-Ygot
Forêt d'Eawy
Ventes-St-Rémy
Neufchâtel-en-Bray
Aumale

Musée de la Pomme
Jardin de Bellevue
Le clos du Coudray
St-Saëns
Jardin Agapanthe
Jardin du Mesnil
La Ferme de Bray
Forges-les-Eaux

OISE

SEINE-MARITIME

Buchy
Bosc-Bordel
Bosc-Roger-sur-Buchy
La Ferté-St-Samson
Yville
Héronchelles
Bois-Guilbert
Sigy-en-Bray
Beauvoir-en-Lyons
Beuvreuil
Blainville-Crevon
Le Héron
Brémontier-Merval
Gournay-en-Bray
Martainville-Epreville
Ry
D 13
La Feuillie
Hêtre de la Bunodière

ROUEN

CÔTE STE-CATHERINE
Bonsecours
Vascœuil
Forêt de Lyons
N.-D.-de-la-Paix
Lyons-la-Forêt
Fleury-la-Forêt
St-Jean
Beauficel-en-Lyons
Rosay-s-Lieure
Bordins
Ménesqueville
Source de Ste-Catherine de Lisors
Abbe de Fontaine-Guérard
Lisors
Abbe de Mortemer
Saint-Denis-le-Ferment

CAEN, LE HAVRE

La côte des Deux-Amants
Écluses d'Amfreville
Écouis
EURE
Neaufles-St-Martin
Gisors

Louviers
Les Andelys
Château-Gaillard
Dangu
Boury-en-Vexin

Gaillon
Château-sur-Epte
Baudemont

VAL D'OISE

Bizy
Vernon
Giverny
Fourges

★★ Recommended
★ Interesting
Ry Worth a visit

Driving tour with departure point

N.-D.-de-la-Mer
Signal des Coutumes

YVELINES

PARIS

LE HAVRE

BEAUVAIS

PONTOISE

159

Gisors★

Gisors is the capital of the Norman Vexin: it was once a frontier town belonging to the dukes of Normandy. The town owes its origins to the castle, which formed part of a line of defence running from Forges-les-Eaux to Vernon and included the castles of Neaufles-St-Martin and Château-sur-Epte.

▸ **Population:** 11,809.
⊙ **Michelin Map:** 304: K-6.
▯ **Info:** 4 rue du Général de Gaulle. ℘02 32 27 60 63. www.tourisme-gisors.fr.
▶ **Location:** Gisors is 76km/ 47mi NW of Paris and 64km/40mi NE of Rouen.
⊛ **Don't Miss:** The château and the Tree of Jesse in St-Gervais-et-St-Protais.
◷ **Timing:** See Gisors in the morning, then tour the Epte Valley.

VISIT
Château Fort★★

Pl. Blanmont. The park is ◷*open daily Apr–Sept 8am–7.30pm; Oct–Mar 8am–5pm. The fortress is open Apr–Sept Wed–Mon 10am, 11am, 2pm, 3.30pm and 5pm; Oct–Nov and Feb–Mar wkds 10.30am, 2.30pm and 4pm.* ◷*Closed Dec–Jan and 1 May.* ⬢€5 (-18 years €3). ℘02 32 27 60 63 or 02 32 55 59 36.

The castle was built as early as 1097 by William II of England, son of the Conqueror. In 1193 it was taken by Philippe Auguste of France. During the Hundred Years' War the castle changed hands several times before returning to the French crown in 1449.

The 11C **keep**, on its 20m/65.6ft artificial mound in the centre of the fortified perimeter and surrounded now by a public garden, is flanked by a watchtower. A staircase leads to the top

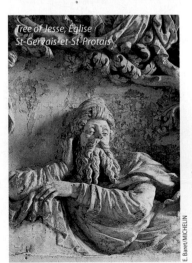

Tree of Jesse, Église St-Gervais-et-St-Protais

E. Baret/MICHELIN

from where there is a fine **view** over the surrounding woodland.

Église St-Gervais-et-St-Protais★

r. de Vienne.

The oldest parts of the church date back to the 12C, but construction continued to the end of the 16C, as is evident both outside and inside. The Gothic chancel was completed in 1249; the side chapels adjoining the ambulatory were added in 1498 and 1507. The transept doors are 16C and Gothic, as is the very tall nave. The monumental west front is Renaissance: the doorway is flanked by two towers, that on the north being built in 1536, that on the south left unfinished in 1591.

In spite of the mixture of architectural styles the church as a whole appears perfectly harmonious.

The large monochrome window in the chapel on the right of the choir dates from the 16C. The chapel below the South Tower contains a charming spiral staircase by Jean Grappin and a huge late 16C Tree of Jesse.

ADDITIONAL SIGHT
Saint-Denis-le-Ferment

7km-4mi NE. Leave Gisors by the D 915, then turn left on the D 16.

The mill of Saint-Paër and its fish farm mark the entrance to this quiet town crossed by the Levrière. In its centre, the church, château and manor are all charmingly authentic. A path (9km/5mi, 3hr), the GR 125, runs along the left bank of the Lévrière, taking you to Hébécourt. It then links, running through woods and fields, the **Château de La Rapée**, **Saint-Paër**, **Bézu-St-Éloi** and then **St-Denis-le-Ferment**. Queen Blanche d'Evreux (also known as Blanche de Navarre), Princess of Navarre, withdrew in 1364 to the Château de Neaufles-Saint-Martin after the death of her husband Philippe VI of Valois; she especially enjoyed this intinerary.

🚗 DRIVING TOUR

Epte Valley
41km/25.5mi. Allow 2hrs.

The road from Gisors to Vernon follows the shady west bank of the Epte, which contrast with the bare slopes hewn out of the chalk bed of the Vexin plateaux.

▷ *From Gisors take D 10 W.*

Neaufles-St-Martin
The village is dominated by a keep standing upon a perfectly preserved artificial mound.

▷ *At the junction turn left onto D 181.*

Dangu
Church. ⏱Can be visited on request at the town hall. ✆02 32 55 22 15.
The main features of the Gothic **church** are the 18C woodwork and painted

pa[...]
Mont[...]
window a[...]
St Lawrence a[...]
fifth son of Anne[...]

▷ *Take the D 146 south [...]*

Château-sur-Epte
Standing on an artificial mound s[...] rounded by a moat are the remains of a massive keep built by William Rufus, King of England from 1087 to 1100, to protect the Norman frontier.

▷ *Return on the D 146. At Bray-et-Lu, turn right.*

Château de Beaudmont
From the ruins of the 11C fortress, standing on its artificial mound, there is a pretty **view** of the valley.

▷ *Continue on the D 5.*

Moulin de Fourges
Built on the banks of the Epte in 1750, the mill has an imposing wheel, which still functions today, turned by the force of the river's waters.

▷ *Continue to Giverny on the D 5.*

Giverny★★
🚶*See Giverny.*

▷ *Drive on to Vernon, by taking the D 313; come back to Gisors on the D 181.*

The History of the Dukedom of Normandy

It was at St-Clair-sur-Epte in 911 that Charles the Simple – a nickname meaning honest and straightforward – met with Rollo, the ruler of the Vikings. Dudon de St-Quentin, Normandy's first historian, recounts that, to ratify the agreement creating the Dukedom of Normandy, the Viking placed his hands between those of the French king. This informal deal, concluded in the manner of tradesmen, carried the same legal weight as a formal exchange of seals and signatures, for a written treaty was never signed. The dukedom is bordered by the River Epte north of the River Seine and by the River Avre to the south. Normandy's boundaries were often fought over throughout history by the kings of France and the dukes of Normandy, who became the kings of England in the late 11C.

...nelling in the chancel, the 16C ...morency Chapel in which a grisaille ...above the altar shows St Denis, ...and, on his knees, William, ...of Montmorency.

...into the valley.

ulation: 622.
chelin Map: 304: I-7.
fo: 36 rue Sadi-Carnot.
℘02 32 51 39 60.
ww.cape-tourisme.fr.
Location: Vernon is 65km/
40.4mi SE of Rouen on A 13.
Parking: Two car parks
are located at each end of
the Clemenceau bridge.
Don't Miss: The Église
Notre-Dame and the park
of the Château of Bizy.
Timing: Guided tours
of the Château de Bizy
take 45min. The park
can be seen in 30min.

Bridge Viewp...

From the bridge there is a ...
Vernon, the wooded islands in the Seine
and the ruined piles on which the 12C
bridge stood. On the right bank are the
towers of Tourelles Castle, which formed
part of the defences of the old bridge.

▷ *Turn left and walk along the Seine.*

The walk takes you by the 18C Bourbon-
Penthièvre house, named for the last
Duke of Vernon. The street of the
same name leads into the **old town**.
Notre-Dame Church stands at the end
of the pretty street with some half-
timbered houses. Note the 16C façade
embellished with Gothic sculptures
at no 15.

Musée A.-G.-Poulain

12 r. du Pont. ♿ *Open Apr–Oct Tue–
Fri 10.30am–6pm; Sept–Mar 2–5.30pm,*
wkd and holidays 2.30–5.30pm
*Closed 1 Jan, 1 May, 14 Jul, 15 Aug, 1
and 11 Nov, 25 Dec. €3.50. €8.50 ticket
combines with Giverny Impressionism
museum. ℘02 32 21 28 09.
www.vernon27.fr/musee.*

A wrought-iron gate that comes from
the castle of Bizy leads you into the
museum's courtyard, housed in restored
buildings from a variety of different eras
(15–18C).

The collections focus on painting,
drawing and sculpture. The collection
includes works by Monet, Rosa Bonheur,
Maurice Denis, Pierre Bonnard, Vuillard
and Steinlen (1859–1923). Do not miss
two works by Claude Monet: Water

Old bridge over the Seine at Vernon

G.Targat/MICHELIN

Château de Bizy

© Mel Longhurst/age fotostock

Lilies and Cliffs at Pourville. The cartoons humorising French society also deserve a look.

Église Notre-Dame★
1 r. du Chapitre.
This 12C collegiate church was remodelled several times before the Renaissance. The 15C west front has a beautiful rose window flanked by galleries. The choir triforium and the clerestory windows combine beautifully. The organ loft and beautiful stained glass windows of the second chapel on the right aisle also date from the 16th century. The organ is 17C.
In rue du Chapitre, on the right side of the church, is a 17C house (nos 3-5). It is one of the oldest houses in Vernon and also serves as the tourist office. There are other interesting old houses in rue Carnot and rue Potard, in particular.

Côte St-Michel★
⊳ *From Vernonnet (north); rue J.-Soret to the church, turn right; follow signs.*
Allow 1hr round-trip on foot.
From the top of the hill there is a good view of Vernon and the Seine Valley.

EXCURSIONS
Château de Bizy★
⊳*2km/1mi W of Vernon by D 181.*
Avenue des Capucins. ⚗ ⸭⸺*Guided tours of the interior (45min) Apr–Oct*

daily except Mon 10am–noon, 2–6pm. ≈€7.80. ℘02 32 51 00 82.
Begun in 1740 by Coutant d'Ivry for the Duke of Belle-Isle, Marshal of France, the château was remodelled several times by successive owners. These included the Duke of Penthièvre, General Le Suire, King Louis-Philippe and Baron Schickler. It is now owned by the family of Albufera.
A Classical colonnaded façade faces the park. Inside, the rooms are accented with beautiful Regency woodwork, 18C Gobelins tapestries woven for Louis XIV, and Empire furniture. The 18C **park** was redesigned in the English style by King Louis-Philippe. Renovation work has restored the splendid *chemin d'eau* (waterway).

Signal des Coutumes
⊳ *8km/5mi from Vernon. Take N 15 out of town and after 5km/3mi, just before Port-Villez, turn right on D 89.*
Notre-Dame-de-la-Mer – From the **look-out point**★ there is a view of the river between Bonnières and Villez.
Carry on along D 89; left at the mairie of Jeufosse and leave the paved road on the right. Outside the hamlet of Les Coutumes, take a paved road to the right, which leads to the edge of the woods.
Signal des Coutumes – There is a lovely, broad **view**★ over the Bonnières meander.

Giverny★★

Claude Monet lived in this village from 1883 until his death in 1926, and attracted many other artists to the area. It was here that he painted the huge canvases of water lilies that can be seen in Paris at the Orangerie Museum and the Marmottan Museum.

VISIT
Maison de Claude Monet★

84, r. Claude-Monet ○ Open 1 Apr– 1 Nov daily 9.30am–6pm. ◎ €6 (owing to the many groups and large crowds, the best time to visit is from end Apr to early Jun, especially late afternoon or lunchtime. ℘02 32 51 28 21. www.fondation-monet.com.

Claude Monet's **garden** (♿*only partially accessible*) slopes gently to the banks of the River Epte. The house displays reproductions of his greatest paintings; the originals hang in musems in Paris and around the world. The tour includes the blue salon, the bedroom with the roll-top desk, the old studio, the yellow dining room with its painted wooden furniture and the tiled kitchen.

The walled garden *(clos normand)*, is planted according to Monet's own design, and *(via a tunnel to the other side of the road)* the Japanese-inspired water garden is fed by the River Epte.

Claude Monet's garden

© Anyka/iStockphoto.com

▶ **Population:** 530.

⚙ **Michelin Map:** 304: J-7 – 2km/1mi SE of Vernon.

ℹ **Info:** An information point is open Apr–Oct daily 10am–7pm, in the car park opposite the Musée des Impressionismes. www.giverny-village.fr. ℘02 32 51 39 60.

◐ **Location:** Giverny is 2km/1mi SW of Vernon, which is (69km/43mi) from Rouen via D 313/D 5.

🅿 **Parking:** Car parks (free) are found on both sides of D 5.

◉ **Don't Miss:** The home of Claude Monet and the Impressionist Museum.

🕐 **Timing:** Give yourself 2hr for each of the museums.

Despite Monet's love for the village, Giverny's inhabitants did not always make work easy for Monet; they required hefty fees before permitting him to paint their haystacks.

Musée des Impressionismes Giverny★

90 r. Claude-Monet. ♿○Open Apr–Oct 10am–6pm (last admission 5.30pm), 1st Sat Jun–Sept till 10pm. ◎€6.50 (7–12 years €3; 13–18 €4.50); no charge 1st Sun of month). ℘02 32 51 94 65. www. mdig.fr. Pass €12 (inc Maison de Claude Monet or Musée de Vernon, 7–12 years €6; €13-18 €8.50 – guided tour once monthly by reservation. Restaurant, tea room, shop and auditorium.

This museum, opened in May 2009 in the former premises of the Musée d'Art Américain *(www.maag.org)*, holds temporary exhibits on the subject of Impressionist art. The museum gardens, composed of sections separated by hedges, burst with bright colour. Designed as a cultural centre, in addition to the collections there are also three galleries and a large auditorium.

Les Andelys★★

Les Andelys, dominated by the impressive ruins of Château-Gaillard, lies in a lovely setting along the Seine. It once consisted of two distinct areas, Le Petit Andely to the west and Le Grand Andely to the east. The latter was the site of a 6C monastery founded by Clotilde, who converted her husband, King Clovis, to Christianity. At a fountain at 29 rue Ste-Clotilde, she is said to have turned water into wine for workmen building the monastery chapel.

▶ **Population:** 9,047.

Michelin Map: 304: I-6

Info: rue Philippe-Auguste. ℰ02 32 54 41 93. http://office-tourisme. ville-andelys.fr.

Location: The two Andelys are linked by avenue de la République and rue du Maréchal-Leclerc. Paris is 100km/62mi away, and Rouen 40km/25mi.

Don't Miss: The view of the Seine Valley from the heights of the château.

Timing: Visit the château in the morning, then enjoy Les Andelys and its surroundings.

Kids: Children will be thrilled by the massive fortress.

A BIT OF HISTORY

In 1196, **Richard the Lionheart**, King of England and Duke of Normandy, decided to bar the King of France's way to Rouen along the Seine Valley by building a massive fortress on the cliff commanding the river at Andely. Within the year Château-Gaillard was erected and Richard cried "See my fine yearling!" **Philippe Auguste**, King of France, did not at first dare attack so formidable a redoubt. But when the vacillating King John succeeded Richard in 1199, the French beseiged the castle, filled in the moat, mined the walls and took the castle by storm on 6 March 1203.

Château-Gaillard★★

Allow 1hr. To reach the château by car: from Grand Andely, follow the signs from rue Louis-Pasteur. On foot (allow 30min ascent): from Petit Andely, follow rue Richard-Cœur-de-Lion, near the tourist office. ⏱Open mid-Mar–mid-Nov Wed–Mon 10am–1pm, 2–6pm (last entry 1hr before closing). ⏱Closed 1 May. ☞€3.15. ℰ02 32 54 41 93 . http://office-tourisme.ville-andelys.fr. From the car park there is a **view**★★ of the castle, the Seine and Les Andelys.

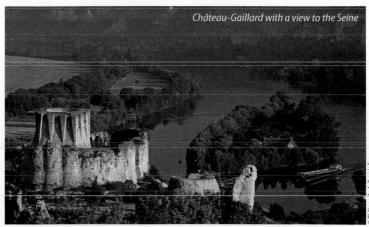
Château-Gaillard with a view to the Seine

© Philippe Body/hemis.fr

CHÂTEAU-GAILLARD

Curtain walls
Curtain walls (no longer standing)

Moat
Outer curtain walls
Officers' residence
Donjon
Governor's residence
MAIN STRONGHOLD
BARBICAN
Moat
Outer bailey
Inner Casemates
Well
Moat
Footbridge
Moat
N

Barbican

The redoubt, separated from the main castle by a deep moat, possessed five towers of which only one, the barbican, remains, encircled by a narrow path.

Castle

The outer ward, the esplanade, is situated between the redoubt and the castle. Around the wall to the left are the foundations of the keep, which rises from the natural rock. At the far end of the wall there is a fine **viewpoint**.

Returning along the bottom of the moat, you pass the casemates (*right*) hollowed out of the rock to store the garrison's food. The keep is round (8m/26ft in internal diameter) with thick walls (5m/16.4ft). Adjoining *(right)* are the ruins of the Governor's residence.

Outside the perimeter wall, a path leads to the edge of the rocky escarpment, which provides an extended view of the Seine Valley.

▶ *Take the one-way descent to rue Richard-Cœur-de-Lion to return to the town.*

ADDITIONAL SIGHTS
Collégiale Notre-Dame★

Grand Andely. ⏱*Open daily Jun–Sept 9am–noon, 2–6pm; Oct–May 9am–noon, 2–5pm.* ☎*02 32 54 41 93.*

A well-balanced façade of twin towers flanked by a square staircase tower fronts the church. The 16C south side is in the Flamboyant style and the 16C and 17C north side is Renaissance in style with round arches, Ionic pilasters,

Collégiale Notre-Dame

© José Antonio Moreno/age fotostock

Village of Gaillon with the turrets of the castle

© JONATHAN/Fotolia.com

balustraded roofs, caryatids and antique-style statues.

Inside, the nave is 13C; the delicately ornamented triforium was remodelled in the 16C and the windows enlarged; the **organ and loft**★ are Renaissance. In the north transept and a nearby chapel are two lovely paintings by Quentin Varin, teacher of Les Andelys native Nicholas Poussin (1594–1665). The Entombment in the south aisle beneath the tower is 16C, the Christ in the Tomb is 14C.

Musée Nicolas-Poussin

R. Ste-Clotilde. Close to the Fontaine Ste-Clotilde, in a street of the same name. ◔*Open 9 Jul–24 Aug Wed–Sun 2–6pm; rest of year Wed–Mon 2–6pm.* ☛*Guided tours available.* ◔*Closed mid Dec–early Jan, 2nd wkd Sept, 1 Jan, 1 May, 25 Dec.* ◉*€2.60 (-10 years, €1.30).* ℘*02 32 54 31 78.*

The famous Classical painter Poussin (1594–1665) was born in Villers, not far from Andelys. This museum devoted to Poussin is in an 18C residence, where copies and a painting by the master, *Coriolanus supplicated by his Mother*, may be found. There is also a 3C mosaic, a few art objects including a beautiful Virgin with Child in painted stone (14C) and a few traditional 17C and 18C pieces of furniture.

Église St-Sauveur

pl. St-Sauveur, Petit Andely. ◔*Open daily 9am–6pm.* ℘*02 32 54 41 93.*

St Saviour's floorplan is a Greek cross and Gothic in style; the chancel is late-12C, the nave early 13C. The wooden porch stands on an early 15C stone foundation. Inside there is an organ dating from 1674.

Musée Normandie-Niémen

r. Raymond-Phelip. ◔*Open Jun–mid-Sept Wed–Mon 10am–noon, 2–6pm; rest of the year Wed–Mon 2–6pm.* ◔*Closed 1 Jan, 1 May, 24, 25, 31 Dec.* ◉*€3.50.* ℘*02 32 54 49 76.*

The Normandie-Niémen squadron of the Free French Air Force fought with the Soviet Union on the Eastern Front from 1943–45.

EXCURSION
Gaillon

▷ *12km/9mi S by the D 316.*

Château - *Restoration, closed to public.* Property of Rouen's archbishops since St Louis, Gaillon was remodelled by Georges d'Amboise, the first great cardinal-minister, in the new Italian style (1497–1510). The structure was the avant-garde monument of its time, bringing the Renaissance to Normandy. The access ramp is to the right, at the top of the D 6015's rise to Rouen. Still under restoration, the entrance pavilion with its towers has Renaissance décor.

Lyons-la-Forêt★

The half-timbered houses, old brick buildings and woodland setting in the heart of the Forêt de Lyons create a picture-book vision of Normandy. Unusually in the French language, the final "s" of Lyons is pronounced, indicating the town's Scandinavian origins.

THE VILLAGE
Halles
pl. Benserade.
The old covered market in the centre of place Benserade was used for scenes in Jean Renoir's film *Madame Bovary*. The fountain appeared in Claude Chabrol's 1990 version of the same novel.
Pretty half-timbered houses surround the square. In the steep street west of the square, **Maurice Ravel** composed *Le Tombeau de Couperin* and completed the orchestration for Moussorgsky's *Pictures at an Exhibition*.

Église St-Denis
r. Bout-de-Bas leads to St-Denis Church, at the edge of the village, on the riverside. ◷*Open only to groups.*
The 12C church was completely renovated in the 15C. The stonework and the timber belfry are admirable, and in the chancel the statue of St Christopher carrying the infant Jesus dates from the 16C.

▶ **Population:** 774.
⚙ **Michelin Map:** 304: I-5.
▤ **Info:** 20 rue de l'Hôtel de Ville. ℘02 32 49 31 65. http://paysdelyons.com.
◗ **Location:** Lyons-la-Forêt is 43km/27mi E of Rouen and 20km/12.5mi N of Andelys.
◉ **Don't Miss:** The château of Vascœuil and the beautiful Forêt de Lyons.

🚗 DRIVING TOUR

FORÊT DE LYONS★★
70km/43.5mi. Allow one day.

The forest covers 10,700ha/26,440 acres and is known for its glorious beech trees. You can also admire an old abbey and two interesting châteaux.

① LYONS TO LES BORDINS

◗ *Leave Lyons to the W via D 6.*

Notre-Dame-de-la-Paix
From this statue there is a fine view of the town of Lyons.

◗ *Take D 169 left.*

Half-timbered houses of Lyons-la-Forêt

© David Tomlinson/Photononstop

Chapelle St-Jean

Behind the 17C chapel a path leads to the Chêne St-Jean (St John's Oak) which has a circumference of 5m/16ft at a height of 1.30m/4ft from the ground.

▷ *Take the second road on the left (D 11) towards Rosay.*

Rosay-sur-Lieure

The **church** and churchyard are in a pleasant setting.

▷ *D 11 goes on to Ménesqueville.*

Ménesqueville

The small 12C country **church,** skilfully restored, contains some very old statues. The stained-glass windows by contemporary artist F E Décorchemont portray the Song of Songs.

▷ *From here, D 12 goes along the pretty Fouillebroc Valley as far as Lisors.*

Lisors

The church contains a 14C crowned Virgin which was found buried in 1936.

▷ *Take D 175; on the right, you will see the ruins of the abbey.*

Abbaye de Mortemer

🚶*Guided tours (45min) available. Unaccompanied access to park year-round 1.30–6pm.* 🅿️*Park and museum €8. Park alone €6.* ✆ *02 32 49 54 34. www.mortemer.fr.*

In the forest stand the ruins of the 12C–13C Cistercian abbey. A **museum** below the conventual building, reconstructed in the 17C, explains monastic life and evokes legends connected with the abbey.

▷ *Across from the abbey, on the left-hand side of D 175, a short path leads to the Croix-Vaubois crossroads.*

Carrefour de la Croix-Vaubois
The monument erected here recalls the foresters who died in the Resistance.

▷ *As you continue along D 175, look for two springs (sources) off to the left.*

Source de Ste-Catherine-de-Lisors
A footbridge spanning the Fouillebroc leads to an oratory, traditionally visited by young girls in search of a husband.

Source du Fouillebroc
This spring is set in pleasant forest surroundings.

Les Bordins Arboretum
Free to visit year round; ⚫guided tours by request. ℰ02 32 49 04 09.
Opened in 1994, this 4,451.5ha/11,000-acre area abounds with trees from across the world, grouped by continent.

② NORTH OF THE FOREST
60km/37mi. Allow about 2hr30min.

▷ *Leave Lyons to the E via D 14.*

Beauficel-en-Lyons
Church. ⊙Guided tours by appointment with Mme Dufour, 1 rte de Fleury, 27480 Beauficel-en-Lyons. ℰ02 32 49 62 51.
The **church** is preceded by a 17C porch and contains beautiful statues, including a 14C virgin in polychrome stone.

▷ *D 14 runs alongside Fleury-la-Forêt Castle (to the right).*

Château de Fleury-la-Forêt
⊙Open Jul–Aug 2–6pm, mid-Mar–end Jun and Sept–mid-Oct wkds and holidays 2–6pm. ⚫Guided tours available. ⚫€7. ℰ02 32 49 63 91. www.chateau-fleury-la-foret.com.
Beyond a wrought-iron gate, an avenue of lime trees leads to the 17C château built of red brick, flint and sandstone. The interior contains interesting displays of dolls, toys and furniture. There is also a huge, richly decorated kitchen.

▷ *Turn left after Bosquentin and follow D 241.*

Hêtre de la Bunodière★
Indicated by a signpost on the right as you leave N 31 to enter the forest, this magnificent beech, at 40m/131ft tall, stands near the Câtelier Reserve. Its circumference measures 3.3m/11ft.

▷ *N 31-E 46 leads back to La Feuillie.*

La Feuillie
At 54m/177ft, the slender church **spire**★ is a bold piece of carpentry.

Le Héron
This pleasant tree-shaded area was designed by La Nôtre.

▷ *Rejoin the D 46 to Vascœuil.*

Château de Vascœuil – Centre d'Art et d'histoire★
⊙Open Jul–Aug 10.30am–12.30pm, 2.30–6.30pm; Apr–Jun and early Sept–early Nov Wed–Sun and holidays 2.30–6pm. ⊙Closed 5 days end Jun–early Jul. ⚫€8 (-18 years €5.50). ℰ02 35 23 62 35. www.chateauvascoeuil.com.
The château is a known cultural centre associated with the memory of Jules Michelet. The **Michelet museum** presents portraits, posters and writings related to the historian and his family, as well as his re-created study. Jules Michelet (1798–1874) wrote a part of his famous *Histoire de France* at Vascœuil. A fierce defender of democracy, he also wrote l'*Histoire de la Révolution*.
Visitors also come especially to Vascœuil for its famous contemporary art exhibitions and collections.
The Crevon waters the gardens, now a **sculpture park**: Volti's well-endowed women, Pompon's pigeon, Dali's *Freedom's Victory*, the exuberant *Ludivine* by Coville, ceramics and mosaics by Léger or Vasarely. Contemporary art exhibitions are held in the 14C–16C **château** and superb 17C **dovecote**. There is a shop and tea room as well.
Église St-Martial – *ℰ02 35 02 11 69. ⚫Guided tour on request, contact Jean-Joseph Le Brozec, r. des Canadiens, weekdays, some Sun.* Here lies the 12C tomb of Hugues de Saint-Jovinien, a holy man.

Écouis★

The village of Écouis centres on the twin towers of its old collegiate church, built between 1310 and 1313 by Enguerrand de Marigny, Superintendent of Finances to Philip the Fair. Opponents accused him of sorcery, and he died on the gibbet in 1315. His artistic patronage may be seen from the remarkable works of art in the church.

COLLÉGIALE NOTRE-DAME★

Open daily 7am–7pm. For a guided tour, make an appointment at the presbytery. ℘02 32 69 43 08.

The brick and stone vaulting replaced roof timbers in the late 18C. The immense choir has beautiful furnishings and remarkable **statues**★ (14C–17C); it terminates in a three-sided apse.

1) Chapel of the Immaculate Conception (16C).
2) Christ on the Cross (13C).
3) St Nicaise.
4) St Ann and the Virgin (14C).
5) Our Lady of Écouis (14C).
6) Statue of St Margaret (14C).
7) Statue of Jean de Marigny, brother of Enguerrand, who was Archbishop of Rouen when he died in 1351.
8) St John Chapel – The wooden vault is a trace of the nave's former vault. Statue of Alips de Mons, wife of Enguerrand de Marigny. Stained glass (14C) of Crucifixion with St John and Mary at the Cross.
9) 14C choir stalls; 16C doors and woodwork.
10) Door of former rood screen.
11) Christ and his Shroud (16C).
12) North side chapel: St Martin, St Francis, St Laurent (14C), St Cecilia.
13) Madonna of the King (14C).
14) St Agnes (14C).
15) St Veronica (14C).
16) Ecce Homo in wood (15C).
17) Annunciation (15C) – The statue of the Virgin is supported by a charming group of small angels reading prophecies relating to the mystery of the Incarnation. The hands and

▶ **Population:** 745.
& **Michelin Map:** 304: I-6.
▪ **Info:** 6 place du Cloître. ℘02 32 69 43 08. www. collegiale-ecouis.asso.fr.
◗ **Location:** Écouis is 12km/ 7.4mi S of Lyons-la-Forêt via D 2.

face of the Virgin, together with the face of Archangel Gabriel, are in marble set into the stone.
18) St John the Baptist (14C).
19) Organ case (17C).

In a **room** on the first floor beautiful works of art are displayed including a cope chest and the chalice of Jean de Marigny (14C).

EXCURSION

Abbaye de Fontaine-Guérard★

◗ *12km/7.4mi NW via N14. Just before Fleury-sur-Andelle, take D 321 left, then the second road on the right. Allow 30min to visit.*

The ruins of the 12C abbey, on the north bank of the Andelle, are both evocative and moving, owing to their isolation and the threat of flooding. Beside the path stands the 15C St Michael's Chapel (left). The abbey church dates from 1218; the square chevet and some apsidal vaulting have survived. The **chapterhouse** (right) is a fine example of early 13C Norman architecture.

Château de Martainville★

This magnificent First Renaissance château is home to a remarkable ethnological musuem devoted to Norman arts and traditions. It offers a complete look at how regional furniture developed from the late MIddle Ages to the Second Empire. The visit is even more fascinating in that the presentation includes all aspects of Normandy's rich culture.

- **Michelin Map:** 304: H-4.
- **Location:** Blainville-Crevon is 20km/12.4mi NE of Rouen via N 31, then D 7.
- **Don't Miss:** The church; the "Emma Bovary" tour. Map in area tourist offices.
- **Timing:** Allow 1hr; marked tour of village (60km/ 37.2mi itinerary). around Ry lets you pass time with Emma Bovary.

VISIT

Open Apr–Sept 10am–12.30pm, 2–6pm, holidays 2–6.30pm; rest of year 10am–12.30pm, 2–5pm, Sun 2–5.30pm, Closed Tue, 1 Jan, 1 May, 1 and 11 Nov and 25 Dec. €3. 02 35 23 44 70. www.musees-haute-normandie.fr.

The elegant brick and stone château, little changed since its construction in 1485–1510, has a massive dovecote (16C) and a half-timbered cart shed (18C).

The château houses the **Musée Départemental des Traditions et Arts Normands** ★, with displays of furniture from Rouen and the Pays de Caux, chests, 17C buffets, 18C cupboards, earthenware and pottery, glass, pewter and copper, regional ceramics and costumes.

🚗 DRIVING TOUR

From Héronchelles to Crevon
Tour of 50km/31mi, about 1hr30min.

> *Leave Martainville E along the D 13.*

Ry is a village of half-timbered and brick houses thought to be Yonville-l'Abbaye, where **Gustave Flaubert** (1821–80) set *Madame Bovary* (1857). Take the kids to the **Galerie Bovary - Musée d'automates** (*Jul–Aug, Tue–Sun 2.30–6pm; May–Jun and Sept–Oct wkds and holidays 2.30–6pm; €5; 02 35 23 61 44*) with 300 automatons playing scenes from *Madame Bovary*. Look also at the 12C **church** with its Renaissance oak **porch** ★ before driving towards Elbeuf-sur-Andelle; you'll turn left on the D 46. This takes you to **Le Héron** with its château and Le Nôtre park; Flaubert is said to have discovered sophisticated society here.

Head north on the D 46, to come to **Héronchelles**, a pretty village with a 16C riverside manor. Continuing on the D 46 to **Yville**; you will admire the beautiful oversized thatched roofs here. Drive even further on the D 46, and take the next right to **Bois-Guilbert**. Right after you enter the village, you will see a grand estate on the left, Bois-Guilbert; it has 7ha/17acres of park, the **jardins de Bois-Guilbert** (*May–Oct, wkds and holidays 3–6pm; by appt; €5, child €3; 02 35 34 86 56).* The 17–18C setting inspired sculptor and landscaper Jean-Marc de Pas to blend unspoiled nature and landscaping to create the Cosmos garden, the Four Elements garden, the Sun garden and the Four Seasons garden. Over 60 sculptures, most in bronze (*Four Seasons, Abbé Pierre, African Woman,* etc.) decorate the park's various green spaces.

Back in your car, you now take the D 38, which you follow by turning left after Bois-Guilbert to head north. At **Bosc-Bordel** there is a nice little 13C church with a 16C wood porch.

Now drive on the D 919 heading for Buchy; taking the D 96 on the left. At **Bosc-Roger-sur-Buchy**, there is a pretty English-style garden,the jardin de Valérianes (*May-Sept, Wed–Sun and holidays 1––6.30pm; €5 (-12 years €2; 02 35 90 64 07),* with 4ha/9a planted

Château de Martainville

G. Targat/MICHELIN

with over 1,000 botanical varieties. Continue on the D 919 to stop off in **Buchy** to visit **Notre-Dame church** with its Renaissance stained glass. Leave Buchy by the D 7. At the intersection take the D 90 for St-Germain-des-Essort, which you cross for a pleasant drive along the Crevon river to Blainville.

The small village of **Blainville-Creon**, in the river valley, is also the birthplace of artist **Marcel Duchamp** (1887–1968). Many artists from the School of Rouen stayed in this town, including Gustave Flaubert (1821–80). Today Blainville-Crevon hosts the annual Archéo-Jazz Festival with dance, cinema, theatre and music.

You won't want to miss the **collegiate church of St. Michael** (*guided tours Jun–Sept Sat–Sun 2–6.30pm; Oct–May,* contact the mairie at *02 35 34 01 60*). Founded in 1488, it has chequered sandstone and silex facing; the interior is Flamboyant. Have a look at the left transept at the monumental late 15C painted wood statue of **St Michael slaying the dragon**.

While you are here you should also visit the **castle** (*wkd 2–6pm; guided tour possible (45min), by appt, reserve three days prior; no charge; 02 35 34 24 82*). The remodelling work going on since 1968 on the medieval castle ruins has unearthed a staircase buried in an artificial mound dating from the 11C, along with about 100m/109yd of curtain wall 5–8m/16–26ft high, dry moats and two towers with well-preserved lower floors belonging to 14C and 15C constructions.

Forges-les-Eaux

In the green heart of the Pays de Bray, Forges-les-Eaux is a spa resort with iron-rich waters reputed to be both refreshing and stimulating.

SIGHTS
Collection Faïence de Forges
In the tourist office. Open Tue–Sun and holidays 10am–noon, 2–5pm. guided tour possible (45min, by appt). €2.50. 02 35 90 52 10. A hundred or so examples of Forges faïence, manufactured until the 19C, are displayed at the town hall.

▶ **Population:** 3,542.

Michelin Map: 304: J-4.

Info: Rue Albert-Bochet. *02 35 90 52 10.* www. forgesleseaux-tourisme.fr.

Location: Forges-les-Eaux is 60km/37mi NE of Rouen.

Don't Miss: Excursions into the Pays de Bray to see the pretty villages.

Timing: After a morning in town, see the Paysde Bray.

Musée de la Résistance et de la Déportation

r. du Marechal-Leclerc. ◷*Open daily 2–6pm.* 💬*possibility of guided tour (1hr30min).* 🎫*€5.* ✆*02 35 90 64 07*
Insignia, arms and uniforms as well as documents recount the dark days of the Occupation in Haute Normandie.

The Spa

Rue de la République boasts some half-timbered façades (17C–18C), and leads onto avenue des Sources, where it passes under the old railway line (now a footpath).
The resort grounds and casino are to the left, just after the bridge. The **park** and spa are managed by the Club Méditerranée in an elegant setting.

Parc Montalent and Épinay Forest

On the other side of avenue des Sources, four pleasant and well-marked **nature trails** wind among the ponds and into the woods.

EXCURSION
La Ferme de Bray

❯ *Leave Forges via D 915 NW; after 8km/5mi, turn left before Sommery and follow the signs. 281 Chemin de Bray.*
♿◷*Open 2–6pm; Easter to All Saints' wkd and holidays and daily Jul–Aug.* 🎫*€6.* ✆*02 35 90 57 27.*
http://ferme.de.bray.free.fr.
On the banks of the Sorson, this restored site shows what a prosperous 17C–18C farm was like. The bread oven, the cider press and the mill are in use. There are regular exhibits in the main house, a spacious 16C building whose façade was redone in the 17C.

🚗 DRIVING TOURS

Le Pays de Bray
60km/37mi. Allow 2hrs.

The Pays de Bray is a lush strip at the centre of the vast bare stretches of the **Caux plateau**. It owes its chief characteristic, known as the Bray "Buttonhole",

to a geological accident, which created a hollow in the surrounding chalk. Running parallel to the valley of the River Seine, the region is a sparsely inhabited patchwork of vales, limestone bluffs, hills, meadows and forests.
Leave Forges-les-Eaux south on the D 921 to come to **La Ferté-St-Samson**. This village is perched just before the main edge of the Bray Buttonhole and from the approach to the church there is an extended view of the depression with its clearly defined rim. In the main square is the 16C house of Henri IV.
From La Ferté take the D9 south. **Sigy-en-Bray** has an abbey church is all that remains of Sigy Abbey, founded in the 11C by Hugh I. It has kept its 12C chancel and seven-sided apse, a 13C portal and the nave vaulting, restored in the 18C. The 15C belltower overlooks a cemetery with a late 15C sandstone calvary.
Take the D 41 east to Argueil, the D 921 south to Fry, then turn left onto the D 1 before the church. The road runs along the southwest Bray escarpment of massive bare mounds crowned with beech trees, called Mont Robert. From the east end of **Beauvoir-en-Lyons**★ (🅿*park beyond the mairie; walk up the street on the left to the church)* there is a **view**★ of the green Bray Valley cutting away in a straight line southeast. In clear weather Beauvais Cathedral is visible.
Return to your car and continue on the D 1; at a crossroads, turn left downhill onto the D 57 for open views of Bray. Pass Elbeouf-en-Bray and then head left for **Brémontier-Merval**. The beautiful 17C Château de Brémontier-Merval is home to an agricultural school; its 100ha/247acre grounds are open to all. Over 500 varieties of apples are grown here.
Return to Elbeuf-en-Bray and take the D 21 for **Gournay-en-Bray** *and* **Ferrières**, the busiest towns in the Pays de Bray. The local dairy industry supplies most of the fresh cheese consumed in France. Collégiale St-Hildevert, a collegiate church, is largely 12C; it has withstood several wars but the late 12C doors have suffered from excessive restoration. Inside, the massive columns are sur-

mounted by carved capitals. The oldest and most worn, at the end of the south aisle, are among the earliest examples of attempts at human portrayal during the Romanesque period.

Take the D 916 north and continue straight on the D8; at St-Etienne, turn left onto the D 84 for **Beuvreuil**, which has a small 11C country **church** (⚏ clo-

sed for repairs) with a wooden porch. The building is decorated with enamelled bricks. Inside are an 11C font stoup, a 15C holy-water stoup, Gothic statues, a 15C altarpiece and a 16C lectern.

▷ *Return to Forges by the D 84 and D 915.*

Neufchâtel-en-Bray

The former capital of the Pays de Bray is today the capital of "bondon", a cylinder-shaped cheese. The other local stars are the "petit-suisse", invented near Gournay-en-Bray, and the *fromage de Neufchâtel*, a farm cheese produced in several shapes.

VISIT
Église Notre-Dame
pl. Notre-Dame.
The doorway dates from the end of the 15C; the early 16C nave contains Renaissance capitals.

The eight windows in the aisles depict local saints: St Radegonde, St Vincent, St Anthony. In the 13C chancel round columns support the pointed vaulting; against a pillar is a gilt wood Virgin crowned.

Fromage de Neufchâtel

G. Targat/ MICHELIN

▶ **Population:** 4,946.
Ⓒ **Michelin Map:** 304: I-3.
🄸 **Info:** 6 place Notre-Dame. ✆02 35 93 22 96. www.neufchatel-en-bray.com.
▷ **Location:** This village is 45km/28mi SW of Dieppe, 50km/31mi NE of Rouen.
Ⓒ **Don't Miss:** Église St-Pierre -et-St-Paul (in Aumale).
Ⓒ **Timing:** Count on a good half-day to see Neufchâtel and its pretty countryside.

Musée J-B-Mathon-A-Durand
Ⓒ*Open mid-Jun–mid Sept Tue–Sun 3–6pm; from early Apr–mid-Jun and mid-Sept–end Oct Sun and holidays 3–6pm.* ⤿ *Guided tour (1hr30min).* Ⓒ*Closed 1 May.* ⬚*€3, no charge Normandy Day or Nuit des musées. (€1.34 + €0.34 /min).* ✆*0899 651 377.*
This museum is set in a half-timbered house built after the destruction of 1940. Its collections are devoted to the Pays de Bray folk art and traditions, smithing and ironwork. An apple mill (1746) is in the garden, along with a press (1837), typical of the region.

🚗 DRIVING TOUR

Northern Pays de Bray
46km/28mi. About 1hr30min.

▷ *Leave Neufchâtel on D1314 to the north.*

The Bray Buttonhole

The movement of the earth's crust during the Tertiary era (64–1.8 million years ago), which brought about the raising of the Alps some 12 million years ago had repercussions as far as the Paris basin. The shocks formed wide, deep undulations in a southeast/northwest direction and subsequently, in the area we call Bray, one of these swelled into a large dome with a steep northeast face.

Erosion relentlessly ate into the limestone surface of the dome, exposing clay laid down in the upper Jurassic Period some 160 million years ago. This elliptical cut, with its clearly defined rim, is known to geologists as a buttonhole, hence the term Bray Buttonhole (*see Forges-les-Eaux*). Continued erosion has given the area irregular, varied landscapes of marshes, *bocage* country, cultivated fields, orchards and great forests.

From the road, which runs north through the so-called Bray Buttonhole formation, there are extensive views of the Béthune Valley *(left)* and Hellet Forest *(north)*.

▷ *Turn left on D 56.*

The road crosses Hellet Forest. From Croixdalle, D 77 *(left)* down the Béthune Valley to Osmoy-St-Valery; it climbs southwest and passes through a gap. The view is of Nappes Forest. On leaving the Mesnil-Follemprise Valley, Bures-en-Bray's belltower appears with Hellet Forest and the Château of Mesnières.

Château de Mesnières

Institution Saint Joseph, 76270 Mesnières-en-Bray. The château is occupied by a private agricultural school. ⏲Open Easter to All Saints' wkd and holidays 2.30–6.30pm; Jul–Aug daily 2.30–6.30pm. ⏲Free access to exterior, guided tour possible. ⏲Closed 11 Nov. ⏲€4 (-12 years free).
This majestic Renaissance château, begun in the late 15C on the site of a medieval castle, lies at a strategic crossing of two royal roads, Paris–Dieppe and Abbeville–Rouen. The beautiful park was designed by Le Nôtre.

Bures-en-Bray

Church. ⏲Guided tours on request from M. Daniel Longin. ✆02 35 93 09 48.
The **church**, partly 12C, has a modern brick façade with porch and a bold twisted wooden spire. In the north transept are an Entombment, a 16C stone altarpiece and a 14C Virgin and Child.

▷ *Uphill after the church take the first road, D 114, left near the café-tobacconist.*

The road follows a terrace at the foot of the southwest face on which the villages have been built.

▷ *At Fresle turn left onto D 97.*

Aumale

The **Église de St-Pierre-et-St-Paul** is both Flamboyant and Renaissance.. The south portal *(damaged)*, is attributed to Jean Goujon (1510–66).

▷ *Take N 29 towards Neufchâtel, turn immediately right onto D 920.*

Foucarmont

The squat concrete **church** (rebuilt 1959–64) yet has wonderful irregular stained-glass windows, with precious stones inlaid in the walls.

▷ *N 28 leads back to Neufchâtel.*

Forêt d'Eawy★★

The Eawy forest (6600ha/16 308acres), together with the Lyons Forest, is the most beautiful beech forest to be found in Normandy.

DRIVING TOUR

Eawy Forest
35km/21mi from St-Saëns. About 4hr30min.

St-Saëns
This small forest town lies next to the Varenne. The church is 19C.

▶ *Take the D 12 for Pommeréval.*

🚹 Ventes-St-Rémy
A signposted path teaches visitors about the forest's trees. There are three itineraries (*tourist office brochure*): local species; forest management and swamps; and conifers and "carcahoux".

▶ *Continue on the D 12, turn left on the D 97, then right on D 48 to Val-Ygot.*

Les V1 du Val-Ygot
Panels explain the 13 concrete buildings, re-created V-1 launchpad (the V-1 flying bomb was the world's first guided missile) and monument to victims of Hitler's secret weapons. There were 117 V-1 sites in Seine-Maritime.

▶ *Take D 99 to Bellencombre. At the town entrance, left and head for Rosay.*

Musée de la Pomme, du Cidre et des Métiers traditionnels
Rosay, ◐*Easter to All Saints' Tue–Fri 2–6pm, Sat 10am–noon, 2–6pm, Sun 3–6pm.* ✆*02 35 94 31 66.*
An eco-museum on traditional professions, and the production of cider.

▶ *From Rosay, take the D 97 to Beaumont-le-Hareng*

Jardins de Bellevue★
Cross Beaumont-le-Hareng; left at bend at church. ⚑◐*10am–6pm.* ●–*Guided*

🚶 **Michelin Map:** 304 H3
📋 **Info:** ✆02 35 34 57 75. www.saintsaens-porte debray-tourisme.com.
📍 **Location:** About 12km/7mi W of Neufchâtel-en-Bray
👁 **Don't Miss:** The Christmas rose collection at the Bellevue gardens.
🚹 **Kids:** Ventes-St-Rémy

tour possible (2hr, by reservation 1 day prior). ●€8. ✆*02 35 33 31 37.*
A 6ha/14acre array of flowers, especially Christmas roses. Superb view at end.

▶ *D 97; at Beauzeville-la-Giffarde, takes the D 225 to Grigneuseville.*

Jardins Agapanthe★
76850 Grigneuseville – access and car park at church. ◐*May–Sept Thu–Tue 2–7pm; Apr–Oct wkd and holidays 2–6pm.* ●–*1hr guided tour.* ◐*Closed 1 Jan, 11 Nov and 25 Dec.* ●€10 (-15 years €5). ✆*02 35 33 32 05.*
A delightful garden of varied intimate spaces; pools, gazebo, tables, seats.

▶ *Continue on D 225 to Biennais, then right for Etaimpuis*

Le Clos du Coudray
Etaimpuis. ⚑◐*Apr–Oct 10am–7pm.* ◐*Closed Nov–Mar.* ●€7.50, price may change. ✆*02 35 34 96 85.*
8000 varieties of plants from abroad.

▶ *Leave Etaimpuis by D 225 to Beuzeville-la-Giffarde, then N 29 to St-Martin- Osmonville, then D 38 to Montérolier.*

Jardin du Mesnil
Montérolier. ◐*May–Oct 2–6pm, Sun except Jun–Sep.* ●–*Guided tour on request.* ●€6. ✆*02 35 34 48 45.*
Flowers, rare bushes, maples, hydrangeas.

▶ *Head back to St-Martin-Osmonville and return N to St-Saëns by the D 38.*

ADDRESSES

🛏 STAY

GISORS

🛏 **Hôtel Moderne** – *1 pl. de la Gare.* 📞*02 32 55 23 51.* 🅿 *- 31 rooms.2 suites* 🚇*€7 .* Family hotel at train station, good for a brief stay.

🛏🍽💰 **Chambre d'hôte Le Four à Pain** – *8 r. des Gruchets, 27140 St-Denis-le-Ferment, 7km/4.3mi NW.* 📞*02 32 55 14 45. 2 rooms.* 🛏. One room is built in an old bread oven in a charming garden; another, bigger room is found in the tastefully renovated farm.

VERNON

🛏🍽 **Hôtel d'Évreux** – *11 pl. d'Évreux.* 📞*02 32 21 16 12. 12 rooms.* 🅿 🚇*€7. Restaurant* 🛏🍽. The Count of Évreux lived in this 17C residence. Chic and elegant.

🛏🍽💰 **Hôtel Normandy** – *1 av. P.-Mendès-France.* 📞 *02 32 51 97 97.* 🅿 *50 rooms.-* 🚇*€10. Restaurant* 🛏🍽*. Closed Sat noon, Mon noon and Sun.* Central; good rooms, functional furniture, cosy lounge and bar. Traditional pubby dining.

GIVERNY

🛏🍽 **Chambre d'hôte Au Bon Maréchal** – *1 r. du Colombier.* 📞*02 32 51 39 70. 3 rooms.* 🛏. A former venue for meetings between Monet and his artist friends. Cosy, comfortable rooms.

🛏🍽 **La Musardière** – *132 r. Cl.-Monet.* 📞*02 32 21 03 18.* 🛏 *10 rooms. €81/136.* 🚇 *€ 9.50. Restaurant* 🛏🍽💰. An old, rustic house (1880s), park. Warm welcome.

LES ANDELYS

🛏🍽 **Chambre d'hôte La Haye Gaillard** – *Côte de Cléry, 27700 Les Andelys.* 📞*02 32 51 66 23. www.lahayegaillard.com.* 🛏 *2 rooms.* 🛏. Farm with comfortable rooms, one in a cleverly-restored dovecot.

🛏 **Chambre d'hôte Mme Vard** – *29 r. de l'Huis, village of Surcy, 27510 Mézières-en-Vexin, 13km/8mi SE of Les Andelys via D 1.* 📞*02 32 52 30 04. Closed Nov–Mar. 4 rooms.* Fresh air and peace; authentic charm of a bustling farm.

LYONS-LA-FORÊT

🛏🍽 **Hôtel Les Lions de Beauclerc**– *7 r. de l'Hôtel-de-Ville.* 📞 *02 32 49 18 90. 6 rooms. €69/97.* 🚇*€9. Restaurant* 🛏🍽. Close to the market; modern comfort and old antiques (adjoining shop). Restaurant and tea room.

🍽 EAT

GISORS

🛏🍽💰 **Le Cappeville** – *17 r. Cappeville.* 📞 *02 32 55 11 08. Closed 12–29 Aug, Wed and Thu.* Dining room in bright lively colours; still has its beams and fireplace. Up-to-date cuisine with authentic accents.

VERNON

🛏🍽 **Le Bistro** – *73 r. Carnot.* 📞*02 32 21 29 19. Closed 1–8 Mar, 21 Jul–15 Aug, Sun and Mon.* This old bar has daily specials of traditional dishes and wine by the glass.

🛏🍽💰 **Les Fleurs** – *71 r. Carnot.* 📞*02 32 51 16 80. Closed 4–13 Mar, 1–27 Aug, Sun eve, Mon. Reservations required.* 15C house, central, with Louis XV furniture. Known for fine food; 2 guest rooms.

GIVERNY

🛏🍽 **Le Moulin de Fourges**– *38 r. du Moulin, 27630 Fourges, 11km/7mi NE.* 📞*02 32 52 12 12. www.moulindefourges.com. Closed Nov–Mar, Sun eve, Mon except Jul–Aug.* A former watermill on the Epte, a place Monet would have loved.

🛏🍽 **Restaurant-Musée Baudy** – *81 r. Claude-Monet.* 📞*02 32 21 10 03. www.giverny.fr. Closed Nov–Mar, Sun eve, Mon except public holidays.* The former hotel residence of Impressionist painters. Specials and salads. Old rose garden.

LES ANDELYS

🛏🍽 **De Paris** – *10 av. de la République.* 📞*02 32 54 00 33.* Attractive early 20C restaurant. Simple rooms are available.

🛏🍽💰 **La Chaîne d'Or** – *27 r. Grande.* 📞*02 32 54 00 31. Closed 1 Jan–4 Feb, Sun eve, Tue lunch, Mon–Tue in Nov–Mar.* Lovely views of Seine. Renowned cuisine. Rooms available.

LYONS-LA-FORÊT

🛏 **Café du Commerce** – *19 pl. Benserade.* 📞 *02 32 49 49 92. Closed Jan and Mon .* Overlooks the 200-year-old market; café-restaurant with outdoor tables.

The Côte Fleurie or "flowering coast" runs from the Pays d'Auge to the east of Calvados, the name evoking Belle Epoque Parisians "summering" at Honfleur or Deauville. Today the vast beaches of fine sand still delight holiday-makers and movie stars alike; the Pays d'Auge itself, straddling Calvados and Orne, produces wonderful dairy products. Camembert is made here, but also Livarot and Pont l'Évèque – fine cheeses, but also the names of the villages making them. Producing apples as well, the Pays d'Auge achieved Appellation d'Origine Contrôlée status for its Calvados in 1942, and for its cider, in 1996.

Côte Fleurie: Subdued chic

The Deauville American Film Festival, considered here to be second only to Cannes, creates a certain image of movie stars and paparazzi. While it is true that there are all-night casinos, elegant seafood restaurants, celebrity homes and artistic history, the Côte Fleurie is only two hours from the French capital, and is also simply a summer home to many Parisians, who come to appreciate its golden sands and local cuisine. Glamour is here, but it is kept discreet; local obsessions do include horses and yachts, but Calvados is drunk more than champagne, and while art galleries abound, there are just as many Sunday painters. The beautiful people – and holiday-makers – are here to relax and rejuvenate, not to be seen.

Pays d'Auge: Authenticity

The Pays d'Auge has long cultivated its verdant countryside to produce Calvados and pommeau from apples, while cider has been the drink of the people since the Middle Ages, although Louis XVI sang its praises. Dairy farming is important here too, close to 50 per cent of the milk production making celebrated Auge cheeses: Camembert, Pont l'Évèque and Livarot, formerly called "the worker's meat". Yet the Pays d'Auge is more than taste treats: preserved villages with half-timbered old quarters, châteaux, Belle Epoque residences, beautiful parks and gardens and places of pilgrimage, all await the visitor.

Highlights

1 A platter heaped with seafood in **Honfleur** (p182)
2 A drive along the south bank of the **Seine** (p187)
3 Exploring contemporary art in a **Trouville** art gallery (p190)
4 Strolling on the Planches in **Deauville**, with sunglasses (p191)
5 Treasure hunting with the kids at **Château de Crèvecoeur** (p203)

Apple orchard near Lisieux, Pays d'Auge

© Francis Cormon/hemis.fr

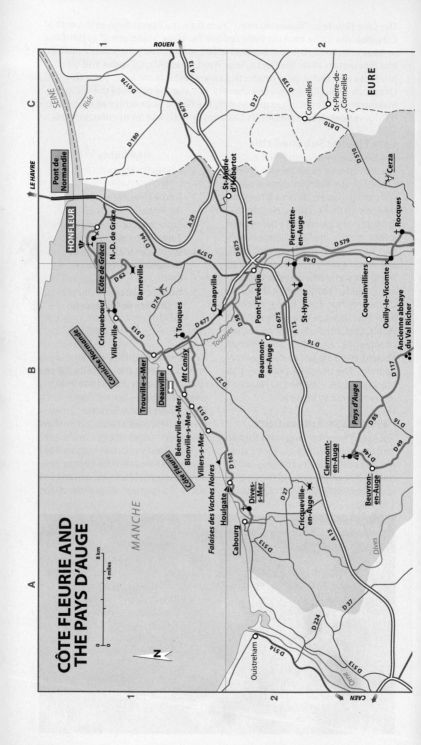

CÔTE FLEURIE AND THE PAYS D'AUGE

MANCHE

LE HAVRE

SEINE

Risle

ROUEN

Pont de Normandie

HONFLEUR

Côte de Grâce

N.-D. de Grâce

Corniche Normande

Cricquebœuf

Villerville

Trouville-s-Mer

Deauville

Mt Canisy

Bénerville-s-Mer

Blonville-s-Mer

Villers-s-Mer

Côte Fleurie

Houlgate

Falaises des Vaches Noires

Cabourg

Dives-s-Mer

Cricqueville-en-Auge

Barneville

Touques

Canapville

Pont-l'Évêque

Touques

St-André-d'Hébertot

Pierrefitte-en-Auge

St-Hymer

Beaumont-en-Auge

Clermont-en-Auge

Beuvron-en-Auge

Cormeilles

St-Pierre-de-Cormeilles

EURE

Cerza

Rocques

Coquainvilliers

Ouilly-le-Vicomte

Ancienne abbaye du Val Richer

Pays d'Auge

Dives

CAEN

Ouistreham

Orne

Pont de Normandie

A 13

D 678

D 180

D 675

D 27

D 139

D 810

D 510

D 144

A 29

D 62

D 74

D 579

A 13

D 675

D 48

D 579

D 513

D 677

D 58

D 675

A 13

D 16

D 27

D 513

D 163

D 117

D 85

D 16

D 146

D 49

A 13

D 513

D 224

D 514

D 513

D 37

N

0   4 miles
0   8 km

EVREUX 3
ROUEN 4

Orbec
Vallée de l'Orbiquet
A 28
ALENÇON
Orbiquet
D 519
D 613
D 4
ORNE
Fervaques
D 64
C
Touques
Lisieux
Domaine de Saint-Hippolyte
St-Germain-de-Livet
D 64
Bellou
D 268
Vimoutiers
D 979
Camembert
Coupesarte
D 579
Livarot
D 579
D 704
D 47
D 511
D 59
D 50
D 613
CALVADOS
D 4
Prieuré St-Michel-de-Crouttes
D 916
Jardins du pays d'Auge
D 101
Crèvecœur-en-Auge
St-Pierre-s-Dives
D 90
D 63
D 613
D 47
D 37
D 613
N 158
D 511
CAEN 3
4
A

HONFLEUR
Deauville
Lisieux
Livarot

★★★ Highly recommended
★★   Recommended
★   Interesting
        Worth a visit
        Driving tour with departure point

Honfleur★★

The lovely town of Honfleur is located on the Seine estuary. The impressive Pont de Normandie has made it easier to get to and from the town, and to visit the Pays d'Auge and the Côte de Grâce. You can spend hours wandering around the old dock (Vieux Bassin), Ste-Catherine Church, the narrow winding streets and port where the fishing fleet unloads fresh fish and shellfish every day. Today, Honfleur can rightly claim to be both a river port and a seaport, as evidenced by the many large liners that choose the welcoming city as a stopover: 220m/722ft-long ships, able to accommodate up to 1 200 passengers in optimal conditions, glide along the quays, where the waters are 7.5–9.5m/24.6–31ft deep.

A BIT OF HISTORY

Canada, a Norman Colony – Ever since the early 16C, navigators had been anchoring briefly along the coast of a land named Gallia Nova by Verrazano, the discoverer of the site of New York. In 1534, **Jacques Cartier** stepped ashore and claimed the territory for France, naming it Canada. François I was less than impressed with the explorer on his return as he brought back no spices, gold or diamonds. Canada was thus left unexplored until the 17C when the experienced navigator **Samuel de Champlain** received orders to colonise this vast territory. He set sail from Honfleur, and in 1608 founded Quebec. On Colbert's advice Louis XIV took an interest in Canada and the country rapidly became a Norman and Percheron colony settled by over 4,000 peasants who made their living by agriculture, fishing, hunting and fur trading.

The Iroquois Indians bitterly opposed the French colonists, who by 1665 had to appeal to France for aid against mounting attacks. A thousand soldiers arrived; simultaneously a decree was issued compelling each man to marry, within a fortnight upon her arrival, one

- ▶ **Population:** 8,163.
- **Michelin Map:** 303: N-3.
- **Info:** Quai Lepaulmier. ✆02 31 89 23 30. www.ot-honfleur.fr.
- **Location:** The city, 25km/15.5mi from Le Havre and 91km/56.5mi from Rouen, lies on the left bank of the Seine, 3km/2mi from the Pont de Normandie.
- **P Parking:** Park on quai de la Tour in the old city.
- **Don't Miss:** Old Honfleur and the wooden Ste-Catherine Church, built by shipwrights.
- **Timing:** Visit Ste-Catherine Quay early in the morning to capture the elongated reflections of the old houses in the still water. In the evening, sunset lights up the *greniers à sel* just opposite.
- **Kids:** The Naturospace offers hundreds of butterflies in an immense greenhouse.

of the women, known as the king's daughters (*filles du roy*), who were sent out from France to help increase the sparse population. The queen took an interest in the selection of the young women, who were to be "not ugly... not repulsive... healthy and strong enough for working on the land".

From Canada, **Cavalier de La Salle** journeyed south to explore and colonise Louisiana in 1682. He established the communication route along the Ohio Valley which was to lead to war with the British and finally the loss by the French of Canada in 1760.

Honfleur, an Artist's Paradise – The character and atmosphere of Honfleur has inspired painters, writers and musicians.

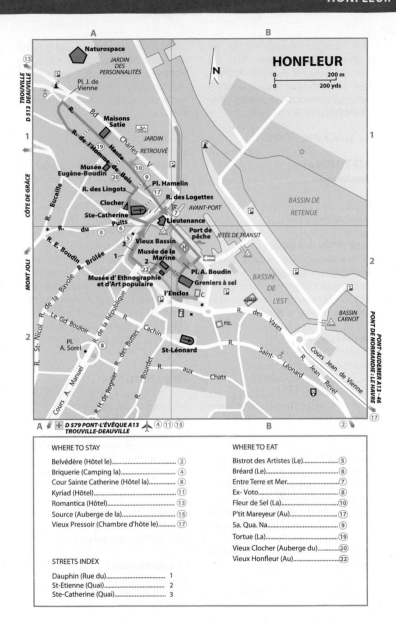

HONFLEUR

0   200 m
0   200 yds

Musset came to stay in St-Gatien in the period when the Normandy coast was fashionable with the Romantics. Honfleur began to fill with painters – not only those who were Norman-born such as Boudin, Hamelin and Lebourg, but also Paul Huet, Daubigny, Corot and others from Paris and foreigners such as Bonington and Jongkind.

It was in the small St-Siméon Inn – "chez La Mère Toutain" – that the Impressionists first met. Ever since artists have continued to visit Honfleur. Baudelaire, who stayed in the town with his mother in her old age, declared, "settling in Honfleur has always been the dearest of my dreams" and while there wrote his *Invitation au Voyage*.

Other Honfleur citizens include the composer Erik Satie (1866–1925), the poet and novelist Henri de Régnier (1864–1936), the author Lucie Delarue-Mardrus, the economist Frédéric Le Play and the historian Albert Sorel.

✿ WALKING TOUR

OLD TOWN★★
Allow 1hr30min.

▶ *Leave from place Arthur-Boudin to the east of the old dock.*

Place Arthur-Boudin
Old slate-shingled houses stand around the square; no 6 is a Louis XIII house with stone and flint chequered decoration. The Saturday-morning flower market brings colour and life to the area.

Greniers à sel
r. de la Ville. &🕒*Open during temporary exhibits or as part of the city's guided tour. Tourist office* 📞*02 31 89 23 30.*
These tile-covered stone buildings were constructed in the 17C in order to store the salt required by the cod fishing fleet.

Rue de la Prison
Opposite the Greniers à sel.
Very picturesque with its line of old timber-framed houses. At the end of the street, on the right, is the former church of St-Étienne, its bell-tower rising up above the old port.
The building now houses the **Musée de la Marine** (Naval Museum).

Musée du Vieux Honfleur
The museum presents three sections – one on the navy, one on popular art and finally the Manoir du Désert.

Musée de la Marine
quai St-Étienne. &🕒*Open same hours and conditions as for the Musée d'Ethnographie et d'Art populaire.* ∞*€3.50 or €4.70 for a combined ticket with the Musée d'Ethnographie.* 📞*02 31 89 14 12.*

The museum, which is housed in Église St-Étienne (deconsecrated), traces the history of the port of Honfleur and contains a large number of scale models and topographical information on the town.

Musée d'Ethnographie et d'Art populaire
r. de la Prison. 🕒*Open Apr–Sept Tue–Sun 10am–noon, 2–6.30pm; mid-Feb–Mar and Oct–mid-Nov Mon and Tue–Fri 2–5.30pm, Sat–Sun 10am–noon, 2.30–5.30pm.* 🕒*Closed 1 May, 14 Jul.* ∞*€3.50 or €4.70 for a combined ticket with the Musée de la Marine.* 📞*02 31 89 14 12. www.musees-basse-normandie.fr.*
Ten Normandy interiors have been reconstructed in this museum located in 16C residences. Note particularly the timbered manor house, the bourgeois dining room, the weavers' and printers' workshop, the bedroom and a shop on the ground floor.

Vieux Bassin★★
The quaysides of the old dock – designed by Duquesne on the orders of Colbert – are picturesque, enhanced by the pleasure boats alongside. The contrast is striking between **St-Étienne Quay,** with its splendid two-storey stone dwellings, and **Ste-Catherine Quay**, where the tall – rising up to seven storeys high – slender houses are faced with slate and timber. The Governor's House (La Lieutenance), next to the swivel bridge, completes the scene.

La Lieutenance
Only a relic now remains of the 16C house in which the king's lieutenant, Governor of Honfleur, once lived. The façade facing the square now incorporates, between two bartizans, Caen Gate, one of the two main entrances to the city in the Middle Ages. From the corner of the passenger quay you get a good view of the house, the old dock and, on the other side, the outer harbour.
Rue de Logettes, a reference to the numerous wooden stalls that once lined the street, leads to place **Ste-Catherine**, in the heart of the neighbourhood of

Old Town street in front of Musée du Vieux Honfleur

© www.calvados-tourisme.com

the same name. In addition to the pretty street and half-timbered houses, the neighbourhood is famous for its unique church and belltower.

Église Ste-Catherine★★

This church is a rare example in western Europe of a building constructed, apart from the foundations, entirely of wood. After the Hundred Years' War all masons and architects were employed on the inevitable post-war reconstruction, but the Honfleur axe masters from the local shipyards determined to thank God immediately for the departure of the English and built a church with their own skills.

The interior has twin naves and side aisles, the timber roof over each nave being supported by wooden pillars. The carved panels ornamenting the gallery are 16C, the organ 18C. There are also many wooden statues.

Clocher de Ste-Catherine★

Open same hours as Musée Eugène-Boudin. 2€ (with combined ticket for Eugène-Boudin, p186). 02 31 89 91 94.
The massive oak belfry, a building covered in chestnut wood, stands apart from the church on a large foundation which contained the bell-ringer's dwelling. Today it is used as an

extension of the Musée Eugène-Boudin and contains religious works.

Rue des Lingots, narrow and winding, goes around the tower; the old cobblestones lead to **rue de l'Homme-de-Bois**, named after a covered wooden head on the house at no **23**.

▷ *Turn left onto rue de l'Homme-de-Bois; 400m/437yd further on, across from the Hôtel-Dieu Chapel, take rue du Trou-Miard to the right, then turn right again onto rue Haute.*

The hospital's old lighthouse, on place Jean-de-Vienne, is now mostly used by seagulls. **Rue Haute**, formerly a pathway outside the fortifications, was home to many local shipbuilders. The composer Erik Satie was born at no **88**, where the timbers are painted red; inside there is an unusual museum. Continue onto **place Hamelin**, birthplace of Alphonse Allais (no **6**), a French humourist of the late 19C.

▷ *End your tour of Honfleur by walking straight on (quai de la Lieutenance and quai de la Quarantaine) to return to place Arthur-Boudin on the right. Or turn and go through the public garden, walking as far as the Seine along the digue de*

185

l'Ouest, where a pleasant pedestrian path has been created on the jetty.

SIGHTS
Musée Eugène-Boudin
r. de l'Homme-de-Bois. Open mid-Mar–end Sept Wed–Mon 10am–noon, 2–6pm; mid-Feb–Mar and Oct–Dec Mon and Wed–Fri 2.30–5.30pm, Sat–Sun and public holidays 10am–noon, 2.30–5.30pm. Closed early Jan–mid-Feb, 1 May, 14 Jul, 25 Dec. €6.50, €9.40 combined with Maisons Satie and Musées du Vieux Honfleur – rates may change; free Nuit des musées. 02 31 89 54 00.

An old Augustinian chapel and a more recent building house this museum, which is chiefly devoted to the painters of Honfleur and of the estuary.

On the first floor is a rich collection of household items from 18C and 19C Normandy. The second and third floors display works by 20C artists who, for the most part, worked in the region: Dufy, Marquet, Friesz, Villon, Lagar, Grau-Sala, Saint-Delis, Gernez, Driès, Herbo, Vallotton, Bigot, etc.

Galleries adjoining the chapel feature 19C paintings by Eugène Boudin (the museum possesses 89 of his paintings and drawings) and by Monet, Jongkind, Dubourg, Isabey, Pécrus, Courbet, Cals. A second holds the Hambourg-Rachet bequest of some 300 canvases (19C–20C) by Derain, Foujita, Garbell, Marie Laurencin, Van Dongen and Hambourg. The third is a drawings room in which about 100 works are rotated each year.

Maisons Satie★
Entrance at 67 bd Charles-V (running parallel to r. Haute). Open May–Sept 10am–7pm; rest of year 11am–6pm. Closed 1 Jan and 25 Dec. €5.60. 02 31 89 11 11.

Wearing headphones, you are guided through a series of stage-like settings recalling the career of Erik Satie (1866–1925) – "born young in an old world". The museum offers the opportunity to hear the music and understand more about the life of the man who came out with such conversational pearls as: "Give me a minute to get my skirt on, and I'll be right with you!"; "Although our information is false, we cannot guarantee it"; "What do you prefer, music or cold-cuts?"; "The piano is like money, it's only pleasant when you've got your hands on it."

Église St-Léonard
S of the Vieux-Bassin, take the rue de la République, then left into the rue Cachin, which leads to the place St-Léonard.

The façade of this church is a bizarre combination of an ornate Flamboyant doorway and a 17C belfry tower.

Inside are two immense shells which have been converted into fonts.

At the entrance to the chancel stand statues of Our Lady of Victory and St Leonard with two prisoners kneeling; note in the chancel the wooden statues of St Peter, St Paul and the four Evangelists. The narthex is furnished with an 18C copper lectern from Villedieu-les-Poêles.

Naturospace★
Opposite the hospital lighthouse, bd Charles V. Open daily Jul–Aug 10am–7pm; Feb–Mar and Oct–Nov 10am–1pm, 2–5.30pm; Apr–Jun and Sept 10am–1pm, 2–7pm (last entry 1hr before closing). Closed Dec–Jan. €8.10 (children €6.30). 02 31 81 77 00. www.naturospace.com.

Inside an enormous greenhouse, 60 species of butterflies from six continents float gracefully in perfect freedom. Surrounded by the whispering of their wings, you stroll among tropical plants and observe cocoons from which, early in the morning, a few caterpillars emerge. Good explanations and special exhibits.

ADDITIONAL SIGHTS
Pont de Normandie★★
3km/2mi E via the D 580. There is a €5 toll for cars, but no charge for pedestrians, cyclists and motorcyclists. Watch out – the wind can be very strong!

Pont de Normandie

© www.calvados-tourisme.com

The bridge was started in 1988 and officially opened in January 1995; it is the third largest bridge to span the Lower Seine after the Pont de Tancarville and the Pont de Brotonne.

Its impact on the economy is three fold: it brings Le Havre and Honfleur closer together by removing the detour via Tancarville Bridge (24km/15mi instead of 60km/37.2mi); it is one of the major motorway links between the Channel Tunnel and the west and south-west of France; and it represents one of the many connections in the so-called **Estuaries Route**, which ties together northern and southern Europe without going through Paris.

The Pont de Normandie, a truly remarkable work of art and a technological feat, was seen as a milestone in the history of civil engineering, since it established the record of the longest cable-stayed bridge (more elegant and cheaper to build than a suspension bridge). Although Lisbon's Vasco da Gama Bridge (1998) is now the longest in Europe, the Pont de Normandie is higher.

This steel and concrete mass, which seems to defy the laws of gravity, is surprisingly light and extremely stable. Careful attention was devoted to the subject of safety: the bridge is designed to withstand winds of up to 440kph/274mph; it can resist shocks caused by the largest cargo boats, which could only col-

lide with the north tower, protected by 9m/30ft of concrete; the road surfacing has in-built sensors triggered off by the presence of black ice; tollbooth operators can monitor traffic continually thanks to surveillance cameras.

Besides the standard lighting for road traffic, the Breton architect **Yann Kersalé** conceived a sophisticated lighting system called *Rhapsody in Blue and White* – a bi-coloured display of static lights outline the two towers (blue on the underside, white on the outside), whereas a row of blue twinkling lights run underneath the deck.

Côte de Grâce★★

The peaceful beauty of this famous hillside, appreciated by all Honfleur enthusiasts, is also appealing to passing tourists.

Calvaire★★
Telescope.

From the cross there is a good **panorama** of the Seine estuary, the Le Havre roadstead, to the right, the Pont de Normandie and, in the distance, Tancarville Bridge.

Chapelle Notre-Dame-de-Grâce

In the centre of the esplanade beneath tall trees stands the small chapel of Our Lady of Grace and within it the statue after which it is named. This graceful

17C building has replaced a sanctuary said to have been founded by Richard II, 4th Duke of Normandy. It was here that navigators and explorers came to pray before leaving on journeys of discovery or colonisation to the North American continent; a borough of Montréal bears this name. The north transept chapel is dedicated to all Canadians of Norman origin. There are numerous small, ex-voto vessels.

Mont-Joli viewpoint

The view complements the one from Calvaire: in the foreground are the town, the port and the coast; to the east is the semicircle of hills. Tancarville Bridge can be seen in the distance.

🚗 DRIVING TOUR

South Bank of the Seine – Honfleur to Rouen★★
130km/81mi. Allow 5hrs.

This charming drive takes you through forests and along roads overlooking the river below.

▶ *Leave Honfleur via cours Jean-de-Vienne and take D 312 towards Berneville and Pont-Audemer.*

The road follows the lower Risle Valley. Beyond Berville, there are many fine views of the estuary. In the spring, the blooming apple orchards turn the landscape into a wonderland.

Pont-Audemer★
See PONT-AUDEMER, p118.

▶ *Take D 810.*

Ste-Opportune-la-Mare
See QUILLEBEUF-SUR-SEINE, p120.

▶ *Take D 95.*

After a section on a crest road, between Val-Anger and Vieux-Port, the Seine Valley comes into view again.

Vieux-Port★
The thatched cottages are half hidden by their orchards.

Aizier
The stone bell tower of the 12C church looks very old. Near the church there is a manhole slab – the remains of a covered way dating from around 2,000 BC.

▶ *From Aizier to Quesney, D 95 and D 65 follow the edge of Brotonne Forest.*

Vatteville-la-Rue
The nave of the church dates from the Renaissance; it bears a black mourning band which was painted on the wall for the funeral of the lord of the manor. The Flamboyant chancel is lit by 16C stained-glass windows.

▶ *Turn left onto D 65, which leads to La Mailleraye (ferry).*

Running alongside the Seine to the right, the road offers views of typical Norman thatched cottages half hidden by trees. After Notre-Dame-de-Bliquetuit, you can see the two ferries which cross at Yainville and Jumièges. Road D 65 then rises in hairpin bends.

Viewpoint★
Picnic area. Viewing table.
To the right can be seen the towers of Jumièges Abbey, particularly impressive at sunset, and to the left the Seine Valley.

▶ *300m/328yd further on, stop on the right in the La Mailleraye lay-by.*

Chêne à la Cuve
100m/110yd from D 913, opposite the 11km post.
Four oak trunks growing from a single bole form a kind of natural vat, 7m/23ft in circumference.

▶ *Take D 313 towards Bourg-Achard and turn right on D 101.*

Moulin de Hauville
🕐*Open Jul–Aug daily 2.30–6.30pm; May–Jun and Sept Sun 2.30–6.30pm.*

€2.50. ℘02 32 56 57 32.

This 13C windmill is one of the few surviving stone mills in Upper Normandy and once belonged to the monks of Jumièges Abbey. Its cap can be orientated according to the direction of the wind and is supported by oak beams. The stone tower and large sails are most impressive. If weather allows, you can see the mill in operation.

▶ *Take D 101 in the other direction and turn left on D 712. Going down the hill, turn onto D 45 (nice views of the forest and the river), then take D 265, which crosses Mauny Forest, then D 64 towards La Bouille.*

Between La Ronce and La Bouille, the road goes along the river's edge.

La Bouille

La Bouille, in a lovely site at the foot of the wooded slopes of the Roumois plateau, has always attracted artists, writers, poets and painters. In the old days, people from Rouen would come here to sample eels stewed in cider, La Bouille cheese and *douillons aux pommes* (apples filled with butter, wrapped in pastry and baked).

Today the village still offers a charming combination of terraces, inns and avenues. Painters set up their easels and sketch the quaint streets and surrounding countryside.

On the quayside, a plaque on one of the houses recalls the critic and novelist **Hector Malot** (1830–1907), born here.

Moulineaux

Church. ⌚*Make appointment at the mairie to visit.* ℘02 35 18 02 45.

The **church** with its slender spire dates from the 13C. Inside there is an attractive woodwork group formed by the pulpit and rood screen (one side of which is Gothic and the other Renaissance). In the apse is the 13C **stained-glass window**★, a gift of Blanche de Castille. Note the 16C tableau of the Flemish School depicting the Crucifixion and a monk in prayer. There is a far-reaching view of the Seine Valley from the cemetery.

▶ *Take D 3, a steep hill.*

Monument Qui Vive

At the crossroads of D 64 and D 67A.

There is a remarkable view (viewing table) of the Seine as it curves round to encircle Roumare Forest.

Road D 64 goes down to the Seine so that one gets a view of the river bend commanded by Robert the Devil's castle and the Rouen industrial suburbs.

Château de Robert le Diable★

⌂ *See Elbeuf – Excursions, p106.*

▶ *Go back to D 64 up a steep climb. Take D 64 right through Londe Forest. At the crossroads known as Le Nouveau Monde, follow D 938 to Orival, to the south.*

Orival★

From Oissel to Orival the road is overhung by curious rocks which are part of the chalk escarpment. Orival Church is an unusual semi-troglodytic 15C building.

▶ *Return to Le Nouveau Monde.*

Roches d'Orival★

🚶 *Park on D 18 by the sign Sentier des Roches; 1hr on foot there and back ⊛ by a steep path which is slippery when wet. At the top turn right onto a path which passes in front of some caves hollowed out of the rocks.*

The path follows the cliff. By a grassy knoll (300m/328yd) there is a **view** of the Seine and of the rock escarpment, broken by a grassy corniche on which the path continues.

▶ *Follow D 18 along the Seine.*

Oissel

Pleasant public garden.

▶ *To return to Rouen, take D 13, then N 138 to the right.*

The pine forest of Rouvray is an oasis of calm, reminiscent of the Landes of southwest France.

Trouville-sur-Mer★★

At Trouville, the cliffs of the Normandy corniche slope away at the mouth of the River Touques, to be replaced by a wonderful beach of fine golden sand. Although modern, the town retains its charm; at the start of the Second Empire (1852), Trouville launched the Côte Fleurie. As in Deauville, the wooden plank promenade *(planches)* runs the full length of the beach. Owing to the comings and goings of the fishermen and the small resident population, Trouville is worth visiting even out of season.

▶ **Population:** 4,928.
Michelin Map: 303: M-3.
Info: 32 quai Fernand-Moureaux, 14360 Trouville-sur-Mer. ℘02 31 14 60 70. www.trouvillesurmer.org.
▶ **Location:** Trouville extends along the north side of the estuary, opposite Deauville, 94km/58.4mi E of Rouen.

VISIT
Corniche★

Make for the corniche road to the north by way of boulevard Aristide-Briand and a left turn.
On the way down there is a magnificent **view** of the Trouville and Deauville beaches and the Côte Fleurie. From the Calvaire de Bon-Secours *(viewing table)* the view is breathtaking.

👥 Aquarium

17 rue de Paris (seafront promenade).
👤◐*Open Jul–Aug daily 10am–7.30pm; Easter–end Jun and Sept–Oct 10am–noon, 2–6.30pm; rest of the year 2–6.30pm.* ◐*Closed 25 Dec.* ◑*€7.50*

(children 3–14 years €5.50).
℘02 31 88 46 04.
www.natur-aquarium.com.
Fresh and salt water fish together with equatorial forest reptiles provide a colourful spectacle.

Musée de Trouville Villa Montebello

64 r. du Général-Leclerc. ◐*Open Wed–Mon 11am–1pm, 2–6pm.* ◐*Closed 1 Jan, 25 Dec.* ◑*€2, no charge Wed.*
℘02 31 88 16 26.
This villa is a fine example of seaside architecture during the Second Empire (1852–70). The museum shows work by artists who brought fame to the town.

Galeries d'exposition

In the tourist office. 👤◐*Check opening times at tourist office* ◐*Closed Tue.*
◑*No charge.* *℘02 31 14 92 06.*
This gallery hosts temporary art exhibitions.

Trouville-sur-Mer

© Veni/iStockphoto.com

Deauville beach

© www.calvados-tourisme.com

Deauville★★

Deauville, a popular resort since the mid-19C, is known for the luxury and refinement of its various establishments and the elegance of its entertainments. Events of the the summer season include racing (including the Grand Prix), the polo world championship, regattas, tennis and golf tournaments, galas, and the international yearling fair. Every year, in early September, the city hosts the prestigious American Film Festival.

VISIT
The Resort
The season in Deauville opens in July and ends with the Deauville Grand Prix on the fourth Sunday in August and the Golden Cup of the international polo championship. Horse racing takes place alternately at La Touques (flat racing) and Clairefontaine (flat racing and steeplechasing) and the international yearling sales are held in Deauville in August. Out of season the resort accommodates numerous conventions as well as seminars.

The coming and going on the **Planches** – a wooden plank promenade running the whole length of the beach – is the most distinctive feature of beach life in Deauville. Lined with elegant buildings such as the Pompeian Baths and the

▶ **Population:** 4,005.

Michelin Map: 303: M-3 – Local map, *see Pays d'Auge, p180.*

Info: Place de la Mairie. ℰ 02 31 14 40 00. www.deauville.org.fr.

Location: Located 94km/59mi from Rouen and 43km/27mi from Le Havre, Deauville lies on the Côte Fleurie. The Touques estuary separates Deauville from the older resort, Trouville.

Don't Miss: The pretty villas as well as the view from Mont Canisy and the coastal road from Honfleur to Cabourg.

Timing: Try to see Deauville in the morning; afternoons bring crowds.

Soleil Bar, where stars and celebrities like to be seen, the Planches draws fashionable strollers.

Between the casino and the Planches, the Centre International de Deauville (C.I.D.) is a remarkable ensemble of suspended gardens, fountains and transparent façades which welcomes all kinds of professional, cultural and festive events.

WHERE TO STAY

Chantilly (Hôtel Le)	②
Continental (Hôtel Le)	④
Épi d'Or (Hôtel L')	⑥
Hélios (Hôtel)	⑧
Normandy-Barrière (Hôtel)	⑫
Patio (Hôtel Le)	⑭

WHERE TO EAT

Bar de la Mer	①
Comptoir et la Table (Le)	②
Dupont avec un thé	③
Flambée (La)	⑤
Galerie de Tourgéville (La)	⑦
Garage (Le)	⑨
Kraal (Le)	⑪
Nautica (Le)	⑬
Orangeraie (L')	⑮
Yearling (Le)	⑰

A walk along the seafront boulevard Eugène-Cornuché will prove that Deauville is not called the "beach of flowers" *(plage fleurie)* for nothing.
The yacht marina on the Touques and the Yacht Club strike an elegant note.
A little **tourist train** will take you on a guided tour of the city (with commentary), and the tourist office has information about walking tours and bicycle trails.

Deauville Port

The port is enclosed on the west side by a breakwater extending from the beach to the mouth of the Touques and on the east by a jetty marking the port entrance to the channel. The deep access channel means that the port is accessible 80 percent of the time. It consists of three docks, entered through a double lock, which provide deep water moorings and ample capacity: 800 berths along 4,000m/4,376yd of quays. At the centre are the slate-roofed marinas, the Deauville harbour master's office, an annexe of the Marina Deauville Club (quai des Marchands, near the lock) and space for shops and hotel services.

🚗 DRIVING TOURS

The mileages given on the following tours are calculated from the Pont des Belges, linking Deauville to Trouville.

In summer, the coast between Honfleur and Cabourg is one of the busiest in France, but is lovely despite the crowds.

Le Mont Canisy★
Round-trip of 25km/15mi (about 1hr).

▷ *Leave Deauville to the SW by the D 513.*

Bénerville Church stands overlooking a crossroads.

▷ *Turn left before the church. 200m/218yds further, at the mairie, go straight and turn left at the crossroads. Continue for 1km/3/4mi.*

Parc Calouste-Gulbenkian
◷*Jul-Aug 2–6pm.* ◷*Closed holidays.* ♒ *€2 (-18 years free).* ♒*02 31 14 02 02 (mairie de Deauville). www.deauville.fr.* This very pretty park was designed in the 1930s for petroleum magnate Calouste Gulbenkian. Sheltered from northern winds and with no buildings facing it, it extends over more than 30ha/74acres. At the entrance, an avenue edged with boxwood and flower beds leads to a wide lawn with ancient trees, opening onto the Auge *bocage*. Don't hesitate to stroll around to get a good idea of the various perspectives and landscapes: Cross-shaped spits symbolise the four rivers of Islam, the fruit garden, vegetable garden and groves of southwest pines. In summer, there are exhibitions and classical music concerts.

▷ *Return to the church and take the street on the right. When you get to the top, turn right towards Mont Canisy. Leave your car in front of the barrier.*

The path leads to the block house where the view extends from the Cap de la Hève to the Orne estuary. The Conservatoire national du littoral offers tours to discover this protected natural site.

▷ *Return to your car and take the road on your right.*

After crossing the modern town of Canisy, the road heads down sharply; views of the Touques valley.

▷ *At the St-Arnoult crossroads, go straight.*

Touques
At the mouth of the river of the same name, the old port of William the Conqueror, the village still has old houses along the Les Ouies stream. The church of St Thomas (12C) owes its name to a visit from St Thomas Becket. The 11C **église St-Pierre** (♒*02 31 88 70 93; www.ville-touques.com*) holds a variety of exhibitions.

The Corniche Normande: From Deauville-Trouville to Honfleur★★
21km/13mi. Allow 1hr.

▷ *Leave Deauville-Trouville to the NE by D 513.*

This pleasant tour passes through magnificent scenery and affords views over the Seine estuary between gaps in the hedges and orchards.
Handsome properties are scattered along the road. Just before Villerville there is a fine view of the oil refineries on the estuary. To the left Le Havre can be recognised by its thermal power station and the belfry of St Joseph's Church.

Villerville⌂
This lively seaside resort, with its nearby meadows and woods, has kept its rural character. Notice the Romanesque belfry on the local church. From the terrace overlooking the beach there is a view of Le Havre and Cap de la Hève. The road is thereafter narrow with hidden bends.

Cricquebœuf
The 12C **church**, with its ivy-covered walls, is a familiar feature on travel posters. The countryside around, with its apple orchards, grazing cows and tranquil ponds, adds to the emblematic beauty.

▷ *In Pennedepie, take D 62; after 2.5km/1.5mi turn right onto D 279.*

Barneville
The church, tucked away in the greenery, is backed by the magnificent park of the 18C château.

▶ *Take D 279 N; after 4km/2.5mi turn left by a château to reach Honfleur via the Côte de Grâce.*

Côte de Grâce★★
♨ *See HONFLEUR – Additional Sights*

Honfleur★★
♨ *See HONFLEUR.*

The Côte Fleurie: From Trouville-Deauville to Cabourg⌂⌂
To Cabourg: 19km/12mi.

▶ *Leave Deauville to the SW by D 513.*

Bénerville-sur-Mer and Blonville-sur-Mer
The hillsides are dotted with villas overlooking a long sandy beach.

Blonville-sur-Mer
Blonville-sur-Mer's sweeping sandy beach stretches to the slopes of Mont Canisy. At Blonville, there is an amusement park near the sea, as well as extensive sports facilities. The Chapelle Notre-Dame de l'Assomption houses some modern frescoes, the work of the artist **Jean-Denis Maillart**.

Villers-sur-Mer⌂⌂
Musée Paléontologique. ♿⏲Open daily Jul–Aug 9am–7pm; Mar–Jun and Sept–Oct 9.30am–12.30pm, 2–6pm; Nov–Feb 9.30am–12.30pm, 2.30–5pm. ⏲Closed Sun afternoon mid Nov–Feb (except school holidays), 1 Jan, 25 Dec. ⊗No charge. ✆02 31 87 01 18. www.villers-sur-mer.fr.
This elegant seaside resort with casino and excellent sports facilities is known for its large beach and its wooded hilly countryside criss-crossed with small paths leading down to the town centre. The beachside promenade incorporates a signpost indicating the passage of the Greenwich meridian.
The **Musée Paléontologique** *(access through the tourist office on place Mermoz)* has exhibits of fossils and stuffed birds from the area together with a stone armchair and seashells which belonged to Ferdinand Postel, artist and photographer who lived in Villers from 1880 to 1917 and who collected fossils along the area's limestone cliffs.
Just before Houlgate, on a downhill hairpin bend, a viewing table offers a **panorama** from the mouth of the River Dives to the mouth of the River Orne.

Falaise des Vaches Noires★
Between Villers-sur-Mer and Houlgate, the Auberville plateau ends in a crumbling and much-eroded cliff face. It is best to walk along the beach at low tide (*about 2hr on foot round-trip*) to enjoy the panorama, which extends from Trouville to Luc-sur-Mer and over most of the Seine bay.
In places large pieces of limestone have broken away from the cliff top and piled up at the base where they have been colonised by seaweed to form fantastic shapes; these are the Black Cows (Vaches Noires). Fossils found on these cliffs form a large part of the collection at the Villers-sur-Mer museum.

Houlgate⌂⌂
Houlgate is set in the verdant Drochon Valley; the shady avenues and the late-19C houses and gardens, in excellent states of conservation, add to the overall charm of this resort, one of the first to appear on the Côte Fleurie, in 1851.
The promenade Rolland-Garros overlooks the fine sandy beach, which is popular for bathing, and continues to the east towards the cliffs of the **Vaches Noires**. The road runs along the coast and, before Dives-sur-Mer, passes in front of a monument commemorating the departure of **Duke William** for the conquest of England.

Dives-sur-Mer★
♨ *See Dives-sur-Mer.*

Cabourg⌂⌂
♨ *See Cabourg.*

▶ *Head to Cabourg via D 45.*

Cabourg ♨ ♨

The large seaside resort of Cabourg, created at the time of the Second Empire (1852–70), centres on the casino and Grand Hôtel on the seafront, from which streets radiate inland, intersecting with two semicircular avenues. Many avenues and streets are lined by attractive houses set in shaded gardens.

A BIT OF HISTORY

Cabourg is famous as the place from which William the Conqueror successfully forced Henry I's troops back into the sea. The holiday towns of Dieppe, Deauville and Trouville are joined by Cabourg, which, benefiting from a rail link, became a tourist destination of choice. By the 1880s, hotels and villas had sprung up around the **Grand Hôtel** on the seafront; Cabourg was truly established.

Marcel Proust went to Cabourg for the first time in 1881, when he was 10. The coastal climate was beneficial to his health (he suffered from asthma), while the town's charm and memories of his childhood drew him to visit frequently as an adult, when he would stay at the Grand Hôtel. *Within a Budding Grove (À l'Ombre des jeunes filles en fleurs)* was a vivid portrayal of the customs of Cabourg and of life in a seaside resort at the turn of the 20C.

EXCURSIONS
Merville-Franceville-Plage
◉ *6km/3.7mi W of Cabourg by D 514.*
When the Allies landed in June 1944, the strongest point in the defences was the Merville Battery.
It was captured by the 6th British Airborne Division. One of the casemates has been converted into a museum, the **Musée de la Batterie** (♿ ◷ *Open daily 15 Mar–15 Oct 9.30am–6.30pm; rest of year 9.30am–5.30pm; ☞€5; ℘02 31 91 47 53. www.batterie-merville.com).*

Ranville
◉ *8km/5mi S of Merville-Franceville-Plage on D 223.*

▸ **Population:** 4,027.
🕭 **Michelin Map:** 303: L-4 – Local map, ☞see *Pays d'Auge, p180.*
🛈 **Info:** Jardins de l'Hôtel de Ville. ℘02 31 06 20 00. www.cabourg.net.
◖ **Location:** Take D 513 from Caen (33km/20.6mi to the SW), Deauville (19km/12mi) and Honfleur (51km/31.7mi) to the E; take D 45 from Lisieux (30km/18.6mi to the SE).
⊙ **Don't Miss:** Magnificent view from promenade Marcel-Proust.
◷ **Timing:** Explore in the morning to avoid crowds.

Ranville was captured at 2.30am on 6 June 1944 by the 13th Battalion of the Lancashire Fuseliers of the 6th British Airborne Division; it was the first village to be liberated on French territory. A war cemetery commemorates these events.

Grand Hôtel Cabourg

H. Le Gac/MICHELIN

Dives-sur-Mer★

If Cabourg is known as a holiday resort, its sister city Dives tends to be associated with history, for it was from here that William the Conqueror, Duc de Normandie, set out to invade England in the 11C.

SIGHTS
Halles★

The magnificent oak frame of the covered market (15C–16C) is in very good condition. Wrought-iron signs identify the stalls of the merchants. On the other side of place de la République stands the 16C Bois-Hibou Manor.

Église Notre-Dame de Dives

This massive church, a centre of pilgrimage until the Religious Wars, is 14C and 15C, except for the transept crossing, a remnant of an 11C sanctuary. Inside, the elegant 15C nave contrasts sharply with the massive pillars and plain arches of the Romanesque transept crossing.

▶ **Population:** 5,864.

Michelin Map: 303: L-4 – Local map, *see Pays d'Auge, p180*.

Info: rue du Général-de-Gaulle. ℘02 31 28 12 50. www.dives-sur-mer.com.

Location: Dives lies across the estuary of the River Dives from Cabourg.

Don't Miss: The old marketplace (Halles) and the church.

Timing: Give yourself an hour to enjoy the town.

The transepts themselves, the chancel and the Lady Chapel, were built in 14C Rayonnant Gothic style.

Village Guillaume-le-Conquérant

This pleasant enclave of art and craft shops is located within the precincts of the old inn of the same name, dating from the 16C.

Lisieux★

Sitting on the east bank of the Touques, Lisieux has become the most important commercial and industrial town in the prosperous Pays d'Auge. The town is renowned for St Theresa of Lisieux and is the second-most important pilgrimage site in France after Lourdes.

A BIT OF HISTORY

Thérèse Martin was born on 2 January 1873 to a well-to-do and very religious family in Alençon; she was an eager and sensitive child who soon showed intelligence and will-power. On the death of his wife, M. Martin brought the family to Lisieux where they lived at Les Buissonnets. At nine years old, Thérèse felt the call of the Church.

The authorities considered her too young and it was only in April 1888, after a pilgrimage to Rome and a

▶ **Population:** 22,700.

Michelin Map: 303: N-5 – Local map, *see Pays d'Auge, p180*.

Info: 11 rue d'Alençon. ℘02 31 48 18 10. www.lisieux-tourisme.com.

Location: 73km/45.4mi E of Evreux via N13 and 36km/XXmi S of Honfleur.

Parking: The basilica is equipped for pilgrimages with ample parking nearby.

Don't Miss: The cathedral of St-Pierre and the CERZA zoo.

Timing: Visit Lisieux in the morning, then tour the countryside in the afternoon.

Kids: The popular game reserve CERZA.

Basilique Ste-Thérèse

S. Sauvignier/MICHELIN

request to the Holy Father, that she entered the Carmelite Order at the age of fifteen and three months. As Sister Theresa of the Child Jesus, she resolved "to save souls and, above all, to pray for the priests". Her gaiety and simplicity cloaked a consuming energy. She wrote the story of her life, *History of a Soul*, finishing the last pages only a few days before entering the Carmelite hospital in which, after an agonising illness, she died in 1897. She was canonised in 1925.

On 19 October 1997, Pope Jean-Paul II proclaimed her a Doctor of the Church, an exceptional honour bestowed on saints of great spiritual influence.

THE PILGRIMAGE
Les Buissonnets

🕐 *Open early Apr–early Oct daily 9am–noon, 2–6pm; end Oct–end Mar 10am–noon, 2–4pm; visit with audioguide.*
🕐 *Closed 1 Jan, 25 Dec.*
🆓 *No charge.* 📞 *02 31 48 55 08.*
www.therese-de-lisieux.fr.

This house is where Thérèse Martin lived from the age of 4 to 15. The tour includes the dining room, Thérèse's bedroom, her father's bedroom and a display of mementoes from her childhood days.

Chapelle du Carmel

🕐 *Open daily Easter–1 Nov, 7.20am–7pm, Nov–Easter 7.20am–6.30pm;*
🆓 *no charge.*

The saint's shrine, a recumbent figure in marble and precious wood, is in the chapel on the right and contains her relics.

Basilique Ste-Thérèse

🕐 *Open Dec–Jan, 9am–5.30pm; Mar and Nov, 9am–6pm; Apr and Oct 9am–6.30pm; May, Jun and Sept 9am–7pm; Jul–Aug 9am–7.30pm.*

This impressive basilica was consecrated on 11 July 1954 and is one of the biggest 20C churches. The **dome** is open to visitors. The construction of the belltower was interrupted in 1975; it ends in a flat roof and contains the great bell, three other bells and a carillon of 44 bells. Notice on the tympanum of the door the carvings by Robert Coin depicting Jesus teaching the Apostles and the Virgin of Mount Carmel. The immense nave is decorated with marble, stained glass and mosaics by Pierre Gaudin, a pupil of Maurice Denis. In the south transept stands a reliquary offered by Pope Pius XI containing the bones of the saint's right arm. The **crypt** (entrance outside, beneath the galleries) is decorated with mosaics (scenes from the life of St Theresa).

Musée-Diorama: Histoire de Sainte-Thérèse

Beneath the north cloister of the basilica. ♿🚶 *25min audio tour.*
🕐 *Open Easter–1 Nov daily 11am–1pm,*

LISIEUX

WHERE TO STAY

Azur (Hôtel)......................................	①
Cerza Safari Lodge..........................	③
Grand Hôtel de l'Espérance............	⑤
Place (Hôtel de la)..........................	⑦
St-Louis (Hôtel)..............................	⑨
Vallée (Camping de la)...................	⑪

WHERE TO EAT

Acacias (Aux)...................................	①
Coupe d'Or (La)...............................	③
Levrette (Auberge de la).................	⑦
Paquine (De la)...............................	⑨
1001 crêpes (Aux)..........................	⑪

*2–6pm; Nov–Dec and Feb–Easter
weekends, school and public holidays
2–5pm.* €3. 02 31 48 55 08.
www.therese-de-lisieux.fr.
This diorama depicts a dozen episodes
in the life of St Theresa.

Cathédrale St-Pierre★

Allow 15min.
Open daily 9.30am–6.30pm.
The cathedral was begun in 1170 and
completed only in the mid-13C.
Exterior – The façade, raised above
the ground on stone steps, is pierced
by three doors and flanked by towers.

Walk round the church by the right to
the south transept's Paradise Door. The
massive buttresses linked by an arch
surmounted by a gallery are 15C.
Interior – The transept is extremely
simple with the lantern rising in a single sweep at the crossing. Walk round
the 13C chancel, to the huge central
chapel which was remodelled in the
pure Flamboyant style on the orders of
Pierre Cauchon, Bishop of Lisieux, after
the trial of Joan of Arc.
It was in this chapel that Thérèse Martin
attended mass. Note the series of 15C
carved low-relief sculptures.

Detail of the timber-framed Vieux Manoir, Orbec

©Michel Mastrojanni/Photononstop/Photolibrary

Musée d'Art et d'Histoire

○Open Wed–Mon 2–6pm. ○Closed 1 Jan, 1 May, 14 Jul, 25 Dec. ✆€3.60. ✆02 31 62 07 70.

Set up in a handsome 16C half-timbered house, a collection of documents and images explains the history, arts and crafts of Lisieux and the Pays d'Auge.

ADDITIONAL SIGHT
▲▲ CERZA★

▶ 12km/7.4mi NE. Leave Lisieux by D 510, E on the plan; 3km/2mi after Hermival-les-Vaux turn right onto D 143.
○Open daily Jul–Aug 9.30am–7pm; Apr–Jun and Sept 9.30am–6.30pm; Oct–Nov and Feb–Mar 10am–5.30pm (last entry 4pm). ✆€16 (children €8). ✆02 31 62 15 76. www.cerza.com.

The **Centre d'Élevage et de Reproduction Zoologique Augeron (CERZA)** provides a pleasant, natural setting for endangered animal species. 52ha/129 acres offer interesting topographical contrasts – valleys and plains, meadows and forests, barren stretches and lush pockets of vegetation, charmingly dotted with small ponds and burbling streams. Signposted routes will take you through the **African Reserve** (a vast area set aside for rhinoceroses, zebras, watussi, ostriches and giraffes) or on a tour of the valley. A great many primates (gelada baboons, macaques, capuchins, gibbons) as well as lemurs live in semi-freedom.

EXCURSIONS
Orbec

▶ Orbec is 18km/11mi southwest of Bernay via D 131 and 20km/12.4mi south of Liseiux via D 516.

Orbec is a small and lively town with a long history, as witnessed by the many old half-timbered houses in the busy shopping street, rue Grande. The town stands quite close to the source of the River Orbiquet in one of the most pleasant valleys in the Auge region. At the entrance to the town stands the famous Pierre Lanquetot factory, which has been producing its delicious Camembert cheeses for the past century.

The **Musée municipal** (107 r. Grande. ○Open May–Sept Wed–Sun 10am–12.30pm, 3–6pm; Easter to end Apr, wkd 10am–12.30pm, 3–6pm; ○Closed public holidays; ✆no charge; ✆02 31 32 58 89) is located in a beautiful 16C timber-framed house, the **Vieux Manoir★**, built for a rich tanner. Carved figures and geometric patterns decorate the exterior.

GR 26 Walk

▶ 4.5km/2.8mi S of Orbec

A small road (chemin de la Folletière-Abenon), follows alongside the Orbiquet river. Leave the car by the bridge and take a path on the left. The GR 26 itinerary (signposted in red and white) leads you on a tour of one of the prettiest valleys in the Pays d'Auge.

Pays d'Auge★★

With its pastures, thatched cottages, manor houses, apple orchards and winding hedgerows, the Pays d'Auge provides a picturesque transition to the beaches of the Côte Fleurie. The heart of traditional rural Normandy, the Auge region is partially covered in original woodland, with a chalk escarpment (30m/98.5ft high), known as the Côte d'Auge, overlooking the Dives Valley and the Caen area.

▶ **Population:** 149,000.

🗓 **Michelin Map:** 303: M-4–N-6.

Info: 11 rue d'Alençon, Lisieux. ✆02 31 48 18 10. www.pays-auge.fr.

▷ **Location:** The Pays d'Auge, between the River Dives on the west and the River Touques on the east, surrounds Lisieux, 36km/ 22.5mi S of Honfleur.

😊 **Don't Miss:** The beautiful château of Crèvecœur-en-Auge, with its half-timbering typical of the region.

🕓 **Timing:** Give yourself 2hr to visit the Manoir des Évêques de Lisieux, 2hr for the Château de Crèvecœur and some extra time to see the gardens.

🚗 DRIVING TOURS

1 CÔTE D'AUGE
66km/41mi. Allow 2hrs.

Lisieux★★
See Lisieux, p196.

▷ *From Lisieux take N 13 west. In La Boissière turn right onto D 59.*

Ancienne Abbaye du Val Richer
Closed to the public.
Following the destruction of the Cistercian abbey during the Revolution, only the 17C hospice remained. François Guizot (1787–1874), a historian and leading politician during the reign of Louis-Philippe (1830–48), retired here after the 1848 revolution until his death in 1874. The Schlumberger brothers, early 20C petroleum engineers, worked here on inventions that would transform the industry (*see Crèvecœur-en-Auge, below).*

▷ *At the crossroads turn left onto D 101 and bear right onto D 117. At the next crossroads turn left onto D 16 and right onto D 85.*

Clermont-en-Auge★
Follow the signs Chapelle de Clermont – Panorama. 🕓*Open Easter–Oct 10am–7pm.*
Leave the car at the start of the avenue leading to the **chapel** *(15min round-trip).* From the east end there is an extensive

panorama★ of the Dives and Vie valleys; in the distance stretches the Caen countryside, bounded by the dark line of the *bocage* hills. The church contains statues of St Marcouf and St Thibeault in polychrome stone in the chancel and on either side of the altar St John the Baptist and St Michael.

Beuvron-en-Auge★
This charming village has kept around 40 lovely old timber-framed houses set around the central square. The former covered market is now a shopping centre. There is a very pretty manor at the south exit from the village, decorated with woodcarvings.

▷ *Take D 49 north through Putot-en-Auge; cross N 175 and pass under the motorway. Fork right to Cricqueville.*

Crèvecœur-en-Auge
The **château** (*closed to the public*), completed in 1584, and its three main buildings with vast roofs, are typically medieval, whereas its chequered stone and brick decoration are Norman.

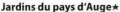

Jardins du pays d'Auge★

Rte des 3-Rois, Cambremer. ○May–Sept 10am–6.30pm; early Oct–15 Nov 10am–5pm, except wkd. ∞€7.20 (5–14-year-olds €5). ℘02 31 63 01 81. www.lesjardinsdupaysdauge.

These beautifully themed gardens are planted on close to 3ha/7acres, with perennials, rare plants and bamboos. The names are evocative as well: the Garden of Scents, the Garden of the Sun, the Garden of the Moon, the Garden of Angels and the Garden of Water... In all about 30 spaces co-exist here, marked out with beautiful constructions typical of the Auge region, which the owners transported here one by one.

◑ *From Sarlabot to Dives there is a beautiful panorama over the Calvados coast.*

2 TRADITIONAL NORMANDY: VALLÉE DE LA TOUQUES

60km/37mi. Allow 2hrs.

◑ *Leave Lisieux via boulevard Herbert-Fournet, D 579 north; right onto D 263.*

Rocques

The village **church** in the centre of its old burial ground has two wooden porches. The chancel and the tower date from the 13C. Inside note the torches and painting of the Brothers of Charity and several polychrome wooden statues.

◑ *Take D 262 NW back to D 579.*

Pont-l'Évêque

Since the 13C Pont-l'Évêque has been famous for its cheese. Only a few old houses remain, mostly in rue St-Michel and rue de Vaucelles. The Aigle d'Or Inn *(68 r. de Vaucelles)* was a post house in the 16C and has retained the Norman courtyard of the period.

The **Église St-Michel** is a fine church in Flamboyant style flanked by a square tower. The modern stained-glass windows (1963–64) are by François Chapuis. An interesting wooden balcony decorates the old **Dominican Convent**, a 16C half-timbered building beside

the Law Courts (Tribunal). The **Hôtel Montpensier**, a building in the Louis XIII style has two corner pavilions.

The 18C Hôtel Brilly (restored) now houses the town hall and the Tourist Information Centre.

◑ *Continue NW to Canapville.*

Canapville

Manoir des Évêques de Lisieux.
&⟳Visit by guided tour (45min) only *Jul–Aug Wed–Mon 2–7pm. ∞€6. ℘02 31 65 24 75.www.manoirdeseveques.fr.*

The 13C–15C **Manoir des Évêques de Lisieux** is one of the most charming country houses in the Pays d'Auge. It consists of the large manor, with three monumental stone chimneys, and the small manor with a bishop's head carved on the entrance post. The 18C ground-floor rooms display Chinese porcelain.

◑ *Take the N 13 towards Pont-l'Évêque, turn right to rejoin D 58.*

Beaumont-en-Auge

This small town, remarkably situated on a spur commanding the Touques Valley, was the birthplace of the mathematician and physicist Pierre **Simon, Marquis de Laplace** (1749–1827). His house and statue are on place de Verdun.

◑ *D 58 south; left on N 175; right on D 280 and pass under the motorway.*

St-Hymer

Pleasantly set in a valley, the village has a 14C **church** with traces of Romanesque in its style. Its belfry is a replica of that of Port-Royal-des-Champs, the famous Jansenist abbey south-west of Paris.

Pierrefitte-en-Auge

Church. ○Contact the Auberge des Deux Tonneaux. ℘02 31 64 09 31.

In the 13C **church** the nave arches are decorated with cameo paintings of landscapes. There is a fine 16C rood beam.

Coquainvilliers

Distillerie Boulard. ♿ 🔊 *Guided tour (30min) possible Apr–Sept 10am–12.30pm, 2–6pm; rest of year, weekdays 10am–12.30pm, 2–6pm.* ∞€3.30. ☎02 31 62 60 54. *www.calvados-boulard.com.*

A guided tour describes the making of apple brandy (Calvados) and traditional distillation techniques.

Ouilly-le-Vicomte

Church. Apply to the mairie to visit. ☎02 31 61 12 64 or to M Aillaume. ☎02 31 62 29 02.

The **church** standing beside the road which spans the Touques is one of the oldest in Normandy, dating from the 10C and 11C.

Parc du château de Boutemont

🕐*Jul–Aug 10am–noon, 3–6pm; Apr–Jun and Sept–Oct Wed–Sun 10am–noon, 3–6pm.* 🔊*Guided tours available (1hr30min by appt).* ∞€8 *(-12 years €3).* ☎02 31 61 12 16.

This pretty French-style park is set around a château built 14–16C. Both are registered as Historical Monuments. The château *(closed to public)* is surrounded by dry moats and consists of a postern, a drawbridge and four corner towers. There is a beautiful view of both château and park from the pretty chapel on the heights behind them.

▶ *Continue east; at the crossroads turn right onto D 579 to Lisieux.*

3 HAUTE VALLÉE DE LA TOUQUES

75km/46.6mi. Allow 3hr round-trip from Lisieux – 👁*see Lisieux.*

▶ *Leave Lisieux via D 579, turn left onto D 64.*

Fervaques

Château. Only the exterior can be visited; call for times. ∞€6 *for a brochure.* ☎02 31 32 33 96.

The 16C and 17C **château** overlooking the Touques is a vast building of brick and stone. Fervaques was the retreat of Delphine de Custine, a friend of the author F R de Chateaubriand (1768–1848), who also stayed there.

▶ *In Les Moutiers-Hubert turn right onto D 64 towards Gacé. At the crossroads turn left onto D 16 and immediately right. Cross the river in Canapville; turn right onto D 33 and continue south. South of Ticheville station cross the railway line. At the next junction turn right onto D 242; after 1km/0.6mi turn right to Vimoutiers.*

Bellou

In the village centre stands Manoir de Bellou, a pleasant 16C timber-framed manor house. The road (D 110) runs southeast through the Moutiers-Hubert Forest and passes the Manoir de Cheffreteau.

Vimoutiers

👁*See Vimoutiers, p205.*

▶ *Take D 579 north and continue along D 579.*

Livarot

Home of the cheese of the same name, this village has some beautiful houses.

▶ *Continue north on D 579; bear right onto D 268.*

Manoir de Coupesarte★

🕐*9am–8pm.* ∞*No charge. Interior closed to visitors.*

This beautiful residence, surrounded by water on three sides, is the main building of the farm. The construction is late 15C or early 16C. Its gracious half-timbered façade has two corner turrets. There is a very beautiful view of the manor's front, from a field to the left after the little lock.

St-Germain-de-Livet★

Château. Feb–Nov, Wed–Mon 11am–6pm. 🔊*Guided tours (1hr) at 11.15am, noon, 2pm, 3pm, 4pm and 5pm (visit to park, last entry 5.30pm).* 🕐*Closed Dec–Jan, early Oct–mid-Oct and 1 May.*

Château de St-Germain-de-Livet

© Francis Cormon/hemis.fr

≈€6.75; no charge 1st Sun of month. ✆02 31 31 00 03.
This delightful **château** consists of a 16C wing, decorated in a highly original stone and brick check pattern, adjoining a 15C half-timbered structure.
The 15C wing contains the guard-room, decorated with 16C **frescoes** (battle scene; Judith bearing the head of Holofernes), and a dining room with Empire-style furniture. On the first floor of the 16C wing are two rooms beautifully tiled in terracotta from the Pays d'Auge, the so-called bedroom of the painter Eugène Delacroix (1798–1863), the gallery with paintings by the Riesener family (19C) and a small round Louis XVI salon.

Crèvecœur-en-Auge

Crèvecœur is a pleasant town situated in the Auge Valley. Some 500m/547yd to the north and to the right of N 13 is the Château de Crèvecœur.

SIGHTS
👤👤 Château★

&🕐Open Jul–Aug daily 11am–7pm; end Mar–end Jun and Sept, 11am–6pm; Oct Sun 2–6pm. ≈€6.50. ✆02 31 63 02 45. www.chateau-de-crevecoeur.com. A mystery visit is organised in the château. As a family, you help the curator to find missing objects. There are six children's learning workshops: from marsh to moat,

▶ **Population:** 525.
⚲ *Michelin Map:* 303: M-5 – Local map, see Pays d'Auge, p180.
🛈 **Info:** Consult tourist offices in Lisieux and the Pays d'Auge.
▶ **Location:** Crèvecœur is on N 13 between Caen (43km/26.7mi W) and Lisieux (20km/12.4mi E).
👁 **Don't Miss:** The wonderful dovecote at the château.
🕐 **Timing:** As the château opens only at 11am, use the early morning to see the manor of Coupesarte.

Manoir de Coupesarte

© Brigitte Merle/Photononstop

about water at Crèvecoeur; daily life in the Middle Ages; a medieval treasure hunt; medicinal and pot plants; and discovery of the ground under their feet.

Encircled by trees and moats, the timber-framed buildings of the **château** – its motte was erected in the 11C – were transformed in the 15C and restored in 1972. They now form a highly picturesque sight: an outer bailey and feudal motte surrounded by a filled-in moat. The 16C gatehouse used to stand beside the former Château de Beuvilliers near Lisieux.

The 16C barn and 15C manor are home to the collections of the **Musée Schlumberger**, named after two Alsatian brothers Conrad and Marcel; in 1928 these geophysicists and petroleum engineers invented the continuous electric logging of boreholes, a technique that was to be extended to countries all over the world.

The museum displays equipment used in oil drilling and prospecting. The **dovecote**, a remarkable construction, is square shaped. Note the projecting eaves formed by the shingled roofing, visible on all four sides of the building. On the side facing winds, is a shelf from which the pigeons are released. The interior woodwork is pierced with 1,500 pigeon-holes *(boulins)*.

The 12C **chapel** features oak framework in the shape of an upturned hull, as well as fragments of a medieval wall painting. The farm buildings contain the second part of the museum, devoted to **Normandy architecture**, which presents examples of traditional timber-framed architecture from the Pays d'Auge. The History Room (Salle d'Histoire) displays miscellaneous objects retracing the history of Crèvecœur-en-Auge over the centuries. If not about in the poultry yard, ask to see the **Crèvecoeur hens**. Feathers ruffled, sporting a pretty crest, these rare birds are the last of a local race.

EXCURSION
Manoir de Coupesarte★

▶ *15km/9mi SE. Leave Crèvecœur-en-Auge by D 16 towards St-Pierre-sur-Dives. At Mesnil-Mauger, turn left onto D 47. Cross Authieux-Papion, then just after St-Julien-le-Faucon, turn right onto D 47. Coupesarte is 1.5km/0.9mi further.*
🕐 *Grounds open daily 9am–7pm.*
No charge. ℘02 31 63 82 12.

This charming half-timbered residence (⚊ *interior closed to the public*) surrounded by water on three sides is the main house of a farm. The construction goes back to the end of the 15C or beginning of the 16C. From the field on the left beyond the small lock there is a good view of the half-timbered façade with its two corner turrets reminiscent of watchtowers.

Vimoutiers

The small town of Vimoutiers is tucked away in the valley of the River Vie between hills covered with apple trees that supply the local cider factories. Vimoutiers has close ties with Marie Harel, who gave us the famous Camembert cheese. A statue to her memory, offered by an American cheesemaker, stands on the town hall square.

▶ **Population:** 4,029.

⊙ **Michelin Map:** 310: K-1.

🔲 **Info:** 21 place Mackau. ℘02 33 67 49 42.

⊙ **Location:** Vimoutiers is 28km/17.5mi S of Lisieux via D 579, and 45km/28mi SW of Bernay.

VISIT

Musée du Camembert

10 av. du Gén. de Gaulle. ⚹ ✦ *Audio-guided tours (20min) Apr–Oct Thu–Mon 2–5.30pm.* ⊚€3. ℘02 33 39 30 29. The exhibition describes the history and manufacturing process of Camembert. Note the collection of Camembert labels. The legend has it that, during the French Revolution, Marie Harel protected a fugitive priest who, in compensation, revealed to her his secret cheese recipe.

EXCURSIONS

Camembert

⊙ *5km/3mi S by D 246.*

Maison du Camembert – ⚹ ⊙*Open May–Aug daily 10am–12.30pm; Apr Wed–Sun 10am–noon, 2–5.30pm; rest of year, contact for info.* ⊚*No charge.* ℘02 33 12 10 37. www.maisonducamembert.com. This modern museum (1992), shaped like an open Camembert cheese box,

lies at the heart of this tiny village, facing the 13C church. Information on the famous cheese and where it is made is displayed. It is also possible to visit a few farms where the cheese is made according to traditional methods.

Prieuré St-Michel de Crouttes★

⊙ *5km/3mi W via the D 916, then take the third road to the right.* ⚹⊙*Open May–Sept Wed–Sun 2–6pm (last admission 30min before closing).* ⊚€6. ℘02 33 39 15 15. www.prieure-saint-michel.com. The origin of this monastic house dates from the 10C. The noble rustic architecture of the buildings is admirably set off by an orchard, gardens and water. Beyond the 18C dairy is the 13C **tithe barn**. One can also see the 18C prior's lodging, the chapel (13C) and the bakery, an 18C timber-framed building. Part of the priory is operated as a bed-and-breakfast, with reception rooms and tea room.

Labels of Camembert cheese

© Hervé Lenain/hemis.fr

ADDRESSES

🛏 STAY

HONFLEUR

🏕 **Camping La Briquerie** – ✆02 31 89 28 32. www.campinglabriquerie.com. Open Apr–Sept. 430 sites. Restaurant 🍴. Set on the edge of a forest, this campground has sites separated by hedges of shrubs or flowers. Some small but well-kept self-catered cottages. Large swimming pool, games-room and miniature golf. Restaurant-bar with meals in season.

🏠 **Chambre d'hôte Le Vieux Pressoir** – Hameau le Clos-Potier, 27210 Conteville, 13.5/ 8.5mi from Honfleur via D 580, rte de Pont-Audemer then left on D 312. ✆02 35 57 60 79. www.la-ferme-du-pressoir.com. 7 rooms. Restaurant 🍴🍴. Set in the countryside, this 18C half-timbered farm will delight those who appreciate calm and simplicity. Every room contains 19C and 20C objects and furniture. Flower garden, duck pond and 300-year-old cider press add to the charm.

🏠 **Kyriad Hôtel** – 62 cours A.-Manuel. ✆02 31 89 41 77. www.kyriad.fr. 50 rooms. 🅿 🍽€9. Restaurant 🍴🍴. At a distance from the city centre, this hotel offers rooms at reasonable prices. Small and functional, they make for an agreeable stay. A garden and a terrace let you bask in the gentle Norman sun.

🏠 **Chambre d'hôte Cour Ste-Catherine** – 74 r. du Puits. ✆02 31 89 42 40. www.giaglis.com. 5 rooms. 🍽. Housed in a 17C convent, this pleasant inn offers five elegant guest rooms, opening onto a flower garden. In the lounge there is some pretty furniture and a fireplace. Breakfast is served in the old cider-press. Charming welcome from the owners.

🏠 **Hôtel Le Belvédère** – 36 r. Émile-Renouf. ✆02 31 89 08 13. www.hotel-belvedere-honfleur.com. Closed Jan. 9 rooms. 🍽€8. Restaurant 🍴🍴. This old town house gets its name from the view from its roof. Peaceful rooms whose cottage setting offers an incomparable view over the Normandy bridge. Pretty garden and good restaurant.

🏠–🏠 **Hôtel Romantica** – ch. Petit-Paris, 14600 Pennedepie, 8km/5mi NE of Honfleur. ✆02 31 81 14 00. www.romantica-honfleur.com. 35 rooms. 🍽€9. Restaurant 🍴🍴. Perched high in the village, this

hotel offers peace and comfort. There is a fine view over the sea from the restaurant. Three swimming pools.

🏠 **Auberge de la Source** – 14600 Barneville-la-Bertran, 5.5km/3.4mi SW of Honfleur. ✆02 31 89 25 02. www.auberge-de-la-source.fr. 16 rooms. 🍽€11. Set in the countryside, this beautiful half-timbered farmhouse has a lovely garden with apple orchards.

TROUVILLE-SUR-MER

🏠 **Hôtel Le Fer à Cheval** – 11 r. Victor-Hugo. ✆02 31 98 30 20. www.hotel-trouville.com. 34 rooms. 🍽€10. These two old villas at the centre of the resort, near the beaches, offer functional rooms. The proprietor, a former baker, offers delicious croissants and pastries at breakfast and afternoon tea.

🏠 **Hôtel Le Trouville** – r. Thiers. ✆02 31 98 45 48. www.hotelletrouville.com. Closed Jan. 15 rooms. 🍽€7. If the façade is a bit tired, the interior is bright and clean. The rooms, two of them for families, have complete bathrooms and new beds. Good value for money.

🏠 **Hôtel les Sablettes** – 15 r. Paul-Besson. ✆02 31 88 10 66. www.trouville-hotel.com. Closed Nov. 18 rooms. 🍽€7. Away from traffic, this hotel offers simple, practical accommodation. Close to the casino and beach.

DEAUVILLE

🏠 **Hôtel Le Patio** – 180 av. de la République. ✆02 31 88 25 07. www.hotel-lepatio.fr. 13 rooms. 🍽. The name tells it all: this century-old edifice with an immaculate façade possesses an enticing, flower-filled patio where breakfasts are served as soon as the weather warms up. The rooms, each one different, are regularly spruced up.

🏠 **Hôtel Hélios** – 10 r. Fossorier. ✆02 31 14 46 46. www.hotelhelios deauville.com. Closed 7–21 Jan. 43 rooms. 🍽€8.50. A practical address at resort centre. Simple rooms freshened up and a small apartment appreciated by families. Mini-swimming pool.

🏠 **Hôtel Le Chantilly** – 120 av. de la République. ✆02 31 88 79 75. 17 rooms, €65/115. 🍽€8.50. This townhouse near the hippodrome has well-looked after rooms. Breakfast in a small dining room.

🏠 **Hôtel L'Époi d'Or** – 23 av. Michel-d'Ornano, 14910 Blonville-sur-Mer. ✆02 31 87 90 48. www.hotel-normand.com. Closed 9

Jan–18 Feb and 18–29 Dec. 40 rooms. ⌧€7.50. Restaurant⌂⊟. Well-renovated pretty Norman-style building. Bright, functional rooms. Enjoy a traditional menu in the lovely restaurant or quick snack in the brasserie.

⌂⊟–⌂⊟⊟ **Hôtel Le Continental** – 1 r. Désiré-Le-Hoc. ℘02 31 88 21 06. www.hotel-continental-deauville.com. Closed 13 Nov–20 Dec. 42 rooms. ⌧€8.50. This hotel, built in 1880, is close to the station. Small, nicely furnished rooms. Pleasant breakfast room.

⌂⊟⊟⊟ **Hôtel Normandy-Barrière** – 38 r. Jean-Mermoz. ℘02 31 98 66 22. www. lucienbarriere.com. 259 rooms. ⌧€30. This elegant timber-framed manor house dating from 1912 is situated in the liveliest part of town: facing the sea, near the casino and the shopping district. A sumptuous hotel that will cater to your every desire. The place to be in this town where everything glitters.

CABOURG

⌂ **Hôtel de Paris** – 39 av. de la Mer. ℘ 02 31 91 31 34.www.hotel-de-paris-cabourg.fr. Closed Jan. 🖻 24 rooms. ⌧ €6.80. Hotel on the city's busiest street, two minutes from the ocean. Bar with outdoor tables.

⌂⊟⊟ **Chambre d'hôte Ferme de l'Oraille** – Chemin de Deraine, 14430 Douville-en-Auge, 7km/4.3mi SE of Dives-sur-Mer via D 45, D 27 between la Maison-Blanche and La Croix d'Heuland. ℘02 31 79 25 49. 2 rooms. ⌧. Restaurant ⌂⊟⊟⊟. At this 18C Norman farm, which still produces dairy products, you can enjoy simple country comfort and farm-fresh food.

LISIEUX

⌂ **Camping de la Vallée** – Route de la Vallée. ℘ 02 31 62 00 40. 1 Apr–30 Sept. Reservation advised. 75 sites. North of Lisieux, 1.5km/1mi from town centre, this campsite is ideal for visiting Lisieux and surrounding area. Weekend bungalow rentals.

⌂ **Hôtel St-Louis** – 4 r. St-Jacques. ℘02 31 62 06 50. www.hotelsaintlouis-lisieux. com. 17 rooms. ⌧€7. New, bright wallpaper, new furniture, improved bathrooms; family hotel with a little garden.

⌂ **La Coupe d'Or** – 49 r. Pont-Mortain. ℘ 02 31 31 16 84. www.la-coupe-dor.com. closed Sun night and Mon noon. 16 rooms. ⌧€8. Restaurant ⌂–⌂⊟⊟. Although in

a busy downtown street, calm reigns in this hotel-restaurant. French billiards and office with Internet access. Decent prices.

⌂⊟ **Hôtel de la Place** – 67 r. Henry-Chéron. ℘02 31 48 27 27. www.lisieux-hotel-delaplace. com. Closed 16 Dec–7 Jan. 33 rooms. ⌧€10. The rooms are of varying sizes, but all have been renovated and are bright and modern.

⌂⊟⊟ **Hôtel Azur** – 15 r. au Char. ℘02 31 62 09 14. www.hotel-azur-lisieux. fr. Closed 15 Dec–15 Jan. 15 rooms. ⌧€9. This hotel occupies a 1960s building. Comfortable rooms. Breakfast served in a winter garden.

⌂⊟⊟ **CERZA Safari Lodge** – CERZA zoological park, D 143, 14100 Hermival-les-Vaux. ℘ 02 31 81 82 30. www.cerzasafarilodge. com. Closed Dec–Mar. 6 yurts, 2 observation teepees in wood. ⌧€6.50. Save on the airfare for an African safari and replace it with this unusual stay in Normandy in a zoological park. Functional but comfortable.

⌂⊟⊟–⌂⊟⊟⊟ **Grand Hôtel de l'Espérance** – 16 bd Ste-Anne. ℘02 31 62 17 53. www.lisieux-hotel.com. Closed 22 Oct–end Mar. 100 rooms. ⌧€10. Large hotel in pure Norman style in town centre. Traditional beams and balconies. Decent rooms, fine dining.

PAYS D'AUGE

⌂⊟ **Chambre d'hôte Le Manoir de Cantepie** –Le Cadran, 14340 Cambremer, 11km/7mi W of Lisieux via N 13, then D 50. ℘02 31 62 87 27. Closed 15 Nov–1 Mar. 3 rooms. Reservations required. ⌧. Splendid 17C manor offering a delightful, elegant stay at a reasonable price.

⌂⊟ **Chambre d'hôte Les Marronniers** – Les Marronniers, 14340 Cambremer. ℘02 31 63 08 28. www.les-marronniers.com. Closed 15 Nov–15 Feb. 4 rooms. ⌧. This charming 17C residence, surrounded by a flower garden, has a superb view over the Dives Valley. The guest rooms are spacious, and breakfast is served on a pleasant terrace.

🍴 EAT

HONFLEUR

⌂ **Ex-Voto** – 8 pl. Albert-Sorel. ℘02 31 89 19 69. Closed Wed, 1 Nov, 25 Dec. Reservations advised. ⌧. One of the few inexpensive yet good-value restaurants in town, this place will make you nostalgic for the neighbourhood bistro. The proprietress concocts special dishes and short orders from fresh market produce. Very few tables, best to reserve.

⊜⊜ **Auberge du Vieux Clocher** – *9 r. de-l'Homme-de-Bois. ℘02 31 89 12 06. Closed 14–30 Jan, 20–30 Jun, 20–30 Oct, 24–25 Dec, Mon and Tue.* Small dining rooms are panelled in wood, with touches of pastel colours, and old plates decorate the walls. Traditional cuisine, with an accent on seafood.

⊜⊜ **La Tortue** – *36 r. de l'Homme-de-Bois. ℘02 31 81 24 60. www.restaurantlatortue.fr.* In a little street of old Honfleur, this regional restaurant has daily specials depending on the catch of the day.

⊜⊜ **Le Bistrot des Artistes** – *14 pl. Berthelot. ℘02 31 89 95 90. Closed Jan, Mar, Oct–Apr and Wed from Oct–Jun.* Antiques, paintings of the sea, photos of Honfleur and leather seating make up the décor of this restaurant with a Parisian bistro flair. Tables near the window have a lovely view of the Vieux Bassin. On the menu: salads and slices of bread with various toppings.

⊜⊜–⊜⊜⊜ **Entre Terre et Mer** – *12 pl. Hamelin. ℘02 31 89 70 60. www. entreterreetmer-honfleur.com. 11 rooms ⊜⊜–⊜⊜⊜. ⊠.* Two pleasant, modern dining areas. One is rustic with wooden beams and rush flooring, the other has tiled floors and is decorated with photographs of Normandy. Serving modern cuisine including both meat and seafood dishes.

⊜⊜ **Au P'tit Mareyeur** – *4 r. Haute. 02 31 98 84 23. www.auptitmareyeur.com. Closed Jan, Mon and Tue. Reservations required.* This tiny restaurant near Honfleur's fishing port is ideal for an intimate meal. Maritime touches add to the cosy feel. Fish and seafood are recommended here.

⊜⊜⊜ **Au Vieux Honfleur** – *13 quai St-Étienne. ℘02 31 89 15 31. www.auvieux honfleur.com. Closed 25 Dec.* This restaurant by the old harbour extends its terrace along the quay when the weather is fine. Savour Norman dishes and seafood while gazing upon the splendid port.

⊜⊜⊜ **La Fleur de Sel** – *17 r. Haute. ℘02 31 89 01 92. www.lafleurdesel-honfleur.com.* The two small dining-rooms with neo-rustic décor at this gourmet restaurant serve good meat and seafood dishes.

⊜⊜⊜ **Le Bréard** – *7 r. du Puits. ℘02 31 89 53 40. www.restaurant-lebreard.com. Closed 31 Jan–4 Feb, 21 Nov–9 Dec, Tue noon, Thu noon, Wed.* Near Ste-Catherine Church, this restaurant has a green façade and two dining rooms. Modern cuisine.

⊜⊜⊜⊜ **Sa. Qua. Na** – *22 pl. Hamelin. ℘ 02 31 89 40 80. www.alexandre-bourdas. com. Closed mid-Jan–end Feb, Wed, Thu and noon on weekdays.* Sa.Qua.Na stands for "savours, quality, nature". Surprising cuisine, both technical and intuitive. Modern décor. Specialities.

TROUVILLE-SUR-MER

⊜ **Le Cap Horn** – *20 r. des Bains. ℘02 31 98 45 06. Closed Mon eve, Tue.* Behind the pretty stone façade are two dining rooms. The upper floor has seaside décor and a terrace. Seafood menu based on the daily catch.

DEAUVILLE

⊜ **Dupont avec un thé** – *20 pl. Morny. ℘02 31 88 20 79. www.patisseriedupont.com.* This shop offers wonderful desserts such as lemon-scented sugar biscuits and coffee-flavoured macaroons. Light meals and a hearty breakfast menu.

⊜⊜ **Bar de la Mer** – *Casino Barrière de Deauville. ℘02 31 88 27 51. www.lucien barriere.com. Closed Nov–15 Feb except public holidays and Fri–Mon during school holidays.* This restaurant, located right on the famous boardwalk, offers a pleasant dining room, an enormous terrace on the beach and a splendid view of the ocean. On the menu: shellfish, grilled meat and salads.

⊜⊜ **Le Comptoir et la Table** – *1 quai de la Marine. ℘ 02 31 88 92 51. Closed 15 days in Nov and Jan.* Wonderful conviviality in this marina restaurant; wood counter and Trouville painting (1947) on the ceiling. Bistro food and great wines.

⊜⊜ **Le Garage** – *118 bis av. de la République. ℘02 31 87 25 25. Closed 11 Dec–7 Jan.* This former garage is now a brasserie. Changing menu and a good choice of seafood.

⊜⊜ **Le Nautica** – *2 r. Désir.-Le Hoc. ℘02 31 88 03 27. Closed Wed out of season, except during school holidays.* The atmosphere of an English pub prevails, with a little touch of the sea, in this brasserie near the train station. The menu offers dishes prepared in the kitchen, smoked salmon and foie gras included.

⊜⊜ **Le Yearling** – *38 av. Hocquart de Turto. ℘02 31 88 33 37. www.le-yearling.fr. Closed 9 Jan–2 Feb, Mon and Tue except Jul–Aug.*

Serving typical French cuisine, its speciality is the grilled Breton lobster served in a *beurre blanc* sauce.

⊜⊜⊜ **La Flambée** – *181 r Gén.-Leclerc.* ℘*02 31 88 28 46. www.laflambee-deauville.com. Closed 2–15 Jan.* Grilled steaks and chops are prepared in the vast open hearth, right before your eyes. There is also more traditional cuisine and, in a tank for your inspection, lobsters.

⊜⊜⊜ **La Galerie de Tourgéville** – *14800 Tourgéville, 6km/3.7mi S of Deauville via D 278 and D 27.* ℘*02 31 87 31 11. www.galeriedetourgeville.com. Closed 1–15 Feb and 1–15 Nov, Mar and Wed.* A restaurant decorated with sundry bric-a-brac and an art gallery. The menu is simple and trendy; the Deauville Parisians simply *adore* it!

⊜⊜⊜ **Le Kraal - La Table d'Auge** – *Pl. du Marché.* ℘*02 31 88 30 58. Reservations advised summer and weekends.* Fresh shellfish, delicious, authentic regional recipes.

CABOURG

⊜ **Dupont avec un Thé** – *6 av. de la Mer.* ℘*02 31 24 60 32. Closed Tue and Wed out of season, noon on Mon, Thu and Fri out of season except school holidays.* A tea salon offering a range of delicious cakes and sweets, notably chocolate and caramel. Branches are located in Dives, Deauville and Trouville.

⊜⊜ **Le Champagne-Ardennes** – *11 pl. du Marché.* ℘*02 31 91 02 29. Closed Mon out of season.* ⊑. Opposite the market, this modest hotel-restaurant is both convenient and well managed. An elegant dining room with a menu specialising in seafood. Upstairs, comfortable guest rooms.

LISIEUX

⊜⊜ **Auberge de La Levrette** – *48 r. de Lisieux, 14140 Saint-Julien-le-Faucon, 20km/12.4mi SW of Lisieux.* ℘*02 31 63 81 20. Closed 26 Jun–2 Jul, 20 Dec–17 Jan, Mon and Tue except public holidays.* Half-timbered house (1550), mechanical music museum. Traditional food.

⊜ **Aux 1001 crêpes** – *16 r. Henry-Chéron.* ℘ *02 31 62 46 88.* On the ground floor of a beautiful 15C wooden building. Low prices for crêpes and salads. Warm welcome.

⊜⊜ **Aux Acacias** – *13 r. de la Résistance.* ℘ *02 31 62 10 95. Closed Sun evening and Mon except holidays, Thu night from Nov–Apr and 25–31 Dec.* Pleasant restaurant with Provençal atmosphere. Traditional cuisine, Norman ingredients.

⊜⊜⊜ **De La Paquine** – *Rte de Moyaux, 14590 Ouilly-du-Houley.* ℘ *02 31 63 63 80. championlapaquine@orange.fr. Closed Sun evening, Tue evening, Wed; 2-17 Mar, 7–22 Sep and 9 Nov–2 Dec.* A flower-decked little inn on entering the village; seasonal menu, warm rustic setting.

PAYS D'AUGE

⊜⊜ **Auberge des Deux Tonneaux** – *14130 Pierrefitte-en-Auge.* ℘ *02 31 64 09 31. www.aubergedesdeuxtonneaux.com. Closed Sun evening and Mon except school holidays.* Beautiful 17C half-timbered house with a thatched roof and terrace overlooking the Touques Valley. Dishes typical of the Pays d'Auge.

🎭 NIGHTLIFE

HONFLEUR

Evenings in Honfleur, the Old Port comes alive. Restaurants, brasseries and bars are clustered on the quais Ste-Catherine, La Quarantaine and St-Etienne. Terraces remain open until 2am in summer.

La Petite Chine – *14-16 r. du Dauphin.* ℘ *02 31 89 36 52. Wed–Mon 10am–7pm. Closed 2 weeks end Jun.* This pretty tea room and pastry shop overlooks the port. 120 types of tea.

Pomme'cannelle – *60 quai Ste-Catherine.* ℘ *02 31 89 55 25. Off-season: 9am–7.30pm; in season: 8am–midnight; closed Dec–Jan.* These ice creams and sherberts must absolutely be tasted: licorice, cinnamon apple, apricot, salty-butter caramel, etc.

🎭 ON THE TOWN

DEAUVILLE

Casino – *R. Edmond-Blanc.* ℘*02 31 14 31 14. www.lucienbarriere.com.* 325 slot machines, punto-banco, and more.

Les Planches – *Le Bois Lauret, 14910 Blonville-sur-Mer, 6km/3.7mi SW of Deauville in the countryside.* ℘*02 31 87 58 09. www.les planches.com. Closed Jan.* All of preppy Paris haunts this disco, known for its Cuban bar, loft and heated pool.

Martine Lambert – *76 bis r. Eugène-Colas.* ℘*02 31 88 94 04.* Made from Norman cows' milk, Martine Lambert's ice cream is subtle and delicious. Her shops are also found in Paris and Trouville.

CABOURG

Bar du Grand Hôtel – *prom. Marcel-Proust.* ℘*02 31 91 01 79.* The Grand Hôtel, with its Belle époque style, huge chandeliers and full draperies, is a monument to nostalgia. You needn't be a guest to have tea here, or better yet, enjoy a snifter of 40-year-old Calvados, while gazing out to sea.

Grand Casino – *prom. Marcel-Proust.* ℰ*02 31 28 19 19.* In addition to its gambling facilities, the casino houses a disco (500 people), a performance hall (500 seats), an Italian-style theatre (up to 500 seats) and a panoramic restaurant facing the ocean. Terrace by the sea.

🛒 SHOPPING

HONFLEUR

Markets – *pl. Ste-Catherine.* Antique market 2nd Sun of each month. Weekly market Sat am featuring local produce and fish. Organic produce market Wed. Evening market Wed in Jul–Aug. Flower market Sat am on place Arthur-Boudin.

Griboulle – *16 r. de l'Homme-de-Bois.* M. Griffoul, nicknamed Gribouille, is an unforgettable local character. He sells Norman shortbread, milk, jam, potted rabbit, preserved pork, cider products, etc. Sample the *pommeau* or Calvados.

La Cave Normande – *13 r. de la Ville and 12 quai Ste-Catherine.* This is where you will find top-quality Calvados as well as cider, perry and *pommeau.*

🏃 LEISURE

HONFLEUR

Centre équestre du Ramier – *ch. du Ramier, 14600 Equemauville, 3.6km/2.2mi SW of Honfleur.* ℰ*02 31 89 49 97. Closed 2 weeks in Sept.* This pretty riding centre has 15 training horses available. Rides last for 1hr–1hr30min.

DEAUVILLE

Le Circuit de Deauville – *rte de Caen, 14800 St-Arnoult, 4km/2.5mi S ofDeauville.* ℰ*02 31 81 31 31 www.dupratconcept.com. From €20.* Sizeable amusement park specialising in motor sports: go-carting. speed boats and jet skis, safety driving courses and more.

CABOURG

Les écuries de la Sablonnière – *av. Guillaume-le-Conquérant, rte de Caen, opposite the Vert Pré campsite.* ℰ*02 31 91 61 70. http://sablonniere.neuf.fr. Open Fri–Wed (daily during school holidays) 9am–12.30pm, 2–6pm.* This club organises horseback rides on the beach and in the hinterland for all levels of experience.

🐾 GUIDED TOURS

HONFLEUR

Honfleur's tourist office offers tours around the town. A tour is the best way to see the famous *greniers à sel* (salt stores). Contact the tourist office.

CALENDAR OF EVENTS

DEAUVILLE

Jun – International Sailing Week and Jumping International. Opening of the horseracing season.

Aug – Musical August (Août musical) music festival, polo championship, horse races, sale of yearlings.

Sept – Festival of American Cinema.

Organic produce market, Honfleur

© www.calvados-tourisme.com

PLAINE DE L'EURE *and Pays d'Ouche*

This region is one of the least-known and most endearing parts of Upper Normandy. Time is suspended here. Only twenty years ago it was still common to see men ploughing their fields by hand and donkeys carrying loads of milk. Hedges enclose and protect little farms, where land is laboured over and crops are dearly earned. Ancient, authentic, the very name of this country, "Ouche", would seem to come from the pre-Celtic "Utica", making this one of the oldest names in Normandy.

Ancient fields

The Eure plain holds fields of cereal crops and pasture, punctuated here and there by curtains of trees or more substantial hints of forest at valley edges. It is difficult to precisely date when the land was first shaped in this way by man, although it is undoubtedly very ancient. The layout of the farms resembles that of Roman latifundia, and is directly inherited from Gallo-Roman villas. Traces do remain and are found regularly from this period, and it is known that the roads crossing this land lie on the old Roman ways.

The French who know Normandy cherish this countryside, which certainly explains the peppering of second homes to be found here.

Pays d'Ouche

The Pays d'Ouche, crossed by the Upper Risle Valley, lies between the Charentonne, Iton and Rouloire rivers. With its clayish soils and calcareous layers acting as sponges to retain moisture, the land is grassy and crisscrossed with hedges: the famous *bocage* country.

Farmers in the Pays d'Ouche traditionally both produce food and gather it. In other words, with a vegetable garden, orchard, poultry yard, and a few animals at pasture on land they generally own, they also gather mushrooms, nuts and berries from the stretches of forest. The day labourers here also often work at the great farms of the Le Neubourg plateau.

Highlights

1 Dream at Diane de Poitier's beloved Château **d'Anet** (p217)

2 Admire craftsmanship of the 13C **St Taurinus** reliquary (p220)

3 See cave mushroom cultivation at **La Champignonnière** (p227)

4 A contemplative moment at **Abbaye du Bec Hellouin** (p228)

5 The **Château du Champ-de-Bataille** gardens (p230)

Chapel, Château d'Anet

© J-C.&D. Pratt/Photononstop

211

PLAINE DE L'EURE AND THE PAYS D'OUCHE

Le Bec-Hellouin	★★ Recommended
Évreux	★ Interesting
Tilly	Worth a visit
⇨	Driving tour with departure point
	Border and area of coverage

0   10 km
0   5 miles

ROUEN

SEINE-MARITIME

EURE

Le Neubourg
Le Tremblay-Omonville
Évreux
Vallée du Rouloir
Conches-en-Ouche
Breteuil-sur-Iton
Chambray
Tilliers-s-Avre
Nonancourt
Verneuil-s-Avre

La Croix-St-Leufroy
Cocherel
Miserey
Le Vieil-Évreux
La Folletière
Obélisque d'Ivry
Forêt d'Ivry
Ézy-s-Eure
Courdemanche
Dreux

Pacy-s-Eure
La Couture-Boussey
Ivry-la-Bataille
Anet
Forêt de Dreux
Mézières-en-Drouais

EURE-ET-LOIR

SEINE

PARIS

CHARTRES   MAINTENON

Dreux★

Dreux is set on the boundary between Normandy and Île-de-France; it is a lively regional market town earning its living from diverse industrial activities. The town is the final resting place of members of the Orléans family, one of France's royal lines; they can be viewed in the crypt of the Royal Chapel of St-Louis where their tombs comprise an impressive collection of 19C sculpture. Nearby, the Eure Valley contains lovely surprises, notably the château of Anet.

▶ **Population:** 32,155.
⟡ **Michelin Map:** 311: E-3.
▤ **Info:** Cour de l'Hôtel-Dieu. ℘02 37 46 01 73. www.ot-dreux.fr.
◖ **Location:** Dreux is 85 km/52.8mi W of Paris via N 12, and 48km/29.8mi E of l'Aigle. The historic centre is on the left bank, and the Grande-Rue (rue Maurice-Violette) is the liveliest street.
◉ **Don't Miss:** The Royal Chapel and the Renaissance Château d'Anet.
◕ **Timing:** You'll need 2hr to see the town, and another 2hr for the Château d'Anet. Make time for a picnic on the château grounds.
👥 **Kids:** The Musée Marcel-Dessal has a children's itinerary.

A BIT OF HISTORY

Dreux rose to importance when the Normans settled west of the River Avre and Dreux Castle defended the French frontier against a belligerent neighbour. The castle, which stood on the hill now occupied by St Louis' Chapel, was besieged many times. It was dismantled on the orders of Henri IV, who razed the town in 1593 after a three-year siege.

In 1556, the Paris Parliament decided that the County of Dreux should in the future be the exclusive property of the French royal family. In 1775, Louis XVI ceded Dreux to his cousin, the Duc de Penthièvre, son of the Comte de Toulouse. Eight years later, when at the king's insistence the duc was forced to give up his magnificent property at Rambouillet, he arranged for the family tombs in the parish church of Rambouillet (subsequently destroyed) to be transferred to the collegiate church adjoining Dreux Castle. When the duc's daughter married Louis Philippe d'Orléans, known as Philippe Égalité, her dowry included the County of Dreux. It was thus that Dreux, which until the Revolution had been a simple family burial place, became the mausoleum of the Orléans family.

SIGHTS
Belfry★

Tourist office: ℘02 37 46 01 73.
At the end of the old Grande-Rue (Maurice-Violette) rises the ornate façade of the Hôtel de ville (town hall), which was built from 1512 to 1537.
The ground and first floors are decorated in the Flamboyant style; the Renaissance second floor shows the skill of a young architect from Dreux, **Clément Métézeau** (1479–1555).

Église St-Pierre

pl. Métézeau, opposite Belfry.
Built in the early 13C and partly damaged during the Hundred Years' War, St Peter's Church was heavily remodelled from the 15C to the 17C.
The façade dates from the 16C. Of the two towers designed to flank it, only the left one was completed. The gate, chancel and left arm of the transept are 13C. The right arm of the transept dates from the 16C to the 17C. The church interior is notable for its fine 15C and 16C **stained-glass windows**, to be found especially in the side chapels *(1st, 2nd and 3rd on the right; 2nd, 3rd and 4th on the left)* and apsidal chapel. The outstanding organ case (1614) is

WHERE TO STAY		WHERE TO EAT	
Beffroi (Hôtel le)	①	Market Pub	①
Dousseine (Hôtel la)	④	Quatre Vents (Aux)	②
Ferme des Luthiers (Chambre d'hôte la)	⑥	Saint Pierre (Le)	④
		Vallée Verte (Auberge de la)	⑥

the work of the local cabinetmaker Toussaint Fortier.

Grande-Rue

The former Grande-Rue, now rue Maurice-Violette, hums with activity most days of the week, particularly during summer festivals. Note at the corner of rue Illiers two 15C half-timbered houses whose upper storeys extend over the street.

Hôtel de Montulé

15 r. Godeau. ℘*02 37 38 87 51. Wed–Mon 2.30–6pm.* ✆*No charge.*
This townhouse built during the reign of Henri IV was a prison under the Revolution; it is today a major art centre, and offers temporary exhibitions.

Chapelle royale St-Louis

2 sq. d'Aumale. ✆*Guided tours possible (45min) Wed–Mon Jul–Aug 9.30am–12.30pm, 1.30–6pm; Apr–Jun and Sept 9.30am–noon, 1.30–5.30pm. Closed 1 Jan, 1 and 11 Nov and 25 Dec.* ✆*€7.70.* ℘*02 37 46 07 06.*
Before the Revolution this site was occupied by the Collegiate Church of St Stephen (St-Étienne). In 1783 it received the remains of members of the Toulouse-Penthièvre families.
In 1816 the dowager Duchess of Orléans, widow of Philippe Égalité, erected a chapel in the Neoclassical style. It was enlarged by her son Louis-Philippe (1773–1850) when he became king, and the exterior was embellished with bell

turrets and Gothic pinnacles. The building as a whole is a monument to the 19C for both the quality of its architecture and the work of talented artists.

The side windows make it possible to admire the stained-glass representations of the patron saints of France and the royal family: (left) St Philip, St Amelia, St Ferdinand (the heads are portraits). The stained glass in the apse illustrates the life of St Louis.

The main crypt contains the tombs of the Princes of Orléans; the recumbent figures form a little museum of 19C statuary by Mercié, Pradier, Dubois, Chapu, Millet, Lenoir, etc.

On the lower level, five extremely rare **glass panes painted with enamels**★★ catch the visitor's attention. They were made in the Sèvres workshops, as was the other glasswork.

The park contains several remains of old fortifications. A fine **view** can be had of the town.

Musée d'Art et d'Histoire Marcel-Dessal

Place du Musée. ⏰*Wed–Fri and Sun–Mon 2–6pm.* ⏰*Closed public holidays (except 14 Jul) and Dec school holidays.* ✆*€2.20 (under 25 years no charge).* ✆*02 37 50 18 61.* *www.musees.regioncentre.fr.*

Set up in a neo-Romanesque chapel, the museum displays furnishings taken from the Collégiale St-Étienne, a 12C church which stood on the site of the Royal Chapel. Shown alongside local archaeological exhibits, dating from Prehistoric, Gallo-Roman and Merovingian times, are exhibits evoking the history of the Dreux region. A set of 18C furniture taken from the Château de Crécy-Couve, formerly owned by the Marquise de Pompadour, is also on show.

The painting gallery displays both ancient and contemporary works. Impressionist and post-Impressionist movements are well represented with canvases by Vlaminck, Montezin and Le Sidaner, arranged around a painting by Claude Monet *(Wisteria).*

Écomusée des vignerons et artisans drouais

68 r. St-Thibault. Guided tours Mon–Sat 10am–noon, 2–6pm, Sun and holidays 3–6pm. ✆*€5.* ✆*02 37 42 62 81.* *www.museedudrouais.com.*

This eco-museum renders homage to Dreux winegrowing: tools, cellars, etc. Medieval garden behind museum is fun for kids; wine appreciation course at nearby Clos St-Thibault.

EXCURSIONS

From Dreux, go 6km/3mi southeast to **Mézières-en-Drouais** for the 🏊🏊 **Lac de Mézières-Écluzelles**, a lake and bird-watching area.

If you go 13km/8mi northwest instead, you come to 🏊🏊**Courdemanche** and the English-style **Rosemary's Garden** (*La Vallée, 10 r. des Ifs, 27320 Courdemanche,* ✆*02 37 48 14 59*).

Finally, 16km/9mi west by the N12 takes you to **Nonancourt** and its 12C fortress; also see the Flamboyant Gothic **Église St-Martin** (*Maison Mouret Grande-Rue, 27320 Nonancourt;* ✆*02 32 58 28 74, or contact M. Guingnier* ✆*06 21 10 19 98*). Just 1km/6mi S from Nonancourt by the D11 is the **Église St-Lubin-des-Joncherets**.

🚗 DRIVING TOUR

DREUX AND IVRY FORESTS

80km/49mi.
Allow 3hrs (including château visit).

▷ *Leave Dreux via D 928 north and take D 161 to the left.*

Outside Dreux, the aqueduct crosses the valley, carrying water from the Avre to Paris. Off to the right, you can see the church in the little town of Montreuil as you drive by, and Dreux Forest off to the left. In Ézy-sur-Eure, an old humpback bridge (Pont St-Jean) crosses the river to Saussay.

Ivry-la-Bataille

The town name refers to a battle on 14 March 1590, when Henri IV defeated the Duc de Mayenne and the Catholic League in the Wars of Religion (1561–98). There are a few quaint timber-framed houses; one (no 5 rue de Garennes) may have lodged Henri IV in 1590; the 11C doorway (end of rue de l'Abbaye), has three sculpted key stones (renovated), and may have been part of Ivry Abbey, destroyed in the Revolution. Diane de Poitiers founded **Église St-Martin**, a 15C–16C church, partly attributed to the famous architect, Philibert Delorme.

⊳ *Take D 833 towards St-André-de-l'Eure.*

In the little village of **Couture-Boussey**, a centre of woodwind manufacture since the 16C, is a **Musée des Instruments à Vent** (◔*Open Tue–Sun 2–6pm;* ◔*closed end Dec–early Jan, 1 May.* ◈*€4;* ☎*02 32 36 28 80; www.lacoutureboussey.com).*

⊳ *Return to Ivry via D 833, continue north on D 836.*

Between Neuilly and the Merey mills, the 16C **Château de la Folletière** (⊶ *closed to the public*) can be seen through the foliage in a park.

⊳ *From Chambine to Pacy, D 836 rises above Eure; nice views upstream.*

Pacy-sur-Eure

There is a monument to Aristide Briand; the beautiful early 13C **Église St-Aubin**, reworked in the 16C, has modern artworks and 16C–17C stone statues.

The kids will like the tourist railroad, the ♟**Chemin de fer touristique à la découverte de la vallée de l'Eure** – (Gare de Pacy-sur-Eure. ☎ *02 32 36 04 63. www.cfve.org. Ask for info, regular trains Jul–Aug, Tue–Wed and Sun early Sept– early Oct, €8.50 (-4 years old free).*

⊳ *Take the right bank for the D 836 to head along the Eure to Anet.*

Château d'Anet★

♟ *Guided tours (45min) Apr–Oct Wed–Mon 2–6pm; Feb–Mar Sat–Sun 2–5.30pm.* ◈*€7.70.* ☎*02 37 41 90 07. www.chateaudanet.com.*

Successive owners since 1840 have endeavoured to maintain Anet's original ornate appearance.

When widow **Diane de Poitiers** (1490–1566) came to court she caught the eye of François I's second son, Henri. At 32 she was beautiful, intelligent and 20 years older; she still fascinated him when he became King Henri II. When in 1559 Henri died in a tournament, Diane had reigned 12 years over king, court, artists and royal finances. She rebuilt Anet, symbol of her power and taste, from 1548 with architect **Philibert Delorme**. Henri's widow Catherine de' Medici took Chenonceau but left her Anet, where Diane died in 1566. The greatest artists embellished the château: sculptors Goujon, Pilon; silversmith Cellini; enameller Limosin; the Fontainebleau tapestry makers.

Entrance Gate – The work of Philibert Delorme. Above the central arch, the tympanum is a casting of Benvenuto Cellini's bronze low relief now in the Louvre (Diane Recumbent). Above the door is a clock, with a stag held at bay by four dogs; the dogs formerly barked and the stag moved to tell the time. The outlying buildings' chimneys bear coffins to evince Diane's constant mourning.

Left Wing of the Main Courtyard – The visit begins on the first floor with Diane's bedroom. The main attraction is the Renaissance bed, decorated with Diane's three crescents. The stained-glass windows include fragments of the original grisailles, a discreet grey element in keeping with Diane's mourning.

The **main stairway**, added by the Duke of Vendôme in the 17C, affords views of both lake and park. The vestibule, also 17C, leads to the Salon Rouge with its French and Italian Renaissance furniture. The Faïence Room, with part of its original tiling, leads to the dining room where two huge atlantes by Puget support the fireplace mantelpiece. Note the central Jean Goujon medallion of Diane snaring the royal stag.

Chapel – Built in 1548 by Philibert Delorme, its layout is a Greek cross. A dome and lantern cover the circular nave, one of the first to be built in France. The skilfully executed diamond-shaped drawing on the coffers produces a surprising optical illusion, the whole cupola seeming to be drawn upwards. The design of the floor tiling recalls this geometrical subtlety. Diane de Poitiers used to attend Mass from the gallery, which communicated with her rooms in the right wing *(demolished)*.

Chapelle funéraire de Diane de Poitiers – *Entrance from place du Château, left of the main entrance.*

The chapel designed by Claude de Foucques, architect to the princes of Lorraine, was begun just before the death of Diane in 1566 and completed in 1577. The white-marble **statue**★ representing Diane kneeling on a tall sarcophagus in black marble, is attributed to Pierre Bontemps; so too is the altarpiece. Since the spoiling of the tomb in 1795, Diane's remains are at rest at the chevet of the Anet parish church.

Évreux★

Évreux, on the River Iton, is the Eure's religious and administrative capital. The city centre was rebuilt after 1945; the town ramparts, former bishop's palace, cathedral and 15C belfry survived. Pleasant stroll in flower gardens along Iton.

A BIT OF HISTORY

5C – Vandals sack the market town.
9C – Vikings destroy the Roman fortified town on present site on Iton.
1119 – Henry I burns the town.
1193 – Philippe Auguste also burns it.
1356 – Jean the Good burns Évreux.
1379 – Charles V's siege.
June 1940 – German air raids.
June 1944 – Allied air raids raze district round the station.

🐾 WALKING TOUR

3km/2mi. 1hr30min (not including the cathedral and the museum).
P *Park at place Clemenceau. See map. Begin at place du Général de Gaulle.*

Place du Général de Gaulle

A castle once stood on this square. Today, there is a fountain that represents the Eure as a woman holding an oar and the city's coat of arms.

Tour de l'Horloge

The elegant 15C clock tower stands on the site of a tower which flanked the town's main gateway.

▶ **Population:** 51,485.
⏚ **Michelin Map:** 304: G-7.
📄 **Info:** 1 ter place du Général de Gaulle. ℰ02 32 24 04 43. www.grandevreux tourisme.fr.
▶ **Location:** Évreux is 96km/60mi W of Paris, 58km/36mi S of Rouen and 48km/30mi NE of Dreux.
P **Parking:** Parking (fee) behind cathedral, near tourist office, near Cloître des Capucins public garden.
😊 **Don't Miss:** The Flamboyant beauty of Notre-Dame Cathedral and the rich collections of the museum.
🕐 **Timing:** Allow yourself 2hr to see the museum.
👫 **Kids:** The Roman ruins at Gisacum will interest them as will the train through the valley of the Dure.

Promenade des remparts

The walk runs beside the River Iton.

Cathédrale Notre-Dame★★

r. Charles-Corbeau. 🕐*Open Mon–Fri 8.30am–7pm, Sat–Sun 9am–7pm.*
The nave's great arches are all that is left of the original church, rebuilt 1119-1193; the choir is from 1260, the chapels are 14C. The lantern tower and Lady Chapel came after the 1356 fire. Note the

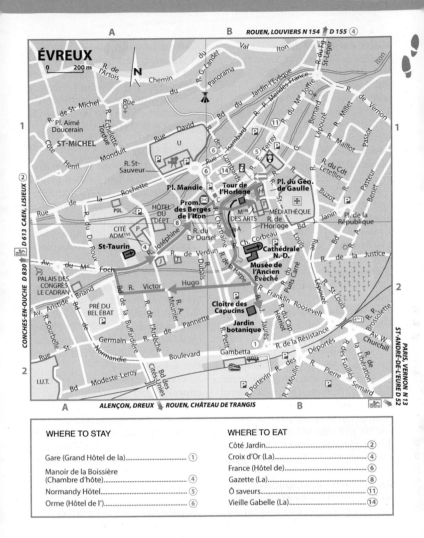

magnificent 16C north transept façade and doorway.

In the 1940 fires, the silver belfry melted; the west towers lost their crowns.

Exterior – *Walk along the north side.*

The aisle windows were redesigned in the 16C in the Flamboyant style of which the north door is a perfect example.

Interior – View the ambulatory chapels' **stained glass**★ (&see Introduction: *Religious architecture, p64)* and **carved wood screens**★ from the transept, between the lantern tower pillars.

Beautiful 18C wrought-iron grill on choir, and the apse windows are perhaps the 14C's most beautiful. Fine Renaissance wood screens at ambulatory entrance. The 15C Treasury Chapel is quite unique: closed off by wrought-iron bars and iron frame.

The fourth chapel **screen**★ is a masterpiece of imagination and craftsmanship; note the lower figures; the chapel glass is early 14C. The central chapel gifted by Louis XI, has 15C windows of considerable documentary interest.

The upper parts depict France's peers at Louis XI's coronation; he is two windows further on.

Musée Ancien Évêché★★

6 r. Charles-Corbeau. ♿ ⏱*Open Tue–Sun 10am–noon, 2–6pm.* ⏱*Closed 1 Jan, 1 May, 1 and 11 Nov, 25 Dec.* ✆*No charge.* ☎*02 32 31 81 90.*

The 15C former bishop's palace looks onto the cathedral; Flamboyant, it has dormer windows, ornamented window pediments and a staircase tower. The Municipal Museum is inside.

The ground floor's first two rooms concern the Eure region and town history and geography.

The former chapter house (Room 3) has a monumental fireplace and medieval and Renaissance collections.

Note the 17C Aubusson tapestries on the Prodigal Son. Room 4 has medieval exhibits: tomb inscriptions in engraved stone, capitals.

The **Archaeological Room**★ in Gallo-Roman rampart ruins, displays domestic and religious objects from the Palaeolithic Age (up to 9,000 BC) to the Gallo-Roman era (AD 1C–4C).

17C and 18C paintings on first floor, and decorative items such as Évreux Hospital apothecary jars in Nevers and Rouen faïence. Contemporary art exhibitions and 19C paintings and objects (Lebourg, Jongkind) on second floor, 20C art on the third, including Hartung and Soulages.

Ancien cloître des Capucins

96 r. de Panette. ⏱*Open daily mid-Apr–mid-Sept 8am–8pm; Mar–mid-Apr and mid-Sept–mid-Oct 8am–7pm; Nov–Feb 8am–5pm.* ✆*No charge.*

Former Capuchin cloisters with four timber-roofed galleries; monolithic columns; moral texts on walls. Garden in cloister close.

Église St-Taurin

Place St-Taurin. ⏱*Open daily Jun–Sept 9am–7pm; Oct–May 9am–8pm.*

This former abbey church established in 660 and dedicated to the first Bishop of Évreux dates back to the 14C and 15C. The well-proportioned 14C chancel is lit by superb 15C windows. Three windows in the apse trace the life of St Taurinus. **Châsse de St-Taurin**★★ – This masterpiece of 13C French craftsmanship in the north transept was given to the abbey by St Louis to contain St Taurinus' relics and was probably made in the abbey workshops. The silver gilt reliquary enriched with enamel is in the form of a miniature chapel and even shows St Taurinus with his crosier.

EXCURSIONS

Take the N 13 for Paris 9km/5mi east, then the road on right for **Vieil-Évreux** and ♟♟**Gisacum - Jardin archéologique** – (✆ *02 32 31 94 78;* ⏱ *Jul–Aug 10.30am–6.30pm; Apr–Jun and Sep 1–6pm; Mar, Oct–Nov Wed–Mon 1–5pm;* ✆*free*), a garden and 1C archaeological dig.

See **Miserey**'s 18C château, 7km/4mi east by the N 13 (towards Paris), then the D 650 on the left.

The park includes Dante-inspired **themed gardens** (✆*02 32 67 00 21;* ⏱*Open daily 1 Apr–mid-Nov; wkd, Mon and holidays 2.30–5.30pm; closed mid Nov–end Mar;* ✆*€6.50*).

To reach **La Croix-Saint-Leufroy**'s **church,** head 17km/10mi north of Evreux, then take the D 316 towards Eure; cross the river and take the D 836 on the left for Louviers.

The church has carved Renaissance baptismal fonts and paintings from the old Croix-St-Ouen abbey *(ask at mairie Tue and Fri 5–7pm - 27490 La Croix-St-Leufroy;* ✆*02 32 67 75 20).*

The last excursion is to **Cocherel**. Drive 25km/15mi northeast of Évreux; you will take the D 316 and after the Eure, you turn right into the D 836. It was in Cocherel that the French statesman **Aristide Briand** (1862–1932) acquired his estates. The "Pligrim of Peace" rests today in the church cemetery *(take the way up off the road leading into hamlet).* His tomb is marked by a soot-coloured granite slab. A statue in his memory also stands on the other side of the Eure bridge. Along the D 57, the Jouy-sur-Eure road, a pyramid recalls Bertrand Du Guesclin's victory at the Battle of Cocherel in 1364, over the forces of Charles II of Navarre.

Conches-en-Ouche★

The town of Conches, on the edge of the woodlands that mark the northern limits of the Pays d'Ouche, is remarkably situated on a spur encircled by the River Rouloir. There is a particularly good view of the town if it is approached along the Rouloir Valley (from Évreux). The keep of the ruined castle is illuminated from April to September.

A BIT OF HISTORY

From Rouergue to the Pays d'Ouche – On his return from the *Reconquista de Iberia* (1034), **Roger de Tosny** made a pilgrimage to Conques, in Rouergue (southwest France) and brought back relics of Ste Foy. This may be the origin of the town's name. Roger dedicated a church to **Ste Foy**; at the end of the 15C it was replaced by the present building.

SIGHTS

Jardin de l'Hôtel de Ville

The Gothic doorway of the town hall – entrance to the former castle – leads to a garden in which stands the ruined keep of the lords of Tosny, surrounded by 12C towers.

From the terrace there is a fine view of the Rouloir valley and the elegant Flamboyant apse of Ste-Foy Church. Below another terrace offers a similar view.

Rue du Val

There are two interesting buildings here. One is the 16C half-timbered **maison Corneille**, home to the family of the famous dramatist (1606–84). At the end of the street, the **hospital** stands on the site of the abbey; the vaulted cellars are open to visitors.

Église Ste-Foy★

r. Ste-Foy. ◑*Open daily 9am–7pm.*
The south tower is crowned by a tall spire of wood and lead, a copy of the one blown down in a storm in 1842. The fine

▶ **Population:** 5,046.
◔ **Michelin Map:** 304: F-28.
🛈 **Info:** Place Aristide-Briand. ℘02 32 30 76 42. www.conches-en-ouche.fr.
▶ **Location:** From Aigle (30km/18.5mi SW) or Évreux (14km/8.5mi NE) take D 830. From Bernay (30km/18.5mi NW) take D 140, and from Rouen (50km/31mi N).
☺ **Don't Miss:** The beautiful windows of the Ste-Foy Church.
◔ **Timing:** Visit Conches in the morning, then stroll along the many paths in the area.

☺ Walking Tours ☺

Pick up a walking guide to the area from the tourist office called *Les Circuits Touristique*; also shows bike and horse riding trails.

---

carved panels of the façade doors are early 16C. Notice the many gargoyles. Inside there are some beautiful statues including that of St Roch (17C) in the south aisle and near the great organ.

Stained-Glass Windows★ – The Renaissance windows, dating from the first half of the 16C, have retained their unity in spite of restoration. Those in the north aisle depict the life of the Virgin. The seven windows (10.5m/34.4ft) in the chancel are divided into two, the upper part illustrating the Life of Christ, the lower to that of Ste Foy and portraits of the donors.

The windows in the south aisle were made in either Île-de-France or at Fontainebleau. The Mystical Wine Press (fifth window) is the best known.

The houses facing the church are 15C and 16C. The vaulted cellars (11C–12C) are open to visitors.

Musée du Terroir Normand

r. Paul-Guilbaud. ⊙*Open Jun–Sept Wed–Sat 10am–noon, 2–5.30pm, Sun 3–6pm.* ⊙*Closed public holidays. P3 (ticket with Musée du Verre).* ℘*02 32 37 92 16. Old farming tools and recreated workshops.*

Musée du Verre

rte de Ste-Marguerite. ♿⊙*See Musée du Terroir Normand.* ℘*02 32 30 90 41.* Glass objects by the "sorcerer of Conche", François Décorchement (1880–1971).

EXCURSIONS

Head 14km/8.5mi S by the D 840 to **Breteuil-sur-Iton.** It is east of Breteuil Forest; the Iton loops here into a lake in the castle's public gardens. William the Conqueror's daughter wed in the **church**. Now head 4km/2mi E to the ♟**Château de Chambray**, knowing

that only the park is open to the public *(contact ℘ 02 32 35 61 70).*

Leaving Conches by the Évreux road, the D 830, you can take 10km/6mi of narrow roads to explore the **Rouloir valley**. At 3km/1.5mi turn left onto a sharp road down through underbrush.

After La Croisille, left on first paved road (D 167). Go 1km/6mi; left at crossroads and down to valley bottom at church of St-Elier in a nice setting. Follow river and you return to see Conches at its prettiest angle.

If you take the D 140 W for 14km/8mi W from Conches, you get to **La Ferrière-sur-Risle** with its 13C–14C **church** and beautiful former **tanneries** *(www.conches-en-ouche.fr).* Take the D 23 N to the verdant Risle valley, the **Val Gallerand**, skirting the Beaumont Forest; you will see superb old Norman farm buildings in the greenery.

L'Aigle

Visit L'Aigle on Tuesday, when it holds France's third-largest market. A major town, L'Aigle is a centre for metalwork, producing pins, needles and more. The historic centre is place St-Martin, with its church.

CHÂTEAU

The château, home to the town hall and **two museums**, was built in 1690 on the site of an 11C fortress, by Fulbert de Beina, Lord of L'Aigle. Legend says he found an eagle's nest here, hence the town name. Mansart (Jules Hardouin 1646–1708) designed this and the Château of Versailles for Louis XIV.

Musée des Instruments de Musique Marcel-Angot

Pl. Fulbert-de-Beina. ℘*02 33 84 44 44. www.ville-laigle.fr.* ⊙*Mon 1.30–5.30pm, Tue–Thu 8.30am–noon, 1.30–5.30pm (Fri till 5.45). Closed holidays.* ⊙*Free.*

Double spiral staircase leads to the first floor to see a collection of musical instruments, the gift of a former

▶ **Population:** 8,508.

⊙ **Michelin Map:** 310: M-2.

🏠 **Info:** Place Fulbert-de-Beina. ℘02 33 24 12 40. www.paysdelaigle.com.

▸ **Location:** L'Aigle lies between the Pays d'Ouche and the Perche, on the road linking Dreux, 59km/37mi to the E, to Argentan. Lisieux is only 56km/35mi NW on D 519.

🅿 **Parking:** You will find parking on the public squares: de la Halle, de l'Europe, de Verdun and de Bois-Landry.

⊗ **Don't Miss:** The Tuesday market; the museum of La Grosse Forge at Aube.

⊙ **Timing:** Give yourself half a day at L'Aigle before visiting the museums at Aube.

♟ **Kids:** The museum of the Comtesse de Ségur (1799–1874), France's most famous children's author.

View of L'Aigle
by Église St-Martin

© Arthur Leroy/Iconotec / Photononstop

bandmaster: wind instruments, string instruments, and more exotic ones such as the serpent, a bass wind instrument descended from the cornett and a distant ancestor of the tuba.

Musée "Juin 44"

Pl. Fulbert-de-Beina. ⏰*Apr–Sept, Tue 10am–noon, 2–6pm, Wed and wkd 2–6pm. Guided tour (30min in French, 40min in English). Closed 1 Jan, 1 and 11 Nov and 25 Dec.* ⬧*€3.60.*
℘*02 33 84 44 44. www.ville-laigle.fr.*
The Battle of Normandy Museum has wax figures of De Gaulle, Churchill, Leclerc, Roosevelt, Stalin, etc. and their recorded voices. The battle is on a 36sq m/387.5sq ft relief map, events traced on dioramas. A small **archaeological museum** has some interesting objects; there is also an exhibition of a **meteorite** that fell on L'Aigle on 26 March 1803. ⬧*No charge.*

SIGHTS
Église St-Martin

Centre of town, presbytery, r. des Emangeards. ℘*02 33 24 08 30.*
An elaborate late 15C square tower contrasts with a small 12C one built of red iron agglomerate *(grison)* and surmounted by a more recent spire. Beautiful modern statues stand in niches between the windows of the south nave, added in the 16C.
Above the high altar (1656) is a beautiful carved wooden altarpiece, consisting of four twisted columns capped by

Corinthian capitals and decorated with vine leaves, bunches of grapes and cherubs. The central composition, attributed to Charles Lebrun (1619–90), a celebrated artist under Louis XIV, shows the Descent from the Cross.

🚗 DRIVING TOUR

PAYS D'OUCHE

75km/46mi. Allow 4hrs.

▷ *Drive N from L'Aigle on the D 930.*

St-Sulpice-sur-Risle

⏰*Open Mon–Fri 3–5pm, telephone beforehand.* ℘*02 33 24 15 76.*
The **church** adjoins the 13C priory, which was partially rebuilt in the 16C. Among its artworks are a 16C tapestry, a 17C painting of St Cecilia, a statue of St Anne and two stained-glass windows from the 13C and 14C.

▷ *Take the road facing the mairie for about 1.5km/1mi; go under the D 918 and continue about 100m/yd. (megaliths on right).*

▷ *Return to L'Aigle by the D 930; take D 12 NW to La Ferté-Frênel at 11km/6mi, where you will see a château.*

▷ *Leave La Ferté-Frênel S by the D 14 for 1km/0.6mi; then left on D 31 to Saint-Evroult-Notre-Dame-du-Bois.*

Saint-Évroult-Notre-Dame-du-Bois

The ruins of this abbey, a great centre of intellectual life in the 11C and 12C, are set in a lovely valley, through which the River Charentonne flows.

Destroyed in the 10C by wars, the Romanesque abbey of Ouche revived in the 11C. It was rebuilt in the 13C in the Gothic style, but little remains.

In front of the main entrance stands a monument to Orderic Vital (1075–1142), an English historian whose work described the abbey in its heyday.

▷ *Leave St-Evroult E by the D 13; go 9km/5mi to Gacé.*

Gacé

Musée de la Dame aux camélias – *pl. du Château. Jun–Aug: guided tours Tue–Sun, 2pm, 2.45pm, 3.30pm, 4.15pm, 5pm. €2.50. 02 33 35 50 24. http://ladameauxcamelias.ifrance.com.* A museum with a modest collection of memorabilia recalling the woman who inspired Verdi's opera, *La Traviata.*

▷ *Go S on the D 932 to Orgères.*

Orgères

In this **church** to St George, an altarpiece and painting, *The Adoration of the Shepherds* is listed as an Historic Monument.

▷ *Continue on the D 932 to Ste-Gauburge-Ste-Colombe, then take the N 26 E to Aube.*

Aube

The **Château des Nouettes**, now a medico-pedagogical institute, was once the residence of Countess Eugène de Ségur.

A "**Comtesse de Ségur**" walking itinerary 9km/5mi long begins from Aube's central square.

Musée de la Comtesse de Ségur

7km/4.3mi SW of L'Aigle by N 26. 3 r. de l'Abbé-Derry. Open mid-Jun–end Sept Thu–Mon 2–6pm, Wed 4–6pm (last entry 5.15pm). Closed public holidays. €4 (6–12 years old €1.50). Ticket combined with Grosse Forge €(children €2). 02 33 24 60 09. www.musee-comtessedesegur.com.

The Russian-born countess (1799–1864), languishing in the country while the count enjoyed other society, produced very late in life a series of tales for her grandchildren. The books met with great success and are still cited, especially *Les Malheurs de Sophie*, but mostly as examples of tedious moralising. The museum's considerable charm lies in its lovely rural setting and frequently changing exhibits evoking 19C children's pastimes as well as aristocratic life and attitudes.

The Musée de la Comtesse de Ségur is in the former presbytery at the foot of the church. It contains exhibits evoking the life and literary career of the countess. Characters from the writer's novels are represented by a collection of dolls and exhibits (toys, games, books, furniture, etc.).

Musée de la Grosse Forge d'Aube

r. de la Vielle-Forge. Open mid-Jun–end Sept Wed–Mon 2–6pm (last entry 5pm). Closed public holidays. Guided tours (45min) 15min past every hour. €4 (6–12 years old €1.50). Ticket combined with Musée de la Comtesse de Ségur €6 (children €2). 02 33 34 14 93.

On the River Risle, as you leave Aube towards L'Aigle, stands the Musée de la Grosse Forge d'Aube, which retraces five centuries of metallurgy. This museum has changed very little since the 17C. Note the furnace for refining metals, the massive camshaft hammer and the wooden bellows (a 1995 replica) operated by a paddle wheel.

There are beautiful models making it possible to better understand the history of metallurgy.

▷ *Return to L'Aigle 4km/2mi away via the N 26.*

Bernay

Bernay developed rapidly around an abbey founded early in the 11C by Judith of Brittany, wife of Duke Richard II. The town, which nestles in the Charentonne Valley, has a number of interesting, renovated, half-timbered houses.

SIGHTS

The principal streets are rue Thiers and du Générale-de-Gaulle, along which the abbey, the museum and the Ste-Croix Church are clustered. The information office is also here.

Boulevard des Monts★

This lovely hillside road north of the centre commands good views of the town and the Charentonne Valley.

Hôtel de ville★

The 17C town hall buildings, which were formerly Bernay Abbey, are in the style of the Maurists, a Benedictine order.

Ancienne église abbatiale

Same as for the municipal museum, below.
The abbey church was begun in 1013 by **Guglielmo da Volpiano**, summoned from Fécamp by Judith of Brittany. In the 15C the semicircular apse was replaced by a polygonal one. Note the carved capitals above the nave and the twin bays in the galleries. The north aisle, rebuilt in the 15C, has diagonal vaulting.

Musée des Beaux-Arts

pl. Guillaume-de-Volpiano Open mid-Jun–mid-Sept Tue–Sun 11am–6pm; rest of the year 2–5.30pm. *Closed 1 Jan, 1 May, 25 Dec.* €3.60 ticket combined with the abbey church (no charge for under-16s, Wed and 1st Sun of month). 02 32 46 63 23.
The museum is housed in the 16C abbot's lodge. Exhibits include a fine collection of Rouen, Nevers and Moustiers faïence and old Norman furniture.

Population: 10,434.

Michelin Map: 304: D-7.

Info: 29 rue Thiers. 02 32 43 32 08. www.bernaytourisme.fr.

Location: Bernay lies at the junction of the Charentonne and the Cosnier rivers. Take N 138 from Rouen (65km/40.5mi NE) or Alençon (92km/57mi SW), or the N 13 from Lisieux (34km/21mi NW) or Évreux (52km/32mi SE).

Don't Miss: The view from boulevard des Monts, the municipal museum, and the lovely château de Beaumesnil.

Timing: Spend a morning in town, then drive along the Risle river.

Kids: The museum has activities for children.

Église Ste-Croix

r. Thiers.
Started in the 14C, the church is heavily restored and contains fine works of art from Le Bec-Hellouin. The remarkable **tombstone** of Guillaume d'Auvillars, Abbot of Bec (1418), stands at the entrance to the sacristy. Sixteen great statues of Apostles and Evangelists from the end of the 14C are in the nave.

Basilique Notre-Dame-de-la-Couture

Access by rue Kléber-Mercier, about 1km/0.6mi S of town centre. Ask for information at the presbytery, 12 rue Alexandre. Open for unaccompanied visits Sat 2–6pm. 02 32 43 06 82.
The interior of this 15C church, established as a basilica in 1950, has wooden vaulting; the statue Notre-Dame de la Couture (16C), highly venerated by pilgrims is placed on a modern altar in the north transept.

DRIVING TOUR

ALONG THE RISLET AND CHARENTONNE RIVERS

65km/40mi. Allow 3hrs.

Near L'Aigle, the pretty, fish-filled **Risle** and the **Charentonne** rivers run almost parallel. There were many watermills in the past, but today only some of them remain, no longer in working order.

▶ *Leave Bernay E by the D 133.*

Menneval

Delightful country church with renovated façade. The local Brotherhood of Charity dates from 1060.

▶ *Continue on the D 133. Less than 2km/1mi after Camfleur, right on D 42.*

Fontaine-l'Abbél

A pretty Norman village with a Louis XIII château and a **church** (o⃥ *closed to the public*). Inside are displayed the banners of the local Brotherhood of Charity.

▶ *Come back on the D 133 that continues to Serquigny.*

Serquigny

The church façade, chequered in blank flint and white stone, has a Romanesque doorway. Inside, the chapel *(left)* and stained-glass windows are Renaissance.

▶ *Continue on the D 133 SE, along the Risle.*

Beaumont-le-Roger

The ruins of the old 13C priory to the Trinity has imposing buttresses visible from the road. The 14C–16C **church** to St Nicholas, badly damaged by the bombings, has been restored; it has both early 15C–16C and modern stained glass.

🚶 Seven trekking paths permit discovery of Beaumont-le-Roger's surrounding area. Contact the tourist office on 📞 *02 32 44 05 79.*

▶ *Leave Beaumont SW by the D 25.*

Château de Beaumesnil★

▶ *13km/8mi SE by D 140.*

🕐 *Open Jul–Aug daily 10.30am–12.30pm, 1.30–6pm; Easter–end Jun Fri–Mon and public holidays 2–6pm; Sept Mon–Wed 2–6pm.* ⊛€7.
📞 *02 32 44 40 09.*
www.chateaubeaumesnil.com.
The château, a masterpiece of the Louis XIII style, is built of brick and stone. The formal gardens and the 60ha/149 acre **park** echo the sumptuous lines of the château.

🚶 The Beaumesnil canton has 17 walking itineraries (*3hr on average – ask at Bernay or Beaumesnil tourist office*).

▶ *Leave Beaumesnil by SW for La Grimoudière, then Landepeureuse, W, then head for Menhir to SW to take the D 49. Turn right for Broglie.*

Brogile

The 18C **château** (o⃥ *private*) is built around a medieval fortress.
The pillars and the choir of the **church** are Romanesque; the rest is 15C and 16C.

Jardin aquatique

♿🕐*Open daily.* ⊛*No charge.*
📞*02 32 44 60 58.*
This charming little water garden is irrigated by the River Charentonne.

▶ *Head alongside the Charentonne in the direction of Bernay, by the D 33.*

👥 Étang Saints-Pères

♿🕐*Open daily.* ⊛*No charge.*
📞*02 32 44 60 58.*
The banks of this little pond offer picnic tables, pedal-boats, walks and recreation facilities.

Ferrières-Saint-Hilaire

This remains of the forge and the forge master's manor still stand.

Saint-Quentin-des-Isles

Below the 19C château, there is a textile plant. A dovecote stands on an island.

Brionne

Medieval Brionne was a Risle Valley stronghold. When William of Normandy besieged it 1047–1050, he met the monks of Bec-Hellouin Abbey, an event that would profoundly affect English religious life.

SIGHTS
Donjon

Park at place du Chevalier-Herluin or by church. Take r. des Canadiens, then right on "sente du Vieux-Château".

Steep path to ruins of one of Normandy's best examples of a square keep (11C). Lovely view of town and Risle Valley. The **Église St-Martin** has a 15C nave; 14C vaulting. The **Musée de la Poupée** *(38 r. de Calleville. ℘ 02 32 45 76 24. Apr–Oct wkd, hols; Jul–Aug 2–6pm. ≪€4)* exhibits antique dolls. Riverside garden in **Jardin de Shaftesbury** *(other side of Risle)*. The tourist office is in an 18C **press**. Visit **La Champignonnière** *(r. de la Briqueterie. ℘ 02 32 57 87 99. By appointment. ≪€3.50)*. Mushrooms grown in a cave.

🚗 DRIVING TOUR

LIEUVEN

55km/34mi. Allow about 2hr30min.

The Lieuven is a region of pastures and cereal crops, between Caux and Auge.

▷ *Leave Brionne N by the D 46. At Authou, continue on the D 137 to St-Georges-du-Vièvre.*

Saint-Grégoire-du-Vièvre

16C figures and rebuses on stone church's southern side.

▷ *Take the D 137 again.*

Saint-Georges-du-Vièvre

🅐 A waymarked Resistance itinerary starts here *(38km/23mi. Brochure from tourist office, 1 r. de Montfort; ℘02 32 56 34 29; www.saintgeorgesduvievre.org).*

▶ **Population:** 4,338.
📍 **Michelin Map:** 304: E-6.
🏨 **Info:** 1 rue du Générale-de-Gaulle. ℘02 32 45 70 51.
🔵 **Location:** Brionne is 40km/25mi NW of Évreux via N 13 and D 130, and nearly the same distance E of Lisieux.
🔍 **Don't Miss:** The square Norman keep and the banks of the Risle.
🕐 **Timing:** After 1–2hr in the village, visit Le Bec-Hellouin and the châteaux of Harcourt and Champ de Bataille nearby.

▷ *Leave St-Georges by the N on the D 29; then left for Saint-Étienne-l'Allier.*

Saint-Ètienne-l'Allier

11C church with interesing 14C recumbant figure. The **monument des Maquisards** *(D 98 and D 29 crossing)*, recalls that the village was one of Normandy's most active Resistance units.

▷ *Leave Saint-Étienne to continue N to Saint-Martin-Saint-Firmin.*

Saint-Martin-Saint-Fermin

The chapel of St Firmin was a major pilgrimage site; there are beautiful wood carvings inside.

🚶 **"Chemin de la Fontaine Fiacre"** – *Leaves from church –7km/4mi. Brochure from Lieuvin tourist offices.* This pretty walk follows the Véronne.

▷ *Take the D 810 to W at St-Siméon, then continue to Lieurey.*

Lieurey

🚶 **"Les chemins de l'eau"** – 250km/155mi of waymarked foot, cycling and horseriding Lieurey-Pont-Audemer paths.

Brochure from Lieuvin tourist offices.

▷ *Continue on D 810 to Cormeilles.*

Cormeilles

Distillerie Busnel – *R. de Lisieux.*
☎*02 32 57 38 80.* ☞ *€2.* Cider distillery.
☜**"Le sentier de la biodiversité"** –
From tourist office, first right; "Les Monts du Bourg". After avenue, left, park at water tower; second left. This route offers a 6km/3mi stroll.

▶ *Return by D 810 to Lieurey; D 137 to St-Georges-du-Vièvre, then SE on D 38.*

Château de Launay

Walk to avenue, right. ☎ *02 32 56 34 29. Guided tour (45min) at 3pm, 4pm, mid-Aug–end Sept.* ☞*€5.*
Note the chateau's **dovecote★**.

▶ *Take the D 38 again.*

Saint-Benoît-des-Ombres

Beyond the small mairie, there is a chapel *(right)* hidden in greenery. Its 15C wooden porch bears a wooden St Benedict.

▶ *Head for St-Victor-d'Epine and D 31; gardens on right after about 2km/1mi*

Jardins du clos Saint-François

St-Victor-d'Épine. ☎*02 32 45 98 90. May–Aug, Fri–Mon 10am–noon, 2–6pm.* ☞*€5.*
English-style garden around thatched cottage. Rose collection.
☜ From the St-Victor-d'Epine mairie, there is the **Circuit de la Grande Boissière**, a 6–9km/3–5mi trekking path.

▶ *D 31 for Berthouville; left on D 26. At Brétigny, take D 48 N, then left on D 38.*

Livet-sur-Authou

Quaint village with half-timbered houses, a castle and a church.

Abbaye du Bec-Hellouin★★

Le Bec-Hellouin Abbey, a medieval religious and cultural centre, produced two great Archbishops of Canterbury for England.

A BIT OF HISTORY

In 1034, the knight **Herluin** found God and founded the Bec Abbey; its pious reputation attracted an Italian scholar, **Lanfranc**, who later became young Duke William's trusted adviser.
Pope Alexander II, a former student of Lanfranc at Bec, appointed him Archbishop of Canterbury, which made him virtual Regent of England whenever William returned to Normandy. On Lanfranc's death in 1093, **Anselm**, the theologian who was now Abbot of Bec, was transferred to Canterbury.
In the 17C, Bec rose to new eminence under **Guillaume de la Tremblaye** (1644–1715), one of the greatest sculptors and architects of his period.

- ▶ **Population:** 415.
- ⓜ **Michelin Map:** 304: E-6.
- Ⓘ **Info:** Place du Mal-Leclerc, 27110 Le Neubourg.
  ☎02 32 35 40 57.
  www.le-neubourg.fr/
  tourisme.
- ▶ **Location:** The abbey is 35km/22mi SW of Rouen and within 40km/25mi of Honfleur (NW), Lisieux (W) and Évreux (SE). Rouen is 52km/32mi NE, Harcourt 10km/6mi SE.
- ⊙ **Don't Miss:** The abbey of Le Bec-Hellouin, the château and gardens at Champ-de-Bataille, and the Harcourt fortress with its arboretum.
- ◷ **Timing:** Spend your morning at the abbey, then go to Champ-de-Bataille or Harcourt in the afternoon.

The monks were driven out during the Revolution and the church, one of the largest in Christendom, was demolished under the empire. In 1948 the site was restored to the Benedictine Order.

VISIT

Abbaye de Bec-Hellouin★★

Open for unaccompanied visits daily 8am–9pm. Guided tours (45min) Wed–Sat and Mon 10.30am, 3pm and 4pm, Sun noon, 3pm and 4pm. €5 (tour). 02 32 43 72 60. www.abbayedubec.com.

New Abbey Church

The new abbey stands in the former Maurist refectory. At the entrance is a 14C statue of the Virgin; the Fathers of the Church are 15C. The altar was presented in 1959 by Aosta, birthplace of Bishop Anselm. Before the high altar lies the 11C sarcophagus of Herluin, founder of Bec. Turn left on leaving to reach the other sights.

Old Abbey Church

Only the column, foundations and fragments of the south transept of the old abbey church remain.

Cloisters

A monumental 18C grand staircase leads to the cloisters. Built between 1640 and 1660, the cloisters were modelled on those of Monte Cassino (Italy). Northeast of the cloisters is a beautiful, 14C Gothic doorway.

Tour St-Nicolas

Closed to the public.
The 15C tower is the most important remainder of the old abbey church. A plaque recalls the abbey's ties with England in the 11C and 12C.

☞ DRIVING TOURS

The Neubourg plain south of the Seine, and the Roumois plateau north are both ideal for the flourishing cereal crops, spreading here amid charming country churches and noble châteaux.

LE ROUMOIS

50km/31mi. Allow 2hr30min.

▷ *Leave Le Bec by Pont-Authou and take the D 38.*

Château de Tilly

Closed to the public.
Lozenge-patterned stone and glazed-brick façade, perimeter wall quartered by pointed turrets.
The winding **staircase**★ in brickwork in the courtyard recalls the Rihour Palace in Lille.

▷ *Come back on the D 124; 4km/2mi further, take D 576 on right.*

Écaquelon

Call in advance if you wish to visit the church: Mme Renverseau. 02 32 42 67 31.
The church contains beautiful 16C wood carvings.

▷ *Take D 582 through Les Epinais and on to Illeville-sur-Montfort. Then D 94 to Rougemontier, right on D 144.*

Routot

Romanesque church; the **maison du Lin** on mairie ground floor tells the story of linen. 02 32 56 21 76. Jul–Aug, 2–6.30pm; Mar–Jun and Sept Wed–Mon, 2–6.30pm. €2.30.

▷ *The D 144 goes to Bouquetot and Bourg-Achard.*

Bouquetot

Call in advance if you wish to visit the church: M. Duval. 02 32 57 35 47.
There is an 11C–12C **church** with statues and 18C paintings. Note the 700-year-old hawthorn.

Bourg-Achard

The **church** has 16C stained glass, and remarkable 15C–16C carved wood. 15C stone Virgin with Bird.

▷ *D 313 to Bourgtheroulde, then take the D 574 to Infreville 1km/0.6mi away.*

Château du Champ-de-Bataille

© Francis Cormon/hemis.fr

Bourgtheroude

Church (*contact mairie prior to visit:* 📞02 35 87 60 70*)* with interesting Renaissance windows. Entrance pavilion and dove-cote remains of 16C château.

Infreville

There is a large 18C rocaille altarpiece in the **church** (*contact mairie prior to visit:* 📞02 35 87 60 70*).*

▶ *To Le Bec: D 438, then D 39, right.*

LE NEUBOURG

50km/31mi. Allow 2hr30min.

▶ *Leave Le Bec by the D 39 heading for Le Neubourg.*

Château du Champ-de-Bataille★

Gardens: 🕐*Open May–Jun and Sept 2–6pm; from Easter–end Apr and early Oct–All Saints' wkd and hols 2–6pm* ◉ *€12. Rooms:* 🎧*Audio-guided tour Jul–Aug daily 3.30–5.30pm. Easter–end Jun, early Sept–All Saints' wkd 3.30–5.30pm.* ◉*€24 (including garden).* 📞*02 32 34 84 34.* *www.chateauduchampdebataille.com.* The name, which means "Castle of the Battlefield", may recall a battle in 935 between forces of the Count of Cotentin and of William Longsword, ancestor of the Conqueror. The 17C château was built by Alexandre de Créqui and occupied by the Harcourt family before it was

looted in 1795. In the 20C it was used as a hospice, a camp for war prisoners and a jail for women. The Duke of Harcourt bought it in 1947 and began restoration, continued by the present owner, Jacques Garcia.

Interior – *Entrance through the main courtyard on the left.* Grand ceremonial rooms presented with the owner's rich collection of furniture and art objects.

Park★★ – A French-style garden of vast proportions has been recreated, offering spectacular perspectives and subtle plantings reflecting 18C philosophical notions of the orders of nature: animal, vegetable, mineral, etc.

🐾**Parcours de découverte du massif du Champ-de-Bataille**. *Contact Le Neubourg tourist office for info.* 📞*02 32 34 84 34.* To take this nature walk (1.5km/1mi), leave your car at the château; from the entrance head round the estate on right to the GR 26 path (about 2km/1mi) that takes you there; by car, take the D 39 for Le Neubourg; before La Mare Auzanne, right (indicated).

▶ *Take the D 39 to Le Neubourg.*

Le Neubourg

50km/31mi. Allow 2hr30min.
The capital of the plain of the same name. The church has a 17C **main altar** decorated with pretty statues.

Musée de l'Ecorché d'anatomie ♿🕐*Open mid-Feb–mid-Dec 2–6.30pm.* 🕐*Closed Mon and Tue, mid-Dec–mid-Feb* and 1 May. €4.50. ℘02 32 35 93 95. www-musee-anatomie.fr. In the early 19C Dr Auzoux, who comes from the region, invented an anatomy model for his medical students that could be taken apart to see muscles, membranes and nerves. This museum shows how he conceived it, along with a room devoted to local fauna.

From Le Neubourg there are five cycling itineraries. Contact the tourist office for information (in converted former train station). The green route through Le Neubourg also offers beautiful cycling excursions.

▷ *Head for Conches-en-Ouche. Leave Le Neubourg by S, taking the D 840.*

Le Tremblay-Omonville

The château has a curious fore part (18C); terraces and imposing service quarters.

▷ *Come back to Le Neubourg and take the D 137 for Brionne.*

Harcourt★

This small town near Le Neubourg is at the intersection of roads leading to the banks of the River Risle and River Charentonne and Beaumont Forest. Not far from the 13C **church** (*open Mon–Tue and Thu–Fri 9am–noon, 1.30–4.30pm, Sat 9am–11.30am; get key at mairie;* ℘02 32 45 02 40) the old wooden marketplace stands intact.

Two waymarked treks (6km/3mi and 20.5km/12mi) leave from the church.

Château d'Harcourt★

Open mid-Jun–mid-Sept daily 10.30am–6.30pm; Mar–mid-Jun and mid-Sept–mid-Nov Wed–Mon 2–6pm. Closed mid-Nov–end Feb. €4. ℘02 32 46 29 70.

Late 12C castle built by Robert II of Harcourt, companion to Richard the Lionheart, modernised in the 14C and made a comfortable residence in the 17C. The imposing mass of the castle stands sheltered by its curtain wall, 20m/65.6ft wide moat, and ramparts flanked by dilapidated towers. Restored medieval entrance and bridge.

Arboretum★

Same as for the château.

Adjoining the main courtyard, a 10ha/25acre arboretum presents over 400 tree species coming from the five continents.

ADDRESSES

STAY

DREUX

Hôtel La Dousseine – *47 route de Sorel, 28260 Anet, 20km/12mi N of Dreux.* ℘02 37 41 49 93. www.dousseine.com. 20 rooms. €6.50. Charmingly discreet location for this hotel; all rooms have views of park; half of the rooms are on the ground floor at garden level.

Hôtel Le Beffroi – *12 pl. Métezeau.* ℘02 37 50 02 03. www.hotelbeffroi.fr. Closed 23 Jul–16 Aug. 15 rooms. €7. To visit the belltower and church of St Peter, you have a front row seat here. Rooms simple but functional; quieter next to the river.

La Ferme des Luthiers – *12 r. Hottetere, 27750 La Couture-Boussey, 26km/16mi N of Dreux.* ℘ 02 32 36 76 06. www.lafermedesluthiers.com.4 rooms. Pretty B&B in what was a sheepfold in the 18C; rustic but comfortable. Family-style Norman cuisine.

ÉVREUX

Chambre d'hôte Manoir de la Boissière – *Hamlet "La Boissaye", 27490 La Croix-St-Leufroy, 16km/10mi NE.* ℘02 32 67 70 85. www.chambres-la-boissiere.com. 5 rooms. This 15C manor is a working farm. The rooms are all different, with family furniture. Pretty duck pond and veranda. Dining by reservation.

Grand Hôtel de la Gare – *61 bd Gambetta.* ℘02 3238 67 45. Restaurant. 29 rooms. €6.50. Just 2 min from the town centre, rooms here offer a reasonable degree of comfort. The restaurant serves traditional food.

Hôtel de l'Orme – *13 r. des Lombards.* ℘02 32 39 34 12. www.hotel-de-lorme.fr. Closed Sat–Sun from Oct–Mar. 39 rooms. €9. In the town centre, this hotel has functional rooms.

LE BEC-HELLOUIN

Chambre d'hôte Château de Boscherville – *27520 Bourgtheroulde, 10km/ 6mi NE.* ℘*02 35 87 62 12. 5 rooms.* Bright, comfortable rooms in this small 18C family château. Jean de La Fontaine stayed here; centuries-old oaks in the park.

Normandy Hôtel – *37 r. Édouard-Feray.* ℘*02 32 33 14 40. www.normandyhotel.eu. 20 rooms.* €9. A step from the Tour de l'Horloge, former relay station with Norman cachet; charming, comfortable rooms. Fireplace in winter, terrace in summer; fine French cuisine.

℉ EAT

DREUX

Market Pub – *19 r. Mérigot.* ℘*02 37 46 18 44. www.restaurant-marketpub.fr. 11.45am– 2pm, 6.45–10pm.* A step away from the market, modern décor and innovative cuisine with top-quality ingredients. Great view of the old town from second-floor.

Aux Quatre Vents – *18 pl. Métezeau.* ℘*02 37 50 03 24. www.aux-quatre-vents.fr. Closed evenings and Sat, except Fri in season.* A family business; traditional recipes in a brasserie-style restaurant. Outdoor tables. Buffet.

Le Saint-Pierre – *19 r. Sénarmont.* ℘*02 37 46 47 00. www.lesaint-pierre.com. Closed 28 Feb–7 Mar, 14–31 Jul, Sun evening, Thu evening and Mon. Lunch menu.* Tucked into little street near church of St Peter. Three dining rooms and pretty pastel colours, bistro furniture. Warm welcome, traditional cuisine, nice price.

Auberge de la Vallée Verte – *6 r. Lucien-Dupuis, 28500 Vernouillet, 2km– 1mi S of Dreux by D 311.* ℘ *02 37 46 04 04. www.aubergevalleeverte.fr. Closed 1–25 Aug, 25 Dec–9 Jan, Sun and Mon. 16 rooms.* . €8. Exposed beams, fireplace and paintings; traditional cooking. Impeccable rooms, bigger in the annex, embellished with a garden.

ÉVREUX

Hôtel de France – *29 r. St-Thomas.* ℘*02 32 39 09 25. Closed Sat lunch, Sun eve and Mon. Reservation advised.* This eatery offers seasonal menus. 16 guest rooms.

La Croix d'Or – *3 r. Joséphine.* ℘*02 32 33 06 07. www.la-croix-dor.fr.* Seafood served in a long, sober dining room or on the veranda is the speciality of this establishment. A local favourite.

La Vielle Gabelle – *3 r. de la Vieille- Gabelle.* ℘ *02 32 39 77 13. Closed 1–24 Aug, Sat lunch, Sun evening and Mon.* Half- timbered façade; two dining rooms, modern cuisine.

La Gazette – *7 r. St-Sauveur.* ℘*02 32 33 43 40. www.restaurant-lagazette.fr. Closed Aug, Sat lunch, Sun.* Well looked-after establishment; modern furnishings, old newspapers lining the walls.

Côté Jardin – *rte de Lisieux, 27180 Parville, 5km/3mi W of Évreux.* ℘*02 32 39 19 19. www.restaurant-cotejardinparville.com. Closed Sun and Mon evenings.* Pretty half- timbered house. Charming dining room; Norman setting, painted pastel.

Ô Saveurs – *1 r. du Maréchal-Joffre.* ℘*02 32 31 61 05. http://osaveurs.wifeo.com. Closed Sun and Mon. Reservation advised.* New restaurant offering traditional Norman cuisine. Two dining rooms, very pleasant terrace. Already popular locally.

LE BEC-HELLOUIN

Le Canterbury – *r. de Canterbury.* ℘*02 32 44 14 59. Closed Sun, Tue eve, Wed.* The aim here is not to impress, but to satisfy. The result: scrupulously well-prepared cuisine served in a fine half-timbered 18C house. Over 60 kinds of Calvados to sample. Small terrace open in fine weather.

☺ ON THE TOWN

ÉVREUX

Le Grand Café – *11 r. de la Harpe.* ℘*02 32 33 14 01.* In pedestrian street on the canal, traditional café with two terraces; view of the cathedral. Brasserie-style meals at lunch and Thu–Sun.

⛒ SHOPPING

ÉVREUX

Chocolatier Auzou – *34 r. Chartraine.* ℘*02 32 33 28 05. Closed 1 Jan, 1 May, Sun in Jul–Aug.* This confectioner's produces several house specialities: Zouzous d'Auzou and macaroons of Grand'Mère Auzou.

The Perche is a region subdivided into two: the Norman Perche and the southern sector, the Perche-Gouët or Lower Perche. The Perche countryside is thick with forests, hedgerows, gentle hills and green dales, while Perche buildings offer interesting architecture. Pays d'Auge manors look like country homes; in the Norman Perche, they resemble small stone fortresses. Although most of these late 15C and early 16C lordly homes are now farmhouses, they still have their towers, elegant turrets and delicately carved façades.

Percheron Horse

The large, powerful Percheron horse is known for gentleness and manoeuvrability. Its capacity to pull heavy loads at a trot long made it ideal for draft work, and especially for coaches from the 17C on. By the 19C it was one of the most common horses in the UK and the United States. However, with the development of motorised vehicles its numbers dropped. In 2009, only 20,000 horses were known of worldwide, and the Perche horse is today considered dangerously close to extinction. French breeders are now attempting to cross it with American stallions to make it a lighter horse for racing.

Cider Country

Cider was originally a peasant's drink. As early as the 16C Rabelais called himself "an apple-gatherer in the Perche countryside", and the Perche countryside has indeed long been one of orchards and cider-making. The 1950s brought modernised farming and the decline of the industry. The drink itself had become

Highlights

1 Climb 155 16C steps to the fortress in **Nogent** (p236)
2 Learn about medieval abbey life in **Thiron-Gardais** (p237)
3 Admire the chapels in **La Ferté-Bernard**'s church (p238)
4 Taste real Norman farm cider in **Le Theil-sur-Huisne** (p240)
5 Visit ancient oaks in **Perche** and **Trappe Forests** (p242)

unfashionable, and the orchards were abandoned. Fortunately, the 1990s brought with them a desire to save this important part of the Perche identity. More than 150 unique Perche apple and pear varieties were rediscovered and logged.

Today orchards are being replanted, local apple varieties are being grafted, and the region has the new ambition of obtaining the coveted AOC label for its unique Perche cider.

Percheron Horse

© Dominique VERNIER/Fotolia.com

PERCHE

N

10 km
5 miles

PARIS

EVREUX
N 154
Nonancourt
D 4
Dampierre-s-Blévy
D 939
EURE-ET-LOIR
D 938
Tillières-s-Avre
D 11
D 30
D 939
EURE
N 12
D 20
Senonches
D 316
D 941
D 939
Forêt de Senonches
Francheville
D 567
D 55
D 926
Verneuil-s-Avre
D 941
La Ferté-Vidame
D 941
Eure
Tourbière des Froux
Forêt humide des Mousseuses
D 4
N 12
Iton
Côteau de la Bandonnière
D 11
Longny-au-Perche
Monceaux-au-Perche
D 8
St-Victor-de-Réno
D 111
D 930
D 918
Autheuil
Forêt de Réno-Valdieu
L'Aigle
D 919
Forêt du Perche
D 32
Tourouvre
La Chapelle-Montligeon
La Vove
Forêt de la Trappe
Abbᵉ de la Trappe
N 12
Loisé
Loisail
D 926
Ste-Céronne-les-Mortagne
Mortagne-au-Perche
D 938
D 932
ORNE
D 932
D 8
N 12
Chêne de la Lambonnière
ALENÇON

CHARTRES

PARIS

LE MANS

SARTHE

Illiers-Combray
Happonvilliers
Yèvres
Brou
Frazé
Thiron-Gardais
Argenvilliers
La Bazoche-Gouët
Frétigny
La Gaudaine
Rougemont
Vichères
Les Étilleux
St-Ulphace
Nogent-le-Rotrou
Margon
Courgenard
Montmirail
St-Maurice-sur-Huisne
Ceton
Courtangis
Courboyer
La Ferté-Bernard
Préaux-du-Perche
Ste-Gauburge
St-Cyr-la-Rosière
La Pierre procureuse
Le-Theil-sur-Huisne
Courcerault
L'Angenardière
St-Germain-de-la-Coudre
Étang et fontaine de la Herse
Bellême
Les Feugerets
St-Martin-du-Vieux-Bellême
Forêt de Bellême
La Perrière
Mamers

Parc naturel régional du Perche

Huisne

Verneuil-sur-Avre
Brou

★ Interesting
† Worth a visit
⇧ Driving tour with departure point

D 941 · D 30E · D 15 · D 923 · D 5 · D 955 · D 338 · D 826 · D 103 · D 112 · D 9 · D 637 · D 118 · D 10 · D 920 · D 955 · D 277 · D 11 · D 923 · A 11 · D 7 · D 36 · D 626 · D 107 · D 7 · D 938 · D 955 · D 2 · D 323 · D 275 · D 7 · D 301 · D 311 · D 918

Nogent-le-Rotrou

The capital of the Perche region lies on the banks of the River Huisne, dominated by its castle. The old town borders the main road (N 23) at the foot of St John's Hill; the new town covers the flat land beside the River Huisne.

A BIT OF HISTORY

Between 925 and 1226 the Gallo-Roman town became a powerful Rotrou family fief; counts of Perche, they gave the town its name (Nogent, from the Gallic *novio-mago,* meaning new market). Nogent was burned in 1449 at Charles VII's command, to prevent the English from capturing it. It was rebuilt soon afterwards, in the Flamboyant or Renaissance style.

SIGHTS

Église Notre-Dame

Corner of rue Gouverneur and rue de Sully ○*Open daily 8am–7pm.*
The building was formerly the chapel of the Hôtel-Dieu (workhouse) and dates from the 13C and 14C. At the end of the north aisle there is a 16C–17C crib; the figures are of painted terracotta.

Famous Names

Poet **Rémi Belleau** (1528–77), born in Nogent-le-Rotrou and one of the founders of the Pléiad group, glorified the art of living; he also described rural landscapes and the beauty of natural shapes. Nogent-le-Rotrou is closely associated with **Maximilien de Béthune**, Duc de Sully (1560–1641), renowned financier of Henri IV. The duke owned Rosny, Sully, La Chapelle-d'Angillon, Henrichemont and Villebon. In 1624 he purchased the château and manor of Nogent from Henri II de Condé.

▸ **Population:** 11,358.
⚇ **Michelin Map:** 311-A-6.
▤ **Info:** 44 rue Villette-Gate. ℘02 37 29 68 86. www.nogentlerotrou-tourisme.fr.
▷ **Location:** Nogent-le-Rotrou is 91km/56.5mi SW of Dreux and 77km/47.8mi S of L'Aigle.
🅿 **Parking:** Park in place de la République.
◈ **Don't Miss:** Château St-Jean; the tomb of Sully.
◔ **Timing:** Take time to tour the surrounding Parc naturel régional du Perche.

Tombeau de Sully

Access is through rue de Sully: courtyard with oratory and tomb. ○*Open daily 9am–4.30pm, closed holidays.*
The doorway pediment to the Hôtel-Dieu (17C) displays Sully's coat of arms and emblems. As Sully was Protestant, his tomb is nearby but not part of the church. Barthélemy Boudin of Chartres sculpted his empty tomb.

Marches St-Jean

Initially only rue du Château led to the fortress; the "Demoiselles d'Armagnac", the duc de Nemours' daughters, had these 155 steps built in the 16C.

Château St-Jean

By the Marches-St-Jean, or by car along rue de Sully, then rue du Château-St-Jean. ○*Open Wed–Mon 10am–noon, 2–6pm; guided tour possible (45min, reserve 1 wk prior).* ○*Closed 1 Jan, 1 May, 1 Nov, 25 Dec.* ⊙€3. ℘02 37 52 18 02. www.chateau-nogentlerotrou.fr.
This impressive castle is on a rocky spur. The Rotrous, counts of Perche, lived in the huge rectangular keep (35m/115ft high), which is supported by unusual buttresses. The enclosing wall with its semicircular towers was built from the 12C–13C. The remarkable gatehouse has two round towers with arrow slits and machicolations. View from courtyard.

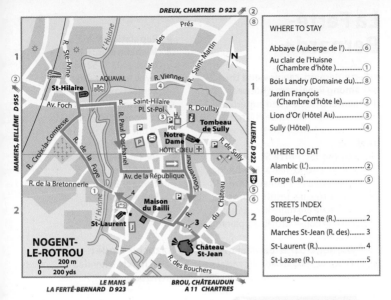

▷ *At foot of r. des Marches-St-Jean, cross r. Gouverneur; take r. Bourg-le-Compte which extends r. St-Laurent.*

Rue Bourg-le-Comte

Several of the houses are of interest: a 13C turreted house (no **2**), which is better seen from rue des Poupardières; a 16C house (no **4**); a Renaissance house with mullioned windows (no **3**).

Maison du Bailli

47 r. St-Laurent. ⏱Exterior only.
Two turrets flank the entrance to the 16C mansion built by Pierre Durant, Bailiff of St Denis' Abbey, and his wife, Blanche Dévrier. The dormer windows are particularly fine.

Église St-Laurent

The building is in the Flamboyant style, surmounted by a tower with a Renaissance top.

⛪Église St-Hilaire

Closed for restoration.
The church (13C–16C) stands beside the River Huisne. Its square tower dates from the 16C. The unusual polygonal chancel (13C) was modelled on the Holy Sepulchre in Jerusalem.

🚗DRIVING TOUR

① NEAR THE PERCHE CAPITAL

50km/31mi. 5hrs (including château).

Head north from Nogent on the D 103; before La Hurie, turn left on D 154 to go to **Frétigny; St Andrew's church** (*℘02 37 49 40 26*), which has 12C–13C frescoes. Now take the D 5 S for **Thiron-Gardais**, to **Tiron Abbey**. Park across from the tourist office and gardens (⏱*abbey: daily 9am–6pm; gardens closed noon–2pm. ◉€3. No charge in winter. ℘02 37 49 49 49*). Founded in 1114, the Benedictine Order of Tiron was influential 12C–13C. The vast church has 14C stalls. Visitors can learn about medieval abbey life in the gardens.

Drive south on the D 5 to **Argenvilliers**, to the 18C **château d'Ourisères** (*park open 10am–5pm, no charge; guided tour of château by appt; ℘02 37 29 43 68*).
From there, take the D 3713 to the **Ferme de Rougemont** where there is an immense view of the region. From here, head for Vichères, take the D 1121, right. Just before Nogent, turn at the chapel on your left for a beautiful view of the countryside around the Perche capital.

La Ferté-Bernard★

In Ferté-Bernard, canals wend their way among Renaissance houses, the fountain, market and superb Flamboyant-Renaissance church.

SIGHTS

Begin by the 15C **Porte St-Julien** *(pl. St-Julien)*, which once had a drawbridge. It takes you to a few Renaissance **old houses** in rue de l'Huisne; *(no 15, caryatid)*. There are more in rue Carnot: a 15C inn and house with lively painted caryatids.

The **Église Notre-Dame-des-Marais★★** *(pl. Sadi-Carnot;* ⁓guided tour; enter by the Flamboyant south portal; ℘02 43 71 21 21)*, built over two centuries, is both Flamboyant and Renaissance. Don't miss the three **absidal chapels★**: 16C windows and one *(right)* has a stunning coffered ceiling; also look out for the sacristy's 15C painted alabaster panels. The 15C–16C **fountain** *(pl. Carnot)*, 16C **market** *(between pl. de la Lice and r. Carnot)* and 12C **St Liphardus' chapel** *(imp du Château, near market)* deserve a visit.

🚗 DRIVING TOUR

7 LE PERCHE-GOUËT
87km/54mi. About a half day.

Meadows and orchards flourish here.

▷ *D 153, via Cherrau; D 136 to Ceton.*

Ceton
St Peter's church has a Romanesque belltower with Gothic choir and nave.

▷ *Take D 637 for Coudray-au-Perche.*

Les Étilleux
⁓ South of the village on D 13, near a tiny farm, take the path up for a view.

▷ *Return to Coudray-au-Perche (D 124), then Authon-du-Perche (D 9) and continue to La Bazoche-Gouët.*

- ▶ **Population:** 9,262
- ♿ **Michelin Map:** B4
  Info: ℘02 37 52 18 02; www.tourisme-laferte bernard.com.
- ▷ **Location:** 40km/24mi E of Mans, 90km/55mi SW of Chartres
- ✆ **Don't Miss:** Discovering the town via its canals – and in a canoe!
- ◷ **Timing:** 1hr for the historic centre.

La Bazoche-Gouët
12C–13C **church**, extended 16C *(access by covered passageway)*.

▷ *Now take the D 338, and after the crossroads with the D 126, the D 94 bis.*

St-Ulphace
Halfway up slope; 15C–16C **church**.

▷ *Continue on D 14.*

Montmirail
Viewed from the terrace, Montmirail **château**'s *(Jul–mid-Aug Wed–Mon 2–7pm; May–Jun and mid-Aug–mid-Sept, Sat and hols 2.30–6.30pm;* ⁓guided tours (40min) 3pm, 4pm, 5pm. ≈€5. ℘02 43 93 72 71)* classical west façade contrasts with the eastern medieval front; the château enjoys a panoramic view of Perche-Gouët. Montmirail also has a 12–16C **church**.

▷ *Take Ferté-Bernard road by the D 36.*

Château de Courtangis
The château is a gracious 16C manor.

▷ *Leave on D 36 for Courgenard.*

Courgenard
Courgenard's church has 16C murals.

▷ *Take D 7 to La Ferté-Bernard.*

Bellême

Bellême, a typical village of the region, overlooks the forest and the beautiful Perche countryside. The town had a particularly turbulent history in the Middle Ages, when Blanche of Castile and the future St Louis (Louis IX, 1214–70) took the fortress by storm in 1229.

SIGHTS
Ville-Close

The **gate**, flanked by two reconstructed towers, together with towers now incorporated into domestic buildings, are the only remains of the 15C ramparts, which once enclosed the town and were built upon 11C fortress foundations.

Rue Ville-Close, on the site of the former citadel, is lined with fine 17C and 18C houses. Outstanding are no **24**, the Governor's house, and especially no **26**, the **Hôtel Bansard des Bois**.

Église St-Sauveur

pl. de la République.
Open Sat–Sun 9am–6pm.
The late 17C St Saviour's Church has a richly decorated interior. Note in particular the imposing high altar and canopy (1712) made of stone and marble, the chancel woodwork from the old abbey of Valdieu, and the windows, each composed of six scenes from the life of Christ. The font, decorated with garlands, stands against a three-panelled altarpiece.

🚗 DRIVING TOUR

2 FORÊT DE BELLÊME

Forêt de Bellême★
35km/21mi. About 3hrs.

This forest (2,400ha/5,930 acres) is one of the most beautiful in the Perche.

▶ *From Bellême take D 938 NW. There is a very pretty* **view** *from road.*

▶ **Population:** 1,576.
🚳 **Michelin Map:** 310: M-4
ℹ **Info:** Bd Bansart-des-Bois. ℘02 33 73 09 69. http://belleme.parc-naturel-perche.fr.
▶ **Location:** Bellême is 22km/ 13.5mi NW of Nogent-le-Rotrou and 17km/10.5mi S of Mortagne-au-Perche.
👁 **Don't Miss:** The old houses of the Ville-Close, and the forest walks.
🕐 **Timing:** Give yourself 1hr to see the town and 3hr to visit the Écomusée at Ste-Gauburge.

Étang et Fontaine de la Herse

A path circles the pool – 15min on foot. A lovely cool spot. Opposite the forester's lodge is a Roman fountain and two stone blocks with Latin inscriptions.

▶ *Backtrack to Colbert crossroads; turn right.*

The forest road (surfaced) affords lovely views.

▶ *At the Creux Valley crossroads, go left to drive along forest edge. Take first right to re-enter the forest. After the Montimer crossroads turn left and head down for 400m/0.2mi.*

Chêne de l'École

This 300-year-old oak is 40m/131ft tall; its circumference is 22m/72ft.

▶ *Return to the Montimer crossroads and continue to La Perrière.*

La Perrière

The name comes from the Latin *petraria* (stone quarry). Many houses are in dark-red ferruginous sandstone *(grison).*
To look at the town's old streets and 15C–17C homes, take the **"sentier découverte"** *(path plan at tourist office).* From the cemetery path near the church there is a **panoramic view★** of the

Perche countryside with Perseigne *(W)* and Écouves Forests *(NW)*. Four **trekking routes** (3, 4, 5 or 12.5km/1, 2, 3 or 7mi) leave from pl. de la Poste or the church *(maps at tourist office).*

▶ *Take the D 210 for Bellavilliers, then D 275 (passing by the D 931) to reach Pervenchères. Continue N by the D 27; after Vauvineux, turn left into marked road for the Chêne de la Lambonnière.*

Chêne de la Lambonnière
This oak, over 500 years old, has a trunk 7.32m/24ft in circumference.

▶ *Return to Pervenchères and continue on D 27 to La Gravelle; take the D 7 (right) to Bellavilliers, then D 310 to St-Martin-du-Vieux-Bellême.*

St-Martin-du-Vieux-Bellême
The village clusters around the 14C–15C church. Three trekking routes (2–4km/1–2mi), from the church to Bellême Forest.

▶ *Take D 955 on left for Bellême.*

3 BELLÊME COUNTRYSIDE
34km/21mi. Allow about 3hrs.

▶ *From Bellême take D 7 south.*

Château des Feugerets
⚲*Closed to public.* A harmonious, well-balanced château design.

▶ *Take the D 7 to St-Germain-de-la-Coudre.*

St-Germain-de-la-Coudre
The church has an 11C crypt. The **Manoir de La Fresnaye** (℘02 33 83 57 64; ◷1 Jul–15 Sep 1–7pm. ◷Closed Sat–Mon – other dates by appt; ⇔€4) has a pretty view from the keep of its 14C–16C manor.

▶ *D 107 for Le Theil-sur-Huisne.*

Le Theil-sur-Huisne
The **Cidrerie traditionnelle du Perche** (at "Tronas" on the D 107. ◷Open Apr–Oct 10am–noon, 3–8pm; Nov–Mar Wed–Sun, 10am–noon, 3–7pm (shop); ⇔No charge. ℘02 37 49 67 30) offers guided tours of cider-making facilities; you can also buy their produce.

▶ *Leave on the D 11 to Saint-Agnan-sur-Eure, then left for Préaux-du-Perche.*

Préaux-du-Perche
The very pretty **church** of St-Germain has architecture ranging 12C–18C. Three **trekking routes** (5.5–17km/3–10mi) depart from the war memorial; a fourth (5km/3mi) leaves from the nature park's car park.

▶ *Take the D 277 W.*

Prieuré de Sainte-Gauburge
At St-Cyr-la-Rosière. ◷Open Apr–Sept 10.30am–6.30pm; Oct–Mar 10.30am–6pm (closed wkd mornings Dec–Jan) ◷Closed 1 Jan, 24–25, 31 Dec. ⇔€5.40. ℘02 33 73 48 06. www.ecomuseeduperche.fr.
The church is now the **Écomusée du Perche**, where past crafts live again. 👥Children's workshops at weekends and school holidays. *Phone to reserve.*
Three **trekking routes** (3.5–13.5km /2–8mi) leave from here to the manors and La Pierre Procureuse.

▶ *From priory, head for Theil, following signs to "La Pierre Procureuse".*

La Pierre Procureuse
This stone roof on a late Neolithic (2,500 BC) dolmen, brings luck if you touch it.

▶ *Backtrack and take road for St-Cyr-la-Rosière, Clémance.*

Manoir de l'Angenardière
⚲*Closed to public.* This manor house, built 15C and 16C, has a rampart.

▶ *Continue to St-Cyr-la-Rosière.*

St-Cyr-la-Rosière
The church has a Romanesque portal and 17C terracotta **Entombment**★.

Mortagne-au-Perche

This pretty village retains a medieval design with the houses clustered together, presenting a jumble of brown-tile roofs contrasting with the lighter-coloured façades. The village was once a stronghold of the Perche region.

VISIT

Jardin Public

These gardens *à la française* offer good views of the Perche countryside. An outstanding equestrian statue by E Frémiet (1824–1910) depicts Neptune as a horse, setting out to conquer Ceres.

Hôpital

Delightful 16C cloisters with panelled vaulting and an 18C chapel are all that remain of the former convent of St Clare.

Porte St-Denis

Musée Percheron , rue du Portail-St-Denis. Open mid-Jun–mid-Sept Tue–Sun 3–6pm. Closed 14 Jul.
No charge. 02 33 25 25 87.
The St-Denis Gate is the sole remnant of the town's fortifications. In the 16C two storeys were added to the original

- **Population:** 4,156.
- **Michelin Map:** 310: M-3.
- **Info:** Halle-aux-Grains. 02 33 85 11 18. www.ot-mortagne auperche.fr.
- **Location:** Mortagne is 35km/21.7mi S of L'Aigle; 74km/46mi SW of Dreux.
- **Don't Miss:** Approaching from the N, on D 930, you will enjoy an excellent view of the town.
- **Timing:** After 1–2hr in town, take one of the described driving tours.

13C Gothic arch and they now house the **Musée Percheron**.

Maison des Comtes du Perche

This 17C house stands on the site of a former manor house. The ground floor houses the public library, and the first floor contains the Musée Alain.

Église Notre-Dame

The church was built between 1495 and 1535 and combines both Flamboyant Gothic and Early Renaissance styles on the exterior decoration.
There is a magnificent 18C **altarpiece**★ in the apse. The stained-glass window

in the third chapel, off the north aisle, recalls the role of local people in the colonisation of Canada in the 17C.

Musée Alain

8 r. du Portail St-Denis. ⏱*Open Tue, Thu–Fri 2–6pm, Wed 9.30am–noon, 1.30–6pm, Sat 10am–noon, 2–5pm.* ⏱*Closed 25 Dec–5 Jan and public holidays.* ⬤*No charge.* ✆*02 33 25 25 87.* French philosopher **Alain** (1868–1951), whose real name was **Émile Chartier**, was born in Mortagne. The museum displays personal belongings.

🚗 DRIVING TOURS

4 FROM MORTAGNE-AU-PERCHE TO LONGNY

50km/31mi. Allow about 1hr30min.

▶ *Leave Mortagne by the D 8, going E.*

Loisé

16C church with monumental tower.

▶ *Continue on the D 8; you pass the Château de la Goyère (left).*

Forêt de Réno-Valdieu★

Forest of very old trees; the most beautiful in the **Série artistique**★*(Degraine crossroads; indicated).* 🚶*Nature walk.*

▶ *Cross forest, take D 29, right.*

Saint-Victor-de-Reno

The church has a Renaissance statue of St Gilles. 🚶*From the church there are walks to Commeauche (4.5km/2mi) and Réno-Valdieu (6km/3.7mi).*

▶ *Return to D 8 to Longny-au-Perche.*

Longny-au-Perche

Pleasant spot on Jambée; good view of 16C **Chapelle de Notre-Dame-de-Pitié** *(r. Gaston-Gibory, right of mairie).* The **Église St-Martin** is 15C–16C.

▶ *D 11, S to Monceaux-au-Perche.*

Monceaux-au-Perche

The **Manoir du Pontgirard** (♿⏱*May–Sept wkd and hols 2.30–6.30pm.* ⬤*€5.* ✆*02 33 73 61 49; http://pontgirard.free. fr)* has fine terraced **gardens.** 🚶*There are three marked walks from the mairie (4km/2mi, 7.5km/4mi, 10.5km/6mi).*

▶ *Take D 11, S to Boissy-Maugis. Cross the Huisne; then 1km/6mi to St-Maurice-sur-Huisne.*

Saint-Maurice-sur-Huisne

At **Jardins des Perrignes** (⏱*Open 15 Apr_15 Jul daily 2–6pm;* ⬤*No charge),* **English gardens** are set around an old manor house

▶ *Head for Courcerault.*

Courcerault

The **Ferme-Musée de la Tonnelière** (⏱*Open Jun–Sept by appt;* ⬤*No charge.* ✆*02 33 83 91 32)* displays old farm and craft tools.

▶ *D 629 N; after 1.5km/1mi turn left.*

Manoir de La Vove

Exterior can be visited all year, Mon and Sat 2–6pm. Park outside. ⬤*No charge.* This is one of the oldest manors in the Perche. Its keep dates back to the 14C.

▶ *Backtrack to D 10 for Mortagne, left; D 5 for La Chapelle-Montligeon, right.*

La Chapelle-Montligeon

A vast neo-Gothic **basilica** (1896) with a view.

▶ *D 5 again N for pretty drive to D 8; turn left to return to Mortagne*

5 THE PERCHE AND TRAPPE FORESTS

54km/33mi. About 2hrs.

These forests are in the **Parc naturel Régional du Perche**★ *(see box opposite).*

▶ *From Mortagne take N 12 north; after 11km/6mi , right on D 290.*

PARC NATUREL RÉGIONAL DU PERCHE

| 0 | 10 | 20 km |
| 0 | 5 | 10 miles |

.... Park border   🛈 Information centre   🚲 Bicycle hire

🐎 Châteaux and manoirs   M Museum or exhibition   🐴 Percheron stables

Parc Naturel Régional du Perche ★

This regional park was created in 1998 to protect and showcase 1 820sq km/702.7sq mi of gentle hills, deep forests, hidden ponds, hedgerows, green valleys and interesting architecture; it also takes numerous initiatives on behalf of sustainable development. The Maison du Parc *(Courboyer, 61340, NOCE. ☎02 33 25 70 10. www.parc-naturel-perche.fr)* has been in the estate of **Courboyer** since 2000. This former manor house's surrounding buildings now house not only the administrative services, but also a shop, a dining space for tasting Perche gourmet specialities and a tourist information centre. Courboyer is a natural emblem for all there is to discover in the Perche, reflecting the rich architectural heritage to be found here in addition to its typical country estate.

Owing to its rich meadows the Perche is devoted to stock raising, particularly the breeding of the draught horses known as **Percherons**.

Autheuil
The Romanesque church (restored) has a fine chancel arch at the transept, and handsome capitals.

▷ *U-turn and D 290 W for Tourouvre.*

Tourouvre
Here you can discover the origins of modern Quebec, at the **Musée de l'Émigration française au Canada★**, which tells how Tourouve inhabitants left for "New France" in the 17C.

▷ *Beyond the church turn right.*

After a steep climb the road enters the **Perche Forest** and, after 2km/1mi, reaches the beautiful Étoile du Perche crossroads. Continue straight ahead and on reaching the Avre Valley turn left to admire the various pools. West of Bresolettes the road enters **Trappe Forest**.

▷ *At junction with D 930, turn right and almost immediately left.*

Abbaye de la Trappe
The 12C abbey was named after an area where hunters caught game using a *trappe*. 🐾Forest walk.

Verneuil-sur-Avre★

Verneuil comprises three districts, the main streets of which are rue de la Madeleine, rue Gambetta and rue Notre-Dame. In the past each district was like a mini-town protected by a fortified wall and a moat, just as the whole town was surrounded by an outer wall and moat. Some fine half-timbered houses and old mansions have been preserved in the town.

▸ **Population:** 6,694.
◔ **Michelin Map:** 304: F-9.
▯ **Info:** 129 place de la Madeleine. ℘02 32 32 17 17.
▷ **Location:** 36km/22.4mi W of Dreux on N 12.
◔ **Timing:** Count on 1 1/2 hr to visit the town.
♟ **Kids:** Don't miss the the the birds at the Bois des Aigles in Bâlines.

WHERE TO STAY

Saumon (Hôtel du).....................⑧

WHERE TO EAT

Collectionneur
Gourmand (Le).......................②
Madeleine (Le).........................④
P'tite Pause nature...................⑨

STREETS INDEX

Poissonnerie (R. de la)................2
Pont-aux-Chèvres (R. du)..........3
Tanneries (R. des).......................4

A BIT OF HISTORY

Verneuil was formerly a fortified city created in the 12C by Henry Beauclerk, Duke of Normandy, third son of William the Conqueror. Together with Tillières and Nonancourt it formed the Avre defence line on the Franco-Norman frontier. In 1204, the town became French under Philippe Auguste, who built the Grise Tower and its defence system.

After many battles with the English, the French victory of 1449 was achieved through the guile of miller Jean Bertin.

SIGHTS

Tour Grise

The sentry walk at the top of this 13C tower is built of red agglomerate (*grison*), from which it takes its name.

To the south, cross the small bridge over the Iton River to view the tower together with a charming little house at its base. The pleasant and relaxing **Fougère Park** lies near the bridge.

The partly ruined **Église St-Jean** has retained its 15C tower and its Gothic doorway.

The term Promenades refers to boulevard Casati and its prolongation. Remains of several of the old outer fortifications are visible. From avenue du Maréchal-Joffre and avenue du Maréchal-Foch are interesting views of the town.

The many old houses are extremely well restored and add to Verneuil's charm. Note for instance the 15C residence at the corner of rue de la Madeleine and rue du Canon, with its chequered walls and turret, which now houses the public library. Between rue Canon and rue Thiers, on rue de la Madeleine, stand a number of attractive stone or timbered houses. The 18C Hôtel Bournonville has wrought-iron balconies. Note also the houses at nos 532 (behind a courtyard), 466 and 401.

A Renaissance house stands at no 136 rue des Tanneries, with a carved wooden door surmounted by wooden statues. At the corner of rue Notre-Dame and rue du Pont-aux-Chèvres stands a 16C town house with decorated turret. On place de Verdun, place de la Madeleine,

16C polychrome tomb, Église de la Madeleine

© Hervé Gyssels/Photononstop

rue de la Poissonerie there are more picturesque old wooden houses.

Église de la Madeleine★

Enter by S side portal. Guided tour of tower only. €2. ℘02 32 32 17 17. *Reservation at tourist office.*

The **tower**★ abutting the church dates from the late 15C–early 16C. The third of the four tiers is surmounted by a richly decorated belfry.

The Renaissance-style porch is flanked by mutilated but beautiful 16C statues of the Virgin and of St Anne. The interior is lit by 15C and 16C stained-glass windows and has several 15C and 16C artworks. The nave ceiling is vaulted in wood.

Église Notre-Dame

pl. Notre-Dame.

The church, built of the red stone known as *grison* in the 12C, has been remodelled and possesses a number of 16C **statues**★ carved by local sculptors. The illustration (below) shows: **1)** St Denis (14C). **2)** St James the Great. **3)** St Christopher. **4)** St Christine. **5)** St Fiacre. **6)** St Susanna. **7)** St Barbara. **8)** St Francis of Assisi.

9) St Benedict. **10)** Joan of Arc, as a Lorraine country girl. **11)** Renaissance *Pietà*. **12)** St Lawrence. **13)** St Augustine. **14)** St Denis with open skull. **15)** St Louis (17C). **16)** Two Prophets (Renaissance woodwork). **17)** St Sebastian (17C woodwork). **18)** 15C chest and altar base. **19)** 11C font. **20)** 14C Trinity (early Norman Renaissance). **21)**Virgin at Calvary (13C). **22)** St John.

EXCURSION
Francheville
◐ *9km/5.6mi NW on D 56.*
Village on River Iton with pretty church. Ironwork museum, the **Musée de la Ferronnerie** *(place Modeste Leroy.* ℘*02 32 60 18 89.* *www.francheville-eure.fr).*

DRIVING TOUR

⑥ **FROM VALLÉE DE L'AVRE TO FORÊT DE SENONCHES**
64km/39mi. Allow 2hrs.

◐ *From Verneuil, drive along the Avre:* *D 839, then D 316 (left) becomes D 102:* *Montigny-sur-Avre and Bérou-la-* *Mulotière for Tillières.*

Tillières-sur-Avre
Tillières was the first Norman fortified town built (1013) to guard the Avre defence line. The church, with its Romanesque nave and panelled vault,

was rebuilt in the 16C. From the garden called the Grand Parterre, there is a fine view of the Avre Valley.

◐ *Head S by D 30 to Brezolles;* *continue on D 939. At Chennevières,* *right for Dampierre-sur-Blévy.*

Dampierre-sur-Blévy
The **Maison de Maître des Forges** *(◐open 10 Jul–20 Aug daily 1–7pm;* ≈*No charge. www.lesforgesde dampierresur-blevy.com)* has a an old 17C forge furnace still in very good condition.

◐ *Continue on D 20 to reach Senoches.*

Senoches
This flower-decked little town has the remains of a 12C **castle** (château), under restoration.
The real treasure is the surrounding 4300ha/10,625 acres of **forest.**
🐾There are about a dozen waymarked treks in the forest *(ask for the map at the tourist office ℘02 37 37 80 11).*
🐾To the southwest, near Manou on the D 140, the site of the **tourbière des Froux** has been protected and turned into a place to learn about the fragile eco-system of the peat bog.

◐ *The D 941 crosses the forest to take* *you to La Ferté-Vidame.*

La Ferté-Vidame
This is a lovely, immense ruined château, set in a vast 18C French-style **park** and forest. Louis de Rouvy, duc de St-Simon – a celebrated memorialist at Louis XIV's court – owned a château here once, but the remains are that of the château of the Marquis Jean Joseph de Laborde, which was subsequently built here in 1770.
The **pavillon Saint-Dominique** *(left at park entrance)* contains two exhibition rooms recounting the lives of the writer and the Marquis de Laborde in La Ferté-Vidame *(◐Visit with diaporama (slide show) Apr–Oct 10am–noon, 2–6pm; rest of the year 10am–noon, 1.30–5.30pm. Closed Mon.* ≈*€2 (under 10s no charge), free on Journées de patrimoine; audio-*

guide rental for tour of park; ℘02 37 37 68 59).

▶ *Return to Verneuil on the D 941.*

ADDRESSES

🏠 STAY

NOGENT-LE-ROTROU

⊝⊝ **Auberge de l'Abbaye** – *15 r. du Commerce, 28480 Thiron-Gardais, 14 km/ 8mi E of Nogent. ℘ 02 37 49 54 18. www.aubergedelabbaye.fr. 7 rooms. ⊆€9. Restaurant* ⊝. Good for exploring around Thiron-Gardais. Simple, comfy rooms.

⊝⊝ **Chambre d'hôte Au Clair de l'Huisne** – *3 r. Bretonnerie . ℘06 11 43 46 72. www. auclairdelhuisne.fr. 3 rooms. ⊆.* Attractive 18C riverside farm with comfortable rooms. Bicycle loan, kayak hire; pool.

⊝⊝ **Domaine du Bois Landry** – *La Graiserie, 28240 Champrond-en-Gâtine. ℘02 37 49 80 01.www.boislandry.com. Seven treehouses for 2 or 4.* Unusual – good beds but no water or electricity.

⊝⊝ **Hôtel Au Lion d'Or** – *28 pl. St-Pol . ℘02 37 52 01 60. www.hotel-chartres-le-mans.com. Closed in Aug.* 🅿 *18 rooms. ⊆€6.50.* Former relay station with nice clean rooms.

⊝⊝ **Hôtel Sully** – *51 r. des Viennes. ℘02 37 52 15 14. www.hotelsullynogent.fr. Closed one week in Aug.* 🅿 *42 rooms. ⊆ €7.* Recent building in quiet neighbourhood; good functional rooms.

LA FERTÉ-BERNARD

⊝⊝ **Chambre d'hôte La Veronnière** – *61260 Le Theil, 8km/5mi NW of La Ferté-Bernard by D 323. ℘02 37 49 76 01. 2 rooms. ⊆.* Environmentally conscious establishment in a stone barn; absolutely fresh ingredients.

BELLÊME

⊝⊝⊝ **Relais Saint-Louis** – *1 bd Bansard-des-Bois. ℘02 33 73 12 21. www.relais-st-louis.com. Closed 15–22 Feb, 12–30 Nov. 9 rooms. ⊆€8. Restaurant* ⊝⊝ Delightful, classically decorated rooms; dining room fireplace, earthy cuisine.

MORTAGNE-AU-PERCHE

⊝⊝ **Chambre d'hôte La Miottière** – *61400 Le Pin-La-Garenne, 12km/7.5mi S. ℘02 33 83 84 01. 3 rooms.* 🅿⌷⌷. Set in the countryside in an area of 53ha/130 acres. Spacious rooms, copious breakfasts.

⊝⊝⊝ **Hôtel Le Tribunal** – *4 pl. du Palais. ℘02 33 25 04 77. 18 rooms. ⊆€9.* Family-run, in a house built 13C–18C. Church and museum nearby.

VERNEUIL-SUR-AVRE

⊝⊝ **Hôtel du Saumon** – *89 pl. de la Madeleine, Verneuil. ℘02 32 32 02 36. www.hoteldusaumon.fr. 29 rooms. ⊆. Restaurant* ⊝⊝. Rooms in the main building decorated with antique furniture.

🍽/EAT

NOGENT-LE-ROTROU

⊝⊝ **L'Alambic** – *20 av. de Paris, 28400 Margon (exit N of Nogent). ℘02 37 52 19 03. Closed Wed evening, Sun evening, Mon, 4–25 Aug, 22–30 Sep and 18–28 Feb.* Former lorry-driver eatery has become a restaurant offering traditional cuisine.

⊝ **La Forge** – *1 r. Alfred-Chasseriaud 28480 Thiron-Gardais. ℘ 02 37 49 42 30. www.a-la-forge.com. Closed Mon and evenings except Fri and Sat.* Artist-chef; his paintings decorate this old 16C abbey forge.

LA FERTÉ-BERNARD

⊝⊝ **Le Dauphin** – *3 r. d'Huisne. ℘02 43 93 00 39. Closed Easter holiday, Aug, Thu evening, Sun evening and Mon.* 16C house with cachet of yesteryear but lively decoration. Up-to-date cuisine.

VERNEUIL-SUR-AVRE

⊝ **P'tite Puse nature**– *15 pl. de la Madeleine. ℘ 02 32 38 58 53. Closed Monday.* Small, charming dining room; big servings made with farm-fresh products.

⊝⊝ **Le Collectionneur Gourmand** – *Ruelle de l'Abreuvoir, 63 r. Gustave Roger. ℘02 32 60 11 11. Closed Mon, Sun evening and Tue noon. Reservations advised.* Bric-a-brac decorates a gourmet restaurant. Look at fascinating old objects while waiting for your food. Tea room in the afternoon.

⊝⊝ **Le Madeleine** – *206 r. de la Madeleine. ℘02 32 37 78 26. Closed Wed.* Nice little traditional restaurant; jazz concerts 1st and 3rd Thu of the month.

CAEN *and the Plages du Débarquement*

The future of the city of Caen was bound to that of England when Duke William conquered that powerful country facing Normandy across the Channel. During the Hundred Years' War, the English occupied and developed the ducal city. Centuries later, on 6 June 1944, Caen found itself at the epicentre of a global power struggle with the Normandy Landings, the decisive battle to liberate France and Europe. Today, Caen's message of peace won it honourable mention in 1999 at the UNESCO Cities for Peace Prize.

Highlights

1 Contemplating **St-Étienne**'s church (p255)

2 Admiring paintings at Caen's **Musée de Beaux-Arts** (p258)

3 D-Day memories at **American Military Cemetery** (p274)

4 Reliving history with the. **Bayeux Tapestry** (p279)

5 Visiting an 18C **Garden of Surprises** (p287)

City of William the Conqueror

The first mention of the name "Caen" was in 1025. Founded in the Roman period, the growing town had been ceded to the Vikings a century before. The Normans were great warriors, and it was one of their greatest, William the Bastard, who in 1066 invaded the British Isles, to become William the Conqueror. From the Conquest onwards, ties between Caen and England were close, and it was the English who developed the ducal city, especially under Henry VI,

who built what is now one of France's oldest universities.

Caen bloomed in the Renaissance, developing an intense intellectual life. Up to the Age of Enlightenment Caen's citizens lived in peace and prosperity, shaping their city. During the 19th century industrial age, rail linked Caen to Paris. With the canal running from the city to the sea, its trading port developed internationally.

Normandy Landings

On 6 June 1944, Caen was the theatre of the decisive battle of World War II. Three million soldiers engaged in the titanic conflict, with Allies landing at five Normandy beaches – code-named Sword, Utah, Gold, Omaha and Juno – and parachuting behind enemy lines. A year later the war was over, but the Allied bombings meant Caen had to rebuild itself almost entirely. In so doing it created the Memorial Museum, a commitment to peace, solidarity and defence of human rights. It is this message that Caen seeks to convey to the world today as a City of Peace.

Le Mémorial, Caen

© www.calvados-tourisme.com

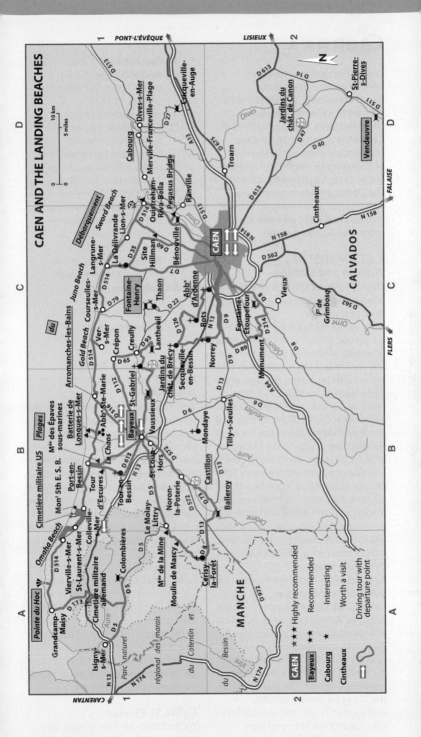

CAEN AND THE LANDING BEACHES

Caen★★★

Caen is the capital of Calvados and the cultural heart of the Basse-Normandie, a lively city with a distinctive identity. The bombs that fell here in 1944 could have left Caen lifeless, but the city proved resilient and drew on the strength of its history to rebuild and recreate. Today Caen is a charming place to visit. It has a modern spirit and a well-regarded university, which was founded in the 15C and now has more than 30,000 students.

A BIT OF HISTORY
William and Matilda

The city achieved importance in the 11C when it became Duke William's favourite place of residence.

After establishing himself as Duke of Normandy, William asked for the hand of Matilda of Flanders, a distant cousin. She replied that she would rather take the veil than be given in marriage to the bastard son of the beautiful Arlette.

One fine day, mad with love and anger, the duke rode headlong to Lille and burst into the palace of the Count of Flanders. According to the Chronicler of Tours, he seized Matilda by her plaits and dragged her round the room, kicking her as he did so. Then he left her gasping for breath and galloped off. Matilda admitted defeat and consented to the marriage. The Pope, however, objected to the cousins' distant kinship. In 1059, through the efforts of **Lanfranc**, the Pope relented.

As an act of penitence the duke and his wife founded two abbeys – the Abbey for Men (Abbaye-aux-Hommes) and the Abbey for Women (Abbaye-aux-Dames). Bayeux remained the episcopal See.

When William departed to conquer England, faithful Matilda became regent of the duchy; in 1068 she was crowned queen of England. She was buried in the Abbey for Women in 1083.

William died in 1087 and was buried in the church of the Abbey for Men.

▶ **Population:** 111,200.
Michelin Map: 303: J-4.
Info: 12 place St-Pierre. ✆02 31 27 14 14. www.tourisme.caen.fr.
Location: At the junction of the rivers Orne and Odon, Caen can be reached by the A 13, some 2.5hr, or 235km/146mi from Paris.
Don't Miss: The Mémorial, the Abbaye-aux-Hommes and the Fine Arts Museum (Musée des Beaux-Arts) housed in the château.
Timing: You need at least 2hr to visit the Mémorial.
Kids: There is an amusement park called Festyland nearby, *see p291.*

WALKING TOUR
Hôtel d'Escoville★

pl. Saint-Pierre.

This mansion, which now houses the tourist office and the Artothèque, was built between 1533 and 1538 by Nicolas Le Valois d'Escoville, a wealthy merchant. The bomb damage incurred in 1944 has been repaired. Behind the plain street façade there is a **courtyard** flanked by two wings at right angles; the harmonious proportions, the arrangement of the various elements and the majestic sculptures make an elegant composition.

The main block facing the entrance is surmounted by an unusual ornament: a large two-storey dormer window supported by flying buttresses projecting from a steep pavilion roof. Climb up to the loggia for a view of the whole courtyard.

▶ *Opposite the Hôtel d'Escoville stands the impressive Église St-Pierre.*

Église St-Pierre★

Open Mon–Sat 7.30am–6pm, Sun 7.30am–12.30pm. 1 Jan, 1 May, Mon of Pentecost, 14 Jul. ✆02 31 93 46 13.

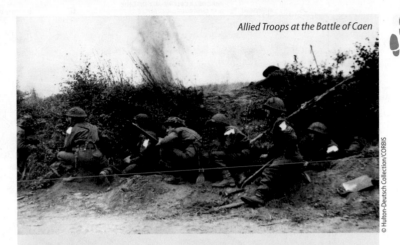

Allied Troops at the Battle of Caen

© Hulton-Deutsch Collection/CORBIS

Battle of Caen

Two Agonising Months – The battle lasted for over two months. On 6 June 1944 there was a heavy bombing raid; fire raged for 11 days and the central area was burnt out. On 9 July the Canadians, who had taken Carpiquet Airfield, entered Caen from the west but the Germans, who had fallen back to the east bank of the Orne in Vaucelles, began to shell the town. The liberation ceremony took place in Vaucelles on 20 July but German shelling lasted another month.

Under the Conqueror's Protection – On 6 June many people sought shelter in St-Étienne Church. During the battle, more than 1,500 refugees camped out in the abbey church. An operating theatre was contrived in the refectory of the Lycée Malherbe, which was housed in the monastery buildings of the Abbey for Men. The dead were buried in the courtyard. Some 4,000 people found accommodation in the Hospice of the Good Saviour (Bon Sauveur) nearby. The Allies were warned of this by the Préfet and the Resistance and these buildings were spared. The quarries at Fleury, 2km/1mi south of Caen, provided the largest refuge. Despite the cold and the damp, whole families lived there until the end of July.

Although only a parish church, St Peter's is richly decorated. Construction started in the 13C, was continued during the 14C and 15C and completed in the 16C in the Renaissance style. The impressive tower (78m/256ft), which dated from 1308, was destroyed during the Battle of Caen in 1944. "The king of Norman belfries" has, however, been rebuilt, as well as the nave into which it fell (all the vaulting has been redone). The west front has been restored to its 14C appearance; the Flamboyant porch is surmounted by a rose window.

The **east end**★★, built between 1518 and 1545, is remarkable for the richness of its Renaissance décor, in which the shapely and graceful furnishings (ornate pinnacles, urns, richly scrolled balustrades, carved pilasters), have replaced the Gothic motifs.

Some of the **capitals**★ *(second and third pillars on the left)* are interesting for their carvings, which are taken from the bestiaries of the period and chivalrous exploits.

The third pillar shows *(from left to right)* Aristotle on horseback threatened with a whip by Campaspe, Alexander the Great's mistress; the Phoenix rising from the flames (Resurrection); Samson breaking the lion's jaw (Redemption); the Pelican in her Piety (Divine Love); Lancelot crossing the Sword Bridge

Maison à pans de bois............ K
Musée de la Poste
et des Techniques
de communication.................. M

STREETS INDEX

Libération (Av. de la).............5
Montoir-Poissonnerie (R.)...8

to rescue his Queen; Virgil suspended in his basket by the daughter of the Roman emperor; the Unicorn (Incarnation), pursued by hunters; Gawain on his deathbed with an arrow wound (image is damaged).

The Renaissance vaulting in the second part of the nave, near the chancel, contrasts with the vaulting in the first part:

each arch is embellished with a hanging keystone, finely carved. The most remarkable keystone, in the fifth arch over the high altar, is 3m/9.8ft high and weighs 3t; it is a larger than life-size figure of St Peter.

The chancel is enclosed by four arches (late 15C–early 16C) surmounted by a **frieze**★★ in the Flamboyant Gothic style

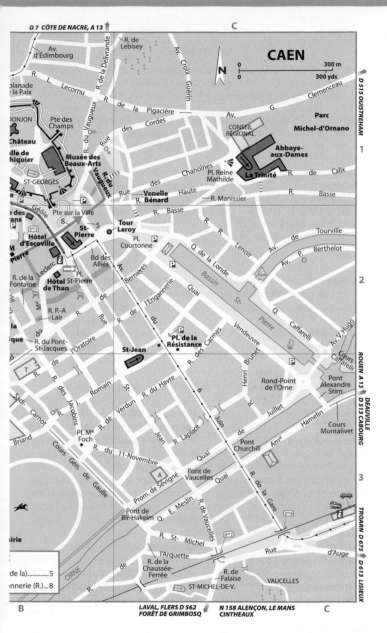

CAEN

N   0 ___ 300 m
    0 ___ 300 yds

with a delicate decoration of flowers and foliage.

The Gothic style prevails up to 2.75m/9ft from the ground but above that level the Renaissance influence increases to predominate in the **vaulting**★★ by Hector Sohier. The vaulting in each chapel is highly ornate; the pendants look like stalactites.

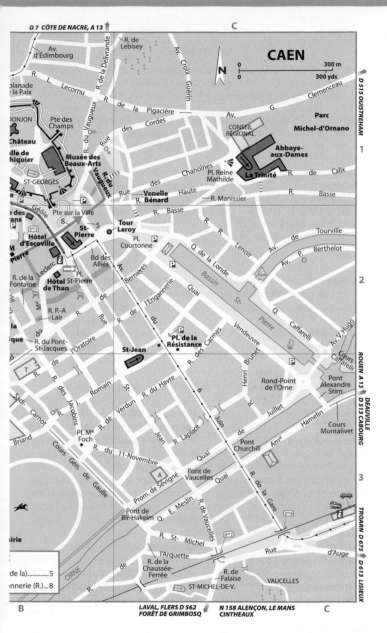 *At the church entrance, turn left onto rue St-Pierre.*

Rue St-Pierre

This is a lively shopping street. Nos **52** (Postal Museum) and **54**, beautiful **half-timbered houses**★ with steep gables, are early 16C; very few have survived in Caen. The profusion of carved

253

Port of Caen

Although the River Orne has always enabled Caen to serve as a port, no major development took place until the middle of the 19C, when Baron Cachin dug a canal parallel to the river. The canal (12km/7.4mi long) was regulated by several locks and served by an outer basin at Ouistreham. Since then the increased output of the Caen steelworks has required the deepening and widening of the canal and the creation of five more docks: St-Pierre for pleasure boats, the New Dock, the Calix Dock, the Hérouville Dock and the Blainville Dock, which came into use in 1974.

Today the transportation of cereals is the chief function of Caen harbour, the largest one in Basse-Normandie, which can receive ships of up to 19 000t fully laden and up to 30,000t partially laden. Because of its broad range of activities, this port is ranked 11th in France. The opening of a cross-Channel car ferry service on 6 June 1986 has established daily links between Caen-Ouistreham and Portsmouth, catering to an estimated one million passengers every year.

decoration and the numerous small statues of saints are in the Gothic style, but there are some Renaissance elements.

Musée de la Poste et des Techniques de Communication

52 r. St-Pierre. ⏰*Open Tue–Sat mid-Jun–mid-Sept 10am–noon, 2–6pm; mid-Sept–mid-Jun 1.30–5.30pm.* ⏰*Closed public holidays.* ⸙€3. ✆*02 31 50 12 20. www.ville-caen.fr/museedelaposte.*

This Postal and Telecommunications Museum, in a lovely half-timbered 16C house, illustrates the history of the postal service through documents and equipment.

Cour des Imprimeurs

Place Pierre-Bouchard.

These early 16C houses used to be home to major printing presses that were in operation here until the early 20C. Take a look at the Flamboyant Gothic windows; their decoration combines vine leaves with curly cabbage leaves.

Rue Froide

In the shadow of St-Saviour's church, this very discreet little street still has interesting houses from the 15C to 19C.

Église St-Sauveur

Place Pierre-Bouchard. ⏰*Open daily 9am–5pm.* ✆*02 31 86 13 11.*

Also known by its old name of Notre-Dame-de-Froide-Rue, St Saviour's church has twin chevets facing rue St-Pierre: Gothic (15C) on the left and Renaissance (1546) on the right. Rue Froide contains interesting old houses, dating from the 15C to the 19C.

▷ *Turn left on rue Paul-Doumer.*

Place de la République

The pedestrian precinct, between place St-Pierre and place de la République, is lively both day and night. Place de la République, which is laid out as a public garden, is bordered by beautiful Louis XIII houses (Hôtel Daumesnil at nos **23–25**) and the modern offices of the Préfecture.

▷ *Turn left on rue Jean-Eudes, continue to rue St-Laurent.*

Notre-Dame-de-la-Gloriette, a former Jesuit church standing on rue St-Laurent, was built between 1684 and 1689.

▷ *Take rue St-Laurent, and head up to place Malherbe.*

Place Malherbe

This square is named after a beautiful restored house where the poet Malherbe is said to have been born in 1555. Heading up toward St-Etienne, la rue Écuyère *(at no 9, pretty Renaissance façade)* then, to the right, little rue aux Fromages *(pedestrian)*, with half-timbered houses on either side, leads to place St-Sauveur.

Place St-Sauveur

A fine collection of 18C houses borders the square, where the pillory stood until the 19C. At the centre is a statue of Louis XIV as a Roman emperor. The north-east side of the square is the site of the old St Saviour's, which was destroyed in 1944.

▷ *Turn left and continue to a traffic circle. Follow rue Guillaume-le-Conquérant, which takes you to the Abbaye-aux-Hommes and the Église St-Étienne (described below).*
To continue the walk, turn right on rue Jean-Marot.

On your way, note the row of attractive houses in rue Jean-Marot; they date from the early 20C.

▷ *Turn left on rue St-Martin.*

Place St-Martin

Note the statue of Constable Bertrand du Guesclin. There is an interesting view of the two towers of St-Étienne.

▷ *Continue NE along the Fossés St-Julien and turn right onto rue de Géôle.*

The 15C half-timbered house (no 31) is called **Maison des Quatrans**.

Rue du Vaugueux

Rue Montoir-Poissonnerie leads to this lovely pedestrian street, which has kept its quaint charm: cobblestones, stone and timber houses, old-fashioned street lights.

▷ *Return to place St-Pierre.*

ABBAYE-AUX-HOMMES★★

Espl. Jean-Marie-Louvel. ⏰*Open 9am–1pm, 2–6.30pm (except during Mass).* ☎*02 31 30 42 81.*
Despite their different styles, St-Étienne church and the monastery buildings of

Église St-Étienne, Abbaye-aux-Hommes

© Robby Verschueren/iStockphoto.com

the Abbey for Men constitute an historical and architectural unit.

Église St-Étienne★★

This is the church of the abbey founded by William the Conqueror; Lanfranc was the first abbot, before being appointed Archbishop of Canterbury and it was probably he who drew up the plans. The church was started in 1066 in the Romanesque style, and was completed in the 13C in Gothic style (east end, choir, spires). The building was damaged during the Wars of Religion in the 16C and painstakingly restored in the early 17C by Dom Jehan de Baillehache, the Prior.
Following the Maurist reforms of the Benedictine order (1663) the abbey enjoyed a period of prosperity until the French Revolution: the church was richly furnished and the monastery was rebuilt. In the 19C St-Étienne became a parish church and the monastery was converted for use as a school. Fortunately, the buildings survived the Battle of Caen unscathed.
Romanesque art has produced few more striking compositions than this plain **west front**; there are no ornate porches, no rose windows, only a gable end resting on four sturdy buttresses and pierced by two rows of round-headed windows and three Romanesque doors. Lanfranc seems to have exercised

the artistic severity of Ravenna and Lombardy in his native country. The austerity of the west front is, however, tempered by the magnificent soaring towers (11C). The first storey is decorated with fluting, the second with single pierced bays and the third with paired bays. The octagonal spires with their turrets and lancets in the Norman Gothic style were added to the two towers in the 13C; the north tower is finer and more delicate in style.

The vast nave is almost bare of ornament except for the great round-headed arches. The construction of the sexpartite vaulting in the 12C altered the arrangement of the clerestory, which is decorated with fretwork typical of the Norman style. At the west end of the church is the organ (1747) flanked by two telamones.

The lantern tower above the transept crossing was constructed in the 11C but rebuilt early in the 17C. The gallery in the north transept houses a large 18C clock in a carved wooden surround. In the 13C the Romanesque chancel was replaced by a Gothic construction, including an ambulatory and radiating chapel; it was the first of the Norman Gothic chancels and subsequently served as a model. With the Gothic style, new decorative motifs were introduced: chevrons on the archivolts, rose windows in the spandrels of the lateral arches, trefoils piercing the tympana of the bays in the galleries, capitals ornamented with crochets and foliage. Note the spacious galleries above the ambulatory and the elegant central arches. The handsome stalls and pulpit are 17C.

In front of the altar is a stone inscribed with an epitaph. The sarcophagus containing the body of William the Conqueror was originally placed beneath the lantern but when the church was sacked by the Huguenots in the 16C, the Conqueror's remains were scattered; all that remains is a femur, which is interred beneath the stone. A monumental 18C paschal candlestick stands on the north side of the altar. The chancel is enclosed by a beautiful 19C wrought-iron screen; the cartouches bear the names and arms of the former abbots, priors and other dignitaries of the abbey.

In the sacristy there hangs an unusual portrait of William the Conqueror, painted in 1708, in which he is made to resemble Henry VIII.

▷ *Leave the church by the chancel door and skirt the handsome* **east end**★★ *of St-Étienne (13C–14C) to reach the gardens in esplanade Louvel, which have been restored to 18C plans.*

Monastery Buildings★

Monastery buildings of the Abbaye-aux-Hommes. ⏱Guided tours (50min), *9.30am, 10.15am, 11am, 2.30pm, 3.15pm, 4pm and 5.15pm. Rest of year 9.30am, 11am, 2.30pm and 4pm.* ⏰*Closed 1 Jan, 1 May, 25 Dec.* ♿ ⌐€2.40, no charge Sun. ✆02 31 30 42 81. www.ville-caen.fr.

These fine buildings were designed early in the 18C by Brother Guillaume de la Tremblaye, the great master builder of the Congregation of St Maur; the **woodwork**★★ is particularly beautiful. The east wing comprises the monks' **warming room**, now a municipal exhibition hall; the **chapter house**, formerly a collegiate chapel and now a registry office, is panelled in light oak and hung with 17C paintings; the chapel **sacristy**, panelled in oak, contains a painting by Charles Lebrun (1619–90) *(Moses Confronting an Egyptian Shepherd)* and a collection of Norman headdresses.

The hall, which features 18C stairs with a wrought-iron banister, leads to the **cloisters** (18C), where the groined vaulting centres on octagonal coffers. From the southeast corner of the cloisters there is a very fine **view**★★ of the towers of St-Étienne and the south side of the church. Fixed to the door into the church is a dark oak timetable of the offices said by the monks (1744).

A doorway leads into the **parlour**, a large oval room with an unusual elliptical vault and beautiful Louis XV wooden doors. The **refectory**, now used for meetings, is sumptuously decorated with late 18C oak panelling and broken barrel vaulting. Some of the paintings above the door and the blind apertures are by Lépicié, Restout and Ruysdael. The wrought-iron banister of the **grand staircase** is decorated with floral motifs. The bold design has no central support. The remarkable Gothic hall in the courtyard, known as the **guard room**★, was built on the remains of a Gallo-Roman structure and is now used for meetings. The panelled ceiling is shaped like an upturned hull. Originally there were two rooms, as the two chimneys suggest.

View of the Abbey★★

Walk through the gardens in esplanade Louvel to reach the east side of place Louis-Guillouard near Old St-Étienne Church (Vieux St-Étienne), an attractive ruin, with the Jesuit church of Notre-Dame-de-la-Gloriette in the background. This is the best view of the 18C monastery buildings flanking the impressive east end of St-Étienne with its bristling bell turrets, flying buttresses, clustering chapels and steep roofs, topped by the lantern tower and the two soaring spires.

ABBAYE-AUX-DAMES★

pl. Reine-Mathilde.
Founded in 1062 by **Queen Matilda**, the Abbey for Women is the sister house to the Abbey for Men. It is located on the northeast side of the old city, about 2km/1mi from the Abbaye-aux-Hommes. From place de la Reine-Mathilde, the towers of St-Étienne Church can just be seen at the end of rue des Chanoines.

Église de la Trinité★★

🚹🕐*Open daily 9am–6.30pm.*
☏*02 31 86 13 11.*
The old abbey church, which dates from the 11C, is a building in the Romanesque style. Its original plan was inspired by that of Benedictine abbeys, characterised by sturdy tiered apsidioles. The spires were replaced early in the 18C by heavy balustrades. The vast nave of nine bays is a fine example of Romanesque art. Broken barrel vaulting marks the transition from the nave into the spacious transept.

Adjoining the south transept is an attractive chapel, which is now used as the chapter house. It was built in the 13C, replacing two Romanesque chapels similar to the two in the north transept. The late 11C groined vaulting in the chancel covers a magnificent span. In the centre of the chancel is Queen Matilda's tomb, a simple monument consisting of a single slab of black marble, which has survived unscathed despite the Wars of Religion and the Revolution.

The crypt *(access by steps in the chapel in the south transept)* is well preserved. The groined vaulting rests on 16 columns, standing close together, which define five bays. An attempt at historiated decoration can be seen on one of the capitals, illustrating the Last Judgement, in which St Michael is portrayed gathering up the dead as they rise from their graves.

Conventual Buildings

🕐*Open daily 2–5.30pm.* 👣*Guided tours (40min) daily 2.30pm, 4pm.*
🕐*Closed 1 Jan, 1 May, 25 Dec.* 🚹
♿*No charge.* ☏*02 31 06 98 98.*
From the French-style garden in the main **courtyard** one can admire the luminous golden façades. The cloisters (only three sides were completed) are a replica of the one in the Abbey for Men. Leading off them is a small oval room, the washroom *(lavabo)*, decorated with stone pilasters and a carved frieze like those in Greek temples; it is furnished with four black-marble basins set in recesses ornamented with a shell. In the **refectory** *(used as a reception room or as a gallery for temporary exhibitions)*, pilasters with Ionic capitals and two columns which flanked the abbess' chair have survived, whereas the oak panelling which covered the lower walls has been removed.

The **Great Hall**, which is the focal point of the whole abbey and leads into the church, is graced by **two flights** of stairs decorated at first-floor level with a cartouche bearing a plant motif; the walls are adorned with portraits of the two last abbesses, Anne de Montmorency and Marie-Aimée de Pontécoulant.

CHÂTEAU★

espl. du Château. Allow 3hr including museums. ℘02 31 27 14 14.

The imposing citadel dominating the mount was begun by William the Conqueror in 1060 and fortified in 1123 by his son, Henry Beauclerk, who added a mighty keep (demolished in 1793). During the 13C, 14C and 15C it was repeatedly enlarged and reinforced.

Throughout the 19C it was used as soldiers' barracks and was severely damaged in the bombardment of Caen in 1944. Since then its massive walls have been restored to their early grandeur.

The line of the ramparts has changed little since the days of William the Conqueror. In some places the walls date from the 12C, but most of them were built in the 15C. The two main gateways are protected by barbicans.

◐ *Enter the castle by the ramp which approaches the south gate opposite Église St-Pierre.*

After passing a round tower, a defensive outwork, one enters the citadel by the town gate *(porte sur la ville)*.

From the terrace *(east)* and the rampart sentry walk there are fine **views**★ of Église St-Pierre and western Caen as far as the Abbey for Men. On the west side of the gate, behind the Normandy Museum, a platform provides an interesting **view**★ over the southwest sector of the town and the belfries of the many churches.

The **north rampart**, the first to be restored under the current programme, can be visited for a remarkable **view**★ of Caen.

The **rampart rooms** *(9.30am–6pm. €5)* offer temporary Musée de Normandie exhibitions. Very contemporary, there is an astonishing view here of the rampart and walkway.

The castle precinct encloses the modern **Musée des Beaux-Arts** *(east)* near the **Porte des Champs** (Field Gate), an interesting example of 14C military architecture; the **Chapelle St-Georges**, a 12C chapel which was altered in the 15C; the **Musée de Normandie** *(west)* in a building that was the residence of the bailiff in the 14C and of the governor of Caen in the 17C and 18C; a rectangular building, incorrectly called the **Salle de l'Échiquier** (Exchequer Hall), which is a rare example of Norman civil architecture in the reign of Henry Beauclerk and was the great hall of the adjoining ducal palace (foundations only visible); adjoining it was the Normandy Exchequer (the Ducal Law Court). Further north lie the foundations of the keep, which was built by Henry Beauclerk and altered in the 13C and 14C; it was a huge square structure, a round tower at each corner, surrounded by a moat which was joined to the castle moat. ☛*You can stroll in the castle moat; descend from the porte des Champs.*

Musée des Beaux-Arts★★

Located within the château, east of St-Pierre gate. ◷Open Wed–Sat and Mon 9.30am–6pm. ◷Closed 1 Jan, Easter Sunday, 1 May, Ascension, 1 Nov, 25 Dec. ☞Temporary exhibits €5.20; no charge 1st Sun of month; permanent collection no charge. ㋡ ℘02 31 30 47 70. www.ville-caen. fr/mba. ㋐ The Café Mancel offers a pleasant break inside the museum, where you can enjoy a meal or a drink (㋙ see Addresses).

Situated within the precinct of William the Conqueror's castle, the Fine Arts Museum displays its collections from a chronological, thematic and geographical point of view. Large religious paintings and imposing historical and allegorical scenes hang in vast halls, bathed in light, whereas works of religious fervour and smaller paintings are displayed in the small cabinets. The large galleries display landscapes, battle scenes and portraits.

The first three rooms on the ground floor are devoted to 15C, 16C and 17C Italian paintings: the *Marriage of the Virgin* by Perugino, with a remarkable new frame, a triptych representing the *Virgin and Child Between St George and St James* by Cima da Conegliano; in a room entirely devoted to Veronese, two paintings are of particular interest: the *Temptation of*

Abraham and Melchizedek *by Rubens, Musée des Beaux-Arts*

St Anthony and *Judith and Holofernes;* also worth noting are *Coriolanus Implored by His Mother* by Il Guercino and *Glaucus and Scylla* by Rosa Salvatore.

The next room deals with 17C French paintings with outstanding works by Philippe de Champaigne *(Louis XIII's Vow)* and religious and mythological paintings by Vouet, Vignon, La Hyre and Le Brun.

Three intimate rooms are devoted to Dutch and Flemish 17C paintings with works such as *A Seascape* by Solomon van Ruysdael, *Virgin and Child* by Roger van der Weyden and *Abraham and Melchizedek* by Rubens.

In the gallery devoted to the 18C are displayed works by French and Italian portrait and landscape painters: Hyacinthe Rigaud *(Portrait of Marie Cadenne)*, François Boucher *(Young Shepherd in a Landscape)*, Locatelli, Lalemand, Tournières.

On the lower level, the various aspects and the evolution of painting during the 19C and the early 20C are depicted through works by Romantic painters (Géricault, Delacroix, Isabey), Realists (Courbet: *The Lady with the Jewels;* Ribot), landscape painters (Corot, Dupré), Impressionists (Vuillard: *Portrait of Suzanne Desprez;* Bonnard, Dufy, Van Dongen: *Portrait of Madame*

T Raulet), and Cubist painters (Gleizes, Villon, Meitzinger). Local artists are also represented: Cals, Fouace, Gernez, Lemaître, Lépine, Lebourg, Rame.

Innovations by contemporary painters such as Tobey *(Appearances)*, Mitchell *(Fields*, 1990), Soulages, Dubuffet *(Migration)*, Vieira da Silva, Szenez, Asse and Deschamps illustrate the different post-war trends: Conceptual art, Abstract landscape, Abstract art, Environmental art. From one end to the other, the museum thus presents an impressive chronology of the history of painting.

Musée de Normandie★

Located within the château, west of the St-Pierre gate. ⏱ *Open Jun–Oct 9.30am–6pm; Nov–May Wed–Mon 9.30am–6pm.* ⏱ *Closed 1 Jan, Easter, 1 May, Ascension, 1 Nov, 25 Dec.* ✆ *02 31 30 47 60. www.ville-caen.fr.*

The history and traditions of Normandy are illustrated by the presentation of the many archaeological and ethnographical exhibits.

The first section is devoted to the prehistoric period up to the arrival of the Vikings in 911 and concentrates on the culture and technology of the era: excavated artefacts, miniature replica of the burial mound at Fontenay-le-

Marmion, statue of a mother goddess found at St-Aubin-sur-Mer, weapons and jewellery found in medieval cemeteries (tomb of a metalworker).

The second section follows the evolution of agriculture: land use (models comparing different types of cultivation and farms), agricultural techniques (display of ploughs, scythes and millstones).

The third section is devoted to crafts and industrial activities: stock breeding, ceramics (jugs, funerary ornaments and decorative ridge tiles), wood (beautifully carved marriage chests), metallurgy (iron and copper work: craftsmen's tools, copperware from Villedieu-les-Poêles), textiles (costumes, headdresses and bridal-ware in silk lace). The last room concentrates on the work of the candlemaker (interesting collection of candles for Easter, funerals and as votive offerings) as well as ceremonial articles belonging to the different brotherhoods (gold thread embroidery and tintenelles, the tiny hand bells used in processions by the Brothers of Charity).

ADDITIONAL SIGHTS
St-Nicolas Cemetery★
r. de Hastings. ⏱*Open daily Mar–Oct 8am–6pm; Nov–Feb 8am–5pm.*
St Nicholas' Church (deconsecrated) was built late in the 11C by the monks of the Abbey for Men and has not been altered since. The west door is protected by a beautiful triple-arched Romanesque porch, an exceptional feature in Normandy.

The church is surrounded by an old graveyard (entrance left of the west front); one may stroll among the mossy tombstones under the shade of the trees and admire the magnificent apse at the east end beneath a steep stone roof.

Église St-Jean
Place St-Ouen.
The fine Flamboyant Gothic building was begun in the 14C, and repaired in the 15C. The belltower, of which the base and first storey are 14C, was inspired by the tower of St Peter but, owing to the instability of the marshy ground, the spire and the belfry were never built, nor

was the central tower; the lower courses of its second storey were capped with a dome.

The vast nave has a remarkable Flamboyant triforium and a highly ornate cylindrical **lantern tower**★ over the transept crossing. The highly venerated statue of Our Lady of Protection dates from the 17C. In the south transept there is an old retable (17C) from the Carmes Convent depicting the Annunciation and bearing statues of St Joseph and St Teresa of Ávila. In 1964 a statue of Joan of Arc was transferred from Oran to a site near the east end of the church in place de la Résistance.

Église St-Julien
1 r. Malfilâtre. For opening hours call ☎*02 31 85 44 53.*
The old church, which was destroyed in 1944, was replaced in 1958 by this modern building. The sanctuary wall, elliptical in shape, forms a huge piece of latticework like that of a stained-glass window.

Le Mémorial★★
Allow 3hr; espl. Général-Eisenhower. ⏱*Open mid-Feb–mid-Nov daily 9am–7pm; 28–31 Dec 9.30am–6pm; rest of the year, Tue–Sun, 9.30am–6pm.* ⏱*Closed 3 weeks in Jan, 1 Jan and 25 Dec.* ⌖ ♿ ⊜€16.50. ☎*02 31 06 06 45. www.memorial-caen.fr. Note that the museum is changing, and new spaces are opening.*
ℹ *Directions to the memorial are signposted from the city centre and from the Péripherique Nord.*
The memorial erected by the city, which in 1944 was at the centre of the Battle of Normandy, takes the form of a Museum for Peace; it is primarily a place of commemoration and of permanent meditation on the links between human rights and the maintenance of peace.

The façade of the sober building of Caen stone, facing esplanade Dwight-Eisenhower, is marked by a fissure that evokes the destruction of the city and the breakthrough of the Allies in the Liberation of France and Europe from the Nazi yoke. It stands on the site of the bunker of W Richter, the German general, who on 6 June faced the British-Canadian forces.

The main events of World War II, the causes and the issues at stake, are presented in the light of the latest historical analysis. A particularly imaginative display on such themes as the inter-war years and the advance of Fascism centres on a spiral ramp. This, together with the use of extensive archive material, including a gripping panoramic projection of D-Day, seen simultaneously from the Allied and the German standpoints, as well as moving testimonies by witnesses of and participants in the drama, confers on this presentation of the recent past the authenticity of living experience.

The film *Hope* uses strong images and original music by Jacques Loussier to trace the alternating outbreaks of war and peace that have followed.

A walk to the Vallée du Mémorial will enable visitors to see the Parc de la Colline aux Oiseaux, in which the Floralies de la Paix has been created. The **Mur de la Liberté** (Wall of Freedom) pays tribute to the hundreds of thousands of American soldiers who fought for freedom in Europe.

Parc floral de la Colline-aux-Oiseaux

Av. Am.-Mountbatten. 02 31 30 48 38. *daily from 10am; closing time depends on the season.* No charge.

Lying northwest of Caen, not far from the Memorial, this park (17ha/42 acres) created in 1994 for the 50th anniversary of the Landings, is actually on a former rubbish tip – hence the name, "Bird Hill". There are themed gardens and a beautiful rose garden.

Jardin des plantes

5 pl. Blot. 02 31 30 48 38. *Daily 2–5pm for the hothouses.* No charge.

A botanical garden and a garden for botanical research, both in the same place, bring together specialised plant collections. The botanical garden for research goes back to the 17C; in particular it includes a tropical hothouse

---

Ouistreham-Riva-Bella

A busy port since medieval times, Ouistreham derives its name from Saxon words meaning "western" *(ouistre)* and "farm" *(ham).*

The name "Riva Bella", or "beautiful coast" in Italian, derives from the name of the first of many residences constructed in the 19C, when the splendid 5km/3mi beach attracted fashionable visitors.

---

where the South American giant water-lily flowers.

OUISTREHAM-RIVA-BELLA★★

15km/9mi – 15min. Leave Caen NE by the D 515, then the D 514.

Jardins du Casino, 14150 Ouistreham-Riva-Bella. 02 31 97 18 63. www.ot-ouistreham.fr. *Jul–Aug 10am–1pm, 2–7pm; Apr–Jun and Sept daily except 1 May 10am–12.30pm, 2–6.30pm; rest of year Mon–Sat except holidays 10am–12.30pm, 2.30–6pm, Sun 2.30–5.30pm.*

Located at the mouth of the Orne and astride the canal from Caen, the combined facilities of the town of Ouistreham and the beach of Riva-Bella make an excellent seaside resort. As the seaport for Caen, the harbour bustles with trawlers, pleasure craft and the cross-Channel ferries plying between Ouistreham and Portsmouth.

Église St-Samson★

Place Lemarignier.

This ancient 12C fortress church was built on the site of a 9C wooden church destroyed by Norsemen.

The gabled west front with its three superimposed tiers of blind arcades above the recessed doorway is particularly remarkable. Step back to get a good view of the late 12C belfry supported by buttresses.

In the nave, note the round piers with gadrooned capitals and the lovely clerestory windows.

Port de Plaisance

Leave the car in place du Général-de-Gaulle.
A large basin on the opposite bank of the canal (Canal de Caen à la Mer) provides berths for many yachts. In season it is a lively and colourful spot.

Plage de Riva-Bella

The beach closest to Caen, this magnificent extent of fine sand invites families from Caen to enjoy the sea as soon as the sun rises.

The resort, which has the French *station nautique* label of certification, authorises all sailing and board sports, on water or sand.There is also a karting track, a horseriding club, a kite-flying club and a miniature golf course.

Lighthouse

Quai Georges-Thierry. ©Open Jul–Aug weekends 2.30–6pm. €2.
From the top of the lighthouse (30m/98.4ft high, 171 steps) there is a good view of the harbour and marina.

Musée du Mur de l'Atlantique – Grand Bunker

Av. du 6-Juin, near the tourist office. ©Open Apr–Sept daily 9am–7pm; Oct–Mar 10am–6pm. © Closed 1 Jan, 25 Dec. €7. ℘02 31 97 28 69.
This museum, located in a former German range-finding station, overlooks the mouth of the River Orne from a height of 17m/55.8ft; it sent firing instructions to the artillery units in Ouistreham. Rooms are arranged as they were in 1944. In the range-finding room, you can study the horizon with the range-finder over a 180° angle and a distance of 45km/28mi.

Musée du Débarquement "no 4 Commando" - Riva-Bella

Pl. Alfred-Thomas. ©Open mid-Mar–Oct daily 10.30am–6pm. €4 (children €1.50). ℘02 31 96 63 10.
The 4th Anglo-French Commando under Commander Philippe Kieffer reduced the enemy strong points on the morning of 6 June. The museum contains original artefacts from the operation.

SOUTH AND EAST OF CAEN

Cintheaux

▶ 15km/9mi. From Caen take N 158 S – allow 30min.
The village, renowned for its late 12C church, stands on the southern edge of the Caen countryside, in an old mining area marked by solitary slag heaps.
The road from Caen to Falaise passes through country laboriously recaptured during the Battle of Normandy between 8 and 17 August 1944 by the Canadian 1st Army (Gaumesnil Cemetery) and its Polish units (Langannerie Cemetery).

Troarn

▶ 14km/8.5mi – allow 30min.
Leave Caen going E and then take N 175. In Troarn take rue de l'Abbaye (second turn on the right after the church).
This little town, which was founded in 1048 by Roger de Montgomery, contains the remains of a 13C abbey.

Vieux

▶ 18km/11mi – 19min. Leave Caen by the SW on the D 405; take the D 8, then the D 147A on the left and the D 212 on the right.
Today it is difficult to imagine that the peaceful village of Vieux was Aregenua, the former capital of the Viducasses, during the Roman period.
The archaeological digs over the past decades have brought to light rich findidngs, presented in a clear and modern way in the **museum** *(Musée et site archéologique; ©Jul–Aug Thu–Tue 10am–6pm; rest of the year 9am–5pm, Sat–Sun 10am–6pm. ©Closed Wed, 1 Jan, 1 May, 1 and 11 Nov, 25 Dec. €4 (under 15 years, no charge). ℘02 31 71 10 20).*
The visit continues on the site itself. While difficult to recreate, it nevertheless has some interesting vestiges, including the sumptuous Villa au Grand Péristyle *(follow the signposting on the site).*

Forêt de Grimbosq

▶ 19km/11mi. Leave Caen S by the D 562, then the D 257.
Themed walks Jul–Aug. Call CPIE Vallée de l'Orne. ℘02 31 79 70 47.

www.cpievdo.fr.

🌿 Crisscrossed with little streams, the superb Grimbosq Forest *(475ha/1,173 acres)* has belonged to the City of Caen since 1973. Its animal park (with deer and boar) is the destination for numerous Caen families, as is the charming St Anne's chapel at the edge of the River Orne. For sports-lovers, there are well-signposted treks (1 1/2hrs to 3hrs) and a fitness circuit leaving from the St-Laurent-de-Condel car park *(on leaving the village, follow the blue "parking" sign to right)*.

🚗 DRIVING TOURS

1️⃣ NORTH OF CAEN
Round-trip of 31km/19.2mi. Allow 1hr.

▶ *From Caen take D 7 and at the top of the hill, turn right on D 401, then D 60 to the left.*

The road bends to the right and there is a panoramic view of Caen.

Bléville-sur-Orne
The blind arcades and oculi which decorate the west front of the church recall the architecture of Tuscany.

La Délivrande *(see p 269).*

▶ *Head back down to Caen by the D 7.*

Epron
This small locality, which was razed in 1944, has been called the Village of the Radio since 1948.

The origin of the nickname was a radio programme that sought to determine which of France's *départements* had been most severely damaged. Calvados was named, and a lottery draw among ten communes fell to Epron. The village was rebuilt thanks to a collection of small change taken up on its behalf.

2️⃣ CHURCHES AND ABBEYS
35km/21mi. Allow 2hrs.

▶ *From Caen take D 9 west towards Bayeux on rue de Bayeux and then rue du Général-Moulin. Halfway up a hill on the outskirts of the town turn right onto the road to the abbey.*

Abbaye d'Ardenne★
🕐*Open Tue–Sun 2–6pm.* 🌿*Guided tour of convent Sat–Sun every 30 min.* 🎫*No charge.* ♿ 🅿 *Leave the car at the main gate (12C).* 📞*02 31 29 37 37. www.imec-archives.com.*

The abbey, which was founded in the 12C by the Premonstratensians, fell into ruin during the 19C but has recently benefited from a major restoration project. An exhibit describing its history can be seen at its sister abbey of Mondaye. In the first courtyard stands a huge 13C tithe barn *(back left)* with aisles covered by a single asymmetrical wooden roof *(restored – open during temporary exhibitions)*. The 13C **abbey church**★ has been damaged on the outside but the nave is a very pure example of the Norman Gothic style. Since 1998, the abbey has housed a major archive of French publications. The abbey church is now a research library.

▶ *Drive west to Rots via Authie.*

Rots
The **church** here has an attractive Romanesque west front; the nave dates from the same period; the chancel is 15C.

▶ *Take D 170 north; in Rosel turn left onto D 126.*

Secqueville-en-Bessin
The 11C **church** has a fine three-storey tower and a 13C spire. The nave and transept are decorated with blind arcading.

▶ *Take D 93 and D 83 south.*

Norrey
Church. 🌿*Guided tour available on written request to M Roland Audes, Mairie, pl. Charles-de-Gaulle, 14740 St-Manvieu-Norrey.* The little Gothic

church has a great square lantern tower but no spire; the interior is richly carved; the chancel was built in the 13C.

▷ *Return to Caen by D 9.*

③ THE BATTLE OF ODON
37km/23mi. Allow 2hrs.

The name of this river recalls the hard-fought battles which took place between 26 June and 4 August 1944 southwest of Caen.

▷ *Leave Caen by the rue de Bayeux, then take D 9.*

The road skirts the airfield which the 12th SS Panzers held for three days, from 4 to 7 July, against the Canadian 3rd Division.

▷ *After another 3km/2mi bear left on D 170; in Cheux turn left behind the church onto D 89; after crossing N 175, at the top of a slight rise, follow D 89 round to the right and straight through Tourville.*

This is the line of the British advance, which began on 26 June in pouring rain at Tilly-sur-Seulles *(northwest)*; the objective was the River Orne to the southeast. A memorial has been erected *(right)* to pay tribute to the men of the 15th Scottish Division who fell here. Just when it seems that the road has reached the floor of the Odon Valley it drops into a rocky ravine, hitherto hidden by thickets; the river has created a second valley within the main one. It is easy to see what a valuable line of defence this natural obstacle would have been and to appreciate the difficulties of the British troops exposed to heavy fire from the Germans on the far side of the valley. In fact the British lost more men crossing the Odon than crossing the Rhine.

The road climbs the opposite slope to a crossroads. The road on the left (D 214) passes straight through Baron-sur-Odon and continues to a T-junction marked by a stone monument surmounted by an iron cross *(right)*. The raised roadway to the right, an old Roman road also known as Duke William's Way, leads to another T-junction where a stele has been set up to commemorate the battles fought by the 43rd Wessex Division. To the south stands **Hill 112** later known as Cornwall Hill.

▷ *Take D 8 to the left towards Caen.*

A monument at the junction with D 36 recalls the operations that took place in July and were marked by fierce duels between armoured vehicles. A night attack on 15 June took place by the light of an artificial moon created by the reflection of searchlights on low cloud.

▷ *Turn left onto D 147A.*

Near a farm on the right the Château de Fontaine-Étoupefour comes into view.

Château de Fontaine-Etoupefour
Access by a track on the right beyond the farm. Guided tours (1hr) Jul– Sept Sun–Wed afternoon. €5. ℘02 31 26 73 20.

Nicolas d'Escoville, who built the Hôtel d'Escoville in Caen, owned this castle. It is surrounded by a moat spanned by a drawbridge, which leads to an elegant 15C gatehouse bristling with turrets and pinnacles. The dining room is hung with three interesting paintings of hunting scenes. On the far side of the paved courtyard stand the ruins of one of the two main blocks (late 16C), currently undergoing restoration.

The refectory houses an exhibit about the battle of Hill 112 in 1944, of which the château was the centre.

▷ *Return to D 8 to reach Caen.*

Plages du Débarquement★★

Normandy Landing Beaches

The choice of Normandy as the landing point for the invasion of Europe was not evident. Defended by the Atlantic Wall, the coast had choppy water and tricky tides. Italy seemed a more likely option, but the invasion, begun in July 1943, proved slow and costly; to the east, the Germans still besieged Leningrad. At the Teheran Conference in late 1943, Churchill, Roosevelt and Stalin agreed on a French front. Men and arms were massed in Britain and intense bombing raids over Germany and France were intended to soften defences. The tour described in this section includes that part of the Calvados coast between the mouths of the Orne and the Vire, also known as the Côte de Nacre, where the D-Day landings took place on 6 June 1944. The marked itineraries, known as Overlord – L'Assaut (Overlord – The Onslaught) and D-Day – Le Choc (D-Day – The Impact), are two of several such itineraries in the Historical Area of the Battle of Normandy.

A BIT OF HISTORY
Operation Overlord

The Normandy Landings, or D-Day, for which the code name during preparations for this massive Allied invasion was Operation Overlord, were commanded by US General Dwight D Eisenhower, with British General (later Field Marshal) Bernard Montgomery in charge of land forces. Transport involved an armada of 7,000 ships and landing craft, and 12,500 aircraft. Some 156,000 troops landed, supported by 195,000 sailors. Preparations were epic: finally, all depended on the tides, to bring landing craft to shore.

See The D-Day Landings on p268 for a more detailed history of events.

- **Michelin Map:** F3-K4.
- **Info:** Port-en-Bessin: ℘02 31 22 45 80. Longues-sur-Mer: ℘02 31 21 46 87.
- **Location:** This section covers the Calvados coast between the mouths of the Orne and the Vire, also known as the Côte de Nacre (Mother-of-Pearl coast) where the Normandy landings took place on D-Day, 6 June 1944.
- **Timing:** Each of the circuits described below takes half a day.

D-Day Landings: A Turning Point

Field Marshal Erwin Rommel, inspecting the Atlantic Wall, pointed out that if the Allies succeeded in breaching it, the Third Reich would fall. Germany fell on 8 May 1945, after a long stuggle, but the end had begun 11 months earlier.

65th Anniversary: 2009

Leaders of France, Great Britain, the USA and Canada met on the beaches of Normandy to mark the June 1944 landings, probably the last commemoration where significant numbers of veterans would be able to take part.

🚗 DRIVING TOURS

1 SWORD BEACH–JUNO BEACH–GOLD BEACH
71km/44mi. Allow 1hr15min.

▷ *From Caen take D 515 northeast.*

The road to Riva-Bella runs down the lower Orne Valley west of the ship canal.

Bénouville
The town hall, which stands alone in a fork in the road near Pegasus Bridge, was occupied by the British 5th Parachute Brigade at 11.45pm on 5 June.

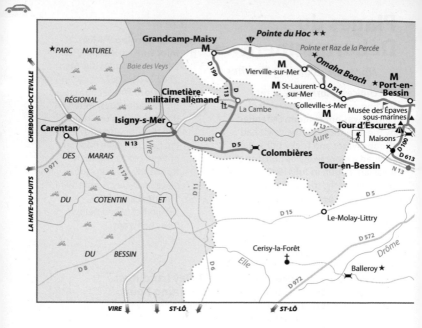

The **château**★ (🕐*end Jun–end Sept 2–6pm;* 🗣*guided tour possible on prior request;* 🕐*closed Tue;* ♿. 💶€2. 𝄞*02 31 95 53 23. www.cg14.fr/chateau_ benouville),* one of the major works by the Parisian architect **Claude-Nicolas Ledoux** (1736–1806), is a fine example of French neoclassical architecture at the end of the 18C.

The interior contains a suite of five rooms and a magnificent **staircase**★★ rising through three landings to the first floor. The château was virtually undamaged in the war.

Pegasus Bridge★

The two Ranville-Bénouville bridges were captured soon after midnight during the night of 5–6 June 1944 by the British 5th Parachute Brigade: **Pegasus** was their emblem.

Major Howard had won the Battle of Pegasus – a field where the Horsa and Hamilcar gliders could land, a mobile bridge made of steel, a house at the water's edge… and the Gondrée family, who waited until **Lord Lovat** (1911–95) and his Green Berets arrived, to the strains of Bill Millin's bagpipes (🕐*see panel, p269).*

Mémorial Pegasus★

Av. du Major-Howard, Ranville. 🕐*Open daily Apr–Sept 9.30am–6.30pm; Feb– Mar and Oct–Nov 10am–1pm, 2–5pm.* ♿. 💶€6. 𝄞*02 31 78 19 44. www.normandy1944.com.*
Near the commemorative stelae stands a museum devoted to life during the Occupation and the Normandy landings.

Ouistreham-Riva-Bella⚓⚓

🕐*See Caen.*

▶ *From Riva-Bella to Asnelles, the D 514 follows the Mother-of-Pearl coast.*

Colleville-Montgomery

At dawn on 6 June the 4th Anglo-French commandos landed here under the command of Captain Kieffer.

In gratitude, the commune of Colleville-sur-Orne added to its name that of General (later Field Marshal) Bernard Montgomery, the victor of El Alamein and commander of the British forces.

South of the town, going towards Biéville-Beauville, a former coastal defence has been transformed into a **memorial** for the Suffolk Regiment. 🕐*Open Jul–mid-Sept Mon–Sat 3–7pm.*

LANDING BEACHES

M Museum or exhibition of the landings

Guided tour(1hr30min–2hr) Tue at 3pm. No charge. 02 31 97 12 61. www.amis-du-suffolk-rgt.com.

Lion-sur-Mer

This seaside resort has a 16C–17C **château**. The **church** has a 11C Romanesque tower and handsome capitals.

Luc-sur-Mer

Luc is a seaside resort known for its bracing air. The spa offers hydro-sodium iodate cures. The beautiful **municipal park**★ (35 r. de la Mer), is an oasis of greenery.

Langrune-sur-Mer

The name of this resort on the Mother-of-Pearl coast is Scandinavian in origin and means green land, probably due to the abundant seaweed, which fills the air with the smell of iodine. The 13C **church** has a handsome belltower similar to the tower of St-Pierre in Caen.

▷ *Take D 7 inland.*

Pegasus Bridge

© Stephen Meese/Dreamstime.com

The D-Day Landings

Dawn of D-Day – The formidable armada, which consisted of 4,266 barges and landing craft, together with hundreds of warships and naval escorts, set sail from the south coast of England on the night of 5 June 1944 (🕮 *for further details, see the Battle of Normandy in the Introduction)*; it was preceded by flotillas of minesweepers to clear a passage through the mine fields in the English Channel.

D-Day Invasion, Omaha Beach

© Bettmann/CORBIS

As the crossing proceeded, airborne troops were flown out and landed in two detachments at either end of the invasion front. The British 6th Division quickly took possession of the Bénouville-Ranville bridge, since named Pegasus Bridge after the airborne insignia, and harried the enemy positions between the River Orne and the River Dives to prevent reinforcements arriving. West of the River Vire the American 101st and 82nd Divisions mounted an attack on key positions such as Ste-Mère-Église or opened up the exits from Utah Beach.

British Sector – Although preliminary bombing and shelling had not destroyed Hitler's Atlantic Wall, they succeeded in disorganising German defences. Land forces were able to reach their objectives, divided into three beachheads.

A German counter-attack was crushed under naval bombardment.

Sword Beach – The Franco-British commandos landed at Colleville-Plage, Lion-sur-Mer and St-Aubin. They captured Riva-Bella and the strongpoints at Lion and Langrune and then linked up with the airborne troops at Pegasus Bridge. The main strength of the British 3rd Division then landed. This area, exposed to the Germans' long-range guns in Le Havre, became the crucial point in the battle.

Juno Beach – The Canadian 3rd Division landed at Bernières and Courseulles, reaching Creully by 5pm. They were the first troops to enter Caen on 9 July 1944.

Gold Beach – The British 50th Division landed at Ver-sur-Mer and Asnelles; by the afternoon they held the area and the artificial Mulberry harbour could be brought into position. The 47th Commandos advanced and captured Port-en-Bessin during the night of 7 June. On 9 June the British sector joined up with the Americans from Omaha Beach. On 12 June, after the capture of Carentan had enabled the troops from Omaha and Utah beaches to join forces, a single beachhead was established.

American Sector – 🕮 The events involved in the landing of American troops at **Omaha Beach** and **Utah Beach** are described under *Omaha Beach* and *Presqu'île du Cotentin*.

La Délivrande

The tall spires of the basilica in La Délivrande, the oldest Marian sanctuary in Normandy, are visible for miles across the Caen countryside and far out to sea. The present **basilica**, Notre-Dame de la Délivrande, is a neo-Gothic 19C building housing a highly venerated statue of the Virgin (late 16C).

At the convent of **Notre-Dame-de-Fidélité** (Our Lady of Fidelity), the last house on the Cresserons road, the chapel chancel is lit by three stained-glass windows (1931), made of crystal and chrome, by **René Lalique**, who was also responsible for the door of the tabernacle.

▷ *Continue on D 7 for 3km/2mi until you reach D 404 leading to Courseulles-sur-Mer. Follow signs for the Musée-Radar up to D 83 on the right.*

Douvre-la-Délivrande

Musée-Radar, rte de Basly.
Open daily mid-Jun–mid-Sept Tue–Sun 10am–6pm; May–mid-Jun holiday weekends 10am–6pm (last entry 30min before closing). €5.50. 02 31 37 74 43.
The **Musée-Radar** retraces the history of radar equipment. Blockhouses, situated on the site of the German radar station at Douvres, have been renovated and provide insight into the daily life of German soldiers stationed along the Atlantic Wall. The role of aerial and maritime search equipment in World War II and their evolution since 1945 is explained with the help of realistic scenery.

St-Aubin-sur-Mer

Bracing seaside resort with an offshore reef for shrimping and crab catching.

Bernières-sur-Mer

The French-Canadian Chaudière Regiment landed on this beach. Press and radio reporters came ashore here and sent the first reports of the landings. The church has a justly famous 13C **belltower**★; the three storeys and the stone spire together measure 67m/220ft.

Courseulles-sur-Mer

It was on this beach west of the locality – a Juno Beach sector – that Winston Churchill set foot on 12 June 1944; on 14 June General De Gaulle went to Bayeux and on 16 June King George VI came to spend a few hours with his troops. A major pleasure port, Courseulles is also a seaside resort.

Centre Juno Beach

Voie des Français-Libres. Open daily Apr–Sept 9.30am–7pm; Mar and Oct 10am–6pm; Feb and Nov–Dec 10am–5pm. Closed 25 Dec. €6.50. 02 31 37 32 17. www.junobeach.org.
At Centre Juno Beach, a short film introduces you to the role of Canadian soldiers and sailors, as well as the heroic performance of Canadian industry in the war effort. Multimedia guideposts and interactive exhibits enliven the displays.

Val-sur-Meregasus

On 6 June 1944 this tiny resort was the main British bridgehead in the Gold Beach sector. A monument com-

---

Bill Millin and his Bagpipes

"Down the road came Lord Lovat's commandos, cocky in their green berets. Bill Millin marched at the head of the column, his pipes blaring out *Blue Bonnets over the Border*. On both sides the firing suddenly ceased, as soldiers gazed at the spectacle. But the shock didn't last long. As the commandos headed across the bridges the Germans began firing again. Bill Millin remembers "just trusting to luck that I did not get hit, as I could not hear very much for the drone of the pipes". The most famous literary work about the Battle of Normandy is undoubtedly *The Longest Day*, written by the late Irish author **Cornelius Ryan** (published by Simon & Schuster in New York).

memorating the landing stands where D 514 meets avenue du Colonel-Harper. The **tower**✶ of St Martin's Church is the original robust 11C Romanesque structure of four storeys.

The **lighthouse** works in conjunction with the lights of Portland and St Catherine's Point in England and at Antifer, Le Havre and Gatteville in France to guide channel shipping. There is an extensive view from the lantern.

America-Gold Beach Museum

2 pl. Amiral-Byrd. ⏱*Open Jul–Aug daily 10.30am–5.30pm; Apr–Jun and Sept Wed–Mon 10.30am–5.30pm.* ⊜*€4.* ✆*02 31 22 58 58.* *www.goldbeachmusee.fr.*

The first exhibit describes pioneering transatlantic flights, notably that of the triple-engine Fokker *America* which landed at Ver in 1927. Homage is also paid to the British troops who landed at Gold Beach on 6 June 1944 to liberate Bayeux. West of Ver-sur-Mer, the cliffs of come into view.

Asnelles

This little resort with its sandy beach lies at the eastern end of the artificial harbour established at Arromanches. From the sea wall there is a good view of the cliffs and the roads (traces of the Mulberry harbour still exist). On the beach stands a monument raised to the memory of the British 231st Infantry Brigade.

West of Asnelles the road climbs to the eastern edge of the Bessin plateau; the Romanesque church in St-Côme comes into view. West of St-Côme, on the right-hand side of the road, a belvedere *(viewing table and parking area)* offers a beautiful **view**✶ down over the harbour and the last remaining elements of the Mulberry harbour.

Arromanches-les-Bains

♿*See Arromanches-les-Bains.*

The road passes through the fields of Bessin. Further on you can see the belltowers of Bayeux.

② LA CÔTE DU BESSIN

▷ *From Bayeux to Port-en-Bessin – 34km/21mi – allow 1hr45min. Leave Bayeux on D 516.*

Arromanches-les-Bains

♿*See Arromanches-les-Bains.*

▷ *After visiting , return to the road you came in on and, about 1km/0.6mi outside of town, turn right on the road to Port-en-Bessin. At Longues-sur-Mer, turn right on D 104 towards the sea.*

Crabs and AVREs and DD Tanks
Ingenious Fighting Machines to Breach the Atlantic Wall

These bizarre fighting machines, known as Hobart's Funnies, formed the 79th Armoured Division, commanded by their foremost inventor Major-General Sir Percy Hobart. The tanks were designed to swim ashore (Duplex Drive: Sherman amphibious tank); to clear a path through the minefields (Crab: Sherman flail tank); to double as flame-throwers (Crocodile: Churchill VII tank); to lay matting on soft sand (Bobbin); and to double as bridges to carry other tanks over obstacles (Ark: Churchill tank). The tanks were a complete surprise to the enemy and after the Normandy landings the 79th Armoured Division pursued its advance, crossing the Rhine and entering Germany.

Eisenhower paid a vibrant tribute to Hobart's Funnies, pointing out that many lives had been saved thanks to the "successful utilisation of our mechanical inventions". A Duplex Drive can still be seen on Canada Beach (Plage du Canada) at Courseulles-sur-Mer.

The Norman Ancestors of Walt Disney?

As is well known, in 1066, Duke William of Normandy sailed across the channel and conquered England. After these historic events, two Norman soldiers who had accompanied his troops, **Hugues d'Isigny** and his son **Robert**, chose to settle on British soil. They were born in Isigny-sur-Mer, a small village near the mouth of the River Vire. Over the years, their surname d'Isigny underwent a series of changes, becoming Disgny, then Disney, which sounded decidedly more Anglo-Saxon. In the 17C, a branch of the Disney family emigrated to Ireland. In 1834, Arundel Elias Disney and his brother Robert, along with their families, embarked on a voyage to North America. Leaving from Liverpool, they arrived on Ellis Island off New York on 3 October, after travelling for a month. That was the start of their American adventures. On 5 December 1901, Elias Disney's fourth child was born in Chicago: he was to become the famous illustrator **Walt Disney**, whose legendary animated cartoon characters like Mickey Mouse and Donald Duck have delighted many a generation of children. He died on 15 December 1966.

Batterie allemande de Longues-sur-Mer★

Half a mile down this road, a surfaced road *(left)* leads to the site of the powerful German battery. In spite of the release by 124 RAF planes of 600t of bombs during the night preceding 6 June, the four German guns began firing at 5.37am on 6 June. The French cruiser *Georges-Leygues* returned fire, followed by the *Montcalm* and the American battleship *Arkansas*.

The Germans were silent for a while but resumed firing in the afternoon; the battery was finally silenced at 7pm by two direct hits from the *Georges-Leygues*. Built on a picturesque cliff, it was composed of four 150mm/5.6in guns with a range of 20km/12.5mi, which enabled it to control Omaha and Gold beaches. The observation post and control room, on the cliff-edge, appeared in a famous scene from the film *The Longest Day* (1962).

Le Chaos

The track descends steeply and is liable to rockfalls; there is a view of the coast from Cap Manvieux in the east to the Pointe de la Percée in the west.

This part of the Bessin coast has eroded into a chaotic jumble.

▷ *Take D 104 south towards Bayeux.*

Abbaye Ste-Marie

◔*Open 1–20 Jul and 10–30 Sept Mon–Fri 2–6pm; Easter–Jul and Oct–All Saints', Thu 2–6pm.* ✏*€4.*
✆*02 31 21 78 41.*

Only the main door and some of the coir and transept remain of the 12C abbey church. Tombstones of the lords of Argouges in the refectory.

▷ *Return north to D 514; continue west to Port-en-Bessin.*

Port-en-Bessin★

From the jetties there is a view of the Bessin coast, Cap Manvieux to Pointe de la Percée. A 17C tower dominates the eastern outer harbour. Good harbour **view** from the clifftop blockhouse; outside Bayeux on the D 6, good **view** of **Château de Maisons** (15C–18C).

③ OMAHA BEACH★

From Bayeux to Carentan 75km/46.6mi. Allow 2hr45min.

▷ *Leave Bayeux by the north 13 going west.*

Tour-en-Bessin

The church has a 12C doorway; the transept spire is 13C, while the Romanesque nave has been renovated. On the arcade columns to the right are scenes of the 12 months of the year.

Pointe du Hoc

© www.calvados-tourisme.com

Tour d'Escures
Park beside D 100; take the private path (left) uphill (15min on foot there and back). Steps on the outside of the wall lead to the top of the round tower (**view**).

Port-en-Bessin★
See p271. From Port-en-Bessin, as far as Grandcamp-Maisy, the road continues through the Bessin region, which is crisscrossed by hedgerows.

Omaha Beach
See Omaha Beach.

Pointe du Hoc★★
From D 514 coming from Bayeux, just after a manor house, turn right to the car park. 1hr on foot.
The Pointe du Hoc was heavily defended by the Germans; their observation post covered the whole area where the American invasion fleet appeared on the morning of 6 June 1944. As the troops landing on **Omaha Beach** would have been particularly vulnerable to attack from this battery, the **Texas** fired 600 salvoes of 35.5cm/14in shells.
The 2nd Battalion of Rangers captured the position by assault at dawn on 6 June, scaling the cliffs with ropes and extendible ladders but with heavy losses – 135 Rangers out of 225. Commandos of the 116th Regiment of the US infantry, assisted by tanks, subdued the German defence. The gaping craters and battered blockhouses give some idea of the intensity of the fighting. Fine **views**★ of the sea and the coast.

Continue west on D 514.

Grandcamp-Maisy
Quai Crampon. Open May–Sept Tue–Sun 9.30am–1pm, 2.30–6.30pm, Mon 2.30–6.30pm; Feb–Apr and Oct Tue–Sun 1–6pm. €4. 02 31 92 33 51.
A little fishing port and marina. A small **museum** describes the exploits of the American Rangers.

Take D 199 and D 113 inland.

Cimetière militaire allemand de la Cambe
This impressive German cemetery with its rectangular lawn (2ha/5 acres) is the last resting place of 21,500 German soldiers who fell in the fighting in 1944.

Château de Colombières
Guided tours (45min) Jul–Aug Mon–Fri 2.30–6.30pm; Sept Sat–Sun 2.30–6.30pm (last entry 30min before closing). Closed public holidays. €5. 02 31 22 51 65. www.chateaudecolombieres.com.
The **château** was HQ for the American press after the Normandy landings.

Isigny-sur-Mer
The town has been famous for the production of milk and butter since the 17C.

Carentan
See Presqu'île du Cotentin.

Arromanches-les-Bains★

A modest seaside resort that owes its fame to the gigantic landing operation of June 1944. In the little port are the remains of a Mulberry harbour, the most extraordinary maritime achievement of the war.

VISIT

Artificial Port★

"As we have no harbour at our disposal, we shall bring ours," said Lord Mountbatten to Churchill. Arromanches was chosen for "Mulberry B", the floating artificial harbour for British troops; "Mulberry A" was for the Americans (&see Omaha Beach).

There were 230 Phoenix caissons (500,000t of concrete; the largest were 70m/229ft long, 20m/65ft high and 15m/49ft wide), 33 pierheads and 18km/11mi of floating roads that crossed the Channel at 6km/3mi an hour. The floating port at Arromanches allowed 9000t of equipment to be landed daily, the same tonnage handled by Le Havre's port prior to the war.

Reinforced after the terrible storm of 19 June 1944 that destroyed the Omaha artificial port, Arromanches still has imposing sections left, including about 20 Phoenix caissons, part of the 8km/4mi jetty closing in the harbour. Concrete floating docks and part of the platform lie on the beach. The best view (preferably at low tide) is from the belvedere situated on the D 514 heading for Asnelles.

▶ **Population:** 610.
& **Michelin Map:** 303: I-3.
⊞ **Info:** Port-en-Bessin: ℘02 31 22 45 80. Longues-sur-Mer: ℘02 31 21 46 87.
◗ **Location:** On the coast, 10km/6.2mi NE of Bayeux via D 516, 38km/23.6mi NE of Caen via D 516 and N 13.
⊛ **Don't Miss:** The remains of the allied artificial "Mulberry" port.
◷ **Timing:** 3hrs for the beach, museum and film.

Musée du Débarquement

Place du 6 juin. ◷*Open May–Aug 9am–7pm; Sept 9am–6pm; Feb and Nov–Dec 10am–12.30pm, 1.30–5pm; Mar and Oct 9.30am–12.30pm, 1.30–5.30pm; Apr 9am–12.30pm, 1.30–6pm.* ◷*Closed 5–25 Jan.* &
⊜*€6.50.* ℘*02 31 22 34 31. www.musee-arromanches.fr.*
The D-Day Landing Museum contains a collection of models, photographs, dioramas, arms and equipment. A large model of the Mulberry port shows how it functioned regardless of the tides. Royal Navy films of the landing are shown.

Arromanches 360°

◷*Open 9.40/10.10am–4.40/5.10/5.40/6.40pm.* ◷*Closed Jan.* &
⊜*€4.20.* ℘*02 31 22 30 30. www.360.com.*
The Price of Freedom mixes archive footage with scenes re-enacted on the landing sites, on a 360-degree screen.

PRINCIPAL UNITS

BREAKWATERS
① Breakwaters made from concrete-filled caissons sunk in the seabed.

PIER-HEADS
② Floating steel pontoons rising and falling with the tides by sliding up and down vertical pillars held to the bottom by suction.

FLOATING PIERS
③ Groups of light metal stages resting on Floats.

Omaha Beach★

Omaha Beach, which until 6 June 1944 existed only as an operational code name, has continued to designate the beaches of St-Laurent-sur-Mer, Colleville-sur-Mer and Vierville-sur-Mer, in memory of the American soldiers of the 1st (5th Corps of the 1st Army) Division, who suffered heavy casualties in the most costly of the D-Day battles.

A BIT OF HISTORY

Normandy Landings – When the American forces landed at Omaha Beach on 6 June 1944, they met an extremely well-organised German defence, aided by a strong coastal current that swept landing craft off course, and beach shingle that proved at first insurmountable to heavy armour. Companies at first baulked, later rallied and by evening the 116th Regiment had taken the Port-en-Bessin-Grandcamp road, enabling the motorised units to gain the plateau.

The austere and desolate appearance, especially of the eastern part, a narrow beach backing on barren cliffs, makes the invasion scene easy to imagine.

🚗 DRIVING TOUR

COLLEVILLE-SUR-MER TO VIERVILLE
9km/5.6mi. Allow 1hr.

Colleville-sur-Mer
The last Germans did not leave the area around Colleville's village church until 10am on 7 June 1944.

▷ *Just before the church, turn right towards the coast.*

Monument to the 5th Engineer Special Brigade
The monument, built on the remains of a blockhouse, commemorates those who died protecting movements between the landing craft and the beach. This is the best belvedere on Omaha Beach.

- **Michelin Map:** 303: G-3.
- **Location:** Omaha Beach is some 20km/12mi northwest of Bayeux.
- **Don't Miss:** The American Cemetery at Colleville-sur-Mer holds some 9,400 crosses and Stars of David, perfectly aligned. Note the extreme youth of the fallen soldiers.
- **Timing:** You will need three hours to see the sights.

American Military Cemetery (de Colleville-sur-Mer)
The 9,385 Carrara marble crosses and Stars of David stand aligned in an impressive site. A memorial stands in the central alley and is surrounded by trees. The commemorative list includes 1,557 names.

A *bélvèdere* (viewing table showing the landing operation) overlooks the sea. The path down to the beach *(30min there and back)* passes a second viewing table.

A monument to the US 1st Infantry Division stands just outside the cemetery.

▷ *Continue west on D 514 to St-Laurent-sur-Mer.*

St-Laurent-sur-Mer
Musée Omaha 6 juin 1944
Av. de la Libération. 🕐*Open daily Jul–Aug 9.30am–7.30pm; mid-May–Jun and 1st 2 weeks Sept 9.30am–7pm; mid-Feb–mid-Mar 10am–12.30pm, 2.30–6pm; mid-Mar –mid-May and mid-Sept–mid-Nov 9.30am–6.30pm. (Last entry 1hr before closing).* ♿ ⊚*€5.80.* ✆*02 31 21 97 44. www.musee-memorial-omaha.com.* This village was not liberated until 7 June after heavy combat. The **museum** describes life under occupation.

▷ *Take D 517 down to the beach: the road runs through a valley.*

American Military Cemetery at Colleville-sur-Mer

©Bryan Busovicki/Bigstockphoto.com

Les Moulins

This site is marked by the **Monument to the D-Day Landing**. Turn right onto the road that runs along the beach and follow it to the end; there, at the foot of the American cemetery, you can look out onto the Ruquet Valley and the road opened by the Engineers unit after the blockhouse was destroyed around 11.30am. Heavy equipment, motorised units and the infantry were able to reach the plateau and then advance to the town of St-Laurent.

▷ *Return to the Monument to the D-Day Landing.*

The first units found shelter here at dawn on 6 June 1944. From a platform erected for the Omaha Beach Monument there is a view of the cliffs the infantry had to scale in order to reach the plateau.

Vierville-sur-Mer

Taking boulevard Maritime westwards, a few hundred metres/yards away is a stele marking the temporary burial place of the remains of soldiers fallen in the battles on the beaches. The village was besieged from the morning of 6 June 1944, and the church seriously damaged after its belltower fell. The road leaves the coast by another "beach exit", only open later in the day. A monument to the United States National Guard forces who fought in the two world wars is at one of the blockhouses the assailants dreaded most.

Musée D Day-Omaha

Rte de Grancamp (D 514).
🕐 *9.30am/10.30am–5/6/7/7.30pm depending on season.* ♿ ∞€5.50 *(children €3).* 📞 *02 31 21 71 80. www.dday-omaha.org.*
This former aircraft hangar displays objects from World War II, including an Enigma machine, aeroplane motors and paratrooper motorcycles.

275

Château de Fontaine-Henry★★

This beautiful building is a fine example of Renaissance architecture. A member of the Harcourt family built it in the 15C and 16C over the dungeons, cellars and foundations of the original 11C–12C fortress.

- ☝ **Michelin Map:** 303: J-4.
- ▶ **Location:** Fontaine-Henry is in the Mue Valley, near the Côte de Nacre and the D-Day beaches, 18km/11mi N of Caen and 25mi/15.5mi E of Bayeux.
- ☺ **Don't Miss:** The stone stalls in the château chapel.
- ⏱ **Timing:** 1hr30min to see the château.

VISIT

☞ *Guided tours (1hr30min) mid-Jun–mid-Sept Wed–Mon 2.30–6.30pm; Easter–mid-Jun and last half Sept Sat–Sun and public holidays 2.30–6.30pm; Oct–2 Nov Sat–Sun and public holidays 2–5.30pm. ⌧€7. ✆06 89 84 85 57/02 31 26 93 67. www.chateau-de-fontaine-henry.com.*

An immense, steeply sloping **slate roof**, taller than the building itself, covers the 16C pavilion on the left. The **main building** is a wonder of delicately worked stonework. Inside is similar stonework, including the **François I staircase**. Furnished throughout, the château has some fine paintings, as well as a rare collection of engravings by **Van der Meulen**. The nave of the 12C chapel was altered in the 16C; don't miss the sculptures inside, as well as the stonework staircase.

EXCURSION

🚶 *Allow 15min on foot there and back. The lane branches off D 170 on a corner, about 500m/550yd from Thaon parish church. This downhill path will take you to the bottom of the valley.*

Ancienne église de Thaon★

Allow 15min there and back.
☞ *Guided tours only Jul–Aug Sun 3–6.30pm; year-round on request. ✆02 31 80 04 76. http://vieilleeglisede thaon.free.fr. ⌧No charge.*

This small 12C Romanesque church is enhanced by its attractive setting in an isolated valley. The belfry, one of the most original in Normandy, is capped by a pyramid roof and deeply recessed twin bays.

Château de Fontaine-Henry

A. de Valroger/MICHELIN

Bayeux★★

Today the Bayeux Tapestry still presents a unique record of the events of 1066 and the Battle of Hastings. Its home, the former capital of the Bessin, was the first French town to be liberated (7 June 1944) in World War II. The town escaped damage during the war, leaving a cathedral and old houses – many tastefully restored – as well as a pedestrian precinct, for explorers in the 21C.

A BIT OF HISTORY

Cradle of the Dukes of Normandy – Bayeux, a Gaulish town, became a Roman centre, then was successively captured by the Bretons, the Saxons and the Vikings.

Rollo, the famous Viking, married Popa, the daughter of Count Béranger, governor of the town. In 905, their son, the future William Longsword, ancestor of William the Conqueror, was born here.

Oath of Bayeux – In the 11C Edward the Confessor ruled over England. He had previously found refuge in Normandy for many years, and Norman accounts claim that he thus chose his cousin, William of Normandy, as his successor. He allegedly sent **Harold**, a powerful favourite of the Saxon nobles, to officially inform the duke.

Harold was shipwrecked on the coast of Picardy and captured by Count Guy of Ponthieu. Freed by **William**, he was received at the Norman court where the duke's daughter, Edwige, was presented as his wife to be.

Harold swore on saintly relics to recognise the duke's right to the English throne. However, when Edward died on 5 January 1066, Harold accepted the English crown.

The Conquest of England – Harold's accession provoked William to set sail with the Norman fleet on 27 September 1066 from Dives-sur-Mer, to fight for his claim to the throne. On 28 September the Normans set foot on English soil

- ▶ **Population:** 14,600.
- ⌖ **Michelin Map:** 303: H-4.
- ⊞ **Info:** Pont St-Jean. ✆ 02 31 51 28 28. www.bayeux-bessin-tourism.com.
- ▷ **Location:** A short distance away from the D-Day beaches of Omaha, Bayeux is midway between Caen (30km/ 18.6mi SW) and Carentan (47km/29.2mi NW).
- ⊛ **Don't Miss:** The Bayeux Tapestry; Notre-Dame Cathedral; Battle of Normandy Museum; gardens of the château of Brécy; Priory of St-Gabriel.
- ⊙ **Timing:** At least 1hr to view the Bayeux Tapestry.
- ♟ **Kids:** The children's audioguide will make the tapestry more interesting for them.

at Pevensey in Sussex and occupied Hastings. Harold dug in on a hill. On 14 October William advanced and emerged victorious by that evening. The Bayeux Tapestry, a propaganda created after the invasion, claims that Harold fell in the fighting with an arrow in his eye.

☜ WALKING TOUR

45min to visit historic centre.
Start from the tourist office.

Rue St-Jean

East of rue St-Martin, partly an attractively restored pedestrian precinct. At no 53 is the Hôtel du Croissant (15C–16C).

▷ *Turn back and head for rue des Teinturiers.*

Quai de l'Aure

Fine view of the river, the water mill in the former tanning district, the arched bridge, the old fish market and the cathedral's towers in the background.

WHERE TO STAY

Argouges (Hôtel d')..............23	
Churchill (Hôtel)..................21	
Les Remparts (Chambre d'Hôte)..........25	
Petit Matin (Chambres d'hôte Le)..........16	
Reine Mathilde (Hôtel)..................19	

WHERE TO EAT

Bristot de Paris (Le)................1	
L' Assiette normande..............12	
Pommier (Le)..................4	
Rapière (La)..................7	
Saint-Martin (Hostellerie)......10	

○ *Take r. Maréchal-Foch; turn right.*

Rue St-Martin

No 6 is the 17C Maison du Cadran, so called for the sundial on the façade. There is a beautiful **half-timbered house**★ with two overhanging upper storeys and slate roof on the corner of r. des Cuisiniers. Just after the rue Franche, right, is the 15C **Hôtel d'Argouges** (wood sculptures).

○ *Turn into rue Franche.*

Rue Franche

Several townhouses: no 5, **Hôtel de Rubercy**, is a 15C–16C turreted manor house; no 7, Hôtel de la Crespellière, after a courtyard, is early 18C.

○ *Turn right into rue de la Juridiction to get to rue des Ursulines.*

Rue des Ursulines

A charming Louis XV hotel opens onto a street dotted with beautiful houses, often hiding behind tall enclosing walls. At no 11, the **Hôtel de Marguerie** (17C) has an imposing stone portal. At the end of the street, at the crossroads and to the right, notice the beautiful hotel with delicately worked window frames.

Rue du Général-de-Dais

No 10, Hôtel de Castilly (18C), in the Louis XV style. No 14, Hôtel de la Tour du Pin (18C), has a majestic Louis XVI façade.

Place Charles-de-Gaulle

On this immense esplanade, a column commemorates General de Gaulle's 14 June 1944 speech: "In our Normandy, glorious and mutilated, Bayeux and its surrounding area witnessed one of the greatest clashes in History…" He had a triumphant return here on 8 July 1960.

○ *From place Charles-de-Gaulle (public garden) head back down to the cathedral by rue de la Maîtrise.*

Cathédrale Notre-Dame★★

Jan–Mar 9am–5pm; Apr–Jun 9am–6pm; Jul–Sept 8.30am–7pm; Oct–Dec 8.30am–6pm; no visits during Mass. Summer guided tours (ask at tourist office).

The cathedral is the seat of the former bishopric of Bayeux, created by St Exupery in the 4C; it became the diocese of Bayeux-Lisieux in 1855, bearing the French title of *"insigne cathédrale"* ("cathedral of note"). The **east end** of this beautiful Romanesque and Norman-Gothic edifice is a graceful com-

© The Art Archive/Corbis

Detail of Norman Conquest of England from The Bayeux Tapestry

Bayeux Tapestry★★★

The **Bayeux Tapestry** *(Tapisserie dite de la Reine Mathilde)* is displayed in the **Centre Guillaume le Conquérant**; the work is the most accurate and lively document to survive from the Middle Ages, providing details on the period's clothes, ships, arms and general lifestyle.

Presentation of the famous tapestry has been organised in two spaces. The masterpiece itself is in a glass case in the dimmed Harold Room.

Wrongly attributed in the 18C to Queen Matilda, the tapestry (in fact an embroidery) was probably commissioned in England soon after the conquest from Saxon embroiderers by Odo of Conteville, Count of Kent and Bishop of Bayeux. In coloured wool on linen, it is 50cm/19in high by 70m/229ft.

The outstanding sections are Harold's embarkation and crossing (4–6), his audience with William (14), crossing the River Couesnon and Mont-St-Michel (17), Harold's Oath (23), the death and burial of Edward the Confessor (26–28), the appearance of Halley's comet, an ill omen for Harold (32), the building of the fleet (36), the Channel crossing and the march to Hastings (38–40), cooking and eating of meals (41–43), the battle and Harold's death (51–58).

The English are distinguished by their moustaches and long hair, the Normans by their short hairstyles, the clergy by their tonsures and the women (three in all) by their flowing garments and veiled heads.

On the first floor, an exhibition makes it possible to understand the origin and history of the tapestry, and to place it in its context. Informative panels and display cases explain the reign of William the Conqueror, as well as the secrets behind the embroidery of the tapestry and the difficulties in preserving it. The visit is organised by themes, easy for young children to understand. At the end of the circuit, the film illustrates the history of the tapestry and the conquest of England.

Centre Guillaume-le-Conquérant, r. de Nesmond. ℘02 31 51 25 50. www.tapisserie-bayeux.fr. Open mid May–Apr and Sept–mid-Nov 9am–6.30pm; May–Aug 9am–7pm; rest of year 9.30am–12.30pm, 2–6pm (last admission 45min before closing). Visit is with an audioguide; special commentary for children. Closed 1st wk Jan, 1 Jan, 25 Dec. €7.80 (children €3.80).

Cathédrale Notre-Dame

© www.calvados-tourisme.com

The 11C **crypt** beneath the choir is divided into three small naves each containing six bays. Above the remarkably delicate foliage of the capitals are 15C frescoes of angel musicians. A recess *(left)* contains the 15C recumbent figure of a canon, his tomb set into the wall. The chapter house is a beautiful late-12C Gothic construction. The vaulting, which was renewed in the 14C, is supported by consoles decorated with monsters or grotesque figures. Paintings and a crucifix thought to have belonged to the Princesse de Lamballe are presented here. The floor of 15C glazed bricks has a labyrinth in its centre. The tiles on the risers at the back of the room depict hunting scenes. The beatification of Ste-Thérèse of Lisieux was signed at the desk.

▶ *On leaving the cathedral, take rue Lambert-Léonard-Leforestier, left.*

Hôtel du Doyen

r. Lambert-Leforestier. ℰ*02 31 92 14 21.* A huge 17C porch leads into the 18C mansion, which houses the collection of the **Baron-Gèrard Museum**, which is closed for repairs until 2012. Themed tours as well as workshops for children are still offered *(call the number above for information).*

▶ *Backtrack and take rue Bienvenu, before the Cathedral.*

Conservatoire de la Dentelle de Bayeux

6 r. du Bienvenu. 🕓*Open Mon–Sat 9.30am–12.30pm, 2 .30–6pm.* ℰ*02 31 92 73 80.* This edifice, called the "Maison d'Adam et Eve" owing to the wood sculptures depicting religious or legendary subjects on its façade, is a shop and workshop where lace-makers continue the generations-old tradition of *point de Bayeux*, the Bayeux pattern. Several beautiful pieces are displayed.

▶ *Take rue de la Chaine, which turns into rue Laitière, to get to rue St-Martin; then take rue St-Jean.*

position. Flying buttresses sustain the choir, flanked with two bell turrets. The central tower dates from the 15C, but its crown, "the bonnet", was redone in the 19C. The portal represents the history of St Thomas Becket, the Archbishop of Canterbury, on the tympanum; his murder in the cathedral was ordered by King Henry II.

The **façade** has two Romanesque towers. The upper windows in the vaulting are 13C, but the wide arches are in the best 12C style. Their justly famous decoration is typical of Norman Romanesque sculpture. In the right transept arm notice, down and to the right, two interesting paintings: *The Life of St Nicholas* and the 15C *Crucifixion*. The tympanum of the left portal represents the Passion *(read from bottom to top)*; that of the right represents the Last Judgement*(read from top to bottom)*.

The three-storey choir, with its ambulatory and radiating chapels, is a magnificent example of Norman Gothic architecture. The stalls are 16C. The high altar is a majestic 18C piece; the six candelabras in chased bronze, the tabernacle and the cross are by Caffieri the Elder. Notice the paintings on the choir vaulting, depicting the first bishops of Bayeux.

The third and fourth chapels on the south side contain 15C frescoes.

ADDITIONAL SIGHTS
Musée-Mémorial de la Bataille de Normandie★

By r. St-Loup, then right on bld du 6-Juin/bld Fabian-Ware. ○*Open May–Sept 9.30am–6.30pm; Oct–Apr 10am–12.30pm, 2–6pm (last entry 1hr before closing).* ○*Closed last 2 weeks in Jan; 1 Jan, 25 and 26 Dec.* ᴑ, ◎€6.50. ☏02 31 51 46 90.

Situated on the line that separated the British and American sectors in 1944, the Memorial Museum recalls the dramatic events of summer 1944. A clear and explicit layout retraces the Battle of Normandy from 7 June to 29 August 1944, alternating chronology and themed spaces (the French Resistance, war correspondents, destroyed towns and cities, civil engineering, etc.). Equipment and uniforms illustrate each phase. A film in the last room *(25min)* is projected at regular intervals, and gives a good summary.

Jardin Botanique

By r. du Dr.-Michel, then the D 6. ○*Open Apr–Sept 9am–8pm; Oct–Mar 9am-5pm.* The garden was created under the second Empire by the famous architect and landscaper, Eugène Buhler. Among the little hills and dales, notice the surprising dimensions of the **weeping beech**: its 40m/131ft diameter has caused it to be classified as a "natural monument" and an "important tree of France". Pond with flowers, glass houses.
👪 A botanical itinerary for children is available at the tourist office.

EXCURSIONS
Abbaye de Mondaye

▶ *11km/6.8mi – allow 45min. From Bayeux take D 6 S. After 8km/5mi turn right onto D 33; follow the signs.*
🔊 *Guided tours (1hr) Jul–Aug 4pm, rest of the year Sun 3.30pm.* ᴑ €5. ☏02 31 92 58 11. www.mondaye.com.
Also called St Martin's Abbey, it was founded in 1215 but rebuilt in the 18C and 19C. The abbey church, which also serves the parish, is in the classical style (early 18C). Its uniformity of design is due to its architect and decorator, **Eustache Restout**, a canon in the Premonstratensian Order. The interior contains some fine pieces: high altar, woodwork in the chancel including a beautiful Crucifixion, the Assumption (a terracotta group in the Lady Chapel) and the Parizot organ (restored).
The 18C conventual buildings – refectory, sacristy (18C woodwork) and library – are open to the public.

Tilly-sur-Seulles

▶ *12km/7mi SW of Bayeux, by the D 6.*
Completely destroyed in June 1944, Tilly saw bloody combat between British troops and the Panzer Lehr in June 1944. A visit to the cemetery gives a good idea of scale (986 British, 232 German graves) as does the **Musée de la Bataille de Tilly** in a former chapel (○*Open May–Sept weekends and holidays 10am–noon, 2–6pm;* ○*closed on certain holidays, call for information;* ᴑ ◎€4, children under-12 free. ☏06 07 59 46 02. http://museetilly.free.fr).

🚗 DRIVING TOUR

① SOUTHWEST OF BAYEUX
Round-trip of 50km/30mi. 3hr30min.

▶ *From Bayeux take D 572 for St-Lô.*

St-Loup-Hors
The 12C–13C church has retained its Romanesque tower and old tombs.

Noron-la-Poterie
This is a well-known centre producing salt glaze ware; some of the workshops are open to the public.

▶ *In La Tuilerie turn left onto D 73, which leads to Balleroy via Castillon.*

Château de Balleroy★
○*Guided tour Jul–Aug daily 10am–6pm; 15 Mar–Jun and Sept–15 Oct Wed–Sun 10am–noon, 2–6pm.*
○*Closed mid-Oct-mid Mar. Visit to Musée des Ballons and park (château closed) 10am–noon, 1.30–5pm, closed*

Château de Balleroy

© www.calvados-tourisme.com

Tue, wkd, 1 Jan, 1 and 11 Nov, 25 Dec. €6.50 (under 7 years, free); €8 combined with museum. 02 31 21 60 61. www.chateau-balleroy.com.

The Château of Balleroy was built between 1626 and 1636 and designed by François Mansart (1598–1666) for the chancellor of Gaston d'Orléons, Jean de Choisy. His descendants, the successive marquises de Balleroy, have occupied it for three centuries. It is today the property of the family of publisher, balloonist and millionaire Malcolm Forbes, who bought it in 1970 and created the Musée des Ballons here. Built in local materials, grey stone and red schiste, the château expresses the style dear to the architect, although it was one of the first of Mansart's private works: the staging of buildings in a perspective of successive courtyards, pyramidal composition of pavilions, etc. The former stables, laid out here and there with interlacing flower beds; and the terrace, flanked by two pavilions, create a setting worthy of the building. The foliage of the romanticised park (135ha/333 acres) and the French-style gardens, complete the theatrical staging.

Interior★ – On the ground floor are the paintings of Albert de Balleroy, a 19C painter of animals: in the Louis XIII salon are hunting scenes and in the smoking-room, portraits. Two of them represent the count: one (on the easel) is by Paul Baudry and the other is signed by Manet (Albert de Balleroy shared an art studio with him in Paris for seven years). In the dining room, the wood paneling is decorated on the theme of the fables of La Fontaine. Of revolutionary design, the staircase suspended on the vaulting leads to the first floor where three bedrooms pay homage to some well-known figures: Queen Victoria, Louis-Philippe, and finally Napoleon and Wellington in a shorthand version of the facts, under the imperturbable eye of Blucher.

The **salon d'honneur** has superb décor, embellished with a collection of royal portraits by Juste d'Egmont; from floor to ceiling it is painted in the French style (the four seasons and the signs of the zodiac).

Musée des Ballons - Hot air and gas balloons, gondolas, trophies, photographs, models, medals and fantasy objects in this museum bring the period of ballooning and dirigibles to life.

Église paroissiale

The church stands before the château entrance. Built in 1651 in the local brown schiste, it is attributed to Mansart. Its octagonal belltower sets it apart. Inside, there is an Annunciation of the 18th century Italian school, over the altar.

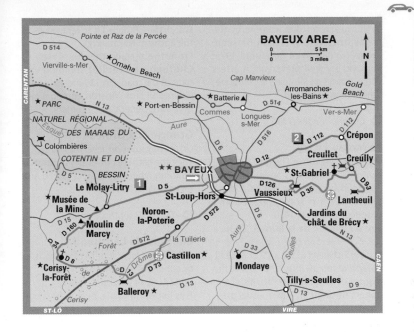

On leaving, turn left onto D 13. At the crossroads take D 13E and D 8 west through Cerisy Forest.

Ancienne Abbaye de Cerisy-la-Forêt★

At the exit from the forest of Cerisy near D 572. Allow 2hr.
Open early Apr–mid Nov 11am–6pm. Guided tours possible (45min) on prior request. Closed Mon (except Jul–Aug). €4. 02 33 57 34 63. www.abbayes-normandes.com

The abbey at Cerisy is a remarkable example of Norman Romanesque architecture. The first monastery dates from around 510. In 1032 Robert I of Normandy, the father of William the Conqueror, founded a new monastery here dedicated to Vigor, former bishop of Bayeux.

Église Abbatiale★ – The nave is remarkable for its height. The choir and especially the **apse★** are striking examples of Romanesque architecture, characterised by delicacy and abundance of light, when most 11C buildings were massive and sombre.

Walk round the church to the east end to admire the **chevet★** with its tiered effect formed by the apse, the choir and the belfry.

Bâtiments conventuels – Following the Revolution, these 13C buildings were used as a stone quarry.

Musée lapidaire – A low chamber with pointed vaulting houses the Archaeological Museum. At the far end of the chamber, on the left, is a dungeon with 15C and 16C graffiti.

Chapelle de l'Abbé – The Abbot's Chapel, built in the 13C with a gift from St Louis, is a good example of Norman Gothic architecture.

Salle de justice – This contains the monks' furniture, as well as documents and manuscripts.

Leave Cerisy by the D 34, to the north and heading for Molay-Littry. The Moulin de Marcy is near the intersection of the D 160 and D 189.

Moulin de Marcy

Le Molay-Littry. Apr–Sept 10am–noon, 2–6pm. Closed Mon. €5 (children €1.50); €7 (children €2) ticket combined with the Musée de la Mine. 02 31 21 42 13.

In this green setting, watered by the Siette, the water mill can be seen; the last miller lived here until 1975. Remarkably well preserved, it offers you a chance to discover a complete, functioning water mill.

▷ *Continue on the D 160.*

Le Molay-Littry

The village was once a busy coal mining centre. The mine was opened in 1743 and flourished until the late 19C. During World War II it was reopened and produced coal until 1950.

The 👥 **Musée de la Mine**★ (🕐*open Apr–Sept Tue–Sun 10am–noon, 2–6pm; 🚪 👁€5 (children €1.50). 🖉02 31 22 89 10; www.ville-molay-littry.fr)* presents the history of mining and the life of the miners through an audio-visual presentation, a reconstruction of a mining gallery, a scale **model**★ of a pithead, and a range of tools.

A tall chimney and significant archaeological vestiges mark the former Frandemiche pit; with informational panels, it is the material link to the presentation at the museum.

▷ *Take D 5 east to return to Bayeux.*

② EAST OF BAYEUX
Round-trip of 34km/21mi. Allow 2hr.

▷ *From Bayeux head for Courseulles-sur-Mer, take D 12 and D 112 towards Ver-sur-Mer.*

Crépon

Admire the Romanesque church with its 15C tower and the prosperous farms.

▷ *Turn right onto D 65.*

Creully

🏃*Guided tours (45min) Jul–Aug Tue–Fri 10.30am–12.30pm, 2.30–5.30pm; early–mid-Sept Tue–Fri by appointment with tourist office.* 👁€4. 🖉02 31 80 18 65.
The **château** is built on the foundations of an 11C castle. The main 12C building is flanked by a 16C round tower adjoining a square keep. During World

War II, the BBC used it to relay news of the Battle of Normandy.

From the terrace there is a view of **Château de Creullet** standing in a loop of the road. On 12 June 1944 King George VI and Winston Churchill met here with General Montgomery.

Grange aux Dîmes
On the Bayeux road, level with no 82.
The tithe barn is a powerfully buttressed building where wheat was stored and taxes were collected.

▷ *Take D 93 south to Lantheuil.*

Château de Lantheuil

🏃*Guided tours Jun–Oct for groups, by appointment only.* 👁€7.
🖉*02 31 80 14 00. Call for hours.*
This imposing castle, built in the reign of Louis XIII, has remained in the same family ever since. The rooms have retained their original décor: woodwork, furniture, sculptures and paintings including a remarkable collection of family portraits.

▷ *Return to Creully; turn left onto D 35. Enter St-Gabriel-Brécy; turn right.*

Ancien Prieuré de St-Gabriel★

Chapel: 🕐*Jul–Aug Wed–Mon 2–6pm; May–Jun. Unaccompanied visits to gardens weekends and school holidays 10am–6pm.* 👁*No charge except for exhibitions.* 🖉*06 89 45 71 63. www.prieuresaintgabriel.fr.*

Ancien Prieuré de St-Gabriel

A. de Valroger/MICHELIN

The old priory of St-Gabriel was founded in the 11C as a daughter house of Fécamp Abbey. The attractive buildings surround a courtyard with a monumental entrance gate. A spiral staircase leads to the **priory room**. The **church** is reduced to the magnificently designed and decorated east end and chancel (11C–12C). Beyond the church is a **garden**, planted with fruit trees and banks of flowers. The 15C **Justice Tower** contained a prison on the lower floor and a lookout at the top.

▷ *Return to D 35; continue west towards Bayeux; then follow the signs south.*

Jardins du Chateau de Brécy★
St-Gabriel-Brécy ◷*Open Easter–Oct Tue, Thu, Sat–Sun and public holidays 2.30–6.30pm.* ∞*€6.* ℘*02 31 80 11 48. www.parcsetjardins.fr.*

The castle is approached through a magnificent great **gateway**★ (17C). The terraced **gardens**★ offer a beautiful perspective, which terminates in a high wrought-iron grill ornately decorated.

▷ *Take D 158; just before the church turn right onto a narrow road; after 2km/1mi turn left onto D 35; after 2km/1mi turn right towards Esquay-sur-Seulles.*

Château de Vaussieux
Vaux-sur-Seulles ⊶*Closed to the public.* In 1778 the American owner of this beautiful 18C mansion gave it to Marshal Broglie to hold manoeuvres designed to intimidate England. The château is an elegant building set in its own park; the outbuildings are half-timbered or of stone.

▷ *Continue onto Esquay-sur-Seulles; take D 126 to return to Bayeux.*

Jardins du Chateau de Canon★

An invitation to time-travel, the gardens of the Château de Canon submerge the visitor in the world of the Age of Enlightenment, in a realm between reason and imagination: Romantic ruins, chinoiseries, grottoes, walled gardens protecting fruit trees, and trees three centuries old and still intact. This is, as Élie de Beaumont, enlightened member of parliament and friend to philosophers, would have wished it.

CHÂTEAU DE CANON
Mézidon-Canon. ◷*Open Easter–31 May Sat–Sun and public holidays 2–6pm.* ♿ ∞*€6 (under 10 years free), €2 for animal circuit.* ℘*02 50 93 65 17. www.opatrimoine.com/chateaudecanon.*
The Château de Canon comes into view at the end of a long avenue bordered with trees and strips of lawn. J.-B. Élie

- ♿ **Michelin Map:** 303 L5.
- **Info:** ℘02 50 93 65 17.
- ▷ **Location:** Mézidon-Canon is 29km/18mi SW of Caen by the D 613 and D47, and 28km/17mi NE of Falaise by the D 511 via St-Pierre-sur-Dives.
- **Don't Miss:** the château's *chartreuses* (walled gardens)
- **Timing:** Allow 1 1/2 hours, to take your time.

de Beaumont, a brilliant lawyer at the Paris Parliament, stewarded the finances of the Comte d'Artois and was a great friend of Voltaire; he created the estate in 1768. The elegant 18C construction is surrounded by service buildings in an L-shape.
Park and gardens★ – The château is embellished with 15ha/37acres of gardens, decorated with statues and follies, which juxtapose the French and English styles Among the main points of inter-

est are the Temple de la Pleureuse, in memory of Mme Élie de Beaumont, who died in 1783. Also of interest is the Miroir d'eau, a body of water surrounded by antique busts; a rare Chinese pavilion; and above all the **chartreuses**★, a series of 12 fruit gardens enclosed by high walls, sheltering a profusion of flowers. Finished in 1780, they are the perfect illustration of the 18C sense of order. In each "room", or enclosed space, fruit trees are trained to grow *en espalier* along the walls, which preserve the sun's heat to ripen the fruit.

The park itself still has a few superb trees, especially 300-year-old Middle Eastern plantains. Some have huts that can be rented for the night (www.coup-decanon.fr).

In the surrounding buildings, which include an 18C cider press, you can buy cider produced on the estate.

Each year in August the park is lively with the evening performances of the **Féeries de Canon**, followed by fireworks over the Miroir d'eau.

👥 To perpetuate the idea of organic, integrated agriculture, such as Élie de Beaumont would have wished it, the château has an organic farm and a wide range of domestic animals, that will delight children.

St-Pierre-sur-Dives★

St-Pierre-sur-Dives developed around an 11C Benedictine abbey founded by William the Conqueror's aunt; the old abbey church still remains.

SIGHTS
Église Abbatiale★
🕐*Open daily.* 📞*02 31 20 97 90.*
Tour St-Michel, was originally a dovecote, doubling as a keep. The **convent buildings** are 17C; the **cloister** is 18C.

Salle capitulaire
23 r. St-Benoist. 🕐*mid-Apr–mid-Oct Mon–Fri 9.30am–12.30pm, 1.30–6pm, Sat 10am–12.30pm, 2.30–5pm. Nov–Mar Mon–Fri 9.30am–12.30pm, 1.30–5.30pm.* 🕐*Closed Sun.* 📞*02 31 20 97 90. www.mairie-saint-pierre-sur-dives.fr.*
13C Gothic chapter house.

👥Jardin conservatoire des fleurs et des légumes du pays d'Auge★
R. St-Benoist across from the tourist office. 🕐*Open daily May–Sept 10am–12.30pm, 2–6pm, Sat 10am–noon, 2–5pm.* 👣*Guided tour Tue 3.30pm and Fri 11am.* 🕐*Closed Sun.* ♿

▶ **Population:** 3,701.
🚗 **Michelin Map:** 303: L-5.
ℹ **Info:** Rue St-Benoist. 📞02 31 20 97 90. www.mairie-saint-pierre-sur-dives.fr.
▶ **Location:** St-Pierre-sur-Dives is 43km/21mi SW of Caen.
🕐 **Timing:** The Monday morning market is one of the largest in Normandy.

💶*€1.50 (under 12 years free), guided tour €2.50 (under 12 years free).* 📞*02 31 20 97 90.*
450 varieties of regional plants, flowers and vegetables are curated here; some of them are on the brink of extinction.

Halles★
📞*02 31 20 97 90. www.mairie-saint-pierre-sur-dives. Closed during events (call for info).* 💶*No charge. Antique and flea market 1st Sun of month; food market Mon morning.*
The 11C–12C market, which was burned down in 1944, has been faithfully rebuilt, even to the use of 290,000 chestnut pegs in its **timber-work**.

Château du Vendeuvre★★

In 1750 Alexandre le Forestier d'Osseville, Count of Vendeuvre, commissioned the architect Jacques-François Blondel to build him a summer residence on the banks of the Dives. The château and its beautiful gardens, with their delightful surprise fountains, continue to delight visitors.

VISIT

🕐 *Open May–Sept 11am–6pm; Apr and Oct–2 Nov Sun and public holidays 2–6pm.* ♿ ⬢*€9.50 (children €7.50).* ✆*02 31 40 93 83. www.vendeuvre.com.*
The château offers five sights: the 👪**Musée du mobilier miniature** (Miniature Furniture Museum), the château interior, the collection of shelters for pets, the garden and the 18C kitchens. Ticket prices depend on how many venues you want to visit.

Musée du mobilier miniature★★

The lovely vaulted rooms of the orangery are the setting for an exceptional collection of miniature furniture, models and masterpieces of skilled craftsmen. About 100 pieces dating from the 16C to the present, are exhibited.

Château★

🕐*Same hours as museum.*
The rooms are attractively furnished. In the dining room, with a great view of the sunset, the table is laid with a linen cloth woven with the family arms and the rear façade of the château. The reception room has lovely carved panelling.
Two popular 18C games are on display: loto and tric-trac on a special table. Note the chair designed for a woman wearing panniers, and in the main bedroom the toiletry set, the pastels in the salon, the study (collection of goose feathers), the smoking room (paraphernalia of an 18C smoker) and the kitchens. Behind the château there is a water garden.

- ♿ **Michelin Map:** 303: L-6.
- 🛈 **Info:** ✆02 31 40 93 83. www.vendeuvre.com.
- ▶ **Location:** The château is 5km/3mi SW of St-Pierre-sur-Dives.
- 👁 **Don't Miss:** The Musée du mobilier miniature, a collection of tiny masterpieces; the park has remarkable water features, including surprise fountains.
- 🕐 **Timing:** You will need 3hr to see the miniature museum and enjoy the garden.
- 👫 **Kids:** There is an amusing collection of shelters for pets.

Fountain at the water garden Château du Vendeuvre

© Hemis/Photoshot

Garden of surprises★

Among the fanciful delights of the garden, the spray of fountains may catch you by surprise. True to the playful spirit that motivated 18C landscape artists, the many wonders include a not-to-be-missed grotto made of 200,000 seashells. Vendeuvre celebrates the **tulip festival** in April, with the wonderful blossoming of tens of thousands of bulbs; the **iris festival** is in May.

ADDRESSES

 STAY

CAEN

⊖ **Hôtel Bernières** – *50 r. de Bernières.* ℘*02 31 86 01 26. www.hotelbernieres. com. 17 rooms.* ⌿€6. Friendly hotel, charming breakfast room, lounge.

⊖ **Hôtel St-Étienne** – *2 r. de l'Académie.* ℘*02 31 86 35 82. www.hotel-saint-etienne. com. 11 rooms.* ⌿€6.50. Dating from 1789, this house is near Abbaye-aux-Hommes. Some rooms with fireplaces.

⊖⊖ **Hôtel des Quatrans** – *17 r. Gémare.* ℘*02 31 86 25 57. www.hotel-des-quatrans. com. 47 rooms.* ⌿€8. Central family hotel with colourful, functional rooms. Rear rooms quieter.

⊖⊖ **Hôtel du Château** – *5 av. du 6-Juin.* ℘*02 31 86 15 37. www.hotel-chateau-caen.com. 24 rooms.* ⌿€8. In the town centre, between marina and château. Rooms small but pleasant.

⊖⊖ **Hôtel du Havre** – *11 r. du Havre.* ℘*02 31 86 19 80. www.hotelduhavre.com. 19 rooms.* ⌿€6. Near La Prairie and racecourse; post-war hotel with modern, quiet rooms.

⊖⊖ **Hôtel la Glycine** – *11 pl. du Commando no. 4, 14970 Bénouville.* ℘*02 31 44 61 94. www.la-glycine.com.* 🅿 *35 rooms.* ⌿€8. *Restaurant*⊖⊖. Near Pegasus Bridge; pleasant lodgings.

⊖⊖⊟–⊖⊖⊟⊟ **Hôtel Moderne** – *116 bld Mar.-Leclerc. t02 31 86 04 23. www.hotel-caen.com. 40 rooms.* ⌿€14. Discreet post-war building. View from breakfast room.

OUISTREHAM-RIVA-BELLA

⊖⊖ **Hôtel de la Plage** – *39 av. Pasteur, 14150 Riva-Bella.* ℘*02 31 96 85 16. www. hotel-ouistreham.com. Closed 12 Nov– 28 Feb. 16 rooms.* 🅿 ⌿€9 .Early 20C quiet Anglo-Norman villa near the beach. Renovated guest rooms.

PLAGES DU DÉBARQUEMENT

⊖ **Chambre d'hôte La Ferme d'Escures** – *Escures village, 14520 Commes.* ℘*02 31 92 52 23.* 🅿⤣*4 rooms.* ⌿. 17C farm near Bayeux, ideal base for touring area. Simple, pleasant rooms; self-catering cottage has its own garden.

⊖ **Chambre d'hôte Le Logis** – *Escures village, 14520 Commes.* ℘*02 31 21 79 56/06 81 86 93 28. http://monsite.wanadoo.fr/ le.logis.* 🅿⤣ *4 rooms.* ⌿. Old houses inhabited by hospitable family. Breakfast in the former stable; comfortable rooms, self-catering cottage.

⊖⊖ **Chambre d'hôte Ferme du Mouchel** – *At "Le Mouchel", 14710 Formigny.* ℘*02 31 22 53 79/06 15 37 50 20. www.ferme-du-mouchel.com.* 🅿⤣ *4 rooms.* ⌿ On a little country road, a pleasant dairy farm, probably from the 16C.

⊖⊖ **Chambre d'hôte La Faisanderie** *Av. du Col.-Courson, 14450 Grandchamp-Maisy.* ℘*02 31 22 70 06.* 🅿⤣ *3 rooms.* ⌿. Vine-covered house at horse farm. Pretty, individual rooms; fireplace in dining room.

⊖⊖ **Chambre d'hôte Le Petit Val** – *24 r. du Camp-Romain, 14480 Banville.* ℘*02 31 37 92 18. www.ferme-le-petitval.com.* 🅿⤣ *5 rooms.* ⌿. Probably 17C, typical Bessin farm, ideal for a nature break. Discreet décor, cosy rooms.

⊖⊖ **Domaine de L'Hostréière**– *r. du Cimetière-Américain, 14170 Colleville-sur-Mer.* ℘*02 31 51 64 64. www.domaine delhostreiere.com. Open Apr–Oct.* ♿🅿 *20 rooms.* ⌿€10.50. Modern rooms, each with terrace, in old farm near US cemetery of St-Laurent-sur-Mer. Gym and swimming pool.

⊖⊖⊟ **Chambre d'hôte Château de Vouilly** – *14230 Vouilly-Église.* ℘*02 31 22 08 59. www.chateau-vouilly.com. Closed 11 Nov–20 Mar.* 🅿 *4 rooms.* ⌿. A moat abounding with fish, handsome gardens, an orangery, imposing drawing rooms and dual-coloured paving in an 18C residence.

⊖⊖⊟ **Chambre d'hôte Manoir de l'Hermerel** – *14230 Géfosse-Fontenay, 7km/ 4.3mi N of Isigny via D 514 then D 199.* ℘*02 31 22 64 12. www.manoir-hermerel.com. Closed 15 Nov–15 Mar.* 🅿 *4 rooms.* ⌿. Fortified 17C farm; visit the 15C Gothic chapel before going to your room.

OMAHA BEACH

⊖ **Chambre d'hôte Ferme du Clos Tassin** *14710 Colleville-sur-Mer, in the village, on D 514.* ℘*02 31 22 41 51. www.clostassin.fr.st. Closed Jan. 5 rooms.* ⤣ ⌿. Farm owners make cider, calvados and pommeau. Taste it in the shop, where meals are taken. Cosy rooms.

🍴🛏 **Hôtel du Casino** – Bld de Chauvigny, 14710 Vierville-sur-Mer. ☎02 31 22 41 02. hotel-du-casino@orange.fr. Closed 15 Nov–15 Mar. 12 rooms. 🅿 🛏€9.50. Restaurant 🍴🛏🍽. Seaside hotel from the 1950s. Ask for a room with a view; enjoy seafood in the dining room.

BAYEUX
🛏 **Chambre d'hôte La Ferme des Châtaigniers** – 14400 Vienne-en-Bessin, 7.5km/4.6mi E of Bayeux via D 126. ☎02 31 92 54 70. 3 rooms.🍴 🛏. Set apart from farmhouse, this converted stable has simple yet pleasant, comfortable rooms.

🛏 **Chambre d'hôte Le Grand Fumichon** – 14400 Vaux-sur-Aure. 3km/2mi N of Bayeux via D 104. ☎02 31 21 78 51. www.fermedefumichon.com. 4 rooms. 🛏. This fortified 17C farm is now a dairy and cider-making farm.

🛏🛏 **Chambre d'hôte Le Manoir de Crépon** – rte d'. 14480 Crépon. ☎02 31 22 21 27. www. manoirdecrepon.com. Closed Jan–Feb. 5 rooms. 🛏.House built 17C–18C. Vast, tastefully furnished rooms.

🛏🛏 **Chambre d'hôte Le Petit Matin** – 2 bis. r. Quincangrogne. ☎02 31 10 09 27/06 08 28 65 59. 🛏🍴. 3 rooms. 🛏. Small hotel near cathedral.

🛏🛏 **Hôtel Reine Mathilde** – 23 r. Larcher. ☎02 31 92 08 13. www.hotel-reinemathilde. com. Closed 1 Dec–31 Jan. 16 rooms. 🛏€7. Family hotel near cathedral. Bar, tearoom, ice-cream shop.

🛏🛏🍽 **Chambre d'hôte Le Moulin de Hard** – At "Le Moulin de Hard", 14400 Subles, 6km/3.7mi SW of Bayeux. ☎02 31 21 37 17/06 13 30 53 28. www.moulin-de-hard.com. 4 rooms.🍴 🛏. Restored 18C watermill near a small river with a beautiful garden. Bikes loaned.

🛏🛏🍽 **Hôtel Ferme de la Rançonnière** – rte d'Arromanches-les-Bains, 14480 Crépon. ☎02 31 22 21 73. www.ranconniere.fr. 🅿 35 rooms. 🛏€12. Restaurant 🍴🛏🍽. Rustic, cosy 15C–18C rooms; breakfast in bed!

🍴 EAT

CAEN
🛏 **Le Bouchon du Vaugueux** – 12 r. Graindorge. ☎02 31 44 26 26. Closed 3 weeks in Aug, Sun and Mon. Reservations required. Popular tavern near château and old Caen. Fixed-price menus.

🛏 **Maître Corbeau** – 8 r. Buquet. ☎02 31 93 93 00. www.maitre-corbeau.com. Closed 3 weeks in Aug, 1 Jan and 25 Dec, Sat noon, Mon noon and Sun. Entirely devoted to cheese: boxes, adverts, implements, etc.

🛏 **Stiffler** – 72 r. St-Jean. ☎02 31 86 08 94. www.stifflertraiteur.com. Closed Mon–Tue 9am–1pm, 2.30–7.30pm, Sun 8am–6pm and school holidays. Closed 27 Jul–18 Aug. Magnificent pastry shop with celebrated charlotte aux fruits de saison.

🛏🛏 **Café Mancel** – At the Château. ☎02 31 86 63 64. www.cafemancel.com. Closed Feb school holiday, Sun evening and Mon. This café and shop has high-quality local produce and also goods from Italy, Flanders, Holland and England.

🛏🛏 **Le Carlotta** – 16 quai Vendeuvre. ☎02 31 86 68 99. reservation@lecarlotta.fr. Closed Sun. Art Deco-inspired brasserie; meats, wide range of seafood.

🛏🛏 **L'Embroche** – 17 r. Porte-au-Berger. ☎02 31 93 71 31. Closed Sat noon, Mon noon and Sun. Reservations advised. 3 specialities: camembert with Calvados, steak with a caramelised balsamic sauce, and tripes Père Michel.

🛏🛏 **L'Insolite** – 16 r. du Vaugueux at foot of château. ☎02 31 43 83 87. www.restaurant-linsolite.com. Closed Sun–Mon except May–Sept. Reservations advised. Half-timbered 16C house with unconventional interior, rustic and retro.

🛏🛏 **Pain et Beurre** – 46 r. Guillaume-le-Conquérant. ☎ 02 31 86 04 57. Closed Sun noon, Sun evening and Mon. Near Abbaye-aux-Hommes. Fine cuisine: authentic and exotic.

🛏🛏 **Saint-Andrew's** – 9 quai de Juillet. ☎02 31 86 26 80. http://restaurant. st.andrew.free.fr. Reservations advised. Good place to eat after a stroll along the Orne. Recalls an English pub, traditional menu.

🛏🛏–🛏🛏🍽 **Auberge de l'Île Enchantée** – 1 r. St-André, 14123 Fleury-sur-Orne. ☎02 31 52 15 52. www.aubergelileen chantee.com. Closed first 2 wks Aug, 24 Feb–8 Mar, 13–28 Jul, Sun eve, Wed eve and Mon. Riverside; warm welcome, gourmet French cuisine.

OUISTREHAM-RIVA-BELLA
🛏🛏 **Le Normandie** – 71 av. Michel-Cabieu. ☎02 31 97 19 57. www.lenormandie.com. Closed 18 Dec–1 Jan, Sun eve and Mon except

Apr–Oct. Also has 22 rooms 🍴🍽🍷. 🍷*€10.* Old Norman house on the port; brightly coloured, well-lit dining room, and an elegant veranda.

🍷🍽 **Le St-Georges** – *51 av. Andry. ✆02 31 97 18 79. www.hotel-le-saint-georges.com. Closed 8–29 Jan, Sun eve, Mon noon. Also has 18 rooms* 🍴🍽🍷. 🍷*€9.* Seaside specialities. Two dining rooms: modern, with large picture windows with panoramic coastal view; traditional with wood ceiling, fireplace.

PLAGES DU DÉBARQUEMENT

🍷 **Café Gondrée** – **Pegasus Bridge** – *12 av. du Cdt-Kieffer, 14970 Bénouville, 9km/5.6mi N of Caen via D 514. ✆02 31 44 62 25. Closed 12 Nov–12 Mar.* 🅿 🍴*€14.* Small, authentic pre-war café, the first house on French soil to be liberated in 1944. Arlette Gondrée, who was four at the time, makes traditional family omelettes with salad.

🍷 **La Flambée** – *2 r. Émile-Demagny, 14230 Isigny-sur-Mer. ✆02 31 51 70 96. Closed 2 weeks Feb–Mar, 2 weeks Sept–Oct, Tue and Wed Oct–Apr.* Fish and meat are grilled over a fire in typical Norman eatery.

🍷 **Les Alizés** – *4 quai Ouest, 14470 Courselles-sur-Mer. ✆02 31 36 14 14. www.les-alizes.net.* Loyal regulars for food; oysters and mussels at any hour; five guest rooms 🍷. 🍷*€6.*

🍷🍽 **Hotel Mercure Omaha Beach** – *On the golf course, 14520 Port-en-Bessin. ✆02 31 22 44 44. www.mercure.com. Closed 17 Dec–15 Jan.* Hotel restaurant, open to public; superb view over Omaha Beach Golf Club. Generous Sunday brunch. Brasserie-restaurant at club house.

🍷🍽 **La Pêcherie** – *pl. du 6-Juin, 14470 Courseulles-sur-Mer. t02 31 37 45 84. www.la-pecherie.fr.* Storm lanterns, oars and port-holes. A few guest rooms resembling ships' cabins 🍴🍽. 🍷*€9.*

🍷🍽 **La Trinquette** – *7 rte du Joncal, 14450 Grandcamp-Maisy. ✆02 31 22 64 90. www.restaurant-la-trinquette.com. Closed Mon and Tue from end Aug–Easter.* ♿ 🅿 Try the local fishermen's dish, *la marmite grandcopaise.*

🍷🍽 **Le Bistrot d'à Côté** – *12 r. Michel-Lefournier, 14520 Port-en-Bessin. ✆02 31 51 79 12. www.barque-bleue.fr. Closed Jan, Tue–Wed from 15 Sept–15 Jun.* Yellow-and-blue dining room; the day's fish and shellfish on a blackboard menu.

🍷🍽 **Le Vauban** – *6 r. du Nord, 14520 Port-en-Bessin. ✆02 31 21 74 83. www.restaurant-levauban.com. Closed mid-Dec–mid-Jan, Tue eve and Wed off-season.* One of the locals' favourite eating places.

🍷🍽 **L'As de Trèfle** – *420 r. Léopold-Hettier, 14990 Bernières-sur-Mer. ✆02 31 97 22 60. asdetrefle3@wanadoo.fr. Closed 6 Jan–10 Feb and Tue except Jul–Aug.* 🅿 Unattractive post-war building, but delicious seafood, well worth the trip.

🍷🍽🍽 **Le Manoir d'Hastings et la Pommeraie** – *18 av. de la Côte-de-Nacre. ✆02 31 44 62 43. www.manoirhastings. com. Closed Sun eve and Mon (except by reservation).* Former 17C priory, enclosed in its garden; several dining rooms including an attic one. A few bedrooms 🍴🍽🍷. 🍷*€12.*

OMAHA BEACH

🍷🍽 **L'Omaha** – *pl. du Monument, 14710 St-Laurent-sur-Mer. ✆02 31 22 41 46. Closed 15 Nov–15 Feb, and some evenings off-season.* Restaurant facing the sea, a stone's throw from Omaha Beach. Plain interior and two summer terraces. Seafood. Souvenirs.

BAYEUX

🍷 **Hostellerie St-Martin** – *pl. Edmond-Paillaud, 14480 Creully. ✆02 31 80 10 11. www.hostelleriesaintmartin.com.* 16C building, formerly village market. Curious décor. Classic cuisine. A dozen bedrooms 🍷. 🍷*€6.*

🍷🍽 **Le Pommier** – *40 r. des Cuisiniers. ✆02 31 21 52 10. www.restaurantlepommier.com. Closed mid-Dec–mid-Jan, Sun, except Jul–Aug.* Restaurant near cathedral; Norman specialities, charming authenticity.

🍷 **Le Bistrot de Paris** – *pl. St-Patrice. ✆02 31 92 00 82.* The daily menu of this bistro-style restaurant is based on the day's market produce. Reasonable prices.

🍷🍽 **Plaisirs des Mets** – *2 r. de Lisieux, St-Pierre-sur-Dives. ✆02 31 90 33 05. www.plaisirs-des-mets.com. Closed Sun, Tue, Wed off-season and Jan.* Restaurant with lovely view of Abbey, in a former bakery; progressive cuisine.

🍷🍽 **Rapière** – *53 r. St-Jean. ✆02 31 21 05 45. Closed 19 Dec–19 Jan, Wed and Thu.* A 15C house in quaint old Bayeux street. Tasty food, Norman produce.

⍣ NIGHTLIFE

CAEN

Caen is a highly convivial and lively town. In the evening, tour the small pubs and restaurants in the Vaugueux district.

Centre dramatique national de Normandie (Comédie de Caen) – *32 r. des Cordes. ✆02 31 46 27 29. www.cdn-normandie.com.* Classical, contemporary theatre; two halls: 300 and 700 seats.

Théâtre de Caen – *135 bld du Mar.-Leclerc. ✆02 31 30 48 00. www.theatre.caen.fr. ticket office: Tue–Sat 1–6.30pm; closed Jul–Aug.* Opera, ballet and contemporary dance; theatre, classical concerts, jazz sessions and traditional music. Concerts free on Sat at 5pm Oct–May, and some evenings in Café Cour.

⍤ SHOPPING

CAEN

Librairie Guillaume – *98 r. St-Pierre. ✆02 31 85 43 13. www.librairie.gen.calv. guillaume@wanadoo.fr. 9.30am–7pm. Closed Mon morning and Sun.* 1902 carved-wood façade. Books on the region and first-rate antique books upstairs.

Poupinet – *8 r. St-Jean. ✆02 31 86 07 25. Tue–Fri 8.30am–1pm, 3–7.45pm, Sat 8.30am–7.45pm, Sun 8.30am–1pm. Closed Jul.* To taste authentic *tripes à la mode de Caen*, you must visit Poupinet. Regional specialities: pâtés, terrines, country-style blood puddings, pork ears in jelly, etc.

Markets – Marché St-Pierre *(Sun am)*, rue de Bayeux *(Tue am)*, boulevard Leroy *(Wed am, Sat am)*, boulevard de la Guérinière *(Thu am)*, Marché St-Sauveur *(Fri am)*, Christmas Market *(Dec)*.

ST-PIERRE-SUR-DIVES

Market – *Les Halles. ✆02 31 20 73 28.* 16C village marketplace; on Monday morning some 150 merchants sell cheese, *charcuterie*, fruit, vegetables and a variety of crafts. On 1st Sun of the month, 8am–6pm, there are antique dealers.

Jardin conservatoire des fleurs et des légumes – *May–Sept Mon 9am–noon.* Exchange of seeds and plantlets.

Marché St-Sauveur, Caen

© www.calvados-tourisme.com

BAYEUX

Markets – *r. St-Jean. Wed 7.30am–2.30pm; pl. St-Patrice. Sat 6.30am–2.30pm.* St-Jean has 25 greengrocers, butchers, fishmongers, etc; St-Patrice has 120 sellers, about half of them with foodstuffs.

Naphtaline – *14–16 parvis de la Cathédrale. ✆02 31 21 50 03. www.naphtaline-bayeux. com.* Two shops in an 18C building: antique and modern lace, Bayeux porcelain, reproduction tapestries. Next door a third shop specialises in medieval items.

⍤ LEISURE

CAEN

Hippodrome de Caen – *La Prairie. ✆02 33 42 41 07. Mar–Jun, Sept–Nov. Closed Jul–Aug.* Racecourse nearly 2km/1mi long, in central Caen. Panoramic view from restaurant (2nd floor). Tours on race mornings (30 times a year). Don't miss it.

Festyland – *rte de Caumont. ✆02 31 75 04 04. www.festyland.com. Check website for hours.* Typical fairground rides, including attractions: *La Vallée aux Dinosaures, Le 1066, Le Carrousel des Arts, Le Valhala, Le Château de Mathilde,* etc. Great for kids.

OMAHA BEACH

Eolia Normandie – *Le Cavey, Omaha Beach sea base, 14710 Colleville-sur-Mer. ✆02 31 22 26 21. www.eolia-normandie.com. Check website for hours and prices.* Guided outings on sand-yachts, wakeboards, catamarans and kayaks.

Due south of the city of Caen and the Invasion Beaches, this area of Basse Normandie is quiet and mostly agricultural, with no major towns nor "must-see" visitor attractions. Anyone who has been to Devon in southwest England will be familiar with the countryside of Le Bocage, where sunken country lanes wind between banks, surmounted by tall thick hedgerows which border woodland pasture and fields. It gained notoriety during the Battle of Normandy in 1944, severely hampering the Allies' tank advances. Covering the Orne and parts of Calvados (famous for its apple brandy) it makes for leisurely picturesque drives.

Highlights

1   Visiting the **castle** where the Conqueror was born (p294)

2   Hiking the **Circuit des Belvédères** for its views (p297)

3   Driving along the beautiful **Vallée de l'Orne** (p300)

4   Taking in the stunning views from the **Roche d'Oëtre** (p301)

5   Watching the equestrian shows at the **Haras du Pin** (p311)

Falaise

William the Conqueror was born here and would be proud that one of his many mighty castles commemorates his legacy. However, even he is overshadowed by the terrible events of 1944 that took place near the town in what is known as the Falaise Gap (or Pocket). Here the retreating German forces were surrounded and fought to the death with tens of thousands of casualties. Today's peaceful bucolic surroundings belie the bloody past.

La Suisse Normande

Don't expect mountains or skiing here, but there are plenty of spectacular cliffs and crags, many fine walking trails and some wonderful hilltop lookout points in Normany's "Little Switzerland". The picturesque River Orne flows through the heart of the area, and is a highly popular destination whether you simply enjoy it from the comfort of your car, or are more daring and take to the water.

Le Pays d'Argentan

The northernmost part of the département of Orne, this area is also watered by the river that forms a major attraction. The area's most popular visitor attraction is also here, the Haras Stud Farm which has plenty of interest whether or not you are a lover of equestrian pursuits. Take time out to visit the Memorial Montormel Museum which is the best place to understand the heroism and horrors of the Battle of Normandy.

Sport and Leisure

With so many rivers, the Suisse-Normande is a natural playground for water sports enthusiasts and many sites offer equipment rentals. At **Clécy**, look for Au fil de l'eau, le Beau Rivage and Lionel Terray; at **Thury-Harcourt**, La Roc qui Beu and the Kayak Club; at **Pont-d'Ouilly**, the Base de Plein Air. Clubs in Pont-d'Ouilly, Clécy and Thury-Harcourt offer opportunities to canoe and kayak along the Orne. On the reservoir at **Rabodanges**, you can also windsurf and waterski.

The area is full of woodland trails and there are also dozens of accessible craggy promontories that provide tremendous views for hikers: the most renowned is the **Roche d'Oëtre**, near Pont-d'Ouilly, which achieves almost Alpine grandeur; others are the Pain de Sucre at Clécy and Mont Pinçon at Thury-Harcourt. None of these requires any climbing ability. However, if you do have that ability, Rochers des Parcs is ideal.

At Pont-d'Ouilly and Notre Dame du Rocher horseriding is available. And at La Route des Crêtes, near Clécy, you can take to the skies strapped to a paraglider.

LE BOCAGE AND THE PAYS D'ARGENTAN

★★ Recommended
★ Interesting
★ Worth a visit

🚩 Driving tour with departure point

Roche d'Oëtre
Falaise
Argentan

MANCHE

CALVADOS

ORNE

Parc naturel régional Normandie-Maine

293

Falaise★

The town's setting in the Ante valley is dominated by the enormous fortress, one of Normandy's first stone castles, where William the Conqueror was born about 1027. In August 1944, Falaise suffered cruelly during the fighting in the Falaise-Chambois pocket (also known as the Falaise Gap). Today the town is a centre for excursions into the Suisse Normande.

TOWN

Église de la Trinité★

The west front of the church features a triangular Gothic porch. On the south side, note the gargoyles and small carved figures. At the east end the Renaissance flying buttresses are highly ornate.

Église St-Gervais

The church dates from the 11C to the 16C; the lantern tower is 12C. Inside, the contrast between the Romanesque south side and the Gothic north is striking.

Porte des Cordeliers

This lovely stone gateway, part of the town wall, is flanked by a round tower and has a 14C–15C porch.

Fontaine d'Arlette

The fountain of the Val d'Ante (Fontaine d'Arlette) provides an impressive view of the castle towering above.

▶ **Population:** 8,475.

Michelin Map: 303: K-6.

Info: Boulevard de la Libération. ℰ02 31 90 17 26. www.falaise-tourisme.com.

Location: Falaise is on N 158 between Caen, 41km/25.5mi to the N and Argentan, 22km/14mi to the SE.

Don't Miss: The château of William the Conqueror.

Timing: Visit the château in the morning, lunch in Falaise and finish the day by touring the valley of the River Laizon.

Kids: Children will enjoy the Automates Avenue exhibit.

Château Guillaume-Le-Conquérant★

Open daily Jul–Aug 10am–7pm; rest of the year 10am–6pm (last visit 1hr before closing). Closed 1 Jan, 25 Dec. €7.50. ℰ02 31 41 61 44. www.chateau-guillaume-leconquerant.fr.

This medieval ensemble (12C–13C), characteristic of defensive Anglo-Norman architecture, has been heavily restored. William the Bastard, Duke of Normandy, was born here in 1027, to a local girl, the beautiful Arlette.

Château Guillaume-Le-Conquérant

O. Forir/MICHELIN

WHERE TO STAY	WHERE TO EAT
Chêne Sec (Chambre d'hôte Le)......................①	Attache (L')...①
Poste (Hôtel de la)................................④	Fine Fourchette (La)..........................④

Inner courtyard

Visitors walking through the Porte St-Nicolas enter a large area of about 1ha/2.5 acres, defined by 15 towers.

Main keep

This rectangular 12C structure is surprisingly large; great impregnable-looking flat buttresses mark the line of the walls. Restauration of the huge *aula,* or main reception room, involved sophisticated techniques: the flooring is made of alternating squares of glass and lead, and the ceiling consists of Teflon stretched over an iron frame. Note the Chapelle St-Prix, a small oratory.

Small keep

This luminous, well-balanced construction commissioned by Henri I Plantagenet in the late 12C was designed to guard the main keep from attack from the rock platform.

Tour Talbot

This impressive round tower, 35m/114.8ft tall with walls 4m/13ft thick, recalls John Talbot, governor of the castle in 1449.

An incredibly deep well (65m/213ft) provides water to the entire castle. The rock platform commands a lovely **view** of the surrounding countryside.

The Battle of the Falaise Gap

Between 12 and 21 August 1944, the last bloody battle of the Normandy campaign was fought near Falaise, the name Falaise Gap referring to the corridor that the Germans sought to maintain to allow their escape. They were unsuccessful and with withdrawal forbidden by Hitler, terrible carnage ensued. In the aftermath of the battle General Eisenhower recorded: *"Falaise was unquestionably one of the greatest 'killing fields' of any of the war areas. Forty-eight hours after the closing of the gap I was conducted through it on foot... It was literally possible to walk for hundreds of yards at a time, stepping on nothing but dead and decaying flesh..."*

Automates Avenue

bld de la Libération. &⦵Open *Jul–Aug daily 10am–6pm; Apr–Jun, Sept and Dec daily 10am–12.30pm,*

1.30–6pm; Oct–Nov and Jan–Mar
Sat–Sun, holidays and school holidays
10am–12.30pm, 1.30–6pm. ☜€6 (4–13
years €4.50). ✆02 31 90 02 43.
Until the 1950s, the Decamps company
decorated the windows of Parisian
department stores with animated scenes,
of which some 300 are displayed.

Musée André-Lemaître

&.◷Same address, ticket booth and
hours as Automates Avenue. ☜€6.
✆02 31 90 02 43.
Local artist **André Lemaître** (1909–95)
is renowned for his paintings of the area
around Falaise and Honfleur.

EXCURSIONS
Faubourg de Guilbray
The **Église Notre-Dame-de-Guibray**
dates from the days of William the Conqueror. The apse and the apsidal chapels
are still pure Romanesque. The organ is
by Parizot (1746).

Versainville

◷ 2.5km/1.6mi. Leave Falaise, heading
north on rue Victor-Hugo. Turn right
after le pont sur l'Ante onto the
Versainville road.
The 18C château (⊶closed to the public)
features a central wing with a peristyle,
linked by a gallery to a huge pavilion
forming the left wing.

Chapelle St-Vigor-de-Mieux

◷ 3km/1.8mi west of Falaise.
◷Open mid-Jun–Sept Tue–Sun
2.30–6pm. ☜€2.50.
Ruined and abandoned, this 15C chapel
has been totally transformed by Japa-
nese artist, Kyoji Takubo, into a work of
art, featuring a roof of coloured glass
and a floor mural on sheets of lead. The
building is called "chapelle des Pommiers" (Chapel of Apples), after the trees
represented on the walls, and is now a
French-Japanese cultural exchange
centre; exhibitions are held in summer.

🚗 DRIVING TOUR

37km/23mi. Allow 3hrs.

▷ Leave Falaise, north on the D 658.

Aubigny
At the entrance to the village, on the
left, stands a late 16C château. The
parish **church** contains statues of six
consecutive lords of Aubigny. Notice
the 13C belfry of **Soulangy** to the left.

▷ Join the D 6 west, in the direction of
Thury-Harcourt. Before Villers-Canivet,
the abbey is signposted on the left.

Abbaye de Villers-Canivet
◷Open May–Jun and Sept Wed–Sun
2–6pm. Guided tours Jul–Aug Wed–
Mon 2–6pm. ☜€4. ✆02 31 90 81 80.
www.villers-canivet.com.
Founded in 1127 by the nuns of Savigny,
and rebuilt in the 18C, the abbey is now
mere ruins, though excavations reveal
its historical importance. The abbey
farm has retained its beautiful fortified
gatehouse and a large tithe barn.

▷ Continue towards Ussy, then right
towards Potigny and Soumont-St-
Quentin and follow the signposts.

Brèche au Diable (The Devil's Gap)
This picturesque **gorge**★ at the foot of
Mont-Joly has been occupied since 3500
BC) according to flints found here. There
are numerous hiking trails.

▷ Head back north towards Ouilly-le-
Tesson and take a right towards d'Assy.

Assy
A magnificent avenue (left) leads to
the **Château d'Assy**, a handsome 18C
mansion with an elegant Corinthian
portico; the chapel dates from the 15C.

▷ Return to Falaise via Rouvres,
Olendon and Épaney.

Clécy★

Tourist centre of the Suisse Normande, the town of Clécy is close to some of the most beautiful spots in the Orne Valley and is the starting point for many hikes.

SIGHT
▲▲ Musée du Chemin de Fer Miniature

Rue d'Ermington, Clécy.
⏱Open early Apr–first two wks Sept Tue–Sun 10am–noon, 2–6pm; Jul and Aug daily 10am–6pm. Last two wks Sept 2–5.30/6pm. Oct Sun only, daily during final week 2–5pm.⛔✕. *€7 (children €5).* *✆02 31 69 07 13. www.chemin-fer-miniature-clecy.com.*

The model railway that is the centre-piece of this museum covers 300sq m/358 sq yd, with backdrops ranging from Switzerland to Flanders. The lights are dimmed to create a magical dusk of illuminated, houses, factories, castles and, of course, trains. The museum is set on a former quarry and a miniature train takes visitors around. In a huge vaulted former lime kiln cellar, cider is now made. A terrace café serves cider and crêpes.

HIKES
None of these walks are strenuous though Le Pain de Sucre and the Circuit des Belvédère do involve ascents.

Bords de l'Orne
From Le Pont du Vey, just outside town, the banks of the Orne, with their *guinguettes*, make for a pretty scene.
A footpath along the river heads south to the Lande viaduct (1km/0.6mi), beside which the Rochers des Parcs attract climbers.

Rochers des Parcs★
🥾*Allow 1hr round-trip. Leave the village of Bo, 5km/3mi southeast of Clécy, on the D 168. At the church a path joins the GR 36 (red and white markings).*
The trail climbs the ridge, revealing stunning views of the Orne, the viaduct and the typical Suisse Normande country-

▶ **Population:** 1,246.
⚲ **Michelin Map:** 303: J-6 –Local map, ⚲*see La Suisse Normande, p301.*
🛈 **Info:** Place du Tripot. ✆02 31 69 79 95. www.suisse-normande.com.
◖ **Location:** Clécy is halfway between Caen (40km/ 24.8mi N) and Flers (23km/ 14.3mi S) via D 562.
⊛ **Don't Miss:** The many scenic walks, with panoramic views.
⏱ **Timing:** Spend the day enjoying the scenery on foot.
▲▲ **Kids:** The Model Railway Museum is a sure bet.

side. At the viaduct, the trail descends towards Vey and Clécy.

Le Pain de Sucre★
🥾*Allow 3hr round-trip. From Clécy take the route de La Serverie. Cross the bridge over the Orne and the level crossing; after 100m/110yd turn right. A sign (left) shows the start of the path to the Pain de Sucre (Sugar Loaf).*
The path *(marked red and white)* climbs up a valley on the right bank of a stream. Cross the stream. Entering the copse, keep to the right of a trail that rises obliquely to the right and leads to the foot of a hillock and a vast **panorama** of the Orne. Going down, on reaching the foot of the hillock, along the slope opposite the one you came by, follow a winding path (well marked) which, passing below the Rochers de la Houle, comes out at the rustic church of Vey.

Circuit des Belvédères★★
🥾*Allow half a day.*
This circuit allows you to make a neat loop, joining the two walks above. Start from La Sauvegarde, or from the church at Bô, and take the GR 36 to Les Rochers des Parcs. The trail leads to Vey, where, near the church, you will find the start of the path to Le Pain de Sucre. Take a well

deserved break at the lookout, retrace your steps a short way down, and follow the path marked yellow (the middle one), that ascends to La Route des Crêtes (the Road of the Peaks). Turn right and follow the road, passing two open areas, one of which may be in use by paragliders. Ignore the first path, down to Vey; instead take the second right, leading down to Sourdeval, a small hamlet where you turn left towards Haut-du-Vey. Follow the yellow signs to La Bruyère and Les Rochers des Parcs, where you will find the GR 36 and your starting point.

L'Éminence

🚶 2hr round-trip. Leave Clécy on the D 168. Around 300m/328yd from the village, up the hill, turn left, past the police station, cross the D 562 towards Grand-Camp, go right into the village and turn left towards Hauts-Vents; the path rises north to l'Éminence, peaking at 254m (833ft). You don't need to climb right up, however, to enjoy a beautiful view of the Normandy countryside and the valley of the Orne.

EXCURSIONS
Route des Crêtes★

▶ 8km/5mi – allow 45min.
From Clécy church take the D 133C towards La Serverie. After the bridge, turn left to St-Rémy; after 1.5km/0.9mi turn sharp right and follow the "Route des Crêtes" (Road of the Peaks).
The road looks down onto the valley, with beautiful views of the meandering River Orne and surrounding areas, particularly the Pain de Sucre and Les Rochers de la Houle.
Follow the wooded slopes and bear left *(beware, sharp bend)*; continue on to St-Omer.

Croix de la Faverie★

🚶 45min round-trip.
Leave from the car park between the post office and the church, and head towards Croix de La Faverie. At the stop sign turn right; then turn left and continue to climb. Follow the signposts to the Croix.
Opposite the cross, a path leads to a grove of pine trees *(picnic site)* with a beautiful **view**: the Rochers des Parcs overlooks the Lande Viaduct.

La Suisse Normande★★

This odd name denotes the area that straddles the **Orne** and **Calvados** regions. It has neither mountains nor lakes in the Swiss sense, and does not even include Normandy's highest points, but nevertheless draws tourists to its attractive landscape. The River Orne winds its way through the ancient rocks of the Armorican Massif, bordered by steep banks surmounted by rocky escarpments.

A BIT OF GEOGRAPHY

Located in the midst of Calvados *bocage* country, some 30km/18.5mi south of Caen, and extending into the Orne *département*, the Suisse Normande lies between the towns of Condé-sur-Noireau, Thury-Harcourt and **Putanges**; some definitions extend the range eastwards to Falaise and the rugged Ante Valley. Besides the Orne valley, the area takes in several small tributaries, including the Noireau, the Vère, the Rouvre and the Baize. Deeply eroded valleys and escarpments appear in stark contrast with the flat plain around Caen.

- **Michelin Map:** 303: J-6 to K-7.
- **Info:** Place du Tripot, Clécy. ℘02 31 69 79 95. 2 Place St-Sauveur, Thury-Harcourt ℘02 31 79 70 45. www.ot-suisse-normande.com.
- **Don't Miss:** The remarkable view of the gorge of the River Rouvre from the belvedere of the Roche d'Oëtre.
- **Timing:** Tour the area in your car before deciding on which of the many hikes to try.

The curious name, Suisse Normande, was coined by tourism promoters in the 19C, as first the train, then the car, brought city-dwellers into the area. Switzerland, then (as now), evoked images of inspiring scenery, clean air, vigorous sports and healthy living. Tourism aside, the Suisse Normande is resolutely rural, with pastures for horses and cattle, fields of rapeseed, winding roads between ancient hedgerows, swathes of forest and picturesque little villages.

Landscape of the Suisse Normande

© www.calvados-tourisme.com

🚗 DRIVING TOUR

Vallée de l'Orne★★
99km/61.5mi. Allow 3hrs.
⊗Nearly all sights require a short walk.
Be sure to wear suitable shoes.

Thury-Harcourt
The town stands on the banks of the Orne and is now a tourist centre for the Suisse Normande to the south. In 1700, Thury became the Harcourt family ancestral seat and was famous for its **château** (*�o━ closed to the public*), burned down by the Germans in 1944.

▷ *From Thury-Harcourt take the D 562 south.*

The road drops down into the valley. Ahead, perched on a hillock, is the small Chapelle de la Bonne-Nouvelle, followed immediately by Caumont with its abandoned sandstone quarry (left) and finally St-Rémy.

St-Rémy
The St-Rémy iron mines, once the most productive in Normandy, were worked from 1875 to 1967, though surface mining had also taken place since medieval times.
👥Musée Les Fosses d'Enfer– (⏱*Open Jul–Aug daily 10am–12.30pm (last entry noon), 2.30–6pm (last entry 5pm); May–Jun and Sept Wed–Mon 2–6pm; Apr and Oct Wed–Mon 2–5.30pm;* ✍*€4.60 (children €2.30);* ✆*02 31 69 67 77. www.musees-basse-normandie.fr*) is a museum on the site of the former mine describing the formation of the earth and the geological basis of all sorts of mineral extraction, especially of energy resources.
About 700m/765yd off the D562 an 11C Romanesque **church,** renovated in the 19C, stands under an enormous yew tree on a promentory; there is a pretty **view** over the Orne valley from the cemetery. The Château de la Maroisière (*o━closed to the public*) dates from the 18C.

Clécy★
👣*See Clécy*

▷ *Leave Clécy along the D 562 south. In Le Fresne turn left onto the D 1.*

The road follows the crest of the ridge separating the valleys of the Orne and Noireau and then joins up with the Béron crest. East of the Rendezvous des Chasseurs (500m/547yd) there is a view north of the Orne valley, and of the Rochers des Parcs. The downhill stretch offers a view (right) of the Roche d'Oëtre, before reaching **Chapelle St-Roch**, a 16C pilgrimage chapel where a *pardon* is held on the Sunday after 15 August. Continue on to **Pont-d'Ouilly**, a busy tourist centre at the confluence of the River Orne and River Noireau.

▷ *Take the D 167.*

Leaving Pont-d'Ouilly, the road passes the foot of a rock whose top is shaped like a lion's head. The road runs along the Orne to Pont-des-Vers.
Take the D 43 to the right. The road climbs, offering glimpses of the beautiful meandering river Rouvre. At Rouvrou, take the sign for « Site de St-Jean ».

Méandre de Rouvrou
🚶*15mn round-trip.*
Follow the road to the war memorial and leave your car there. The monument has been built in the neck of the winding river meander, surrounded by a copse of shady pines.

▷ *Head in the direction of Ségrie-Fontaine, then towards Bréel.*

Ségrie-Fontaine
Maison de la rivière et du paysage
♿⏱*Open Apr–Sept Mon–Fri 9.30am–5.30pm (Jul–Aug until 6pm), Sat–Sun 2–7pm; rest of the year Mon–Fri 9.30am–5.30pm.* ✆*02 33 62 34 65. www.cpie-collinesnormandes.org.*
The Ségrie-Fontaine Nature Centre gives details of four walks along the river and gorge.

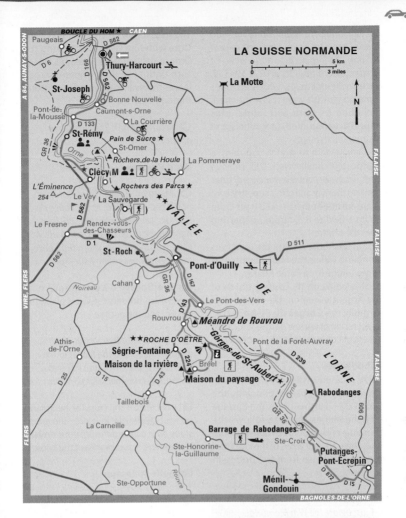

LA SUISSE NORMANDE

BOUCLE DU HOM ★   CAEN

Paugeais
Thury-Harcourt
St-Joseph
Bonne Nouvelle
Pont-de-la-Mousse
Caumont-s-Orne
La Courrière
St-Rémy
Pain de Sucre ★
St-Omer
Rochers.de la Houle
La Pommeraye
Clécy M
L'Éminence
254
Le Vey
Rochers des Parcs ★
La Sauvegarde
VALLÉE
Le Fresne
Rendez-vous-des-Chasseurs
St-Roch
Pont-d'Ouilly
D 511
DE
Noireau
Cahan
Le Pont-des-Vers
Rouvrou
Méandre de Rouvrou
Athis-de-l'Orne
★★ROCHE D'OËTRE
Gorges de St-Aubert ★
Pont de la Forêt-Auvray
L'ORNE
Ségrie-Fontaine
Maison de la rivière
Bréel
Maison du paysage
Rabodanges
Taillebois
La Carneille
Barrage de Rabodanges
Ste-Croix
Putanges-Pont-Écrepin
Ste-Honorine-la-Guillaume
Ste-Opportune
Ménil-Gondouin

BAGNOLES-DE-L'ORNE

La Motte

N

0   5 km
0   3 miles

◆ At Bréel, take the D 229, then the D 329 left.

Roche d'Oëtre★★

The Roche d'Oëtre enjoys a superb **setting**, dominating the Gorge de la Rouvre with its steep escarpment. This is the highest point in La Suisse Normande and the view of this mighty cliff from the viewpoint indicator is breathtaking. To the right of the indicator, note, beneath the main lookout point, a rocky ridge in the shape of a human profile.

Relax and learn more about the site in the well equipped modern **Visitor Information Centre** (🕐 *Open daily,*

Roche d'Oëtre

S. Sauvignier/MICHELIN

Apr–Jun and Sept 10am–6pm; Jul–Aug 10am–7pm, Oct 10am–5pm; rest of year 2–5pm; ⬡free access to the view, €4 interpretive centre; ♿✕ ☏02 31 59 13 13, www.roche-doetre.fr), which includes films on various aspects of the area, including its flora and fauna, plus impressive multimedia terminals and an interactive map.

🐾 If you want to stretch your legs, a signposted circular walk *(1hr, steep in parts, walking shoes recommended)* goes down to the river and offers superb views. There are three other marked trails (from 600m/655yd to 8.5km/5mi) departing from the centre.

East of the Roche d'Oëtre the road runs along the valley; the final viewpoint is at the bridge in La Forêt-Auvray.

At this point on its course, north of the Argentan region, the Orne flows through, the **Gorges de St-Aubert**★, a succession of narrow gorges which are accessible only on foot (♨see below).

Rabodanges

A 17C moated castle (⚬━ *closed to the public)* is set in a park overlooking the Orne valley. Further on, at the Barrage de Rabodanges, the road follows the shoreline of the 95ha/235 acre artificial lake. There are fine views of the lake from the road and also from the bridge in Ste-Croix.

▷ *At Ste-Croix, turn left onto the C 1 just before the War Memorial.*

Putanges-Pont-Écrepin

This little town on the Orne is the departure point for walking the 🔺 **Gorges de St-Aubert**.
Take the D 121 to the dam. From the car park, a steep path leads to the trail head, off to the right.

Boucle du Hom★
5km/3mi.

▷ *Leave Thury-Harcourt northwest on the D 6. After around 1.5km/1mi, take the D 212 right.*

The road follows the west bank of the Orne with fine views overlooking the Orne and its verdant riverbanks.
Turn right at Le Hom where the road leaves the river, to enter a deep cutting through the rock.

▷ *Return towards Thury-Harcourt on the D 6.*

Mont Pinçon★

▷ *14km/9mi. Leave Thury-Harcourt northwest on the D 6. At the Vallée de Hamars, turn left onto the D 36, then right on the D 108 at the crossroads. At Plessis-Grimault, turn sharp right onto the D 54, towards Aunay-sur-Odon.*

The **Pré-Bocage** is a picturesque rural area which borders the Caen plain, the Bessin, and the *bocage*.

▷ *The road climbs to an altitude of 365m/1,200ft. At the top, near the television transmitter, turn left and continue for another 600m/1,970ft.*

🔺 Leave the car and cross the heathland on foot (☂*Beware in winter, the rough stony path can be difficult)*; your reward is an extensive **panorama** of the *bocage*.

Chapelle St-Joseph

▷ *17km/10.5mi. Leave Thury on the D 6 towards Bayeux; after a bridge, turn left onto the D 166. The road climbs up through the valley of the Orne. Turn right at Mesnil-Roger to St-Martin-de-Sallen, and turn right onto a narrow road leading uphill, from which a single-track road leads off to the right to the Chapelle St-Joseph.*

From behind the chapel, there is a beautiful **panorama**★ of the Orne Valley and the heights of the Suisse Normande.

▷ *Return to St-Martin-de-Sallen and take the next road on the right to rejoin the D 6 to Thury.*

Aunay-sur-Odon

This small modern town, rebuilt entirely in 1947–50 as a result of the Allied bombardments of 1944, is an ideal base for several excursions, notably in the Suisse Normande.

🚗 **DRIVING TOUR**

LE BOCAGE
Villers-Bocage
▷ *7km/4mi north of Aunay-sur-Odon on the D 6.*

Like Aunay-sur-Odon, the town of Villers-Bocage was completely rebuilt after the war, but its style is much more daring, radical even, with an interesting mix of modern buildings, not least the Église St-Martin, built of stone and concrete.

▷ *Take the D 71 west.*

Caumont-l'Éventé
The exposed hilltop situation of this small town explains its unusual name, as well as a lot of storm damage. Abandoned in the late 19C the old slate quarries of **Souterroscope des ardoisières** (⏰*Open Apr–Aug daily 10/11am–5/7pm, Feb–Mar and Sept–mid-Nov Tue–Sun 11am–5pm, mid-Nov–mid-Dec Sun only 11am–5pm.* ⬦€9.75. ☎02 31 71 15 15, www.souterroscope-ardoisieres.fr) were dug by hand. Today they provide a window into a subterranean world. Only a small part of the quarries are accessible but these include vast chambers, a lake and a sound-and-light show with fountains. Information boards and a small museum relate to the underworld of fauna, geology and caving and includes an interesting collection of minerals. Wear warm clothes and sturdy shoes, the constant temperature underground is 12 degrees C.

▷ *Leave town south on the D 53.*

ℹ **Info:** R. de Verdun - Aunay-sur-Odon. ☎02 31 77 60 32. Pl. Charles de Gaulle, Villiers-Bocage. ☎02 31 77 16 14. www.ot-paysprebocage.fr

🚫 **Don't Miss:** Going underground at Caumont-l'Éventé; the bird shows at the zoo.

St-Martin-des-Besaces, Musée La Percée du Bocage
⏰*Open Wed–Mon Apr–Sept 10am–6pm.* ⬦€5. ☎02 31 67 52 78. www.laperceedubocage.com.
This gripping museum (its name means Bocage Breakout) tells the story of how the British army liberated the area in July 1944. It includes a graphic diorama, a large collection of contemporary photos, documents and relics from the battle, a superb audio-visual display, and moving accounts from combatants.

▷ *Leave St-Martin-des-Besaces south east on the D 165, then follow the signs in the direction of la Cabosse.*

🐾 Zoo de Jurques
⏰*Open mid-Feb–Oct daily 10am–6/7pm (mid-Mar–early Apr and late Sept–late Oct Sat–Sun only).* ⬦ €14 (children €8.50). ☎02 31 77 80 58. www.zoodejurques.fr. Set in a wooded 15ha/37 acre park, the zoo is home to dozens of species of animals in near-wild conditions. It specialises in endangered creatures, including snow leopards, Siberian tigers and three very rare white lions. Other highlights include its birds of prey, feeding times for the wolves and penguins, and its parrot **shows**★. Look out too for the reptiles and mini-farm.

▷ *Return to Aunay on the D 114 which passes through the Bois de Buron.*

Vire

Vire stands on a small hill overlooking the rolling Normandy *bocage*. The town grew up around its castle in the 8C. In the 12C Henry Beauclerc (King Henry I of England, fourth son of William the Conqueror), strengthened the castle's fortifications and built the keep. In the 13C the population increased and trade flourished, but the Wars of Religion (1561–98) led to decline and in 1630 Cardinal Richelieu dismantled the castle. The 17C and 18C brought another period of prosperity. Vire is an important road junction and as such it was almost annihilated in 1944.

SIGHTS

Église Notre-Dame
pl. Notre-Dame.

This 13C–15C Gothic church was erected on the site of a 13C Romanesque chapel built by Henry Beauclerc. The 13C porch is flanked by a slate-roofed tower. The belltower is surmounted by a balustrade; its spire succumbed to lightning in the 15C. In the south transept is a gilded Baroque altarpiece and a 19C *pietà* by a sculptor from Lisieux. The church suffered heavily during wars and the French Revolution, but has been well restored.

Tour de l'Horloge

© www.calvados-tourisme.com

▶ **Population:** 12,815.
🚗 **Michelin Map:** 303: G-6.
🚌 **Info:** Square de la Résistance, 14500 Vire. ℘02 31 66 28 50. www.vire-tourisme.com.
▶ **Location:** On the route between Caen and Fougères.

Les Vaux de Vire

Access via rue du Valhérel. The Vaux de Vire refers to where the steep-sided Vire and Virenne valleys meet. It is a popular place for walking and intriguingly gave its name to a local collection of 15C satirical drinking songs. The clipped form *"vau de vire"* was in common use by around 1500. This was subsequently conflated to *"voix de ville"* and eventually became part of the English language as vaudeville.

Tour de l'Horloge

pl. du 6 Juin. 🕐*Open Jul–mid-Sept Tue–Thu 2–6pm, Fri–Sat 10am–12.30pm, 2–6pm.*

The old main gate (13C) to the fortified town is flanked by twin towers and surmounted by a 15C belfry, built to include both a clock *(horloge)* and a bell. A niche holds a wooden statue of the Virgin dating from the 16C.

EXCURSIONS

Plan d'Eau de la Dathée

▷ *7km/4.3mi S on D 577, then turn right onto D 76.*

There are good views and a walk (7km/4.3mi) round the shore, as well as a water sports centre, a bird reserve and picnic area.

Le Bény-Bocage

▷ *15km/9mi north on the D 577 (the Caen road).*

The streets of this pleasant village, which boasts a beautiful market hall, are often decked with flowers. Nearby is the Vallée de la Souleuvre, which is very popular for horseriding

Viaduc de la Souleuvre

▶ *6 km/3.8mi west of Bény-Bocage on the D 56, signposted to La Ferrière-Harang.*

Built in 1869 to plans by Gustave Eiffel for the Vire–Caen railway, the viaduct was all but destroyed in World War II and abandoned. Partially rebuilt, It is now a famous bungee jumping point *(http://normandie.ajhackett)*.

Saint-Sever-Calvados

▶ *13km/8mi west of Vire, on the D 524, on th edge of the Forêt de St-Sever.*

The church takes its name from Sever, a slave who in the 6C, having converted his pagan master, was offered land, where he established a religious community. Eventually appointed Bishop of Avranches, he returned to the abbey built in his name to die, and his tomb became a place of pilgrimage. In the 11C, the establishment became a Benedictine abbey.

The abbey church we see today was built in the 13C and 14C though it suffered a partial destruction of the nave in 1821. The separate belltower dates from the 17C. The transept crossing is dominated by a graceful lantern; the choir is lit by large lancet windows, two of which retain their 13C stained glass. Note, on the south side, the 15C window.

🚗 DRIVING TOUR

17km/11mi. Allow 1hr15min.

FORÊT DE ST-SEVER

Comprising 618ha/1,528 acres of oak, beech, pine, fir and larch, the forest lies south of Vire

▶ *Leave St-Sever on the southbound road to St-Pois. At the end of the village, take the forest road left.*

The road goes deep into the forest and at a crossroads is the small chapel, La Vierge à la Vilaine. A little further on, anglers can fish in the pond of Vieux-Château. Continue on and you will find a series of slightly raised ponds. After

S. Sauvignier/MICHELIN

Vire Chitterlings

This well-known local speciality *(andouille)* is prepared to a traditional recipe.

The stomach and the smaller intestines of the pig are cleaned, chopped, salted and marinated and then stuffed into the larger intestine, which is smoked over a beechwood fire for several weeks.

The black colour produced by the process is proof of authenticity. The sausage-like chitterlings are then cooked in water and tied off.

the ponds, the road rises slightly (🔍 *a footpath branches off right, leading to the ruins of the old castle*), then passes through open countryside before arriving at a crossroads.

▶ *Turn right onto the D 299. This road rejoins the D 81 where you turn left.*

Ermitage/ Monastere du Carmel

During the early 16C reign of Louis XIII, a small colony of hermits established itself in this retreat, living according to the rules of the Camaldolese, a religious order founded in the village of Camaldoli in Tuscany in 1010. The monks lived here until the French Revolution. Of the original settlement, only the monastery gate (1776), and the Chapel of Our Lady of the Angels, almost entirely paved with granite tombstones, remain.

The buildings have been occupied since 1984 by a group of Carmelite nuns from Avranches, hence its current name. The public are welcome to attend services.

Flers

Situated in the heart of a *bocage* –
a region of traditional hedgerows –
Flers' traditonal way of life was
producing textiles, based on local
linen and hemp. This has given
way to new industries, notably
mechanical engineering and
electrical appliances.

Musée du Château

av. du Château. ○Open Apr–Oct
Mon–Fri 10am–noon, 2–6pm,
Sat–Sun 2–6pm. ○Closed 1 May,
13 Jul.€2.50. 02 33 64 66 49.
www.flers-agglomeration.fr.

The present castle, with a moat on
three sides, has a 16C main building
by the alchemist **Nicolas Grosparmy**,
lord of Flers from 1527 to 1541, with
an 18C classical main façade. The first-
floor rooms contain the painting and
decorative art sections. In the gallery
devoted to the regional schools of the
19C there are works from the Barbizon
School by Corot and Daubigny, pre-
Impressionists such as Boudin and
Lépine, and Impressionists including
Caillebotte.

EXCURSION
Museé de Tinchebray et prison royale

Prison royale, 34 Grande-Rue, corner r.
de la Prison. Guided tours Jul–Aug
Wed–Sun 2.30–6.30pm. €4.
02 33 64 23 55.

The old *prison royale* now houses a local
ethnography museum. The revolutionary tribunal was set up on the first floor.
Two cells have fireplaces; prisoners were
allowed coal, if they paid for it. The thick
walls and wooden doors with impressive locks bear graffiti – some dates
from 1793.

DRIVING TOUR

Around Mont de Cerisy
Round-trip of 24km/15mi. Allow 3hrs.

▷ *Take the D 924 west.*

▶ **Population:** 16,947.
Michelin Map: 310: F-2.
Info: 2 pl. du Dr-Vayssières.
02 33 65 06 75.
www.flers-agglomeration.fr.
Location: Flers is at the
crossroads of the Paris–
Granville and Caen–Laval
routes: 92km/57.5mi S of
Caen via D 562; 58km/36mi
N of Mayenne via D 962
and D 23; 30km/18.6mi
SE of Vire; 44km/27mi W
of Argentan via D 924.
Don't Miss: The view
from the château at
Mont de Cerisy.
Timing: You need half
a day to see Flers and
its surroundings.

La Lande-Patry

Two giant yews dating back over 1,000
years grow in this old cemetery

▷ *Continue southeast on D 18 to*
Cerisy-Belle-Étoile.

Mont de Cerisy★

○Open daily 9am–6pm.

A road bordered by rhododendrons,
climbs up the slope to the ruined
castle, which commands extensive
views★ over the countryside, as far as
the foothills of the Suisse Normande.
The plateau is the venue for the local
Rhododendron Festival.

▷ *Turn around, go back to the D 18*
and continue straight on.

Les Vaux

After passing between Mont de Cerisy
(left) and Rocher de St-Pierre *(right)*, the
road ends in the old hamlet of St-Pierre
where a small Roman bridge spans the
river.

▷ *Return to Flers via St-Pierre-*
d'Entremont and Caligny.

Argentan

The small town of Argentan looks down from its hillside site onto the confluence of the River Orne and the River Ure. The itinerary known as L'Encerclement (The Encircling Movement) – one of eight trails in the Historical Area of the Battle of Normandy – goes through the town. France's most renowned stud farm, the Haras du Pin, lies nearby.

A BIT OF HISTORY

Kingly Disputes and Lacemaking – It was in Argentan in the 12C that the papal legates assembled to settle the disagreement between the English king, Henry II Plantagenet, and his chancellor, Thomas Becket, Archbishop of Canterbury. Ironically Becket's assassins also set out from here to accomplish their dark deed.

Although Colbert, Louis XIV's minister, chose nearby Alençon to set up the Royal French Lace Workshop, he did not entirely neglect the lacemakers of Argentan. The rediscovery of 18C lace patterns for the Point d'Argentan in 1874

▶ **Population:** 15,465.
Ⓜ **Michelin Map:** 310: I-2.
🇮 **Info:** Chapelle St-Nicholas, 6 place du Marché, 61200 Argentan. ℘02 33 67 12 48. www.argentan.fr.
◗ **Location:** Argentan lies on the River Orne, surrounded by forests, between Flers and Alençon, each 45km/28mi away.
◉ **Don't Miss:** The Château of Bourg-St-Léonard.
◷ **Timing:** Allow 1 day.

enabled the characteristic Argentan pattern to regain its popularity.

TOWN
Église St-Martin

r. St-Martin. ☜*Guided tours Jun–Sept by appointment with the tourist office.* ℘*02 33 67 12 48.*

The church, which was damaged in 1944, is dominated by an octagonal tower surmounted by a decapitated spire. The overall style is Flamboyant

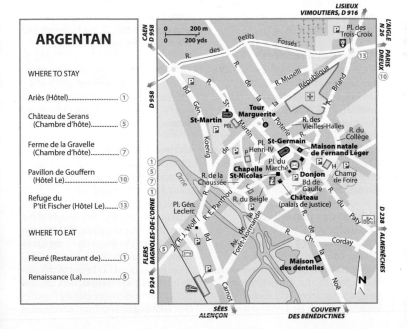

Gothic but includes several Renaissance innovations.

Église St-Germain★

pl. du Marché. ○*Open Jun–mid-Sept Mon, Wed, Thu and Fri 9am–noon, 2–6pm, Tue 2–6pm, Sun 3–6pm.* ○*Closed public holidays.* ℘*02 33 67 12 48 (tourist office).*
The church, badly damaged by shelling in 1944, was built in the Flamboyant style from the 15C to the 17C.
Walk round the church clockwise to view the unusual pentagonal east end (16C) and the unusual circular chapels at the ends of the transepts. At the base of the belfry a fine Flamboyant **porch** opens on to rue St-Germain.

Château

○➞*Closed to the public.*
The castle now serves as the Law Courts. This imposing rectangular building, flanked by two square towers, was built in 1370 by Pierre II, Count of Alençon.

Ancienne chapelle St-Nicolas

pl. du Marché.
Built in 1773, this chapel belonged to the castle. The Tourist Information Centre occupies the ground floor, and the first floor *(open on request)* houses a beautiful carved 17C altarpiece.

Maison des dentelles

34 r. de la Noë. ♿○*Open Apr–mid-Oct Tue–Sat 9am–11.30am, 2–5.30pm, Sun 3–5.30pm.* ◉*€3.* ➞*Guided tours available.* ℘*02 33 67 50 78.*
The town's lace museum presents a charming introduction to the history of local lacemaking right up to the present day. A number of dresses and other outfits are on show, many the work of famous designers.

Abbaye des Bénédictines

2 r. de l'Abbé. ♿○*Open Mon–Sat 2.30–4pm.* ◉*€2.* ○*Closed one week late Dec–Jan.* ℘*02 33 67 12 01.*
This enclosed order of nuns has exclusive rights to the Argentan stitch, a needlepoint lace style comprising a variety of motifs on a honeycomb-like background. There are no workshops, but you can ask to see specimens illustrating stages in the development of Argentan lace and samples of old and modern needlepoint lace.

🚗 DRIVING TOURS

Pays d'Argentan

Around Argentan is a plain circled by woods: Écouves to the south, Gouffern to the north. The Orne Valley, separating this region from the Pays d'Auge, entered into military history in August 1944.

1 BANKS OF THE RIVER ORNE

32km/20mi. 1hr round-trip from Argentan.

▷ *Leave Argentan southwest on the D 924.*

Écouché

At the crossroads marking the start of the town, stands a tank, acting as a war memorial.
The imposing 15C–16C **church** (○*Open Jul–Aug daily 2.30–5pm, if closed, ask the Syndicat d'Initiative for the key;* ℘*02 33 36 88 82)* was never completed and the ruined 13C nave never rebuilt. The Renaissance triforium in the transepts and the chancel are worthy of note.

▷ *Leave Écouché heading northwest on la Grande-Rue, in the direction of Falaise. Where the town ends, follow the road left, which leads to the Château de Serans.*

Château de Serans

○*Open May–Sept daily; Oct–Apr Sat–Sun and hols only 2–6pm.* ◉*€4. Rooms available.* ℘*02 33 36 69 42. www.atelierbalias.com.*
Built in the early 19C, in the style of the villas of the Veneto, since 1991 this castle has been the property of the Greek painter, Balias (b.1943). This versatile artist has applied his talent to the castle interiors and exteriors, with unusual bas-reliefs and contemporary frescoes that take inspiration from neoclassical

and ancient designs. The castle grounds are home to a sculpture park.

◯ *Return on the D 771, then head in the direction of Ménil-Glaise.*

Ménil-Glaise★

The **view**★ from the bridge takes in the rock escarpment crowned by a castle on the south bank of the Orne; there is another good view from a terrace.

◯ *Turn round; continue straight ahead passing (left) the path from the bridge and (right) the Batilly road; turn left onto the D 924 to Argentan, 9km/5.6mi south.*

② LE VAUDOBIN

🚶 *12km/7.4mi – plus 15min walk (round-trip);* 😣 *Beware slippery paths.*

◯ *From Argentan take the D 916 northeast; after 7km/4.3mi (beyond Gouffern Forest) turn left and cross La Londe. Park near the quarry; take the path left of the quarry entrance.*

🚶The path crosses the Meillon stream, bears left round a large rock and climbs uphill past a rock bearing fossil imprints. From the top of the grassy mound there

is a view of the Meillon Gorge and the Dives Valley.

③ FOREST AND CHÂTEAUX

68km/42.5mi. Allow one day.

◯ *Leave Argentan to the northeast via N 26, then take D 113 to the left.*

As you leave Argentan, the road crosses Gouffern Forest, then winds back down into the Dives Valley.

Chambois

A stele near a central crossroads recalls the joining up of the Polish 1st Armoured Division (attached to the 1st Canadian Army) and American 3rd Army troops on 19 August 1944 to cut off the retreat of the German 7th Army.
The huge rectangular **keep** *(donjon)* buttressed by four towers is a good example of 12C military architecture. The church has an 11C stone spire and a fine Descent from the Cross.

◯ *Take D 16 up hill to Montormel.*

Mémorial de Montormel

&🚗⚭*Visit by guided tour (1hr) only daily May–Sept 9.30am–6pm; Apr 10am–5pm; Oct–mid-Dec and mid-*

Jan–Mar Wed and Sat–Sun 10am–5pm.
€5. ℘02 33 67 38 61.
www.memorial-montormel.org.

This museum and memorial commemorates the Battle of Normandy, and in particular, the **Battle of the Falaise Gap** (see p295) which raged from 12 to 21 August 1944, resulting in 10,000 to 12,000 deaths (some estimates put the figures much higher). Field Marshall Montgomery declared that it marked the "beginning of the end of the war". From here there is a superb panoramic **view**★ over the plain.

Two galleries are of particular interest: in one, a large relief map describes the battle; the other is devoted to the soldiers of the Polish 1st Armoured Division. Its eye-witness accounts are harrowing.

Le Bourg-St-Léonard★

11km/7mi E by N 26. Château.
Guided visit (45min) Jul–Aug daily 2.30–5.30pm; May–Jun and 1st 3 weekends Sept and holidays 2.30–4.30pm. €3. ℘02 33 36 68 68.
This elegant 18C château was built by the chief of the Treasury under Louis XV. The interior is embellished with panelling, tapestries and 18C furniture. Take a walk to enjoy the views from the paths in the huge English-style park.

Haras National du Pin★

From France's most famous stud farm, (see opposite) you can see the outline of the Écouves Forest.

Almenêches

The Renaissance church here was once part of a Benedictine **abbey**. The altars are decorated with sculptures representing historical events, including the canonisation of St-Opportune, a local abbess.

Château de Médavy

Open Jul–Aug daily 2.30–7pm, call for other times of the year. €6.
℘02 33 35 05 09.
Surrounded by a moat fed by the Orne, and by formal gardens, this 18C château was rebuilt for a French Marshal on the ruins of an ancient fortress. All that remains of the latter are two 15C towers, one of which houses a chapel with a beautiful marble altar. An extensive restoration project is currently under way, and will last several years. At the same time the owners are refurnishing the château. Don't miss the Russian winter sled, the Atlas Hall, the great staircase, and the remarkable parquet floor in the grand salon.

Château d'Ô

Open Aug, call for days and times.
℘02 33 39 55 79.
This late 15C château combines the Flamboyant Gothic and Renaissance styles. For generations the château belonged to the Ô (pronounced the same as *eau*) family, who were royal courtiers. The name is appropriate, as the sloping roofs, slim turrets, delicate ornamentation and brick-and-stone façade reflect beautifully in the water of the moat.

▷ *Take the D 958 in the direction of Argentan. After 3.5km/2mi, turn left onto the D 745, then right onto the D 752.*

Château de Sassy

Open Easter–Sept. Guided tours (45min) daily mid-Jun–mid-Sept 10.30am–12.30pm, 2–6pm; Easter–mid-Jun and last half Sept Sat–Sun and public holidays 3–6pm. €7.
℘02 33 35 32 66.
Building began in 1760, was interrupted by the Revolution and continued in 1817. The main salon holds several 17C tapestries. The **chapel**, partly hidden by trees, contains a 15C Flemish oak altarpiece carved with scenes from the Passion. The **terraces** and **gardens** of the château are delightful.

▷ *Continue on the D 752.*

St-Christophe-le-Jajolet

The village church is a place of pilgrimage to St Christopher, the patron saint of travellers. On the day of pilgrimage *(last Sun in Jul and first Sun of Oct)* a procession of cars files past.

Haras National du Pin★

Le Pin Stud Farm, "the equestrian Versailles", dating from 1665, enjoys a magnificent setting amid woods and meadows; its grounds were designed by the king's landscape architect, André Le Nôtre. Nearby Gacé was home to the heroine of La Dame aux Camélias, who inspired Verdi's opera *La Traviata*.

- **Michelin Map:** 310: J-2.
- **Info:** Association Haras du Pin Tourisme. ℘02 33 36 68 68. www.haras-national-du-pin.com.
- **Location:** The Haras is some 15km/9mi E of Argentan via D 926.
- **Don't Miss:** The Cour d'Honneur on Thursdays, with stallions and carriage teams.

VISIT

Open daily Apr–Sept 10am–6pm; school holidays (other than the Jul–Aug holiday) 10.30am–noon, 2–5pm; rest of the year 2–5pm. Closed 1 Jan, 25 Dec. ⚒✕ €10. Display of horsemanship Jun–Sept Thu (Jul–Aug also Tue) 3pm. €6. ℘02 33 36 68 68. www.haras-national-du-pin.com.

Three magnificent woodland rides converge on the horseshoe-shaped *cour* (courtyard), surrounded by splendid buildings. It is named the Cour Colbert, after Jean-Baptiste Colbert, chief minister of Louis XIV, who founded the stables in 1665. The château *(only open certain days offseason, see website)* holds offices and reception rooms. Guided tours take visitors through the stables to see the 40 or so horses, the 19C carriage collection and to explore the equestrian world, past and present, through its modern interactive visitor centre. The harness room, paddocks and forge are also open on certain days in the summer *(see website)*.

EXCURSIONS

St-Germain-de-Clairefeuille

10km/6mi SE (via Nonant-le-Pin).
The church is distinguished by its magnificent woodwork including 13 **painted panels**★ of the Life of Our Lord by the early 16C Flemish School.

Gacé

13km/8mi N. Head towards Exmes on the D 26, then turn right onto the D 14.

Severely damaged during the battles of 1944 Gacé was fortunate to retain its imposing brick **Château** *(Guided tours Jun–Aug Tue–Sun every 45 min 2–5pm last tour 2.45pm; €2.50. ℘02 33 35 50 24)*, built between the 15C and 18C. The town is famous for being the home of Marie Duplessis, immortalised as "the Lady of the Camelias" in the novel *La Dame aux Camélias*, by Alexander Dumas *fils* (the younger) and is the basis for Verdi's *La Traviata*. She is celebrated in a special museum as part of the castle tour.

DRIVING TOUR

VUE SUR LA DIVES

23km/14mi. Allow 1hr30min.

This short tour takes in beautiful countryside, calling at **Exmes**, the historic capital of the Argentan, and the nearby 15C **Manoir d'Argentelles**.
Take the D 926 east and, at the Tête-au-Loup, turn left onto the D 26 on the edge of the woods.
After visiting Exmes and its Romanesque parish church, continue on the D 26, then take the D 305 south to Villebadin. The views around here are particularly fine. At the end of the village, turn left to the Manoir d'Argentelles *(open Easter–Sept Sun afternoons)*.
At the first crossroads turn right towards the D 305 and rejoin it to the left. Cross the D 14 to return to the D26.

⬡STAY

FALAISE

⊜⊜ **Chambre d'hôte Le Chêne Sec** – *Pertheville-Ners, 9km/5.6mi E of Falaise.* ✆*02 31 90 17 55. 2 rooms.* The bedrooms in this peaceful, elegant 15C manor house feature exposed beams, stone walls and country furniture. Restaurant (⊜⊜).

⊜⊜⊟ **Hôtel de la Poste** – *38 r. G. Clemenceau.* ✆*02 31 90 13 14.* The bedrooms in this 1960s building have been recently refurbished and are well kept; those at the rear are quieter. The restaurant (⊜⊜) serves traditional dishes.

LA SUISSE NORMANDE

⊜ **Chambre d'hôte La Ferme du Vey** – *Le Vey.* ✆*02 31 69 71 02. www.ogites.com/ ferme-du-vey. 3 rooms.* This working cattle farm offers comfortable rooms in an outbuilding. Friendly owner.

ARGENTAN

⊜ **Le Refuge du P'tit Fischer** – *1 pl. des Trois-Croix.* ✆*02 33 67 05 43. 17 rooms.* At the entrance to Argentan, on a busy street, this hotel offers modern, fuctional rooms on three storeys, well soundproofed. Brasserie-style restaurant.

⊜ **Arlès** – *Z.A. Beurrerie, 1km/0.6mi via 4 on map.* ✆*02 33 39 13 13. 43 rooms.* Simple and functional accommodation, set on a busy road (but well insulated against noise), with a bistro-style dining room (⊜⊜).

⊜⊜⊟ **Chambre d'hôte Château de Serans** – *Écouché, 10km/6mi SW.* ✆*02 33 36 69 42. www.atelierbalias.com. 2 rooms.* This fascinating château, graced with contemporary art by the current owner, offers two bedrooms with beautiful views of the estate.

⊜⊜ **Chambre d'hôte Ferme de la Gravelle** – *41 r. de la Gravelle, Sarceaux, 2.5km/1.5mi W.* ✆*02 33 67 04 47. 3 rooms.* ⊠. Set in a small rural village. There is a peaceful atmosphere in this country house. Rooms are pretty and a gîte is also available. Restaurant (⊜⊜).

⊜⊜ **Pavillon de Gouffern** – *Silly-en-Gouffern, 11km/7mi E.* ✆*02 33 36 64 26. www.pavillondegouffern.com. 20 rooms.* The exterior of this former 19C hunting lodge, is rustic, with typical Norman half-timbering, the renovated interior is chic and contemporary. Restaurant (⊜⊜⊟).

⬡EAT

FALAISE

⊜⊜ **L'Attache** – *rte de Caen, 1.5km/ 0.9mi N.* ✆*02 31 90 05 38.* A former coaching inn with a charming façade and attractive interior. The focus is on local cuisine with the occasional heirloom variety of herbs and vegetables.

⊜⊜⊟ **La Fine Fourchette** – *52 r. Clemenceau.* ✆*02 31 90 08 59. www.fine-fourchette.fr.* Modern cuisine on five set menus is served in two bright and cheery semi-formal dining rooms.

CLÉCY

⊜ **La Guinguette à tartines** – *1 Le bord de l'Orne.* ✆*02 31 69 89 38. http://la-guinguette-a-tartine.com. Open Mar–Sept.* Set on the banks of the Orne; snacks, salads and simple dishes are served in a relaxed atmosphere.

LA SUISSE NORMANDE

⊜⊜ **Au Poisson Vivant** – *Pont-Érambourg, Pierre-du-Regard, 9km/5.5mi W of Pont-d'Ouilly.* ✆*02 31 69 01 58. Closed Mon and Tue.* Set in a former dance hall this small dining room is lengthened by a veranda and decorated in 1930s style.

⊜⊜ **Auberge Saint-Christophe** – *Pont-d'Ouilly, 12km/7.5miSE of Clécy.* ✆*02 31 69 81 23. www.auberge-st-christophe.fr.* This old house, covered in Virginia creeper, sits on a quiet country road very close to the River Orne. Rustic dining room, regional cuisine. Bright cheerful modern rooms (⊜⊜).

⊜⊜ **Relais de la Poste** – *Rte de Caen, nr Thury-Harcourt.* ✆*02 31 79 72 12. www.hotel-relaisdelaposte.com.* This Caen-stone house has an elegant dining room serving traditional cuisine with an extensive wine list. Comfortable characterful rooms (⊜⊜⊟); lovely garden.

ARGENTAN

⊜⊜ **Restaurant de Fleuré** – *61200 Fleuré, 6.5km/4mi SW.* ✆*02 33 36 10 85. Closed Sun eve, Thu eve, Mon.* This family restaurant is a local favourite with carefully prepared cuisine and a cordial ambience.

⊜⊜ **Hostellerie La Renaissance** – *20 av. de la 2e Division-Blindée.* ✆*02 33 36 14 20. www.hotel-larenaissance.com. Closed Sun eve.* Hotel restaurant with a quiet, friendly atmosphere and a choice of prixe-fixe menus.

Created in 1975 and spread over the two regions of Basse-Normandie and the Pays de Loire, the **Parc naturel régional Normandie-Maine** covers 2,350sq km/907sq mi and includes 150 communes from the Orne, Manche, Mayenne and Sarthe *départements*. Lying on the boundaries of both Normandy and Maine, the park can be divided into an upper stretch *(haut pays)*, featuring crests and wooded escarpments in the Alpes Mancelles, and a lower stretch *(bas pays)*, characterised by a *bocage* landscape, the rolling hills of Saosnois and open fields around Sées and Alençon.

Alençon

Just outside the park boundary, the main town of this region, Alençon became famous in the 17C for its lace, once in high demand throughout Europe. Lace-making as a serious commercial enterprise has long gone and the town now has a thriving plastics industry in its place. Unlike many towns in the region, however, Alençon retains much of its historic fabric, escaping the Battle of Normandy with only minor damage.

Alpes Mancelles

Just south of Alençon, this picturesque region of small villages, hills and river valleys clad in woodland, heather and broom, spans the Normandy and Pays de Loire border. It follows the twists and turns of the Sarthe River valley as far as Fresnay-sur-Sarthe. The villages of St-Céneri-le-Géri and St-Léonard des Bois are particularly attractive and the latter has plenty to offer outdoor enthusiasts.

Highlights

1 Admire **Alençon** lace at the town museum (p316)
2 Take a trip along the **Sarthe River valley** (p320)
3 Marvel at the medieval crafts-manship of **Sées** Cathedral (p321)
4 March up the grand staircase of the Château de **Carrouges** (p323)
5 Stroll through the historic town centre of **Domfront** (p325)

Around Carrouges

This is the centre of the national park with the Château de Carrouges being the region's single biggest visitor attraction in every sense. The little hilltop town makes a good base. Nearby, don't miss the fascinating Champ de la Pierre gardens.

Half-timbered houses in Domfront

© Leroy Arthur/age fotostock

ALENÇON AND THE PARC RÉGIONAL NORMANDIE-MAINE

Carrouges	★★	Recommended
Alençon	★	Interesting
Domfront		Worth a visit
⟶		Driving tour with departure point

Around Domfront

The charming historic town of Domfront with its half-timbered houses is the best stopover for exploring the west of the Parc. From here you can make an excursion to the attractive town of Mortain, to the west, with its lovely waterfalls.

Sport & Leisure

If you like messing about in boats, you can navigate a good stretch of the River Sarthe through the Alpes Mancelles by canoe or kayak. Try Alpes Mancelles Aventures in St-Léonard-des-Bois. If you prefer wheels to water, hire mountain bikes from Espace VTT FFC, also in

St-Léonard-des-Bois. Also near here is the Parc aventure du Gasseau, offering an excellent Acrobranche course navigating the treetops while suspended on wires. Horseriding is popular in many areas, particularly the Écouves Forest. Pamper yourself by taking one of the many hydrotherapy treatments available at Bagnoles-de-l'Orne. Untypical of the region, this posh spa town attracts wealthy clients from all over France and is not the sort of place you want to visit on a tight budget. Even if you have an aversion to spas, however, it's worth a quick visit to admire the town's early 20C Belle Époque architecture.

Alençon★

A royal lace-making town under Louis XIV, Alençon has a rich architectural heritage, a Fine Arts Museum with a collection of lacework and paintings from the 15C–19C; and waterways and gardens surrounding the pedestrianised town centre. Alençon was liberated on 12 August 1944 due to the decisive role of the French 2nd Armoured Division in the Battle of the Falaise-Mortain Pocket.

SIGHTS
Maison d'Ozé
pl. de la Magdalena.
Now home to the tourist office, this attractive 15C house, according to local lore, sheltered the future king, Henri IV, in 1576. It is named after the first prefect of Orne (who held the post 1800–1815), though it belonged to the Le Coustelier family.

Église Notre-Dame★
Grand-Rue. ⏱*Open daily 9am–noon, 2–5.30pm.* ◆*Guided tours available Jun–Aug; ask at the tourist office.*
The beautiful 14C–15C Flamboyant Gothic Church of Our Lady was begun during the Hundred Years' War. The tower, transept and chancel were

Descent from the Cross, Église Notre-Dame

E. Lambère/MICHELIN

▶ **Population:** 28,935.
⚙ **Michelin Map:** 310: J-4.
▯ **Info:** Maison d'Ozé, place de la Madeleine. ℘02 33 80 66 33. www.paysdalencon tourisme.com. 19 ave. de docteur Riant, Fresnay-sur-Sarthe. ℘02 43 33 28 04. www.ot-alpes-mancelles.com
◗ **Location:** From Alençon, roads lead to Paris (195km/122mi E via N 12), and to Brittany, Belgium and Spain. The A 28 leads to Le Mans (58km/36mi to the S) and to Rouen (160km/100mi to the N).
⊚ **Don't Miss:** The little villages of the Alpes Mancelles, especially St-Léonard-des-Bois and St-Céneri-le-Gérei.
🕐 **Timing:** Take a half-day in the town, then enjoy the lovely countryside in the forest of Perseigne or in the Alpes Mancelles.

rebuilt in the 18C. The elegant three-sided **porch**★, built by Jean Lemoine from 1490 to 1506, is an example of the purest Flamboyant style. All the decoration is concentrated on the upper parts of the church. The Transfiguration in the central gable shows Christ with the prophets Moses and Elijah; below are the apostles Peter, James and John, with their backs to the street.

Inside, the sweeping lines of the nave rise to the highly decorated rib **vaulting**. The lines of the triforium merge with those of the clerestory to form a unified whole. Note the **stained glass**★ by the master-glaziers of Alençon and the Maine region. The glass in the clerestory windows dates from 1530.

The first chapel off the north aisle is where Marie-Françoise-Thérèse Martin (1873–97), better known as St Theresa of Lisieux, was baptised.

Halle au Blés

r. des Filles Notre-Dame. ○*Open daily 9am–noon, 2–6pm. www.ville-alencon.fr.*
The old circular grain market, built 1812, was covered towards the end of the 19C with a glass dome, which the ladies of the town nicknamed "the hoopskirt of Alençon". It functions today as a cultural centre and its outline is an emblem of the city.

Musée des Beaux-Arts et de la Dentelle★

Cour carré de la Dentelle. ♿○*Open Jul–mid-Sept daily 10am–noon, 2–6pm; rest of the year Tue–Sun 10am–noon, 2–6pm.* ○*Closed 1 Jan, 1 May, 25 Dec.* ⊜*€4 (free first Sun of month).* ℘*02 33 32 40 07.*
Located in the old 17C Jesuit college, the Museum of Fine Arts and Lace houses

From Venice Lace to Alençon Lace

Lace-making began in Alençon during the 16C but took off in the mid-17C, after it perfected the art of imitating the finest Venetian techniques – then regarded as the best in Europe. Louis XIV's minister, Colbert, established a Royal Workshop and an industry developed, employing around 8,000 people. So there would be no competition from Venice, or indeed anywhere else, Colbert banned all imported lace. The Alençon lace-makers subsequently developed their own style, Point d'Alençon lace, an even more delicate stitch than that of the Venetians. The industry survived the Revolution and reached new heights under Napoléon I. From 1880 onwards, however, mechanical lace making and changes in fashion meant the decline of Alençon hand-made lace. Today, the last vestiges of the craft are kept alive by the Atelier National du Point d'Alençon (*closed to the public*), created by the State in 1976, to uphold lace needlepoint traditions, and who still supply needlework to the highest government establishments.

L'Encerclement

The itinerary known as L'Encerclement (The Encircling Movement), one of several in the Historical Area of the Battle of Normandy, runs from Alençon to L'Aigle, tracing the progress of the 2nd Armoured Division under General Leclerc.

Find out about this and other routes at http://www.normandie-tourisme.fr. by entering "Battle of Normandy" in the search box.

paintings from the 15C to the 19C as well as collections of lace. The French and Nordic Schools of the 17C are well represented, with canvases by Philippe de Champaigne, Jean Jouvenet, Allegrain, Voet, Ryckaert and Wyck. There is also a fine selection of 19C French painting with works by Boudin, Courbet, Fantin-Latour, Lacombe, Laurens, Legros and Veyrassat.

The presentation of the **lace collection**★ offers a broad review of the principal lace-making centres in Italy and France. Its display of Alençon lace, which uses a needlepoint technique unique in France, includes the elegant creations of the Alençon lace-makers from the 17C to the present day.

There is also a collection of Cambodian objects brought back by **Adhémar Leclère** (1853–1917), a native of Alençon and 19C governor of Cambodia.

Ancien Château
49 r. du Château.
From place Foch, you can see the 14C and 15C towers of the old castle, built by Jean II le Beau, first Duke of Alençon and an ally of Joan of Arc.

The central tower, known as the crowned tower, has an unexpected outline: the main tower with machicolations is itself crowned by a slimmer, round tower. The other two towers, which defend the main gate, can be seen from rue du Château.

Église St-Léonard
pl. Marguerite-de-Lorraine. Enquire at the presbytery. ℰ *02 33 26 20 89.*
The rebuilding of the present church was begun in 1489 by René, second Duke of Alençon, and was completed in 1505 by his widow, Marguerite de Lorraine.

Nearby *(no 10 rue Porte-de-la-Barre)* is a 15C house (Maison à l'Étal) with a slate-hung façade.

Hôtel de Guise
The local Prefecture and Départment offices now occupy this beautiful 17C building, which, despite its name, was formerly a military headquarters.

Maison de la famille Martin - Chapelle Ste-Thérèse
r. St-Blaise. ○ *Open Jun–Sept daily 9am–noon, 2–6pm; Oct–Dec and Feb–May Tue–Sun 9.30am–noon, 2–5pm.* ○*Visit by guided tour (30–45min).* ℰ *02 33 26 09 87. www.famillemartin-therese-alencon.com.*
This is the birthplace and childhood home of Thérèse Martin (1873–1897) who became St Theresa of Lisieux in 2008. A double staircase leads to the chapel, which adjoins the house.

EXCURSIONS
Fresnay-sur-Sarthe
▷ *21km/13mi S of Alençon.*
Fresnay occupies a picturesque site, perched high above the River Sarthe. The town centre is a preserved network of narrow streets bordered by beautiful medieval houses. It is also a centre for excursions into the Alpes Mancelles or Sillé Forest.

La Belle Échappée
8 r. de la Forêt de Perseigne, La Fresnaye-sur-Chédouet. ⴠ○*Open April–Sept Wed–Sun 10am–noon, 2–7pm; Oct–Mar Sat–Sun 10am–12.30pm, 2–6.30pm (last entrance 1hr before closing).* ○*Closed 25 Dec–2 Jan.* ⴤ*€5.* ℰ*02 43 34 39 11.*
The name means "the beautiful journey" and the exhibits and exhibitions in this museum of cycling celebrate the history

of this popular national sport and of its many great French champions.

🚗 DRIVING TOURS

FORÊT DE PERSEIGNE★
Round-trip 53km/33mi. About 3hrs.

◐ *Leave Alençon heading southeast on the D 311 in the direction of Chartres.*

Bordered by the former provinces of Perche and Champagne Le Mans, the Perseigne Forest, comprising mainly oak, beech and fir, covers more than 5,000ha/12,000 acres and is marked by deep valleys.

The route initially bypasses the forest to the north before penetrating its depths via the D 236. On leaving the hamlet of Buisson, turn left on the D 236; 4 km/2.5mi further on, turn right at a sharp bend to Aillières-Beauvoir, then go right again towards Ancinnes, on the forest road leading to Croix-Pergeline. At the last intersection (note the boundary marker stone), take the road left to Gros-Houx. The road leads downhill into a valley where you can walk through a beautiful series of oak, beech and fir copses. At the Trois-Ponts junction, follow the road up the hill; to the left is the picturesque vallée d'Enfer (Hell's Valley), at the bottom of which is a meander-

ing stream. Climb the belvedere tower (30m/90ft high) to enjoy the views from the highest point (349m/1,145ft) in the Sarthe district.

🚶 *There are 8km/5mi of waymarked paths round the belvedere and in Hell's Valley.*

◐ *Take the D 234 southeast to the twin villages of Aillières-Beauvoir then the D 116 south via Villaines-la-Carelle. At the crossroads with the D 311 continue southwest on the D 310.*

Chapelle Notre-Dame-de-Toutes-Aides
The doorway of this graceful pilgrimage chapel is surmounted by a Virgin and Child. Above the 17C altarpiece is an Assumption; below is a painting of the Annunciation.

◐ *In St-Rémy-du-Val turn right in front of the church onto the road to Neufchâtel-en-Saosnois (D 117). Turn left onto the D 165. From Ancinnes take the D 19 to Alençon.*

THE ALPES MANCELLES★
See map p314. 82km/51mi – approx 3hr round-trip from Alençon (excluding the Misère Valley).

The Alpes Mancelles is a particularly picturesque part of the Normandie-

St-Céneri-le-Gérei

© Musat Christian/Dreamstime.com

Maine Regional Park on the border with the Pays de Loire.

◆ *On leaving Alençon take the N 12 west via St-Denis-sur-Sarthon; in Lentillère turn left towards Champfrémont; then bear right to Mont des Avaloirs.*

Mont des Avaloirs
A belvedere marks the summit (417m/1 368ft); this is one of the highest points in western France.

◆ *At the second crossroads turn left onto the D 204 and then fork right onto the D 255. In St-Julien-des-Églantiers turn right onto the D 245, right again onto the D 218 and right again onto the D 20.*

Corniche de Pail
The road, which climbs slowly, provides a view over the Mayenne basin.

◆ *In Pré-en-Pail take the N 12 east and the D 144 south via St-Pierre-des-Nids.*

St-Céneri-le-Gérei★
This picturesque village, often listed as one of the most beautiful in France, has a charming setting with a hilltop Romanesque church, a bridge spanning the Sarthon and ancient stone houses.

For many years it has been a centre and source of inspiration for artists, painters and sculptors and there is an artists' exhibition centre here.

◆ *From St-Céneri-le-Gérei take the D 56 south; turn right onto the D 146.*

St-Léonard-des-Bois★
This attractive village is an ideal excursion centre for the Alpes Mancelles and is home to several outdoor pursuits operators (◆ *see Introduction*) .

Vallée de Misère★
🚶 *1hr30min round-trip.*
From the church square take the path at the corner by the Hôtel Bon Laboureur. At the crossroads marked by a stone cross take a path uphill. Beyond Le Champ-des-Pasfore turn left. At the next crossroads turn left onto a path marked in red and white. From a bench there is a fine **view**★ of the wild Misère Valley, St-Léonard and the Manoir de Linthe further downstream.

◆ *From St-Léonard-des-Bois take the D 146 north. Turn right onto the D 56; in Moulins-le-Carbonnel turn left onto the D 150, which becomes the D 315, and will take you back to Alençon.*

Sées★

The quiet old cathedral town of Sées, with its several religious communities, has been the seat of an episcopal See since St Latuin converted the district to Christianity in the year 400. Its historic centre has been sensitively restored.

SIGHTS
Cathedral★★
Allow 15min. ⏰*Open daily 9am–6.30pm.* ♿. ☎*02 33 28 74 79.*
The cathedral is one of the finest examples of 13C and 14C Norman Gothic in the country.
Exterior – The porch on the west front is disfigured by heavy buttresses, added in the 16C when the cathedral began to lean alarmingly.
Interior – In the **chancel**★★ and the **transepts**★★ the triforium is a fascinating example of Gothic art, lit by magnificent 13C **stained glass**★★ and rose windows in the transept. In the south transept is the "Beau Dieu" Carrara marble bust by Bernini (1678), one of the last works of the Italian Baroque master. Note, too, the beautiful marble altar from the Louis XVI period, executed by Brousseau, the architect of the diocese. One side of the gilded bronze represents the Entombment, the other scene carved into the marble relates to the discovery of the relics of the two saints, Gervais and Protais.

- ▶ **Population:** 4,967.
- ⬡ **Michelin Map:** 310: K-3.
- ▯ **Info:** place du Général de Gaulle. ☎02 33 28 74 79.
- ◐ **Location:** 22km/13.5mi SE of Argentan, or 19km/11.8mi N of Alençon, near the Forêt d'Écouves.
- ⬡ **Don't Miss:** The chancel of the cathedral; Forêt d'Écouves.
- ⏰ **Timing:** Take a day to see the town and enjoy the forest.

Musée départemental d'Art religieux
pl. du Gén. de Gaulle. ⏰*Open Jul–Sept Wed–Mon 10am–6pm.* ◉*€2.* ☎*02 33 81 23 00.*
The museum, in the former canons' residence, presents a varied collection (12C–19C) of religious art and objects.

Ancien évêché (Palais d'Argentré)
The Old Bishops' Palace was built for Bishop Argentré in 1778.
The beautiful wrought-iron gate has an escutcheon and foliated scrolls.

Ancienne abbaye St-Martin
⚊*Closed to the public.*
The old abbey is now a children's home. However, through the great main gate

Sées on Bastille Day, the cathedral in the background
© Kaos02/Sime/Photononstop

the gracious 18C abbot's lodging can be glimpsed.

Église Notre-Dame-de-la-Place

Guided tour available from the tourist office. ℘02 33 27 81 76.
The organ loft is Renaissance, and twelve bas-relief sculptures, which illustrate scenes from the New Testament, date from the 16C.

Anciennes halles

This unusual covered market, a rotunda with a peristyle, dates from the 19C.

Basilique de l'Immaculée-Conception

◷*Open daily 9am–7pm.*
Built in 1872 in Gothic-Revival style, and featuring murals enriched with gold-leaf, the Basilica has a calm meditative atmosphere.
Opposite stands la tour d'Argentan, a remnant of the city's 12C fortifications.

🚗 DRIVING TOUR

Écouves Forest★

29km/18mi. About 2hr15min.

This itinerary explores a diversity of forests (oak, beech, fir, pine, spruce).

◐ *Past Sées, the D 908 leads into the forest via Choux.*

⊛ Guided tours on foot or on horseback through the forest massifs (Écouves, Andaines, Bellême and Perche-Trappe, Réno-Valdieu, Moulins-Bonsmoulins) are available on request one month in advance from the Office National des Forêts. ℘02 33 82 55 00. www.onf.fr.
As you reach the top of the hill, turn left onto the D 226 for views over the Argentan countryside.
*The various visitor facliities include a Fitness Trail at Chêne-au-Verdier and a Discovery Trail at the Rendez-Vous crossroads. The forest is home to kites and deer.

Carrefour de la Croix-de-Médavy

The Sherman tank (*Valois*) at this crossroads belonged to the 2nd French Armoured Division (*2e division blindée, 2eDB*) under the command of General Leclerc. At the other side of the crossroads, a board recalls the battles fought by the 2eDB during the Battle of Normandy.

SÉES

WHERE TO STAY

Ferme équestre des Tertres
(Chambre d'hôte)...................... ①

Île de Sées (Hôtel)......................... ④

Roses et les Pivoines
(Chambre d'hôte Les)................ ⑥

WHERE TO EAT

Cheval Blanc (Le)........................ ①

Normandy (Au)............................ ④

The **Signal d'Écouves** is, with the Mont des Avaloirs, the highest point (417m/1 368.6ft) in western France.

Carrefour de la Croix-Madame

Turn left onto the path to Sapaie-Pichon and keep following the trees marked with yellow stripes. ◀◀ *1hr 30min approx round-trip.*
Fine vistas can be enjoyed on this trail.

◯ *Return to your car and follow the D 204.*

The road descends quickly, with fine views. After the Chêne-au-Verdier crossroads there are beautiful woodlands.

◯ *At the Rochers-du-Vignage crossroads, turn right onto the D 26 then immediately right onto a forest track.*

Rochers du Vignage★

🏃 *1hr45min round-trip.*
The path *(marked with yellow stripes)* leaves the forest road to follow a low rock crest from which there are outstanding views over the forest. The path reaches the Chêne-au-Verdier, runs parallel with the Aubert forest road for around 300m/yd, forks right, then returns downhill to the forest road and back to your car.

◯ *Follow the D 26 towards Alençon.*

At the exit to the forest, at the junction with a forest trail is a monument and cemetery, some 200m/yd south, both commemorating the 2eDB.

Carrouges

Located in the centre of the Parc naturel régional Normandie-Maine, this immense château and park (10ha/25 acres), belonged to a famous Norman family, Le Veneur de Tillières, for almost five centuries. in 1936 it was bought by the nation. The town is a good base for exploring the region, and its Maison du Parc visitor centre is an indispensable source of information.

Château de Carrouges★★

◀◀*Guided tours (45min, last tour 45min before closing); mid-Jun–Aug 9.30am–noon, 2–6.30pm; Apr–mid-Jun and Sept 10am–noon, 2–6pm; rest of the year 10am–noon, 2–5pm.* ⊙*Closed 1 Jan, 1 May, 1 and 11 Nov, 25 Dec.* ⊚€7. ℘02 33 27 20 32. www.monuments-nationaux.fr
From the park with its fine trees and elegant flower beds there are good views of the château.
The **Conservatoire botanique des pommiers de Bretagne et de Normandie** includes 152 varieties of apple trees. The 16C **gatehouse**★ is an

▶ **Population:** 735.
⚬ **Michelin Map:** 310: I-3.
🯄 **Info:** Rue du Crochet.
  ℘02 33 31 02 88.
◗ **Location:** Set on a high point NW of the Écouves forest, Carrouges is 26km/16mi E de Bagnoles-de-l'Orne and 30km/18.5mi NE of Alençon.
⊛ **Don't Miss:** The majestic grand staircase at the château.
⊙ **Timing:** Allow at least 90min to see the château.

elegant brick building with decorative geometric patterns. Surrounded by a moat, the château is austere but imposing; its buildings are arranged around an inner courtyard. The stables and domestic quarters occupy the ground floor; the apartments and state rooms occupy the first floor.
The **kitchen** presents an imposing array of copper pans. The **Louis XI Bedroom** was named after the king's visit on 11 August 1473.

Château de Carrouges

G. Targat/MICHELIN

The panelling is adorned with delicate panels of foliage highlighted in a different colour.

In the principal **antechamber** the chimney breast is decorated with a hunting scene. The remarkable fireplace in the **dining room** is flanked by two polished granite piers with Corinthian capitals. The sideboards are Louis XIV; note the Restoration chairs.

The **portrait gallery** with its Louis XIII chairs assembles past lords and owners. The **drawing room** occupies part of one of the corner towers. The straw-coloured panelling dates from the late 17C or early 18C.

The visit ends with the monumental great **staircase**★ and its brickwork vaulting and round-headed arches as they wind up and round the square stairwell.

Maison du Parc

⊙*Open Jun–Sept Wed–Mon 10.30am–6.30pm; rest of the year Tue–Fri 10.30–noon, 2–5pm.* ℘*02 33 81 75 75.* *www.parc-naturel-normandie-maine.fr.*
This is the principal visitor centre for the **Parc naturel régional Normandie-Maine** with interesting exhibitions and interpretations of the park, and provides a comprehensive information service whatever your interests. The park can be explored by car, on foot (2,499km/1,553mi of signposted paths) or by bike (via four themed itineraries). Details and maps are available here.

The centre occupies the restored buildings of a 15C chapter of canons, and is an outbuilding of the château. Next door is the **Conservatoire botanique des pommiers de Bretagne et de Normandie**, a collection of the 152 apple varieties to be found in the two regions.

EXCURSIONS
Goult

▶ *13km/8mi E of Carrouges via D908, then left on D 204.*

A road lying between two farooms leads to the **Chapelle St-Michel**, all that remains of the La-Lande-de-Goult Priory, once a stop on the medieval pilgrimage route to Mont-St-Michel.

The 12C Romanesque porch has remarkable capitals carved with complex designs of birds and mythical beasts, as well as hunting scenes. From the cross, there is a fine view of the Écouves forest. Nearby earthworks indicate remains of a Roman military camp.

Tourbière (peat bogs) des Petits-Riaux – follow the signposts. Guided walks are organised by the park rangers – enquire at the Maison du Parc.

A discovery trail *(1.4 km/0.9mi)*, partly on a boardwalk, allows visitors to safely explore this fragile ecological treasure, which includes a spongy carpet of sphagnum moss, ferns and all sorts of amazing carnivorous plants such as round-leaved sundew (Drosera).

Le Champ de la Pierre

◉ *8km/5mi northwest via the D 908 and the D 909.* ◷*Open mid-Jul–Sept 10am–noon, 2.30–6.30pm.* ◉*€3.50; blast furnace additional €3.* ℘*02 33 27 21 70. http://lechampdelapierre.com.* Created in the late 18C, this delightful romantic 4ha/10 acre "Jardin remarquable" is full of pretty features and surprises. Take the bridle path lined by lime and beech trees to the lakeside where you will find an 18C blast furnace and forges. This metal-working industry was the mainstay of the local community for nearly three centuries until being abandoned around the mid-19C. It made fixings, locks and general hardware; one of its notable commissions being the superb main gates for the Château Carrouges. The iron ore came from the bois de Ranes and the charcoal from the forêt d'Ecouves.

A maze leads to a Temple of Diana and there is also a rose garden and a vegetable garden.

Domfront★

Domfront lies spread along a rocky ridge over a gorge carved by the River Varenne, affording a panorama of the Passais *bocage* country. In addition to its **strategic site★** on the old route between Mont-St-Michel and Paris, the town features historic ruins and a well-restored town centre.

A BIT OF HISTORY
Under English Rule

In 1092 the townspeople of Domfront rose up against their overlord Roger de Montgomery and rallied to **Henry Beauclerc**, the son of William the Conqueror.

In 1100 Henry became king of England and Domfront an English possession. In the 12C Henry II Plantagenet and his queen, Eleanor of Aquitaine, often visited with their brilliant court.

In August 1170 papal legates met here to attempt to reconcile Henry and his estranged Archbishop of Canterbury, Thomas Becket. Domfront passed from English to French hands, and back again, during the Hundred Years' War. It became French for good in 1450.

Matignon's Siege – In 1574 Gabriel, Comte de Montgomery (1530–74), who had mortally wounded the French king

▶ **Population:** 953.
◔ **Michelin Map:** 310: F-3.
▯ **Info:** 12 place de la Roirie. ℘02 33 38 53 97. www.ot-domfront.com.
◐ **Location:** Domfront lies between Mayenne (36km/22.4mi S) and Flers (22km/13.5mi N).
◈ **Don't Miss:** The Old Town and its half-timbered houses; Notre-Dame-sur-l'Eau.
◔ **Timing:** Several bike tours have been mapped by the tourist office.

Henri II in a tournament, defended Domfront against the royal forces under the Comte de Matignon. Montgomery surrendered, believing that his life would be spared, but was executed on the orders of Henri's widow, Catherine de' Medici.

OLD TOWN CENTRE★
Allow 30min.

The old town is enclosed by a wall and 13 of the original 24 towers. The best preserved are those on the south side; one is still crowned with machicolations. For a good view walk along rue des

Fossés-Plisson. Several 16C stone houses, formerly inhabited by noble or well-to-do families, have been restored.

Grande-Rue

This sloping street, now a pedestrian zone, has kept its original paving.

Rue du Docteur-Barrabé

There are some lovely timber-framed houses, notably no 40 and at the corner of ruelle Porte-Cadin.

Église St-Julien

This modern church (1924) in neo-Byzantine style is dominated by a tall cement belfry. Inside, an immense mosaic depicts Christ in Majesty. The area around the church, in particular rue St-Julien and place du Commerce, is a pleasant area for a stroll.

Hôtel de Ville - Musée

○ *Open Mon–Fri 9am–noon, 1.30–4.45pm (request admission from the Secretariat).* & ℘ *02 33 30 60 60. www.domfront.com.*

In the town hall, the **Salle Charles-Léandre** houses paintings and drawings by local artist Charles Léandre (1862–1941).

Terre-plein nord des remparts (City Walls north)

From la place du Panorama is a beautiful (partial) view into the deep Varenne valley, better known by the townfolk as the "val des Rochers".

ADDITIONAL SIGHTS
Jardin public du Donjon★

Cross the bridge over the old moat to the public gardens, laid out on the site of the fortress destroyed in 1608.

Of Henry Beauclerc's 1092 fortress there remain two imposing sections of the keep's walls and two towers from the flattened curtain wall.

Inside the curtain walls stand the ruins of the late 11C Chapelle St-Symphorien. Eleanor of Aquitaine's daughter was born in Domfront and christened in this very chapel. Skirt the ruins of the keep to reach the terrace which affords a **panorama★** of the Passais countryside. A view indicator points out the three rivers; Mayenne, Varenne and Égrenne.

Église Notre-Dame-sur-l'Eau★

Under the château on the Varenne River.
This charming Romanesque Church of Our Lady on the Water (late 11C) was badly damaged in the 19C when five

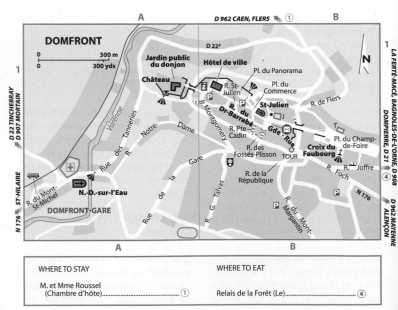

WHERE TO STAY	WHERE TO EAT
M. et Mme Roussel (Chambre d'hôte)..............①	Relais de la Forêt (Le)..............④

of its seven nave bays were destroyed to make way for a road. Following war damage in 1944 the church was restored. According to legend, at Christmas 1166, Thomas Becket, Archbishop of Canterbury, celebrated Mass in this church while in exile in France.

Several 12C frescoes have been uncovered in the south transept representing the Doctors of the Church (theologians who expounded the Christian doctrine). A Gothic canopy covers a recumbent figure with a lion at its feet.

Croix du Faubourg

From the foot of the Calvary, there is a **panorama**★ similar to the one from the public gardens, but it extends further east towards Andaines Forest.

EXCURSION
Dompierre

◗ *9 km/5.6mi northeast on the D 21.*

The wealth of this village was based on iron working and its **Museum of Wire and Iron** (*Open May–Sept Sun 3–6pm, Jul and Aug Tue–Sun 3–6pm; €3. 02 33 38 03 25*) has displays not only on iron but on other traditional local trades such as cotton spinning, shoe-making, lace-making and farming.

To see traces of the industrial past still in situ, pick up the leaflet from the museum, which details a 10km/6mi walk around Dompierre's old mineworks. It is marked in yellow and takes around 3hr.

🚗 DRIVING TOUR

NORTHWEST OF DOMFRONT
Round-trip of 35km/22mi. About 2hrs.

◗ *Leave Domfront on the D 22 and pick up the scenic narrow D 907.*

Lonlay-l'Abbaye

The church, once part of an 11C abbey, enjoys a pleasant country setting. It was damaged in 1944. The 15C porch opens directly into the transept; the south arm

is typical of Romanesque construction and decoration. The Gothic chancel and its granite pillars have been restored.

◗ *5km/3mi west of the village turn left onto the D 134.*

La Fosse-Arthour

From the high rocks to the left is a view down into the 70m/230ft deep gorge of La Fosse-Arthour. The River Sonce runs swiftly between the gorge before opening out into a swirling pool then continuing on its way in a series of small cascades.

The gorge is the subject of many local legends, the most popular being that it is named after the mythical King Arthur, said to have ended his days here.

Fishing and canoeing are popular along this stretch of water.

◗ *Take the D 134 south towards St-Georges-de-Rouelley; at the first junction turn left onto the Rouellé road. In Rouellé turn left onto the D 907 to Domfront. After 1.5km/0.9mi turn right onto a narrow unsurfaced road, towards the end, which leads to the Manor ruins.*

Manoir de la Saucerie

Open mid-Jul–early Aug 10.30am–1pm, 2.30–6.30pm. €3; 02 33 38 99 08.

The name comes from Robert le Saucier who was a favourite servant of Eleanor of Aquitaine; at the end of the 12C she gave him the land on which the current manor stands.

The Manoir is a most unusual and attractive building with a fortified appearance, though it has never seen battle. In fact it is a small Châtelet (gatehouse) flanked by two round towers with loopholes and is all that remains of the original 16C manor house. Its unusual picturesque stone, brick and timber upper storey and roof construction is said to be unique in France.

◗ *Return to the D 907 for Domfront.*

Bagnoles-de-l'Orne★

In addition to its healing waters, the spa town of Bagnoles-de-l'Orne has a lovely serene lakeside setting★. The lake is formed by the Vée, a tributary of the Mayenne, before it enters a deep gorge cut through the massif of the Andaines Forest. It is best appreciated by taking a stroll from Tessé-la-Madeleine to the Roc au Chien.

▶ **Population:** 2,561.
Michelin Map: 310: G-3.
Info: Place du Marché. ℘02 33 37 85 66. www.bagnolesdelorne.com.
▶ **Location:** Bagnoles is 2km/1mi N of the N 176, which links Alençon (47km/29mi SW) to Mont-St-Michel (90km/56mi W). The town comprises two distinct parts: to the W Bagnoles-Château and E, Bagnoles-Lac.
Parking: Near the château, the museum, the casino and the place du Marché.
Don't Miss: Roc au Chien.
Timing: Half a day for the spa waters.
Kids: Forêt des Andaines.

BAGNOLS-LAC
Parc de l'établissement thermal★
The park surrounding the spa building is planted with pines, oaks and chestnut trees. The Allée du Dante on the east bank of the Vée, which is often crowded with bathers, leads from the lake to the spa building. Other alleys in the park wind towards Capuchin's Leap and to the pictureque site known as the Abri Janolin. Shops along rue des Casions line the lake front.

Musée départemental des Sapeurs-Pompiers de l'Orne
16 av. Albert-Christophle.
&Ⓞ*Open daily Apr–Oct 2–6pm (last entry 30min before closing).*
€3.80. ℘02 33 38 10 34.
A deconsecrated church houses the Fire Brigade Museum with its collection of horse-drawn hand pumps, the oldest pre-dating 1790, plus badges, medals, helmets, uniforooms, breathing apparatus, radios and other equipment.

BAGNOLS-CHÂTEAU
Le Roc au Chien★
Tours by tourist train (30min) Jun–Sept Mon–Fri 3.15 and 4.30pm; Mar–May and Oct Sat–Sun and public holidays 3.15 and 4.30pm. €5.60. ℘02 33 30 72 70.
www.bagnolesdelorne.com.
45min round-trip. Start from the church and walk up the avenue du Château; the main gateway opens on to the avenue and the public park of Tessé

that holds an arboretum containing 150 different tree species, a bird-watching trail, a children's playground and other amusements. The château, built in the 19C in neo-medieval style, now houses the town hall.
Take the avenue on the right, which overlooks the Bagnoles Gorge and leads to the rocky promontory, the Roc au Chien, where there is a lovely **view**★ of Bagnoles beside the lake *(left)* and the spa building and its park *(right)*.

EXCURSIONS
Château de Couterne
▷ *1.5km/0.9mi south of Bagnoles on the D 335. Park the car by the bridge.*
⊶*The interior is closed to the public.*
The massive brick and granite château (16C and 18C) is reflected in the waters of the Vée.

La Ferté-Macé
▷ *6km/4mi north via the D 916.*
This small town has retained a number of 18C and 19C buildings and houses that recall its past role in the textile industry. It is also famous for *tripes en brochettes*, tripe skewered on hazel wood sticks.

WHERE TO STAY

Bois Joli (Hôtel)... ③
Nouvel Hôtel... ⑤
Ô Gayot (Hôtel).. ⑦
Source
  (Chambre d'hôte Auberge de la)........... ⑨

WHERE TO EAT

Bon Accueil (Au)... ①
Maison de la Trippe.................................... ⑨
Terrasse (La).. ⑫

There is a large tourist complex, including a leisure park (pedalos, windsurfing, fishing, climbing, swimming, golf, etc.) and a dozen holiday houses. A lively market is held on Thursday mornings. An 11C Romanesque tower is all that remains of the old parish church, demolished in 1861.

The **hôtel de ville** (town hall) houses works by the local artist **Charles Léandre**, as well as fascinating 19C paintings celebrating the postal service and local manufacturing.

♈ Musée du Jouet

32 r. de la Victoire. ◔*Open Jul–Aug daily 3–6pm; Apr–Jun and Sept Sat–Sun and public holidays 3–6pm.* ◉*€3.30 (under 6 years no charge).* ℘*02 33 37 47 00 or 02 33 37 04 08.*

This museum of 19C and 20C games and toys has been set up in the former municipal baths.

Rânes

▶ *13km/8mi from La Ferté-Macé via D 916.*

Rebuilt in the 18C, the castle, which now houses the local *gendarmerie*, has retained its 15C two-storeyed keep, complete with crenellations and machicolations. Enjoy the panoramic view from the top.

🏃 HIKES

The Andaines Forest (℗*see driving tours below*) is ideal for walks and hikes. We offer two suggestions below (for more ideas visit the tourist office).

Circuit de St-Ortaire et du chêne Hippolyte

🏃 *4.5km/2.8mi – allow 1hr45min.*
Start near the Market Square. Walk beside the train tracks. The first place you come to is the Priory of St Ortaire, an ancient establishment founded by Jean de Valois, dedicated to the

saints Radegund and Ortaire. A little further on, in the heart of the forest, is a giant 300-year-old oak (known as the Hippolyte) with a girth of around 5.25m/17ft and a height of 30m/98ft.

Gorges de Villiers★

◗ *12km/7.5mi southeast, near St-Ouen-le-Brisoult.*

🚶 There are several well marked walking trails in this beautiful gorge, which has been created by the River Gourbe. The Chapelle St-Antoine trail takes around an hour. It initially leads to the river, passing over an impressive scree slope; look out for the small cave of the fairy, Gisele, who, according to local lore, protects travellers. Near the bridge, across the Gourbe, is a hot spring, which in Roman times attracted a cult following. The trail crosses the river and climbs up to a wide path. Go right on here and this takes you back into the forest. Set in a beautiful glade, the chapelle St-Antoine (built 1875) appears in a beautiful glade. Walk back along the river to the starting point of your walk.

🚗 DRIVING TOUR

Vallée de la Cour

11km/6mi northeast. ◗ *Take the D 916, turn right onto the D 387 and then right again, after 600m/yd onto the D 20, then follow the signs.*

🏞 A road leads to a lake where there is good fishing.

Forêt des Andaines

Part of the Normandie-Maine Regional Nature Park the forest offers pleasant walks and, if you're lucky (and quiet), a glimpse of deer, stag or roe deer.
Popular places include the slender **Tour de Bonvouloir** observation tower; the **Chapelle Ste-Geneviève**, a picnic site; and, best of all, the heavy-horse shows at **Ferme du Cheval de Trait** (*Juvigny-sous-Andaine;* ♿ 🕐*shows Jul–Aug Wed–Thu, Sat–Sun; Apr–Jun and Sept–Oct check the website.*
🎫*€10 (5–12 years €4).* 🍴 🐴*Book for lunch on the farm;* 📞*02 33 38 27 78. www.chevaldetrait.com.*

Mortain★

This small, well-kept town is built halfway up a hillside in an attractive setting★ where the River Cance, cutting through the last of Basse-Normandie's southern hills, emerges on to the vast wooded Sélune basin, leaving in its wake a rock-strewn countryside. The name of the town is derived from the word Maurus and could refer to the Moors who served in the Roman army.
During the Middle Ages Mortain was the capital of the county held by Robert, the stepbrother of William the Conqueror. The town has been rebuilt over the ruins left by the Battle of Normandy.

SIGHTS
Grande Cascade★

🅿 *Use the car park at avenue de l'Abbaye-Blanche (at a bend in the road)*

▸ **Population:** 2,191.
⬡ **Michelin Map:** 303: G-8.
🔲 **Info:** Rue du Bourglopin.
📞02 33 59 19 74.
www.ville-mortain.fr.
◗ **Location:** Mortain is 25km/15.5mi S of Vire via D 577 and D 977. Avranches is 42km/26mi W via D 5.
🔎 **Don't Miss:** The picturesque Grande and Petite Cascades and the "Chrismal" treasury at St-Évroult Church.
🕐 **Timing:** You will need at least a half day to tour the Cascades, which involve considerable walking; and the Abbaye Blanche.

and take the path downhill, or park in rue du Bassin (signposted) and take the path that follows the river bank. The waterfall (25m/82ft) is created by the River Cance flowing through a wooded gorge; the foaming waters are reminiscent of the mountain streams of the Pyrenees or the Alps.

Petite Cascade★

🚶 *45min round-trip. From place du Château take the downhill path south (left) along the wall of the Caisse d'Épargne (signpost).*

The path crosses the River Cance and follows the bank upstream past the Needle Rock. It then crosses the Cançon stream on stepping stones before reaching the waterfall (35m/114.8ft) in a rock amphitheatre.

Petite Chapelle★

From Mortain take the road south towards Rancoudray; in front of the Gendarmerie turn left. Park in the car park at the top of the hill; walk up the avenue of fir trees.

To the left and beyond the chapel there is a belvedere providing a **view**★ of the wooded heights of Mortain and Lande-Pourrie, with an indicator to identify the various points of interest. On a clear day Mont-St-Michel and the Breton coast are visible on the horizon *(right)*.

Abbaye Blanche

At edge of town, going towards Villedieu-Sourdeval. ⏰*Open Apr–Dec Wed–Mon 10am–noon, 2.30–7pm.* ☏*02 33 79 47 47.*

This 12C former monastery, now a nunnery, sits amid a landscape of rocky outcrops. It was founded in the 12C by Adeline and her brother Vital, chaplain to Count Robert, stepbrother of William the Conqueror.

The chapter house is composed of two bays with pointed vaulting.

The cloister gallery, unlike other Romanesque cloisters in the region, which have twinned columns or clusters as at Mont-St-Michel, consists of a simple

WHERE TO STAY
Logis
  (Chambre d'hôte le)...①
Temps de Vivre
  (Hôtel le).........................③
WHERE TO EAT
Grange (La).......................④

row of single columns. The vaulting is of timberwork.

The church displays the usual features of the Cistercian plan: flat east end with an oculus and transept chapels. The diagonal ribs are a precursor of the Gothic style. The groined vaulting of the Lay Sisters' Refectory is supported by two central columns.

The storerooms have two barrel vaults of four bays each; the capitals are carved with foliage and scrolls.

Collégiale St-Évroult

Town centre. ⏰*Open daily 9am–7pm. To see the treasury, ask at the tourist office Jul–Aug.* ☏*02 33 59 19 74.*

This old collegiate church, reconstructed in the 13C, is built of sandstone in a severe Gothic style. The 13C belfry is plain and simple. The door in the second bay shows all the fine decorative elements known to Norman Romanesque. The single arch relies neither on columns nor capitals. The chancel stalls have carved misericords representing satyr-like figures.

The **treasury** contains the **Chrismal**, an exceptional 7C casket (portable reliquary) of Anglo-Irish origin, made of beechwood, lined with copper and engraved with runic inscriptions and images of sacred personages.

EXCURSIONS
Barenton
▶ *9 km/5.6mi southeast. Leave Mortain on the road to Domfront.*
Near Barenton in the Normandie-Maine Regional Park is **La Maison de la Pomme et de la Poire** cider and perry farm (⊙*open Apr–Oct 10am–noon/12.30pm and 2–6/6.30pm; *⊜*general admission free, guided tour €2.50. ℘02 33 59 56 22.www.parc-naturel-normandie-maine.fr.)*
Here you can learn all about the making of cider, perry and calvados and its wider economic importance to the region, take a tour of the orchards and, of course, enjoy a tasting at the end of your visit.
Children can join in the fun too with a special interpretive trail of their own

Ger
The town is famous for its distinctive brown pottery which reached its zenith in the 19C, employing 700 workers. Production concentrated on stoneware pots, fired at very high temperature (1260°C), which were sold through western France. The industry has now all but gone, though you can explore its history at the nearby regional Museum of Pottery, located on the road to Flers some 15km/9.5mi from Mortain.

▶ *From Mortain take D 157, then D 60 on the left, heading towards Le Placître.*

Musée régional de la Poterie★
3 r. du Musée-Le Placître. &⊙*Open Jul–Aug 11am–7pm; Apr–Jun and Sept 2–6pm, Easter and All Souls' school holidays 2–6pm (last ticket 1hr before closing). *⊜*€4.20 (children €1.75). ℘02 33 79 35 36. www.sitesetmusees.cg50.fr.*
The museum comprises 12 buildings:a potter's house, three long tunnel-

kilns from the 17C and 18C, a drying device for pots, various workshops, a bakery, etc. There is an interesting **demonstration**★of manufacturing techniques. Pottery is still made on the premises and is available for sale.

🚗 DRIVING TOUR

Vallée de la Sée
Round-trip of 58km/36mi. Allow 3hrs. From Mortain take D 977 N towards Vire.

North of La Tournerie, where the road winds downhill, there is a view of the vast Sourdeval basin, through which runs the River Sée.

▶ *In Sourdeval turn left onto the D 911.*

The road follows the curves of the narrow **Sée Valley**★, offering a new view at each bend.

Moulin de la Sée
Brouains. &⊙*Open Jul–Aug Mon–Fri 9am–7pm, Sat–Sun and public holidays 11am–7pm; Mar–Jun and Sept–Oct Mon–Fri 9am–12.30pm, 2–6pm, Sat–Sun and public holidays 2–6pm (last entry 30min before closing). *⊜*€5. ℘02 33 59 20 50.*
This mill is also known as the Écomusée de la Vallée de Brouains, a museum devoted to rivers and related activities, including fish breeding (the River Sée is one of France's finest salmon runs), the development of hydraulic energy, and the development of water-powered industries, from pewter ware to stainless steel cutlery.

▶ *After passing the church in Chérencé-le-Roussel, turn right onto the D 33.*

St-Pois
From here there are fine views south of the Sée Valley.

▶ *In St-Pois turn right, then right again onto the D 39 which climbs uphill.*

St-Michel-de-Montjoie

At the southwest entrance to the village, a terrace affords a fine view which, on a clear day, extends to Mont-St-Michel. The village is known for its granite quarry (*northwest off the D 282 towards Gast*) and for its mineral water, Eau de Montjoie.

The **Musée du Granit** (*open Jun–mid-Sept daily 2–6pm; May Sun 2–6pm, last entry 5pm; €4.20. 02 33 59 02 22*) explains the local history of quarrying and displays objects fashioned from the quarry – capitals, pediments, sarcophagi, balusters, millstones – in a wooded park.

Return to Chérencé-le-Roussel. Turn left onto the D 33 to return to Mortain.

Sillé-le-Guillaume

Occupying a strategically important site, which protected northern Maine from Norman invasion, the small town of Sillé-le-Guillaume had a rich and eventful past.

Château

Guided tours available. €2.50. 02 43 20 10 32 (tourist office). www.tourisme.sille-le-guillaume.fr.
At the end of the Hundred Years' War, the English sacked the 11C fortress. The 15C castle was built on the ruins.

Église Notre-Dame

The church stands upon the site of a former Romanesque church of which the **crypt** and the south transept gable remain. A beautiful 13C door (restored in the 15C) is decorated with a statue of the Virgin and Child.

🚗 DRIVING TOUR

LA FORÊT DE SILLÉ

30km/19mi. Allow 1hr.

Leave Sillé-le-Guillaume northeast on the D 310.

This short tour takes you into the forest, which is popular with walkers.

Take the D 105 towards Sillé-Plage then left on the D 203E.

- ▶ **Population:** 2,360.
- 🚲 **Michelin Map:** 310: I-5.
- 🅸 **Info:** Maison du lac et de la forêt, Forêt de Sillé. 02 43 20 19 97
- ▶ **Location:** Sillé-le-Guillaume is 35km/22mi NW of Le Mans and 17km/10.5mi SW of Fresnay-sur-Sarthe.

Sillé-Plage is a popular lake with a beach where you can swim and enjoy water sports. The information office (*see box, above*) is a useful resource. On the Coco-Plage part of the beach are the remains of an ancient medieval castle. Continue around the lake, in the direction of Sillé-le-Guillaume and take the forest road right towards Grand-Ligne which leads via a crossroads to **Croix-de-la-Mare**. A 45min round-trip walk leads to the highest point in the forest, marked by a cross (erected by a penitent after the French Revolution) and a chapel dating from 1862.

At the Croix de Mare crossroads take the D 103 towards bis-Rouessé Vasse, then the D-310 back to Sillé-le-Guillaume.

ADDRESSES

🛏 STAY

ALENÇON

Hôtel Marmotte – *Les Grouas, 61250 Valframbert, 1km/0.6mi N of Alençon.* &02 33 27 42 64. *46 rooms. Restaurant*. The rooms in this traditional family hotel offer contemporary furnishings and modern plumbing. A good base to explore the area.

Chambre d'hôte La Garencière – *72610 Champfleur, 6.5km/4mi SE of Alençon.* &02 33 31 75 84. *5 rooms. Restaurant*. Prettily decorated bedrooms. A covered swimming pool looks onto the countryside, and there is a billiards room.

Chambre d'hôte Le Moulin de Linthe – *rte de Sougé-le-Ganelon, 72130 St-Léonard-des-Bois.* &02 43 33 79 22. *www.moulindelinthe.fr. 5 rooms.* The bedrooms have character in this picturesque old mill, still with paddle wheel.

Château de Sarceaux – *61250 Valframbert.* &02 33 28 85 11. *www.chateau-de-sarceaux.com. 5 rooms.* A large park with a pond surrounds this 17C–19C château. South-facing rooms are elegantly decorated with antique furniture and family portraits. Candlelit dinners in the dining room, with classic cuisine.

Mercure – *187 av. Gén-Leclerc, 2.6km/1.6mi SW.* &02 33 28 64 64. *53 rooms.* ⊿€10. Fairly recent building in a small commercial park. Rooms are practical and well soundproofed, those on the first floor are modern and renovated.

CARROUGES

Gite de Mary – *St. Martin des Landes (3km de Carrouges.* &02 33 28 84 21, http://gite.de.mary.pagesperso-orange.fr. This well-equipped cottage, sleeping 8, is in an idyllic country location.

St-Pierre – *61150 Rânes.* &02 33 39 75 14. *12 rooms.* This small hotel with a warm welcome features typical colourful rustic rooms, The restaurant ((*closed Tue)* specialises in local food, tripe and frog legs.

SÉES

Chambre d'hôte Ferme Équestre des Tertres – *61500 La Chapelle-près-Sées, 4km/2.5mi S of Sées.* &02 33 27 74 67. *www.fedestertres.com. 5 rooms.* This farm is the starting point for horse rides through the Écouves Forest. Hikers can follow waymarked trails; other guests could try a barouche ride. Stylish bedrooms with robust furniture.

Chambre d'hôte Les Roses et les Pivoines – *26 r. du Dr-Homey.* t02 33 26 17 02. *2 rooms.* ⊿.This beautiful, quiet and cosy mansion houses two very comfortable rooms with antique furniture and floral fabrics. The largest, in the 18C wing, has a stone fireplace. A very friendly welcome is assured.

Hôtel Île de Sées – *61500 Macé, 5.5km/3.5mi NW of Sées.* &02 33 27 98 65. *www.ile-sees.fr. 16 rooms.* This former dairy is set in a park amid peaceful countryside. Dark woodwork adds warmth to the interior decoration. Nice rooms decorated in pastel shades.

DOMFRONT

Chambre d'hôte M et Mme Roussel – *"La Roculière", 61700 St-Bômer-les-Forges, 10km/6mi N.* &02 33 37 60 60. *4 rooms.* A pretty farm with rooms to match.

BAGNOLES-DE-L'ORNE

Ô Gayot – *2 av. de la Ferté-Macé.* &02 33 38 44 01. *www.hotel-ogayot-bagnoles-orne.federal-hotel.com.16 rooms.* This recently renovated town centre hotel offers minimalist rooms, bar, tea room, gourmet shop, and modern bistro serving contemporary cuisine ( ). Terrace.

Auberge de la Source– *La Peras, 61600 La Ferté-Macé, 5km/3mi NW.* &02 33 37 28 23. *5 rooms.* This new building is in old Norman-style with bricks and half-timbering. Rooms have excellent beds and parquet floors. The restaurant ( ) serves regional fare and has an open fire.

Nouvel Hôtel – *ave. du Dr-Pierre-Noal, 61140 Tessé-la-Madeleine, 0.5km/0.3mi S.* &02 33 30 75 00. *www.nouvel-hotel-bagnoles.fr. 30 rooms.* This lovely, thoroughly renovated villa dating from 1900 lies close to the thermal spa. Modern rooms are decorated in warm colours. Covered terrace.

MORTAIN

Hôtel de la Poste – *place des Arcades.* &02 33 59 00 05. *25 rooms.* Opposite the Collegiate Church, this pleasant hotel is gradually renovating its rooms. Choose those with a view of the valley. Seasonal menus in the restaurant ( ).

🍽 **Hôtel Le Temps de Vivre** – *12 r. St-Martin, Sourdeval.* 📞*02 33 59 60 41.* *www.logishotels.com. 10 rooms.* On the village square, next to the cinema, the stone façade is bedecked with flowers. Rooms are small but newly refurbished and well kept. Pleasant restaurant (🍽🍽).

♈ EAT

ALENÇON

🍽 **Auberge Normande** – *Le Pont-du-Londeau, 61250 Valframbert.* 📞*02 33 29 43 29. Closed Sun eve and Mon. Reservations advised.* Often fully booked for lunch, as the locals appreciate the updated regional cuisine and reasonable prices.

🍽 **Le Saint-Léo** – *pl. de l'Église, 72130 St-Léonard-des-Bois.* 📞*02 43 33 81 34. Closed Wed off-season and Tue.* A simple, convivial stop in this picturesque village in the Alpes Mancelles. The dining room faces the Sarthe and offers fresh local fare with an accent on galettes and crêpes.

🍽🍽 **Au Petit Vatel** – *72 pl. Cdt-Desmeules.* 📞*02 33 26 23 78. Closed late Jul–early Aug, Sun eve, Wed.* Traditional fare with regional touches. One menu is devoted entirely to Norman specialities.

SÉES

🍽🍽 **Au Normandy** – *20 pl. du Gén.-de-Gaulle.* 📞*02 33 27 80 67. Closed Wed.* Behind a 17C façade lies a dining room with blackened beams and a welcoming atmosphere. The menus have regional accents, but the pizza and crêpes also provide good quality comfort food.

CARROUGES

🍽 **La Gourmandie** – *19 av. du Maréchal-Leclerc.* 📞*02 33 29 10 37. Closed Sun and weekday evenings in winter.* Choose from their delicious galettes and crêpes or the *plat du jour.*

🍽🍽 **Le Jean-Anne** – *2 r. de la Fée-d'Argouges, Rânes. 11km/6mi NE.* 📞*02 33 39 75 16. Closed Sun eve, Mon.* With views of the castle, this husband-and-wife-run restaurant serves bourgeoise cuisine.

DOMFRONT

🍽 **Bistrot St Julien** – *2 pl. St-Julien.* 📞*02 33 37 14 60.* This Bordeaux-style bistro with a sunny terrace is as good for a sandwich or salad for lunch, as it is for a nice plate of roast lamb with rosemary for dinner.

🍽 **L'Échauguette** – *12 Grande rue.* 📞*02 31 37 71 71.* The salads, pizzas, galettes and crêpes taste even better here when taken on the shady terrace looking over the back garden.

🍽🍽 **Le Relais de la Forêt** – *Le Bourg, Dompierre, 9km/5.6mi NE.* 📞*02 33 30 44 21. Closed Mon–Thu eves.* Slightly old-fashioned décor; expect local seasonal produce, accompanied by local cider.

🍽🍽🍽 **Auberge du Grand Gousier** – *1 pl.de a Liberté.* 📞*02 33 38 37 25. www.grandgousier.com.* Enjoy fine local cuisine such as monkfish in red wine, or veal sweetbreads with shallots and basil, in this charming cosy half-timbered house.

BAGNOLES-DE-L'ORNE

🍽 **Maison de la Trippe** – *20 pl. du Gén.-Leclerc, La Ferté-Macé.* 📞*02 33 37 11 85. Open Tue–Sun 7am–7.30pm (closed Sun pm).* Offal is the house speciality at this small daytime restaurant and shop.

🍽🍽 **La Terrasse** – *r. des Casinos.* 📞*02 33 37 81 44. Closed Sun eve, Mon.* Excellent regional cuisine with fish specialities are served in an inviting rustic interior with a sheltered terrace.

🍽🍽 – 🍽🍽🍽 **Le Bois Joli** – *12 av. Philippe-du-Rozier.* 📞*02 33 37 92 77. www.hotelboisjoli.com.* Overlooking the lake, this beautiful Anglo-Norman villa, built in 1900, offers a choice of three prixe-fixe gourmet menus.

🍽🍽🍽 **Au Bon Accueil** – *23 pl. St-Michel, Juvigny-sous-Andaine.* 📞*02 33 38 10 04. www.aubonaccueil-normand.com. Closed Sun eve, Mon.* This elegant establishment serves fine, light regional cuisine using the freshest local produce.

MORTAIN

🍽🍽 **La Grange** – *Bellefontaine, 7km/4.3mi N.* 📞*02 33 59 01 93. www.village-enchante. fr.* Situated at the entrance to the village, this charming barn conversion is a delight if rather touristy. The menu features snacks, salads, simple grills and fixed-price meals.

THE NORTH OF THE MAYENNE

The northern portion of the Mayenne *département* that extends into Normandy is also known as the lower Maine or the black Maine, remnants of a former province. Through it flows the River Mayenne, on which sit the ancient fortress cities of Laval and Mayenne. The navigable river system once formed a vital transport artery, defended by picturesque forts and castles; today, marinas line the river banks. The landscape, part of the Amoricain Massif, is rocky and forested, crisscrossed with hedgerows planted to contain the marshy soil, and dotted with gardens, orchards and pastures where horses graze.

Highlights

1 The imposing château at **Lassay-les-Chateâteaux** (p340)

2 The extensive remains of the Roman past at **Jublains** (p340)

3 The Chapelle St-Créspin of La Basilique **Évron** (p342)

4 **Laval** Old Town, for its history, art, architecture (p346)

5 Milking a visit to the Lactopôle at **Laval** for all it's worth (p349)

Around the Mayenne

Laval is both a thriving modern city and one that enjoys the title "city of art and history". Its delightful old town, made up of medieval and Renaissance buildings, clusters under the castle on the bank of the Mayenne River. The terraced **Perrine gardens**, noted for their magnificent trees and water features, offer views of the town and river. Tucked away among the surrounding countryside are abbeys, castles and Roman ruins, ideal for driving tours.

Mayenne is the main city of this region, with an old Carolingian core and the eponymous river flowing through the heart of town. It is a good base from which to explore the many picturesque villages and surrounding countryside. Chief among these are the ancient market town of **Lassay-les Châteaux**, with its splendid little-visited castle, and the well-preserved town of **Évron**, set among forests and lakes at the foot of the Coëvrons hills.

At the little village of **Pontmain**, a magnificent basilica marks the site of an apparition of the Virgin and the beautiful **La Pellerine gardens** bloom all summer long. The 11C keep at **Ste-Suzanne**, set on a commanding promontory above the River Erve, offers splendid views of this village, voted one of the most beautiful in France. For the archaeologically inclined the most impressive sight in the Mayenne is probably the remains of the ancient Roman garrison town at **Jublains**, with its fortress, temple, amphitheatre and public baths.

Lassay-les-Château

Laval by the Mayenne

© Kevin O'Hara/age fotostock

Mayenne

Historically Mayenne was a fortified "bridgehead" town, defending the river, which has been navigable to Laval since the 17C. Its strategic importance was reinforced in June 1944, when the town had been nearly levelled, but thanks to the heroism of American Sergeant Mack Racken, the bridge remained intact. It was the only bridge still spanning the River Mayenne and allowed the Allies to march on Paris.

▶ **Population:** 299,000.
Michelin Map: 310: E-5.
Info: Quai de Waiblingen. *02 43 04 19 37.* www.mairie-mayenne.net.
▶ **Location:** Mayenne is on the route from Le Mans (104km/64.5mi SE) to Mont-St-Michel. It is also between Caen (120km/74mi N) and Laval (32km/20mi S).
Don't Miss: The pretty villages in the forest of Mayenne.
Timing: Take a day to see the town, and to enjoy the many nautical activities on the Mayenne River.

SIGHTS

Château Carolingien

pl. Juhel. Open Jun–Sept daily 10am–7pm; Feb–May and Oct–Dec Tue–Sun and public hols 10am–12.30pm, 2–5/6pm. Closed 1 May, 25 Dec. €4. 02 43 00 17 17. www.museeduchateaudemayenne.fr.
During construction work on a new cultural centre in 1993, workers discovered an old fortress dating from the time of the Carolingian kings (751–987), and archaeologists were called in. The new museum presents artefacts from 15 years of digs, in lively displays. The present castle, reinforced several times in the 11C–15C, stands on the hill on the west bank of the river. It suffered frequent sieges, most famously when William the Conqueror took it by cunning, rather than by force.
The perimeter wall remains, giving the castle a feudal appearance. The promenade between the curtain walls and the town gardens commands a fine **view**★ of the town.

Basilique Notre-Dame

This church has been remodelled several times. The west front, along with the pillars and arches in the nave, are 12C; the transept walls and windows are 16C. The church was rebuilt at the end of the 19C in the Gothic style.

Église St-Martin

Located opposite the château, on the hillside on the other side of the river. Open Easter–Oct daily 9.30am–5pm.

In the 11C the church belonged to Marmoutiers Abbey in Tours, and both the apse and transept date from this period.
The modern stained glass, like that in the Basilique Notre-Dame, is by the master glazier Maurice Rocher.

EXCURSIONS

Ambrières-les-Vallées

▶ *12km/7.5mi north on the D 23.*
This ancient medieval settlement perches on a rocky peak.
Near the town hall, the **Musée des Tisserands mayennais** (Mayenne Weavers Museum. Open Jul–Aug, Tue–Sun 2.30–6.30pm. €3. 02 43 04 96 19) tells the story of how cloth and canvas weaving was vital to the prosperity of the region. Housed in three former 18C weavers' cottages, it traces all the production stages of sheets, clothing, ships' sails and more. The cellar-workshop, with period tools, a large loom and furnishings, gives a good idea of the workers' lot during this time. Audio-visuals complement the visit.

Ernée

▶ *24km/15mi west via the N 12.*
At the town entrance, on the edge of the road, sheltered by trees, stands the

Mayenne with the castle and Basilique Notre-Dame

© Nicolas Thibaut/Photononstop

chapel of Charné. It is all that remains of the ancient village of Charné, which was abandoned centuries ago, when the people moved to the new town of Ernée. It features a Gothic choir and transept, and Romanesque tower. Note the 15C polychrome wood-carved statue of the Virgin.

Balzac set part of his novel *Les Chouans* in and around Ernée.

🚗 DRIVING TOUR

Forêt de Mayenne

50km/30mi.

▷ *Leave Mayenne to the south west on the D 104.*

Fontaine-Daniel

A beautiful lake overlooked by a lovely chapel, flower-decked houses and a former Cistercian abbey all contribute to the charm of Fontaine-Daniel.

The village was created around a fabric manufacturer's known as the **Toiles de Mayenne**.

Founded in 1806, it was installed in the grounds of the old Cistercian Abbey (which had lost its property during the Revolution), and has produced nationally acclaimed upholstery fabrics here ever since. An exhibition centre and shop (◐*Open Mon–Sat 9am–12.30pm, 1.30/2–6pm.* ◐*Closed public holidays.* ✆*02 43 00 34 80. www.toilesdemayenne. com)* displays its high-quality fabrics.

River Mayenne

Cruises depart daily in summer; the standard cruise lasts 2hr (€8.50), there is also a 1hr mini-cruise €6), or you could make a night of it by going on a dinner cruise. Alternatively you can explore the river independently by hiring a pedalo or electric motorboat from the Base Nautique Halte Fluviale at Quai Waiblingen. Visit www.paysdemayenne-tourisme.fr for more details on both cruising and hiring boats. For canoe and kayak rentals, visit www.kayakmayenne.fr.

▷ *The D 104 and D 123 lead to St-Germain-le-Guillaume, then Chailland on the D 165.*

Chailland

This small town is dominated by a rocky outcrop, on top of which stands an over-size statue of the Virgin.

▷ *Turn right before the church.*

The road bypasses the rocky outcrop and passes between the Château de la Touche and a pond, before entering the oak-and-elm coppiced Mayenne Forest, which is privately owned. Gradually the forest subsides to thickets.

Lassay-les-Châteaux★

On the edge of this ancient market town stands an imposing fortress. Some of its buildings have recently been restored, revealing some splendid red-granite façades such as that of the Maison du Bailly.

THE CHÂTEAU★

Guided tours (1hr) Jun–Sept daily 2.30–6.30pm; Easter–May Sat–Sun and public holidays 2.30–6.30pm. €6. 02 43 04 71 22.

The castle, which dominates the village, features eight pepper-pot towers linked by a strong curtain wall. It was built in 1458 in place of an older building, dismantled in 1417 during the Hundred Years' War. A prime example of military architecture under the reign of Charles VII, the castle has links with King Henri IV, the writer and poet Victor Hugo and the chemist A L de Lavoisier, who was a prisoner here during the Revolution. During World War II the castle was used as a German command post.

▶ **Population:** 2,450.
🚗 **Michelin Map:** 310: G-4.
🅸 **Info:** 8 rue du Château. 02 43 04 74 33.
▷ **Location:** On the D 34 between Bagnoles-de-l'Orne (17km/10.6mi NE) and Mayenne (19km/12mi SW).
☺ **Don't Miss:** For a good overall view of the castle take the path under the stone bridge at the foot of the towers.
🕐 **Timing:** Allow time to take a walk in the surrounding countryside among the hedgerows (*bocage*).

The working drawbridge, which spans the moat, leads to the barbican, a fortified structure defending the entrance. The two towers guarding the drawbridge are linked by living quarters, in which 16C and 17C weapons and furniture are displayed. The casemates can be seen at the foot of the barbican. The tour ends with a stroll in the park.

Ville Romaine de Jublains★

This archaeological site, comprising baths, the ruins of a fort, a temple and theatre are the best Gallo-Roman period remains in the region and offers a valuable insight into local life under the Romans.

A BIT OF HISTORY

Following the conquest of Gaul by Julius Caesar (50 BC), the Romans divided the country into districts and built towns; the town of Noviodunum (Jublains) was built at an ancient crossroads as an important link in the road network of the Roman Empire. Its main role, as a sanctuary, is shown by the alignment of the public buildings along the axis of the temple.

▶ **Population:** 689.
🚗 **Michelin Map:** 310: G-5
🅸 **Info:** 02 43 04 3033. www.jublains.fr.
▷ **Location:** The remains of the Roman city are 10km/6mi SE of Mayenne; 14km/8.5mi NW of Évron.
☺ **Don't Miss:** The remarkably preserved theatre.
🕐 **Timing:** If you are near Jublains in late July or early August, try to attend a musical performance organised by Les Nuits de la Mayenne (www.nuitsde lamayenne.com).

Fortresse gallo-romaine

© Nicolas Thibaut/Photononstop

SIGHTS
Musée départemental d'Archéologie
Situated at the entry to the fortress, 13 r. de la Libération. ○*Open May–Sept daily 9am–6pm; Oct–Apr Wed–Mon 9.30am–12.30pm, 1.30–5.30pm.* ○*Closed mid-Dec–early Jan.* ⟨⟩ ⟨⟩€4.50. ℘02 43 04 30 16. www.jublains.fr.
This modern museum not only interprets the adjacent Roman site, but also other archaeological themes of the Mayenne region, in particular the palaeolithic site at Saulges with its decorated cave, the Gaulish and Gallo-Roman sanctuaries and the development of the Roman town, then called Noviodunum. A large-scale model gives a good idea of what the town looked like in ancient times.

Fortresse gallo-romaine
This consists of three concentric parts. The central building – the oldest part of the fortress, dating from the early 3C – is a massive rectangular storehouse with four angle towers. During the late 3C crisis (invasions, military anarchy and peasant rebellions), which shook the Roman Empire, the storehouse was surrounded by a rampart of raised earth and a moat. This moat was later filled in, and fortified walls were erected in around AD 290, just before the whole site was abandoned.

Les Thermes (Public Baths)
Below the church; entrance through the Syndicat d'Initiative. ⟨⟩○*Same opening times, etc. as museum.*
The building, which dates from the late 1C, was altered in the 3C and transformed into a Christian church at the end of the Gallo-Roman period. The layout of the baths and main rooms is shown on a plan: the cold bath *(frigidarium)* paved in blue schist; the warm room *(tepidarium)*; and the sweating room *(laconicum)*. The hot bath *(cella soliaris)* is situated beyond the excavated part.

Theatre
The theatre was offered to the town by a rich Gaul, Orgetorix (c. 81–83).

Temple
The temple can be visited freely; brochures are distributed at the museum or at the Syndicat d'Initiative.
The temple is situated at the other end of the Roman town, 800m/yd from the theatre. Its proportions were vast (each side 80m/262.5ft long). It was built of limestone brought in from the Loire region.

Évron★

This small town at the foot of the Coëvrons possesses one of the finest churches in the Mayenne, visible from up to 10km/6mi away. In the 19C the town's linen mills prospered; today it is classified as a "station verte de vacances" – recognised for the beauty of its surroundings.

BASILIQUE NOTRE-DAME★

pl. de la Basilique. ◔*Open daily.*
◔*Guided tours (1hr) of the basilica, crypt and St-Crespin Chapel Jul–Aug Tue–Sat 2pm, 3pm, 4pm, departing from the information point.* ✍€4.
℘02 43 66 85 04. www.evron.fr.
A massive square 11C tower, embellished with corner buttresses and turrets, links the Romanesque part of the nave to the 18C abbey buildings. The nave's four original bays are Romanesque, while the remainder of the basilica was rebuilt in the 14C in the Flamboyant Gothic style. Note the fine 16C organ case and in the trefoil the fragments of a fresco depicting the Nursing Virgin.

The bare Romanesque nave enhances the sense of space, soaring height and luminosity and contrasts with the Gothic decoration elsewhere (restored 1979).

Chancel

Slender columns, pure lines and subtle decoration give the chancel

▸ **Population:** 7,152.
◔ **Michelin Map:** 310: G-6.
▯ **Info:** 4 Place de la Basilique. ℘02 43 01 63 75. www.evron.fr.
▷ **Location:** Évron, surrounded by forests and lakes, is 26km/16mi SE of Mayenne via D 7, and 33km/20.5mi NW of Laval via D 20, then N 157.
☺ **Don't Miss:** The St-Crespin chapel in the Notre-Dame Basilica.
◔ **Timing:** After an hour or so of seeing the town, make an excursion into the surrounding countryside.

considerable elegance. The overall effect is embellished by five windows with 14C stained glass, restored in 1901. During repair work to the chancel paving, a crypt and several sarcophagi were discovered, one dating to the 10C.

Chapelle St-Créspin★★

This 12C chapel opens off the north side of the ambulatory. Christ is shown in a mandorla surrounded by the symbols of the Evangelists. Four lovely Aubusson tapestries represent Abraham's Sacrifice of Isaac, Hagar and Ishmael in the desert; Lot and his daughters leaving Sodom; and Jacob's Dream.

At the altar is a large 13C statue of Our Lady of the Thorn (the full name of the basilique is Notre-Dame-de-l'Épine) in wood plated with silver. Beneath a remarkable 13C crucifix, a cabinet contains two outstanding pieces of metalwork: a delightful 15C silver Virgin and a 16C reliquary.

🚗 DRIVING TOURS

Le Bois de Mirebeau
Allow 1hr45min.

▷ *35km/22mi. From Évron take the D 20 north.*

Frescoes in Chapelle St-Créspin
S. Sauvignier/MICHELIN

As the road climbs there are views to the west over woods and lakes.

▷ *Beyond Ste-Gemmes-le-Robert turn right onto the Mont Rochard road, which is sometimes in poor repair.*

Le Gros Roc

From this rocky escarpment, surrounded by vegetation, there is an extensive view over the *bocage* countryside.

▷ *Turn left onto the D 241 just before a bridge.*

The road passes the **Château de Montesson**, encircled by a moat; its lodge is crowned by an unusual roof and the adjoining round tower also has a highly original onion-domed roof.

▷ *In Hambers, opposite the church, turn left onto the D 236. After 2.5km/1.5mi turn left again onto the narrow road leading to the Butte de Montaigu.*

Butte de Montaigu★

Allow 15min on foot there and back from the car park.

The butte (mound or hillock), crowned by an old chapel, is only 290m/952ft high but, because of its isolation, makes an excellent viewpoint from which to see the hills of the Coëvrons rising to the southeast: Évron, Ste-Suzanne on its rocky spike, to the south; Mayenne and its forest to the northwest; the forests of Andaines and Pail to the north and northeast.

▷ *Return to the D 236 and continue south through Chellé. At the T-junction turn left onto the D 7 at the entrance to the village of Mézangers; turn right to the Château du Rocher (where you must park and walk).*

Château du Rocher★

Allow 30min on foot there and back. The château itself is closed to visitors.
🕐*Open: grounds mid-Jun–Sept daily 10am–noon, 2–6pm.*

A gallery of five low rounded arches runs the length of the Renaissance façade. Delicate sculptures adorn the buildings. The more austere 15C façade faces the lake in the park.

▷ *Return to the D 7 and continue south to return to Évron.*

Les Bois des Vallons

36km/22.5mi. Allow about 1hr.

▷ *From Évron take the D 32 west. On the west side of Brée, turn right onto the D 557. On approaching St-Ouen-des-Vallons, turn right to the Château de la Roche-Pichemer.*

Château de la Roche-Pichemer

🕐*Open Jul–mid-Aug 2–6pm.*
Park near the moat, outside the gate.

The château consists of two main Renaissance wings built at right angles and covered with tall slate roofs. Massive square pavilions project from each corner, considerably enhancing the building, which is fronted by formal gardens.

▷ *From St-Ouen-des-Vallons take the D 129 and D 24 south via Montsûrs to La Chapelle-Rainsouin.*

La Chapelle-Rainsouin

A room off the church chancel contains a beautiful 16C polychrome stone **Entombment**★.

▷ *Take the D 20 NE. In Châtres-la-Forêt turn right onto the D 562. Continue on, and turn right again to the Château de Monteclerc.*

Château de Monteclerc

⊶*Closed to the public. Leave the car at the beginning of the avenue.*

This plain but elegant building, dating from the beginning of the 17C, stands at the far end of a vast courtyard. The drawbridge lodge has a rounded roof crowned by a lantern turret.

▷ *Return to Châtres-la-Forêt; turn right onto the D 20 to return to Évron.*

Ste-Suzanne★

In the 11C the viscounts of Beaumont built this peaceful village, nicknamed "pearl of the Maine", in a **picturesque setting**★ on a rocky promontory commanding the north bank of the Erve. It is one of the most important strongholds in the region and was the only one to successfully resist William the Conqueror.

SIGHTS
Tour d'orientation
Via rue du Grenier à Sel.
From the top of the tower you can see the old town nestled around its 11C keep, the new town beyond the ramparts, and the surrounding countryside.

Promenade de la Poterne
This 3km/2mi walk along the ramparts starts at the Tour du Guet (watchtower), and passes the castle and the Porte de Fer (Iron Gate). The second half of the walk, ending at the Porte du Guichet (Wicket Gate), provides distant views *(northeast)* of the Coëvrons Hills and *(north)* of Mont Rochard and the Butte de Montaigu, topped by St Michael's Chapel. Before you set off, pick up a leaflet from the tourist office for points of interest en route.

Parish church
Go inside to see the graceful 16C polychrome wood statue of Ste-Suzanne, and a 14C stone Virgin and Child statue.

▲▲ Musée de l'Auditoire
7 Grande-Rue. ○*Open Jul–Aug daily and May, Jun and Sept Sat–Sun 2.30–6.30pm.* ☞*€4 (children €2.50).* ℘*02 43 01 42 65.*
http://museeauditoire.jimdo.com.
Housed partly in a courthouse dating from the 17C and (as from 2012) also in an ancient mill house, this exhibition looks back on the medieval town of Ste-Suzanne.

▶ **Population:** 960.
◔ **Michelin Map:** 310: G-6.
▯ **Info:** 1 rue du Chenil. ℘02 43 01 43 60. www.ste-suzanne.fr.
◑ **Location:** Ste-Suzanne is 50km/31mi E of Le Mans, 32km/20mi W of Laval.
◉ **Don't Miss:** The view from the castle keep.
◷ **Timing:** Half a day.
▲▲ **Kids:** The Théatrales Pitchoun runs a summer programme for children.

Château de Ste-Suzanne
○*Open Jul–Aug daily 10am–7pm, May, Jun and Sept public hols and weekends 10am–1pm, 2–7pm; rest of the year daily 9.45am–12.30pm, 1.30–5.15pm.* ○*Closed 1 Jan, 25 Dec.* ☞*€4.* ℘*02 43 01 40 77.* *www.ciap.lamayenne.fr.*
The second floor of this handsome early 17C château is devoted to an architectural and regional heritage centre, and features a remarkable **timberwork roof** in the shape of an upturned ship's keel. There is a great **view**★ from the castle keep.

EXCURSIONS
La Ferté-Clairbois – domaine du Chevalier
▶ *2km/1.25mi south of Ste-Suzanne, towards Sablé.* ○*Open Jul–Aug daily. See website for details of shows.* ☞*€6–16.* ℘*02 43 01 42 15.* *www.ferteclairbois.com.*
This medieval recreation of a small castle is brought to life by costumed actors who re-enact chivalrous days of old, including medieval banquets, tournaments and horseriding spectacles.

Dolmen des Erves
▶ *3km/2mi on the D 143, Assé-le-Béranger road.*
This megalithic monument, now restored, dates from the 4th millennium BC.

DRIVING TOUR

LA FORÊT DE LA GRANDE-CHARNIE

26km/16mi. Allow 1hr30min.

▷ *Leave Ste-Suzanne northeast on the D 9. After 1km/1/2mi, turn right onto a minor road 700m/yd further on. Leave your car beside the houses.*

Point de vue du Tertre Gane

Cross a picnic area in the woods to get to a viewing platform strewn with boulders. From here there is a panorama of Ste-Suzanne and the surrounding plain.

▷ *Return to your car, go as far as "La Foussillère" retirement home and then turn right. After crossing the D 210, turn right taking the road up the hill.*

Signal de Viviers

The road ends at the edge of a steep wooded area with La Grande-Charnie forest ahead. The path to the left, takes you to you can reach a rock surmounted by a statue of Sacré-Cœur; through the gaps in the trees you can see the Coëvrons hills.

A long descent leads to Torcé-Viviers en Charnie. Turn left at the end of the hill, go through the village and turn left on to the D 210. After 5.5 km/3.5mi, take a right turn onto the D 156 and D 7.

Pontmain

Legend has it that here, on the border with Brittany, on 17 January 1871, during the Franco–Prussian War, the Virgin appeared to several of the village children, including Eugène and Joseph Barbedette, offering a message of hope. An armistice was declared 11 days later.

SIGHTS
Grange Barbedette

It was from this thatched barn that some of the village children, and then the other villagers, allegedly saw the Virgin in the sky above the house of Augustin Guidecoq on the far side of the square.

Basilique

The vast neo-Gothic basilica was built at the end of the 19C. The ten stained-glass windows in the chancel depict the Virgin's Apparition at Pontmain, at Lourdes, and at La Salette, as well as scenes from the life of Christ.

Chapelle & Musée des Missionaires Oblats

Behind the basilica is the Mission of the Oblate Fathers of Mary Immaculate. The interior of the chapel (built in 1953) is surprisingly attractive, illuminated by a golden light diffused by stained-glass windows. There is also a museum (Open Sun and public holidays 2.30–6pm. Other days on request. ℰ02 43 30 27 51).

▸ **Population:** 879.
◔ **Michelin Map:** 310: C–4.
▤ **Info:** 5 rue de la Grange. ℰ02 43 05 07 74.
▷ **Location:** Pontmain is 16km/10mi NE of Fougères, 45km/28mi NW of Mayenne, 6km/4mi SW of Landivy and 35km/22mi SW of Mortain.
◉ **Don't Miss:** The excursion to the lovely garden of la Pellerine.

EXCURSION
Jardin de la Pellerine★

▷ *21km/13mi S of Pontmain, on the N 12 between Fougères to the W and Ernée to the E. La Larderie, La Pellerine.* Open May–Oct Thu–Fri 10am–6.30pm, Sat–Sun and public holidays 2–6.30pm. €6. ℰ02 43 05 93 31.

Lovely gardens surround a 17C house:roses, shrubs, arbours and ponds with aquatic plants, including water lilies, on a 2ha/5-acre site.

Laval★

The first thing that strikes any visitor to Laval is the River Mayenne, which flows gently through the centre of town, under the river bridges and creating fords, as it has since the city was founded in the year 1000. Laval has a picturesque château, many venerable half-timbered houses, and has produced many distinguished citizens (see box, p348).

OLD TOWN★
Place de la Trémoille

The square is named after the last of the local lords, guillotined during the Revolution. On the east side stands the Renaissance façade of the 16C **Nouveau Château** built for the Count of Laval; it was enlarged in the 19C and now houses the law courts.

Vieux Château★

Pl. de La Trémoille. ◑Open Tue–Sat Jun–Sept 10am–12.30pm, 1.30–6pm; Oct–May 10am–12pm, 2–6pm, Sun 2–6pm all year. Unaccompanied visit ◉*1.* ●*Guided tours Tue–Sat 2–5pm, Sun 2–6pm (last departure 1hr before closing)* ◉*€2.* ✆*02 43 53 39 89. www.laval-tourisme.com.*

To the right of the railings in front of the law courts stands a handsome 17C porch, next to an early 16C half-timbered house. Through the porch is the courtyard of the Old Castle, enclosed by ramparts; from here there is a picturesque **view**★ of the old town. In its present state the bulk of the castle dates from the 13C and 15C; the windows and dormers in white tufa, carved with scrolls in the Italian style, were added in the 16C. The crypt and the keep (12C–13C) are the oldest parts.

Donjon

Originally separated from the courtyard by a moat, the keep was later incorporated between the two wings of the castle. Within the keep, the most interesting feature is the extraordinary **timber roof**★★, which was built c.1100 to an ingenious circular design. Great

beams, radiating from the centre like the spokes of a wheel, project beyond the walls (which are over 2m/6.6ft thick) to support the wooden defensive gallery that projects out to defend the gate and the base of the walls.

Musée d'Art naïf★

Within the Old Castle. ◑Same hours as for the Vieux Château. ◉*€1.*

The Museum of Naïve Painting, which can be visited separately from the castle and the keep, displays a number of canvases by painters from France and around the world. A reconstruction of the studio of Henri Rousseau, born locally (see below and box, p348) contains mementoes of the artist.

Rue des Orfèvres

The narrow street that runs south into Grande-Rue is lined with beautiful 16C overhanging houses and 18C mansions. At the T-junction stands the Renaissance house (1550) of the Master of the Royal Hunt (Grand Veneur).

Grande-Rue

This was the main street of the medieval city; it descends to the River Mayenne between rows of old houses, some half-timbered with projecting upper storeys, others in stone with Renaissance decoration.

▶ **Population:** 148,964.
◔ **Michelin Map:** 310: E-6.
▯ **Info:** 1 allée du Vieux-St-Louis. ✆02 43 49 46 46. www.laval-tourisme.com.
▷ **Location:** Laval is 32km/20mi S of Mayenne by D 162. Le Mans is 86km/53.4mi to the E on N 157.
◓ **Timing:** Allow about an hour to see the Old Town, not including visits to the château, museums and churches.
◉ **Don't Miss:** A walk along the docks to see the old *bateau-lavoir* St-Julien.

> *Turn right onto rue de Chapelle.*

The street climbs between medieval and Renaissance houses to a charming statue of St René in a niche *(right)* at the top.

> *Go straight ahead onto rue des Serruriers.*

South of the Beucheresse Gate are two slightly askew half-timbered houses.

Porte Beucheresse

In former days this 14C gate, then called Porte des Bûcherons, opened directly into the forest; its two round towers, topped with machicolations, were once part of the town walls. Henri Rousseau was born in the south tower, where his father worked as a tinsmith.

Cathédrale

The building has been altered many times but the nave and the transept crossing are covered with Angevin vaulting, characterised by curved rib vaulting in which the keystones are at different heights.

The walls are hung with Aubusson tapestries (early 17C) depicting the story of Judith and Holofernes in six panels. On the left pillar near the chancel is a beautiful triptych painted by the

Antwerp Mannerist School in the 16C; when closed it presents the Martyrdom of St John the Apostle, and when open, three scenes from the life of John the Baptist. In the north transept there is an imposing revolving door, which was carved in the 18C.

On leaving the cathedral, walk round the east end to admire the northeast door (facing the law courts), which is decorated with 17C terracotta statues.

Rue de la Trinité

Look out for the 16C house along here, adorned with statues of the Virgin and the Saints.

QUAYS★

The quays on the east bank provide the best overall **views**★ of Laval across the River Mayenne. From the **Pont Vieux**, a 13C humpback bridge, there is a more detailed view of the old town.

Intriguing relics of the past, **bateaux-lavoirs** (floating public wash houses), are moored along quai Paul Boudet. One of these, the **St-Julien** (○ *open Jul–Aug Tue–Sun 2–6pm*), has been restored.

Jardin de la Perrine★

These public gardens are home to many kinds of tall trees, ponds, waterfalls, lawns, a rose garden and flower

Famous Citizens

Laval is the birthplace of many exceptional men. **Ambroise Paré** (1517–90) was the first to practise the ligature of arteries during amputations and is deserving of his reputation as the father of surgery: yet he was modest about his success, "I dress their wounds, God cures them."

Henri Rousseau (1844–1910), whose nickname was Le Douanier (the Customs Officer), was originally a tax collector in Paris. He was the archetype of the modern naïve artist and was known for the meticulous approach which he brought to his paintings of lush jungles, wild beasts and exotic figures.

Alfred Jarry (1873–1907) was the inventor of pataphysics, the science of imaginary solutions, and the forerunner of the Surrealists. He created the grotesque satirical character of *Père Ubu, King of Poland*, when he was still in his teens. Jarry died destitute and largely unappreciated. Today, however, he is honoured as one of the creators of the Theatre of the Absurd.

Alain Gerbault (1893–1941) was a renowned tennis player, as well as a sailor. In 1923 he made the transatlantic crossing single-handed; he died in the Polynesian islands. His second boat, the *Fire-Crest II*, is exhibited in the Jardin de la Perrine.

Jean Cottereau (1757-1794), called Jean Chouan, led Royalist troops during the French Revolution. In 1793 the Royalists occupied Laval and beneath its walls defeated the Republican army of General Lechelle. The name **Chouan** was adopted from their rallying cry, the hoot of the tawny owl *(chat-huant)*.

beds. The views from the terraces are excellent.

Musée des Sciences

21 r. Douanier-Rousseau; ○*Open daily except public holidays 10am–noon, 2–6pm.* ○*Closed between exhibits;* ✎€2 *(1st Sun of month no charge).* ☏*02 43 49 47 81. www.ccsti-laval.org.* This Science and Culture Museum is housed in an imposing building. In addition to scientific subjects it also includes archaeological exhibits from local excavations. Don't miss the 19C astronomical clock in its own carved wooden case.

OTHER SIGHTS
Notre-Dame-d'Avesnières Basilica

▶ *1.5km/1mi S, via the quai d'Avesnières.* This ancient sanctuary dedicated to the Virgin Mary was made into a basilica in 1898. The Romanesque **east end**★ is best seen from the Pont d'Avesnières. The attractive Gothic-Renaissance spire is an identical copy, made in 1871, of the original, which was erected in 1538.

The fine Romanesque chancel consists of three storeys of arches and bays. The modern stained glass is by Max Ingrand.

Église St-Vénérand

The nave of the church is flanked by double aisles. The north front, facing the street, has a Flamboyant **door**★ decorated with an attractive 17C terracotta figure of the Virgin.

Tour Renaise

This 15C round machicolated tower was part of the old city walls.

Église Notre-Dame-des-Cordeliers★

Built between 1397 and 1407, this former Franciscan monastery chapel contains a remarkable set of seven 17C **altarpieces**★★. Six of them can be seen in the north aisle *(lighting is essential; token available from the tourist office);* they were carved out of tufa and marble by the local architect **Pierre Corbineau** (1600–78).

👥 Lactopôle André-Besnier★★

10 r. Adolphe-Beck. ⏰Open year-round Mon–Fri 9am–12pm, 2–6pm. Guided tours 10am, 2.30pm at weekends and public hols. ⓘ €10 (children €6.50). ♿ ☎02 43 59 51 90. www.lactopole.com.
Everything you ever wanted know about milk, cheese and other dairy products is answered in this exhibition, which claims to be the biggest of its kind in the world. Looking nostalgically at the past – it counts Marie Antoinette's milk churn among its 2,500 or so exhibits – it also deals with present-day issues and looks at future trends in this industry, which is of such importance to Normandy

Ancienne Église de Pritz

▶ 2km/1mi N. Leave Laval by allée de la Résistance, rue du Vieux-St-Louis and D 104. ⚠Closed to the public.
This simple ancient church stands on the right-hand side of the road in a garden in the hamlet of Pritz. It dates from about the year 1,000 and was altered and enlarged in the Romanesque period.

EXCURSIONS
Abbaye de Clermont

▶ 16km/10mi west on the D57; turn right at the Chapelle-du-Chêne, then take the D115. ♿ ⏰Open daily Mar–mid Sept 9am–6.30pm; rest of year 9.30am–4.30pm. ⓘ €4. ☎02 43 02 11 96.
The ruins of this once great house stand in open country watered by many streams. The abbey was founded in 1152, on lands gifted by the Count of Laval. It housed a thriving monastic community until the Revolution.
The square east end of the **church** comes into view before the dilapidated west front and the austere Romanesque porch with its three round-headed openings. South of the church is the **cloister garth**. The wooden cloister galleries have not survived, but the **lay brothers' range** (west) contains the cellar and the refectory.

Entrammes Gallo-Roman Baths

▶ 13km/8mi south of Laval via the N 162. 🚶Guided tours (1hr) daily Jul–Aug 10.30am–12.30pm, 2.30–6.30pm; May–Jun and 1 Sept– mid-Sept Sun and public hols only, 3–6pm ♿ ⓘ€3.50 ☎02 39 90 20 72 (out of season ☎02 43 49 46 46). www.laval-tourisme.com.
During restoration work inside the church in 1987, remains of the former town's **Gallo-Roman baths** were discovered in a remarkable state of preservation. These included Roman walls, up to 8.5m/28ft high, four bathrooms in a row, arcades and various religious finds including a sarcophagus. An audiovisual presentation also interprets the site. The town's claim to more recent historical fame is that, until 1959, the famous Port-Salut cheese was made here by Trappist monks, in the **Abbaye du Port-du-Salut** (1.6km/1mi west). The cheese is still sold today, under the label "Entrammes", available locally. Two **chapels** of the abbey are open to the public.

Parné-sur-Roc

▶ 14km/8.5mi south of Laval via the N 162, then the D 21.
The 11C parish church contains some interesting **mural paintings** (late 15C to early 16C). On the left mural is the silhouette of the resurrected Christ against a background of red stars and a Madonna Dolorosa; the right mural depicts the saints Cosmas and Damian, popular in the Middle Ages. These Greek twins were physicians, thought to have been martyred in the year 287.

ADDRESSES

🛏 STAY

LASSAY-LES-CHÂTEAUX

🛏 **La Ferme de la Prémoudière** – *St-Denis-de-Villenette, 11.5km/7mi north.* 𝄞*02 33 37 23 27. www.lapremoudiere.com. 5 rooms.* These attractively converted farm buildings provide the best of both worlds, combining B&B and self-catering. There is a kitchenette for guests' use, pre-prepared farm-fresh meals to buy, and a communal breakfast area. Rooms are basic but cheerful.

STE-SUZANNE

🛏–🛏🛏 **Hôtel Beauséjour** – *4–6, rue de la Libération.* 𝄞*02 43 01 40 41. www.hotelstesuzanne.com.* Set in an old building facing directly onto the street, this small hotel has fairly basic but comfortable rooms and a pleasant beamed dining room.

🛏🛏 **Relais du Gué de Selle** – *rte de Mayenne, Évron–Mézangers, 5km/3mi N.* 𝄞*02 43 91 20 00. www.relais-du-gue-de-selle.com. 24 rooms.* This restored farm has cosy pastel-coloured rooms, a lovely garden and a small swimming pool. Beneath a boat-shaped beamed roof, its formal dining room (🛏🛏–🛏🛏🛏) serves classic cuisine with a bistro menu at lunchtime.

LAVAL

🛏 **Camping Village Vacances Pêche** – *Villiers-Charlemagne, 20km/12.5mi S of Laval via N 162.* 𝄞*02 43 07 71 68. www.sudmayenne.com. Open Apr–Oct. 20 sites each 100sq m/120sq yd. Reservations advised.* Campers have their own bathroom and you can rent small chalets with individual terraces. Keen anglers will enjoy themselves here; the lake abounds in pike, pike-perch and carp.

🛏🛏 **Marin'Hotel** – *102 av. Robert-Buron.* 𝄞*02 43 53 09 63. www.marin-hotel.fr. 25 rooms.* This no-frills hotel is opposite the train station in a thoroughly modernised old building. Rooms are functional and well soundproofed from the street noise. The breakfast room has a nautical theme.

🛏🛏–🛏🛏🛏 **Best Western Hôtel de Paris** – *22 r. de la Paix.* 𝄞*02 43 53 76 20. www.hotel-laval.fr. 50 rooms.* Situated right in the town centre, close to the shopping area this hotel offers simple well soundproofed rooms with white roughcast walls and coloured wood furniture. Rates are significantly cheaper at weekends.

🛏🛏🛏🛏 **Chambre d'hôte Chateau Le Bas du Gast** – *6 r. de la Halle-aux-Toiles, across from the Salle Polyvalente.* 𝄞*02 43 49 22 79. www.chateaulebasdugast.fr. 4 rooms.* In the centre of Laval's old quarter, this 17C–18C château is surrounded by a beautiful garden featuring trimmed box hedges. The oak parquet flooring and period furniture in the vestibule set the scene and atmosphere as soon as you enter. The spacious guest rooms have been thoughtfully decorated.

MAYENNE

🛏–🛏🛏 **Campanile** – *Za De L'huilerie.* 𝄞*02 43 00 71 71. www.campanile-mayenne.fr. 38 rooms.* Cheap and cheerful good-value no-frills chain hotel with spotless rooms, in the city centre.

🛏🛏–🛏🛏🛏 **Hôtel la Tour des Anglais** – *13 bis, place Juhel.* 𝄞*02 43 04 34 56. http://latourdesanglais.com. 21 rooms.* This centrally located hotel compensates for its basic rooms with a breathtaking view of the river and town from its historic tower, parts of which date back over 1,000 years; once a fortress and a prison, it is now a lounge bar. Guests can also relax in the terraced gardens.

🛏🛏🛏 **Hôtel Beau Rivage** – *rte de Ste Baudelle, Moulay, 1.6km/1mi south.* 𝄞*02 43 00 49 13. www.restaurantbeaurivage.com.* The hotel occupies a former riverside dance hall in a lovely grassy spot, with a terrace shaded by a large horse chestnut tree. A veranda seating 80, with sliding windows, looks onto the river *(see below, EAT).* Reserve one of their new smartly refurbished rooms.

🍴 EAT

MAYENNE

🍴🍴 **Beau Rivage** – *rte de St-Baudelle, Moulay, 1.6km/1mi south.* 𝄞*02 43 00 49 13. www.restaurantbeaurivage.com. Closed Sun eve and Mon.* The River Mayenne flows just below the shaded terrace of this beautifully sited hotel restaurant. In cool weather you can relax in the spacious dining room with exposed timber work and watch meat and fish being grilled in the brick-built fireplace.

🍴🍴 **La Marjolaine** – *Le Bas-Mont, Moulay, 1.6km/1mi south.* 𝄞*02 43 00 48 42. www.lamarjolaine.fr. Closed early Jan, Feb school holidays, Mon lunch and Sun eve.* This splendid old stone house stands in its own grassy grounds with a swimming pool. In the evening, dine on refined modern cuisine, either inside the cosy dining room, or out on the terrace. There is a good selection of wines. At lunchtime, a bistro menu is served. 23 comfortable, spacious guest rooms (⊜⊜–⊜⊜⊜).

⊜⊜–⊜⊜⊜ **La Forge** – *Fontaine-Daniel, 5km/3 mi southwest.* ℰ*02 43 00 34 85. www.restaurantlaforge.fr. Closed third wk Aug–first wk Sept; Sun eve and Mon.* The old forge in the centre of this charming village has been transformed into a contemporary restaurant, serving inventive dishes focusing on textures, herbs and aromatic plants.

LAVAL

⊜⊜ **Le Johannesburg** – *5 r. de la Trinité, Old Laval, near the Cathedral.* ℰ*02 43 53 21 21. Closed last week Jul, 1st 2 weeks Aug.* Behind a 17C façade, formerly housing a Cistercian abbey, this building has been converted into a beautifully decorated pub tucked away in a deep cellar. One of the most pleasant spots in Laval for a beer, it specialises in stone-grilled steaks. Live music.

⊜⊜–⊜⊜⊜ **À La Bonne Auberge** – *170 r. de Bretagne.* ℰ*02 43 69 07 81. www.alabonneauberge.com. Closed last wk Feb, first three wks Aug.* The pastel-coloured decoration of the dining room gives this inn an intimate, muted atmosphere. The veranda adds light and an impression of space. Well-prepared cuisine at reasonable prices. Selection of comfortable rooms (⊜⊜–⊜⊜⊜).

⊜⊜–⊜⊜⊜ **L'Antiquaire** – *5 r. Béliers.* ℰ*02 43 53 66 76. www.restaurant-lantiquaire.com. Closed last wk Feb, last fortnight Jul–first wk Aug, Sat lunch, Sun evening and Wed.* This restaurant occupies the ground floor of an old Laval house in the old town. It has a cosy dining room, with turn-of-the-20C British décor in tones of red. Generous portions of traditional cuisine, showing flashes of modern creativity.

⊜⊜–⊜⊜⊜ **L'Édelweiss** – *99 av. R-Buron.* ℰ*02 43 53 1100. www.restaurant-edelweiss-laval.fr. Closed late Feb, last fortnight Jul–first fortnight Aug, Sun eve, Mon and holidays.* Next to the train station, this is a contemporary dining room in pastel tones, where you can enjoy traditional and modern cuisine from a wide range of menus in a friendly setting, without fuss.

⊜⊜–⊜⊜⊜ **La Table Ronde** – *Pl. de la Mairie, Changé, 4km/2.5mi N of Laval via the D 104.* ℰ*02 43 53 43 33. Closed 1 week in Feb, 3 weeks in Aug, Sun eve, Wed eve and Mon.* Opposite the château. Upstairs is a gastronomical restaurant with Louis XVI-style chairs and formally laid tables; downstairs is a bistro.

⊜⊜⊜ **Bistro de Paris** – *67 r. du Val de Mayenne.* ℰ*02 43 56 98 29. www.lebistro-de-paris.com. Closed Aug, Sat lunch, Sun eve, Mon.* In the heart of the historic centre, the locally renowned Bistro de Paris has a classic façade and elegant atmospheric Art Nouveau brasserie decor. Refined brasserie food is on the menu.

⊜⊜⊜ **Gerbe de Blé** – *83 r. Victor-Boissel.* ℰ*02 43 53 14 10. www.gerbedeble.com. Closed 1st fortnight Aug, Sat lunch.* This renowned family-run establishment is well worth a detour. Traditional dishes are made using only regional and seasonal ingredients. The relaxed dining room has contemporary décor in cream tones with pale beams. The elegant but cosy bedrooms (⊜⊜⊜) are ideal for a stopover after a feast here.

⭍ SHOPPING

LAVAL

Abbaye de la Coudre – *r. St-Benoît.* ℰ*02 43 02 85 85. www.abbaye-coudre.com. Closed Easter, 25 Dec.* Beneath exposed rafters illuminated by lightwells in the roof, the abbey shop offers all kinds of food and drink products made by monastic communities from near and far: jams and conserves, beer and wine, coffee from Cameroon, biscuits, Bonneval chocolate, honey, nougat and caramels. The speciality of the house is Trappist cheese aged in the abbey cellars.

CALENDAR OF EVENTS

LAVAL

Mayenne Nights – *mid-Jul–mid-Aug.* Shows and performances of music and theatre at three major sites: Ste-Suzanne, Jublains and Laval. ℰ*02 43 53 63 90. www.nuitsdelamayenne.com.*

Tucked into the bottom of the Cotentin Peninsula on its western side, lies the fabulous Bay of Mont-St-Michel which, along with the world-famous abbey dedicated to the Archangel Michael, was added to the list of UNESCO World Heritage Sites in 1979. Situated at the junction of the regions of Normandy and Brittany, there is a great diversity of landscape on offer, both maritime and urban, with headlands and plentiful viewpoints from which to enjoy the extensive vistas.

Highlights

1   The view from the **Rampart Walk at Granville** (p354)
2   Excursion to the **Îles Chausey** (p357)
3   Visit to **Mont-St-Michel** (p358)
4   Driving tour of **Mont-St-Michel Bay** (p364)
5   Visit to the **Abbaye de Hambye** (p372)

The Tides

The bay experiences the highest tides in Europe, which are the source of many local legends. The author Victor Hugo compared the speed of the tide with that of a galloping horse.

There is approximately 14m/46ft between high and low tide, and due to the aforementioned rapidity with which it covers the sand flats, it is no wonder that the pilgrims, known as "miquelots", crossing them named the Abbey "St Michael in peril on the sea". Even today it is very dangerous to try to reach the abbey from the nearby coast and it is essential to approach it by the designated route only.

However, there are beneficial effects of the tides. The creation of polders led to the establishing of salt-marsh meadows, locally known as "herbus", which are well suited to grazing the 7,000 sheep of the area. The result is salt-flavoured meat or "agneau de pre-salé" which is a speciality of the region and can be found in local restaurants whose trade is derived in large part from visitors to Mont-St-Michel and the bay.

History

Much of the history of the bay is bound up with the abbey, which dates from the early medieval period, and the pilgrimages that have taken place over the years. Once located on a small rocky island, the area between the mainland and the island became silted up and engineering works have been carried out to reverse this process. A new hydraulic dam will use the waters of the River Couesnon to flush away the silt and restore island status to Mont-St-Michel. Instead of visitors crossing the causeway, which helped to create

Sailing around the Îles Chausey

G.Targat/MICHELIN

GRANVILLE AND THE BAY OF MONT-ST-MICHEL

LE MONT-ST-MICHEL ★★★	Highly recommended
Abb⁰ de Hambye ★★	Recommended
Granville ★	Interesting
Carolles	Worth a visit
🚩	Driving tour with departure point

Iles Chausey

Grande Île

Pointe du Roc

Granville

St-Pair-s-Mer

Jullouville

Carolles

Edenville

Pignon Butor

Cabane Vauban

St-Jean-le-Thomas

Bec d'Andaine

Genêts

Baie du Mont-St-Michel

LE MONT-ST-MICHEL

Beauvoir

Courtils

Ossuaire allemand

Pontorson

Avranches

Abb⁰ de la Lucerne

Champrépus

Villedieu-les-Poêles

Abb⁰ de Hambye

Mont Robin

Sienne

CALVADOS

MANCHE

Sée

Sélune

Ducey

La Roche-qui-Boit

Vezins

St-Hilaire-du-Harcouët

St-James

Cimetière américain de Bretagne

V⁰ du Beuvron

Couesnon

CAEN

COUTANCES

RENNES

RENNES

FOUGÈRES

DOMFRONT

the silt build up, they will now cross an elevated bridge by shuttle, thus allowing the water to flow naturally beneath. The main towns of the area, Avranches at the head of the bay and Granville at its eastern extremity, both have interesting histories. Avranches was where Henry II made his public penance for the murder of Thomas Becket. In more recent times it was from here that General Patton launched the attack that was to cripple the German Army and allow the Americans to advance.

Today

The area is primarily agricultural, with sheep farming, cereal production, fishing and shellfish farming being the main industries. The bay acts as a nursery for flat fish such as plaice and sole and is one of the largest producers of shellfish in France, with about 10,000 tonnes of mussels and 3,000 tonnes of oysters produced here every year. Of course, tourism has become vitally important to the region and the abbey attracts more than 3 million visitors per year.

Granville★

This lively seaside resort, set on a rocky promontory, is also a busy port with an active fishing fleet and a marina. Granville is also the departure point for ferries to the Chausey and Channel Islands.

A BIT OF HISTORY

In the 15C, the English fortified the rocky promontory as a base from which to attack Mont-St-Michel, then occupied by the Normans. The town was recaptured permanently by the knights of Mont-St-Michel in 1442. Prosperity came with deep-sea fishing in the 18C, and Granville flourished with the rising popularity of sea bathing in the 19C.

WALKING TOURS

UPPER TOWN

Allow 2hrs.

The Main Gate (Grand Porte) with its drawbridge remains the principal entrance to the fortified upper part of town, which holds all Granville's military and religious past within its ramparts.

Église Notre-Dame

pl. du Parvis, Upper Town.

The oldest parts of this austere granite church go back to the 15C. The nave and the west front were erected in the 17C and 18C. The 14C statue, in the north chapel, of Our Lady of Cape Lihou is greatly venerated locally.

Pointe du Roc

This is an exceptional **site**★. The point which marks the northern limit of Mont-

---

- ▶ **Population:** 13,087
- **Michelin Map:** 303: C-6.
- **Info:** 4 cours Jonville. ℰ02 33 91 30 03. www.ville-granville.fr.
- **Location:** As the crow flies, Granville is 150km/93mi from Paris; 106km/65.8mi from Cherbourg; 109km/67.7mi from Caen; 50km/31mi from Mont-St-Michel.
- **Don't Miss:** A look at haute couture in the Villa Dior.
- **Timing:** Try to fit in a day trip to the Îles Chausey.
- **Kids:** There is an aquarium children will enjoy.

St-Michel Bay is linked to the mainland only by a narrow rocky isthmus. In the 15C the English dug a trench, known as Tranchée aux Anglais, as part of their fortifications.

The walk (the path starts from the harbour) to the lighthouse offers a fine view of the sea and the rocks.

Roc des Harmonies – Aquarium

Enter from 1 bld Vaufleury. Open Apr–Sept daily 10am–7pm; Oct–Mar 10am–12.30pm, 2–6.30pm (last entry 1hr before closing). Closed Mon in Mar. €8.50. ℰ02 33 50 19 83. www.aquarium-du-roc.com.

The **tanks** contain fish from local waters – note the sea perch with its powerful jaws – as well as exotic and freshwater species.

RAMPART WALK★

Park on the parvis of Notre-Dame Church.

Go through the Grand'Porte and over the drawbridge. Turn right onto rue Lecarpentier to follow the south rampart to place de l'Isthme.

*The **view**★ from the square extends, on a clear day, to the coast of Brittany.*

On the Water

Granville is famous for its traditional fishing vessels, such as *la bisquine*, a sailing ship that challenged those of Cancale during fierce regattas as early as the 1850s. Today, cruises are offered aboard some of these, superbly restored by ardent craftsmen.

WHERE TO STAY	
Bains (Hôtel des)	①
Mercure Le Grand Large	③

WHERE TO EAT	
Échauguette (Crêperie Grill l')	①
Terra Nova (Le)	④

◐ *Continue along the inside of the ramparts by rue du Nord. The view is spectacular in stormy weather. The Chausey Islands lie to the northwest. Turn left onto rue des Plâtriers to reach rue St-Jean, then turn right.*

Note, at no 7 rue St-Jean, an old house with a ground-floor shop and then, at no 3, a house dating from 1612.

Musée du Vieux Granville
In the fortified gatehouse, Grand'Porte. ⏱Open Apr–Sept Wed–Mon 10am– noon, 2–6pm (6.30pm Jul–Aug); Oct– Mar, Wed and Sat–Sun, 2–6pm (last entry 30min before closing). ⏹Closed 1 May, 1 Nov and Jan. ⬤€2.70 (€1.70 low season). ✆02 33 50 44 10. www.ville-granville.fr.

On the first floor is a collection of Norman costumes and headdresses as well as household furnishings, notably the **toiles de Hambaye**, pieces of canvas or gunny sacks painted in stylised decoration, and used as bed curtains. On the second floor are exhibitions about the sea.

The Carnival at Granville

This long-standing tradition was originated by local fishermen. Before leaving for long fishing expeditions in Newfoundland, cod fishermen would go out to spend their money in the streets of the city, dressing up in various costumes for the occasion. Today the Carnival takes place during Shrove Tuesday celebrations (the day before the beginning of Lent); it lasts for four days and includes a funfair with a procession of floats, an orchestra and majorettes. On the last day the residents, dressed up and masked, pay a visit to their friends; a Carnival effigy is burned on the beach, marking the end of festivities.

Musée Richard-Anacréon

pl. de l'Isthme. Open Feb–May and Oct–Dec, Tue–Sun 2–6pm; Jun–Sept, Tue–Sun, 11am–6pm. Closed 1 and 8 May, Mon and when exhibits are being changed. €3. 02 33 51 02 94.
This museum of modern art presents a permanent collection of works by major 20C artists including Derain, Utrillo, Signac and Van Dongen, as well as temporary exhibits. A yearly exhibit of rare books draws bibliophiles.

LOWER TOWN
La Plage

The narrow beach at the foot of shale cliffs is overlooked by the Plat-Gousset breakwater promenade.

Jardin public Christian-Dior et Villa des Rhumbs

Garden open daily 9am–9pm (5pm in low season). No charge. Museum open mid-May–mid-Sept daily 10am–6.30pm and 22 Oct–26 Feb 2–5.30. €6. 02 33 61 48 21.
This public garden and museum are located in the childhood home of the famous couturier. From the upper terrace you look down on the Granville promontory, north towards Regnéville and out to the Chausey Islands. The cliff path passes the cemetery to reach the great expanse of Donville Beach. Low tide reveals numerous stakes used for growing mussels.

EXCURSION
Îles Chausey
See Îles Chausey.

St-Pair-sur-Mer

St-Pair has a breakwater promenade protecting a beach of golden sand, which is perfect for children. The **church** is said to have been founded in the 6C by two local Evangelists, St-Pair and St-Scubilien. The building consists of the Romanesque belfry and the bay beneath, the 14C chancel and a 19C neo-Gothic nave and transepts.

Jullouville

8.5km/5mi. Leave Granville by the D 911.

This resort, which is really an extension of St-Pair-sur-Mer, is famous for its fine sandy guarded beach, which is much appreciated by families. In summer it is possible to catamaran, kayak or wind-surf, while in low season there is sand yachting. Two clubs for children complete this range of activities.
There is a pleasant walk along the sea front which is lined with 19C villas, palms and mimosas. When you reach the Pignon Butor the view extends north as far as the Pointe du Roc at Granville. There is also a small beach at Edenville that extends towards Carolles.

Abbaye de La Lucerne

12km/7.5 mi SE of Granville via D 973, then D 580 until just before St-Pierre-Langers. It is on the road between Sartilly and St-Léger-en-Avranchin.

The sizeable restored ruins of Lucerne Abbey stand in a fine parkland setting in the Thar Valley. Founded in 1143, construction started in 1164.

Abbey Church

♿🕐 *Open mid-Mar–Sept Mon–Sat 10am–noon, 2–6.30pm, Sun 2–6.30pm; mid-Oct–mid-Nov and Christmas school holidays Mon–Sat 10am–noon, 2–5pm, Sun 2–5pm.* 🕐 *Closed during religious holidays.* 📢 *Guided tours available afternoons Jul–Aug daily, Sept Sat–Sun.* ♒€5. 📞*02 33 48 83 56. www.abbaye-lucerne.fr.*

The doorway in the 12C façade is Romanesque. The transept crossing (restored) supports a late-12C Gothic square **belltower**★. The south transept houses a fine 18C **organ**★ with 33 stops.

Cloisters and Conventual Buildings

The arcades of the northwest corner and the entrance to the chapter house still stand. In the southwest corner, is a 12C *lavatorium,* with four Romanesque arcades. Note the old tithe barn and the dovecote.

Îles Chausey★

According to legend, the Chausey Islands were part of the ancient Scissy Forest submerged by the sea in 709. The islands are a popular day excursion *(1hr by boat)* and are uninhabited except for Grande Île, which has a population of up to 400 in summer, and only a dozen in winter.

👆 **Michelin Map:** 303: B-6.
🔷 **Location:** The islands are 17km/10.5mi from Granville.
👁 **Don't Miss:** The remarkable spectacle of the high tide.
🕐 **Timing:** The excursion takes a day; you can spend the night.

VISIT

La Grande Île★

The Island (2km/1mi long by 700m/2,297ft at its widest point) is the largest, and the only one accessible to visitors. Spring flowers are especially lovely. The **lighthouse** stands 37m/121.4ft above the sea.

Fort

The fort was built between 1860 and 1866 against a British attack that never came. It now serves as a shelter for local fishermen.

🔷 *Go round the fort. The path goes past an old cemetery with four tombs.*

Vieux Fort

The Old Fort was rebuilt in 1923. Below it, on the beach at Plage de Port Homard, the enormous tidal range is 14m/46ft.

The Moines and the Éléphant

These granite rocks, which can be reached at low tide, are thought to resemble monks and an elephant.
More than 200 rocks, known locally as *grunes,* are revealed when the tide is out. Sailors should get some advice and double-check charts before setting out on an adventure.

Mont-St-Michel★★★

Why is the world fascinated by Mont-St-Michel? No doubt it is not just the beauty of the architecture and the length of the mount's history. Perhaps it is the sense of mystery in the movement of the tides that separate this rocky outcrop from the mainland, or the play of twilight on the water and walls, or the cry of gulls gliding above the salty grass marsh. It is impossible to take the measure of Mont-St-Michel without including its unique natural setting: the rock and the bay of this UNESCO World Heritage Site are truly one.

A BIT OF HISTORY

An amazing achievement – The abbey dates back to the early 8C when the Archangel Michael appeared to Aubert, Bishop of Avranches. He founded an oratory on the island, then known as Mount Tombe. In the Carolingian era (8C–10C) the oratory was replaced by an abbey. From then until the 16C a series of increasingly splendid buildings, in the Romanesque and then the Gothic style, succeeded one another on this mount dedicated to the Archangel Michael. The abbey was remarkably well fortified and never fell to the enemy.

The construction is an amazing achievement. The blocks of granite were transported from the Chausey Islands and Brittany, then hoisted up to the foot of the building. The crest of the hill was very narrow, so the foundations had to be built up from the lower slopes.

Pilgrimages – Pilgrims flocked to the mount, even during periods of attrition like the Hundred Years' War. The English, who had possession of the area, granted safe conduct to the faithful in return for payment. People of all sorts made the journey: nobles, rich citizens and beggars who lived on alms and were granted free accommodation by the monks. Hotels and souvenir shops flourished. The pilgrims bought med-

▶ **Population:** 41

Michelin Map: 303: C-8.

Info: Corps de garde des Bourgeois. ✆02 33 60 14 30. www.ot-montsaint michel.com, www.abbaye-saintmichel.com.

Location: Mont-St-Michel is at the northern limit of D 976, which connects with D 175 at Pontorson, 10km/6mi S, which in turn leads to Avranches (21km/13mi NE) via N 175 and major national arteries.

Parking: Car parks (€4 per day per vehicle) stretch over 2km/1mi of dykes. Arrive early in the morning to get a space closer to the mount, or park as near as you can along the access road if just there to admire the Mount or take photos. During very high tides, car parks are inundated and you must park along the access road. Attendants are there to help.

Don't Miss: Try to catch the miraculous spectacle of sunset over the bay from the steps of the church.

Timing: In the summer, night visits are organised, to musical accompaniment (Mon–Sat 7–11.30pm; last entry at 10.30pm). ✆02 33 89 80 00.

Kids: The Maison de la Baie offers guided tours of the bay covering a large distance (check beforehand). The nature centre at Relais de Vains-St-Léonard explains the fauna and flora of the bay (see Relais des Genêts p366). Alligator Bay (see p367) displays alligators, crocodiles, turtles, etc.

View towards Mont-St-Michel

© Philippe Devanne/Fotolia.com

als bearing the effigy of St Michael and lead amulets which they filled with sand from the beach. In periods of widespread disaster the pilgrimage incited such excesses of fervour that the church authorities were obliged to intervene. Of the many thousands of people crossing the bay, some drowned, others perished in the quicksands. The deaths led to the lengthening of the prayer to St Michael in Peril from the Sea.

Decline – The abbey came to be held *in commendam* (by lay abbots who received the revenue without exercising the duties) and discipline among the monks grew lax. In the 17C the Maurists, monks from St Maur, were made responsible for reforming the monastery, but they only made some disappointing architectural changes and tinkered with the stonework. Further dilapidation ensued when the abbey became a prison.

From being the local Bastille before the Revolution, it was converted afterwards into a national prison for political prisoners, who included Barbès, Blanqui and Raspail. In 1874 the abbey and the ramparts passed into the care of the Historic Monuments Department (Service des Monuments Historiques). Since 1966 a few monks have again been in residence conducting the services in the abbey church.

THE ABBEY★★★

⏰*Open daily 2 May–Aug 9am–7pm (last admission 1hr before closing); Sept–Apr 9.30am–6pm.* 💬*Guided tours (1hr).* ⏰*Closed 1 Jan, 1 May, 25 Dec.* ⬚*€8.50 (under 18 years no charge); no charge to attend Mass, during which visits are not allowed: Tue–Sun noon–12.15pm.* ✆*02 33 89 80 00. www.monum.fr.*

The tour, which is given in French and English plus other languages during the high season, passes through a maze of corridors and stairs floor by floor, not from building to building or period by period.

Outer Defences of the Abbey

A flight of steps, the Grand Degré, once cut off by a swing door, leads up to the abbey. At the top on the right is the entrance to the gardens; more steps lead up to the ramparts.

Through the arch of an old door is a fortified courtyard overlooked by the fort, which consists of two tall towers linked by machicolations. Even this military structure shows the builder's artistic sense: the wall is attractively constructed of alternate courses of pink and grey granite. Beneath a flattened barrel vault a steep and ill-lit staircase, the Escalier du Gouffre (Abyss Steps), leads down to the beautiful door that opens into the guard room, also called the Porterie.

Salle des Gardes or Porterie

This gatehouse was the focal point of the abbey. Poor pilgrims passed through it on their way from the Merveille Court to the Almonry.

Abbey Steps

An impressive flight of 90 steps rises between the abbatial buildings *(left)* and the abbey church *(right)*; it is spanned by a fortified bridge (15C).

The stairs stop outside the south door of the church on a terrace called the Saut Gautier **(Gautier Leap)**, after a prisoner who is supposed to have hurled himself over the edge. The tour starts here.

West Platform

This spacious terrace, which was created by the demolition of the last three bays of the church, provides an extensive **view**★ of the Bay of Mont-St-Michel.

Church★★

The exterior of the church, particularly the east end, with its buttresses, flying buttresses, bell turrets and balustrades, is a masterpiece of light and graceful architecture. The interior reveals the marked contrast between the severe, sombre Romanesque nave and the elegant, luminous Gothic chancel.

La Merveille★★★

The name, which means the Marvel, applies to the superb Gothic buildings on the north face of the mount. The eastern block, the first to be built between 1211 and 1218, comprises, from top to bottom, the refectory, the Guests' Hall and the Almonry; the western block, built between 1218 and 1228, consists of the cloisters, the Knights' Hall and the cellar.

Stages of Construction

Romanesque Abbey

© Florian Monheim/age fotostock

La Merveille

11C–12C: Between 1017 and 1144 a church was built on the top of the mount. The previous Carolingian building was incorporated as a crypt – Notre-Dame-sous-Terre (Our Lady Underground) – to support the platform on which the last three bays of the Romanesque nave were built. Other crypts were constructed to support the transepts and the chancel, which projected beyond the natural rock. The convent buildings were constructed on the west face and on either side of the nave. The entrance to the abbey faced west.

Gothic Abbey

13C–16C: This period saw the construction of:

- ♦ The magnificent Merveille buildings (1211–28) on the north side, used by the monks and pilgrims and for receiving important guests.
- ♦ The abbatial buildings (13C–15C) on the south side, comprising the administrative offices, the abbot's lodging and the garrison's quarters.
- ♦ The main gatehouse and the outer defences (14C) on the east side, protecting the entrance, which was moved to this side of the mount.
- ♦ The chancel of the Romanesque church had collapsed and was rebuilt in the Flamboyant Gothic style (1446–1521) above a new crypt.

Alterations

18C–19C: In 1780 the last three bays of the nave and the Romanesque façade were demolished. The present belltower (1897) is surmounted by a beautiful spire that rises to 157m/515ft and terminates in a statue of St Michael (1879) by Emmanuel Frémiet. The 4.5m/15ft tall archangel, in position for over 100 years, was recently restored after lightning struck off St Michael's sword.

Restoring the Bay

A project to restore the Bay of St-Michel is in full swing. The entire project is extremely complex, but its ultimate aim is to reverse the silting-up that has gone on for years, due to human intervention and the construction of the 1877 causeway, among other factors. In the first stage, begun in 2006, a dam is being constructed on the River Couesnon to restrain the influx of sand. Finally, the current causeway will be dismantled and replaced by another 1000m causeway plus 750m bridge extension, planned for 2014, which will allow tidal water to swirl freely around the bay. Tourist access to the mount will not be interrupted during these major works. For more information, you can consult the website www.projetmontsaintmichel.fr or visit the new **tourist information center** in the new car park (○*Open Jul–Aug daily 10am–7pm, Apr–Jun and Sept daily 10am–12.30pm, 2–6pm, Oct–mid-Nov and 2nd week Feb–Mar Wed–Sun 2–8pm*).

From May 2012, car parks will be located further inland and shuttle buses will ferry tourists to and from the Mount while works continue.

MONT-ST-MICHEL

0   50 m

FONTAINE ST-AUBERT

CHAPELLE ST-AUBERT

Jardins de l'abbaye

Tour du Nord

Échauguette du Nord

Bastillon de la Tour Boucle

Tour Claudine

Grand degré extérieur

LA-MERVEILLE

Réfectoire

Châtelet

Logis Tiphaine

Tour Cholet/ Demi-Lune

CLOÎTRE

Église abbatiale

Église paroissiale St-Pierre

Tour Basse

Terrasse de l'Ouest

Musée historique

Bâtiments abbatiaux

Chemin de ronde

Grande-Rue

Remparts

Terrasse du Saut Gautier

Grand degré intérieur

Musée de la Mer et de l'Écologie

TOUR GABRIEL

Tour de la Liberté

TOUR DES FANILS

Porte du Roi

Maison de l'Arcade

Corps de garde des Bourgeois

Tour du Roi

Porte de l'Avancée

WHERE TO STAY	WHERE TO EAT	
St-Pierre (Auberge)............③	Mère Poulard (La)................②	Sirène (La)............................④

From the outside the buildings look like a fortress, although their religious connections are indicated by the simple nobility of the design. The interior is a perfect example of the evolution of the Gothic style, from an almost Romanesque simplicity in the lower halls, through the elegance of the Guests' Hall, the majesty of the Knights' Hall and the mysterious luminosity of the Refectory, to the cloisters, which are a masterpiece of delicacy and line.

Cloisters★★★

The cloisters seem to be suspended between the sea and the sky. The gallery arcades display heavily undercut sculpture of foliage ornamented with the occasional animal or human figure (particularly human heads); there are also a few religious symbols. The double row of arches rests on delightfully slim single columns arranged in quincunx to enhance the impression of lightness. The different colours of the various materials

add to the overall charm. The *lavatorium* (washroom) on the right of the entrance recalls the ceremonial washing of the feet every Thursday.

Refectory★★

The effect is mysterious; the chamber is full of light, although it appears to have only two windows in the end wall.

To admit so much light without weakening the solid side walls that support the wooden roof and are lined with a row of slim niches, the architect introduced a very narrow aperture high up in each recess. The vaulted ceiling is panelled with wood and the acoustics are excellent.

Old Romanesque Abbey

The rib vaulting marks the transition from Romanesque to Gothic. The tour includes the Monks' Walk and part of the dormitory.

Great Wheel

The wheel belongs to the period when the abbey was used as a prison. It was used to haul provisions and was operated by five or six men turning the wheel from within as if on a treadmill.

Crypts

The transepts and chancel of the church are supported by three undercrofts or crypts; the most moving is **Notre-Dame-sous-Terre** *(accessible only during guided tours)*: the Carolingian structure that stands where St Aubert officiated, is a simple rectangle (8x9m/26.9x29.5ft), divided into two small naves by a couple of arches resting on a central pillar. The place is awe-inspiring because of the complete silence that prevails and because of the memory of events which took place here more than 1,000 years ago. The most impressive is the **Crypte des Gros Piliers**★ (Great Pillared Crypt), which has ten pillars (5m/16.4ft in circumference) made of granite from the Chausey Islands.

Guests' Hall★

Here the abbot received royalty (Louis IX, Louis XI, François I) and other important visitors. The hall (35m/114.8ft long) has a Gothic ceiling supported on a central row of slim columns; the effect is graceful and elegant. At one time it was divided down the middle by a huge curtain of tapestries; on one side was the kitchen quarters (two chimneys) and on the other the great dining hall (one chimney).

Knights' Hall★

The name of this hall may refer to the military order of St Michael, which was founded in 1469 by Louis XI with the abbey as its seat.

The hall is vast and majestic (26x18m/85.3x59ft) and divided into four sections by three rows of stout columns.

It was the monks' workroom or *scriptorium* where they illuminated manuscripts, and read and studied religious or secular texts, and for this reason it was heated by two great fireplaces. The almonry and cellar occupy the rooms on the lower floor.

Cellar

This was the storeroom; it was divided into three by two rows of square pillars supporting the groined vaulting.

Almonry

This is a Gothic room with a Romanesque vault supported on a row of columns.

Abbey Gardens★

🕐*Closed in winter and in bad weather.*
A pleasant place for a stroll with a view of the west side of the mount and St Aubert's Chapel.

Cloisters

©Jameson Weston/iStockphoto.com

THE VILLAGE
⊙ The cobbled streets are uneven and steep here, and the abbey is a labyrinth of corridors and cloisters. Wear the most comfortable shoes you own.

Outer Defences
The outer gate opens into the first fortified courtyard. On the left stands the Citizens' Guard room (16C) occupied by the tourist office; on the right are the Michelettes, English mortars captured in a sortie during the Hundred Years' War.

A second gate leads into a second courtyard. The third gate (15C), complete with machicolations and portcullis, is called the King's Gate because it was the lodging of the token contingent maintained by the king to assert his rights; this gate opens onto the Grande-Rue where the abbot's soldiers lodged in the fine arcaded house *(right)*.

Grande-Rue★
This picturesque narrow street climbs steeply between old (15C–16C) houses and ends in a flight of steps. In summer it is crowded with stalls of souvenir merchants just as in the Middle Ages.

Ramparts★★
These are 13C–15C. The sentry walk offers fine views of the bay; from the North Tower the Tombelaine Rock, which Philippe Auguste had fortified, is clearly visible.

👥 Musée de la Mer et de l'Écologie
⊙ Open all year 9am–6pm. ◉ €9 (children €4.50). *☏ 02 33 60 85 12.*
Films and an audio-guided tour explain the environment of the mount, including the tides, the dangers in the bay and the silting-up process. There are also 150 models of old boats.

👥 Musée historique
⊙ Same hours and conditions as for the Musée de la Mer. *☏ 02 33 60 07 01.*
This historical museum retraces the history of the Mount back 1,000 years, using a sound and light show and with glass cases of old objects and weapons. The tour ends in the dungeons.

Église paroissiale St-Pierre
The 11C parish church has been much altered. The apse spans a narrow street. The church contains a crucifix and other furnishings from the abbey; the chapel in the south aisle houses a statue of St Michael covered in silver; in the chapel to the right of the altar there is a 15C statue of the Virgin and Child and another of St Anne and the Virgin as a child.

Logis Tiphaine
⊙ Same hours and conditions as for the Musée de la Mer. *☏ 02 33 60 23 34.*
When the 14C warrior Bertrand du Guesclin was captain of the Mount, he had this house built (1365) for his wife Tiphaine Raguenel, an attractive and educated woman from Dinan, while he went off to the wars in Spain. The house was heavily restored in the 19C.

🚗 DRIVING TOURS

Mont-St-Michel Bay★★

▷ About 100km/62mi of coastline border the bay.

The islands, cliffs, beaches and dunes form a series of ecosystems that are home to many species of flora and fauna. Travelling along the coast, you will be rewarded by stunning views of Mont-St-Michel, and you can enjoy walks along pleasant paths rambling between the polders and grassy fields.

Tall Tales and Natural Phenomena
Pilgrims liked to tell frightening tales of the perils of Mont-St-Michel, but the natural phenomena of the site are now well understood. What used to be called quicksand is really the effect of swathes of firm sand sitting on top of pockets of more liquid sand.

The fearsome fog that occasionally envelops the whole bay with such speed can now be predicted by weather forecasters, and there is no

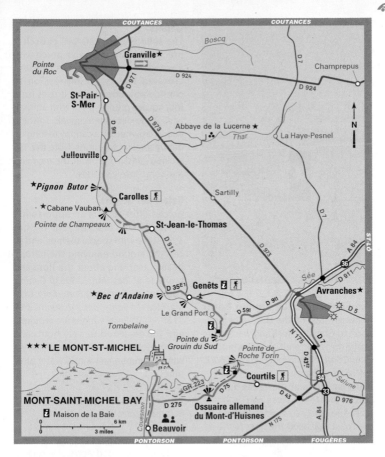

longer a need to ring the church bell to warn of its imminence. And the tide racing in faster than a galloping horse? Although there are specific points where the action of the spring tide combines with geological features to create a movement of water at a speed of up to 25–30kph/15.5–18.6mph, the average rate of speed of the incoming tide is 3.7kph/2.3mph – about the speed of a person walking.

From Granville to Mont-St-Michel
40km/25mi. Allow 2hr30min.

Between Granville and Carolles, there is a wide open view of the bay.

St-Pair-sur-Mer
See Granville.

Jullouville
The town is renowned for its fine sand beach. A pleasant walk leads along the seafront, passing 19C houses scattered among pine trees. The view extends from Pignon Butor to the Point du Roc.

Carolles
The village is set on the last headland before the sandy expanse of Mont-St-Michel Bay. As you drive between Carolles and St-Jean-le-Thomas, there is a splendid **view** ★★ of the bay. Don't hesitate to stop the car to enjoy it.
In the vicinity there are also several attractive walks with fine views.
The **Vallée des Peintres** (Artists' Valley) is an attractive spot, green and rock-strewn (Car park at Carolles-Plage, N of Carolles).

Vauban Hut near Carolle

© Philippe Bosseboeuf/Fotolia.com

The **view**★ from **Le Pignon Butor** *(viewing table)* on the clifftop extends north to Granville Rock and west to the Pointe du Grouin and Cancale in Brittany *(1km/0.6mi – 1hr on foot there and back, NW of the village).*

The path through the **Vallée du Lude** crosses an area of gorse and broom to reach the lonely cove, Port du Lude, on the coast. *Follow the signs to the car park, 1hr on foot there and back.*

▷ *South of Carolles on D 911 beyond the small bridge turn right; park at the end of the road; take the downhill path (left) which then climbs (right) towards the cliff.*

The **view**★ from the Vauban Hut, a stone building standing on a rocky mound, includes Mont-St-Michel in the middle of the bay.

St-Jean-le-Thomas

This seaside resort is very busy in the summer months.

▷ *On entering Genêts turn right.*

Bec d'Andaine★

There is a good **view** of Mont-St-Michel from this beach backed by dunes.

Genêts

The solid granite 12C–14C **church** is preceded by an attractive porch with a wooden roof. Inside, the transept crossing leaves an impression of considerable strength, as it rises from four square granite piers with animal- and foliage-decorated capitals. The high altar is crowned by a canopy resting on gently swelling columns. Note the 13C stained-glass window at the east end and some lovely statues.

Relais des Genêts

Guides offer visitors an opportunity to join walking tours through the bay area, some with special themes, and all centred around enjoying the natural beauty, learning about the flora and fauna *(4 pl. des Halles, 50530 Genêts; ⊙Open Apr–Sept daily 9am–6pm; Oct–Mar Mon–Fri 9am–1pm, 2–5.30pm. ℘02 33 89 64 00).* Reservations are required, and you are asked to wear boots and warm clothing in winter, and carry a wind-breaker, a snack and water at all times.

▷ *On leaving Genêts turn right before the calvary.*

The coastal road goes through Le Grand Port and offers good views, at very close quarters, of Mont-St-Michel, especially from the **Pointe du Grouin du Sud** (Grouin du Sud Point). The famous salt-marshes can also be seen.

Maison de la Baie-Relais de Vains-St-Léonard (Bay Centre)

Relais de Vains Saint-Léonard, rte du Grouin du Sud, 50300 Vains. ⊙Open Jul–Aug 10am–7pm; Apr–Jun and school holidays 2–6pm; Sept 10am–6pm. Guided tours (1hr30min). ⊙Closed Christmas holidays. ⊛€4.20 (7–15 years €1.75). ℘02 33 89 06 06. http://manche.fr/patrimoine.

Before undertaking a walking tour of the bay, lead your children through this multimedia exhibition to introduce them to the flora and fauna they will encounter.

Take D 591 and D 911 to Avranches.

Avranches★
See Avranches.

At Bas-Courtils, turn left onto D 75; after 2km/1mi turn right onto D 107.

Ossuaire Allemand du Mont-d'Huisnes
This circular construction with 68 compartments, built in 1963, contains the remains of 11,887 German soldiers who fell in France. From the belvedere there is a good view of Mont-St-Michel.

Continue along D 275.

The coastal road skirts the salt-marshes where flocks of sheep are put out to graze on the special grass. The lambs (*agneau de pre-salé*) are prized for their succulent tender meat. Again there are fine views of Mont-St-Michel.

Alligator Bay
Located at the entrance to Beauvoir, on the edge of D 976. 62 rte Mont-St-Michel. Open Apr–Sept daily 10am–7pm; Feb–Mar and Oct–Nov daily 2–6pm; Dec–Jan Sat–Sun and school holidays 2–6pm. €11.50 (children 4–12 years €7.50, 13–18 years €9.50). 02 33 68 11 18. www.alligator-bay.com.
Thrills are guaranteed at this reptile breeding centre where you can see a wide variety of tortoises, snakes and crocodiles.

Pontorson

Pontorson is a favourite stopping place for visitors on their way to Mont-St-Michel. The town is named after a local baron, Orson, who in 1031 built a bridge (*pont* in French) over the Couesnon.

VISIT
Église Notre-Dame
Open daily.
The 11C church is said to have been founded by **William the Conqueror** to thank the Virgin for saving his army from the Couesnon quicksands. The episode is portrayed in a stained-glass window and also in scene 17 in the Bayeux Tapestry. The church was given pointed vaulting at a later date and has been remodelled several times. The massive rough granite west front has kept its Romanesque appearance, with a great arch, only slightly pointed. Note the tympanum on the south doorway, carved with a man and a bird. A Gothic arch opens into the chapel of St Saviour, where there is a fine 15C altarpiece: the Broken Saints. Despite being mutilated during the Wars of Religion and the Revolution, it is a work of great richness.

- **Population:** 4,094.
- **Michelin Map:** 303: C-8.
- **Info:** Place de l'Hôtel-de-Ville. 02 33 60 20 65. www.mont-saint-michel-baie.com.
- **Location:** Pontorson is 9km/5.6mi S of Mont-St-Michel on D 976.
- **Don't Miss:** The chapel of the St-James American Military Cemetery.

EXCURSION
St-James
15km/9mi E by D 30.
This is one of western Normandy's oldest cities, founded by William the Conqueror in 1067. Several old streets and 15C ramparts recall the historic past. The **Cimetière américain et Mémorial de Bretagne** is on the outskirts of St-James (*take D 230 in the direction of Louvigné*). This cemetery holds the graves of more than 4,400 Americans. In the chapel are regimental colours, stained-glass windows, coats of arms and maps that commemorate the events of 1944.

Avranches★

The pretty and lively city of Avranches is one of the oldest towns in Normandy; its origins date back to early antiquity. St Aubert, Bishop of Avranches in the 8C, instigated the foundation of Mont-St-Michel and the two centres are therefore closely linked not only geographically but historically. The surrounding area is known for the Avranchin breed of sheep.

SIGHTS

The museum, the Plate-forme and the town hall (Mont-St-Michel manuscripts) are located around the site of the former episcopal palace, while the botanical gardens are slightly down the hill. The Basilica of saints Gervais and Protais is a short walk from the town hall.
Entry to the Basilica Treasury is included in the museum and manuscript ticket. The Patton Monument is a 20-minute walk down rue de la Constitution.

Jardin des Plantes

pl. Carnot. ◷*Open 8.30am–dusk.*
The botanical gardens were once the property of a Capuchin monastery that was destroyed during the Revolution. From the terrace at the far end of the garden is a **panorama**★ of the bay.

La Plate-forme

From place Daniel-Huet, walk along the garden of the Sous-Préfecture to reach the site of the old cathedral. This little square contains the paving stone on which Henry II made public penance in

- ▶ **Population:** 8,179.
- ⚅ **Michelin Map:** 303: D-7.
- ▯ **Info:** 2 rue Général de Gaule. ℘02 33 58 00 22. www.ot-avranches.com.
- ◖ **Location:** The town, on a granite spur, has a commanding view of Mont-St-Michel, 25km/15.5mi to the W. It can be reached by A 84, linking Villedieu-les-Poêles (23km/14.3mi) to the NE and Rennes, 87km/54mi to the SW.
- ▣ **Parking:** In the town centre, near the museum, Plate-forme and gardens.
- ⊘ **Don't Miss:** The superb view of Mont-St-Michel from the Jardin des Plantes.
- ◷ **Timing:** One can easily spend a half-day at Avranches.
- ▲▲ **Kids:** At the Scriptorial, children are welcomed with a special tour led by the elf Titivillus.

1172. From the terrace there is a wide **view**★ embracing Mont-St-Michel.

Monument Patton

This memorial commemorates the deployment of General Patton's troops towards Brittany and the Basse-Normandie (in July 1944 with the American 3rd Army). The square on which it stands is now American territory.

Henry II Repents (12C)

Relations between the King of England, **Henry Plantagenet**, who was also Duke of Normandy, and his Archbishop of Canterbury, **Thomas Becket**, became very bitter. It is said that one day the king cried, "Will no one rid me of this turbulent priest?" Four knights took the words as a command and, on 29 December 1170, Thomas Becket was murdered in Canterbury Cathedral.

The Pope excommunicated Henry II, who begged absolution. Robert of Torigni, Abbot of Mont-St-Michel, held a council attended by the king at Avranches, and so it was that at the door of the cathedral (collapsed in 1794) Henry II, barefoot and dressed only in a shirt, made public penance on his knees on 22 May 1172.

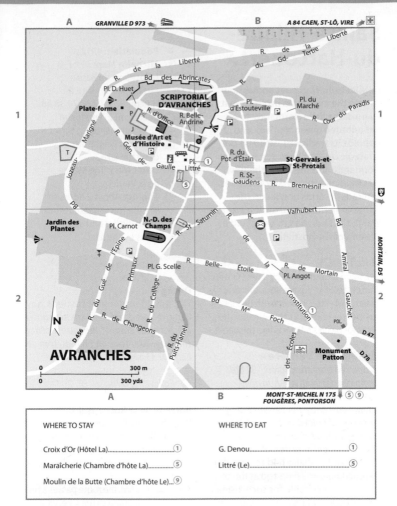

AVRANCHES

WHERE TO STAY		WHERE TO EAT	
Croix d'Or (Hôtel La)	①	G. Denou	①
Maraîcherie (Chambre d'hôte La)	⑤	Littré (Le)	⑤
Moulin de la Butte (Chambre d'hôte Le)	⑨		

Musée d'Art et d'Histoire

pl. Jean de St-Avit. ◷*Open Jun– Sept daily 10am–12.30pm, 2–6pm.* ◉*€1.50.* ℘*02 33 58 00 22. www.ville-avranches.fr.* The museum contains varied collections illustrating the history of the town.

Scriptorial – Musée Manuscrits du Mont-St-Michel★★

pl. d'Éstouteville. ♿◷*Open Jul–Aug daily 10am–7pm; May–Jun and Sept, Tue–Sun 10am–12.30 and 2–5pm; Oct– Dec and Feb–Apr Tue–Fri 10am– 12.30pm, 2–5pm, Sat–Sun 10am– 12.30pm, 2–6pm (last ticket 1hr before closing).* ◷*Closed 1 May, 1 Nov, 25 Dec.* ◉*€7 (children €3).* ℘*02 33 79 57 00. www.scriptorial.fr.*

The Scriptorial houses a collection of precious 8C–15C **manuscripts**★★.

Basilique St-Gervais-et-St-Protais Treasury

pl. St-Gervais. ◷*Open Jul–Sept daily 10am–noon, 2–6pm; Jun Mon–Sat 10am–noon, 2–6pm, Sun 2–6pm.* ◉*No charge.* ℘*02 33 58 00 22. www.ville-avranches.fr.*

This vast late 19C basilica contains several gold objects, including a gold and silver **reliquary** containing the skull of St Aubert, the 8C bishop, which legend says was pierced by St Michael's finger.

Sainte-Hilaire-du-Harcouërt★

St-Hilaire-du-Harcouët knows how to gain the maximum profit from its charms: the little Normandy town has adopted green tourism, and upholds its traditions. Sited on the strategic frontier between Brittany, Normandy and the Loire, the town was built and fortified by Harcouët, comrade-in-arms of William the Conqueror. Destroyed during World War II, the town had to be rebuilt at the end of the hostilities.

- ▶ **Population:** 4,112.
- **Michelin Map:** 303: F-8
- **Info:** Place du Bassin 50 600 Saint Hilaire du Harcouët. ✆02 33 79 38 88.
- **Location:** 27km/16.9m SE of Avranches.
- **Parking:** On the street or by the lake.
- **Don't Miss:** The Musée de la Verrière.
- **Timing:** About 2 hours to see the town and museum.
- **Kids:** Picnics and sports areas by the lake.

THE TOWN

The town is dominated by a neo-Gothic church (1855). Just below the priory, a stretch of water, graced with two lakes, has been created in the Airon valley. Areas for picnics or sports line the banks.

Musée de la Verrière★

Signposted from the church – 37 bld Gambetta. ⊙Open Jul–Aug daily 11am–7pm; May–Jun, Sept–Oct 11am–6.30pm (last entry 1 hr before closing). Possibility of guided visits. ⊜ €3 (under 12s free). ✆02 33 49 67 06.

The nuns of the order of St Francis D'Assisi and St Claire had to abandon the building some time ago as the convent was not suitable for such a small number. Nowadays it houses an exhibition about the principle Norman Cistercian abbeys, as well as an important collection of sacred art.

The centre also presents an excellent view of the cloistered life of the nuns: the visit is brought to life by video evidence, pictures and waxwork models based on the faces of the nuns themselves.

🚗 DRIVING TOUR

La Route des Barrages

50km/31mi. Allow 1hr30min.

▶ *Leave St-Hilaire by the D 976, direction Avranches.*

Ducey

The 17C Montgomery castle is now being restored. ⊙*For information about guided visits contact the tourist office. Jul–Aug, Tue, Thur and Sat at 3pm. ⊜ €2. ✆02 33 60 21 53.*

▶ *Follow the D 78.*

Barrage de la Roche-qui-Boit

Unfortunately it is not possible to visit this small dam, dating from 1919.

At the junction with the D 582, turn left onto the road marked "le Rocher, accès au lac".

After 2km/1.25m, the route passes a holiday village, leading to the lake, which is very pleasant and well shaded.

▶ *Return to the D 582 and turn left.*

The road leads you back to a view of the valley. After the bridge over the river, take a small road on the right, which climbs rapidly to the Auberge du Lac, on the ridge of the Vézins dam.

Barrage de Vézins

Visits are currently suspended due to heightened security. This curved structure (1931) with multiple buttresses has created a long artificial lake.

Villedieu-les-Poêles★

The town occupies a bend in the River Sienne and is an important road junction. It takes part of its name (*poêle* means pot or frying pan) from the making of pots and pans – a local activity here since the 12C. By 1740, there were 139 workshops in the town.

From making the great round-bellied copper milk churns *(cannes)*, the local factories now make copper and aluminium boilers for domestic and industrial use. The town has retained its medieval appearance with many attractive inner courtyards, stepped streets, alleys and old houses.

SIGHTS
Église Notre-Dame

This 15C church in the Flamboyant Gothic style was built on the site of a 12C church. The square transept tower over the crossing is emblazoned with various heraldic emblems. The chancel contains an 18C gilt wooden tabernacle.

Atelier du Cuivre

54 r. Général Huard. &▪ *Guided tours (45min).* ○*Open Sept–Jun Mon–Fri*

▶ **Population:** 3,895.
⚙ **Michelin Map:** 303: E-6.
🛈 **Info:** Place des Costils.
   📞02 33 61 05 69.
   www.ot-villedieu.fr.
▶ **Location:** From Granville, Villedieu is 26km/16mi E.
▪ **Kids:** The zoo in Champrepus.

9am–noon, 1.30–5.30pm, Sat and Jul–Aug until 6pm. ○*Closed public holidays.* ≈*€5.20 (combined ticket with the Maison de l'Étain €9).* 📞*02 33 51 31 85. www.atelierducuivre.com.* The story of copper working in Villedieu is explained: the copper deposits, techniques of copper working and a tour.

Musée de la Poeserie and Maison de la Dentellière

25 r. Général Huard, cour du Foyer. ○*Open Apr–15 Nov Sun–Mon 2–6.30pm, Tue–Sat 10–12.30 and 2–6.30pm.* ○*Closed Easter Sun and Mon, Pentecost Mon, 14 Jul, 25 Dec.* ≈*€4 (combined ticket with the Musée du Meuble normand €5).* 📞*02 33 69 33 44.*
A reconstruction of an old workshop shows the copperware-making process.

VILLEDIEU-LES-PÔELES

WHERE TO STAY

Abbaye (Auberge de l').......... ①

Fruitier (Le)............................. ③

WHERE TO EAT

Acherie
   (Manoir de l')...................... ①

Ferme de Malte (La).............. ④

The lace-maker's house displays Villedieu lace, popular in the 18C.

Fonderie de Cloches★

r. du Pont-Chicnon. ⟨symbols⟩*Guided tour (1hr) mid-Jul–Aug daily 9am–6pm; Sept–mid-Nov and mid-Feb–mid-Jul Tue–Sat 10am–12.30pm, 2–5.30pm.* ⟨symbol⟩*€4.90.* ℰ*02 33 61 00 56. www.cornille-havard.com.*
The foundry still produces bells for belfries, ships and other public buildings, exported worldwide.

Maison de l'Étain

15 r. Général Huard. ⟨symbol⟩*Open May–Sept Mon–Sat 9am–noon, 1.30–5.30pm; Mar–Apr and Oct Tue–Sat 1.30–5.30pm.* ⟨symbol⟩*€3.50 (combined ticket with the Atelier du Cuivre €9).* ⟨symbol⟩*Closed public holidays.* ℰ*02 33 51 05 08.*
In a house dating to the middle ages, an exhibit illustrates the art of pewter-working in the past.

Musée du Meuble normand

9 r. du Reculé. ⟨symbol⟩*See Musée de la Poeslerie.* ℰ*02 33 61 11 78.*
The collection of Norman furniture dates from 1680 to 1930.

EXCURSIONS
Abbaye de Hambaye★★

▷ *12km/7.5mi N of Villedieu by D 9 and D 51.* ⟨symbol⟩*Guided tour (45min, last tour 30min before closing) Apr–Oct Wed–Mon 10am–noon, 2–6pm.* ⟨symbol⟩*€4.20.* ℰ*02 33 61 76 92.*
Beside the River Sienne are the majestic ruins of Hambye Abbey, which was founded around 1145. The **church**★ is imposing, although it lacks a roof, a west front and the first bay of the nave. The narrow 13C nave was extended in the 14C by three bays.
The exceptionally large Gothic chancel has pointed arches, an ambulatory and radiating chapels. The tombstones are those of Jeanne Paynel, last descendant of the founders of Hambaye, and her husband, Louis d'Estouteville. The lay brothers' refectory (now used as a conference room) is furnished with 17C

Rouen tapestries and a collection of old furniture.

Mont Robin

▷*13km/8mi N by D 999. About 2km/1mi beyond Percy turn right towards Tessy-sur-Vire and right again almost immediately to Mount Robin.*
From this point (276m/906ft) there is an expansive **view** east in the direction of the Suisse Normande.

▲▲ Parc zoologique de Champrepus

▷*8km/5mi W by D 924 toward Granville. Picnic area and adventure playground.* ⟨symbols⟩*Open Apr–Sept daily 10am–7pm; Feb–Mar and Oct Sat–Sun 11am–6pm.* ⟨symbol⟩*€12.80 (3–12 years €7, 13–19 €10.80).* ℰ*02 33 61 30 74. www.zoo-champrepus.com.*
Over 80 species are presented in a pleasantly shaded setting of parkland covering 6ha/15 acres. There is also an amusement park and snack shops.

ADDRESSES

🏠 STAY

GRANVILLE

⊖ **Chambre d'hôte Le Hamel** – *"Le Hamel", 50380 St-Aubin-des-Préaux, 8km/5mi from Granville.* ℰ*02 33 51 42 65. 4 rooms. Closed last 2 weeks Sept.* ⟨symbols⟩. An old stone farm building in a peaceful, verdant setting with spacious, comfortable rooms. Lounge and breakfast room with a fireplace that is welcome on cold days.

⊖⊖ **Chambre d'hôte Manoir de la Croix** – *50530 Montviron – 8 km/5mi south of l'abbaye de la Lucerne by the D 35 then the D 105.* ℰ *02 33 60 68 30 . www. manoirdelacroix.com.* ⟨symbol⟩ *Reservation obligatory.4 rooms.* ⟨symbol⟩. This 19C residence has a tree-planted garden. There are very large suites furnished with collections of period furniture, and two other cosy rooms.

⊖⊖ **Hôtel des Bains** – *19 r. Clemenceau.* ℰ*02 33 50 17 31. www.hoteldesbains-granville.com. 54 rooms.* ⟨symbol⟩. Right on the coast in the bay of Mont-St-Michel; ask for a room with a view, or one equipped with a relaxing jacuzzi.

⊜⊜⊜**Mercure Le Grand Large** – *5 r. de la Falaise. ℰ02 33 91 19 19. www.mercure-granville.com. ⅍ 51 rooms. ⊇€12.* Looking down from the beach from the clifftop, this hotel, associated with a thalosso-therapy centre, offers duplex or studio accommodation, mostly with sea views.

ÎLES CHAUSEY

⊜⊜ **Hôtel Fort et des Îles** – *50400 Îles Chausey. ℰ02 33 50 25 02. www.hotel-chasey.com. Closed 10ct–7 Apr. 8 rooms.* Reservations essential. *Restaurant⊜⊜.* The sounds of wind and waves will lull you in this white house set in a flower garden. Its the only hotel on the island, with a few simple rooms. Local seafood can be enjoyed in the dining room.

MONT-ST-MICHEL

⊜ **Chambre d'hôte Amaryllis** – *Le Bas-Pays, 50170 Beauvoir, 2.5km/1.5mi S of Mont-St-Michel dir. Pontorson. ℰ02 33 60 09 42. 5 rooms. ⊇.* This stone house was renovated specifically as a B&B. The impeccably clean rooms feature well-equipped bathrooms and a furnished terrace.

⊜ **Hôtel La Tour Brette** – *8 r. Couesnon, 50170 Pontorson, 9km/5.6mi S of Mont-St-Michel. ℰ02 33 60 10 69. http://fraysse.phpnet.org. Closed Wed except Jul–Aug. 10 rooms. ⊇. Restaurant⊜.* This well-situated little hotel owes its name to an old tower that protected Normandy from the dukes of Brittany. Rooms are small but recently renovated.

⊜⊜ **Chambre d'hôte Mme Gillet Hélène** – *3 Le Val-St-Revert, 35610 Roz-sur-Couesnon, 15km/9mi SW of Mont-St-Michel via D 797, the coast road to St-Malo. ℰ02 99 80 27 85. 4 rooms. ⊇.* This 17C family house overlooks the bay and offers a beautiful view of Mont-St-Michel and the surrounding countryside. Four rooms where an old-world charm lingers on: three on the sea side and a more recent one with a terrace facing the garden.

⊜⊜ **Hôtel Bretagne** – *59 r. Couesnon, 50170 Pontorson, 8km/5mi S of Mont-St-Michel via D 976. ℰ02 33 60 10 55. www.lhotel restaurantdebretagne.fr. 12 rooms. ⊇. Restaurant⊜.* This regional-style house has lovely 18C wood panels, a grey-marble fireplace and a plate-warming radiator. Cosy, typically British bar and spacious, pleasantly furnished rooms.

⊜⊜ **Hôtel Les Vieilles Digues** – *68, rte du Mont-St-Michel, 50170 Beauvoir, 3 km/2mi south of Mont-St-Michel in direction of Pontorso. ℰ02 33 58 55 30. Closed Dec– Jan. ▣ 7 rooms. ⊇.* This pretty stone house has large bright rooms, well furnished, view of Mont-St-Michel on request. Pleasant half-timbered breakfast room and landscaped garden.

⊜⊜⊜ **Hôtel de la Digue** – *La Digue. ℰ02 33 60 14 02. www.ladigue.eu. ▣ 35 rooms. ⊇ €14. Restaurant⊜⊜.* This coastal hotel has been a relais since 1877. Functional rooms. Dining room with a view of Mont-St-Michel. Traditional cooking using seafood.

⊜⊜⊜⊜ **Âuberge St-Pierre** – *Grande-Rue. ℰ02 33 60 14 03. www.auberge-saint-pierre.fr. 21 rooms. ⊇€14. Restaurant⊜⊜.* This half-timbered inn has a restaurant and small, well-kept bedrooms. Choose between a brasserie on the road side, a dining room upstairs, or the terrace.

AVRANCHES

⊜ **Le Moulin de la Butte** – *11 r. du Moulin-de-la-Butte, 50170 Huisnes-sur-Mer, 18km/11mi SW. ℰ02 33 58 52 62. www.lemoulinde labutte.fr. 5 rooms. ⋈ ⊇.* At the entrance to the village, opposite Mont-St-Michel, this large, modern house has light, spacious rooms.

⊜⊜ **Chambre d'hôte La Maraîcherie** – *1 La Maraîcherie, 50300 Le Val-St-Père, 5km/3mi SE. ℰ02 33 58 10 87. 3 rooms. ⋈ ⊇.* The former stables of this pretty 18C farm, next to the bay of Mont-St-Michel, have been transformed into guest rooms furnished in Norman style.

⊜⊜⊜ **Hôtel La Croix d'Or** – *83 r. de la Constitution. ℰ02 33 58 04 88. www.hotel delacroixdor.fr. Closed Jan and Sun eve from 15 Oct–25 Mar. 27 rooms. ⊇. ▣.* This low, half-timbered house extends into an attractive garden full of flowers in season. Some guest rooms overlook the garden.

VILLEDIEU-LES-POÊLES

⊜⊜ **Auberge de l'Abbaye** – *50450 Hambye. ℰ02 33 61 42 19 - aubergede labbaye@wanadoo.fr. Closed 9–31 Jan, Sun eve and Mon. 6 small rooms. ⊇ €9.* You cannot fail to notice this large hotel near the abbey. The dining room is bright with floral decoration and coloured net curtains. Classic cuisine.

Le Fruitier – *Pl. Costils.* ☎*02 33 90 51 00. www.hotel-le-fruitier-villedieu.com.* ⌷€8.50. *Closed 23 Dec–21 Jan, Mon lunch, Thur lunch, Sunday eve except Jul–Aug.* Functional and well-presented rooms and apartments in this family hotel near the tourist office. Traditional and tasty cooking.

⏍ EAT

GRANVILLE

Au Marquis de Tombelaine – *25 rte de la Falaise, 50530. Champeaux, 3km/2mi southeast of Carolles by the D 911.* ☎ *02 33 61 85 94. www.aumarquisdetombelaine.com. Closed 6–30 Jan.* 6 rooms. ⌷€8. The two parts of the hotel are separated by the coast road. On one side is the restaurant, with meals served in a rustic setting and on the other are six rooms enjoying a view of the Bay.

Crêperie l'Échauguette – *24 r. St-Jean.* ☎*02 33 50 51 87.* Nestling in one of the narrow streets of old Granville, you can enjoy buckwheat galettes and pancakes.

La Citadelle – *34 r. du Port.* ☎*02 33 50 34 10. www.restaurant-la-citadelle.com. Closed Wed.* Before setting off for the islands, stop and have a meal here in the dining room with its blue-wood panelling or sit on the small raised terrace. Specialities are seafood, including lobster.

Le Terra Nova – *Pl. du Mar.-Foch.* ☎*02 33 50 00 79. www.casino-granville.com. Closed Mon and Tue.* ♿ This restaurant occupies part of the Casino. There is a view of the sea from the dining room and in good weather you can see the Channel Islands.

MONT-ST-MICHEL

La Gourmandise – *21 rte du Mont-St-Michel, 50170 Beauvoir, 4km/2.5mi S of Mont-St-Michel.* ☎*02 33 58 42 83. Closed Nov–Mar and Tue except Jul–Aug.* This Breton house transformed into a crêperie enlivens the village. Simple décor, lit by large bay windows. The extensive menu offers a choice of crêpes, etc.

Auberge de la Baie – *44 rte de la Rive, 50170 Ardevon, 3km/2mi SE of Mont-St-Michel, direction Avranches, via D 275.* ☎*02 33 68 26 70. www.aubergedelabaie.fr. Closed Nov and Tue–Wed except Jul–Aug.* This restaurant on a main road is a welcome break from the bustling tourism of Mont-St-Michel, at least for an hour or two. On the menu: traditional and regional dishes, plus a short list of galettes.

La Promenade – *pl. du Casino, 50610 Jullouville.* ☎*02 33 90 80 20. www.la-promenade.fr. Closed Mon–Tue. Reservations advised.* It would be difficult to find a better view of Mont-St-Michel Bay than at this elegant restaurant-tearoom on the ground floor of the former casino hotel (1881). Handsome antique furniture.

La Sirène – *16 Grande-Rue.* ☎*02 33 60 08 60.* Take the spiral staircase to enter the crêperie in this 14C house that was an inn for many years. The frosted-glass windows confirm the genuine flavour of the place.

Pré-Salé – *Restaurant of the Hôtel Mercure, BP 8 rte de Mont St Michel 50170, 2 km/1.25mi south of Mont-St-Michel by the D 976.* ☎*02 33 60 14 18. www.le-mont-saint-michel.com. Closed 12 Nov–6 Feb.* On the banks of the River Couesnon the Mercure Hotel invites you into a well-lit, renovated dining room. Taste the famous meat from sheep that graze on the local salty pastures.

La Mère Poulard – *Grande-Rue, BP 18 50170, Mont-St-Michel.* ☎*02 33 89 68 68. www.merepoulard.com.* This hotel-restaurant is famous for Mother Poulard's omelette, which rubs shoulders with appetising regional recipes.

AVRANCHES

G Denou – *9 pl. Littré.* ☎*02 33 58 05 74. Closed Mon, end Jan–start Feb, 2 weeks in Jun, 2 weeks in Oct.* This pleasant tearoom is great for a quick lunch: sandwiches, *crêpes* and more.

Le Littré – *8 r. du Dr-Gilbert.* ☎*02 33 58 01 66. Closed last 2 weeks Jun, Sun and Mon.* The regulars occupy low chairs in the bar, but you can sit comfortably at a table in one of the two dining rooms.

VILLEDIEU-LES-POÊLES

Manoir de l'Acherie – *37 r. Michel de l'Epinay, 50800 Ste-Cécile, 4km/2.5mi E.* ☎*02 33 51 13 87. www.manoir-acherie.fr. Closed Mon and Sun eve mid-Oct–Apr.* Enjoy a meal (or a night) in this beautiful 17C manor house. The restaurant fare is plentiful, with grills sizzling on a wood fire.

Restaurant La Ferme de Malte – *11 r. Jules Tétrel.* ☎*02 33 91 35 91. www.lafermedemalte.fr.* A touch of luxury at this comfortable, highly rated restaurant in the town.

LA PRESQU'ILE DU COTENTIN

The pronounced thrust of the Cotentin Peninsula, or La Presqu'Ile du Cotentin, into the Atlantic corresponds with an equally uncharacteristic landscape: the austere surroundings of La Hague are more like Brittany than Normandy. Geographically speaking, the area can be divided into three parts: the Cotentin Pass is the lower plain, the Val de Saire includes the river valley and the whole northeast part of the peninsula, the Cap de la Hague is the granite spine jutting out into the sea. The wooded hinterland was the cradle of Norman adventurers who once controlled the central Mediterranean area.

Geography

Surrounded on three sides by the sea, and separated from the mainland by swamps, the peninsula extends from south of Granville in the west to Carentan in the east, passing through Cherbourg in the north, from which it gets the name by which it is most commonly known in English: the Cherbourg Peninsula. The whole Peninsula lies within the Manche *département* of the Basse-Normandie Region. Off the west coast lie the Channel Islands known to the French as Les Îles Anglo-Normand and, of course, in the east are the westernmost of the beaches used for the Allied Landings in 1944.

Today

The Peninsula is very rural and agriculture is one of the most important economic activities, with dairy farming and vegetable growing being the most prominent. Cider and Calvados are also produced here from locally grown apples. Being a coastal region, fishing is also much in evidence and the oysters

Highlights

1 Visit to **Coutances Cathedral** (p381)
2 The **Cité de la Mer** at Cherbourg (p397)
3 Crossing to the **Île de Tatihou** (p402)
4 **Parc Animalier** at St-Martin (p404)
5 **Paratrooper** dummy at Ste-Mère-Église (p406)

from St-Vaast-la-Hougue are renowned throughout France.

There are two important nuclear facilities in the area, one at Flamanville, but better known is the plant at La Hague where there is a nuclear waste reprocessing and storage site.

Like many rural regions tourism is becoming increasingly important, especially to the D-Day beaches, the nearby town of St-Mère-Église and, of course, the various war cemeteries.

Cap de la Hague

© Jakez//iStockphoto.com

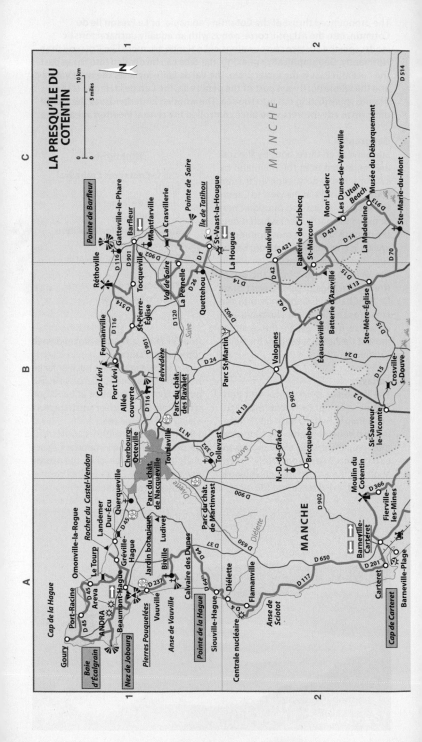

LA PRESQU'ÎLE DU COTENTIN

MANCHE

Baie d'Écalgrain
Nez de Jobourg
Pointe de la Hague
Cap de la Hague
Goury
Port-Racine
Omonville-la-Rogue
Le Tourp
Areva
ANDRA
Beaumont-Hague
Pierres Pouquelées
Vauville
Anse de Vauville
Biville
Calvaire des Dunes
Ludivet
Jardin botanique
Gréville-Hague
Landemer
Querqueville
Rocher du Castel-Vendon
Parc du chât. de Nacqueville
Octeville
Cherbourg
Cap Lévi
Port Lévi
Allée couverte
Belvédère
Fermanville
Réthoville
St-Pierre-Église
Tocqueville
Gatteville-le-Phare
Barfleur
Montfarville
La Crasvillerie
Pointe de Barfleur
Pointe de Saire
Île de Tatihou
St-Vaast-la-Hougue
La Hougue
Val de Saire
La Pernelle
Quettehou
Saire
Parc du chât. des Ravalet
D 24
Parc St-Martin
Valognes
Douve
N 13
Briquebec
N.-D.-de-Grâce
St-Sauveur-le-Vicomte
Moulin du Cotentin
Flerville-les-Mines
Carteret
Barneville-Carteret
Cap de Carteret
Barneville-Plage
D 201
D 650
D 117
Flamanville
Centrale nucléaire
Siouville-Hague
Anse de Sciotot
Diélette
Parc du chât. de Martinvast
Toutaville
Tollevast
Douve
Douve
Divette
Diélette
Quinéville
Batterie de Crisbecq
St-Marcouf
Mon Leclerc
Les Dunes-de-Varreville
Utah Beach
Musée du Débarquement
La Madeleine
Ste-Marie-du-Mont
Ste-Mère-Église
Batterie d'Azeville
Écausseville
Crosville-s-Douve
D 421
D 14
D 15
D 70
D 42
N 13
D 24
D 2
D 15
D 902
D 900
D 650
D 366
MANCHE
MANCHE
D 514

N

10 km
5 miles

CALVADOS

CAEN
N 13
D 5
D 5
D 15
D 514
D 5
D 11
D 6
D 6
Jardin d'Elle
Les Sources-
d'Elle
D 972
Vire
Toute
Canal de Vire
N 174
D 8
D 974
St-Lô
Vre de la Vire
N 174
D 11
N 174
Torigni-
s-Vire
D 186
CAEN
N 174
D 53
La Chapelle-
sur-Vire
D 551
Roches de Ham
D 28
D 28
A 84
AVRANCHES

Douve
N 13
Les Ponts d'Ouve
Carentan
des Marais
Taute
N 13
D 29
du Cotentin
et du Bessin
Centre
W. Harvey
Marchésieux
Rémilly-s-Lozon
D 900
Hauteville-
la-Guichard
D 38
Soulles
D 972
D 53
D 52
Savigny
D 972

Naturel
D 903
D 971
Régional
D 903
D 24
Maison
des marais
St-Martin-
d'Aubigny
D 900
D 971
Coutances
Jardins d'Argences
Saussey
D 7
Sienne
B

Parc
D 903
D 24
Mont Castre
130
Ay
D 900
Gratot
D 971
Coutances
D 650
D 73
D 73
D 971
AVRANCHES

D 900
La Haye-
du-Puits
D 900
Lessay
Fermel de l'âne
Pirou
D 2
D 94
D 650
Tourville-
sur-Sienne
Regnéville-
s-Mer
D 73

131
Mont de Doville
D 903
Créances
D 94
Pirou-Plage
D 650
Agon-
Coutainville
Pointe
d'Agon

Canville-
la-Rocque
D 903
D 650
Portbail

★★ Recommmended

★ Interesting

Worth a visit

Driving tour with departure point

Coutances

Valognes

Carentan

377

St-Lô

In 1944 St-Lô acquired the sad title of Capital of Ruins. On 19 July, the day the town was liberated, only the battered towers of the collegiate church and a few houses in the suburbs remained standing. Since then St-Lô has been rebuilt and it is now the site of one of the largest stud farms in France.

A BIT OF HISTORY

Key Town – St-Lô, a vital communications centre, was destined to play a strategic role in the Battle of Normandy. Owing to its position at a crossroads, the town underwent heavy bombing from 6 June, aimed at dispersing enemy forces. The battle for St-Lô began early in July in the middle of the War of the Hedgerows to capture the Lessay-St-Lô road, the base for Operation Cobra.

The town, which was the centre of German resistance, fell on 19 July. A monument, erected in memory of Major Howie of the American army, recalls a moving episode in the town's liberation. Howie had wanted to be one of the first to enter St-Lô, but he was

▶ **Population:** 19,092.
○ **Michelin Map:** 303: L-5.
▯ **Info:** rue de la Poterne - Plage Verte. ℘02 14 29 00 17. www.saint-lo-agglo.fr
○ **Location:** St-Lô lies between Coutances (29km/18mi W) and Bayeux (37km/23mi NE).
○ **Don't Miss:** The outdoor pulpit at the Église Notre-Dame.
○ **Timing:** In late summer, attend the Thursday exhibition at the stud farm.
▲▲ **Kids:** Haras national stud farm.

killed on 18 July. To fulfil his wish, the first Allied troops to enter St-Lô carried his coffin in with them, setting it down in the ruins of the belfry of Holy Cross Church.

A week later, after an unprecedented aerial bombardment – when 5,000 tonnes of bombs fell on an area of 11sq km/4sq mi – the German front

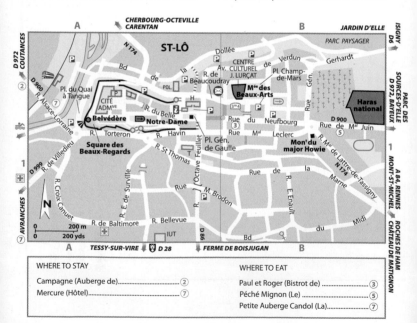

WHERE TO STAY		WHERE TO EAT	
Campagne (Auberge de)............②		Paul et Roger (Bistrot de)............③	
Mercure (Hôtel)............⑦		Péché Mignon (Le)............⑤	
		Petite Auberge Candol (La)............⑦	

broke in the west and the Avranches breakthrough was launched.

Reconstruction – A new town has arisen from the ruins, planned so that one can now clearly see the outline of the rocky spur, ringed by ramparts and towers, which have become the landmark. The oldest district, the Enclos, in the upper part of the town includes the Préfecture and administrative buildings, which make an interesting post-war architectural group.

The extremely modern tower in place Général de Gaulle is an amazing contrast to the former prison porch nearby, now a memorial to Resistance fighters and the victims of Nazism.

SIGHTS
Église Notre-Dame
r. de la Chancellerie (facing the Préfecture) ⏱️*Open daily 8.30am–7pm.*
The west front of the church (13C–17C) and the two towers have been shored up, but otherwise left as they were in 1944 as a witness to the ferocity of the bombardment.

In St Thomas Becket's chapel, note the large window by Max Ingrand. There is an outside pulpit against the north wall, level with the chancel.

Belvédère
From the tower overlooking the spur on which the town stands there is a view of the Vire Valley and the *bocage*.

Hôpital-Mémorial France-États-Unis
By rue de Villedieu to the SW.
The hospital was built jointly by the two nations and has a Fernand Léger mosaic on one of its façades.

Musée des Beaux-Arts
In the Centre Culturel Jean-Lurçat, pl. Champ-de-Mars. ♿⏱️*Open Wed–Sun 2–6pm.* 🚫*Closed 1 Jan, Easter Sun and Mon, 1 May, Ascension, 1 Nov, 25 Dec.* 🎫*€2.55.* 📞*02 33 72 52 55.*
The museum has a good collection of tapestries as well as 19C French painting: Boudin, Miller and Corot.

🐴 Haras national★
437 r. du Maréchal-Juin, dir. Bayeux. ♿🚌*Guided tours hourly (1hr).* ⏱️*Open Jul–Aug Mon–Sat 11am, 2.30–4.30pm, Sun 2.30–4.30pm; Jun and Sept Sat–Tue 2.30–4.30pm; May Fri–Sun 2.30–4.30pm.* 🎫*€6 (12–16 years €2.50). Presentation of stallions at 3pm every Thu from the last Thu of Jul to 1st Thu of Sept.* 🎫*€6 (children €6–16).* 📞*02 33 55 29 09.*
The St-Lô stud, the biggest of the 23 national studs, specialises in breeds such as Norman cobs, trotters and French saddle-horses. Every Thursday in season, the stables hold a **presentation**★ of the stallions.

Hôpital-mémorial France-États-Unis
route de Villedieu, west of the town.
This edifice exists thanks to a Franco-American initiative. In the entrance, a huge mosaic by Fernand Léger celebrates the friendship between the Allies.

Musée du Bocage normand - ferme de Boisjugan
bld de la Commune, 50000 St-Lô, on the road south to Vire. ⏱️*Jun–Sept Wed–Fri 10am–12pm, 2–6pm, Sat–Sun and hols 2–6pm; Mar–May and Oct, Wed–Sun and hols. 2–6pm; Jan–Feb, Nov–Dec,*

St-Lô and the Unicorn

Strolling through the streets of St-Lô, the attentive visitor will glimpse many versions of the unicorn, a handsome white horse with a goat's beard, cloven hooves and a narwhal's spiralled horn growing from his forehead. Considered as shy, wary creatures embodying purity, chastity and loyalty, unicorns in the Middle Ages came to symbolise the Virgin Mary. The devotion of the inhabitants of St-Lô for the Virgin may account for the presence of a unicorn on the city's coat of arms, in rue de la Porte-au-Lait, and even leaping from a stone fountain on the corner of rue Leturc and rue du Neufbourg.

Thur–Sun and hols 2–6pm. Closed 1 Jan, 1 May, 25 Dec. €4.75 (under 12 no charge).t02 33 56 26 98. Situated around a huge square courtyard, the restored buildings of this large farm (dating from the 17C–19C) showcase a modern and interactive interpretation of rural life. Emblematic rooms featuring country life have been recreated – the butter-making facility, the stables and valet's room, the cow byre and workshop. The creation of these collections allows visitors to follow the evolution of methodology in agricultural life and raising animals. One floor is dedicated to the latter activity, a tradition in Normandy. A video completes the visit.

EXCURSIONS
Parc des Sources-d'Elle
At Rouxeville, 14 km/8.75m east of St-Lô by the D 11, on the the left near the road to Caumont-l'Éventé. Mar–Oct. 7.30am–7pm. €2. 02 33 56 17 90. With no lack of fish, fishermen are happy in this huge 37 ha/91 acre park, boasting eight lakes and splendid rhododendron shrubberies.

Jardin d'Elle
At Villiers-Fossard, 6km/3.75m north east of St-Lô by the D 6. Open Feb–Nov, 9am–12pm, 2–6.30pm, Sun and hols 2–6.30pm. Ticket Office closes 1hr30 mins before closing. €6 (8–14-year-olds €3). 02 33 05 88 64. www.dellenormandie.com.
More than 2,500 varieties of plants, trees and bushes are spread among a multitude of small themed gardens. You can lose yourself in this labyrinth of greenery, abundant with flowers, some scented, in which all the plants are indentified, which is a good way of encouraging you to stop in the garden centre, which is located at the entrance and exit of the garden.

DRIVING TOUR

Vallée de la Vire
20km/12.5mi.

Leave St-Lô SE on the N 174.

Torigni-sur-Vire
Château des Matignon. Guided tours (1hr30min) Jul–Aug daily 2.30–6pm (last entry 5pm); last 2 weeks of Jun and 1st 2 weeks of Sept Sat–Sun and public holidays 2.30–6pm. €3.50. 02 33 56 71 44.
Since the 19C the **Château des Matignon** has consisted of only the west wing (restored). The main staircase (17C) leads to the reception rooms, which contain a very fine collection of

View of the Vire River Valley from the Roches de Ham

G. Targat/MICHELIN

tapestries, Louis XIII, Louis XV and Louis XVI furniture and works by the wildlife artist Arthur Le Duc. The park includes three ponds encircled by shaded paths.

○ *From Torini take N 174 north; after 5km/3mi turn left onto D 286.*

Roches de Ham★★
Alt 80m/262.5ft.
From the magnificent escarpment (above the river) there is a **view** of a beautiful bend in the River Vire.

○ *Return downhill; turn right onto D 551 and right again; pass through Troisgots and descend towards La Chapelle-sur-Vire.*

La Chapelle-sur-Vire
This small village has been a centre of pilgrimage since the 12C. In the church stand a statue of Our Lady of Vire (15C) and a low relief of St Anne, the Virgin and Child.

○ *Continue along D 159.*

The shaded road crosses the River Vire, then follows its course.

○ *At the crossroads with D 511, turn right.*

There is a view of the **Château de l'Angotière** (⚮ *closed to the public*).

Coutances★★

Coutances is perched on a hillock crowned by a magnificent cathedral, miraculously saved from the bombardments that destroyed two-thirds of the town in June 1944. The name of this religious and judicial centre of the Cotentin Peninsula recalls the Roman Emperor Constantins-Chlorus (293–306). In the 14C Coutances acquired an aqueduct *(ancien aqueduc)* of which only three arches remain standing to the northwest of the town on the Coutainville road.

▲▲ CATHÉDRALE★★★
Guided tours for children (6–12 years); call or enquire within. Tour of the cathedral, art project, stone-carving, visit to cathedral tower. ○*Open Mon–Fri 9.30am–6.30pm, Sat 10am–12.30pm, 2–6pm, Sun 10am–1pm.* ℘*02 33 19 08 10. http://cathedralecoutances.free.fr/.*
One of the best views of the cathedral is when arriving at Coutances from the south; the elegance of the proportions and the purity of the lines are starkly outlined against the sky.
Geoffroy de Montbray, one of those great prelate knights Duke William

▶ **Population:** 9,436.
⚭ **Michelin Map:** 303: D-5.
⚏ **Info:** Place Georges-Leclerc. ℘02 33 19 08 10. www.tourisme-coutances.fr.
○ **Location:** Coutances is at a crossroads: D 972 links it to St-Lô (29km/18mi E), D 900 heads towards Cherbourg (77km/48mi N) and D 971 leads to Granville (29km/18mi S). The coast is 10min to the W.
⚭ **Don't Miss:** The cathedral, a miracle of Gothic architecture, and the display of old Nativity crèches at the manor of Saussey.
○ **Timing:** Take 2hrs to see the town and cathedral, before embarking on one of the excursions in the area.
▲▲ **Kids:** The cathedral offers guided tours for children in July–August.

gathered round him, completed the first nave in 1056. Then, thanks to the generosity of the sons of Tancrède

Under the lantern tower of Cathédrale de Coutances

M.-O. Bernard/MICHELIN

de Hauteville, whose amazing Mediterranean adventure had just begun, he built the chancel, transept, central tower and the façade with its twin octagonal towers reminiscent of those at Jumièges.

In 1218, after the town had been burned down, a new Gothic cathedral was mounted on the remains of the 11C church, involving prodigious adaptations of style, as can be seen from the way the Romanesque towers of the old façade were incorporated into a new rectangular front and surmounted by spires.

Exterior

Above the great window a beautiful gallery crowns the façade, whereas on either side rise the towers, quartered at their highest, octagonal level, by graceful elongated pierced turrets. The profusion of ascending lines, so remarkable in their detail, culminates in the flight of the spires, which rise to 78m/256ft. The bold turreted lantern tower at the transept crossing is noteworthy for its slender ribbing and fine, narrow windows.

Interior

Pause at the beginning of the nave for a remarkable general view of this singular building with its upswept lines: to right and left wide arcades are lined above by galleries where the lower windows, surmounted by blind rose windows, have been blocked up; above again, along the bottom of the clerestory windows, a second balustrade of a different design lines the walls.

Dominating the transept crossing is the octagonal **lantern tower**★★★. It is 41m/134.5ft high at its apex and the best example of its type in Normandy. At the base of the south transept pillar stands the beautiful and deeply venerated 14C statue of Our Lady of Coutances, which miraculously survived the 1944 bombing of St Nicholas' Church. The north transept contains the oldest, 13C stained-glass windows; the south, a 14C window, in sombre tones, of the Last Judgement. The chancel, with the same architectural simplicity as the nave, is later in date and wider. As you walk round the two ambulatories, note the false triforium formed from two arches, each covering twin bays. The radiating chapels are shallow and the ribs of their vaulting combine with the corresponding ambulatory bay rib to form a single arch. The central apsidal chapel, known as the Circata, was enlarged during a late 14C rebuilding by Sylvestre de la Cervelle. Above the

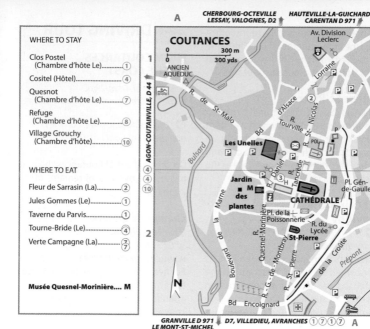

slender painted columns small figures and animals peer out from the foliage of the capitals.

Upper Storeys★★

Guided tour (1hr30min), reserve beforehand (children under 10 years not permitted). Jul–Aug Sun–Fri 11am, 3pm, Sun 3pm; Jun and 1st 3 weeks Sept Tue and Sun 3pm. 02 33 19 08 10. €7.

The walk, which explores the Romanesque parts of the original building, starts at a west front tower, continues through the attic of the aisle then on to the third-floor galleries to finish at the top of the lantern tower. The **panorama** extends from Granville, over the Chausey Islands to Jersey and on a clear day even Mount Pinçon is visible.

ADDITIONAL SIGHTS

Jardin des Plantes★

r. Quesnel-Morinière. Open daily Jul–Aug 9am–11.30pm; Apr–Jun and Sept 9am–8pm; Oct–Mar 9am–5pm. Sound and light show in Jul–Aug. No charge. 02 33 19 08 10.

The garden's entrance is flanked by an old cider press on one side and the Quesnel-Morinière Museum on the other. The terraced promenade traverses the sloping gardens with their many flower beds and pine trees.

Musée Quesnel-Morinière

2 quai Quesnel-Morinière. Open Jul–Aug 10am–noon, 2–6pm; Sun 2–5pm; Sept–Jun Wed–Sat and Mon 10am–noon, 2–5pm, Sun 2–5pm. Closed 1 Jan, Pentecost Mon, 25 Dec and Tue. €2.50 (under 18s and Sun afternoon no charge). 02 33 07 07 88.

The museum is in the former Hôtel Poupinel, which was bought in 1675 by the king's counsellor of the same name. The collections are mainly local: regional pottery and paintings by local artists. Outstanding, however, are Rubens' Lions and Dogs Fighting and the Last Supper by Simon Vouet. The popular arts and traditions section includes 18C–20C costumes from the Coutances area, 18C–19C regional pottery, headdresses, furniture and kitchen utensils.

Les Unelles

A new steel frame and glass-walled building adjoins the former seminary buildings which have been transformed to house an arts centre, the tourist office and the local authority offices. The name is derived from the Unelli whose capital was Cosedia, present day Coutances.

Église St-Pierre

This fine 15C–16C church, built by Bishop Geoffroy Herbert, was given a lantern tower over the transept crossing. In accordance with Renaissance custom, it was decorated ever more richly as the height increased.

EXCURSIONS
Savigny

▷ *11 km/7m east by the D 972, then right towards Savigny.*

Savigny's Romanesque church (12C) is renowned for its 14C frescoes. On the left hand wall of the nave, one depiction of the Last Supper *(Cene)* is particularly well preserved. In the chancel, four scenes illustrate the martyrdom of St Barbe; the last one on the left dates from the 19C. Visit the sacristy behind the altar, where you can see a large sculpted relief of Christ, from the 11C *(guided visits in summer, Fri 3–5pm).*

Hauteville-la-Guichard

▷ *15km/9mi NE. Leave Coutances to the N on D 971 heading for St-Sauveur-Landelin, then turn right onto D 53. Just after Moncuit, turn left towards Hauteville (D 435).*

The **Musée Tancrède de Hauteville** (◔*Open Jul–Aug Tue–Sun 2–6pm, last 2 weeks Jun and 1st 2 weeks Sept Sun 2–6pm. Rest of year, last Sun of each month. ◔Closed public holidays and Dec–Jan. ⊛€4; ℘02 33 19 19 19)* plunges you into the heart of the Norman conquest of Sicily and southern Italy at the beginning of the 11C. Tancrède and his 12 children (the most famous were Robert Guiscard and Roger I of Sicily) were the true founders of Norman power in the Mediterranean. Incredibly well organised and extremely cunning, they created a powerful state remarkable for its military achievements as well as its cultural influence.

🚗 DRIVING TOUR

FROM COUTANCES TO THE COAST

Round-trip of 47km/29mi. Allow 1hr30min.

▷ *Leave Coutances west on the D 44 and then turn right onto D 244.*

On the way out of Coutances the road passes the overgrown remains of the aqueduct.

Château de Gratot★

◔*Open daily 10am–7pm. ⊛€3.* ℘*02 31 45 18 49.* *www.chateaugratot.com.*

For five centuries the château belonged to the Argouges family. Long abandoned, it has been restored and converted into an arts centre.

A small three-arched bridge over the moat leads to the entrance gatehouse and then the inner courtyard. Within the courtyard from left to right are the 18C pavilion and the 17C main building, flanked by the Round Tower, and the Fairy's Tower with the North Tower to the rear.

Maison seigneuriale

Two flights of steps lead to the entrance of the now roofless former living quarters. The ground floor was lit by tall windows, the upper floor by dormers.

Tour ronde

This early 15C round tower is quite medieval in appearance. The narrowing of the staircase as it moved upwards was devised to hinder an attack as only one person could pass at a time.

The entrance to the basement is at the foot of this tower.

Caves

The groined vaulting of these fine cellars is supported by stout piers. The masonry is composed of stones placed edgewise. The late 15C tower, now called the Fairy's Tower, is reinforced by a powerful buttress. It is octagonal at the base but becomes square at the top and is crowned by a saddleback roof.

Tour d'angle

This corner tower, the only part of the medieval castle that remains, probably dates from the late 13C or the early 14C; the door has been walled up.

Communs

One of the rooms in these 16C outbuildings hosts an exhibition on the château, its construction and restoration.

▶ *In St-Malo-de-la-Lande take D 68 towards Tourville-sur-Sienne then turn right onto D 272 to Agon-Coutainville.*

Agon-Coutainville

Coutainville is one of the more popular resorts on the west coast of the Cotentin Peninsula, bounded by the Channel to the west and the Sienne estuary to the east. At low tide these great wet sandy stretches are popular with those looking for shrimps, cockles and clams.

▶ *Take the road leading to the Pointe d'Agon.*

Pointe d'Agon

The line of stones on the right-hand side of the road is a memorial to the author **Fernand Lechanteur** (1910–71), who wrote in the Norman dialect. From the headland there is a good view of this part of the Channel coast and especially of the port of Regnéville on the other side of the estuary.

▶ *Return to Agon-Coutainville, then follow the road to the hamlet, rue d'Agon.*

The D 72 road soon overlooks the silted up port of Regnéville.

Tourville-sur-Sienne

The roadside statue is of Admiral de Tourville, who lost the Battle of La Hougue (1692). From the terraced

cemetery *(road from the statue)* there is a good view of Regnéville harbour, closed off by the sandy headland, Montmarin belfry, the Rocher de Granville, and in clear weather, the Chausey Islands.

▶ *Drive to Pont-de-la-Roque along D 650, then to Regnéville-sur-Mer along D 49.*

Regnéville-sur-Mer

From the 13C **church**, follow signposts to the **Musée du Littoral et de la Chaux** *(14 rte des Fours-à-Chaux;* ◷*Open year round, call for precise hours.* ⬮€4.20. ✆02 33 46 82 18), set up in the former Rey lime kilns. This splendidly restored example of mid-19C industrial architecture presents traditional activities connected with the Channel coast.

▶ *Leave Regnéville on D 49 towards Montmartin-sur-Mer, then Hyenville (D 73). Continue on D 73 until you cross D 7 and drive towards Coutances via Saussey.*

Manoir de Saussey★

◷*Open Easter–Sept daily 2–6.30pm (last entry 30min before closing).* ⬮€6. ✆02 33 45 19 65.
The 17C buildings are enhanced by a pretty rose garden, an orchard, a vegetable patch and a series of delightful flower beds. Note the collection of **Nativity scenes** and a lovely exhibition of **glassware**.

▶ *Go back to D 7 and follow signs to the Manoir d'Argences.*

Jardins d'Argences

◷*Open mid-May–mid-Oct daily 2–6pm.* ⬮€5.50. ✆02 33 07 92 04.
The grounds surrounding this manor house (15C–18C) are enchanting and laid out along a series of pretty itineraries.

▶ *Drive back to Coutances.*

Lessay★

Lessay grew up round a Benedictine abbey founded in 1056 by a Norman lord. The first monks came from Le Bec-Hellouin. The town is particularly lively in September during the Holy Cross Fair, which originated in the 13C. Attended by about 400,000 people, it is one of the oldest and most important in France.

- ▶ **Population:** 2,046.
- **Michelin Map:** 303: C-4.
- **Info:** 11 place Saint-Cloud. 02 33 45 14 34. www.canton-lessay.com.
- ▶ **Location:** Lessay lies between Coutances, 21km/13mi to the S on D 2, and Valognes, 36km/ 22.4mi N on D 900.
- **Don't Miss:** The impressive view of the abbey nave.
- **Timing:** In July and August, concerts are held at the abbey.
- **Kids:** There are several nature trails; ask at the tourist office.

ABBEY CHURCH★★

Av. Paul Jeanson. ○*Open daily 9am–6pm, except during services. Allow 30min.* ○*No charge.* ○*Guided tours (1hr) Jul–Aug Wed 3pm (check dates at tourist office).* ○*€4.*

The magnificent Romanesque abbey church, damaged during the war, was reconstructed between 1945 and 1957, using original building materials wherever possible; the result is one of the most perfect examples of Romanesque architecture in Normandy.

Building of the original church began in 1098 with construction of the apse, chancel transept and two bays of the nave, with their vaulting; the remaining bays of the nave were completed several years later.

Exterior

The full beauty of the lines of the apse, abutting on a flat gable, can best be seen from the War Memorial Square. The rather squat square belfry with its Hague schist slates is also worth noting.

Interior

The seven broad bays of the nave and the transepts are roofed with pointed vaulting; there is rib-vaulting in the aisles. The gallery in front of the clerestory windows passes round the entire building in the thickness of the walls. The chancel terminates in an ovenvaulted apse lit by two rose windows. A 15C chapel with a cobbled floor *(right of the chancel)* contains the baptistry and the font. The new windows are inspired by Irish manuscripts.

EXCURSIONS

Créances

▶ *3 km/2mi southwest.*

This commune owes its fame to its marshland and notably to its famous carrots grown in sand (Red Label). The *mielles*, sandy areas close to the sea, provide perfect conditions for growing this sweet fleshed carrot, which has such a tender skin that it does not need to be peeled. The sand provides excellent drainage, with nearby seaweed acting as fertiliser. The beach, a huge stretch of sand, bordered with gorse lined dunes, is much loved by kite fliers, sand buggy enthusiasts, windsurfers and shore fishermen.

Ferme de l'âne - Asinerie de la Devise

▶ *2 r. de la Devise (between Créances and Pirou-Bourg, on the D 72).*
○*Open daily10am–noon, 2–7pm during school hols; rest of the year by reservation only.* ○*€20 per team (4 adults maximum, several teams possible).*
02 33 45 95 51 / 06 76 65 27 98.

Discover the varying breeds of donkeys in France (the soft grey coloured Cotentin donkey, the Large Black from Berry, the Poitou donkey, the Pyrenees donkey, and so forth), together with their

La Foire de Sainte-Croix

Lessay is extraordinarily lively during the days of the Holy Cross Fair (second weekend in September). The origins of the fair are lost in the 11C – it is supposed that the Benedictines were the first sponsors. Friday is fair day for horses, donkeys, dogs, ferrets and fowl; Saturday welcomes cattle, sheep and goats. More than 1,500 exhibitors attend and dozens of carnival rides are set up alongside. To feed the 400,000 visitors, about 2 800 local lambs are grilled along an alleyway reserved for this purpose.

way of life. The farm visit is completed with a donkey car ride of 2.8km/1.5mi *(I hour)* on the paths around Lessay, and in the regional national park: you can also discover more about the environment by taking a donkey cart out on your own.

Château de Pirou★

▶ *10km/6mi SW of Lessay. Allow 1hr.*
🕒 *Open daily Apr–Sept 10am–noon, 2–6.30pm; mid-Oct–Nov and Feb–Mar 10am–noon, 2–5pm.* ➳€5.

The 12C fortress, which once stood on the coast beside an anchorage, since silted up, is one of the oldest Norman castles and served as an outpost for the defence of Coutances under the lords of Pirou who owned it from the 11C to the 14C. These lords were related to the House of Hauteville, of which several members contributed to the formation of the Norman kingdom of Sicily.

The castle passed to other noble families until the late 18C, when it was used as a hideout for smugglers dealing in tobacco from Jersey, before finally becoming a farm in the 19thC.

Three fortified gatehouses – there were originally five – lead to the old sheepfold, the outer bailey and then to the castle itself, a massive structure encircled by a moat, whose towers are constructed directly on the top of the ramparts, with no overhang.

The courtyard is bordered to the left with outhouses. As you progress you will see firstly the bakers (with a monumental chimney, and a huge oven), the press room, the chapel and the Plés room, where justice was dispensed. Here a **tapestry** is displayed, similar in style to the Bayeux Tapestry, recounting the conquest of southern Italy and Sicily by the Cotentin Normans. The original tapestry can be seen only in July and

Château de Pirou

S. Sauvignier/MICHELIN

The Legendary Geese of Pirou

When the Norse invaders failed to take the Pirou fortress they decided to lay siege to it. After several days of waiting they realised that there was no longer any sign of activity within the castle but, being suspicious, they decided to delay a little longer before making the final assault. Imagine their surprise when they found that the only remaining occupant was a bedridden old man, who informed them that the lord, his wife and other occupants of the castle had transformed themselves into geese, to escape from the hands of their attackers. Indeed, the Norsemen recollected having seen a skein of wild geese flying over the castle walls the previous evening. According to Norse traditions, the human form could only be reassumed once certain magic words had been recited backwards. The geese came back to look for their book of magic spells but, alas, the Norsemen had set fire to the castle. Legend has it that the geese return every year in the hope of finding their book of spells, which explains why there are so many skeins of geese in the vicinity of the castle.

August; otherwise a copy is on display. After the last room a staircase leads to the ramparts.

There is a lovely view of the surrounding countryside from the top of the castle's square tower, which dominates the entrance.

Barneville-Carteret★

This popular seaside resort, the closest port to the Channel Islands, is lively, the dunes windswept, and the long beach is of fine sand.

SIGHTS

The resort was created in 1965 by the coming together of the communes of Barneville and Carteret. It is now based around three relatively distant centres: Barneville-Bourg, Barneville-Plage and Carteret. It is best to have some means of transport to move from one to another.

Carteret★

This is the oldest area, along with Barneville-Bourg. Even in the 1820s, the 19C writer Jules Barbey d'Aurevilly *(see p405)* spent family holidays here. Chateaubriand visited in 1842. At the end of the 19C, the fashion for sea bathing

Pirou-Plage

▶ *2km/1.25mi SW of Pirou by the D 650.*
This small resort has a 6km/3.75mi expanse of fine sand (swimming supervised in summer) running alongside the promenade and a seawater swimming pool. Fishing, windsurfing and water sports are all available here.

▶ **Population:** 2,299.
Michelin Map: 303: B-3 – Local map, *see Presqu'île du Cotentin, p376.*
Info: 10 rue des Écoles. ✆ 02 33 04 90 58. www.barneville-carteret.fr.
Location: Valovnes is 28km/17.5mi NE, Cherbourg 37km/23mi NE via D 650 and Caen 120km/74.5mi to the E.
Don't Miss: You may want to tour Carteret on the tourist train, before trying some of the hikes and walks giving views over the sea.
Timing: The Saturday morning market is worth your time.
Kids: The tourist train.

dramatically changed this fishing village into a spa resort. Carteret still has a sense of quiet charm, thanks, in the main, to the villas that were built there around the beginning of the 20C. Most of them are built above the port.

Finally, the magnificent **rocky head-land ★★** which, to the north, shelters the Gerfleur estuary, and its beach (beware of strong currents offshore), and is hidden in a ravine, makes Carteret one of the most agreeable coastal resorts of the Cotentin Peninsula.

Ports – Carteret port remains very active. Today there are twenty or so fishing vessels, which trawl for sole and ray, set pots for lobster and crab, and drag net for whelks and Coquilles St-Jacques. When they return, the port comes to life and visitors can enjoy this authentic snapshot of life that adds to the charm of the resort. In addition, Carteret possesses a yacht harbour with 300 moorings and an embarkation point for the Channel Islands.

Beaches – Above and beyond Barneville beach (see Barneville-Plage, p390), which is family orientated and has a life guard, the resort has two other beaches which are quite different in style. Carteret, facing south, has cabins set in the shade of the cliffs, forming a continuation of the port, and is also guarded. This is not the case for the Vieille-Église beach, which is situated at the foot of the dunes, from the north of the Carteret headland to the Rozel point. Wild, and made rather dangerous by violent currents, this is the favoured spot for windsurfers and speed sailors.

Le train touristique du Cotentin: Carteret-Porbail – *59 r. Hauvet, 50270 Barneville-Carteret. ℰ 06 30 35 15 71/02 33 04 94 54. http://ttcotentin. monsite-orange.fr/. ⏱ Jul–Aug, Sun and hols, Coastal train departs at 3pm; market train, departs 10am Tue from Carteret for the market at Portbail and Thur from Portbail for the market at Carteret. €8 (4–12 years €4).*

👥 This train, dating from the 1930s, runs 10km/6mi on a former rail track along the beaches and the surrounding dunes and heathland. Known as the coast train during the weekend, it becomes the market train twice a week.

Barneville-Bourg

Just behind the dunes and beaches lie shops and banks. The town's Saturday morning market attracts the surrounding population, who come to buy their provisions from local suppliers. The market is held next to the church, surrounded by granite mansions which are 16C – the oldest in the area.

Église St-Germain

The 11C church of St-Germain of Auxerre, standing high on the town's central

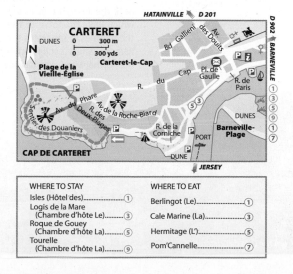

WHERE TO STAY

Isles (Hôtel des)	①
Logis de la Mare (Chambre d'hôte Le)	③
Roque de Gouey (Chambre d'hôte La)	⑤
Tourelle (Chambre d'hôte La)	⑨

WHERE TO EAT

Berlingot (Le)	①
Cale Marine (La)	③
Hermitage (L')	⑤
Pom'Cannelle	⑦

hill, was given a fortified tower in the 15C. A late 19C restoration disfigured the chancel, which lost its ceiling, but the arches and capitals of the Romanesque nave have delightful **decoration**★. On one of these capitals, note the figure portraying the Prophet Daniel confronting a fierce lion. The monument on the way out of Barneville commemorates the cutting-off of the Cotentin Peninsula on 18 June 1944 during the Battle of Normandy.

Barneville-Plage

The seafront boulevard bordered by villas leads to the popular beach.

🐾 WALKING TOUR

Cap de Carteret★★

Allow a total of 2hr for these two walks.
🚶Follow the signs La Corniche and le Phare; park near the roundabout by Carteret beach. Take sentier des Douaniers *(left)*, which is very narrow and requires care. The view changes constantly on the way to Carteret's second beach, the extensive Plage de la Vieille-Église.
🚶Take the road leading down to this beach to return inland. At the crossroads either turn right up to the **lighthouse** *(phare)* for an overall view or turn left *(avenue de la Roche-Biard)* to a viewing table: **views**★ of the coast, the Channel Islands and inland.

▶ *Alternatively, continue straight ahead at the crossroads to return to your car.*

🚗 DRIVING TOUR

52km/32.5mi.

▶ *Leave Barneville-Carteret by the road for Coutances. At La Picauderie, turn right onto the D 50 which goes to the harbour at Portbail.*

Portbail

🏠 *26 r. Philippe-lebel – ℰ02 33 04 03 07. www.portbail.fr.*
The former port was improved to provide a yachting basin with 200 moorings, and a new port is planned for 2012. This, plus two beaches of fine sand 2km/1mi away, and a sailing school, have made the area the place of choice among the resorts of the Cotentin. Sea fishing competitions, sand yachting, golf and horseriding complete the range of activities on offer.
Église Notre-Dame – ℰ02 33 04 03 07.
🐾*Guided tours* ⏱ *Jul–Aug Tue–Sun 10.30am–12.30pm, 3.30–6.30pm; Sept–Jun, arrange at the tourist office.* ⊛ *€2. Ticket combined with visit to baptistry (no charge for children).* Now disused, the church is a building from the start of the Roman era, dominated by a 15C tower. The columns and the chapels decorated with interlacing patterns and animals form one of the main attractions of the interior. To the left of the altar, there is a 16C statue of St Jacques made from multicoloured stone. The church also hosts temporary exhibitions. As you leave, note the 13 arch bridge to your right which links the town to the port and the beaches. It separates the southern harbour, which is still functioning, from the northern one, which is now polder.

View from the Cap de Carteret

C. Brett/MICHELIN

Baptistry – *℘02 33 04 03 07.* €2 *combined ticket with the church.* Excavations have revealed the remains of the ancient baptistry. From the original hexagonal structure only the lower parts of the exterior walls remain, with fragments of blue schist, the font, and water drainage systems.

◯ *Follow the signs to St-Sauveur-le-Vicomte passing St-Lô-d'Ourville. At the crossroads of the D 15and the D 903, follow the direction La Haye-du-Puits and take second road on the left towards Canville-la-Rocque.*

Canville-la-Rocque
Église St-Malo – the north chapel of the church has frescoes from the 16C. This is well conserved, illustrating the history of the Pendu-dépendu. This legend relates the tale of a young man who was falsely accused of a crime and hung by the roadside in St-Jacques-de-Compostelle. On their return from pilgrimage, his parents found him still hanging there, but still alive. Justice was served and he was taken down, to be replaced by the guilty party. Note also the 17C fonts, the door panels and the stalls.

◯ *Rejoin the D 903 and turn left*

La Haye-du-Puits
5 r. Émile-Poirier. ℘02 33 46 01 42. www.ot-lahayedupuits.com.
Still dominated by its redoubtable dungeon from the 11C *(no visits allowed)*, the town was heavily damaged during the liberation of Normandy in 1944. The town is at the heart of an area that has been long renowned for witchcraft.

◯ *Cross the town and continue on the D 903 towards Carentan. Shortly before Lithaire, turn right (sign "Lac du Mont-Castre") and follow the signage.*

Mont Castre★
Dubbed "Hill 122" during the Battle for Normandy, Mont Castre cost the 90th division of the US infantry dear, with a loss of more than 2000 men.

Aside from these memories, follow the road after the houses, which leads to an area for relaxation and discovery on Mont Castre. A huge lake has been created in a former quarry.

There are several possibilities for circular tours, one of which is a panoramic walk *(1hr)*, which includes a Gallic covered alley, dating from 1500 BC, the ruins of a Roman lookout post and the remains of a former 11C church in Lithaire.

◯ *Returning on the D 903, go to Lithaire where you take several left-hand turns in the direction of Neufmesnil (D 67).*

A circuit of 11km/6.9mi, marked in yellow. Use the car park of the church at Doville.

Mont de Doville
This mount, which is 131m/430ft high, deserves its name, if you believe in its Scandinavian origin – "Bald Escarpment". Also known as "Mont Colquin", it is one of the principal hills of the area along with Mont Castre and Mont Etenclin. From the orientation table there is a panoramic view of the countryside around La Haye-du-Puits and the marshland of La Sangsurière (a nature reserve).

◯ *Rejoin the D 137, then the D 127 to the north. After Besneville, follow the signs to Fierville-les-Mines.*

Fierville-les-Mines
Moulin à vent du Cotentin – *℘02 33 53 38 04. www.moulin-du-cotentin. com.* guided tours (30min). €3.70 (6–12-year-olds €1.10). This 18C windmill, restored in 1997 with a mechanism imported from the Vendée, is the only working example in the Cotentin and continues to produce wheat, buckwheat and spelt wheat flour. The tour gives an understanding of the complexities of this work. You can buy the wheat produced here.

◯ *Return to Barneville-Carteret following the D 50, the D 130 then the D 42.*

Pointe de la Hague★★

Some of the highest cliffs in Europe, interspersed with small sandy beaches and charming ports, all linked by the Customs Path, which is well known to walkers. This "end of the world" place with its dramatic cliffs is renowned for its spectacular scenery as well as the beauty of its gardens, which have a tropical feel. Although often associated with the nuclear power industry the name of La Hague is particularly associated with the generosity of nature.

▶ **Population:** 1,367.
- **Michelin Map:** 303: AB1/2.
- **Info:** 45 r. Jallot, 50440 Beaumont-Hague. ℰ02 33 52 74 94. www.lahague.org.
- **Location:** La pointe de La Hague is at the extreme north west of the Cotentin Peninsula. 29 km/18mi northwest of Cherbourg by the D 901, and 49 km/31 mi north of Barneville-Carteret by the D 650 and the D 37.
- **Don't Miss:** the dunes between Carteret and Hatainville.
- **Timing:** Allow a day to do both tours.

🚗 DRIVING TOURS

West Coast★★

45km/28mi. Allow 1hr30min.

▷ *Leave Carteret and drive north on the D 201.*

Between Carteret and Hatainville, the road wanders along the highest dunes on the Normandy coast. The dunes separate grassy hollows known as *"mielles"*, where rare and brightly coloured plants grow, such as the blue of sea lime-grass to the bright pink of the pyramidal orchid.

▷ *Continue towards Surtainville and Le Rozel.*

Between Le Rozel and Flamanville, the road runs above Sciotot cove. You can see the Flamanville headland to the North. Cliffs replace the dunes.

Flamanville
Centre nucléaire de production d'électricité de Flamanville
⚠ *For security reasons, the nuclear power station no longer receives visitors.* This nuclear power station, occupying 120ha/296 acres, stands in part on the granite bedrock, and in part on an artificial platform that juts into the ocean. Two production units have

an installed capacity of 1,300 million kWh each. Each unit produces 9,000 million kWh.
Between Flamanville and Le Rozel the road overlooks a small bay, the **Anse de Sciotot**. Cap de Flamanville and, to the south, the Pointe du Rozel, are visible. The cliffs become lower, giving way to dunes. Between Hatainville and Carteret the road runs along the dunes, the highest on the Norman coast. The grass covered hollows between the dunes are known locally as *mielles*.

▷ *Continue towards the north.*

Diélette
The small port of Diélette, at the foot of the dark cliffs, is the only refuge between Goury and Carteret. As the tide goes out, a beach of fine sand appears between its two breakwaters.

Siouville-Hague
Siouville's long gently sloping beach is the spot for surfing on this coast. The waves are ideal for learning to surf, windsurf, and kite surf safely, as well as for experienced surfers. Competitions for water sports, such as the French championships for skimboard, the Siouville Surf Open, etc. take place here. If

offers walkers the chance to enjoy the sight of acrobatic men and women enjoying their various water sports.

Biville★

The village is set on a plateau overlooking the desolate shoreline of Vauville Bay. The Blessed **Thomas Hélye** (1187–1257), a native of Biville, lies in the 13C chancel. On the north side is a 19C bronze group showing Thomas Hélye with some of his followers.

The arrival of the Allies and the liberation of the region is commemorated in a stained-glass window by Barillet (1944) *(first on the right in the nave)*.

○ *Walk along the street beside the church; by a fence, make some sharp turns and take the path which passes in front of a chapel dedicated to the Virgin and continue to the Calvary.*

Calvaire des Dunes★

🏃 *45min on foot there and back.*

○ *At the end of the street next to the church, go through the gate and take the path which passes by a little chapel and leads up to the cross.*

From the foot of the cross there is a panoramic view: in the foreground the desolate landscape of Vauville Bay stretches from the Nez de Jobourg to the cliffs at Flamanville.

○ *Continue towards Vauville.*

Beyond the village of Petit Thot the road affords a good **view**★ of the moorland around the bay of Vauville.

Vauville

The **Botanical Garden**★ *(&⊙Open Apr–Sept daily 2–6pm; Oct Tue and Fri–Sun 2–6pm; ∞€6; ℘02 33 10 00 00; http://jardin-vauville.fr) in the grounds of the manor specialises in evergreen plants.*

The 12C church and the 17C manor make an attractive picture.

Réserve naturelle de la mare de Vauville – *Entry at the side of the Muni-*

cipal Camping de Vauville –footpath with information boards or guided visit (∞ €5) organised by le Groupe ornithologique normand. ℘02 33 08 44 56. Binoculars advised.

🐾🧍Created in 1976 and managed since 1983 by the Normandy Ornithology Group, this nature reserve, possessing a huge 62 ha/153acres natural water lake, cut off from the sea by a cordon of dunes and ringed with reeds, allows visitors to discover an exceptionally rich flora and fauna; numerous species of birds (marsh snipes, mallard ducks, reed warblers, etc.), invertebrates and amphibians.

Pierres Pouquelées★

45min round-trip on foot from D 318.

🔲 Leave the car 200m/220yd before the first houses of Vauville and walk inland up a path on the right. When it reaches the plateau turn left to reach the Pierres Pouquelées gallery grave. Continue right to a small rise from which there is a **panorama**★ of the coast from the Nez de Jobourg to the Flamanville cliffs.

La côte Nord et La baie d'Écalgrain

55km/35mi. Allow 2hr45mins.

The road rejoins the north coast, near-Gruchy, then follows the road west along the Bay d'Écalgrain before returning to Beaumont-Hague.

Beaumont-Hague

This was the home town of the 17C smuggling family, the Jallot de Beaumont.

○ *Leave Beaumont-Hague going east on the D 245, then take the D 237 left and the D 45 until Gréville-Hague (4.5 km/2.8mi).*

Gréville-Hague

The small church was a model for the painter **Jean-François Millet** (1814–75) in his works of Norman landscapes. The artist's bust sits on a rock at the crossroads and the **house** where he was born in **Gruchy** is open to the public

(guided tours (45min) Jul–Aug daily 11am–7pm; Jun and Sept 11am–6pm; Apr–May and school holidays except Christmas 2–6pm (last entry 1hr before closing); €4.20. 02 33 01 81 91).

▷ From Gréville-Hague, take the D 237 to the right for Gruchy.

Rocher du Castel-Vendon★
Allow 1hr round-trip on foot.
Leave the car at the entrance to the village and continue on foot to the public wash-house by a sunken road that then becomes a footpath: parts of this itinerary are difficult.
The path follows the right-hand side of the valley. From a rocky promontory, there is a **view** of the coast from Cap Lévy to Pointe Jardeheu. In the foreground stands the granite rock spine called the Rocher du Castel-Vendon.
Leaving Gruchy by car, leave the D 45 for a moment to make a detour via **Quervière Bay**. Take the road towards **Éculleville**, then take a left, just before a sign marked "Baie de Quervière". At the end of the road, park and enjoy the **panorama**.

▷ Return to the D 45.

Omonville-la-Rogue
Manoir du Tourpa – daily 2 Jul–4 Sept 10.30am–7pm; 12 Feb–8 Apr, 8 May–1 Jul and 5 Sept–16 Dec 2–6pm, Sun and hols 10.30–6pm; 9 Apr–7 May 10.30–6pm. 21–31 Dec, 1 Jan. No charge. 02 33 01 85 89. www.letourp.com.
This magnificent manor house (15C and 16C), was bought back by the coastal Conservatoire and has been completely restored to create a major tourist and cultural centre for the north of the Cotentin. The Tourp exhibitions remind visitors of the beauty of its rich and varying landscape, the variety of its fauna and flora, and the history of a region with strong traditions. The huge outhouses of the manor are grouped around a large enclosed courtyard.

Omonville-la-Petite
A pretty little country graveyard surrounds the church: the poet Jacques Prévert (1900–77) lies here beside his ancestors. (to the left of the entrance).

Maison de Jacques Prévert – Open daily Jul–Aug 11am–7pm; Jun and Sept 11am–6pm; Apr–May and school holidays except Christmas 2–6pm (last entry 1hr before closing); €4.20; 02 33 52 72 38). Parking on the square in front of the church (300m/yd on foot). Bought in 1971 by Prévert, this house was his last refuge before his death in 1977. Annual temporary exhibitions recreate his, and his painter and writer friends', work. A film portrays the life of the poet.

 Towards l'anse St-Martin – leave from Prévert's house and after 5km/3mi, follows yellow signs (1h30min on foot, there and back). Straight after Prévert's house, take the the road sloping uphill to the left. At the next intersection, turn at the panel marked "Hameau Henry" then take a left straight away after leaving the village, before the wash house. The walk passes by the Mont-Clin cross, which offers a 360 degree view over St-Martin bay and the surrounding area. At the hamlet of Guillemins-de-Bas, note the head of a policeman sculpted on the roof of the last house, placed there to scoff at the customs men who were on the hunt for smugglers. Bas-Monterie farm, his hide-out, can be seen just before the hamlet of Fours. The path opens out onto the gorgeous beach of St-Martin cove where several boats usually lie at anchor. Return on the tarmac road to the left and turn right 300m/yd further on to get back to Omonville-la-Petite church.

Port-Racine★
The climb towards St-Germain-des-Vaux reveals this liliputian harbour, considered to be the smallest active port in France. The name of Port-Racine comes from a ship's captain who had established his base here, under Napoleon I.

▷ From the lower parking place,

a road (600m/656yd) leads to a pleasant shaded garden.

Jardin en hommage à Jacques Prévert

🕐*Open Jul–Aug daily 11am–7pm; Easter–Jun and Sept Sat–Thu 2–7pm.* 🎟*€5.* 📞*02 33 52 74 94 (Beaumont-Hague tourist office).*

Prévert loved this calm and verdant valley, fed by a river. Since 1981, one of his close friends, Gérard Fusberti, has brought these charming places to life with little scarlet bridges and benches, and examples of his poetry placed here and there. Leaving for Goury, you pass through heathland, which is littered with numerous rocks. Upon entering Auderville on the right, the descent to Goury offers a good view of La Hague.

Goury★

The small harbour is an important coast-guard and lifeboat station.

👥 Ludiver – Observatoire – Planétarium de La Hague

1700 r. de la Libération. ♿🕐*Open Jul–Aug daily 11am–6.30pm, planetarium shows at 11.30am, 3pm and 4.30pm (last entry 1hr before closing); rest of the year Sun–Fri 2–6pm, show at 3pm.* 🕐*Closed Jan, Easter Mon, 1 May, 1 and 11 Nov, 24–25, 31 Dec.* 🎟*€7.50 (children €5.50).* 📞*02 33 78 13 80. www.ludiver.com.*

Set on the Tonneville and Flotteman-ville-Hague plateau (180m/591ft), this new centre comprises a museum on astronomy and the universe, a plan-etarium with a seating capacity of 80 and an interior amphitheatre where the images of a 600mm/23.6in telescope are projected live to the public.

▷ *Return to Goury and take the D 401.*

Baie d'Écalgrain★★

This desolate beach, backed by heath-land, is one of the area's wild beauty spots. To the left of Alderney are Guern-sey and Sark.

▷ *From Dannery, take D 202, right to the Nez de Jobourg.*

Nez de Jobourg★★

Off D 901 in Beaumont-Hague. 🕐*The information centre at the Avra Centre for storage of nuclear waste is open Mon–Fri 8.30am–noon, 1.30–5pm. Guided tour (2hr) Mon–Fri by reservation.* 🎟*No charge; identification required. Parking inside site.* 📞*03 33 01 69 00. www.andra.fr.*

The long, rocky and barren promon-tory is now a bird sanctuary (seagulls). Walk along the **Nez de Voidries**. From the Auberge des Grottes there is a view north of Écalgrain Bay, the lighthouse off Cap de la Hague and the Channel Islands: Alderney, the nearest, Sark, Guernsey and Jersey. Farther south the Nez de Jobourg itself comes into view, separated from the Nez de Voidries by Senneval Bay.

▷ *Return to Dannery, then rejoin the D 901 and turn right.*

ANDRA – Centre de stockage de la Manche

🕐*Office open Mon–Fri 8.30am–noon, 1.30–5pm. Guided visit (identification required).* 🎟*No charge.* 📞*02 33 01 69 00. www.andra.fr .*

This storehouse for radioactive waste, opened in 1969, received 527,000 m3 of so-called "parcels", up to 1994. From 1991 to 1997 works were carried out to make the site water tight, to ensure that the waste was contained and the envi-ronment protected.

Usine Areva

🚫*For security reasons visits are suspended. Tours of the coastline are available.* 📞*02 33 02 73 04.*

This factory by the D 901 processes nuclear fuel. Facing the factory, take the D 403, which descends steeply. Between Herqueville and Beaumont the road is rather rough. There is a great view from the place known as "13 Winds", which looks down on Vauville harbour and the cliffs of Flamanville.

Cherbourg-Octeville★

Cherbourg is a seafaring town with the largest artificial harbour in the world. Here, on the northern shore of the Cotentin Peninsula, this city has beautiful monuments and is known for its remarkable breakwater.

A BIT OF HISTORY

Titanic Undertakings – The great military architect **Vauban** (1633–1707) saw the possibilities of Cherbourg as an Atlantic port. An attempt in 1776 to create an offshore barrier by submerging 90 huge timber cones filled with rubble failed when the sea washed it all away. However, over time all of the material that had accumulated on the sea bed began to form an artificial island. A fortified breakwater was eventually completed in 1853.

Today the breakwater remains essential for maintaining a safe haven against often violent storms.

Frogmen at Work – The capture of Cherbourg on 26 and 27 June 1944 marked a decisive stage in the Battle of Normandy, allowing for the landing of heavy equipment on a large scale. When the American 7th Corps took Cherbourg they found the harbour completely devastated and mined. Mines were cleared by Royal Navy frogmen, so that Cherbourg could supply the Allied armies. The undersea pipeline **PLUTO** (**P**ipe **L**ine **U**nder **T**he **O**cean) from the Isle of Wight emerged at Cherbourg, bringing gasoline to the Allies from 12 August 1944.

SIGHTS

Six historic trails wind through the city, with explanatory markers in French and English. They start across from the SNCF train station, across from St-Trinité and from the former Transatlantique station.

▶ **Population:** 42,328.
◔ **Michelin Map:** 303: C-2.
▤ **Info:** 2 quai Alexandre III, 50100 Cherbourg-Octeville. 𝒫02 33 93 52 02. www.cotentin-tourisme.com; www.ville-cherbourg.fr.
◑ **Location:** The N 13 ends in Cherbourg, after passing through Caen (123km/77mi SE) and Bayeux (96km/60mi).
◉ **Don't Miss:** The Cité de la Mer and a boat tour of the port area.
◷ **Timing:** Count on 3hr to see the Cité de la Mer.
👥 **Kids:** See the aquarium and the submarine at Cité de la Mer.

Muséum d'histoire naturelle d'archéologie et d'ethnographie

Rond point Leclerc, Parc Emmanuel Liais. ◷*Same as Musée Thomas-Henry.* *No charge.* 𝒫02 33 53 51 61.
On the ground floor are exhibits of shells, mammals and birds. Upstairs Egypt, Asia, Africa, Oceania and the Americas are represented.

Place Napoléon

A bronze statue of the emperor dominates the square. Nearby is the **Église de la Trinité**, a Flamboyant Gothic church.

Musée Thomas-Henry

4 r. Vastel. ◷*Open May–Sept Tue–Sat 10am–noon, 2–6pm, Sun–Mon 2–6pm; Oct–Apr Wed–Sun 2–6pm.* ◷*Closed public holidays.* *No charge.* 𝒫02 33 23 39 30.
The first gallery is devoted to paintings with Cherbourg and the sea as themes. The 15C–19C paintings are on display in the other galleries, including Fra Angelico's altarpiece panel, *The Conversion of St Augustine* and Filippo Lippi's *Entombment*. The local artist **Jean-François Millet** (1814–75) is well represented.

Cité de la Mer★★

Gare Maritime Transatlantique, facing the marina. ♿🕐*Contact for hours.* ☞*€18 Apr–Sept, €15.50 Oct–Dec and Feb–Mar.* ☎*02 33 20 26 69.* www.citedelamer.com.

The Art Deco former hall of the transatlantic passenger station has information kiosks, but the core of the museum lies in adjacent wings with basins and tanks that present marine

Le Redoutable, Cité de la Mer

©SIPA PRESSE_E.Travers/Cité de la Mer

fauna and flora. *Le Redoutable*, the first French nuclear submarine, is here.

Quai de France

Behind the Cité de la Mer the port also regularly handles cruise ships such as the *Queen Mary II* at the Gare Maritime Transatlantique on the Quai de France. Information about the arrivals and departures of these ships can be obtained from the tourist office (*℘ 02 33 93 52 02 or www.otcherbourgcotentin.fr*).

Boat Trip Round the Roadstead

Ticket booth and embarkation point at Cité de la Mer. ≈Guided tours 6 Jul–3 Aug 2pm, 3.30pm, 5pm; Aug 11.30am, 2pm, 3.30pm, 5pm, 6.30pm; Apr–5 Jul and Sept 1.30pm, 3pm, 4.30pm.* ≈€13.* ℘02 33 20 09 00.

The roadstead is a sheltered offshore anchorage. Visitors sail past the central fort of the seawall, which Napoleon called his pyramid, and the military port.

Fort du Roule

A road winds up to the fort on Roule Hill (112m/367ft). In June 1944, the Germans entrenched here offered fierce resistance before surrendering. The ramparts offer a good **panorama**★ *(viewing table).*

Musée de la Libération

av. Étienne-Lecarpentier, Fort du Roule. ♿⏱*Same as Musée Thomas-Henry.* ≈€3.80.* ℘02 33 20 14 12.

The museum retraces the dark years of French history from 1940 to 1944 as well as hopeful events such as the D-Day landing, the liberation of Cherbourg and the rebuilding of the port.

EXCURSIONS
Tourlaville

▶*5km/3mi E. From Cherbourg take avenue de l'Amiral-Lemonnier SE. In Tourlaville, at the crossroads before the Hôtel Terminus, turn right onto rue des Alliés. 800m/875yd farther on at the junction with D 63 turn right again onto D 32. Park the car and continue on foot.*

The Park of the Château des Ravalet★

♿⏱*Open daily May–Aug 8am–8pm; Mar–Apr and Sept–Oct 8am–6.30 pm; Nov– Feb 8.30am–5pm.* ≈Guided tours (1h30min) offered Jul–Aug on Mon.* ≈No charge.* ℘02 33 87 88 98. www.ville-cherbourg.fr.

The park of this lovely Renaissance château includes tropical plants, lovely stretches of water and fine beech trees.

Martinvast
▷ *10 km/6.25mi south of Cherbourg by the D 900.*

Château de Martinvast
🕐 *Open Mon–Fri 10am–noon, 2–6pm, Sat–Sun and public holidays 2–6pm.*
🕐 *Closed Sat Nov–Mar.* ⊚€6. ☎*02 33 87 20 80. www.chateau-martinvast.fr.*
Although the château is not open to the public, its attractive **park** offers seven signposted trails.

Tollevast
▷ *10km/6.25mi south of Cherbourg by the D 900, then left towards Hardinvast.*
Église –You need to take your time, and if possible binoculars, to discover this small Romanesque church (12C). At first sight, there is nothing exceptional about it, apart from the harmony that its sober architecture exudes. Its main interest lies in the abundant sculpted décor that is found on the masonry on the exterior, the tops of the columns of the western porch, and the diagonally ribbed chalice forms of the chancel.

👥 Ludiver – Observatoire – Planétarium de La Hague
▷ *Leave Cherbourg going west on the D 901, in the direction of Équeurdreville-Hainneville. At the roundabout, take the Cap de La Hague direction for 4km/2.5mi. At the intersection, go towards Tonneville and follow the signs.*
🕐 *Open all year except January. See website for details of opening times.*
⊚ *€7.50 (children 7–18 €5.50).*
☎*02 33 78 13 80. www.ludiver.com.*
Set on Flottemanville-Hague and Tonneville plateau (180m/590ft), the aim of this centre is the discovery of the sky, stars and planets. The site incorporates a museography area dedicated to the universe, a planetarium with 80 places (Jul–Aug 11.30am, 3pm, 4.30pm; rest of the year 3pm), an inside amphitheatre (images from a 600mm/23.6 in telescope are projected live to the public). The observation site is blessed with ideal conditions, because atmospheric and light pollution is minimal here.

▷ *Return towards the coast and pass under the D901.*

Querqueville
▷ *7.5km/4.5mi northeast of Cherbourg via D 901.*
Beside the parish church stands the 10C **Chapelle St-Germain** *(left)*, the oldest religious building in the Cotentin area. From behind the church *(path between the chapel and the church)* there is a view over the Cherbourg roadstead stretching from Cap Lévy *(east)* to Pointe Jardeheu *(west)*.

Château de Nacqueville
▷ *9.5km/6mi northwest of Cherbourg by the D 901, the D 45, then left to La Rivière.* 🔊 *Guided tours (1hr)*
🕐 *May–Sept Tue, Thur, Fri, Sun and public holidays noon–5pm; park closes at 6pm.* ⊚ *€6.* ☎*02 33 03 21 12. http://naqueville.com.*
This beautiful 16C edifice, built as a fortified manor, covered with ivy, makes a romantic sight, standing by a pool in a **park**★ of oak trees and flowering shrubs. The park was created by an English landscape designer in 1830 and is resplendent with rhododendrons, azaleas and hydrangeas.
Only the great hall with a beautiful Renaissance fireplace is open to the public.

Landemer
▷ *10km/6mi to the northwest of Cherbourg by the D 901 and the D 45. Le manoir is situated at the entrance to Landemer, next to the road, on the left.*
Manoir de Dur-Écu 🕐 *Jul–Sept Tue–Thur 11am–1pm, 3–7pm.* ⊚*€4 (under 18 no charge).* ☎*06 10 58 68 41.*
A 16C manor house with bizarre groups of towers, built on 9C foundations. Only the courtyards and the *pigeonnier* can be visited but there is also a maze in the cornfield next to the manor.
After Landemer, the road goes into the ravin du Hubiland and soon, on the right, you will have a beautiful view of the lighthouse at Cap Levi at the Pointe Jardeheu.

Barfleur★

This charming fishing port, with its granite houses and quays, is one of the most beautiful villages of France. Tradition has it that the boat that carried William, Duke of Normandy, to England was built here. A bronze plaque placed in 1966 at the foot of the jetty marks his departure (1066).

SIGHTS
Église St-Nicholas
Set in a cemetery on a rocky promentory, this squat 17C church has the appearance of a fort. In the south transept is a remarkable 16C *Pietà* while in the north transept above the font is a stained-glass window depicting Ste-Marie-Madeleine Postel (1756–1846).

Maison de Julie Postel
La Bretonne hamlet. ♿🕐*Open 9am–7pm.* ✆*No charge.* ✆*02 33 54 02 17.*
Julie Postel was born in Barfleur in 1756. As Sister Marie-Madeleine she founded the Sisters of the Christian Schools of Mercy (La Congrégation des Sœurs de la Miséricorde), now called Sisters of Ste-Marie-Madeleine Postel.

🚗DRIVING TOURS

Pointe de Barfleur
4km/2.5mi N by D 116 and D 10.

🐾 Reach the Pointe by the GR 223 Coastal Footpath or by the D 116 to Gatteville and right onto the D 10.

Gatteville-le-Phare
The church, rebuilt in the 18C, still has its original 12C belfry. The Mariners' Chapel (Chapelle des Marins), in the square, is built over a Merovingian necropolis.

Phare
🕐*Open May–Aug 10am–noon, 2–7pm; Apr and Sept 10am–noon, 2–6pm; Mar and Oct 10am–noon, 2–5pm; Feb and Nov–Dec 10am–noon, 2–4pm.* 🕐*Closed*

▶ **Population:** 653.
🗺 **Michelin Map:** 303: E-1.
ℹ **Info:** 2 rond-point Guillaume-le-Conquerant. ✆02 33 54 02 48. www.ville-barfleur.fr.
◖ **Location:** Barfleur is reached from Cherbourg (29km/18mi to the W) via D 116, which follows the coast, or by D 901, which is more direct.
◉ **Don't Miss:** The view from the top of the Gatteville lighthouse, and the arrival of the day's catch from fishing boats in the port.
🕐 **Timing:** The area requires at least a half day of your time.

Jan, 1 May, 25 Dec, and if winds are too high. ✆*€2.* ✆*02 33 23 17 97.*
The lighthouse, on the northeastern extremity of the Cotentin Peninsula, is one of the tallest in France (71m/233ft). The light, with a range of 56km/35mi, and the radio beacon, installed in a small 18C tower, guide ships into Le Havre. From the top (365 steps) there is a **panorama**★★ stretching over the east coast of the Cotentin Peninsula, St-Marcouf Islands, Veys Bay and, in clear weather, the cliffs at Grandcamp. The shallow waters and swift currents have caused many shipwrecks, including the *White Ship* in 1120, with Henry's heir, William Atheling, and 300 members of the Anglo-Norman nobility on board.

Montfarville
◖*2km/1mi S by D 155.*
This 18C granite church has a chapel and belfry dating from the 13C and a highly colourful **interior**★. The paintings on the vaulting are by a local artist, Guillaume Fouace.

The North Coast From Barfleur to Cherbourg★★
38km/23.6mi. Allow 1hr30min.

▶ *Leave Barfleur by the D 901.*

Tocqueville

This was the family seat of **Alexis de Tocqueville** (1805–59) the author of *Democracy in the United States* and *The Ancien Régime and the Revolution*.

Réthoville

Moulin de Marie Ravenel –*Guided visit.* ♿ ⏱ *Jul–Aug Tue–Sun 2–7pm; May–Jun and Sept weekends and hols only 2–7pm.* ⊛€2 *(under 14 no charge).* 🕿*02 33 54 37 20/02 33 54 56 18. www. tourisme-fermanville.new.fr.* This 18C mill was the residence of the miller/poetess Marie Ravenel in the 19C

▶ *Take the D 514 to rejoin the D 901 in the direction of St-Pierre-Église.*

St-Pierre-Église

The fortified 17C church has a 12C Romanesque doorway. The 18C **château** was the family home of the Abbé de St-Pierre (1658–1743), the author of a plan for peace entitled *Projet de Paix Perpétuelle.*

▶ *Leave St-Pierre-Église by the D 210 in the direction of Fermanville.*

Fermanville

A flower bedecked village, with granite houses which are typical of the region. **Vallée des Moulins** – ▪️Leave from the tourist office car park; 8km/5mi – waymarked in yellow.

▶ *Leave Fermanville by the small road signposted "Phare du cap Lévi". 600m/yd after leaving the hamlet of La Bourdette, a surfaced path on the right leads to the Cap Lévi Semaphore.*

Cap Lévi

Encirling a harbour near to Fermanville, Cap Lévi has three buildings which are dedicated to coastal watch, unique in Europe.
Sémaphore du cap Lévi – ⏱*Sun–Thu 30 Apr–30 Jun, 5 Jul–27 Sept 2–7pm (guided visit at 3pm).* ⊛€3. 🕿*02 33 54 61 12.* Destined to give assistance to ships in distress, by bringing them help, this semaphore is the only one in France that is open to the public.

▶ *Rejoin the road to the Lighthouse.*

Phare – reconstructed in granite in 1946, it has a height of 28m/90ft.

▶ *Return to Fermanville then take a turn to the right which is the fort road that runs along the small port.*

Port-Lévi – Small anchorage port.

▶ *Drive in the direction of Fermanville and follow the signs for "Port-Lévi".*

Fort du cap Lévi – ♿ ⏱*Closed Jan, 25 Dec.* ⊛*No charge.* 🕿*02 33 23 68 68.* Constructed in the 19C to defend this coastline, which faces England. The fort today houses a chambre d'hôte (℅*see Barfleur addresses).*

▶ *Just after the harbour in Brick, turn left, in front of the Maison Rouge auberge, the steeply climbing Maupertus road.*

Belvédère★

There is a magnificent view of the coast and Cherbourg in the distance.

▶ *Return to the D 116; continue west; in Bretteville take the D 320 left towards Le Theil.*

Allée Couverte (Gallery Grave)

This collective burial chamber consists of a double row of upright stones supporting flat slabs laid horizontally.

▶ *Return to Bretteville; take D 116 west.*

On approaching Cherbourg one can see the roadstead (offshore anchorage area) and Pelée Island, which serves as an anchor for the mole. With the great breakwater, this divides the harbour from the sea. To the left is Roule Fort.

St-Vaast-la-Hougue

Among the good reasons to visit this popular seaside resort with a marina and a mild climate are the delicious *huîtres* (oysters).

SIGHTS
Phare
The lighthouse is situated at the end of the large granite jetty. The Chapelle des Marins was a landmark for sailors.

Fort
Follow the direction of La Hougue. The road along the Grande Plage is bordered by tamarisks and at the end of the beach the keep of the fort stands proud.

EXCURSION
Île de Tatihou★
Crossing (10min) every 30min (high tide) and every hour (low tide). ○ *Apr–Sept 10am–6pm; rest of the year Sat 2–5.30pm. Max. 500 visitors per day; book in advance.* ○ *€8.60 return fare (ticket includes visit to the museum and the Tour Vauban).* ○ *02 33 23 19 92. http://manche.fr/tatihou.*
An amphibious vehicle takes visitors over to Tatihou. The **Musée maritime départemental** has sections on naval architecture and objects from the site of the Battle of La Hougue (1692).

🚗 DRIVING TOUR

Le Val de Saire
40km/25mi. Allow 2hr30min.

▷ *Take D 1 north towards Réville; after crossing the bridge turn right to the Pointe de Saire.*

Quettehou
The 13C granite **church** is flanked by a tall 15C belfry. From the cemetery there is a view of Morsalines Bay, the Hougue Fort and the Pointe de Saire.

▷ *Leave Quettehou by the D 902 north*

Population: 2,128.
Michelin Map: 303: E-2.
Info: 1 place du Général-de-Gaulle. ○02 33 23 19 32. www.saint-vaast-reville.com.
Location: St-Vaast is 12km/7.5mi S of Barfleur; 18km/11mi NE of Valognes.
Don't Miss: Vauban's Tower.

---

and turn left onto the D 26.

The circuit offers beautiful views of the Cotentin coast and countryside.

▷ *At Valcanville, take the D 125. At the crossroads with the D 238, turn left to La Pernelle, then at 300m/328yd follow the signs "Église, panorama".*

La Pernelle
Beyond the rebuilt church of **La Pernelle** is a former German blockhouse, once an observatory, which commands a **panorama**★★ *(viewing table)* extending from the Gatteville lighthouse (north) to the Grandcamp cliffs (south) by way of the Pointe de Saire, Tatihou Island, Hougue Fort and the St-Marcouf Islands.

▷ *Traversez la D 902 puis empruntez la D 328 jusqu'à Jonville.*

Pointe de Saire
Beyond the hamlet of Jonville, by the sea, is an old blockhouse that offers a good **view**★ of the attractive rock-strewn beaches of Pointe de Saire and of Tatihou Island with St-Vaast in the background.

▷ *Continue north on D 1.*

Beyond Réville the road passes **La Crasvillerie**, a delightful 16C manor house. As you approach Barfleur, the countryside gradually changes, becoming more like the neighbouring region of Brittany, with houses made of granite hewn from local rocks, rocky bays and gnarled trees bent by the wind. Gatteville lighthouse stands to the north.

Valognes★

Valognes is an important road junction at the heart of the Cotentin Peninsula and is the market town for the surrounding agricultural area. The aristocratic town described by Barbey d'Aurevilly was partially destroyed in June 1944; it has been rebuilt in the modern style and expanded. Several traces of the past have survived including Gallo-Roman ruins, 11C–18C churches, and private mansions built in the 18C when local high society made Valognes the Versailles of Normandy.

▶ **Population:** 7,196.

Michelin Map: 303: D-2.

Info: Place du Château. ℘02 33 40 11 55. www.ot-cotentin-bocage-valognais.fr.

Location: Valonges is at a major crossroads: Cherbourg is 20km/12.5mi N, Barnville-Carteret 29km/18mi SW, St-Sauveur-le-Vicomte is 16km/10mi SW.

Don't Miss: In Jul–Aug, tours led by expert guides trained by the Ministry of Culture. Contact Le Clos de Cotentin. ℘02 33 95 01 26 or the tourist office.

SIGHTS

Hôtel de Beaumont★

11 r. Barbey-d'Aurevilly. Guided tours (1hr) Jul–mid-Sept daily 10.30am–noon, 2.30–6.30pm; weekends of Easter, Pentecost, 1 May and the Ascension 2.30–6.30pm (last entry 1hr before closing); rest of the year open for groups (20+) only. €6. ℘02 33 40 12 30. www.hoteldebeaumont.fr. This noble 18C residence, miraculously spared by the bombings, has a splendid front in dressed stone. Inside, the sweeping flight of steps with a double winding stairwell gives access to the upper floor by a stone arch ending in mid-air. The terraces are laid out as formal gardens.

Hôtel de Grandval-Caligny

32 r. des Religieuses. Guided tours (45min) on request 1 day in advance to Mme Fauvel. 1 May 1–15 Sept Mon–Sat 11am–noon, 2.30–6pm. €4. ℘06 68 36 45 95.

Hôtel de Beaumont

A. de Valroger/MICHELIN

The 19C novelist **Jules Barbey d'Aurevilly** once lived in this handsome 17C–18C mansion.
Note the staircase with its wrought-iron banister, the Empire-style ceramic stove in the dining room, and the alcoved bedrooms.

Musée Régional du Cidre

r. du petit-Versailles and r. Pelouze.
🕐 *Open Apr–14 Jun and 15–30 Sept Wed–Sun 2–6pm; 15 Jun–14 Sept daily 11am–7pm; Nov hols 1–5pm. Oct–Mar open for group bookings only (✆ 02 33 95 82 00). ☞ €4. ✆ 02 33 40 22 73. www. mairie-valognes.fr.*

The Cider Museum is in the **Maison du Grand Quartier**, one of a group that housed a 15C–18C linen factory.

Musée de l'Eau-de-Vie et des Vieux Métiers

🕐 *Open same hours as Cider Museum.*
Housed in the **Hôtel de Thieuville** (16C–19C), this museum displays equipment for distillation, stonemasonry, iron and copper work from the 11C to the 20C.

EXCURSIONS
Bricquebec

▷ *From Valognes, go west on the D 902 about 13km/8mi.* 🔍 *Guided tours (1hr30min) of the castle.* 🕐 *Jul–Aug Wed–Mon 2–6.30pm. ☞ €1.80. ✆ 02 33 87 22 50 (town hall).*

The town is known for its old **castle** and its Trappist monastery. The inner courtyard of the castle is still enclosed by a fortified wall. The 14C **keep** is a handsome polygonal tower (23m/75.5ft high). The sentry walk between the keep and the clock tower offers a view of the town. The **Tour de l'Horloge** (Clock Tower) houses a small regional museum where there is a collection of old furniture, some medals and mineral samples. There is also a restored 13C crypt.

Musée À la Recherche du Temps Perdu

▷ *In Bricquebec, take the D 902 in the direction of Barneville-Carteret, turn left into the D 900 in direction of St-Sauveur-le-Vicomte and follow the signage.*

✆ *02 33 10 27 73.* 🕐 *Jul–Aug 9.30am–noon, 2–7pm; from Easter till end Jun and Sept–Oct weekends and hols 2–7pm. ☞ €4. (10–16 years €2).*

👥 Located in a former farm, this museum retraces the history of rural life in the first half of the 20C. A class room from the 1940s, a grocer's shop from the 1930s, with a postman leaning on the counter, a funeral procession following a coffin, have all been created. There are also other memories documented: those of a doctor who practised in Bricquebec from 1905 to 1936, and communion offerings.

▷ *From Bricquebec take D 50 and D 121 north; just before the Calvary turn left onto a path.*

Abbaye Notre-Dame-de-Grâce

From Bricquebec, 2km/1mi via D 50, then D 121 and the road to the left, just before a stone cross. The abbey is not open for tours but it is possible to attend services, watch an audio-visual presentation at 3pm and purchase items. ✆ 02 33 87 56 10.

The Trappist monastery, which is occupied by a community of Cistercian monks, was founded in 1824 by Abbot Dom Augustin Onfroy, a local priest.

Parc animalier St-Martin

Montaigu-la-Brisette, at 12km/7.5mi to the NE of Valognes by the D 902.
🕐 *Open daily Apr–Oct 9am–6pm; Oct–Mar 10am–4pm.* 🕐 *When it snows and 25 Dec. May close early in winter due to bad weather. ☞ €13. (3–10 years €9). ✆ 02 33 40 40 98.*
www.espace-zoologique.com

👥 The exhibits in this park, which is located in the heart of the forest, come from all five continents: from Bactrian camels (Asia), to the amusing maras, a type of hare from Patagonia; watusi cattle from Africa, to llamas, not forgetting the baboon colony which delouse themselves all day, nor the multicoloured macaws and arrogant ostriches.

St-Sauveur-le-Vicomte

St-Sauveur-le-Vicomte, standing on the banks of the Douve in the heart of Cotentin, is closely associated with the 19C writer **Jules Barbey d'Aurevilly** and Ste-Marie-Madeleine Postel, who founded the Sisters of the Christian Schools of Mercy in the 19C.

- ▸ **Population:** 2,118.
- **Michelin Map:** 303: C-3.
- **Info:** Le Vieux Château. ℘02 33 21 50 44. www.ville-saint-sauveur-le-vicomte.fr.
- **Location:** St-Sauveur-le-Vicomte is 15km/9.6mi S of Valognes on D 2 and 19km/12mi E of Barneville-Carteret via D 650 and D 15.
- **Don't Miss:** The keep of the Vieux Château.
- **Timing:** You will need 3hr to see the château and the abbey.

SIGHTS

Château

Guided tour (1hr) Jul–Aug Tue–Sun 3pm, 4.30pm. Gardens open all year. €2. ℘02 33 21 50 44.

The bust at the entrance is that of Jules Barbey d'Aurevilly, by Rodin. This 12C castle was the ancestral home of two Norman families, the Néels and the Harcourts. The castle has suffered many a siege, notably by the English in 1356 and the French in 1375. Louis XIV had the castle converted into a hospice in 1691.

Église

Only the transept dates from the 13C. The rest of the church was rebuilt in the 15C. At the entrance to the chancel are a 16C *Ecce Homo (left)* and a 15C statue of St James of Compostela *(right)*.

Musée Barbey-d'Aurevilly

64 r. Bottin-Desylles. Enter the castle precinct (which now contains an old people's home), climb the stairs (left) beyond the vault. Open Wed–Mon Jul–Aug 11am–6pm; mid-Apr–Jun and Sept–Oct 1–6pm. Guided tours available. €4.20. ℘02 33 41 65 18.

The museum contains mementoes of Jules Barbey d'Aurevilly (1809–89), a critic and writer of popular fantastical novels who was born in the town and is buried in the castle cemetery.

Abbaye

Open daily 9.30am–noon, 2–6pm. No charge. Guided tours available on request. ℘02 33 21 63 20.

The abbey was founded in the 10C by Néel de Néhon, Vicomte de St-Sauveur.

The Hundred Years' War ruined the abbey and forced the monks into exile. At the Revolution the building was further dismantled. In 1832 it was bought by Mother Marie-Madeleine Postel to serve as the mother house for the order, which she had founded in Cherbourg in 1807. Although damaged in World War II, the abbey was repaired between 1945–50.

Abbatiale – The plain round-headed windows in the south aisle of the abbey church date from the Romanesque period. The tomb of Ste-Marie-Madeleine Postel lies in the north transept.

Parc – The well-tended park with its fine trees and colourful flower beds is a pleasant place for a stroll.

EXCURSION

Château de Crosville-sur-Douve

Proceed towards Valognes for 5km/3mi and in Rauville-la-Place take D 15 towards Pont-l'Abbé, then follow the signposts. Open Easter–Oct and 1–24 Dec daily 2–6pm. €6 (includes the garden). ℘02 33 41 67 25.

The oldest part of this imposing 17C château is the round, machicolated tower with its staircase turret.

Ste-Mère-Église

This town entered modern history brutally on the night of 5–6 June 1944 when troops from the American 82nd Airborne Division landed to assist the 101st Division in clearing the exits from Utah Beach. Ste-Mère-Église was liberated on 6 June but fighting continued until tanks advanced into the town from Utah Beach the following day.

SIGHTS
Église
The solid 11C–13C church was damaged particularly during the dislodging of German snipers from the belfry. A dummy at the end of a parachute hangs from the steeple as a reminder of Private John Steele's ordeal: dropped over the area during the night of 6 June 1944, he was caught dangling from the steeple by his parachute. He played dead for two hours, a few feet from a bell that never stopped ringing. The Germans eventually unhooked him.

Borne O de la Voie de la Liberté
In front of the town hall.
This is the first of the 12,000 symbolic milestones *(bornes)* along the Road of Liberty followed by General Patton's 20th Corps of the American Third Army to Metz and Bastogne.

Musée Airborne★
14 r. Eisenhower. &Open daily Apr–Sept 9am–6.45pm; Oct–Nov, Feb–Mar and Christmas school holidays 9.30am–noon, 2–6pm. €7. 02 33 41 41 35. www.musee-airborne.com.*
A parachute-shaped building in a large park at the entrance to the town houses the Airborne Museum, which contains mementoes of the fighting on D-Day.

Ferme-Musée du Cotentin
chemin de Beauvais. &Open daily Jul–Aug 11am–7pm (last entry 1hr before closing); Jun and Sept 11am–6pm; Apr–May and school holidays (except Christmas) 2–6pm. €4.20. 02 33 95 40 20.*

▸ **Population:** 1,629.
Michelin Map: 303:E-3.
Info: 6 rue Eisenhower. 02 33 21 00 33.
Location: The N 13 between Bayeux (59km/37mi E) and Valognes (16km/10mi NW) passes by Ste-Mère-Église. www.sainte-mere-eglise.info/.
Don't Miss: Look up to the church steeple at the paratrooper dangling there.
Timing: Take 2hr to see the village and the Airborne Museum.
Kids: The Cotentin Farm Museum.

Housed in the Beauvais farm (16C), this Cotentin Farm Museum recreates rural life of the early years of the 20C.

🚗 DRIVING TOUR

In the footsteps of the American landings
43km/27mi. Allow 2hr15min.

Écausseville
Hangar à dirigeables – *Cross the town and follow the red signs "Hangar"* &Guided visit Jul–Aug daily 10am–6pm; Jun and Sept Sat–Thu 2–6pm; Apr–May and Oct Wed, Sat–Sun 2–6pm. €2 (under 12 no charge). 02 33 54 01 02. www.aerobase.fr.*
This huge hangar in the middle of nowhere offers rare evidence of infrastructures used for air combat during the 1914–18 war. Built in the last year of the war, it formed part of the air station of Montebourg-Écausseville, whose mission was to spot German submarines and mines in order to provide safe passage for maritime convoys. Its 150m/164yd length and 30m/33yd width houses airships. After the abandonment by the Navy of these dirigibles in 1936, it served as a storage centre for

tanks and cannons, and spare parts for ships and planes, etc.

▶ *Head north to Montebourg, then follow the D42 to Quinéville.*

Quinéville
This is a family seaside resort. Good view of St-Vaast roadstead from the square near the church.

Mémorial de la Liberté retrouvée
18 av. des Plages, Quinéville.
♿ ⏰ *Open last week Mar–11 Nov daily 10am–7pm.* ⊚ *€6.* ☏ *02 33 95 95 95. www.memorial-quineville.com.*
This museum recreates daily life during the dark days of the Occupation. There is a village street, a blockhouse, and miscellaneous documentary material from the period.

▶ *Follow the coastal route south D 421 to Gougins.*

Gaps in the cordons of dunes provide views that change, along the coast, from the cliffs of Grandcamp to the fort of La Hougue and Saire point. Single storey granite houses with slate roofs, are a forerunner of the Sairea valley.

▶ *At Gougins, turn right onto the D 69 towards la batterie de Crisbecq.*

St-Marcouf
Batterie de Crisbecq – ⏰*Daily Jul–Aug, 10am–9pm; May–Jun and Sept 10am–6pm; Apr and Oct–Nov 11am–6pm.* ⊚*€ 6 (under 12s €3.50). A reduction is given on showing a Normandy Pass.* ☏ *06 68 41 09 04. www.batterie-marcouf.com.*
The St-Marcouf Battery had vital strategic interest, because its 210mm guns could sweep the Utah beaches. It was therefore the target of terrible attacks aimed at neutralising and removing the position.
Crisbecq was struck by hundreds of tonnes of bombs, which reduced the major arms to silence, but did not destroy the pillboxes. On 8 June 1944, during a fierce attack by American troops, Lieutenant Ohmsen requested

that the Azeville battery fire above him to ease the vice he was caught in. The garrison held until the morning of 12 June. Resistance was strong and only 78 out of more than 350 men survived the battle, before reaching Cherbourg. The shattered pillbox on the left is impressive, but it was the Americans who shelled it, after the surrender.

▶ *Continue 1.6 km1mi on the D 69, then turn left into the D 269. At 1km/0.6mi, follow the directions for Azeville.*

Azeville
Batterie – *Guided visit (1hr15min).* ⏰*Open daily Jul–Aug 10am–9pm; May–Jun and Sept 10am–6pm; Apr and Oct–Nov 11am–6pm (last entry 1hr before closing).* ⊚*€6.50 (under 12s 3.50 €). Reduction of €1 with Normandy Pass.* ☏*02 33 40 63 05. www.batterie-marcouf.com.*
Away from the coast, and less exposed than the Crisbecq, this battery has been built near to the village to allow the camouflage of certain pillboxes which were installed in houses. Equipped with 105mm cannons, the battery had no view of the sea, and its garrison lived the good life for a long time with a "casino" – a hut with a bar, stage and dancing girls and even a water reservoir which served as a swimming pool. Exceptionally well preserved, it has notably maintained the core of its underground galleries.

▶ *Return and follow the D 420 until Ravenoville, where you turn right onto the D 14 for 300m/yd. Turn left on the D 15, until Ravenoville-Plage. Follow the dunes on the D 421, southeast.*

Les Dunes-de-Varreville
In an opening in the dunes, 100m/110yd from the route des Alliés, a rose granite **monument** in the form of a ship's prow and bearing the cross of Lorraine commemorates the landing of the 2nd French Armoured Division under General Leclerc on 1 August 1944.

▶ *Continue on the D 421.*

Utah Beach

Despite murderous fire from the German coastal batteries, the troops of the American 4th Division (7th Corps) disembarked on 6 June near La Madeleine and Les Dunes-de-Varreville and managed to make contact with the airborne troops of the 82nd and 101st Divisions, who had landed in the region of Ste-Mère-Église. Three weeks later the whole of the Cotentin Peninsula had been liberated.

At **La Madeleine** there is a milestone – the first on the Road to Liberty – erected in 1947 to honour soldiers killed during the landings and a memorial to the 4th Division. A German blockhouse *(left)* is now a monument to the dead of the 1st Engineer Special Brigade; a stele and a crypt commemorate the American 90th Division. On an area of dunes, presented by the commune of Ste-Marie-du-Mont as official American territory, there stands a huge stele erected on the 40th anniversary of the landings by the Americans, in homage to those who died at Utah Beach.

Musée du Débarquement

Ste-Marie-du-Mont. &⌚*Open daily Jun–Sept 9.30am–7pm (last entry 45min before closing); Apr–May and Oct 10am–6pm; Feb–Mar and 1st 2 weeks Nov 10am–5.30pm; mid-Nov–Dec and school and public holidays Sat–Sun 10am–12.30pm, 2–5.30pm.* ⊘*Closed 25 Dec.* ⊜*€7.50.* ℘*02 33 71 53 35. www.utah-beach.com.*
Utah Beach D-Day Museum is undergoing an extensive expansion programme. The museum will display its magnificent collection in an entirely new exhibition space. This will include a hangar to house a full-scale replica of the B-26 *Dinah Might*, whose crew from the 533rd Squadron parachuted safely during the Landings but were later captured.

▷ *Take the D 913until Ste-Marie-du-Mont (5.5km/3.4mi).*

Ste-Marie-du-Mont

The impressive **church** is identified by its square 14C tower, of which the top storey is a Renaissance addition. A roadside monument honours 800 Danish sailors who took part in the **D-Day landings**.

Carentan

Carentan is an important cattle market town and one of the largest centres of the regional dairy industry. Known as the gateway to the Cotentin Peninsula it is surrounded by the magnificent wet pastureland of the Marais, much appreciated by the cattle and horses of the region.

SIGHTS

The octagonal spire of the belfry of the **Église Notre-Dame** (12C–15C) dominates the whole region. The fine stone house at the corner of rue de l'Église and place Guillaume-de-Cerisay was described by Balzac under

▸ **Population:** 6,058.

⊙ **Michelin Map:** 303:E-4.

▯ **Info:** Bd de Verdun, 50500 Carentan, ℘02 33 71 23 50. www.ot-carentan.fr.

▷ **Location:** Carentan marks the entry to the Cotentin Peninsula. Bayeux is 44km/27.5mi East and Cherbourg (51km/32mi NW).

⊙ **Don't Miss:** the spire of Église Nôtre-Dame.

⌚ **Timing:** Allow at least half a day to see the town and do the driving tour.

the name Hôtel de Dey in his work *Le Réquisitionnaire*.

The arcades of the old covered market in **place de la République** date from the late 14C. The **hôtel de ville** (town hall) occupies a 17C–19C convent.

The port, situated to the northeast of town, was inaugerated in 1982 at the end of the canal that links with the sea in the Baie des Veys.

🚗 DRIVING TOUR

Parc naturel régional des marais du cotentin et du Bessin

40km/25mi. Allow 2hr30min.

▷ *Leave Carentan by the D 913 in the direction of St-Côme-du-Mont.*

Les Ponts d'Ouve★ – Maison du Parc

50500 St-Côme-du-Mont. ◷*Open daily all year* ⊚*€6.* ✆*02 33 71 65 30. www.parc-cotentin-bessin.fr.*

Near Carentan is a visitor centre for the Marais du Cotentin et du Bessin Park. In addition to the exhibits indoors on flora and fauna, there is a **discovery trail** through the park with informative panels. There are observation areas set up for bird-watchers.

The nature park, formerly known as the Marais de Carentan, was inaugurated in June 1991. With a total area of 145,000ha/358,000 acres these wetlands stretch from the Bay of Veys on the east coast of the Cotentin Peninsula to Lessay haven on the west coast. This area of marshland *bocage* with its many canals is rich in plant and animal life.

▷ *Return to Carentin, leave the town by the D 971, then turn left on the D 29. Keep going for 13km/8mi, then right on the D 8.*

Rémilly-sur-Lozon

The village is renowned for its reed work, which developed considerably in the 19C.

Château de Montfort – **L'art du bois.** ♿ ◷*Open daily Jul–Aug 2.30–7pm;*

Apr–Jun and Sept–Oct Sat–Sun 2.30–7pm. ⊚*€3.50 (6–12 years €2).* ✆*02 33 55 30 11.* Visitors first fall for the charm of this former castle, dating from 15C, then enjoy exploring a restored outbuilding that houses an astonishing exhibition of sculptures in balsa wood. A passionate wood worker, Gilbert Housset has amused himself by creating life-size models of his motorbike, a tractor, aircraft engines, clothes, etc.

▷ *Take the D 94 in the direction of Marchésieux (2.5km/1.6mi).*

Marchésieux

In this southern section of the Parc, this commune, with several interesting features, has a church decorated with remarkable 14C frescoes.

Maison des marais – *Signed on the D 900 at the entry to St-Lô and Périers.* ◷*Open daily Jul–Aug 2.30–6.30pm; Easter–Jun and Sept–All Saints' Sun and hols 2.30–6.30pm.* ⊚*€3.05 (under 14 years €0.80).* ✆*02 33 07 15 20. www. musees-basse-normandie.fr.*

Remarkably restored, this large house illustrates perfectly what traditional accommodation was like in the marshlands, that is to say, built on a foundation of stone by adding layers or levees of earth, without any wooden structure. The region has preserved several thousand, most of which date from the 19C.

▷ *Leave Marchésieux to the SW and follow the D 433 until Le Bourg-d'Aubigny. Turn right on the D 142.*

St-Martin-d'Aubigny

Maison de la brique de Basse-Normandie – ◷*Open daily Jul–Aug 2.30–6.30pm; mid-Jun–end Jun and Sept Sun 2.30–6.30pm.*⊚ *€3 (8–12 years €0.75).* ✆*02 33 07 61 95.* With a chimney, a vast flame oven, drying rooms… the brickworks has kept the core of its installations and offers the opportunity to discover an activity about which not much is known.

ADDRESSES

🏨 STAY

ST-LÔ

⊜⊜ **Chambre d'hôte Château de Dampierre** – *14350 Dampierre, 9km/5.6mi from Torigny-sur-Vire via D 13, then right on D 53.* ☎*02 31 67 31 81. 15 rooms.* ☐ ☑. A magnificent tree-lined approach leads to this 16C manor. Well-kept rooms overlooking the moat, the gatehouse and a superb dovecot, in the midst of the *bocage* countryside.

⊜⊜⊜ **Auberge de Campagne** – *Château de la Roque, 50180 Hébécrevon, 7.5km/4.7mi W of St-Lô towards Coutances, then towards Périers via D 900.* ☎*02 33 57 33 20. www. chateau-de-la-roque.fr. 15 rooms.* ☑*€10. Closed mid Dec–mid Jan.* This beautiful 16C–17C residence appears at the end of a poplar-lined approach. Tastefully decorated rooms, lovely park for strolls, spa, sauna and plenty of activities on offer. The *restaurant*⊜⊜ offers fine local cuisine in its dining room, which displays exposed beams. Friendly welcome.

⊜⊜⊜ **Hôtel Mercure** – *1 av. Briovère.* ☎*02 33 05 10 84. www.mercure.com. 67 rooms.* ☑ *€13.* Restaurant ⊜⊜. Opposite the ramparts two hotels have united to become a contemporary establishment. The new and refurbished rooms are comfortable. The restaurant has traditional cooking with a regional accent.

COUTANCES

⊜ **Chambre d'hôte Village Grouchy** – *11 r. du Vieux-Lavoir, 50560 Blainville-sur-Mer, 2km/1mi N of Agon-Coutainville via D 72.* ☎*02 33 47 20 31. Closed Mar. 5 rooms.* ☐ ☑. This little village used to comprise exclusively fishermen's homes. In this house, large bedrooms with wood panelling make for a fine halt right by the sea. A summer kitchen is at guests' disposal in the garden.

⊜⊜ **Chambre d'hôte Le Quesnot** – *3 r. du Mont-César, 50660 Montchaton, 6.5km/4mi SW of Coutances via D 20 then D 72.* ☎*02 33 45 05 88. www.chambres-hotes-montchaton.fr. Closed 15 Nov–Easter. 3 rooms.* ☑*€9.* Guests have the use of a small 18C stone-built house with its own terrace and tiny garden and a view of a little church perched on a promontory. Modern bedrooms above the large country-style dining room.

⊜⊜ **Chambre d'hôte Le Clos Postel** – *5 rte d'Urville, Village d'Urville, 50590 Regneville-sur-Mer, 10km/6mi SW of Coutances via D 20, rte de Montmartin-sur-Mer and D 49.* ☎*02 33 07 12 38. Closed Dec–Jan. 4 rooms.* ☐ ☑. This fomer presbytery has been totally restored and benefits from a great view of the Baie de la Seine. A calming atmosphere prevails in the garden. The four well-kept rooms (two of them in the old pigeon house) offer plenty of comfort.

⊜⊜ **Hôtel Cositel** –*rue de Saint Malo.* ☎*02 33 19 15 00. www.cositel.fr. Closed Dec–Jan. 55 rooms.* ☑*€9.50.* Modern construction in the town. Rooms are functional; the bistro offers light fare.

BARNEVILLE-CARTERET

⊜⊜ **Chambre d'hôte La Roque de Gouey** – *16 r. Gilles-Poërier, 50580 Portbail, 8km/5mi SE of Barneville.* ☎*02 33 04 80 27.* ☐. *6 rooms.* ☑. Simply decorated rooms; pleasant garden area.

⊜⊜ **Chambre d'hôte La Tourelle** – *5 r. du Pic-Maillet, in Barneville-Bourg.* ☎*02 33 04 90 22.* ☐. *5 rooms.* ☑. This 16C house faces the village church: an old-fashioned place offering good breakfasts.

⊜⊜⊜ **Chambre d'hôte Le Logis de la Mare** – *Village de La Mare-du-Parc, 50270 Surtainville, 11 km/6.9mi north of Carteret by the D 650, then the D 66 to the left.* ☎*02 33 04 35 50. www.logisdelamareduparc. com. 5 rooms.* ☑ In this extensive lovely 18C house are five very large well-equipped comfortable en-suite rooms. Four on the first floor for 2 or 3 people and one on the ground floor accessible for people of reduced mobility, with an adapted bathroom.

⊜⊜⊜ **Hôtel des Îles** – *9 bld Maritime.* ☎*02 33 04 96 76. 31 rooms.* ☑*€12.* Maritime décor characterises this hotel with spacious rooms.

CHERBOURG-OCTEVILLE

⊜ **Hôtel Angleterre** – *8 r. P.-Talluau.* ☎*02 33 53 70 06. www.hotelangleterre-fr. com. 23 rooms.* ☑. Situated in a quiet part of the town centre, a simple hotel with a white façade. Rooms are a bit small, but renovated and perked up with pastel colours. Reasonable prices.

⊜ **La Croix de Malte** – *5 r. des Halles.* ☎*02 33 43 19 16. Closed 15 days at Christmas. 24 rooms.* ☑. A stone's throw from the theatre and the casino. The rooms, furnished in pine, are well soundproofed. Ask for one of the larger rooms when you reserve.

⊜⊜ **Chambre d'hôte Manoir St-Jean** – *Le hameau St-Jean, 50110 Tourlaville, 1km/ 0.6mi beyond the châtau des Ravalet via D 322 and the road marked centre aéré, rte de Brix.* ✆*02 33 22 00 86. www.manoir-saint-jean.com. 3 rooms.* 🍴; 🖵. Located on the edge of the châtau des Ravalet park, this converted 18C farmhouse overlooks the green Trotebec Valley. You will be well taken care of by the owner, who has great knowledge of the natural and cultural wealth of her region. Two self-catering cottages.

⊜⊜ **Hôtel Ambassadeur** – *22 quai de Caligny. 50100 Cherbourg.* ✆*02 33 43 10 00. www.ambassadeurhotel.com. 40 rooms.* 🖵.This hotel overlooks the port, providing a view of constant activity. But the rooms are well soundproofed. Reasonable prices.

⊜⊜⊜ **Hôtel Renaissance** – *4 r. de l'Église.* ✆*02 33 43 23 90. www.hotel-renaissance-cherbourg.com. 12 rooms.* 🖵. This hotel has bright, soundproofed rooms and modern bathrooms.

ST-VAAST-LA-HOUGUE

⊜ **Chambre d'hôte La Ferme de Cabourg** – *10 rte du Martinet, 50760 Réville, 3.5km/2.2mi N of St-Vaast via D 1, then D 328 dir. Jonville.* ✆*02 33 54 48 42. 3 rooms.* 🍴. A poplar-lined alley leads to this fortified 15C farm. The guest rooms are nice and bright.

⊜⊜ **Hôtel de France et Fuchsias** – *20 r. du Mar.-Foch.* ✆*02 33 54 40 41. www.france-fuchsias.com. Closed 2 Jan 2–12 Feb and Mon Sept–May, Tue Nov–Mar. 35 rooms.* 🖵. *Restaurant*⊜⊜. When the fuchsias are in bloom they cover the walls of this 100-year-old hotel set back from the harbour. Some rooms overlook the garden. Meals in the dining room, on the veranda or the terrace.

VALOGNES

⊜ **Chambre d'hôte Le Haut Pitois** – *50700 Lieusaint, 2km/1mi S of Valognes via D 2, small road to left on leaving the village.* ✆*02 33 40 19 92. 4 rooms.* 🍴🖵. A superb woodland road leads to this former farm in a calm setting. The rooms, located upstairs in an outbuilding (2 can sleep 4 or 5 people) are sparse but functional with complete bathrooms. Ideal for a tight budget and for families.

⊜⊜ **Grand Hôtel du Louvre** – *28 r. des Réligieuses.* ✆*02 33 40 00 07. www.grandhoteldulouvre.com. Closed 28 Dec 6, 23 Dec–15 Jan and 4–12 Mar. 18 rooms.* 🅿 🖵. *Restaurant*⊜⊜. Near the centre of town, this hotel has character: Barbey d'Aurevilly, a 19C Gothic novelist, stayed in room no 4. Rooms, reached by a spiral staircase, have been renovated but retain their 19C character, as does the dining room.

STE-MÈRE-ÉGLISE

⊜ **Chambre d'hôte La Dannevillerie** – *50630 Le Vast, 5km/3mi NW of Quettehou via D 902 and D 26, then 2km/1mi further on, take the road on the right before Le Vast.* ✆*02 33 41 23 22. www.ladannevillerie.com. 3 rooms.* 🍴🖵. Nestling in the Val de Saire, this farm offers peace and repose. Delicious breakfasts.

⊜⊜ **Château de Quinéville** – *18 rue de l'Église, 50310 Quinéville.* ✆*02 33 21 42 67. www.chateau-de-quineville.com. Closed Jan–Mar. 30 rooms.* 🅿 🖵. *Restaurant*⊜⊜. Rooms in the former stables are more modern than those in the 18C château. The garden has Roman ruins, a 14C tower and a pond. Attractive dining room, traditional fare.

⌁/ EAT

ST-LÔ

⊜ **Bistrot de Paul et Roger** – *40 r. du Neufbourg.* ✆*02 33 57 19 00 . Closed 1st week Aug, Sun and Mon lunch.* In the middle of this crazy bric-à-brac of glazed tiles, Louis XVI chairs, old posters and black-and-white photographs, don't miss the priceless collection of old radio sets. Copious cuisine.

⊜⊜ **La Petite Auberge** Candol – *1216 rte de Candol, exit towards Canisy.* ✆*02 33 05 34 11. www.aubergedecandol.fr. Closed Mon and Tue.* After long years of travel, the chef has settled here to create delicious seafood dishes served on the terrace or close to the fireplace.

⊜⊜ **Le Péché Mignon** – *84 r. du Maréchal-Juin.* ✆*02 33 72 23 77. http://le-peche-mignon.monsite-orange.fr/. Closed Sun eve and Mon, except for group bookings.* Near the Haras national, the owner/chef prepares regional dishes adapted to today's tastes. Two dining rooms, including a more modern one with brightly coloured tablecloths.

COUTANCES

Le Jules Gommes – *34 r. du Vaudredoux, 50590 Regneville-sur-Mer, 10km/6mi SW of Coutances via D 20, rte de Montmartin-sur-Mer and then D 49.* ℘*02 33 45 32 04. www.le-jules-gommes.com. Closed Mon–Tue except school holidays. Reservation required at weekends.* This establishment, which shares its name with a late 19C three-masted schooner, positively exudes charm. Handsome rustic interior featuring exposed stone, a fireplace and watercolours. Both seafood and inland cuisine, crêpes, and a pub featuring a healthy choice of ales and whiskies.

La Verte Campagne – *Le Hameau Chevalier, 50660 Trelly, 13km/8mi S of Coutances via D 7, D 49, then D 539 and a minor road.* ℘*02 33 47 65 33. www.laverte campagne.com. Closed 22 Nov–15 Dec.* This 18C farm, covered with Virginia creeper in summer, has retained its authentic charm: wide ceiling beams, stone walls and old fireplaces. This renowned restaurant serves dishes prepared with care. A few rooms available upstairs.

Le Tourne-Bride – *85 r. d'Argouges, 50200 Gratot.* ℘*02 33 45 11 00. Closed 1–15 Jul, Feb holidays, Sun eve and Mon.* The proprietors of this former post-coach relay, Martine and Denis Poisson, offer a warm and attentive welcome. In the two rustic-style dining rooms, the menu focuses on traditional Norman cuisine, with produce straight from the sea and the local fields.

BARNEVILLE-CARTERET

Le Berlingot – *rte de Bricquebec, (D 902), Hameau Costard, 50270 Sortosville-en-Beaumont, 7km/4.3mi NE of Barneville.* ℘*02 33 53 87 16. Closed mid-Nov–Mar, Tue and Wed out of season.* This restaurant, specialising in crêpes, is popular with locals. The meat dishes are also good.

La Cale Marine – *Port de Carteret - 2 prom. Abbé-Lebouteiller.* ℘ *02 33 53 82 50. Closed from mid-Nov till beginning of Feb.* Called "la Cala Kiki" by the locals, this café-brasserie is appreciated for its terrace ideally situated opposite the fishing quay with its floats and lobster pots, and also for its moules marinière. Nothing sophisticated, but a pleasant stop to have a meal and enjoy the sun in the company of seagulls awaiting the return of the fish from the high seas.

L'Hermitage – *4 prom. A.-Leboutellier, 50270 Carteret.* ℘*02 33 04 46 39. www.hotel-hermitage-carteret.com. Closed 4 weeks mid-Nov–mid Dec, 5–25 Jan.* Great for seafood. Terrace facing the port. Rooms and self catering apartments with an exceptional view of the sea are available.

Pom'Cannelle – *10 r. du Gén.-Leclerc (à côté de la Poste), 50250 La Haye-du-Puits.* ℘*02 33 46 45 57. www.restaurantpom cannelle.fr. Closed Mon and Wed eve 15 Sept–15 Jun).* Crêpes and country cooking, fish and seafood, home-made duck foie-gras, duck cutlet with camembert cream, etc., all served in a pleasant environment with matching colour scheme. Revealed beams and wooden panelling complete the attractive décor.

CHERBOURG-OCTEVILLE

L'Antidote – *41 r. au Blé.* ℘*02 33 78 01 28. Closed Sun–Mon. Reservations advised.* A pleasant terrace and a wood-panelled dining room. The specialities include rillets de saumon de Cherbourg (a salmon patty), black pudding with pineapple, ginger and apples, and foie gras. Warm welcome.

Café de Paris – *40 quai Caligny.* ℘*02 33 43 12 36. Closed Mon lunch and Sun, three weeks in Nov and three weeks in Mar.* This bistro-style restaurant is bright and warm. Enjoy a selection of seafood while admiring the view of the harbour in one of the two dining rooms.

Sel et Poivre – *17 r. du Port.* ℘*02 33 01 24 09.* A pinch of salt, a dusting of pepper and a good dollop of know-how bring out the best in typical local fare served in a charming dining room.

Le Faitout – *25 r. Tour-Carrée.* ℘*02 33 04 25 04. www.restaurant-le-faitout. com. Closed last 2 weeks Dec. Reservations required.* An attractive retro façade, and a handsome wood-panelled décor, like that of a ship, inside. Traditional cuisine and Norman specialities.

Le Pily – *39 Grande Rue.* ℘*02 33 10 19 29. www.restaurant-le-pily.com. Closed Sat lunch, Wed and Sun evening.* Warm welcome in a fashionable plum and cream coloured dining room, with a cosy lounge area. Delicious contemporary cuisine.

ST-VAAST-LA-HOUGUE

⊝⊜ **Crêperie Léoncie** – *27 quai Vauban.* ✆*02 33 44 42 50.* You had better book ahead for this little place with a good reputation. Try the delicious crêpes with scallops or with three kinds of apples.

⊝⊜ **Le Chasse Marée** – *8 pl. du Gén. de Gaulle.* ✆*02 33 23 14 08. Closed mid-Dec–Jan, Mon lunch in Jul–Aug, Sun eve and Mon–Tue from Sept–Jun.* The dishes are mostly locally caught seafood. On the walls, the pennants of prestigious yacht clubs (mainly British) and old marine photos form an appropriate setting for the refined cuisine.

VALOGNES

⊝ **L'Agriculture** – *18 r. Léopold-Delisle.* ✆*02 33 95 02 02. www.hotel-agriculture.com.* In the centre of Valognes, this vine-covered building sits on a quiet little square. The interior is charming and rustic. Delicious house specialities. Guest rooms are modern and comfortable.

STE-MÈRE-ÉGLISE

⊝⊜ **L'Estaminet** – *pl. de l'Église, 50480 Ste-Marie-du-Mont-Village.* ✆*02 33 71 57 01. Closed Jan, Tue eve and Wed Oct–May.* Stop on the tiny, charming square next to the church, which on 6 June 1944 was stormed by thousands of Allied vehicles on their way from Utah Beach. This lovely Norman inn is the right place to recover from an emotional visit to the beaches. Seafood on the menu. A few rooms.

⊝⊜ **Le John Steele** – *4 r. du Cap-de-Laine, 50480 Ste-Mère-Église.* ✆*02 33 41 41 16. http://auberge-hotel-restaurant.auberge johnsteele.com. Closed Sun eve and Mon Oct–Jun.* Situated near the famous church, this inn (1730) pays homage to the soldier John Steele. Typically Norman dining room with exposed beams and stone walls. Regional cuisine. A few simple rooms.

🛒 SHOPPING

COUTANCES

Market – *pl. du Gén. de Gaulle, 50560 Blainville-sur-Mer.* An extremely animated and colourful market. Country produce of every kind can be found here, including, *naturellement*, the local cheese: le Coutances.

Beach huts in Gouville-sur-Mer
© Clément Philippe/age fotostock

🏃 LEISURE

COUTANCES

Several beaches are found on this part of the west coast, within 12–15km/7.5–9mi of Coutances. From north to south: **Anneville-sur-Mer**, a little beach with fine sand, set in the dunes; **Gouville-sur-Mer**, a beach 6km/4mi long with several acres of oyster beds (👁*for a guided tour of the oyster beds,* ✆*02 33 47 84 33)*; **Blainville-sur-Mer**, another beach with a reputation for oysters, also offers fishing and a wide sand beach much appreciated by families; **Agon-Coutainville** is the furthest south, and you will find here a golf course, a casino and all sorts of sports and nautical activities.

CHERBOURG-OCTEVILLE

Station Voile Nautisme et Tourisme de Cherbourg Hague – *r. du Diablotin, quartier Chantereyne.* ✆ *02 33 78 19 29.* This club offers many activities: canoeing, kayaking, sailing, diving, beach sports, mountain biking, paragliding, hang-gliding, etc. Lessons and equipment rentals are available.

🎭 ON THE TOWN

CHERBOURG-OCTEVILLE

Cherbourg is a sailors' town and under its peaceful daytime atmosphere runs a fun-loving, wild streak that surfaces after midnight.

Café du Théâtre – *8 pl. du Gén.-de-Gaulle.* ✆*02 33 43 01 49. www.lecafedutheatre. com. Closed Sun.* A great place to meet after a movie or show, or just to hang out. A glass-enclosed terrace lets you enjoy the view over the public square in all weathers. A lounge with red plush seats recalls the days when this was a theatre. Reasonably priced, traditional cuisine.

Casino de Cherbourg – *18 quai Alexandre III.* ✆*02 33 43 00 56.* Built in 1827, this casino is the oldest in France. Gamblers can try their luck, but others might prefer the leather armchairs of the elegant bar, or the 1950s style pub "Fifty's Diner". The disco plays golden oldies.

THE CHANNEL ISLANDS

The nine Channel Islands are divided into two territories known as **Bailiwicks**. The **Bailiwick of Jersey** includes Jersey plus the two uninhabited rocky islets of the Minquiers and the Ecréhous; the **Bailiwick of Guernsey** includes Guernsey, Alderney, Sark and Herm, plus the tiny privately owned isles of Brecqhou and Jethou. All the principal islands encourage tourism, maintaining marinas to attract sailors, ensuring clean beaches for surfers and swimmers, and conserving the countryside, to the delight of bird-watchers, walkers and cyclists.

Highlights

1. **St Peter Port**, Guernsey (p421), particularly **Hauteville House**.
2. Go wild in Jersey's near-natural **Durrell Wildlife Park** (p433)
3. Imagine Nazi occupation in the **Jersey War Tunnels** (p434)
4. Explore the fine fort of **Mont-Orgueil Castle** (p440)
5. Get away from it all on beautiful natural, car-free **Sark** (p442)

Governance

The Channel Islands have been associated with the English crown since the Norman conquest, despite the fact that they lie much nearer to the French coast – Jersey is a mere 22km/14mi from the Cotentin Peninsula, but 160km/100mi south of Britain – and were largely French-speaking until the 20C. However, English is now the universal language of the islands; the native tongue is a dialect of Norman French, the language of William the Conqueror, and is rarely heard. However, beneath the apparent English atmosphere lie 1,000 years of Norman tradition and sturdy independence.

The original Norman laws and systems have been renewed and modified by subsequent monarchs, though in matters of defence and international relations, the islands are subject to decisions made by the Home Office.

The most significant constitutional change in recent years was in 2008, when Sark discarded its feudal system and introduced a (largely) democratic constitution.

The islands yesterday and today

The islands are rich in prehistoric tombs and monuments indicating human habitation from 7500–2500 BC. They were annexed by the Normans in 933 and later attached to the English crown by William the Conqueror. Some customs and traditions and the Norman-French dialect heard on these islands, which have only been universally English-speaking since the early 20C, date back to this period. In 1204 King John was forced to cede Normandy to the French, but the Channel Islanders chose to remain loyal to the English Crown in return for certain privileges, one of which was an independent parliament. Despite this, the French tried repeatedly to capture the island. Threats of invasion by Napoleon account for the many Martello defence towers built along the coasts. The islands were occupied by the Germans from 1940–45, the only British territory to fall to the enemy during World War II, and the islanders suffered considerable hardship during this period.

By contrast today the Channel Islands are known for their high standard of living compared to the rest of the UK, benefitting from a VAT-exempt economy and lower rates of income tax. This has encouraged the islands to become a tax haven for wealthy British citizens, and a buoyant industry in financial services has developed. Farming, however, still plays an important part in the local economy and maintains a supply to mainland Britain of early vegetables (potatoes, tomatoes, grapes), cut flowers and rich Channel Island milk.

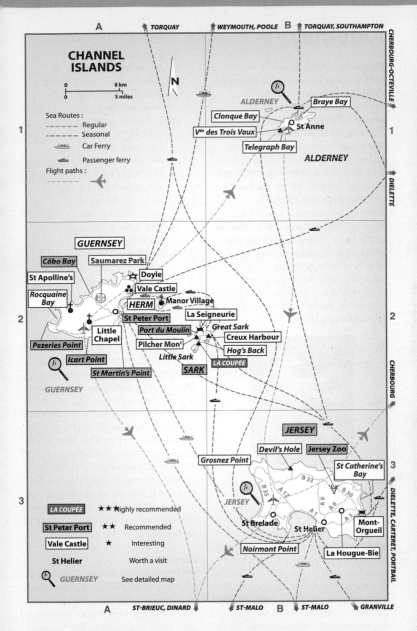

Channel Islands

A   TORQUAY   WEYMOUTH, POOLE   B   TORQUAY, SOUTHAMPTON

CHANNEL ISLANDS

0   8 km
0   5 miles

N

Sea Routes :
— — —   Regular
— — —   Seasonal
   Car Ferry
   Passenger ferry
Flight paths :

CHERBOURG-OCTEVILLE

DIELETTE

ALDERNEY

Braye Bay
Clonque Bay
St Anne
V^de des Trois Vaux
Telegraph Bay
ALDERNEY

GUERNSEY

Cóbo Bay
Saumarez Park
Doyle
St Apolline's
Vale Castle
Rocquaine Bay
Manor Village
HERM
La Seigneurie
St Peter Port
Great Sark
Little Chapel
Port du Moulin
Creux Harbour
Pezeries Point
Pilcher Mon¹
Hog's Back
Icart Point
Little Sark
LA COUPÉE
St Martin's Point
SARK
GUERNSEY

CHERBOURG

JERSEY

Devil's Hole   Jersey Zoo
Grosnez Point
St Catherine's Bay
B 33
JERSEY
B 35
B 30
A 9
A 6
LA COUPÉE   ★★ Highly recommended
A 12
A 3
St Peter Port   ★★ Recommended
St Brelade
Mont-Orgueil
Vale Castle   ★ Interesting
St Helier
A 1
St Helier   Worth a visit
GUERNSEY   See detailed map
Noirmont Point
La Hougue-Bie

DIELETTE, CARTERET, PORTBAIL

A   ST-BRIEUC, DINARD   ST-MALO   B   ST-MALO   GRANVILLE

Geography

Owing to their situation and the Gulf Stream, the islands enjoy a mild climate that nurtures spring flowers and semi-tropical plants. Long sandy beaches contrast with rugged cliffs, and quiet country lanes meander between traditional granite houses. Tidal currents in the islands are among the strongest in the world; at low tide, when the sea may retreat as much as 12m/39ft, huge areas of rocky reefs are exposed, greatly increasing the land mass and making it possible to walk further out (up to 3km/2mi).

The islands are served by ferries from France and England, and by flights to Jersey, Guernsey and Alderney. Scheduled ferries also connect the islands.

Alderney

Measuring a mere 5.6km/3.5mi long by 2.4km/1.5mi wide, Alderney slopes gently from a plateau in the southwest, to a tongue of low-lying land in the northeast. There is one main settlement, St Anne, also known as The Town. Alderney is a haven for nature lovers: flora includes wild broom, thrift, sea campion, ox-eye daisies, wild orchids and the bastard toadflax (Thesium humifusum); among the fauna are black rabbits and, even rarer, blonde hedgehogs. Bird-watchers can spy hoopoes and golden orioles, birds of prey and the occasional white stork or purple heron. Seabirds include fulmars, guillemots and kittiwakes, as well as colonies of gannets and puffins.

▶ **Population:** 2,294.

Michelin Map: 503.

Info: Lower Victoria Street, St Anne. ℘01481 822333. www.alderney.net.

Location: Alderney is the most northerly of the Channel Islands and lies 12km/7.5mi W of the Cherbourg Peninsula, separated from the Cap de la Hague headland by the treacherous tidal current known as the Alderney Race.

Don't Miss: The best beaches are in the bays of Braye, Clonque and Telegraph. Also try the cliff walk from Haize to Giffoine.

A BIT OF HISTORY

Owing to its key position, nearest to England, France and the Channel shipping lanes, Alderney has frequently been fortified. The Romans seem to have used it as a naval base; there are traces of a late-Roman fort at the Convent. The first English fortifications were initiated by Henry VIII on the hill south of Longis Bay. In the Napoleonic period, the British strengthened existing defences and sent a garrison of 300.

Between 1847 and 1858, alarmed by the development of a French naval base at Cherbourg, the British Government created a safe harbour at Braye by constructing a huge breakwater and built a chain of ten forts along the north coast.

In June 1940 almost all the population left the island and the livestock was evacuated to Guernsey. During their five-year occupation, the Germans re-fortified most of the Victorian forts and built masses of ugly concrete fortifications. They also built three labour camps and a concentration camp, which mainly held Russian prisoners. When the islanders returned late in 1945 they found their possessions gone and their houses derelict or destroyed. It took ten years and substantial government aid to make good the damage.

Constitution

Alderney is part of the Bailiwick of Guernsey. Since the introduction of the new constitution on 1 January 1949, the budget and other financial matters have to be approved by the States of Guernsey. Otherwise, all island business is decided by the Committees of the States of Alderney, which consists of ten elected members and an elected president, who serve for four years. The court consists of six Jurats under a chairman, all of whom are appointed by the Home Office.

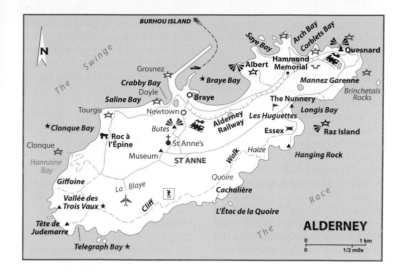

ALDERNEY

ST ANNE

St Anne, with its cobbled streets and smart whitewashed granite houses, lies about half a mile from the north coast on the edge of the best agricultural land, known as La Blaye.

The original medieval settlement was centred on **Marais Square**. As in ancient times, narrow lanes or *venelles* lead out to the un-enclosed fields divided into *riages*, each consisting of a number of strips: Alderney is one of the few places in Britain still to use this archaic system of managing open agricultural land.

Another settlement grew up at **Le Huret**, where the people assembled to decide when to gather the seaweed *(vraic)* used to fertilise the land. In the 15C more houses were built to the east of the square and the Blaye was extended to support a population of 700. In the 18C the huge profits made from privateering led to a building boom; thatch was replaced by tiles, the first Court House was built and the governor improved the communal buildings as well as his own residence. The northern part of the town – **Queen Elizabeth II Street**, **Victoria Street**, **Ollivier Street** – developed in the early Victorian era.

Workmen's cottages were built at Newtown and elsewhere. Many attractive houses and gardens line the green lanes, such as La Vallée, which run from St Anne down to the north coast.

St Anne's Church

Consecrated in 1850, this church was designed by Sir Gilbert Scott in the transitional style from Norman to Early English cruciform and is known as the "Cathedral of the Channel Islands". English was then replacing Norman French as the local language; the lectern holds two Bibles, and the texts in the apse and near the door appear in both languages.

During the war the church was used as a store and the bells were removed; two were recovered on the island and the other four were found in Cherbourg. The churchyard gates in Victoria Street, erected as a memorial to Prince Albert, were removed by the Germans but replaced by a local resident.

Alderney Museum

🕑 Open Apr–Oct Mon–Fri 10am–noon, 2–4pm, Sat–Sun 10am–noon. ♿ ♋£2. ✆01481 823 222.

The Alderney Society's museum, installed in a former school founded in 1790 by Jean Le Mesurier, governor of the island, presents island geology; flora and fauna; archaeology, particularly finds from the Iron Age settlement at Les Huguettes; domestic and military history, including the Victorian fortifications and the German occupation.

The **Clock Tower** (1767) standing nearby is all that remains of the old church, which was pulled down when the present one was built.

The elegant Royal Connaught Square, renamed in 1905 after a visit by the Duke of Connaught, third son of Queen Victoria, was the town centre in the 18C. **Island Hall** (north side), a handsome granite building which is now a community centre and library, was enlarged in 1763 by Governor John Le Mesurier to become Government House. Mouriaux House was completed in 1779 by the governor as his private residence.

Alderney Courthouse

Guided tours Mon–Fri 9.30am–12.30pm, 2–5pm. Ask at Court Office. ℘01481 822 817.

The present building in Queen Elizabeth II Street dates from 1850. Both the court and the States of Alderney hold their sessions in the first-floor courtroom.

The name of Victoria Street, the main shopping street, was changed from rue du Grosnez to celebrate Queen Victoria's visit in 1854.

The Butes recreation ground provides fine views of Braye Bay (northeast), across Crabby Bay and The Swinge to the Casquets (northwest) and the English Channel.

DRIVING TOURS

1 TOUR OF THE ISLAND

14km/8.5mi. Allow one day.

It is possible to walk round the whole island following the clifftop footpath (you can also drive around).

Braye

The harbour is protected by Fort Grosnez (1853) which was built at the same time as the massive **breakwater** (914m/1,000yd long plus another 548.5m/600yd submerged).

The first quay, the Old Jetty, was built in 1736 by the governor to provide a safe landing-stage for the privateers and smugglers he protected. The modern concrete jetty dates from the turn of the 20C.

Burhou Island

For permission to spend the night, contact the Harbour Office. ℘01481 822 620. £20 per night; *Bring water.* Closed 15 Mar–Jul (breeding season). The Voyager *makes trips around the island and reefs daily with a knowledgeable crew. Tickets from McAllister's Wet Fish Shop, Victoria St.* ℘01481 823 666.

The island, which lies northwest across The Swinge (about 2km/1mi), is riddled with rabbit warrens and supports large colonies of puffins, razorbills, gannets and storm petrels as well as other seabirds. Tours visit the puffins on Burhou, including the impressive gannet colonies on Les Étacs and Ortac and the Atlantic seal colony near Burhou Reef. A hut provides simple accommodation for an overnight stay for hardy bird-watchers.

Alderney Railway
(Petit chemin de fer)

Operates bank holidays and weekends in summer 2.30pm, 3.30pm. Call for fares. ℘01481 823 580. *www.alderneyrailway.com.*

Opened in 1847, the railway was built to transport the blocks of granite from the quarry to the port for breakwaters and forts. Today, it is the only train in the Channel Islands and runs from Braye Road Station to Mannez station at the eastern end of the island. Two 1959 London Underground carriages serve as coaches.

Braye Bay★

The largest bay on the island offers a sandy beach with good bathing and a fine view of the harbour. Skirting the beach is a strip of grass, Le Banquage, where the seaweed (vraic, *gathered for manure and fuel*) was left to dry.

Corblets Bay with a view to Mannez Lighthouse

© Amanda Hart/iStockphoto.com

Fort Albert

Mount Touraille, at the east end of Braye Bay, is crowned by Fort Albert (1853). There is a fine view inland to St Anne, westwards across Braye Bay to Fort Grosnez and the breakwater with Fort Tourgis in the background, and eastwards over the northern end of the island.

Hammond Memorial

At the fork in the road E of Fort Albert.
Slave labourers from France, Spain, Ukraine, Russia and North Africa, who worked and died during the Nazi occupation under the auspices of the infamous Organisation Todt – are recalled by plaques inscribed in their languages. There were four camps on Alderney which each held 1,500 men, including the only concentration camp on British soil, Lager Sylt, near the old telegraph tower at La Foulère. Many Jews and Russians lost their lives here but little is known about the camp's precise activities. Controversially, the States (Alderney's governing body) do not commemorate the sites of the four camps, possibly to dissociate themselves from accusations of collaboration.

North Coast

Three excellent sandy bathing bays cluster round the most northerly headland beneath the walls of Fort Château à l'Étoc (1854), now converted into private flats: **Saye Bay**, nearly symmetrical in shape; **Arch Bay**, named after the tunnel through which the carts collecting seaweed reached the shore; **Corblets Bay**, overlooked by Fort Corblets (1855), now a private house with a splendid view.

Mannez Garenne

The low-lying northern end of the island, known as Mannez Garenne (Warren), is dominated by the remains of a German observation tower.

Mannez Lighthouse

Guided tours (weather permitting) Easter–Sept Sat–Sun and bank holidays. £2. Steep steps; children under 1m/3.3ft tall may not ascend. 01481 823 077 or 01481 823 737.
Built in 1912, the lighthouse stands 37m/121ft high and casts its beam nearly 27.5km/17mi. From the lantern platform there is a magnificent **view**★ of the coast and the Race and, on a clear day, of the nuclear power station on the French coast. Many ships have come to grief on this coast.
Three mid-19C forts command the coastline: Les Homeaux Florains, now in ruins; Fort Quesnard, on the east side of Cats Bay, and Fort Houmet Herbe.

Raz Island

A causeway, covered at high tide, runs out to Raz Island in Longis Bay. Its fort

(1853) has been partially restored and there is a fine **view** southwest of Essex Castle and Hanging Rock.

Longis Bay

The retreating tide reveals a broad stretch of sand, backed by a German tank trap which provides excellent shelter for sunbathing. The shallow bay was the island's natural harbour from prehistoric times until it silted up early in the 18C. Traces of an Iron Age settlement were discovered at **Les Huguettes** in 1968; the finds are displayed in the Alderney Museum. Various relics indicate the existence of a Roman naval base protected by a fort.

The Nunnery

Parts of this building, thought to be the oldest on the island, date back to the 4C. It became a garrison and British soldiers based here in the 18C gave it its present name. It is now private dwellings owned by the States of Alderney.

Essex Castle

The present structure, which takes its name from a previous castle on the site, was built in 1840 to be used first as a barracks and then as a military hospital; it is now private property.

Hanging Rock

The tilt of this 15m/49ft rocky column projecting from the cliff face at a 45-degree angle is jokingly said by locals to have been caused by the people of Guernsey trying to tow Alderney away.

2 Cliff Walk

From Haize around to Giffoine there is a magnificent walk served by several footpaths running inland back to St Anne. The view of the steep cliffs plunging into the rock-strewn sea is spectacular.

Cachalière

A path leads down past the old quarry to an abandoned pier. From here the rocks of **L'Étac de la Quoire** can be reached at low tide.

Telegraph Bay★

Access to the tower is by a path and steps, which are not recommended as they are steep and difficult. Beware being cut off from the steps by the tide.
The Telegraph Tower (1811), which provided communication with Jersey and Guernsey, has given its name to the bay below. Except at high tide, there is excellent bathing, sheltered from all but a south wind. There is also a good view of La Nache and Fourquie rocks.

Tête de Judemarre

The headland provides a fine **view** of the rock-bound coast and of the islands of Guernsey, Herm and Sark.

Vallée des Trois Vaux★

This deep cleft is in fact three valleys meeting on a shingle beach.

Giffoine

From the cliff it is possible to see the gannets on their nests in the colony on Les Étacs. The remains of a German coastal battery crown the headland above Hannaine Bay, where sandy spits between the rocks provide reasonable bathing. There are fine **view** of Burhou, Ortac and the Casquets to the north.

Clonque Bay★

A path descends the gorse-and-heather-clad slope above the attractive bay. A causeway runs out to Fort Clonque (1855), now flats; two futher causeways enabled horse-drawn *vraic* (*see above*) carts to reach the seaweed beds.
Just south of Fort Tourgis (1855), at the northern end of the bay, is the best-preserved burial chamber on the island, **Roc à l'Épine**, a capstone supported by two upright stones. Alderney once had many such megaliths, sadly destroyed when the Victorian fortifications were built.

Saline Bay

The shore, exposed to heavy seas so that bathing can be hazardous, is commanded by Fort Doyle, now a youth centre; beyond lies **Crabby Bay** in the lee of Fort Grosnez.

Guernsey★

Smaller and less sophisticated than Jersey, Guernsey has its own particular charm and a slower tempo. Visitors come for the Regency elegance of St Peter Port, its wild, dramatic southern cliffs, and the bathing, swimming and surfing on the sandy beaches and rocky promontories of the west and north coasts.

ST PETER PORT★★

The island capital is built on the east coast overlooking an anchorage protected from high seas by Herm and Sark. The medieval town by the shore was rebuilt after bombardment during the Civil War (1642–46).

Profits from privateering in the late 18C produced a delightful Regency town. Guernsey's popularity as a tourist destination was assured when Queen Victoria visited in 1846.

As you walk up Market Street, to the right is the covered market comprising Les Halles, with the Assembly Rooms above, completed in 1782. Opposite is the Doric-style meat market (1822). Les Arcades, 1830 (on the left), is very handsome despite the loss of the final bay. The Fish Market was finished in 1877. Finally, the Vegetable Market was constructed in 1879.

The large modern harbour bustles with car and passenger ferries, fishing boats and private yachts. Stroll out to White Rock or visit the castle for a fine **view** of the town, the harbour and the neighbouring islands.

▶ **Population:** 61,029.
◔ **Michelin Map:** 503.
▯ **Info:** North Plantation, St Peter Port, GY1 2LQ Guernsey. ℘01481 723 552. www.visitguernsey.com.
◗ **Location:** Guernsey is the second largest of the Channel Islands (63sq km/24sq mi). The south coast, higher, rocky and ragged, contrasts with the sandy bays of the rest of the coast.
⊚ **Don't Miss:** A stroll down the streets of St Peter Port, a swim in Côbo Bay, and the panoramic view from Icart Point in the south.
◔ **Timing:** You'll need a half-day at St Peter Port, plus a day or two to tour the island by car or bicycle, with time for swimming, of course.
♦♦ **Kids:** The Folk Museum; the Aquarium.

Hauteville House★★

38 Hauteville. ↗↙Guided tours (1hr) May–Sept Mon–Sat 10am–4pm; Apr noon–4pm. ⊜£6. ℘01481 721 911. www.victorhugo.gg/hauteville-house.
Victor Hugo was exiled from his native France for political reasons in 1851. After time in Brussels and Jersey, he bought this impressive white house in 1856.

During his 14 years' residence Hugo redecorated the interior, doing much of the work himself, sometimes with eccentric results; note the position of mirrors, placed so as to enhance the effect of various features.

Hugo used to work on his poems and novels standing at a small table in the **Glass Room,** on the third floor overlooking the sea. From the **Lookout** where he sometimes slept, he could see the house up the road (La Fallue, 1 Beauregard Lane) in which his faithful mistress, Juliette Drouot, lived from November 1856 to 1864.

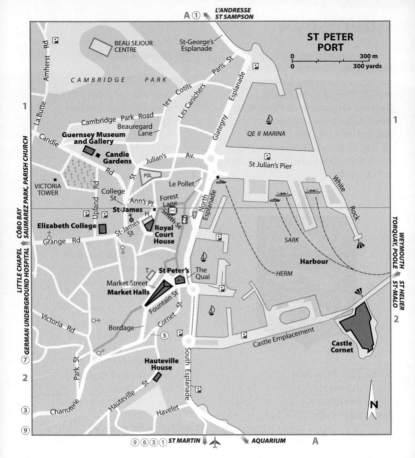

Castle Cornet museums★

Allow 2hr. ◷*Open Apr–Oct daily 10am–5pm.* ⊜*£9; after 4pm £1.* ✗. ☎*01481 721 657 (castle),* ☎*01481 726 518 (Guernsey Museum). www. museums.guernsey.net.*

An exhibition in the Main Guard relates the **Story of Castle Cornet** from prehistoric to present times. The original castle (c.1206) was reinforced under Elizabeth I and again under Victoria. The castle suffered its greatest misfortune in 1672 when a lightning strike ignited the gunpowder store in the old tower keep. On the Saluting Platform in the outer bailey the ceremony of the **noonday gun** takes place daily.

From the citadel there is a fine **view**★ of the harbour and town *(west)*, St Sampson, Vale Castle and Alderney *(35km/21.7mi north)*, Herm, Sark and the French coast *(east)* and Jersey *(south)*. The **Maritime Museum** relates the island's maritime history from the Gallo-Roman period to the present day. The **201 Squadron Museum** recounts the story of the island's RAF squadron.

A **Militia Museum**, housed in the hospital building (1746), contains arte-facts of the Royal Guernsey Militia, which was disbanded in 1939. Collections of weapons are housed in the **Armoury**. The **Royal Guernsey Light Infantry Museum** is on the ground floor of the building and tells the story of Guernsey-men who fought in the Great War.

St Peter's Church★

The Town Church, as St Peter's is known, was begun by William the Conqueror in 1048, and completed around 1475. The nave and west door are part of the original Norman structure, which doubled as a fort.

Elizabeth College
Founded in 1563 by Elizabeth I, the Mock Tudor-style building dates from 1826–29.

Guernsey Tapestry★
St James, College Street. ○*Open Easter–Oct Mon–Sat 10am–4.30pm; rest of year Thu only 10am–4pm.* *£4.75.* *01481 725 277.* *www.guernseytapestry.org.gg.*
Designed to celebrate the Millennium, this tapestry of ten panels was created in two years by the inhabitants of the ten parishes of the island, and traces the history of Guernsey over the last thousand years.

Royal Court House
○*Open Sept–Jul Mon–Fri 9.30am– 12.30pm, 2.30–4.30pm. Parliament: debates last Wed and Thu of month (except Dec, when 2nd Wed of month and Aug when closed). Details of debates available from the Greffe (Registrar's Office).* *No charge.* *01481 725 277.*
The elegant neoclassical church of **St James**' is now a concert hall. The law courts and the States of Deliberation hold their sittings in the elegant **Royal Court House** (1792); its archives go back 400 years.

Guernsey Museum and Art Gallery
&○*Open Apr–Oct 10am–5pm; Nov– Dec and Feb–Mar 10am–4pm. Living history show 11.15am Thu.* ○*Closed 25–26 Dec.* *£5.50.* *01481 726 518.* *www.museums.guernsey.net.*
A cluster of modern octagonal structures and a former Victorian bandstand, now housing the charming Café Victoria tearoom, is home to the Lukis collection of archaeological artefacts, retrieved from La Varde chambered tomb in 1811, and the Wilfred Carey Collection of paintings, prints and ceramics. Currently being redeveloped, in 2012/2013 there will be a new art gallery, a Discovery

Room and a "Cabinet of Curiosities", drawing on some of the museum's historic collections.

Candie Gardens
Extending below the museum and the Priaulx Library, these splendid Pleasure Gardens were laid out in 1898 and have recently been renovated

EXCURSIONS
Saumarez Park★
▶ *In Castel, 3.5km/2.2mi west on the Route De Côbo.*
The trees and shrubs of this beautiful park are matched by the formal rose gardens; the pond is alive with wildfowl. The house (**St John's Residential Home**) dates from 1721.

▲▲ Guernsey Folk and Costume Museum★
Saumarez Park, Castel. ○*Open daily May–Aug 9.30am–5.30pm, Mar–Apr and Sept–Oct 10am–5pm.* *£4 (children £1.50).* *& P* *01481 255 384.* *www.nationaltrust-gsy.org.gg.*
Housed within the farmstead buildings of Saumarez House a series of Victorian interiors are recreated. Its collection, recently expanded, includes costumes, agricultural implements and other rural artefacts dating from the 17C to the current day.

Parish Church
▶ *3.5km/2.2mi west on Rectory Road.*
Early documents list the castle's 12C church of St Mary (**Ste-Marie-du-Castel** or Our Lady of Deliverance) as belonging to the abbey of Mont-St-Michel in 1155; before then, the site may have had a pre-Christian sanctuary and Roman fort. There are fine **views** from here, to the coast and across to Vale Church.

St Andrew
German Underground Hospital and Ammunition Store
La Vassalerie Rd. ○*Open May–Sept daily 10am–noon, 2–4pm (Jul–Aug 4.30pm); Mar and Nov, Sun and Thu 2–3pm. Oct daily 2–4pm.* *£4 (children £2).* *01481 239 100. Wear warm clothes.*

This huge project took nearly three and a half years to build and consists of a series of tunnels, dug out by hundreds of slave workers, down into the granite bedrock. Today the miles of hollow corridors and interlocking wards are eerily vacant, with some departments (operating room, store, etc.) open to visitors.

Little Chapel★

▷ *Les Vauxbelets, 1km/0.6mi from Underground Hospital. www.thelittle chapel.org.*
Possibly the smallest chapel in the world, measuring roughly 3m (9ft) by 2m (6ft), this little jewel was originally built by a Salesian monk, Brother Déodat, in March 1914. It is his miniature version of the famous grotto and basilica at Lourdes, beautifully decorated with seashells, pebbles and colourful pieces of broken china. Now part of Blanchelande Girls College it is open free of charge in daylight hours.

🚗 DRIVING TOURS

1 CLOS DU VALLE: ST PETER PORT TO VALE CHURCH

8km/5mi. Allow half a day.

Until 1806 the northern part of Guernsey, known as Clos du Valle, was cut off by the Braye du Valle, a tidal channel of mudflats and saltmarsh. The channel was filled in and the reclaimed land (121ha/300 acres) is now covered with glasshouses.

▷ *Leave St Peter Port by the coast road (Glategny Esplanade) north towards St Sampson. Turn left in Belle Grève Bay onto Le Grand Bouet and then take the second right.*

Guernsey's second port, St Sampson, lies at the eastern end of the Braye du Valle. Its church, **St Sampson**, is the oldest church in Guernsey, allegedly built where the saint came ashore (c.550), either from Llantwit Major in South Wales or from Dol in Brittany.

Its churchyard overlooks the disused Longue Hougue Quarry.

▷ *From the bridge take Vale Avenue north and bear left onto the main road (Route du Braye). Oatlands Craft Centre is located opposite a garden centre.*

Oatlands Village

Braye Rd, St Sampson. ⏱*Open daily 9.30am–5pm.* ♿ 🅿 📞*01481 294 525.*
Oatlands brick kilns, built in 1892 and recently restored, stand as reminders of a thriving brick-making industry. The site now includes several shops, a Brasserie and café and children's play area.

Vale Castle★

The medieval castle, now in ruins, was built on the site of an Iron Age hillfort (c.600 BC) on the only high point in Clos du Valle. There is a fine **view** inland, along the east coast and out to sea to the reef, Alderney *(north)*, Herm and Sark *(west)*, and Jersey *(south)*.

Bordeaux Harbour provides mooring for fishing boats and the only safe swimming in the area.

◐ *Follow the main road north; as it curves gently left, turn right onto the minor road; bear left; park by the dilapidated glasshouses (right) opposite the passage tomb.*

Dehus Dolmen

◷*Open daily sunrise–sunset. Light switch on the left as you enter.*
This passage grave has four side chambers covered by seven capstones: crouch down to see Le Gardien du

Tombeau, the figure of an archer *(switch for spotlight).*

◐ *Several minor roads meander north to the coast.*

The **Beaucette Quarry Marina** was created by a blast in an old quarry, opening a breach to the sea.
From **Fort Doyle** there is a **view**★ of the Casquets reef and Alderney *(north)*, the French coast, Herm and Sark *(west)*.
Fort Le Marchant is the most northerly point in Guernsey. It offers a fine view, particularly of **L'Ancresse Common**, the only extensive open space on the island, used for recreation; and of **L'Ancresse Bay**, popular for bathing and surfing.
La Varde Dolmen is the largest passage grave in Guernsey. **Les Fouaillages** burial ground is 7,000 years old.

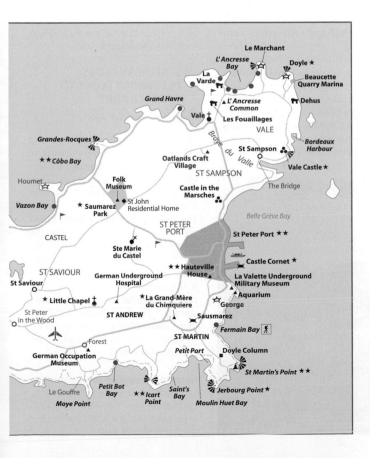

Vale Church was consecrated in 1117 on the site of an earlier chapel dedicated to St Magloire, who, with St Sampson, brought Christianity to Guernsey in the 6C.

2 WEST COAST: LE GRAND HAVRE TO PEZERIES POINT

15km/10mi. Allow half a day.

The **Grand Havre**, a large inlet at the west end of the Braye du Valle, is best admired from the Rousse headland, with its tower and jetty. A more extensive horizon is visible from the German gun battery on the granite headland, the **Grandes Rocques**.

Côbo Bay★★ is a charming combination of sand and rocks, safe for bathing. The huge beach between Fort Houmet *(north)* and Fort le Crocq *(south)* at **Vazon Bay** is also excellent for swimming.

In the Grande-Rue at Perelle, **St Apolline's Chapel**★ received its charter in 1394. It is decorated with a **fresco** *(light switch)* of *The Last Supper*.

Le Trépied Dolmen burial chamber at Le Cationoc was excavated in 1840 by Frederic Lukis, whose finds are in the Guernsey Museum. In past centuries the site was used for witches' Sabbaths. The tall defensive tower on the L'Erée Headland is called Fort Saumarez. To

the south stands **Le Creux ès Faies Dolmen**, a passage grave dating from 2000 BC to 1800 BC.

The grand sweep of **Rocquaine Bay**★ is interrupted by the "Cup and Saucer", originally a medieval fort. It is painted white as a navigation mark.

Fort Grey Shipwreck Museum

Open Apr–Oct daily 10am–4.30pm. £4. 01481 265 036. www.museums. gov.gg.

This small museum is dedicated to the many shipwrecks in Guernsey waters, with exhibits from more than 100 wrecks between 1750 and 1978

The picturesque harbour of Portelet, full of fishing boats, is backed by the houses of the Hanois Lighthouse keepers. Nearby is the **Table des Pions**, a famous local "fairy ring". **Pezeries Point**★★ is the most westerly point in all the Channel Islands, a remote and unfrequented place. Its fort was built in the Napoleonic era.

3 SOUTHERN CLIFFS: PLEINMONT POINT TO ST PETER PORT

26km/16mi. Allow half a day.

The cliffs along the south coast and round to St Peter Port provide some of the wildest and most dramatic scenery on the island *(beware the cliff face, which can be unstable and dangerous)*; a footpath runs to the town.

The headland at **Pleinmont Point** provides an extensive **view**: along the southern cliffs *(east)*, out to the Hanois Lighthouse and its reefs *(west)*, across Rocquaine Bay to Lihou Island *(north)*.

A footpath stretches all along the clifftops, past the watch houses before coming out by the Aquarium in St Peter Port. **La Moye Point**, the smallest of the three promontories on the south coast, is wild and beautiful.

German Occupation Museum

Les Houards Forest, south of the church. Open daily Apr–Oct 10am–5pm; rest of year restricted opening times. £5. P 01481 238 205.

Coastline near Petit Bot Bay

© Alan Smithers/iStockphoto.com

Artefacts from the Nazi occupation: includes weaponry, uniforms, vehicles, personal effects, etc.

Petit Bot Bay, with good bathing and a sandy beach at low tide, lies at the foot of a green valley guarded by a defensive tower (1780).

▶ *Return uphill to the main road; turn right down rue de la Villette, which turns inland to rejoin the valley leading down to Moulin Huet Bay.*

Icart Point★★ is the highest and most southerly headland with very fine **views**★ of the coast.

On the east side is **Saint's Bay**, a favourite mooring for fishermen. A stream runs down a beautiful valley to **Moulin Huet Bay**★, where it plunges down the cliff face into the sea.

The swimming here is good, but even better at neighbouring **Petit Port** *(east)*. St Martin is of little interest but, near the car park, **St Martin's Point**★★ commands is a magnificent view down to the lighthouse on the point, north up the coast to St Peter Port, and seaward to the other islands.

▶ *Follow the path along the cliff.*

Jerbourg Point★ is Guernsey's southeastern extremity: excavations have revealed Neolithic remains. The Château de Jerbourg protected islanders in the Middle Ages when the French occupied Castle Cornet.

Fermain Bay *(access on foot from the car park or cliff path from Jerbourg; in summer, the bay is accessible by boat from St Peter Port)*, with its pebbled cove, backed by densely wooded cliffs and an 18C defensive tower, offers a sandy beach and good bathing at low tide.

▶ *Continue east on the main road; on a left-hand curve, turn left beyond the main gate into the shaded car park.*

Sausmarez Manor

&. *House:* ☜ *guided tours* ⏰ *Daily late Mar–Oct 10.30am, 11.30am; Jun–Sept also 2pm. Extra tour 11am Fri and Sat (unless there is a wedding).* ⌾£7. *Subtropical Garden & Art Park Sculpture Garden:* ⏰ *Open daily 10am–5pm year round.* ⌾£6.
&.✕ ✆ 01481 235 571.
www.sausmarezmanor.co.uk.

The elegant Queen Anne house was built in 1714–18 by Sir Edmund Andros, the Seigneur of Sausmarez and former Governor of New York. The interior displays handsome family furniture, portraits and mementoes of the family's 750 years on the island.

The wooded **grounds** are planted with tall bamboo and camellias and include **Subtropical Gardens**, a **Sculpture Park**, a ride-on railway, a pitch-and-putt golf course and a putting green. At the gate into St Martin's churchyard stands a Stone Age menhir, **La Grand'mère du Chimquière**★ carved to represent a female figure. The church itself dates from 1225 to 1250; the south porch was added in the 1520s.

▶ *Return to the main road; turn right to Jerbourg.*

La Valette Underground Military Museum

⏰ *Open mid-Mar–mid-Nov daily 10am–5pm.* ⌾£5. ✆ 01481 722 300.
The museum occupies five tunnels that were excavated to hold fuel tanks for refuelling U-boats, Displays relate to the Guernsey Militia, plus German artefacts and mementoes of the occupation.

▲▲ **Guernsey Aquarium**

⏰ *Open daily 10am–6pm (Sun and bank holidays 5pm).* ⏰ *Closed 1 Jan, 25–26 Dec.* &. ⌾£4.50 (children £3.50). ✆ 01481 723 301.
This is home to local sea fish, European freshwater fish and tropical fish. Also on display are frogs, toads, terrapins and basilisks.

Herm

The broad sandy beaches on Herm's north coast contrast with the steep cliffs at the southern end of the island. Herm has neither roads nor cars, and walkers enjoy a profusion of wild flowers, dunes, trees and cliffs. The deep fringe of rocks offshore is most impressive at low tide. Southwest, across a narrow channel, the islet of Jethou (private property leased from the British Crown) rises like a hillock and is home to thousands of seabirds.

▶ **Population:** 97.
ⓒ **Michelin Map:** 503.
🗓 **Info:** North Plantation, St Peter Port, Guernsey. ☎01481 723 552. www.herm-island.com.
◖ **Location:** Herm is 2.4km/ 1.5mi long, 0.8km/0.5mi wide, and is 5km/3 mi, from Guernsey, a 20-min boat ride away.
◉ **Don't Miss:** The view from Grand Monceau.
🕑 **Timing:** Allow one day.

A BIT OF HISTORY

Prehistoric tombs made of granite slabs found in the north of the island are evidence of human settlement in 2000 BC. In the 6C Christianity was introduced by St Magloire, who founded monasteries in Sark and Jersey. In the 17C pirates used the island as a base but it remained largely deserted. In 1947 the Crown sold Herm to Guernsey and in 1949 Major Peter Wood and his wife

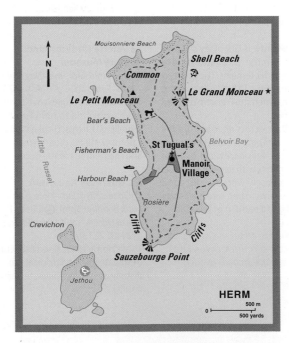

became tenants. In 1987 the lease was transferred to their family company. The island has been developed for tourism, maintaining its great natural beauty.

VISIT
Le Manoir Village

A surfaced road climbs up to the tiny hamlet next to the 18C manor house with its square tower. **St Tugual's Chapel** was built in the 11C.

The northern end of the island is composed of sand dunes, known as The Common, covered by prickly vegetation and fringed by sandy beaches, notably Bear's Beach, Mouisonnière Beach and **Shell Beach**, so called because it is composed of millions of shells deposited by the Gulf Stream. From the hillock of **Le Grand Monceau**★ there is a splendid panoramic view of the sands, the rocks and the islands. North on the horizon lies Alderney; to the east the French coast. **Le Petit Monceau** beyond is a smaller hillock, overlooking Bear's Beach.

The southern end of the island is composed of steep granite cliffs dropping sheer into the sea. In **Belvoir Bay** nestles a small sheltered bathing beach. The southern headland, Sauzebourge Point, provides a view of Jethou *(southwest)* with Guernsey in the background *(west)* and Sark *(southeast)*.

Jersey★★

Victor Hugo, who spent three years in Jersey (1852–55) was enchanted by the island: "It possesses a unique and exquisite beauty. It is a garden of flowers cradled by the sea. Woods, meadows and gardens seem to mingle with the rocks and reefs in the sea." In addition to the delights of the beaches and the countryside, today's visitors can enjoy a wide range of more sophisticated pleasures with a calendar full of vibrant festivals and events and a lively nightlife.

▶ **Population:** 87,186.
⬥ **Michelin Map:** 503.
▤ **Info:** Liberation Place, St Helier, Jersey JE1 1BB. ✆01534 448 800. www.jersey.com.
▶ **Location:** Measuring 116sq km/44.7sq mi, Jersey lies 19km/12mi W of France's Cotentin Peninsula.
⊛ **Don't Miss:** Walking the north and east coasts.
⧑ **Kids:** Durrell WIldlife Park; Living Legend amusement park.

A BIT OF HISTORY

The tombs and prehistoric monuments found on the island indicate human habitation between 7500 and 2500 BC. The Roman presence was brief, and in the 6C St Helier arrived and established Christianity. The dominant influence is that of the Normans who invaded in the 10C and left a rich heritage of customs and traditions.

After 1204, when King John was forced to cede mainland Normandy to France, the French made repeated attempts to recover the Channel Islands: the last attempt occurred in 1781 when Baron de Rullecourt, a soldier of fortune, landed by night in St Clement's Bay. Under the command of Major Peirson, aged just 24, the militia and British forces defeated the enemy in what came to be known as the **Battle of Jersey**; both leaders were mortally wounded.

Constitution

Jersey is divided into 12 parishes, which together with two groups of islets, the Minquiers to the south and the Ecréhous to the northeast, make up the Bailiwick of Jersey. The parliament, known as the States of Jersey, with 53 elected members, is presided over by the bailiff, who is appointed by the Crown. The three other officers and the Dean of Jersey, an Anglican clergyman, also Crown appointees, may speak in the assembly, but only the 12 senators, 12 constables and 29 deputies, elected to serve for a period of three to six years, may vote.

Economy

Agriculture has long sustained the islanders: wheat and rye, turnips and parsnips, four-horned sheep supplying wool for the famous Jersey stockings and knitwear (dating back to the 17C), apples for cider, table grapes grown under glass and Doyenne de Comice pears. The mild climate continues

to favour the cultivation of flowers (daffodils, freesias, carnations and lavender) and vegetables for export, most notable Jersey Royal potatoes. Some crops are grown in the open fields, others under glass. Unique to Jersey is the giant cabbage *(Brassica oleracea longata)*, which grows up to 3m/10ft tall. In recent years, the tourism and financial services industries have been driven by competitive young residents who have benefited from an excellent local education.

ST HELIER

St Helier is a lively town, the main commercial centre on Jersey and the seat of government, situated in a sheltered position on the south side of the island.

It is named after St Helier, one of the first Christian missionaries to land in Jersey, murdered by pirates c.555, after living as a hermit there for 15 years. The scant local population was swelled by refugees fleeing the St Bartholomew Day Massacre (1572) and the Revolution (1789) in France.

The shops in the pedestrian precinct formed by **King** and **Queen Streets** are a popular attraction.

Royal Square

The gilded-lead statue of George II, dressed as a Roman emperor, looks down on this charming small square with its spreading chestnut trees; from this point are measured the distances to all the milestones on the island. It was here that the Battle of Jersey erupted. Bordering the south side are the granite buildings of the **Royal Court House**. At the east end of the range of buildings are the **States Chambers** *(entrance round the corner)* where the Jersey Parliament sits in session (*Sept–Jul: for hours, contact the Visitor Service Centre on Halkett Place.* *01534 441 020. www. gov.je).*

Central Market

This Victorian granite building (1882) is furnished with cast-iron grilles at the windows and entrances, and covered

Famous Sons and Daughters

The most famous name connected with Jersey is **Lillie Langtry** (1853–1929): the Jersey Lily who became an actress and a close friend of Edward VII and captivated British high society with her beauty; she is buried in St Saviour's churchyard.

The fashionable 19C painter, **Sir John Everett Millais** (1829–96), who won acclaim with his painting entitled *Bubbles*, grew up in Jersey and belonged to an old island family. So too did **Elinor Glyn** (1864–1943), who became a novelist and Hollywood scriptwriter. The well-known French firm that makes Martell brandy was started by **Jean Martell** from St Brelade.

with a glass (actually perspex) roof supported by iron columns. Its bustling stalls are arranged around a fountain. The central fish market is around the corner in Beresford Street.

St Helier Parish Church

The foundation of the present pink-granite church with its square tower pre-dates the Conquest. It continues to be the seat of the Dean of Jersey – hence the epithet "Cathedral of Jersey". The altar cross and candlesticks were a gift from Queen Elizabeth, the Queen Mother.

Elizabeth Castle

Access on foot by a causeway at low tide (30min); otherwise by amphibious vehicle (Castle Ferry) from West Park Slipway. ○*Open Apr–Oct daily 10am–5.30pm.* ▧*£9 (ferry £2.50).* ◗*Guided tour (1hr).* ♫*01534 723 971 (Castle). www.jerseyheritage.org.*

In the 12C William Fitz-Hamon, one of Henry II's courtiers, founded an abbey on St Helier's Isle in St Aubin's Bay. The castle buildings were completed shortly before Sir Walter Raleigh was appointed governor (1600), and called Fort Isabella Bellissima in honour of

Queen Elizabeth I. It was considerably reinforced during the Civil War (1642–46) while occupied by Royalists who, after resisting the repeated assaults from Parliamentary forces on the island, surrendered after a 50-day siege. The young Prince of Wales stayed here when fleeing from England in 1646, and again three years later when returning to be proclaimed King Charles II. During World War II the Germans added to the fortifications by installing a roving searchlight, bunkers and gun batteries. In 1996 Queen Elizabeth II handed the castle, together with Mont-Orgueil, over to the islanders.

The guard room displays the various stages in the construction of the castle. The **Militia Museum** contains mementoes of the Royal Jersey Regiment. From the keep, known as the Mount, there is a fine **view**★ of the castle itself and also of St Aubin's Fort across the bay.

South of the castle a breakwater extends past the chapel on the rock where, according to legend, St Helier lived as a hermit *(procession on or about 16 July, St Helier's Day).*

Jersey Museum & Art Gallery★

The Weighbridge. ⚒ ⊙ *Open Apr–Oct daily 10am–5pm, Nov–Dec 10am–4pm.* ⊙ *Closed 24–26 and 31 Dec.* ⊛ *£8.* ℘ *01534 633 300.*
www.jerseyheritagetrust.org.
The island's principal museum and gallery is housed in a former 18C merchant's house and adjoining warehouse.

The **ground-floor** area is shared by temporary exhibitions and films about Jersey. The treadmill, which was turned by 12 men and operated a pepper mill, was used in St Helier prison during the 19C. By the stairs are displayed a number of silver toiletry articles from the set which accompanied Lillie Langtry on her travels. On the **first floor**, the history of the

island from the Stone Age to the present is unfurled as a series of tableaux.

The **second floor** displays the Barreau-Le Maistre collection of fine art with paintings, drawings and watercolours by local artists or of topographical interest: Sir John Everett Millais PRA (1829–96), PJ Ouless (1817–85), "the Jersey Turner" J Le Capelain (1812–48) and the illustrator Edmund Blampied (1886–1966). Works by **Sir Francis Cook** (1907–78) bequeathed to the Jersey Heritage Trust are on permanent display in their own gallery, a converted Methodist Chapel, in Augrès *(A 8, Route de Trinité).* The **third-floor** rooms recreate domestic interiors (1861) typical of a middle-class Jersey family.

New North Quay

The most prominent landmark is the world's largest **steam clock** (11m/36ft high), modelled on a traditional paddle steamer of a type that once shuttled between the islands and Southampton. It was inaugurated in August 1997 as part of the development of the St Helier waterfront.

♟♟ Maritime Museum

New North Quay. ⚒ ⊙ *Open Apr–Oct daily 10am–5pm.* ⊛ *£8 (children £5).* ℘ *01534 811 043.*
www.jerseyheritagetrust.org.
Installed in converted 19C warehouses, the Jersey **Maritime Museum** has changing displays relating to the fishing, shipbuilding and trading industries, and to piracy.

The **Jersey Occupation Tapestry**★ comprises 12 panels (2x1m/6x3ft) illustrating the story of the occupation from the outbreak of war to the Liberation: each scene, based on archive photographs and contemporary film footage, has been embroidered by a separate parish.

Fort Regent

Access by escalators in Pier Road. ⚒ ⊙ *Open summer Mon–Fri 6.30am–9.30pm (hours vary for facilities), Sat–Sun 8.15am–5pm, bank holidays 10am–5pm; for winter hours, contact*

Visitor Services Centre. 🅿. 🐚*Prices depend on activity.* 🕐*Closed 1 Jan, 25–26 Dec.* ✆*01534 449 800. www.gov.je.*

The massive fortifications of Fort Regent, were built in 1806 to protect Jersey from invasion by Napoleon. Within, topped by a shallow white dome, is a modern leisure centre operated by the government and providing a variety of sports facilities. The rampart walk provides splendid **views**★ of the town and St Aubin's Bay *(west)*.

EXCURSIONS
🏛🧍 Durrell Wildlife Park★★

❍ *From St Helier take the A 8 N to Mont de la Trinité; at rue Asplet turn right onto the B 31 towards Trinity Church; this road soon becomes rue des Picots passing in front of the zoo (right).*

🕐*Open daily 9.30am–6pm (last Sun Oct–last Sun Mar 5pm) 9.30am–5pm.* 🕐*Closed 25 Dec.* 🐚*£12.90 (children £9.40).* ♿✕🅿 ✆*01534 860 000. www.durrellwildlife.org.*

This pioneering wildlife park, formerly known as Jersey Zoo, was founded by the naturalist **Gerald Durrell** (1925–95) in 1963 as a unique centre for research and breeding of rare and endangered species. Today its rolling parkland (10ha/25acres) provides suitable environments for around 1,000 animals with exotic species of plants providing both food and natural cover.

Residents include babirusas from Indonesia, spectacled bears from the forest uplands of Bolivia and Peru (the only bear indigenous to South America), snow leopards and cheetahs, and an extensive list of birds. Most popular, however, are the primates: a dynasty of lowland gorillas descended from the silverback Jambo (1961–92), orangutans from Sumatra and lemurs from Madagascar, marmosets and tamarins from Brazil, some of which roam freely in the thick shrubbery.

Tortoises, terrapins, snakes, frogs, toads and lizards, happy to lounge in their warmed enclosures among sprigs of flowering orchids, thrive in the Gaherty Reptile Breeding Centre.

Eric Young Orchid Foundation★

Victoria Village, Trinity. 🕐*Open Feb– last Sun before Christmas Wed–Sat 10am–4pm.* 🐚*£4.* ♿ ✆*01534 861 963. www.ericyoungorchidfoundation.co.uk.*

A fabulous show of prize orchids is presented here. Displays are regularly reorganised to ensure constant shows of species, the groups arranged to allow close study of their distinctive blooms.

🏛🧍Pallot Steam, Motor and General Museum

Rue du Bechet,Trinity. 🕐*Open Apr–Oct Mon–Sat 10am–5pm. Steam train runs Thu, also Tue in high season.* 🐚*£5 (children £1.50).* ✆*01534 865 307. www.pallotmuseum.co.uk.*

A fascinating collection of steam engines and organs, farm machinery, motor vehicles, vintage bicycles, locomotives and rolling stock, and lots more besides, that were the passion of the island engineer extraordinaire "Don" Pallot (1910–96). Not only did he refurbish, recondition and assemble this mechanical heritage collection, he also invented several implements to make the life of the Jersey farmer easier.

Jersey War Tunnels★

❍ *5km/3mi W. Les Charrières Malorey, Saint Lawrence, Saint Helier, JE3 1FU. Leave St Helier on St Aubin's Road; at Bel Royal, turn right.*

🕐*Open Mar–Nov daily 10am–6pm (last entry 4.30pm). Closes half-day Liberation Day and Battle of Flowers Day (last entry 12.30pm).* 🐚*£10.90.* ♿✕ ✆*01534 860 808. www.jerseywartunnels.com.*

This large complex of tunnels is kept as a compelling memorial to the forced labourers (Spaniards, Moroccans, Alsatian Jews, Poles, Frenchmen, Russians) who worked on its construction for three and a half years under the severest conditions. Note that some visitors may find the visit rather harrowing, others may suffer from claustrophobia. Hohlgangsanlagen 8 was intended as a secure, bomb-proof artillery barracks. In January 1944, still incomplete, it was converted into a hospital designed to treat the wounded from Hitler's intended invasion of the British mainland. It was equipped with an operating theatre, five 100-bed wards, X-ray room, mortuary, stores, kitchen, staff quarters, etc. Wartime films, archive photographs, newspaper cuttings, letters and memorabilia document the personal suffering and trauma of those caught up in the events.

The **Occupation Walk** opposite the complex leads to an area fortified by anti-aircraft gun positions, crawl trenches, barbed wire entanglements and personnel shelters *(leaflet available from the Visitor Centre)*.

Moulin de Quétivel

Open May–mid-Sept Sat 10am–4pm. £2. 01534 483 193. *www.nationaltrustjersey.org.je.*

The **mill** (pre-1309), on a bend in St Peter's Valley, is one of several powered by the rushing water of streams until steam power made them obsolete. During the German occupation the machinery was restored but was largely destroyed by fire in 1969. Since 1979, re-equipped with parts from other disused Jersey mills, Quétivel has ground locally grown grain and produces stone-ground flour for sale.

Jersey Living Legend Village

Take the A 11, St Peter's Valley Road, to the C 112, then follow signs. *Open Apr–Oct daily 9.30am–5pm, Mar and Nov Sat–Wed 9.30am–5pm. Jersey Experience £7.50 (children £5), additional charges for golf and karting.* 01534 485 496. *www.jerseyslivinglegend.co.je.*

The centrepiece of this complex is the Jersey Experience, a multi-sensory special effects adventure into Jersey's heritage and history, starring famous island residents – John *(Bergerac)* Nettles is the main character – in a time-travelling yarn. There are also two 18-hole Adventure Golf courses, the Jersey Karting Complex, shops and places to eat.

La Hougue Bie★

From St Helier take either the A 6 (Route Bagatelle) or the A 7 (St Saviour's Hill) NW; at Five Oaks take the A 7 (Princes Tower Road) to the entrance to La Hougue Bie (left). *Open early Apr–Oct daily 10am–5pm (last entry 4pm). £7.* 01534 853 823. *www.jerseyheritagetrust.org.*

A tiny park, encircled by trees, is dominated by a high circular mound. Its strange name may be derived from the old Norse word *haugr* (meaning barrow) and *bie*, a shorthand for Hambye, a Norman lord who, in the Middle Ages, came to rid Jersey of a dragon. Whatever, it is has come to denote one of Europe's finest passage graves.

During the German occupation, the site was heavily fortified, as it provides an excellent **view** over outlying countryside.

Neolithic Tomb★

This cruciform passage burial chamber, excavated in 1924, dates from 3500 BC. Similar tombs have been discovered in England and Brittany.

The grave was originally built above ground with upright stones and roofed with granite slabs, before being covered by a mound of earth and rubble (12m/40ft). A passage (10m/33ft long) leads to the funeral chamber (3x9m/10x30ft), which is covered with huge capstones (the heaviest weighing 25t). The central granite pillar is a modern addition to support the large capstones, which were found to be cracked.

Archaeology and Geology Museum

The artefacts here are from local excavations – notably from La Cotte de St Brelade, a sea cave in the Ouaisné headland and the Belle Hougue caves on the north coast: remains of mammoths, objects belonging to Neolithic farmers and hunters, Bronze Age metal objects found in St Lawrence, etc. The geology section presents samples of the various rocks and minerals found on the island.

Chapels

The mound is surmounted by two medieval chapels: the **Chapel of Our Lady of the Dawn** (Notre-Dame-de-la-Clarté) dates from the 12C; the altar (late medieval) came from Mont-Orgueil Castle. The abutting **Jerusalem Chapel** was built in 1520 by Dean Richard Mabon after a pilgrimage to Jerusalem. The interior bears traces of frescoes of two archangels.

German Occupation Museum

A German bunker, built in 1942 as a communications centre, houses radio equipment, weapons, medals, original documents (orders and propaganda) and photographs of the period.

 DRIVING TOURS

1 THE SOUTH COAST

18km/11mi. Allow about 2hrs.

▶ *From St Helier take the A 1 (Route de St Aubin) west.*

Millbrook

The Villa Millbrook was once home to Sir Jesse Boot, first Baron Trent of Nottingham, founder of Boots the Chemists, who is buried at St Brelade. From the outside **St Matthew's Church** (⏰*Open Sun–Fri 9am–6pm;* 🅿 ✆*01534 502 864. www.glasschurch.org)* is unprepossessing but in 1934 **René Lalique** (1860–1945), the French glass specialist, was invited by Lord Trent's widow to redecorate the interior with his own style of distinctive **glasswork**★. Thereafter, St Matthew's became known as the **Glass Church**. The entrance doors are made of panels presenting a row of four angels. The flowering lily appears in the windows, screens and in the Lady Chapel. The luminescent, ethereal quality is most apparent at dusk when the lights are switched on.

▶ *Follow the main road (Route de La Haule) and then the A 1 (Route de La Neuve).*

St Aubin

The little town, which faces east across St Aubin's Bay, is particularly picturesque with its long sandy beach, fishermen's cottages and tall granite merchants' houses, lining steep, narrow streets or clinging to the cliffs along the shore. St Aubin was invoked as protector against pirates.

The local church (1892) has a fine stained-glass window made by William Morris & Co. **St Aubin's Fort** on the island *(access at low tide)* was built in the reign of Henry VIII, 1509–47.

The Corbière Walk from St Helier to Corbière follows the line of the old **Jersey Railway**, which opened in 1870.

▶ *Turn left off the main road onto the B 57 (Route de Noirmont) for access to the promontory and Portelet Bay.*

Noirmont Point★

Beyond the pebble beach nestling in **Belcroute** stretches the headland, still scarred by the remains of substantial German fortifications (1941 and 1943–44) including the 12m/40ft deep **Command Bunker** (⏰*Open May–early Oct most Suns and some Sats, see website for details.* ✎*£2.50. www.ciosjersey.org.uk).* Stand on top of the most advanced bastion to get fine views of the rocks immediately below and westwards round to the Île au Guerdain.

▶ *Return to the main road, the A 13 (Route des Genets) and then fork left onto the B 66 (Mont Sohier).*

St Brelade★

This favourite seaside resort is situated in a sheltered bay; its sandy beaches and usually safe waters (*certain areas can be dangerous)* are ideal for swimming and water-skiing. **Winston Churchill Memorial Park** backs the bay.

At the western end of the beach, behind a screen of trees, lies the parish church and a medieval chapel, surrounded by a graveyard.

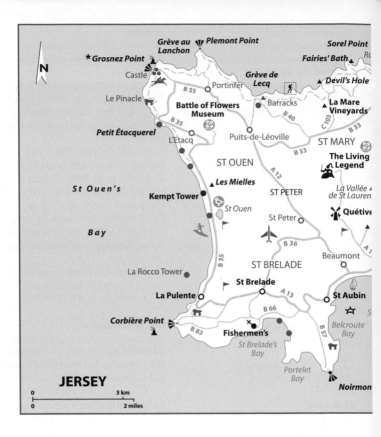

Map of Jersey showing: Grève au Lanchon, Plemont Point, Sorel Point, Grosznez Point, Castle, Fairies' Bath, Ro, Portinfer, Grève de Lecq, Devil's Hole, Le Pinacle, B 55, Barracks, La Mare Vineyards, Battle of Flowers Museum, B 40, C 103, Petit Étacquerel, B 35, L'Etacq, Puits-de-Léoville, ST MARY, B 33, ST OUEN, B 33, The Living Legend, St Ouen's, Les Mielles, ST PETER, La Vallée de St Lauren, Kempt Tower, St Ouen, Quétive, A 12, Bay, St Peter, B 36, Beaumont, La Rocco Tower, B 35, ST BRELADE, La Pulente, St Brelade, A 13, St Aubin, Corbière Point, B 66, Belcroute Bay, B 83, Fishermen's, B 57, St Brelade's Bay, Portelet Bay, JERSEY, Noirmon, 0 — 3 km, 0 — 2 miles

Parish Church

🖉 *Light switch inside on the left of the entrance.*

The cherished church of St Brelade is built of granite from the cliffs of La Moye. The chancel, nave and belfry date from the 11C. In the 12C the church became cruciform with the addition of a transept; the aisles were added later. The altar is a solid slab of stone, marked with five crosses representing the five wounds of the Crucifixion. The 15C font is made of granite from the Chausey Islands, which lie south of Jersey and belong to France.

Fishermen's Chapel

🖉 *Light switch inside on the left of the entrance.*

Built of the same granite as the church, the chapel interior is decorated with delicate medieval **frescoes**★.

At the east end is an Annunciation c.1375; the other paintings are from a second phase of work c.1425: the south wall (right of the altar) shows *Adam and Eve* followed by *The Annunciation* and *The Adoration of the Magi*; the west wall bears *The Last Judgement*; on the north wall fragments have been deciphered as scenes from *The Passion*.

The paintings probably owe their survival to the fact that from c.1550 to the mid-19C the chapel was used as an armoury and as a carpenter's shop, thus avoiding the attentions of the Reformation.

Behind the chapel a short flight of steps leads to a path through the churchyard to the beach; this is the only surviving example of a *perquage*: once commonplace in medieval Europe, these paths were escape routes from a church, traditionally a place of sanctuary, to the shore and away out to sea.

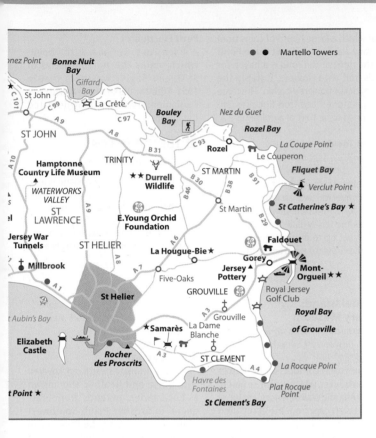

◐ Continue along the road back into town; turn left onto the A 13 (Route Orange); bear left down B 83 (Route du Sud) to Corbière.

Point de Corbière★

All that remains of the terminus of the Jersey Railway is the concrete platform. As the road descends, a magnificent view is steadily revealed of the rock-strewn point and the white lighthouse rising from its islet: an excellent place to watch the sun set over the Atlantic. Before the lighthouse *(access on foot at low tide but closed to the public)* was built in 1874, this was a perilous stretch of water where a number of ships foundered; in clear weather the light carries 28km/17.4mi.

② THE WEST COAST

13km/8mi. Allow 1hr.

◐ *Follow the road round to the junction with the B 35 (rue de Sergente); turn left towards the coast.*

St Ouen's Bay

The deep surf which rolls into the bay makes it a favourite spot for experienced surfboarders and windsurfers. The firm sand attracts car and motorcycle racing fans.

In the middle of the bay sits **La Rocco Tower**, the last round tower to be built in Jersey (1800).

Beyond the beach, the landscape is wild and uncultivated, the vegetation sparse. **La Pulente** used to be the main centre for gathering seaweed *(vraic)*, which was traditionally used as fertiliser. La Sergenté, also known as the Beehive Hut, is an important Neolithic tomb, near which a large hoard of coins from Brittany was found. The **St Ouen Pond** on the right of the road is a haven for birds and wild flowers, notably the Jersey or lax-flowered orchid. The three upright stones, Les Trois Rocques, are presumed to be part of a dolmen.

Kempt Tower

🕐*Open May–Sept daily 2–5pm.* ⊜*£2.* 🅿 ✆*01534 483 651.*
This defensive tower, built in 1834, has been converted into an interpretation centre for a nature reserve called **Les Mielles** (the Jersey dialect word for sand dunes), set up to monitor and protect indigenous plants, birds and butterflies.

▷ *Continue for 500m/yd along the bay.*

Channel Islands Military Museum

🕐*Open mid-Apr–Oct daily 9.30am–5.30pm (last entry 4.30pm).* ⊜*£4.* ♿ ✆*01534 862 137.*
The rooms and corridors of this former German bunker, which was once part of Hitler's Atlantic Wall defences, are full of artefacts left over from the occupation

▷ *Follow the B 35 (Route des Laveurs); turn left onto the C 114 (Mont des Corvées).*

Battle of Flowers Museum

♿🕐*Open Easter–Oct daily 10am–5pm (last entry 4.30pm).* ⊜*£4.50 (children £2).* 🅿 ✆*01534 482 408.*
The **Battle of Flowers**, held on the second Thursday in August along Victoria Avenue in St Helier, was started in 1902 to celebrate the coronation of Edward VII and is the island's most famous festival with 27 floats up to 13.7m/45ft long, taking part in 2011. Traditionally, the floats were broken up after the parade and the crowd pelted one another with the flowers, then mostly hydrangeas. Today it is mostly chrysanthemums. If you're not on the island for the battle then this museum is the next best thing.

▷ *Return to the coastal road; bear right onto the B 35 (Route de l'Étacq).*

Petit Étacquerel

A defensive tower guards the point, which marks the northern end of St Ouen's Bay. It was here that in 1651 Admiral Blake landed with the Parliamentary forces that defeated the Royalists.

③ THE NORTH COAST

38km/24mi. Allow 3hr30min.

The northern coast of the island is less densely populated. Cliff paths, which stretch from Plémont Bay to Sorel Point and beyond, provide spectacular views of the uneven coastline and the open sea to France, Guernsey and Alderney.

▷ *Continue north by bearing left onto the B 55 (Route de l'Ouest); bear left again to reach the car park and lookout point at Grosnez.*

Grosnez Point★

An area of desolate heathland, covered with gorse and heather and known as Les Landes, extends from Étacquerel to Grosnez Point. Southwest of the racecourse sits **Le Pinacle**, an impressive rock associated with pagan rituals from Neolithic to Roman times. The scant remains of **Grosnez Castle** (c.1373–1540) offer magnificent views out to sea, of Sark and the other islands (northwest).

▷ *Return to the B 55; in Portinfer turn left onto the C 105 (Route de Plémont); fork left to Grève au Lançon; eventually the road skirts the holiday village to end in a car park from where a footpath runs along the coast to Grève de Lecq.*

Steep cliffs containing caves shelter the attractive small bay of **Grève au Lançon**, which has a sandy beach at low tide. The rocky promontory **Plémont Point** projects into the sea giving a fine view of the cliffs.

▷ *Return along the C 105 (Route de Plémont); turn left onto the B 55 (Route de Vinchelez) from Grosnez, which leads* to Léoville in the parish of St Mary. Turn left onto the B 65 (Mont de la Grève de Lecq).

Grève de Lecq

The defensive tower on the attractive sandy bay was built in 1780; the conical hill behind is from an Iron Age fortification.

Grève de Lecq barracks were built between 1810 and 1815 to accommodate the 150 British soldiers who manned the gun batteries on the slopes around the bay.

Today they function as a **history and interpretive centre** for Jersey's north coast. (*Open May–Sept Wed–Sat 10am–5pm, Sun 1–5pm.* ☏01534 482 238. www.nationaltrustjersey.org.je). Original features include two prison cells and the ablutions block with outdoor *pissoirs*. In spring and early summer the area is abloom with wild flowers: gorse, daffodils, bluebells and foxgloves. The water's edge is broken by jagged rocks locally known as **Paternoster Rocks** after the many prayers uttered by passing fishermen, remembering colleagues who perished there. Far out to sea is the French coast.

▶ *From Grève de Lecq continue on the B 40 (Mont de Ste-Marie); turn left onto the B 33 (La Verte Rue) and left before the West View Hotel onto the C 103.*

La Mare Vineyards

Open: Visitor Centre and shop third wk Apr–Oct daily 10am–5pm. Guided tours Mon–Fri 10.40am–3.45pm, Sat–Sun 11.15am–3.30pm. £8.50. ☏01534 481 178. www.lamarevineyards.com.

This is the only vineyard in Jersey, planted on the estate of an 18C farmhouse. Guided tours take visitors around the vineyards, the orchards, the Cognac-style distillery and the chocolate production kitchen. An audio-visual presentation shows behind the scenes, there is a tour of the winery, and, of course, a tasting of the wines, liqueurs and apple brandy.

▶ *Continue along the C 103 to the Priory Inn.*

Devil's Hole★

🚶 *Park by the inn and take the path down to the cliff.*

This blow hole is an impressive sight, made more dramatic by the amplified thunder of the sea entering the cave below.

▶ *Minor roads run east to St John's Parish and north to the coast.*

Sorel Point

The section of road, **Route du Nord,** is dedicated to the islanders who suffered during the German occupation. It runs from Sorel Point where a deep pool known as the Fairies' Bath is revealed in the rocks at low tide.

Hamptonne Country Life Museum★

La Rue de la Patente, St Lawrence.
Open daily early/mid-Apr–early Nov 10am–5pm. £7 (children £4.50). ☏01534 863 955. www.jerseyheritagetrust.org.

Six hundred years of Jersey's rural heritage is brought to life in these old farm buildings with the help of lively costumed characters.

▶ *Go back the way you came. Just before St John's Church, turn right onto the B 52 and then take the C 99.*

Bonne Nuit Bay

Once a haunt of smugglers and pirates this is a favourite place for swimming and sailing. The fort, La Crête, at the east end was built in 1835.

▶ *From here a footpath follows the coast to Bouley Bay; to reach Bouley Bay by car, take C 98, B 63, C 97 (rue des Platons).*

Bouley Bay

This deep sandy bay protected by a jetty and backed by high granite cliffs, is a safe, popular place for swimming.

Take the C 102, then left on the B 31.

④ ROZEL BAY TO ST HELIER

21km/13mi. Allow 1hr 30min.

Rozel Bay

Part of the bay is taken up by a fishing port where the boats go aground at low tide. Above the bay, at the northern end, traces of a great earth rampart survive from the Castel de Rozel, an Iron Age settlement. At the opposite end sits Le Couperon, a Neolithic passage grave (2500 BC).

The road turns inland before returning to the coast above Fliquet Bay and finally meandering down to the water line.
Fliquet Bay is a rocky bay between La Coupe and Verclut points: an ideal place for geologists to decipher the volcanic evolution of the island.

Either follow the road to St Martin or make a detour via country roads – B 38 (Grande Route de Rozel), B 91 (rue des Pelles), B 91 (Route du Villot), B 29 (Mont des Ormes) to Verclut Point (left) and to Gorey Harbour (right).

St Catherine's Bay★

From the lighthouse there is a magnificent **view**★★ of sandy bays and rocky promontories southwards. Out to sea lie the Ecréhou islets, once a favoured place for smugglers, now a popular spot for a Sunday picnic.

Bear right off the coast road (Route d'Anne Port).

Faldouet Dolmen

This 15m/49ft long dolmen dates from 2500 BC. Digs have revealed vases, stone pendants and polished stone axes.

Gorey

This little port at the northern end of Grouville Bay is dominated by Mont-Orgueil Castle on a rocky spur. Attractive old houses line the quay and yachts add colour in summer.

Mont-Orgueil Castle★★

Open Apr–Oct daily 10am–6pm; Nov–Mar Fri–Mon 10am–4pm.
Closed 1 Jan, 24–26 and 31 Dec.
£10.50. ✕ *℘01534 853 292.*
www.jerseyheritagetrust.org.

Gorey Castle received its present name in the early 15C from Henry V's brother, Thomas, Duke of Clarence, who was so impressed by the castle's position and its defensive strength that he called it Mount Pride (Mont-Orgueil in French). Over the centuries the castle has served as a residence for the lords and governors of the island – including **Sir Walter Raleigh**, 1600–03) – a prison for English political prisoners, and a refuge for a spy network during the French Revolution.

The oldest buildings date back to the early 13C when King John lost control of Normandy and built a castle to defend the island from invasion.

The **view**★★ from the top is extensive: down to Port Gorey, south over Grouville Bay, north to the rocks of Petit Portelet and west to the French coast.

Within the castle's network of staircases, towers and rooms is a series of waxwork tableaux, illustrating significant events in the history of Mont-Orgueil; life-size wooden soldiers guard the castle from attack, "the wounded man" statue shows the fate that could befall those fighting to save the castle from invasion, and in the basement is a witchcraft exhibit.

Take the A 3 along the waterfront.

Royal Bay of Grouville

Grouville is graced with Jersey's finest bay, a magnificent crescent of sand stretching from Gorey Harbour to La Rocque Point. The Seymour and Icho Martello towers (1811) may be reached on foot at low tide. Grouville's **Church** has an unusual 15C granite font.

Jersey Pottery★

Open daily 9am–5.30pm, Sun from 10am. *Closed 1 Jan, 25 Dec.* ♿ P
℘01534 850 850. www.jerseypottery.com.
A paved garden, hung with baskets

of flowers and refreshed by fountains, surrounds the workshops where the distinctive pottery is produced. You can watch the craftsmen at work *(except Mon)*, and the showroom displays the full range of products for sale.

St Clement

St Clement is Jersey's smallest parish, and it was here that Victor Hugo wrote *Les Châtiments* and *Les Contemplations*, before departing to Guernsey in 1855. The dolmen at Mont Ubé, the 3.4m/11ft menhir known as **La Dame Blanche**, and a tall granite outcrop called Rocqueberg suggest that this section of the island was inhabited by Neolithic man.

The oldest extant parts of the present church date from the 12C; the wall paintings date from the 15C *(St Michael Slaying the Dragon; The Legend of the Three Living* and *Three Dead Kings)*.

St Clement's Bay

This sandy bay stretches from Plat Rocque Point, past Le Hocq Point, (marked by a defensive tower), to Le Nez Point (3km/2mi).

From the A 4 (Grande Route de St Clement) turn onto B 48 (rue du Pontille), which leads onto A 5 (St Clement's Road), to reach Samarès Manor (right).

Samarès Manor

Open early Apr–mid-Oct daily 9.30am–5pm. Gardens and manor £6.95. **Manor house:** *guided tour (40min) Mon–Sat. £3.55.* ♿✕🅿
📞 01534 870 551.
www.samaresmanor.com.

The name Samarès is probably derived from the Norman *salse marais*, the salt pans that provided the lord of the manor with a significant part of his revenue. Today it is the manor gardens that help earn his keep, created in the 1920s by millionaire shipping magnate and philanthropist, Sir James Knott. The **Herb Garden** is claimed to be the most spectacular in the UK. Also in the grounds is a rare medieval **Colombier** (dovecote), which goes back to at least the 16C, and probably well beyond that. The house is notable for its Norman undercroft and wood-panelled dining room. The **Jersey Rural Life and Carriage Museum** holds a fine collection of carriages, carts and agricultural equipment.

Continue west on the coast road.

Le Rocher des Proscrits

On the east side of the White Horse Inn, a slipway descends to the beach and a group of rocks, Le Rocher des Proscrits (The Rock of the Exiles), where **Victor Hugo** used to meet regularly with fellow exiles.

Sark★★

Offering peace and tranquillity and a traditional way of life without cars, Sark is the smallest independent state in the British Commonwealth and, until 2008, was the last feudal fief in Europe. Its two parts – Great Sark and Little Sark – are linked by La Coupée, a high narrow neck of land that inspired Turner and Swinburne. The island consists of a green plateau bounded by high granite cliffs dropping sheer into the sea or flanking sheltered bays

▶ **Population:** 600.
🕑 **Michelin Map:** 503.
▤ **Information:** The Avenue 📞 01481 832 345. www.sark.info.
▷ **Location:** 12km/7.5mi E of Guernsey, 19km/12mi NW of Jersey. The island is 5.6km/3.5mi long by 2.4km/1.5mi wide.
◉ **Don't Miss:** The magnificent view from the heights of La Coupée.

and sandy beaches. Sark is a haven for wildlife – marine creatures in the rock pools and caves; a wide range of bird species; wild flowers in spring and summer.

A BIT OF HISTORY

Little is known of the island's history before it became part of the Duchy of Normandy, aside from the fact that in the middle of the 6C, St Magloire landed here from Brittany with 62 companions and founded a monastery. In 1042 Sark was given to the abbey of Mont-St-Michel by William the Conqueror. After centuries of intermittent invasions and lawlessness, during which the monks fled, Sark came under English control in the 16C. In 1565 Elizabeth I granted Sark to Helier de Carteret, Lord of the Manor of St Ouen in Jersey, on condition that he establish a colony of 40 settlers prepared to defend the island.

He divided the land into 40 holdings, attributing one to each of the 40 families who had accompanied him from Jersey. Half of the current island population can still trace their descent from these colonists.

The island of Brecqhou (just off the west coast across the Gouliot Passage), a dependent of the fiefdom of Sark since 1565, was acquired in 1993 by the reclusive multi-millionaire British twins Sir David and Sir Frederick Barclay.

Constitution

In 2008, in order to comply with the European Convention on Human Rights, Sark dismantled its 443-year-old feudal system of government. In its place it introduced a 30-member chamber, with 28 members elected in island-wide elections, plus one hereditary member and one member appointed for life. At its head is the hereditary lord *(seigneur)*, while the life member is the *seneschal*, in Sark's case, the local judge.

GREAT SARK
Maseline Harbour

The lighthouse (1912) looks over the harbour from the cliffs on Point Robert.

Creux Harbour★

Opposite the tunnel to Maseline Harbour is a second tunnel to Creux Harbour, dry at low tide.

La Collinette

A short tunnel leads to Harbour Hill (0.8km/0.5mi); at the top is the crossroads called La Collinette.

Ahead stretches **The Avenue**, the main street lined with shops. The small barrel-roofed building on the left at the far end is the two-cell island prison built in 1856. Beyond is **Le Manoir**, built by the first seigneur, bearing the De Carteret arms. **St Peter's Church** dates from the 19C.

La Seigneurie★

🕑*Open (grounds only) Easter–Nov Mon–Sat 10am–5pm.* ♿ ⬤*£2. www.sark.info.*

The residence of the seigneur of Sark stands on the site of St Magloire's 6C monastery. Begun in 1565, it was considerably enlarged in 1730. The square tower, built in 1860, provides a splendid view of the island. The house is sheltered from the wind by a screen of trees and high walls. The gardens are luxuriant with flowers and shrubs.

Port du Moulin★★

A road along the north side of the Seigneurie becomes a path along the clifftop. Follow the Window and Bay sign to the **Window in the Rock**, which the Rev William Collings, then lord of Sark, had made in the 1850s to provide an impressive **view** of Port du Moulin.

▷ *Return to the fork in the path and take the other branch to Port du Moulin.*

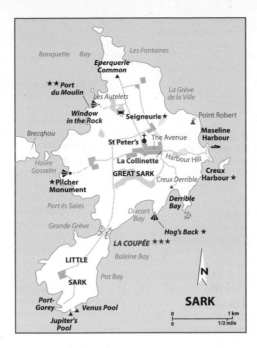

Popular with bathers, the bay is flanked by strangely shaped rocks. On the right stand **Les Autelets**, three granite columns, accessible as the sea retreats.

Derrible Bay

At Petit Dixcart turn left onto a stony path, then right onto a path beside a field; a left fork leads down through the trees to Derrible Bay, which at low tide has a large sandy beach.

Part way down, a turning to the right leads to the **Creux Derrible**, an enormous hole in the granite cliffs *(⊙take care in poor light).*

Return to the first fork and bear left; at the seaward end of the ridge known as the **Hog's Back**★ stands an ancient cannon, where a magnificent **view** includes *(left)* Derrible Bay and Derrible Point, *(right)* Dixcart Bay with La Coupée and Little Sark in the background.

La Coupée★★★

On either side of the narrow isthmus joining Great Sark and Little Sark steep cliffs drop into the sea. The view is magnificent: Brecqhou, Jethou, Herm and Guernsey to the right; Jersey and the French coast to the left. Grande Grève Bay is a good place for bathing.

Little Sark

On the southern headland lie abandoned 19C silver mines. A footpath to the left of the old mine chimney runs down to **Venus Pool**, visible at low tide, when visitors *(⊙check the time of high tide)* can walk from the Venus Pool westward round the headland via Jupiter's Pool, several caves and the rocks in Plat Rue Bay, to **Port Gorey**, which served the silver mines. The clifftop path provides a fine view down into Port Gorey.

ADDRESSES

🛏 STAY

ALDERNEY

⊜⊜ **The Victoria Hotel** – *Victoria Gilbert Street. ☎01481 822 754. www.victoriahotelalderney.com. 6 rooms.* This small family-run hotel in a recently refurbished Victorian terraced house is set in the conservation area of St Anne's. Cosy and spacious bedrooms.

⊝🛏 – ⊝🛏🛏 **Farm Court** – *Les Mouriaux.* ℘*01481 822 075. www.farmcourt-alderney. co.uk. 9 rooms.* In a quiet location on the edge of St Anne's, this attractive complex of renovated farm buildings is set around a lovely cobbled courtyard garden. Rooms are large with contemporary and antique furnishings.

GUERNSEY

⊝ – ⊝🛏🛏 **Dove Cottage at Maison Bel Air** – *Le Chêne, Forest.* ℘*01481 238 503. www.maisonbelair.com. Closed Dec–Feb. 6 rooms.* Cosy modernised self-catering two-bedroom cottage in lovely grounds overlooking Petit Bot Bay.

⊝🛏 **Hôtel La Michèle** – *Les Hubits, St Martins.* ℘*01481 238 065. www.la michelehotel.com. 16 rooms. Restaurant (residents only ⊝🛏).* Near Fermain Bay, comfortable, well-equipped rooms. Relaxing lounge, lawned gardens with , terrace and outdoor swimming pool.

⊝🛏 **Sunnydene Country Hotel** – *r. des Marettes.* ℘*01481 236 870. www. sunnydenecountryhotel.co.uk. Open Easter– Oct. 20 rooms.* Comfortable family lounge, swimming pool, pretty garden and putting course. Traditional but unfussy rooms.

⊝🛏🛏 **Hôtel La Frégate** – *Les Cotils, St Peter Port.* ℘*01481 724 624. www.lafregatehotel.com. 22 rooms. Restaurant ⊝🛏🛏.* Enjoy a panoramic view over St Peter Port at this welcoming luxury boutique hotel, set in a peaceful location.

HERM

⊝🛏🛏🛏 **The White House Hotel** – *GY1 3HR Herm.* ℘*01481 722 159. www. herm-island.com/hotels. Open Apr–mid-Oct. 40 rooms.* Splendid views of the harbour and beach. Choice of rooms in the main house or in the cottages, and of formal or informal dining (half-board compulsory). Garden with a summer swimming pool.

JERSEY

⊝ – ⊝🛏 **Chambre d'hôte Au Caprice** – *Route de la Houle, La Houle, St Aubin.* ℘*01534 722 083. www.aucapricejersey.com. Open mid-Mar–Oct. 12 rooms.* Set in a modern house, very close to a long sandy beach, the comfortable cottage-style rooms are spacious.

⊝ – ⊝🛏 **Chambre d'hôte La Bonne Vie** – *Roseville St, St Helier.* ℘*01534 735 955. www.labonnevie-guesthouse-jersey.com. 10 rooms.* Situated close to the beach and the town centre, this flower-decked Victorian house is meticulously looked after. Warm welcome and sweet guest rooms with flowery cushions, curtains and quilts.

⊝🛏 **Old Bank House** – *Main Rd, Gorey Village, Grouville.* ℘*01534 854 285. www.oldbankhousejersey.com. 18 rooms.* This small unpretentious hotel on the coast road has a terrace garden where you can take snacks and tea. Bedrooms are modern and plain.

⊝🛏 – ⊝🛏🛏 **Harbour View Guesthouse** – *Le Boulevard, St Aubin's Harbour, St Brelade.* ℘*01534 741 585. www.harbourviewjersey.com. 14 rooms.* Set right on the quayside overlooking picturesque St Aubins Harbour, this attractive rustic-style guesthouse has a convivial atmosphere and offers large modern bedrooms.

⊝🛏 – ⊝🛏🛏 **Prince of Wales** – *Grève de Lecq, St Ouen.* ℘*01534 482 278. www.princeofwalesjersey.com. 14 rooms.* This large detached mid–late 20C hotel overlooks one of Jersey's most idyllic sandy bays. Rooms are comfortable if bland.

⊝🛏🛏 **The Moorings Hotel** – *Gorey Pier.* ℘*01534 853 633. www.the mooringshotel.com. 15 rooms.* This small, unpretentious and welcoming hotel enjoys a fine location, facing the harbour just below Mont-Orgueil Castle.

⊝🛏🛏 **Somerville Hotel** – *Mt du Blvd, St Aubin.* ℘*01534 741 226. www. dolanhotels.com. 56 rooms.* This grand turn-of-the-20C classic seaside hotel overlooks St Aubin with beautiful views of the bay. It has lovely gardens and terraces and many facilities including an outdoor pool. Bedrooms are large and luxurious.

⊝🛏🛏🛏 **Windmills Hotel** – *Mont Gras D'eau, St Brelade.* ℘*01534 744 202. www.windmillshotel.com. 40 rooms.* Discreetly set in luxuriant gardens on the heights above St Brelade's Bay, The Windmills has superb sea views and a lovely pool surrounded by luxuriant terraced gardens.

SARK

⊝🛏 **Le Vieux Clos Guest House** – *rue de Mouline.* ℘*01481 832 341. www.levieuxclos. co.uk. 6 rooms.* This Georgian-style house is set on one of the highest parts of the island and was home to generations of Sark doctors. Its bedrooms are homely yet elegant, its pride and joy is its beautiful secluded garden.

🍴 EAT

GUERNSEY

🍴🍷 **Hotel Fleur du Jardin** – *Kings Mills, Castel.* 📞*01481 257 996. www.fleurdujardin. com.* This beautifully converted 15C house serves contemporary cuisine in gastropub surroundings at reasonable prices. The hotel comprises 15 very chic bedrooms (🍷🍷).

🍷🍴 **L'Escalier** – *6 Tower Hill, St Peter Port.* 📞*01481 710 088. www.harbourguides.com/ lescalier. Closed Mon.* This intimate, Anglo-French family-run restaurant is just a short walk from the town centre.

🍷🍴 **The Absolute End** – *Longstore, St Peter Port, GY1 2BG, N.* 📞*01481 723 822. Closed Jan and Sun.* A favourite with locals for its excellent seafood. Comfortable bar upstairs.

🍷🍴 **The Auberge** – *Jerbourg Rd, St Martins.* 📞*01481 238 485. www.theauberge.gg.* From the garden and the terrace, diners enjoy a splendid view over the sea and the neighbouring islands. Modern cuisine.

🍷🍴 **The Pavilion Brasserie** – *Le Gron, St Saviour.* 📞*01481 264 165. www.thepavilion. co.gg. Closed Jan, Mon, Christmas.* Creative dishes and delicious seafood are served in rustic laid-back surroundings. Highly recommended.

JERSEY

🍴 **Spinnakers Cafe** – *Gorey Village.* 📞*01534 850 831. www.jerseypottery.com. Open 9am–5pm (Fri 7pm).* Near to, and run by the Jersey Pottery company, this lively colourful café-restaurant serves high-quality homemade soups, sandwiches, salads, grills and seafood. Specials on the daily blackboard.

🍷🍴 **Old Court House Inn** – *St Aubin's Harbour, St Aubin.* 📞*01534 746 433. www.oldcourthousejersey.com.* This 15–17C inn, full of nooks and crannies, and with ancient blackened beams, has a number of dining areas, There are two main dining rooms, one a former tribunal, another the reconstructed stern of a galleon looking onto the harbour (as does the terrace). The kitchen specialises in seafood dishes. Its spacious attractive traditional-modern bedrooms (🍷🍷–🍷🍷🍷) are good value.

🍷🍴–🍷🍴🍷 **The Grill** – *The Royal Yacht Hotel, Weighbridge, St Helier.* 📞*01534 720 511. www.theroyalyacht.com.* This stylish bistro-style space is the place to come for a simple, perfectly cooked steak and an excellent glass of wine, with impeccable service.

🍷🍴🍷 **Green Island** – *Green Island, St Clement.* 📞*01534 857 787. http://green island.je. Closed Sun eve and Mon.* This attractive informal beachside restaurant is popular with both local people and visitors. A Mediterranean influence is evident throughout – in the décor, the ambience and the style of cooking.The menu is based on locally caught fish.

🍷🍴🍷 **Sumas** – *Gorey Hill.* 📞*01534 853 291. www.sumasrestaurant.com.* This elegant restaurant is a favourite of locals and tourists alike, who come for modern British dishes with Mediterranean flair. Book a table on the glorious terrace to enjoy views of Mont-Orgueil Castle and the harbour.

🍷🍴🍷🍷 **Bohemia** – *The Club Hotel & Spa, Green Street, St Helier.* 📞*01534 880 588. www.bohemiajersey.com.* Jersey's top restaurant, holder of a Michelin star since 2005, produces food that is well-judged and clever, without being gimmicky, and has added a Chef's Table in the heart of the kitchen.

🍷🍴🍷🍷 **Tassili** – *The Esplanade, Grand Jersey Hotel, St Helier.* 📞*01534 722 301. www.grandjersey.com. Closed Sun, Mon.* This Michelin-starred restaurant showcases the very best of Jersey's local and seasonal produce in an opulent setting within an intimate ambience.

SARK

🍷 **Café de la Seigneurie** – *Open Easter to the end of October, 10am–5pm.* Near to the La Seigneurie gardens (🌿*see p442*). Stop for a spot of tea, a snack or even a light lunch.

🍷🍴–🍷🍴🍷 **La Sablonnerie** – *Little Sark.* 📞*01481 832 061. Open Easter–mid-Oct.* A country lane leads to this hotel, set in a 16C farm, with an acclaimed restaurant,serving classic unfussy dishes, by candlelight in the evening. An open fireplace contributes to the rural atmosphere. Spacious bedrooms (🍷🍷🍴).

INDEX

INDEX

INDEX

INDEX

INDEX

INDEX

INDEX

MAPS AND PLANS

MAP LEGEND

	Sight	Seaside resort	Winter sports resort	Spa
Highly recommended	★★★	�له☆☆	❋❋❋	‡‡‡
Recommended	★★	☆☆	❋❋	‡‡
Interesting	★	☆	❋	‡

Selected monuments and sights

◉ ⇉	Tour - Departure point
⛪ ✝	Catholic church
⛪ ✝	Protestant church, other temple
✡ ◻ ☾	Synagogue - Mosque
▬	Building
■	Statue, small building
ⵜ	Calvary, wayside cross
◎	Fountain
●━■━	Rampart - Tower - Gate
✕	Château, castle, historic house
∴	Ruins
◡	Dam
☼	Factory, power plant
☆	Fort
∩	Cave
▱	Troglodyte dwelling
⛗	Prehistoric site
▼	Viewing table
ⱽ	Viewpoint
▲	Other place of interest

Sports and recreation

🏇	Racecourse
⛸	Skating rink
≋ ▱	Outdoor, indoor swimming pool
🎪	Multiplex Cinema
⟁	Marina, sailing centre
⛺	Trail refuge hut
▭━■━■━▭	Cable cars, gondolas
▭┼┼┼┼┼▭	Funicular, rack railway
🚂	Tourist train
◆	Recreation area, park
🐎	Theme, amusement park
ⱶ	Wildlife park, zoo
❀	Gardens, park, arboretum
☙	Bird sanctuary, aviary
🚶	Walking tour, footpath
☺	Of special interest to children

Abbreviations

A	Agricultural office (Chambre d'agriculture)	**P**	Local authority offices (Préfecture, sous-préfecture)
C	Chamber of Commerce (Chambre de commerce)	**POL.**	Police station (Police)
H	Town hall (Hôtel de ville)	🛡	Police station (Gendarmerie)
J	Law courts (Palais de justice)	**T**	Theatre (Théâtre)
M	Museum (Musée)	**U**	University (Université)

Additional symbols

🅱	Tourist information	⊗	Post office
═ ═	Motorway or other primary route	⊘	Telephone
❶ ❶	Junction: complete, limited	⊠	Covered market
▭━▭ ═	Pedestrian street	⁘✕⁘	Barracks
┴═════┴	Unsuitable for traffic, street subject to restrictions	△	Drawbridge
┉┉┉ ┈┈	Steps – Footpath	⋃	Quarry
≋ 🚉	Train station – Auto-train station	✗	Mine
🚌 🚐	Coach (bus) station	🅱 🅵	Car ferry (river or lake)
─┴─	Tram	⛴	Ferry service: cars and passengers
Ⓜ	Metro, underground	⛵	Foot passengers only
🅿	Park-and-Ride	③	Access route number common to Michelin maps and town plans
♿	Access for the disabled	Bert (R.)...	Main shopping street
		AZ B	Map co-ordinates

COMPANION PUBLICATIONS

REGIONAL AND LOCAL MAPS

To make the most of your journey, travel with Michelin maps at a scale of 1:200 000: **Regional maps nos 512 and 518** and the new local maps, which are illustrated on the map of France below. And remember to travel with the latest edition of the **map of France no 721** (1:1 000 000), also available in atlas format: spiral bound, hard back, and the new mini-atlas – perfect for your glove compartment.

INTERNET

Michelin is pleased to offer a route-planning service on the Internet: **www.travel.viamichelin.com** or **www.viamichelin.com**
Choose the shortest route, a route without tolls, or the Michelin recommended route to your destination; you can also access information about hotels and restaurants from *The Red Guide*, and tourist sites from *The Green Guide*.

The Michelin Adventure

It all started with rubber balls! This was the product made by a small company based in Clermont-Ferrand that André and Edouard Michelin inherited, back in 1880. The brothers quickly saw the potential for a new means of transport and their first success was the invention of detachable pneumatic tires for bicycles. However, the automobile was to provide the greatest scope for their creative talents. Throughout the 20th century, Michelin never ceased developing and creating ever more reliable and high-performance tires, not only for vehicles ranging from trucks to F1 but also for underground transit systems and airplanes.

From early on, Michelin provided its customers with tools and services to facilitate mobility and make traveling a more pleasurable and more frequent experience. As early as 1900, the Michelin Guide supplied motorists with a host of useful information related to vehicle maintenance, accommodation and restaurants, and was to become a benchmark for good food. At the same time, the Travel Information Bureau offered travelers personalised tips and itineraries.

The publication of the first collection of roadmaps, in 1910, was an instant hit! In 1926, the first regional guide to France was published, devoted to the principal sites of Brittany, and before long each region of France had its own Green Guide. The collection was later extended to more far-flung destinations, including New York in 1968 and Taiwan in 2011.

In the 21st century, with the growth of digital technology, the challenge for Michelin maps and guides is to continue to develop alongside the company's tire activities. Now, as before, Michelin is committed to improving the mobility of travelers.

MICHELIN TODAY

WORLD NUMBER ONE TIRE MANUFACTURER

- 70 production sites in 18 countries
- 111,000 employees from all cultures and on every continent
- 6,000 people employed in research and development

Moving
for a world

Moving forward means developing tires with better road grip and shorter braking distances, whatever the state of the road.

CORRECT TIRE PRESSURE

RIGHT PRESSURE

- Safety
- Longevity
- Optimum fuel consumption

-0,5 bar

- Durability reduced by 20% (- 8,000 km)

-1 bar

- Risk of blowouts
- Increased fuel consumption
- Longer braking distances on wet surfaces

forward together
where mobility is safer

It also involves helping motorists take care of their safety and their tires. To do so, Michelin organises "Fill Up With Air" campaigns all over the world to remind us that correct tire pressure is vital.

WEAR

DETECTING TIRE WEAR

The legal minimum depth of tire tread is 1.6mm. Tire manufacturers equip their tires with tread wear indicators, which are small blocks of rubber moulded into the base of the main grooves at a depth of 1.6mm.

Tires are the only point of contact between the vehicle and road.

The photo below shows the actual contact zone.

If the tread depth is less than 1.6mm, tires are considered to be worn and dangerous on wet surfaces.

NEW TIRE

WORN TIRE
(1,6 mm tread)

Moving forward
means sustainable mobility

By 2050, Michelin aims to cut the quantity of raw materials used in its tire manufacturing process by half and to have developed renewable energy in its facilities. The design of MICHELIN tires has already saved billions of litres of fuel and, by extension, billions of tons of CO2.

Similarly, Michelin prints its maps and guides on paper produced from sustainably managed forests and is diversifying its publishing media by offering digital solutions to make traveling easier, more fuel efficient and more enjoyable!

The group's whole-hearted commitment to eco-design on a daily basis is demonstrated by ISO 14001 certification.

Like you, Michelin is committed to preserving our planet.

Chat with Bibendum

Go to
www.michelin.com/corporate/en
Find out more about
Michelin's history and the
latest news.

QUIZ

Michelin develops tires for all types of vehicles.
See if you can match the right tire with the right vehicle...

Solution : A-6 / B-4 / C-2 / D-1 / E-3 / F-7 / G-5

Michelin Apa Publications Ltd

58 Borough High Street, London SE1 1XF, United Kingdom

No part of this publication may be reproduced in any form
without the prior permission of the publisher.

© 2012 Michelin Apa Publications Ltd
ISBN 978-1-907099-62-5
Printed: December 2011
Printed and bound in Germany

The regions of Normandie Vallée de la Seine

Eastern Normandy. See the map opposite.

For western Normandy, known as Normandie Cotentin, see the inside front cover.